S0-AVG-561

TUTT LIBRARY

A gift to

COLORADO COLLEGE
1 8 7 4

WITHDRAWN
from

James Work McCreery
and
Mary A. McCreery
Book Fund

SIBELIUS

SIBELIUS

ANDREW BARNETT

YALE UNIVERSITY PRESS
NEW HAVEN AND LONDON

WITHDRAW

COLORADO COLLEGE LIBRAR
COLORADO SPRINGS, COLORADO

Copyright © 2007 Andrew Barnett

All rights reserved. This book may not be reproduced in whole or in part, in any form (beyond that copying permitted by Sections 107 and 108 of the U.S. Copyright Law and except by reviewers for the public press), without written permission from the publishers.

For information about this and other Yale University Press publications please contact:
U.S. Office: sales.press@yale.edu   yalebooks.com
Europe Office: sales@yaleup.co.uk   www.yalebooks.co.uk

Set in Sabon MT by Carnegie Book Production, Lancaster
Printed in Great Britain by St Edmundsbury Press Ltd, Bury St Edmunds

ISBN 978-0-300-11159-0

Library of Congress Control Number: 2007932450

A catalogue record for this book is available from the British Library

10 9 8 7 6 5 4 3 2 1

ML
410
.S54
B37
2007

In memory of Michael Bitten
1961–2005

—

CONTENTS

LIST OF ILLUSTRATIONS

between pages 240 and 241

1. Jean Sibelius with his sister Linda (left) and brother Christian (centre), probably in 1876. (Anna Helena Snellman, d. 1879)
2. Christian Gustaf Sibelius, the composer's father. (Photographer unknown)
3. Maria Charlotta Sibelius, the composer's mother. (Photographer unknown)
4. Korpo gård. (Photographer unknown)
5. Jean Sibelius, 1889. (Photographer unknown)
6. Christian Sibelius, the composer's brother, around 1889. (Photographer unknown)
7. Pehr Sibelius, the composer's uncle. (Photographer unknown)
8. Jean Sibelius, 1896. (Daniel Nyblin, Helsinki)
9. Axel Carpelan. (Photographer unknown)
10. Sibelius standing in front of the fireplace at Ainola, 1905. (Photographer unknown)
11. Jean Sibelius with Aino and three of their daughters at Ainola in the second decade of the twentieth century. (Eric Sundström, Helsinki)
12. Jean Sibelius, 1915. (Eric Sundström, Helsinki)
13. Jean Sibelius rehearsing for his 50th birthday concert in Helsinki, 1915. (Photographer unknown)
14. Jean Sibelius playing the piano, 1927. (Suomen Kuvalehti)
15. Sibelius acknowledging applause at his 70th birthday concert at the Exhibition Hall in Helsinki, 1935. (Photographer unknown)
16. Jean Sibelius, c. 1935. (Helander)
17. Jean Sibelius, 1930s. (International Magazine Service, Stockholm)
18. Jean and Aino Sibelius, 1945. (International Magazine Service, Stockholm)

All photographs are reproduced by kind permission of the Sibelius Museum, Turku

PREFACE AND ACKNOWLEDGEMENTS

In the early 1960s Erik Tawaststjerna started to write a ground-breaking biography of Sibelius that was to occupy him for several decades. The Finnish and Swedish editions run to five volumes apiece and capture the spirit of Sibelius's era as no comparable work has done before or since. At that time, however, the available information about some aspects of Sibelius's life and work, in particular the music written before he made his breakthrough with *Kullervo* (1892), was incomplete. One can only admire and wonder at Tawaststjerna's perspicacity in correctly dating some of the early chamber pieces on the basis of their musical style, despite the almost total lack of corroborative evidence available to him.

In later life, Sibelius was selective – to say the least – about the information he released concerning his early chamber music. None of the works had been published, and, either from forgetfulness or on purpose, he often made confusing or even blatantly inaccurate statements about his own works. Biographers had no option but to take his remarks at face value, as they had no access to the manuscript sources. This situation changed dramatically in 1982, when the Sibelius family donated all of the manuscripts kept at the composer's home, Ainola, to Helsinki University. It is important to remember that this collection was by no means complete: Sibelius himself had destroyed many manuscripts in the 1940s. Other important manuscript collections were held by the publishers Wilhelm Hansen in Copenhagen (these were subsequently acquired by Helsinki University) and Robert Lienau in Leipzig, and by the Sibelius Museum in Turku. The Ainola collection was examined in minute detail and catalogued by Kari Kilpeläinen; his indispensable reference work appeared in 1991. Until then it had been impossible to produce a thorough catalogue of Sibelius's works, an omission repaired when Prof. Fabian Dahlström's thematic-bibliographic catalogue was issued in 2003. These two works have dramatically transformed our view of Sibelius's music, especially with regard to his early period, and exciting new information is still coming to light. Performers, too, have increasingly taken an interest in Sibelius's music, foremost among them the pianist Folke Gräsbeck, who has devoted years of painstaking research to these works and has championed them untiringly in the concert hall and on record. As Dahlström has observed: 'It is of the greatest importance that performers, too, were able to see the manuscripts. That which an archivist may overlook can become readily apparent when one actually plays a work … [There are works] that have proved to be vibrant music but which, at one time, were classified as nothing more than sketches. And the deeper we dig, the more we perform these pieces, the clearer the picture becomes.'[1]

The flow of background material has kept pace with the musical revelations. Since the mid-1990s a wealth of new information has entered the public domain. Much of Sibelius's correspondence has been published, edited by SuviSirkku Talas and Glenda Dawn Goss, followed in 2005 by Fabian Dahlström's edition of his diaries. Vesa Sirén's volume *Aina poltti sikaria* (*He Always Smoked a Cigar*, 2000) is a biography with a difference: it interweaves the story of Sibelius's life with compelling reminiscences about the composer from his family and friends.

The present volume aims to place Sibelius's music in context by discussing *all* of his surviving works. This immediately raises procedural problems: how complete or extensive does a piece need to be in order to qualify as a 'work'? In solving this question I have been assisted immeasurably by Swedish record company BIS's project to record all of Sibelius's music, an undertaking which at the time of writing (2006) is approaching completion and with which I have been closely involved since the mid-1980s. The lengthy examination of manuscripts and fragments, and discussions both with the musicians involved and with my colleagues at BIS Records, have been an immensely rewarding part of this undertaking. If a work is included in the BIS edition, it will be discussed in this volume.

When discussing a large body of musical works of which the original titles are in a multitude of languages it would no doubt be possible to construct a system of inalienable rules in order to ensure a consistent, standardized approach. In my view this would be not only unnecessarily rigid but even downright foolhardy. Some of the works are known internationally in Finnish, some in Swedish, and yet others have over the years acquired a variety of widely accepted English designations, either from the publishers or unofficially. I have thus allowed myself to be guided by common practice, instinct and taste. There is no point in calling a major work by a Finnish or Swedish title that an English-speaking reader who knows neither language cannot understand or remember. For a lesser-known piece, however, the original title may add nuance and colour and is well worth retaining. By and large I have left titles unchanged if they are readily understandable from the original; this applies to many of the French or Italian titles that are in any case close to the English translation. In the case of less familiar works – principally choral pieces and songs, where a number of alternative English titles may exist, some more poetic than accurate – I have generally kept to the Finnish or Swedish names, though with an English translation provided where appropriate.

Many of the early pieces and fragments were left untitled by the composer. Most of these works have been provided with 'working titles' by the musicians who have performed and recorded them, and such 'unofficial' titles are indicated in square brackets. They are based on the music's style and character, and correspond to the types of title that Sibelius himself allocated to similar pieces. As they are an unobtrusive and convenient way to identify a significant body of works, I have chosen to retain them.

Where quotations are taken from Finnish or Swedish originals, the translations are where possible my own and thus may differ from those found in other biographies. An exception is made, however, if the entire source work has been published in English translation.

This book draws on many exciting new developments in Sibelius research and I am most grateful to the eminent scholars who have shared their findings and discoveries with me. In particular I should like to express my appreciation to Fabian Dahlström; to Kari Kilpeläinen, Timo Virtanen and their colleagues at the National Library of Finland; and to Markku Hartikainen, Vesa Sirén and Eija Kurki, all of whom have helped me to form a more detailed and accurate overview of Sibelius's life, work and times.

There can be few more enlightening ways to get beneath the skin of a piece of music than to attend a recording and interact with the musicians who have chosen to bring it to life, and this is especially true of works that are being recorded (and in some cases played) for the very first time. Of the many performers whose insights have been a source of inspiration I should like to express my particular gratitude to: Folke Gräsbeck; Osmo Vänskä; Jaakko Kuusisto; Matti Hyökki, Antti Lindqvist and the YL Male Voice Choir; the members of the Tempera Quartet (Laura Vikman, Silva Koskela, Tiila Kangas and Ulla Lampela); and the players (and management) of the Lahti Symphony Orchestra.

My collaboration with BIS Records in Sweden has opened many doors for me and I am especially indebted to Robert von Bahr, the firm's managing director, who has given me unwavering support for more than twenty years. His colleague Robert Suff, producer of many outstanding Sibelius recordings, has also provided invaluable assistance on both a conceptual and a practical level.

Malcolm Gerratt and the staff of Yale University Press have been constructive and much appreciated partners throughout this project. Sibelius's heirs have kindly given their consent for the reproduction of music examples from works in manuscript, and Sibelius's publishers

– Breitkopf & Härtel, Edition Wilhelm Hansen, Fennica Gehrman Oy, Robert Lienau and Muntra Musikanter – have granted permission to print the other music extracts. I am also grateful to Inger Jakobsson-Wärn of the Sibelius Museum in Turku for supplying the photographs.

I should like to thank Edward Clark, president of the UK Sibelius Society, for his co-operation and encouragement; Leif Hasselgren, Ian Maxwell, Geoff Hayes, Anjali Dhar and John Davis for their innumerable valuable suggestions and constructive comments; Matthew Harvey, whose Sibelius-themed paintings have provided much inspiration; and, last but not least, my wife Kyllikki for her constant support and patience.

NOTE ON SPELLINGS AND ABBREVIATIONS

Many places in the south and west of Finland have both Finnish and Swedish names, and in Sibelius's lifetime the Swedish names were used far more commonly than they are today. Nowadays, in a volume not specifically intended for Swedish readers, the use of Swedish names for many towns and cities that have since become predominantly Finnish-speaking (e.g. Tavastehus [Hämeenlinna], Åbo [Turku]) seems old-fashioned to the point of affectation, and so I have generally used the Finnish forms. Some districts in Finland remain mostly Swedish-speaking, especially around the south-west coast, and for such locations it seems appropriate to retain the Swedish spellings. In any case, some places in these areas have no widely used Finnish names, (though developments in Swedish orthography have resulted in some changes – e.g. Hafträsk is nowadays spelt Havträsk).

Some of Sibelius's works are so closely associated with their place of composition that its name is commonly included in the work title: the 'Hafträsk', 'Korpo' and 'Lovisa' Trios. In such cases I have chosen to retain the Swedish spelling as used by Sibelius both for the location and for the musical work, even though Lovisa [Finnish: Loviisa] now has a majority of Finnish speakers.

Below are some Finnish place names used in this book and their Swedish equivalents:

Finnish	Swedish
Helsinki	Helsingfors
Turku	Åbo
Tampere	Tammerfors
Hämeenlinna	Tavastehus
Järvenpää	Träskända
Lahti	Lahtis
Loviisa	Lovisa
Korppoo	Korpo
Vaasa	Vasa
Pori	Björneborg
Oulu	Uleåborg

Finnish	*Swedish*
Viipuri	Viborg
Tottisalmi	Tottesund
Kerava	Kervo
Lohja	Lojo
Tammisaari	Ekenäs
Hanko	Hangö
Kallio	Berghäll

JS, JSW AND HUL

In 1982 the Sibelius family donated a major collection of manuscripts to Helsinki University Library (HUL, now the National Library of Finland). Many of these works are now known by JS numbers, referring to an alphabetical list of Jean Sibelius's compositions without opus number used in Fabian Dahlström's *Jean Sibelius: Thematisch-bibliographisches Verzeichnis seiner Werke* (Breitkopf & Härtel 2003). The abbreviation JSW stands for *Jean Sibelius Werke* (*Jean Sibelius Works*), the name of the critical edition of the complete works and arrangements by Sibelius that is currently in progress at Breitkopf & Härtel. Additional surviving pieces and fragments not included in the JS list are located principally in the collection of the National Library of Finland and can be identified by their numbers in the HUL manuscript collection, as catalogued by Kari Kilpeläinen in *The Jean Sibelius Musical Manuscripts at Helsinki University Library – A Complete Catalogue* (Breitkopf & Härtel, 1991).

CHAPTER 1

SIBELIUS'S CHILDHOOD AND YOUTH: 1865–1885

1865–82

In 1860 a recently qualified doctor named Christian Sibelius arrived in the small town of Hämeenlinna. He had trained in Helsinki, but his family came from Lovisa, a coastal town to the east of the capital, where his widowed mother Katarina owned a house near the church (the house still exists and is now a museum devoted to Sibelius). His family was fairly large by today's standards; he was the middle child of five, with three brothers and a sister. Their father Johan, born in Lappträsk – a few miles north of Lovisa – in 1785, had moved to Lovisa as a teenager in 1801, initially working as a shopkeeper's assistant, and died in 1844, having risen to a position of some social prominence (it was Johan who, following the fashionable trend, Latinized the family name 'Sibbe' to form 'Sibelius'). Christian's oldest brother, also called Johan, became a sea captain, commanding and owning a share in a cargo ship named the *Ukko* (named after the chief of the gods in the *Kalevala*, the Finnish national epic poem), whilst the second, Pehr, moved to Turku where his ventures included working as a seed merchant. The last and youngest brother, Edvard, was a surveyor by profession; he suffered ill health for much of his life and fell victim to tuberculosis. Their younger sister Evelina was religious and idealistic, but also known for her love of music. Pehr Sibelius too was an enthusiastic amateur musician and instrument collector who even tried his hand at composing; he was also a keen astronomer. None of Christian's brothers ever married, and nor did his sister Evelina.

By all accounts a gregarious man, Christian Sibelius was soon accepted into the town's social scene. He wasted little time in proposing to a young lady half his age, Maria Borg, a priest's daughter who had recently moved to Hämeenlinna with her sisters and widowed mother. Maria was one of eight children, although two of them had died young. Apparently the introduction had been effected by the local headmaster, Gustaf Eurén – who, like Christian Sibelius, belonged to the circle of men who gathered to dine and socialize at the Seurahuone Hotel (prophetic, perhaps, of Jean Sibelius's famous gatherings at the Hotel Kämp in Helsinki).

Music also played a part in Maria's family. She herself was an amateur pianist and her sister Julia even taught the instrument. Their father Gabriel – who had been a headmaster in Hämeenlinna and Turku before he became a priest – had died in 1855, leaving their mother Juliana, who by all accounts was a down-to-earth and realistic, at times formidable lady.

Christian Sibelius and Maria Borg were married on 7th March 1862 – by a local vicar named Wegelius – and the modest house that Christian was renting in Residensgatan [Residenssikatu] (nowadays Hallituskatu; the house itself is now a museum) became the Sibelius family's home.

The large families of the mid-nineteenth century meant that births and deaths were numerous. In this respect 1863 was a year of mixed fortunes for the Sibelius family. On 11th April Christian's younger brother Edvard died, but on 27th November of that year Maria Sibelius gave birth to a daughter, Linda. In 1864 Captain Johan Sibelius, Christian's eldest brother, also passed away: according to family legend, he died in Havana from yellow fever. The following year, to be precise at 12.30 on 8th December, Christian and Maria could celebrate their first son. 'Come and welcome our son', wrote Christian Sibelius to his brother Pehr on 4th January 1866, 'his name is Johan Christian Julius. We'll start to call him Janne in memory of our late brother. ... Maria and the children are doing well.'

The year 1867 was fateful. The winter was unusually long and harsh, and this had a disastrous effect upon the food crops. Famine was nothing new in Hämeenlinna of that period: both 1862 and 1865 had been difficult years in this respect, but the winter of 1867–68 was worse still. Typhus was rife and Christian Sibelius set up a twenty-bed isolation hospital but, in the summer of 1868, he himself contracted the disease and, on 31st July, he died. His death revealed how severely he had overspent in the preceding years. Sibelius's father had employed two maids and two manservants – lavish indeed for a small family in a small house.

Although the Sibelius family was not devoid of financial acumen – Johan the sea captain had been one of the founders and leading lights of the Lovisa Savings Bank, for instance, and Pehr was familiar with business and accounting – Christian seems not to have inherited any. During his studies in Helsinki he had been a popular figure at gatherings – where he entertained his friends with playing the guitar and singing Bellman songs – and had spent too much. After his marriage, too, the easy-going and sociable doctor had shown little aptitude for controlling his family's finances (a characteristic that his famous son would share), and he had also lent money unwisely. Virtually all the Sibelius family's possessions were sold to pay debts, but they were nonetheless declared bankrupt.

Maria Sibelius had two small children to support and was pregnant with a third: another boy, named Christian after his father, was born on 27th March 1869. The passing of Dr Sibelius naturally had a devastating effect upon the young family. Linda Sibelius later recalled: 'Janne, Kitti [Christian] and I became fatherless at such an early age that we didn't really understand how great a loss our father's death was. Mother was then only twenty-six. For her it was very difficult. Luckily we had our dear grandmother and other relatives who were very kind to us. We could attend good schools, and everything was arranged very well for us.' Janne was only two when his father died, and could have understood little of what was happening. 'Little Janne was heard to say to his mother one day: "Won't daddy ever come back, however many times I call out Dear, Dear Daddy!"', his aunt Evelina wrote to her brother Pehr. Janne had only hazy memories of his father but in later life he did tell his secretary, Santeri Levas, how he sat on the floor at home next to the coffin and played with his father's hunting horn. As the coffin was carried out, he sang in a loud voice the children's song 'Spring min snälla ren' ('Run, my dear reindeer').

The rented house in Residensgatan had to be vacated but luckily their maternal grandmother, Juliana Borg, was on hand to provide support. Mrs Borg, along with her unmarried children Julia, Tekla and Axel, was then living in Bryggerigatan [Prykikatu] by the lakeside in the south-east corner of the town. Maria Sibelius and her children moved in too, and lived there for several years.

Hämeenlinna was to remain Sibelius's home for around twenty years. In those days it was still a small community of 2,000–3,000 people. A Russian garrison was based there, and the town's potential prosperity had recently been augmented by the opening in 1862 of a railway link to Helsinki, some 60 miles to the south; the station was across a bridge on the eastern side of town. It was probably through this rail link that the typhus outbreak that killed Christian Sibelius arrived in Hämeenlinna. When Sibelius was a child, the town was predominantly made up of traditional Finnish wooden buildings, many built in the aftermath of a devastating fire in 1831; very few of these remain today. In the impressive marketplace in the town centre stood the church, dating from 1798 (its exterior was reworked in 1892). As yet there was no heavy industry, although the town was already an educational and administrative centre; it was also a conspicuous focus of culture and music.

Sibelius's early contacts with the world of music were intimately bound up with his family circumstances. The family had a square piano and, as a small child, Janne would listen intently whenever anyone played it. When he was roughly five years old he seems to have begun to pick out tunes on the piano and also, in a modest way, to improvise.

Improvisation was indeed a character trait of Sibelius as a small child. Contemporary accounts tell how, while the other children were playing, he would sometimes sink into his own dream world in which the lakes, forests and creatures around him played a prominent role. He also displayed unusual imagination when inventing the excuses and stories that all small children are prone to tell.

In 1871 Juliana Borg sold her house in Bryggerigatan and the family moved to the first of two rented houses – in Residensgatan, just a stone's throw east of the house in which Sibelius was born. Janne started school in the autumn of 1872, when he was enrolled in a Swedish-language school run by Eva Savonius. Meanwhile, at home, his aunt Julia – whom he described as 'quite nice but a dreadful ninny' – was on hand to give him piano lessons. Her tuition was a mixed blessing: she apparently rapped him on the knuckles every time he played a wrong note – a teaching method totally incompatible with Janne's character. He soon resorted to improvisation and amused himself by teasing and criticizing his aunt's other pupils. On the other hand, it seems to have been at this time (if not before) that he learned to read music.

During the summer holidays, Janne and his family visited his paternal grandmother and aunt Evelina – along with Sibelius's father's cousin, Adolf Sucksdorff, 'Uncle Isu', and his family. 'For me, Lovisa represented sun and happiness. Hämeenlinna was where I went to school, Lovisa was freedom,' Sibelius later recalled. Despite its modest size Lovisa was at that time a prosperous community and it is no surprise that the young boy felt at ease in its relaxed seaside atmosphere.

Both of Sibelius's grandfathers had died before he was born and, in his father's generation, the Sibelius family had lost three sons within five years. It therefore fell to Pehr Sibelius's lot to assume a 'paternal' responsibility in the family. Janne wrote to Pehr regularly, and the surviving correspondence contains much valuable information about his early life and music. From her home in Lovisa Evelina, too, was a source of great encouragement and support for the three young Sibelius children. One might have expected Janne to grow very close to the aunts and uncles on his mother's side of the family, but this seems not to have been the case. Even with his mother, his relationship was respectful rather than spontaneous and warm (though he did later tell Karl Ekman that 'My mother was the good angel of our home. She devoted herself entirely to the care of her children; she lived for us and with us. An unusually warmhearted being.'

In 1873 the family moved again, to the corner of Kaserngatan [Kasarmikatu]. A more significant move, however, came in 1874 when Mrs Borg bought the house in Västra Slottsgatan [Läntinen Linnankatu] that she was to occupy until her death. This house, facing the Stjärnparken [Tähtipuisto] park (nowadays the Sibelius Park), was to be Sibelius's home for eleven of his most formative years. It was also in 1874 that Janne changed schools. The decision had evidently already been made that he would eventually attend the Hämeenlinna Normaalilyseo (grammar school) but this school was Finnish-speaking – the first of its kind to be so in Finland – and the first language of the Sibelius and Borg families was Swedish. It thus seemed prudent to send him to a primary school where he could also improve his Finnish and so he duly started a year of study at Lucina Hagman's Finnish-speaking preparatory school.

When trying to imagine the early life of a person who later became famous in one particular area of activity, it is all too easy to assume that that activity dominated his or her childhood years to the exclusion of everything else. It is therefore enlightening to read, in the earliest of Sibelius's surviving letters (1874–77), of him enthusiastically playing with the toolbox, toy soldiers, stamp albums and so on that he received as gifts from his family. He also enjoyed nature walks and swimming, and as a teenager he experimented with hunting and fishing. In later life Sibelius told Otto Andersson that his first composition was a piano piece for children's theatre, called *Ökenscen* (*Desert Scene*), but no other traces of such a work have survived. As a boy Sibelius is known to have entertained his aunt Evelina with a piano improvisation called *Aunt Evelina's Life in Music*. It is often claimed that his first surviving composition dates from this period too: *Vattendroppar* (*Water Drops*) JS 216, a tiny piece for violin and cello *pizzicato* lasting a mere 24 bars. In fact nobody knows when this piece was composed and many respected Sibelius scholars – among them Fabian Dahlström – suspect that it was written around 1881.

In 1876 Janne started secondary school at the Normaalilyseo, which then occupied a single-storey stone building just yards from where he lived (in 1888 it relocated to a new and much larger building across the park from Sibelius's house, although the original building still survives). A dreamer like Sibelius was anything but a model pupil. Though he showed a keen interest in literature, he was too much of a free spirit to respond well to academic schooling. According to his family and friends, the problems would start as soon as school was over for the day: 'While other children were doing their homework, Janne was playing the violin or piano ... if he did get his books out, he seemed to find it impossible to concentrate on them, because his head was always full of notes.' And the next morning he would have 'difficulties getting to school on time because he could never find his clothes. The night before his shoes had been tossed just anywhere, his socks were lost, and there were buttons missing from his jacket. Then he had to try and find his books, for Janne had no idea where any particular volume could possibly be. Finally, there was the search for his cap, usually involving the whole family.' As a result, 'his teachers at the Normal Lyceum shook their heads over him, wondering what would become of him.'

In the spring of 1879 Janne fell awkwardly while disembarking from a boat, and broke his right arm. Although the break healed well, he continued to suffer from stiffness in his right arm, which was henceforth slightly shorter than his left. This naturally caused some difficulties when he started to play the violin.

It was in the autumn of 1881 that Janne started formal violin lessons under a local bandmaster in Hämeenlinna, Gustaf Levander. He wrote to uncle Pehr on 21st September: 'I have now begun to take violin lessons from Director Levander', and later told his biographer Karl Ekman: 'music grasped me with a power that rapidly relegated all my other interests to the background. That was when I began to study the violin in earnest.' From the rapidity with which he started to play in various ensembles, we may well assume that Janne was not a complete beginner when he started his lessons, and his letters to Pehr bear out this supposition. A letter from the summer of 1881 suggests that he was an experienced enough player to judge the quality of the instrument: 'Thank you, dearest uncle, for the violin that you sent me on loan; after the days when I have been without one, the violin sounds really good. It is quite a good violin,' and later in the letter of 21st September he reveals why he had temporarily been without an instrument of his own: 'I have taken my violin away from Karl Stenroth as you wanted me to do, and when Aunt goes to Åbo [Turku], I will return your violin to you.'

The early 1880s also saw Janne's first serious attempts at composition. To understand these pieces we must bear in mind that, by and large, they were written for performance by Janne himself along with his family and friends, and it is thus no surprise that the violin features prominently. We should also bear in mind that in many cases information about their origins is sketchy. Many of these pieces were probably not performed – at least not in public – and Janne, although he became a distinguished player by Hämeenlinna standards, was not yet a celebrity. If we accept that *Water Drops* really had been composed in 1875 or thereabouts, the next piece to have survived is a duet for two violins with the intriguing title *Luftslott* (*Castles in the Air*), JS 65. Divided into four sections in a slow–fast–slow–

fast pattern and playing for some six minutes, *Castles in the Air* contains some characteristic musical ideas. Already in the first bars of the opening *Adagio* we hear a tritone (A to E flat). Later Sibelius makes effective use of triplet rhythms and even a descending fifth at the end of a phrase. The faster sections recall central European dance music: we know that Sibelius played violin duets by the Moravian composer Georg Müller together with his schoolfriend August Ringvall no later than January 1882. *Castles in the Air* is believed to date from 1881 and so it is quite possible that he was here influenced by Müller's pieces. Nonetheless, Sibelius's inexperience is readily apparent; melodically and rhythmically the piece is clumsy, and structurally it does not really hang together.

There had been enough musical boys among Janne's schoolfriends for a choir and orchestra to be set up, and just before Christmas 1881 he wrote to his uncle Pehr that he had joined the orchestra as a second violinist. Thereupon Pehr lent him some sheet music, and he wrote again in January to thank his uncle. The music in question may have been Müller's duets.

At Christmas 1882 Pehr suggested that Janne should devote more time to playing the piano, in order to develop greater fluency in reading music, and in the new year his nephew took this advice. But much of Janne's spare time was absorbed by another type of musical study. In the late summer of 1882 his aunt Evelina gave him a book on the theory of harmony for which he thanked her profusely. He does not mention the author's name, but in later life recalled that he had studied Adolf Marx's *Kompositionslehre* and so this may well have been the volume in question. In early 1884 he added Johann Lobe's *Lehrbuch der musikalischen Komposition* to his collection, which he described as 'a very interesting study'.

A [*Menuetto*] *in D minor*, possibly from as early as 1882, seems to be Sibelius's earliest surviving piece for conventional piano trio (i.e. violin, cello and piano). Presumably the undemanding cello part was intended either for the young Christian Sibelius or uncle Pehr; although both played the instrument, we do not know how competent they were at this time.

1883

In 1883 the Sibelius family spent the summer holiday in rented rooms at Kantala, a villa in Kalalahti near Sääksmäki. Janne's uncle Otto sailed from Tampere and Janne often went swimming, rowing, hunting or fishing. In July he wrote to uncle Pehr that he had been playing the violin for only an hour or two per day, but a few weeks later he was busy composing a three-movement *Trio*, JS 205, and a *Menuetto in F major*, JS 126, both for two violins and piano.

Sibelius himself wrote that the *Trio* was 'in G major', but in fact this is true of only part of its first movement. This movement moves from A minor via G major to D minor, the second migrates from C major to F major, and the third from D major to D minor. Such a relaxed approach to conventional tonal relationships is a characteristic feature of Sibelius's earliest multi-movement works. Formally and harmonically the trio represents a big step forward from *Castles in the Air*. It is still not especially advanced music, but its melodies are skilfully wrought and very elegant. There is much in the piece that recalls dance music of the type found in Müller's duets. We should bear in mind that dances of various kinds – minuets, waltzes, mazurkas, polkas, polonaises and so on – are a vastly underestimated category of Sibelius's output, and an essential component of his style throughout his long career. Although the *Menuetto* is stylistically very similar to the *Trio*, it is by no means sure that it was intended for the same piece: above a score fragment for the finale of the *Trio* there is the title 'Partitur Trios' ('Score Trios'), which would suggest that Janne had been planning a second work of which the *Menuetto* would have formed part; moreover, Janne mentions 'another trio' in his letter to Pehr of 25th August. The technical demands of the violin writing, even in these early pieces, far surpass what could be expected of a pupil who had only learnt the instrument for two years, again suggesting that he had already gained some proficiency through private studies before he started his lessons under Levander.

Another work for piano trio that cannot be dated with accuracy is the the [*Andante*]–*Adagio*–*Allegro maestoso in A minor and E flat major*, written some time in the period 1883–85. It is of sufficient length to serve as the first movement of a longer work but, although the two initial slow sections function excellently as an introduction, the *Allegro maestoso* is not in sonata form. For this reason alone it seems reasonable to assume that the piece was composed before the *Piano Trio in A minor*, the first movement of which does use sonata form.

1884

In early 1884 at the latest, Christian Sibelius started cello lessons. Little is known about his cello studies, but by 24th February Janne could report to Pehr: 'Kitti is playing diligently and has made good progress'; to judge from the music that Janne wrote for him, he must have developed into a reasonably accomplished player. Linda, meanwhile, learned to play the piano well enough to hold her own with her brothers in the family piano trio. All three Sibelius children inherited different characteristics from their parents. Janne had his mother's artistic sensibility and his father's gregarious nature. Christian (with whom Janne always enjoyed a particularly close and harmonious relationship) was more level-headed and down-to-earth, whilst Linda exhibited compulsive, even fanatical traits that ultimately developed into mental illness.

The *Piano Trio in A minor*, JS 206, occupied Janne during the early part of 1884. Originally he seems to have planned the work as a four-movement quartet for two violins, cello and piano, as is shown by a manuscript fragment in which a second violin part is crossed out and there are sketches for a finale.[1] The major innovation in the first movement is Sibelius's use of sonata form; presumably he had now read enough books on musical theory to feel confident enough to apply what he had learnt. Still entirely self-taught as a composer, he was eager to put into practice the knowledge he had gained from Marx and Lobe. The entire trio has clear echoes of such composers as Haydn, Schubert and Mendelssohn, whose music would have been familiar to Sibelius from performances in Hämeenlinna. Much of the first movement has a steadfast if unsubtle march-like character, whilst the expansive, elegiac slow movement contains passages of great beauty. The last complete movement is a minuet, and whilst it is not inconceivable that Sibelius would have envisaged a minuet as a final movement, this one has such an inconclusive ending that it does not fulfil this function very effectively. The material that Sibelius had sketched for the finale seems not to have been fully worked through at this stage. At some point he put the movement aside, although he returned to the material some months later and used it in the finale of his *Piano Quartet in D minor*.

There remain some unanswered questions about the work's origin. In February 1884 Sibelius wrote to Pehr that he had already composed 'a quartet for two violins, cello and piano; [and] a trio for violin, cello and piano is not yet harmonized'. The quartet that he mentions must be the preliminary version of the *Trio in A minor*, as the *Piano Quartet in D minor* was written much later that year. What, then, is the 'trio for violin, cello and piano'? The terminology of Sibelius's letter suggests that it was not merely a trio version of the same work. He might, of course, have been referring to a shorter piece such as the above-mentioned [*Andante*]–*Adagio–Allegro maestoso in A minor and E flat major*. Another possible candidate is a rather bland fragment for piano trio, [*Moderato*] *in A minor* (1885),[2] which has neither a clear beginning nor a clear ending but is comparable in style to the slow movement of the larger trio; on the other hand, Kari Kilpeläinen's paper analysis dates that fragment to 1885.

Why, in any case, did Sibelius decide to turn the quartet into a trio? During his Hämeenlinna years – and beyond, too, in the case of works for friends and family – he tended to compose for the players and instruments that were at his disposal. Possibly one of his violinist friends moved from

Hämeenlinna in early 1884 and Sibelius preferred to rework the composition rather than wait for a replacement. Only a few months later, however, another good violinist must have been found for the *Piano Quartet in D minor*. In any case, Hämeenlinna had its fair share of competent musicians. In addition to Sibelius's own family members and his violin-playing schoolfriend August Ringvall, he could call upon the members of the town's string quartet, in which he himself played second violin. Its leader was Anna Tigerstedt, the daughter of Dr Theodor Tigerstedt, the town's physician. Janne's violin teacher, Gustaf Levander, played the viola, and the local pharmacist, Hugo Elfsberg, was the ensemble's cellist. Elfsberg's wife was a competent enough pianist to join the quartet when necessary. The Hämeenlinna quartet survived until the end of 1884, when the Elfsbergs moved to Helsinki.

The four-movement *Violin Sonata in A minor*, JS 177, was probably Sibelius's first completed work for violin and piano. He wrote the date 17th July 1884 on the main title page, but 1883 on the violin part, suggesting that the piano accompaniment was added after the violin part was already complete. Again, the relationship of keys between the movements is unconventional: A minor, A minor, B minor and a concluding rondo in D major. This piece is more ambitious in scale than the *Trio* from the previous year, but it too is to a large extent modelled on central European music, both the Viennese classics and also dance music. The first movement contains some very effective display writing for the violin, whilst the theme of the *Andantino* second movement could almost have been borrowed from the minuet of Haydn's *Symphony No. 94* (the 'Surprise' Symphony). As Folke Gräsbeck has pointed out, Sibelius's own minuet in the sonata sounds 'more rustic and Nordic than Viennese classical'. The high-spirited finale, however, returns to the world of Schubert or even Bizet: it has affinities with the *Galop* from the latter's *Jeux d'enfants*.

The manuscript of the *Piano Quartet in D minor*, JS 157, is dated 31st August 1884. Here Sibelius continues to write in an essentially Viennese classical style, but the themes have a more clearly defined profile, the use of sonata form is more confident and the expressive range far wider. Moreover, the melodic material throughout the work is shared with admirable even-handedness between the instruments. Whereas the first movement of the *Piano Trio in A minor* had been a relatively naïve, march-like piece, the corresponding movement in the *Piano Quartet* is an almost Beethovenian concert *allegro* on a grand scale, complete with a grand introduction that already establishes the principle of contrast between a dance-like motif (from which the main theme of the movement is derived) and a harmonically almost static, rising motif. A subsidiary idea in this movement bears a close resemblance to Fredrik Pacius's well-known setting of Runeberg's *Vårt land*, which would later become the Finnish national anthem. The second and third movements are in E flat major. The seemingly endless cantilena of the *Adagio* second movement is irresistible. The ghosts of Schubert and Mendelssohn are never far away in the third movement, an elegant minuet, nor indeed in the E minor rondo finale (especially in its *Più lento quasi adagio* episode). Towards the end of the finale Sibelius experiments with some unexpected, almost stuttering syncopations (a distant pre-echo, perhaps, of the final chords of the *Fifth Symphony*). As noted above, this movement is partly based on the sketches for a finale to the *Trio in A minor*. As the music shares the classical urbanity of the other movements of the *Piano Quartet* rather than continuing in the almost bucolic artlessness of the *A minor Trio*, however, it would seem probable that Sibelius wrote much of this movement, too, in the summer.

The *Piano Trio* and *Piano Quartet* serve well as illustrations of the confusion that has long reigned about Sibelius's early music. Around the time of his fiftieth birthday, Sibelius allowed Erik Furuhjelm to reproduce short extracts from the trio's first movement and the quartet's E minor finale in his biography, and claimed that they had been written in 1881–82. The title 'Fragment for Piano Quartet in E minor' duly appeared in various Sibelius literature throughout the twentieth century. Following the 1982 donation to Helsinki University, Kari Kilpeläinen could establish that these 'fragments' were parts of complete works, and – after analysing the handwriting and paper – could establish a reliable date for them.

The earliest of Sibelius's instrumental character pieces are gentle, mellifluous works: an *Andantino in C major* for cello and piano from 1884 (JS 40), and an *Andante grazioso in D major* for violin and piano from the same period or soon afterwards (JS 35); both have the reflective, almost sentimental warmth found in the slow movement of the *Piano Quartet*.

1885

1885 marked a turning point in Sibelius's life, for that was the year in which he passed the school-leaving exam ('studenten') that was a requirement for university entry. Despite the need to devote some energy to his schoolwork, though, he still found time to compose. His earliest surviving work for string quartet is the *Molto moderato–Scherzo*, JS 134, and even this is not a 'pure' string quartet piece, as the scherzo section also exists in a version for piano solo (with two alternative trios) from the following year. The *Molto moderato* introduction, seventeen bars long, is followed by an elegant and good-humoured scherzo in the Viennese classical style. The writing focuses principally on the first violin part, raising suspicions that

Sibelius wrote the piece for his own use. The piece is found in a 29-page collection of manuscript sketches that also contains complete drafts of the *String Quartet in E flat major*[3] from the spring of 1885 – presumably from the May/June period, after Sibelius had sat his examinations. Immediately after the *Molto moderato–Scherzo* in the manuscript sketchbook we find fragments of a *[Scherzo] in B minor* (the first half, plus the first violin part of the second half); the composer Kalevi Aho has produced a performing version by adding the three missing instrumental parts in the second half. Despite its brevity, the piece has a restless, *moto perpetuo* character that looks forward towards *Lemminkäinen's Return* a decade later.

The same book of sketches continues with a lengthy, dramatic *Allegro con brio* for a projected violin sonata in D major. In this piece Sibelius again demonstrates his firm grasp of sonata form. Although the violin still presents the lion's share of the musical material, the piano's role is more than purely that of an accompanying instrument. Unfortunately no other movements for this sonata have been found; the sonata movement is instead followed in the sketchbook by an *[Allegro] in C major* for piano trio that breaks off abruptly; possibly it was planned as a sonata exposition. The thematic invention in this trio is not especially memorable, however, and it is understandable that Sibelius chose not to pursue it further.

The major work from early 1885 is the *String Quartet in E flat major*, JS 184, dated 31st (*sic*!) June 1885. This four-movement work is less ambitious in scale than the *D minor Piano Quartet*; its middle two movements in particular are of modest proportions. Its tonal scheme (E flat major; G minor; B flat major; E flat major), however, is less idiosyncratic than those found in Sibelius's earlier multi-movement works. There is much in this piece that recalls Haydn, especially in its sonata-form first movement. The slow movement shows Sibelius experimenting with note values and rhythm in a way that would later become one of his trademarks: the rapid demi- and hemidemisemiquavers within the slow pulse of the *Andante molto* tempo even anticipate the slow movement of the *Second Symphony*. The brief scherzo is an elegant minuet, whilst the finale too has a dance character: it is a sprightly polonaise.

Apparently from the same period is Sibelius's first surviving work for solo piano, a concert mazurka in D flat major marked *Con moto, sempre una corda*, JS 52. The fair copy is marked 'Minne af J.S. 1885' ('Souvenir of J.S. 1885'), but we do not know for whom it was composed; Folke Gräsbeck has suggested that it may have been a farewell present for a schoolfriend.

After he left school, Sibelius had some months to fill before setting off for a new life in the capital. He spent his summer holidays at Kalalahti and in July wrote to uncle Pehr about playing his violin outdoors on the rocks, and how he 'imagined that the entire slope was an orchestra. The crows were the oboes, the magpies the bassoons, the sea gulls the clarinets, the thrushes the violas, the chiffchaffs the violins, the pigeons the violoncellos, the pine thrushes the flutes, the cock on the farm the concertmaster, and the pig the percussionist. You can just imagine that I was in a dangerous position and had to make a speedy retreat because the violas started dirtying me; I moved to another place a little lower down, but it was even worse. They tried very hard to drown me out, but they were beaten.'

One of the most fascinating projects that he undertook was the composition of an 'opera'. This was a joint venture with Walter von Konow, one of his closest schoolfriends, whose family came from Lahis gård in Sääksmäki. In an essay to commemorate Sibelius's sixtieth birthday, from the collection *Aulos*, von Konow later recalled how they became friends when they were just six years old. They loved to be outside amid nature and dreamed up fantastic stories of elves and trolls, and often read the fairy-tales of Hans Christian Andersen and Zachris Topelius. The schoolfriends used to mount theatrical shows, with Sibelius directing from the piano: '... we planned a long, wonderful saga from our world of dreams; for which I should write the text and Janne the music.' On 4th August 1885 Sibelius wrote to Pehr: 'I have begun to compose the music to Walter Konow's opera *Ljunga Wirginia*.' No trace has survived of the libretto; if the author kept it, it may have been lost when his house, close to Turku castle, was destroyed in a Russian air raid at the turn of the year 1939–40. The music was not identified until January 2001, when Folke Gräsbeck found the title on a preliminary sketch for the first movement. Even though Sibelius calls it an opera, neither the fair copy nor the numerous sketches contain any trace of vocal parts.

The score consists of six movements for violin, cello and piano four hands, and is Sibelius's earliest surviving attempt at writing music with a dramatic purpose. The first five movements are intact, but only the violin part has survived for the final section of the last movement; this has been completed by Kalevi Aho. The nineteen-year-old composer seems to have consciously avoided the Viennese Classical style that characterizes his other major works from 1885 and aimed instead for a freer, more theatrical manner – at times reminiscent of Weber or Rossini, although Sibelius would almost certainly not have been familiar with their work at this early stage in his career.

The lack of a libretto makes it impossible to speculate about the plot of this 'opera', or even about the implications of its title. Much of the work's musical weight is concentrated in the first, second and sixth movements. The first movement, with its opening 'fanfares', has something of the character of an overture and is linked by a violin recitative to the furious tarantella of the second movement, which in turn eventually winds down into the chorale-like third movement. Next comes a relaxed, good-humoured intermezzo, whilst the very brief, aphoristic fifth movement leads into the energetic finale, a sequence of propulsive ideas that culminates in an intense, infectious dance in the folk style.

CHAPTER 2

CHAMBER MUSIC FROM HELSINKI, KORPO AND LOVISA: 1885–1889

Janne paid a brief visit to Lovisa in early September 1885, where he stayed with 'Uncle Isu' Sucksdorff, a wholesaler and bookseller who helped him with practical matters such as the acquisition of violin strings. While there he played in a concert including a flute quartet by Schubert and a solo violin piece, Alexandre Artôt's *Souvenir de Bellini*, and was flattered to be presented with a bouquet by the daughter of a family friend, a young lady named Ellen Hackzell. Within days, however, it was time for him to move on and start his new life as a student in Helsinki.

The Finnish capital with its a population of some 60,000 may have been small by European standards, and its musical establishment may have been relatively recently established, but warring factions had already developed. On the one hand there was the 38-year-old Martin Wegelius, who had founded the Music Institute (now the Sibelius Academy) in 1882. He was a versatile musician – a pianist, composer, conductor and critic – who had studied in Vienna, Leipzig and Munich and who would direct the Music Institute until his death. Having grown up in a home where religious pedantry competed with a fondness for music and literature, Wegelius became a notorious disciplinarian who even regarded absence through illness as a form of truancy. On the other hand he was to prove a good friend to Sibelius and take a kindly, even paternal interest in his development. Wegelius was a capable administrator who could take the credit for many international musicians (including Busoni) coming to Helsinki. He was also an obsessive Wagnerian, with a particular fondness for *Die Meistersinger*; he wrote a 323-page biography of Wagner and also established the first Finnish Wagner Society.

If Wegelius was still a relatively young man, his fierce rival Robert Kajanus was a decade younger still. In 1882, having fallen out with

Wegelius, who was unwilling to offer him work at the newly established Music Institute, Kajanus founded the Helsinki Orchestral Society (or Philharmonic Society orchestra, now the Helsinki Philharmonic Orchestra), the first professional symphony orchestra in the Nordic countries. Kajanus was to conduct this orchestra for the rest of his life, and it owed its survival through many politically and financially precarious years to his energy and enthusiasm. He had studied in Helsinki, Leipzig and Paris, and was already established as a composer whose works included several impressive orchestral scores, not least *Kullervo's Funeral March* (1880) on a subject from the *Kalevala*. As a composer Kajanus's achievements surpassed those of Wegelius although their music does betray their one shared interest: a love of Wagner. In 1885, as a spin-off from the Orchestral Society, Kajanus founded an orchestral school to rival that of Wegelius. It is as a conductor, however, that Kajanus is most often remembered today, especially for his pioneering performances – and in the early 1930s also recordings – of the music of Sibelius. Temperamentally, Kajanus and Sibelius were quite similar: as a child, Kajanus had been a solitary dreamer who loved nature deeply but was too impatient to excel academically.

The older generation was represented by the German-born Richard Faltin, Kajanus's teacher. After studies in his home town of Danzig and subsequently in Dessau and Leipzig, Faltin had moved in 1856 to Viipuri, where he set up a choir and orchestra. He arrived in Helsinki in 1869 and achieved distinction as a teacher, organ virtuoso, composer (especially of songs) and conductor; he had also succeeded Fredrik Pacius as director of music at Helsinki University. Pacius himself, the 'grand old man' of Finnish music, was still alive and active as a composer, though by then in his mid-seventies.

Although his family was sufficiently aware of his musical interest to allow him to enrol at the Music Institute, Sibelius still needed a 'proper' career and, having considered working in an office or studying pharmacy, he eventually took his uncle Axel Borg's advice – incidentally following the examples of Tchaikovsky and Joseph Martin Kraus – and settled on law. He enrolled at Helsinki University, but right from the outset it was clear that his efforts at the law faculty were low on his list of priorities. If he had been hoping that the move to the capital would liberate him from the shackles of a houseful of female relatives, he was to be partially disappointed: his mother and sister Linda moved to Helsinki with him, as Linda was also pursuing her education. They rented an expensive apartment at Kaivopuisto (Brunnsparken), villa No. 19, on the city's southern shoreline. His brother Christian remained in Hämeenlinna with his grandmother and aunts for several more years to complete his schooling.

For Janne the new home had one further disadvantage: there was no piano in it. On the other hand, it must have been an overwhelming experience for the young composer to move to the relative sophistication and bustle of a city some twenty times larger than Hämeenlinna. No doubt this environment encouraged him to assert his independence – and this soon made itself felt in his studies. He spent hardly any time at the university but devoted himself all the more enthusiastically to music. Despite having limited access to a piano, he wrote three short pieces for the instrument – an [Andante] in E flat major, JS 74, a [Menuetto] in A minor, JS 5 and a [Tempo di valse] in A major, JS 2 – apparently his earliest surviving waltz – in a manuscript that also contains some contrapuntal exercises.[1] At the Music Institute his violin teacher was Mitrofan Vasiliev, son of a music professor from Berlin, whom he described in a letter to Pehr as 'a middle-aged man with dark eyes and black hair and he is pale and thin'. Sibelius admired his teacher greatly and the feeling was mutual, as Vasiliev reportedly called his pupil 'a musical genius'. In December 1885 Janne made his first appearance before the Helsinki public as a violinist, playing Jacob Dont's Allegretto and Scherzo together with other students from the Institute.

1886

As 1885 gave way to 1886, Pehr Sibelius gave Janne a very fine violin, which had been in the family for some years since Johan Sibelius, the sea captain, had acquired it at a flea market in St Petersburg. The violin is believed to be the work of no less a master than the great Austro-German instrument maker Jacob Stainer, though its authenticity cannot be proved. Janne used this instrument throughout his active performing career and it is now in regular use in the possession of his grand-daughter Satu Jalas Risito.

From Martin Wegelius's point of view Sibelius's by then appreciable catalogue of chamber works set him apart from his fellow students, as did the considerable knowledge he had gleaned from his own studies of compositional theory. Wegelius not only taught Sibelius theory, counterpoint and harmony but also developed a keen personal interest in and friendship with his pupil.

It was during the spring term of 1886 that the truth about his university studies emerged. He sat a Finnish language examination in the autumn, but apparently neither took a paper in law nor showed any inclination to do so. It took a visit from his uncle Otto Borg to put things into perspective. On a visit to the capital from Mikkeli, Otto found a book on the history of the Nordic countries untouched on Janne's desk. 'After all, Janne, it would be best for you to devote yourself entirely to music, seeing that study does not interest you any more than this,' his uncle conceded. Sibelius did retain one tie with the university, however: as a violinist in the university orchestra.

Even at this early stage, Sibelius had developed the habit of borrowing money from his family. He asked uncle Pehr for a loan before he even arrived in Helsinki, for example (letter of 4th August 1885), and for another the following March (31st March 1886). To support his second request he mentioned that he had applied for a scholarship and quoted two testimonials, one from Richard Faltin ('The student J.S. has today played an audition for me on the violin and demonstrated his very promising talent. He has both musical talent in general and unusually fine pitch. The skill he has achieved on the said instrument is already quite considerable') and the other from Martin Wegelius ('The student Jean Sibelius, enrolled since the 15th of September at the Music Institute, has mainly studied violin performance and music theory there and made great progress in both subjects, and he has distinguished himself by his exceptional musical talent...'). Wegelius's testimonial required a word of explanation, and Sibelius now admitted: 'Jean Sibelius is my music name.' This decision may have been based on nothing more than the desire to put to good use some visiting cards he had found bearing the name 'Jean Sibelius' that had belonged to his late uncle Johan, the sea captain.

Sibelius used the freedom of student life to establish several bad habits. He had secretly experimented with smoking as a schoolboy in Hämeenlinna, sneaking upstairs to the attic where he would not be discovered, but in Helsinki he did not need to be so clandestine. He also experimented with alcohol, although he had to be careful not to offend his mother's religious sensibilities.

It may have been at this time that Sibelius composed an appealing rondo for violin and piano, [*Moderato*]–*Presto*–[*Tempo I*] *in A minor*, JS 7, although it is impossible to date the piece with precision. The same applies to two separate piano arrangements – one with a trio in E minor, the other with a trio in A major – of the *Scherzo* for string quartet from the spring of 1885; the piano versions omit the original *Molto moderato* introduction from the quartet piece. Principally, however, Sibelius's goal at this period was to become a virtuoso concert violinist. On Vasiliev's instructions he had already been learning pieces by Pierre Rode and Giovanni Battista Viotti. In May he played David's *Concerto in E minor* (with piano accompaniment) at the Music Institute, and the following day he took part in a performance of Mozart's *String Quartet No. 21*. In *Nya Pressen* there was a positive review of his performance of the David concerto, penned by one Karl Flodin: 'Jean Sibelius possesses a highly developed technique and in general played faultlessly.'

Flodin had studied under Richard Faltin and was a capable pianist (he was later to accompany his wife, the soprano Adée Leander-Flodin, in performances of Sibelius's songs, and even recorded *Den första kyssen* in 1904). He was one of the earliest serious music critics in Finland and commanded great respect. In 1925 he recalled his first encounter with Sibelius: 'There was something peculiarly fascinating about his slender figure. It was as if his straightforward nature always wanted to meet one with open arms. But you were never sure whether there was not, after all, some mockery behind it. His speech overflowed with paradoxes and metaphors, without allowing you to realize what was serious and what only played on the surface... His eyes gazed as if through a dull mist, but when his imagination began to play restlessly, his look became deeper and glittered with a blue brilliancy.'[2]

It comes as no surprise that the young student found time to devote attention to some of the young ladies at the Music Institute – including Emi (Naomi) Bergroth, who was lodging with Wegelius. Despite having grown up in a house full of women, however, Sibelius's early attempts were embarrassingly awkward. One of Emi Bergroth's friends, Karin Palander, later recalled: 'Wherever we two would go, "Sibbe" was somewhere close by, trying to become acquainted. We only called him Sibbe among ourselves, because in those days one didn't so readily use the familiar form of address... "What a pretty friend you have," Sibelius said to me once, happening to blow a kiss towards her [Emi's] window. But Emi Bergroth had plenty of admirers, and was not especially fond of Sibelius. We didn't have any idea of his future greatness.' Martin Wegelius was in a better position to judge his star pupil's prospects. Sibelius finished the spring term with good marks, and on an outing for the pupils and staff of the Music Institute, the authoritarian teacher declared his belief that Sibelius would achieve everything that he, Wegelius, had only dreamt of. Karin Palander continued: 'Wegelius was deeply moved and, when he had finished, threw his glass violently against the rocks. Only then did we, his fellow students, comprehend what a great talent he must have had, as our revered director, who was parsimonious with his praise, was in such awe of his future and his potential.'

Sibelius's first year at the Helsinki Music Institute focused primarily on theoretical studies and violin playing, but the summer holidays in 1886 offered him a valuable outlet for his compositional ambitions. That summer Jean and his family stayed at Vidix gård (Vidix manor) in the tiny village of Hafträsk on Norrskata island, north of Korpo in the Turku archipelago. Uncle Pehr had shipped a square piano from Turku, and the whole family made music with enthusiasm: Jean and Pehr played the violin, Christian the cello, and Linda, aunt Evelina and Maria the piano. In 1915, Sibelius told Otto Andersson how he used to like to play the violin while walking on the shore, even when the weather was stormy, and his works from this period reflect something of this passion. Foremost among them is the four-movement *Piano Trio in A minor, 'Hafträsk'*, JS 207, which – especially in its first movement – combines the freshness of the young Sibelius with a Beethovenian breadth and grandeur. The seriousness with which Sibelius approached his task is indicated by the fact that he immediately made substantial revisions to the movement. Folke Gräsbeck, who prepared the edition used in modern concert performances, writes: 'The parts for the first movement presented particular problems. Several older drafts exist for a rather long, amorphous version, but an improved version (not least in formal terms) has only survived as fragments. Among these fragments, however, is the cello part for the whole movement in a fair copy by the composer's brother Christian and, by using this as a starting point, we have assembled a version that uses as much as possible of the composer's revision.' The relaxed, easy-going slow movement has the character of a barcarolle, perhaps a reminiscence of the family's boating excursions that summer. Whereas Sibelius's earlier multi-movement works had usually featured a minuet as the third movement, here we find a fast, almost symphonic scherzo that combines its infectious high spirits with a certain robust earthiness. Most of the thematic material of the rondo finale has a skipping 6/8 metre, but effective contrast is provided by a steady yet intense chordal idea – a bold stroke that anticipates the finale of the *Piano Quintet* and the first of the *Six Impromptus* for piano. The concluding bars, as undemonstrative as they are unexpected, look ineffective on paper but in a good performance come across as a masterstroke of gentle humour.

Other works from the Hafträsk summer include an [*Andantino*] *in A major* for piano trio. The piece is not quite complete but, with the addition of just one bar at the end of the B section, it can be played according to an ABA pattern. Both the dignified, hymn-like opening theme and the more expressive second theme are well worth rescuing. The manuscript contains sketches for the *'Hafträsk' Trio*'s first movement, and the stylistic similarity to the *'Hafträsk' Trio* is undeniable.[3] The third work in the same manuscript is a solemn [*Minuet*] *in D minor* for violin and piano that is clearly better suited for concert performance than for dancing; Folke Gräsbeck has suggested that it was probably composed for a musical soirée at the beginning the holiday period.

An [*Andantino in A minor*], JS 8, in ABA form, also for violin and piano, may come from the same period; it has a barcarolle-like metre similar to the slow movement of the *'Hafträsk' Trio*. It is tempting to believe that the *Allegro in D major*, JS 27, for piano trio, an ebullient polka-like piece, must have been composed during the holiday as well, such is the *joie de vivre* that it radiates.

Back in Helsinki for the autumn term of 1886, Sibelius started to spread his wings a little further, and to enjoy student life with more abandon. He started a close friendship with Adolf Paul. Paul, a pianist, novelist, dramatist and poet, had moved to Finland from Scania (Skåne) in southern Sweden at the age of nine, but was to spend much of his adult life after 1889 in Germany – indeed, many of his dramatic works are in German. It was probably at this period that Sibelius – following in his father's footsteps – started to develop a taste for life's luxuries, among them alcohol and cigars. He continued to appear as a violinist, playing works by Vieuxtemps and Bériot with piano accompaniment.

At some point during 1886 Sibelius composed a piece for solo violin, the highly demanding [*Étude*] *in D major*, JS 55. The double stoppings and runs in this piece would seem to anticipate the solo writing in the *Violin Concerto*, but it is by no means a concert piece and it is probable that Sibelius wrote it as an exercise for his own use. The manuscript for the violin étude also contains a sketch for the set of [*Eleven Variations on a harmonic formula*] *in D major* for piano – a far more appealing prospect for public performance. The manuscript does not establish a definitive order for the inner variations (although it clearly identifies the beginning of the work and the euphoric polonaise that ends it), and some detective work by Folke Gräsbeck was necessary to arrive at a convincing performing version. As Gräsbeck observes, the work is 'dominated by youthful exuberance and sparkling good humour... If the variations were indeed conceived as theoretical exercises, the end result still approaches the status of genuinely inspired piano music.'

1887

In early 1887 the Sibelius family was in Lovisa, where they spent some time with the Sucksdorffs. The salon in the Sucksdorff house was equipped with both a piano and a harmonium, and it was probably then that Sibelius composed an exquisite *Andante cantabile in E flat major*, JS 30b, for this unusual combination of instruments. The piece is dedicated to uncle Isu's much younger wife Betty and to a family friend, Elise Majander, and is a fine example of the 'souvenirs' that Sibelius wrote for friends and family. Structurally it is unremarkable – a brief introduction leads to a lied form with trio – but the main theme, suave and leisurely with a hint of wistfulness, is very agreeable. The *Andante cantabile* also exists in a slightly modified version for solo piano, JS 30a, and it seems probable that the piano version was prepared in Korpo the following summer. While with the Sucksdorffs, Sibelius also wrote a longer piece – the *Quartet in G minor* for violin, cello, harmonium and piano, JS 158, which he also dedicated to Betty Sucksdorff. This very appealing quartet, in only one movement, is around nine minutes in length and clearly episodic in structure. In character the main theme is predominantly warm and mellifluous; one of the episodes has a *staccato* character that brings to mind the violin and cello *pizzicati* of *Vattendroppar*, whilst another (sharing a theme with the [*Catalogue of Themes, 50 Short Pieces*] for piano, a composition exercise that Sibelius would soon deliver to Wegelius), resembles a hesitant waltz.

A group of five pieces for violin and piano – [*Allegretto*] in G major, JS 86, [*Tempo di valse*] in B minor, JS 89, [*Mazurka*] in A major, JS 84, [*Andante molto*] in C major, JS 49, and [*Aubade*] in A major, JS 3 – cannot be dated with precision; Kari Kilpeläinen has dated some of the sketches for them to 1886. As they are stylistically more advanced than the exercises that Jean would produce over the next few months, it is possible that they were written for performance with the Sucksdorffs. The violin parts for all five were copied into the same manuscript,[4] which has led Kilpeläinen to speculate that they 'have perhaps been played as a suite, or were intended to form one'. The [*Allegretto*] has something of the *cantabile* quality of the later *Nocturne* from the music to *King Christian II*. The piano part for the seductive, urbane [*Tempo di valse*] is not quite complete but a performance version was prepared by the violinist, conductor and composer Jaakko Kuusisto in 1999. Syncopations dominate the brief, aphoristic [*Mazurka*], whilst by contrast the [*Andante molto*] has an emphatic, rhetorical grandeur. The brief and gentle [*Aubade*], in which 'many "birdsong" trills in the violin part have a counterpart in the piano's demisemiquaver ornamentations'[5] is not an obvious way to conclude such a notional suite of pieces, but we shall probably never discover the composer's precise intentions.

From around the same time comes a tiny [*Scherzino*] in F major, JS 78, also for violin and piano. The fair copy of this piece is on the same page as the [*Mazurka*] in A major, and it might therefore also have been intended for the same 'suite'.

CHARACTERISTICS OF SIBELIUS'S STYLE

Sibelius did not start his official studies of composition – under Martin Wegelius – until early 1887. By this time, however, his vocabulary as a composer already included many of his characteristic devices. This applies to both melody and harmony. Many of the features in question are not in themselves especially distinctive, but they became ingrained in the Sibelian style in a very individual and pervasive way.

Melodically, two features already stand out. The interval of a descending fifth, often at the end of a phrase, has long been recognized as a Sibelian trademark of prime importance. By the time of the *'Hafträsk' Trio* from the summer of 1886, however, this was already in much evidence: it appears prominently in both the first and the second movements. Even earlier, it had put in a passing appearance in the [*Andante*]–*Adagio*–*Allegro maestoso* for piano trio (violin part, bars 87–88).

In a ground-breaking article about *Finlandia*, Harri Miettunen has pointed out that this tone poem is based on a motif that is found in one form or another in most of Sibelius's works. 'The motif is a four-note cell consisting of three adjacent tones. It is most apparent in the opening of the hymn section [of *Finlandia*]: a step down from the central note and back, and a step up. The motif also appears without its first note. At first sight, this may seem too simple a figure to be considered a motif proper, let alone a major element in Sibelius's output as a whole, but he uses it with a logic that is quite unparalleled ... Its endless variations obscure its presence; one does not really notice it until one understands the principle ... One form of the motif is identical to the ornament known as the *gruppetto*, which has its own symbol, very similar to a supine letter S or its mirror image, depending on which way the *gruppetto* is to be played. Could this be Sibelius's musical signature, akin to B–A–C–H (B flat, A, C, B natural) or D–Es–C–H (D, E flat, C, B natural)?'

The origins of this 'S-motif' lie very early in Sibelius's output: it occurs at the start of *Castles in the Air* and again, in almost complete form (without its last note), as the basis of the second theme of the first movement of the *String Quartet in E flat major* of 1885. By the time of the *Adagio in F minor* for string quartet, JS 14 (1888–89), it was more easily recognizable, although still rather concealed in the texture (first violin, start of bars 27 and 29). Before long the 'S-motif' was a dominant feature – for instance of the first movement of the *Piano Quintet* and in the *String Trio in G minor*, JS 210 and, as Miettunen points out, it remained a constantly recurring feature of Sibelius's music all through his career. The actual sound of an 'S-motif', and thus its expressive message, can vary greatly according to the harmonic and rhythmic context: it can be cold and bleak (the clarinet solo that opens the *First Symphony*, or in *Tapiola*), hymn-like (its most prominent occurrence in *Finlandia*), frantically busy (the scherzo of the *Second Symphony*), warm and nostalgic (*Lied*, Op. 97 No. 2); it can add a touch of unexpected colour (the glockenspiel in the *Fourth Symphony*) or even convey primeval gloom (*Pohjola's Daughter*). It seems unlikely that the 'S-motif' was consciously employed for its symbolic meaning, but it is at least as central to Sibelius's style as the famous 'Grieg motif' (octave-seventh-dominant, as at the start of his *Piano Concerto*) was for the Norwegian composer.

Numerous rhythmic elements deserve mention. One is the use of a dotted rhythm on the penultimate beat of a motif, in 4/4-time and usually preceded by several notes of equal duration. This is frequently used in music of a celebratory, dignified or chivalrous character (second theme of the *Alla marcia* from *Karelia*, *Andante festivo*). The dotted rhythm is already present in music written in Hämeenlinna – in the first movement (bar 23ff.) of *Ljunga Wirginia* (1885). It is seen even more clearly in the *Moderato–Maestoso in E flat major* for violin and piano, JS 132 (1887–88), a baroque-style student exercise written for Wegelius. A similar dotted rhythm in the [*Andante*]–*Adagio–Allegro maestoso* for piano trio (1883–85), by contrast, serves as an emphatic up-beat.

The second distinctive rhythm is a syncopated short–long–short pattern. This is used in a wide variety of ways: at one extreme, common until the mid-1890s but also found on occasion later in his career, it may appear as part of the main rhythm of a theme, often in music of a bright and happy character (finale of the 'Korpo' *Trio*, first movement of the *Piano Sonata*, the *Intermezzo* from *Karelia* or the fifth of the *Six Humoresques* for violin and orchestra), and at the other – its most common manifestation in Sibelius's mature music – it can form an *ostinato* accompaniment, often on a pedal point (slow movement of the *Violin Concerto*, the *Nocturne* from *Belshazzar's Feast* or the song *Norden*). A variation of this is the steady syncopated accompaniments found in *Pohjola's Daughter* or the slow movement of the *Fourth Symphony*.

At a very early stage, triplets became an essential weapon in Sibelius's armoury. His use of triplets can be traced back to the Hämeenlinna years, to *Castles in the Air*; in the *Piano Trio in A minor* of 1884 they play a crucial role in the second theme of the first movement. Triplets also form a variant of the dotted up-beat in the [*Andante*]–*Adagio–Allegro maestoso* for piano trio (1883–85). Like the short–long–short rhythms, they fulfilled a number of different requirements: they served as fanfares (in the *Prelude* for brass (JS 83), or in the *Alla marcia* from *Karelia*), they added rhythmic or decorative interest to otherwise rather regular passages (the main theme of the *Moderato–Allegro appassionato* for string quartet (JS 131), or the opening bars of *The Wood-Nymph*), or they combined with duple rhythms in rhythmically ambivalent hemiola patterns (the finale of the 'Korpo' *Trio*). What is often referred to as a 'Sibelius triplet' is a development of the ornamental function: it is a quick triplet found between longer notes that are separated by a wide interval: the triplet softens and bridges the gap. The most famous examples of this are found in the main theme of *The Swan of Tuonela* and in the first movement of the *Second Symphony* but the device is regularly found throughout Sibelius's mature output.

Slow, grand 3/2 rhythms – of the type that lend such an unmistakable *gravitas* to the polyphonic string passage near the beginning of the

Seventh Symphony – first made an appearance in the first movement of the *Trånaden* suite from 1887, and before long were determining the course of entire movements – such as the first movement of the *Piano Quintet* of 1890. Before that, Sibelius tried similar slow writing in a two- or four-beat pulse in the slow movement of the *Trio for Two Violins and Piano* of 1883 and in the third movement of *Ljunga Wirginia*. He did not abandon the two- or four-beat variety entirely, however; even as late as 1925 this sort of writing is found in the scene where Miranda is lulled to sleep in the incidental music to *The Tempest*.

It goes without saying that when several of these devices are combined – as in the first theme of *The Wood-Nymph*, where triplets and the dotted rhythm are juxtaposed, or indeed the *Moderato–Maestoso*, JS 132, which combines the short-long-short pattern with the dotted rhythm – the identity of the composer is especially easy to recognize.

In his teaching Wegelius applied Ludwig Bußler's theory of composition, according to which the pupil should first learn to master the smallest units, for example two-bar-long exercises, and then gradually increase the size of the structural units. This is the procedure followed in the [*Catalogue of Themes, 50 Short Pieces*] for piano,[6] which was therefore probably written as an exercise. The first fourteen sketches are each two bars long, Nos 15–30 are each four bars long, Nos 31–48 are each eight bars long whilst No. 50 runs to 32 bars. A few of the later numbers elaborate material heard in earlier ones, and one theme (heard in Nos 5 and 26) is also found in the *Harmonium Quartet* (which raises the possibility that he may have started work on the catalogue before the Christmas holiday, perhaps so that he would have something to show Wegelius at the first lesson; the date '1887' is written on the cover page) but otherwise none of the themes was directly re-used in any other composition – surprising, because some have distinct promise. A set of [*Four Themes*] for string quartet was presumably also written as an exercise for Wegelius.

In the spring of 1887 Sibelius also applied himself to his violin playing – not only in chamber music and as an orchestral player but also as a soloist. At one concert he performed the second and third movements of Mendelssohn's *Concerto in E major* but the performance was not a success, and Richard Faltin complained both about his tone and his intonation. In chamber music Sibelius resumed his collaboration with his brother Christian, who had also come to Helsinki to begin his medical studies.

One wonders if Sibelius managed to attend a performance of *Loreley*, the third and last opera by the venerable Fredrik Pacius, which was premièred on 28th April. Admittedly Pacius's work had more in common with the grand opera style and an earlier era of German romanticism than with the

Wagnerian style favoured by Wegelius, but it was nevertheless well received by the conservative Helsinki public. Pacius's music, much indebted to Weber and his teacher Spohr, did not directly influence Sibelius, although they had a mutual admiration of Beethoven (and Sibelius's father had been a choir member at the première of Pacius's masterpiece, the opera *Kung Karls jakt* [*The Hunt of King Charles*], in Helsinki in 1852). It was principally Pacius's influence, however, that led younger Finnish composers to turn to Germany rather than Russia when they went to study abroad, and this was the route that Sibelius would follow.

Early in the summer Sibelius paid a visit to his schoolfriend Walter von Konow at Lahis gård. They seem to have resurrected their operatic plans, and a *Scherzo in E minor for violin, cello and piano four hands*, JS 165, is believed to be a pendant to *Ljunga Wirginia* from two years earlier. This sparkling and decidedly untheatrical concert piece, with two trio sections, has not quite survived intact, but completions to the piano parts by Timo Hongisto and Kalevi Aho have allowed a performing edition to be created.

Following the success of the family holiday at Hafträsk the previous summer, Pehr and Evelina Sibelius took it upon themselves to arrange another visit to the same area in 1887. This time the family rented a cottage in the village of Korpo kyrkby, on a rocky hillock overlooking both the church (an imposing stone structure built between the thirteenth and fifteenth centuries) and the neo-classical manor house of Korpo gård. Some friends of the family, a Dr Fredrik Wilenius and his wife Ina, had rented accommodation at the manor house itself and were staying there together with their sixteen-year-old niece, Ruth Ringbom (aunt of the composer and conductor Nils-Eric Ringbom). The Sibelius family were naturally more than willing to join their friends in music-making: Mrs Wilenius was a capable pianist, which was convenient as Sibelius's sister Linda did not spend the entire summer in Korpo, whilst Ruth Ringbom played the violin. She also seems to have been rather fond of Jean's brother Christian, and the feeling was mutual. Some time later Christian even proposed marriage, but Ruth refused – a decision she apparently regretted for the rest of her life.

Mrs Wilenius had made sure that there was plenty of music to be played at the group's evening soirées; she had brought copies of Beethoven's piano trios as well as music by Schubert, Fesca (probably Alexander Fesca [1820–49]) and Karl Reissiger. Not that she need have worried: Jean was composing with unstoppable momentum, and had a particular interest in writing and playing music for piano trio. Fortified by nothing stronger than coffee, he would compose at night, each day bringing some newly written pages to be tried out in the music room at Korpo gård. Although Sibelius must have been keen to put into practice what he had learnt from

Wegelius over the previous months, however, it is worth remembering that these pieces were not written in an academic context, and it is unlikely that Sibelius showed them to his teacher. 'I guarded my double life jealously', Sibelius later told Karl Ekman, 'so that exceedingly few got to know of the works in which I expressed my innermost strivings.'

The principal result of his efforts is a work that might well be judged to reflect the warmth and light of a Finnish summer night: the great *Piano Trio in D major*, the '*Korpo*' *Trio*, JS 209. Of Sibelius's early chamber pieces, few – if any – have a more urgent claim on the repertoire. Its abundant and luxuriant melodies are no longer so indebted to Mozart, Schubert, and Haydn, but develop the Beethovenian style that had been clearly evident in the first movement of the '*Hafträsk*' *Trio* of the previous summer.

Structurally, too, it is hard to overestimate the significance of the '*Korpo*' *Trio*, as it is the earliest major work by Sibelius to experiment with the principle of formal compression that was to become an essential element of his later music. The first movement is more or less in sonata form, complete with slow introduction. Instead of the expected development section, however, Sibelius writes a fugal passage; this can be seem as an early example of the composer's compression technique, comparable especially with the *First Symphony* in which the development and recapitulation in the first movement are conflated. It should be noted that the main theme of the '*Korpo*' *Trio*'s first movement is in any case not especially well suited to further development: when a similar idea appears in the first movement of the *Third Symphony* it represents the result of such a process rather than its starting point.

The second movement, marked 'Fantasia', combines a beautiful, rhapsodic slow movement with a scherzo and a dignified, elegant trio. Its main theme takes inspiration from Mozart and Schubert but retains a character of Nordic romanticism. The next passage is of especial importance: the music is constructed from short–long–short rhythms and triplets, and the melody of the triplets is based on the interval of a second – almost an 'S-motif'. The following year Sibelius would use a very similar motif starting with two triplet groups in his *Suite in E major* for violin and piano, and from there it would migrate to music of ever more serious character, for instance the choral song *Sydämeni laulu* and the first version of the *Violin Concerto*. Later on, the trio movement acquires a hymn-like character, reminiscent of the hymn *Härlig är jorden*, and rather similar to other works by Nordic composers such as Niels W. Gade's *First Symphony* (1841–42), which Sibelius could possibly have heard or studied, and Grieg's *Symphony in C minor* (1863–64) which he would certainly not have known. This is followed by an extended, improvisatory transition where

Sibelius seems to be listening to nature's innermost voices: there are eerie harmonics that must have sounded very radical to Dr and Mrs Wilenius, and rising and falling fourths from the piano – an interval that is often associated with Sibelius's Symbolist works of the 1890s, but here sounds more like a harbinger of the Expressionism in the third movement of the *Fourth Symphony*.

All such associations are forgotten as we launch into the rondo finale, which follows without a break. Its dance-like main theme, again based on short–long–short syncopations and triplets, has a folk-like quality, though the other themes of this movement are more urbane in character: the second theme is especially elegant, whilst the third demonstrates how the young composer could use a skilfully written accompaniment to lend vitality to a melody which is not in itself especially quick. He had practised this in the finale of the 'Hafträsk' Trio and the same technique is used to monumental effect in the finale of the *Fifth Symphony*.

This formal advance goes hand in hand with a growing use of thematic and rhythmic motifs that have, as Sibelius was later to put it, an 'inner relationship'. The main theme of the first movement combines the classical discipline of semiquaver/quaver patterns – a hallmark of the first movement of the *Third Symphony* – with a melodic and rhythmic shape that hints at the corresponding movement of the *Second*;[7] the second group, by contrast, has almost the luxuriance of Rachmaninov. The characteristi-cally Sibelian triplets (rising and falling with a wave-like motion) that accompany the second group of the first movement, for example, find an echo in the accompaniment of one of the slow movement's principal ideas, and also find an echo in the finale. Another example is the main motif of the mercurial scherzo, which opens with six triplets from the violin that point forward to the main theme of the finale. For a young man who had received only a few months of formal composition lessons, the trio is a remarkable achievement.

A siciliano-like *Andantino in G minor* for piano trio, JS 43, can be provisionally dated to the Korpo summer on account of the type of manuscript paper used. Technically straightforward and stylistically far less bold than the 'Korpo' Trio, it is nevertheless a charming piece well suited to a domestic chamber-music environment.

If the 'Korpo' Trio was the indisputable musical highlight of Jean's summer holiday in Korpo – as well as being, by some margin, his most impressive piece to date – it was by no means the only large-scale work that he produced there. The five-movement suite for piano and recitation *Trånaden* (Longing), JS 203, to texts from *Suckarnas mystèr* (*Mystery of the Sighs*) by Erik Johan Stagnelius, was dedicated to Ina Wilenius. In the outer movements, which use related thematic material, we find the first example of Sibelius's use of a dignified, noble 3/2 metre, which was later to become a notable characteristic feature of his music. The poetry here is philosophical and elevated: 'Two laws govern human life... The force of desire is the first. The compulsion to renounce is the second... and eternal duality and unity appear in the mystery of sighs.'[8] Sibelius responds to these lofty ideas with a theme that, despite its grandeur, resembles a slow waltz; it even contains an anticipation of *Valse triste*. The middle movements, each related to a specific aspect of nature, are more pictorial. The expressive range that Sibelius could draw from the piano is evident from the second, *Ser du hafvet?* (*Do you see the sea?*): at first the main theme has a wonderfully ominous, stormy character, but before long it bursts forth in splendour and light. The principal idea of the third movement, *Hör du vinden?* (*Do you hear the wind?*), is a beautiful, Romantic melody, surrounded by gentle gusts of onomatopœic sextuplets, whilst in the fourth, *Hvad är våren?* (*What is the spring?*), the depiction of spring in both the poetry and the music is more heavy-hearted than one might have expected. Formally, *Trånaden*, like *Ljunga Wirginia* two years earlier, is a free fantasy. It is uncertain whether the recitation was intended to accompany the music or, as Erik Tawaststjerna suggested, to be heard in alternation (it would be hard for a speaker to be heard above many of the louder pages). It must be admitted that the music is uneven but, at its best, it is both inventive and memorable – an impressive gift indeed for Mrs Wilenius.

Ina Wilenius was also the dedicatee of a much simpler piano piece written that summer, *Au crépuscule*, JS 47, an F sharp minor souvenir in lied form. This is one of the few instrumental miniatures from Sibelius's early period to bear a descriptive title, though it is hard to find any specific 'twilight' association in the music itself. It was presumably also around this time that Sibelius made the harmonically more advanced solo piano version – *Andante in E flat major*, JS 30a – of the piece for harmonium and piano that he had written a few months earlier in Lovisa. An [*Aubade*] *in A flat major*, JS 46, completes Sibelius's output of solo piano music from Korpo; its date can be confirmed from sketches for the finale of the 'Korpo' Trio on the same manuscript.[9]

Ruth Ringbom, too, received a souvenir from Sibelius: the *Andante cantabile in G major* for violin and piano, JS 33, an attractive miniature in lied form that is technically not too challenging. Another work for violin and piano, an [*Andante elegiaco*] *in F sharp minor* shares not only its key but also its atmosphere – described by Folke Gräsbeck as one of 'remote, Slavic melancholy' – with *Au crépuscule*, but the violin piece remained incomplete: the manuscript breaks off at the beginning of a waltz-like trio section in A major.

An *Andante molto in F minor* for cello and piano, JS 36, was written for Christian and can probably also be dated to the summer holiday; it may be the piece to which Christian referred in a letter as 'a consertino [*sic*] for cello'.[10] This exceptionally well-crafted piece is longer than most of Sibelius's souvenirs, and the virtuoso writing in the cadenza-like middle section – anticipating the later cello piece *Malinconia* – shows that Christian must by then have been a proficient player. Further evidence of this comes in the [*Theme and Variations*] *in D minor* for solo cello, JS 196, Sibelius's largest surviving work in variation form and in all probability the first Finnish work for solo cello. A brief introduction leads to the theme itself, which has the character of a berceuse, and subsequently passes through seven variations and a coda which range from neo-baroque to virtuosic in character. A third cello piece from Korpo, the *Tempo di valse in G minor*, JS 193, is sadly incomplete: only a sketched cello part survives. Shortly after the holidays, Sibelius wrote to Pehr of his plans to have a 'Walse fantastique' (*sic*!), Op. 1, performed by the cello virtuoso Jaromír Hřimalý, who was making a concert tour of Finland that 1887; it is quite possible that the G minor waltz was the piece to which he was referring. As far as we know, however, Hřimalý did not perform Sibelius's piece.

The same letter to Pehr contains a reference that seems rather strange: 'When my big trio is eventually performed, it will take place with tableaux, because otherwise it cannot be understood.' This is almost certainly a reference to the 'Korpo' Trio, but no traces of a programme for this work have survived (and, at least for a modern listener, nor are they necessary).

It is possible that the *Serenata*, JS 169, and the *Minuet and Allegro*, JS 128, for two violins and cello, were intended to belong together – perhaps as the last three movements of a piece for which the first movement was never composed (in which case the presence of a link passage between the *Minuet* and *Allegro* would serve as further testimony to Sibelius' structural experimentation, though it is considerably simpler than the corresponding passage in the 'Korpo' Trio). These substantial movements exploit the string instruments' lyrical qualities, and the technically simple second violin parts suggest that they were intended for Ruth Ringbom. The *Serenata* begins with a densely scored eight-bar introduction, followed by a sensual, Italianate melody, accompanied by cello *pizzicati* that anticipate the beginning of the slow movement of the *Second Symphony*. The *Minuet* is a boisterous, down-to-earth piece, although there is a dramatic change of mood in the trio section, with its drone-like bass line and a startling, cadenza-like flourish from the first violin.[11] After a repeat of the minuet, a brief coda leads into the C major *Allegro*, lusty and tuneful from the first bar to the last.

A [Duo] in E minor for violin and cello, JS 68, was also written in 1887, very possibly during the summer holidays. In this piece, outer sections in a quasi-baroque style frame two brief interludes with a decidedly Mediterranean character.

Sibelius did not spend all of his time composing and playing at Korpo gård itself, but managed to combine music with outdoor activities as well. According to one story he took a trip by rowing boat to visit his childhood friend Gösta Arrhenius at Gunnarsnäs, and played his violin all the way.

In the autumn term Sibelius changed violin teacher. His new tutor was a temperamental Hungarian, Hermann Csillag, who earned Sibelius's respect as a 'first-rate violinist and excellent teacher' with 'a large and broad tone. His technique is very assured and his playing, crystal clear.'[12]

Socially, too, Sibelius was beginning to spread his wings. His association with the young Armas Järnefelt, who joined the Music Institute in the autumn (like Sibelius, he had turned to music after initial law studies), was to prove especially fortuitous. They became close friends, and Sibelius soon accepted his new colleague's invitation to visit his home and family. It was not just that Armas was the son of a general and therefore a member of a distinguished and prominent family – although this must have impressed Sibelius, who for many years nurtured the hope that his own family might have had noble antecedents. The Järnefelt family were high achievers and were known for Fennoman tendencies – a robust advocacy of the Finnish language and of specifically Finnish culture: apart from Armas, who made a name for himself as a composer and conductor, two of his brothers became illustrious representatives of their chosen genres – Arvid as a writer (though at that time he was still studying law) and Eero as a painter. The oldest brother, Kasper, became a teacher and translator. All of them were to play a significant role in Sibelius's life. But, more importantly, they had a young and beautiful sister, Aino.

According to a later account by Armas Järnefelt, Sibelius and Aino met on Jean's first visit to the Järnefelt family home. Aino happened to be listening to the young men playing music (she herself even remembered dancing to it). Her presence made Sibelius nervous and he made a mistake. He jumped up to apologize; their eyes met, and they immediately fell in love.

On the face of it the Järnefelts were unlikely champions of the Fennoman cause. Lieutenant-General Alexander Järnefelt was a career soldier who had served in the war between Russia and Turkey in 1877–78. In the 1880s he had been governor of the province of Mikkeli and later of Kuopio, and in November 1888 assumed the same position in Vaasa on the west coast. Not far from Vaasa the family acquired a grand summer house by the sea,

Tottesund Manor, which had been built in 1800 and boasted a (reputedly haunted) formal garden modelled on that of Versailles. Sibelius described the General's character as 'grave, haughtily reserved, a thorough aristocrat in his zeal for the Finnish people'.

His wife Elisabeth came from a prominent Baltic artistic family; she had grown up in St Petersburg, and Russian – not Finnish – was her first language. She was 'lively, friendly, liberal-minded, full of sympathy for the lower classes…, devoted to literature and art', welcomed her sons' free-thinking friends into her home and later developed an enthusiasm for Tolstoy. Between 1859 and 1875 she bore nine children, four sons and five daughters, although the youngest two died very young and the oldest of the girls, Liida, had died in 1885 at the age of 19. The family had set up home at Mikonkatu 17 in central Helsinki. Sibelius noticed that Alexander and Elisabeth were very different; in fact they had by then grown irreconcilably apart, with contrasting interests and attitudes. Aino evidently enjoyed a good relationship with both of her parents (indeed she sometimes served as a mediator between them) but they did not offer her the same opportunities for higher education that her brothers had enjoyed.

In the Järnefelt brothers Sibelius found congenial and talented companions who shared and in many ways helped to fashion his own cultural outlook. His contacts with them paved the way for his exploration of the potential of Finnish culture and of the *Kalevala* in his music. At this time Arvid was collaborating with the writer Johannes Brofeldt (better known as Juhani Aho, a name he adopted in 1907; like Sibelius, he took a fancy to Aino Järnefelt, but unlike him he also took an interest in her mother Elisabeth!) and the journalist Eero Erkko with the aim of establishing a Finnish-language newspaper, which eventually came into being with the name *Päivälehti*. They could not have realized at this stage how significant an impact Sibelius's music would have on their cause.

If Sibelius had misled Erik Furuhjelm by a year or two concerning the dates of the *Trio in A minor* and *Piano Quartet in D minor*, he was even further from the truth when discussing a piece he called 'Sonata' in D minor, which he claimed to have composed in 1881–83. This work is now known as the *Suite in D minor*, JS 187. With its six short movements, none of which is in sonata form, it is certainly not a sonata in the conventional, classical mould. Stylistically the piece is far more advanced than his other music from 1881–83, and Kari Kilpeläinen's analysis of the handwriting and paper used has shown that the suite was probably written in 1887–88. By that time Sibelius had produced enough large-scale chamber pieces to know what he would feel justified in calling a sonata. So why, almost three decades later, did he apparently provide such misleading information to Furuhjelm? Presumably – feeling safe in the knowledge that the suite would not be performed in the foreseeable future – Sibelius permitted himself some latitude with the truth in order to give the impression that he had been more of a youthful prodigy than had in fact been the case. Furuhjelm was not so easily deceived, however: he states that the work is 'not a sonata in the real sense, but a skilfully prepared melody cycle of modest proportions'. Some years later, indeed, the composer himself added the title 'Suite' to the manuscript.

Much of the weight of the *Suite in D minor* is concentrated in its outer movements, which are longer and more serious in tone than the others. The first movement has a gentle melancholy that is intensified by the violin playing *con sordino*, whilst the last is a virtuosic display piece with a brief, intense trio. Of the inner movements – all in major keys – two are stylized dances. The third movement is a hauntingly beautiful (and all too brief) *Andantino*, very much in the style of the souvenirs that Sibelius wrote around 1887. The composer crossed out the entire fifth movement in the manuscript, but reinstating this brief but heartfelt *Moderato* maintains the alternation of slow and fast movements and, arguably, lends greater weight to the suite as a whole.

1888

Jean spent Christmas 1887 and New Year with the von Konows at Lahis gård before returning to the Music Institute. He was now well established as a talented student who enjoyed an active and stimulating social life. This period of his life (1887–89) presents a particular problem when it comes to in determining the chronology of his works – not least because it was extremely productive. Moreover, many of the works are of small scale, or fragments, and give little clue as to their intended purpose. Kari Kilpeläinen's paper and handwriting analyses of Sibelius's manuscripts are invaluable but there are limits to what they can reveal. In the descriptions below, the works are categorized as student exercises, dances (mostly for piano solo), and souvenirs and sketches for independent compositions. Naturally there is some overlap between the groups: some of the student exercises, for instance, are also dances. The souvenirs are often the pieces about which most is known, as information about the dedicatee or circumstances of their origin has sometimes been preserved. Otherwise we can be certain of very little.

The works from the academic year 1888–89 tend to exhibit a growing desire to experiment with larger formal structures. No doubt this can be put down to an increasing level of formal awareness as a result of his studies under Wegelius. The music also *sounds* different: a new fullness and intensity of texture – often seen in passages with 'screaming', long-held notes – becomes a hallmark of Sibelius's chamber pieces from 1889 until 1893. Some of the innocence of Sibelius's earlier music is lost in the process, and it is hard to escape the notion that, in some of the chamber pieces from now until around 1893, the composer's ambitions in formal terms and his new-found focus on sonority had not yet found a comfortable balance with the thematic invention itself. Such a balance would only be fully restored when Sibelius fell under the spell of the *Kalevala* and of Finnish folk music.

Piano music

Student exercises: Among the pieces that can be assumed to be student exercises, some are of very tiny proportions – although the invention and craftsmanship are of high quality. This applies for instance to a *Tempo di Menuetto in F sharp minor*, an *Allegro in E major*, a surprisingly deeply felt [*Moderato*] *in F minor* (with a falling fifth at the end of the phrases, a characteristic use of triplets and unmistakably Sibelian harmonies), a playful *Vivace in E flat major* and an *Andantino in C major* with syncopated accompaniment and echoes of Grieg in both melody and harmony. All five are believed to date from 1888 and are found in the same manuscript.[13]

Three more, slightly longer pieces are found in a single manuscript from the same year.[14] For a student exercise, the *Andantino in B major*, JS 44, exhibits great delicacy and refinement, its melody lent special poignancy by the flattened mediant (G natural) in the second and third bars. Neither this nor its companion piece, the gently lilting *Allegretto in B flat minor*, JS 18, would sound out of place alongside Sibelius's piano miniatures from the period of the First World War. Sibelius crossed out the last piece, a tempestuous *Allegro in F minor* that might have been planned as an experiment with piano sonorities and the use of grace notes.

The *Largo in A major*, JS 117 (1888) and the slightly Elgarian *Adagio in D major*, JS 11 (1888), have the character and proportions of sonata movements, and were presumably composed for Wegelius; the same applies to the rondo-form *Vivace in D minor*, JS 221 (1888), which features tarantella rhythms, though of a more cultivated, polite character than in *Ljunga Wirginia* three years earlier. A C minor [*Interludium*] (1888), found in a manuscript that otherwise contains violin compositions,[15] sounds like an introduction to the following [*Maestoso*], to which it is motivically related (they are moreover in the same key). An academic purpose can likewise be assumed for [*Three Fugue Expositions*] *in D minor* (1888–89). The fugue theme itself is the same in each of these three fragments, and not dissimilar to that of Bach's *Fugue in A minor*, BWV 865, from *The Well-Tempered Clavier*, Book I.

Dances: A [*Waltz*] *in E major* (1888) begins promisingly, then changes character and becomes a mazurka. The *Più lento–Tempo di valse*, JS 150 (1888), is more substantial; after its slow introduction there are several sparkling waltz sections in a Viennese style. A separate but obviously related [*Waltz, Fragment*] *in F minor* (1888) is presumably a rejected *minore* section intended for the same piece. The *Allegretto in G minor*, JS 24 (1888), is also in 3/4 but its rhythmic patterns are closer to the style of a mazurka. A wholly different type of dance idiom is explored in the irrepressible Viennese-style [*Polka in E flat major*], JS 75 (1888–89) – Sibelius at his most exuberant.

Souvenirs and sketches: In the *Moderato–Presto*, JS 133 (1888), we find extreme contrasts between the Bach-like solemnity of the *Moderato* and the sudden flurries of energy in the *Presto* sections. The constant changes of mood give the piece the character of an improvisation. A turbulent [*Allegro, Fragment*] *in E major* (1888) breaks off after just six bars, and was probably a sketch for the song *Upp genom luften* (*Up through the air*), JS 213, for mixed choir and piano.

Works for chamber ensemble

Student exercises: Not having written a string quartet work of any magnitude since the *Quartet in E flat major* in 1885, Sibelius seems to have followed Wegelius's principles and started with short pieces. A manuscript believed to date from 1888[16] includes a group of three such miniatures alongside various sketches for string quartet. Both the *Alla marcia in E minor*, JS 16, and the *Presto in F major*, JS 154, are in lied form without trio. The *Alla marcia* is essentially a robust, confident piece (its opening *pizzicati* anticipate the *Polka* from the *Suite mignonne* of 1921) but both the melodic shape and rhythmic pattern from the first violin in the seventh and eighth bars foreshadow the slow movement of the *Fourth Symphony*. The high-spirited *Presto* contains some characteristic Sibelian triplets but it is the third piece in the group, the *Theme and Variations in G minor*, JS 197, that is the most ambitious. The theme itself (first violin) is an unpretentious idea, eight bars in length. Even in this rather short piece, Sibelius can find ample contrast of texture and mood despite retaining both the key of G minor and the 2/4 time signature in all five variations.

The [*33 Small Pieces*] for string quartet (1888–89) find Sibelius at his most uninhibited – surprisingly so in view of their presumed status as exercises. In some ways this set can be seen as a pendant to the [*Catalogue of Themes, 50 Short Pieces*] for piano from 1887 but, whereas some of the piano themes are truly tiny fragments (a mere two bars), even the shortest of the quartet pieces has a clearly defined musical personality. The set is a collection of sketches, character pieces and dances, ranging in length from 8 to 22 bars. The seventh of the set sounds almost like Dvořák (*American Quartet*), whilst No. 12 anticipates Prokofiev (*Romeo and Juliet*), and No. 20 is a miniature funeral march. The charming grace notes of No. 21 found an echo many years later in the fourth movement of *Voces intimae*. The second half of No. 32 contains a rhythmic motif on a repeated note that would recur in several larger-scale works[17] and can be seen as a triple-time variant of the trumpet idea in the *Allegro* section of *Finlandia*. Naturally there is no significant thematic development in these tiny pieces, but on the whole they sound delightfully spontaneous, and most of them have such infectious melodies that it is astonishing that Sibelius did not re-use them in larger works. Only occasionally does the young composer misjudge the medium – such as in No. 30, a rather noisy march which, with its multiple stoppings in the violins and viola, seems to reach an uneasy compromise between folk music and quasi-orchestral sonority.

Souvenirs, single movements and sketches: On 1st February 1888 Jean wrote to uncle Pehr that he had started to compose for string quartet. The previous autumn he and his brother had formed a string quartet together with Richard Faltin (son of the university's director of music) and the violist Ernst Lindelöf. Faltin and Jean took turns as leader, and sometimes also as viola player (Lindelöf would then play second violin). The group met each week at the Sibelius family's Kaivopuisto apartment, in a small top-floor room built, tower-like, on one side of the house. They played quartets by Haydn, Mozart and Beethoven, so it comes as no surprise that Jean should now start to compose for such an ensemble again. It would seem highly probable that the *Allegretto in D major*, JS 20, a charmingly lyrical piece not unlike the character pieces for violin and piano from the period of the First World War, and the *Andantino in C major*, JS 39, which opens with a rising motif on the viola almost identical to the first notes of the *Karelia Overture*, were written for such gatherings. A further indication that the *Andantino* was probably not written as an academic exercise is that it was also incorporated into an unfinished melodrama, *Den lilla sjöjungfrun* (*The Little Mermaid*), which will be discussed in more detail later.

The *Andante–Allegro* for piano quintet, JS 31 (1888–89), is a complete sonata exposition with a generous and very varied selection of themes. Had the movement (or even an entire quintet) been completed, the work would have been on the very grandest scale. Sibelius does not hesitate to demand the maximum possible sonority from his players – a foretaste of the orchestral composer – but also contrasts these stirring outpourings of passion with moments of great intimacy and naïvety. Could this impassioned work really be just a student exercise for Wegelius? Or might Sibelius have abandoned the project because its emotional range was simply too wide?

A significant manuscript[18] gathers together three pieces for string quartet. The first of them is the sonata-form *Allegro in E minor*, JS 28 which, were one to judge from its suspenseful opening chords, could have been written much later in Sibelius's career. The saturated string textures later in the piece, however, fit in with the presumed date of 1889; the piece occupies very much the same stylistic world as the *Andante–Allegro* for piano quintet. Characteristically the triplet figures assume rhythmic and textural importance. The second piece is a relaxed, gently undulating scherzo and trio comprising the *Allegretto in A major*, JS 17, and *Più lento in F major*, JS 149. Finally, in the intense *Adagio in F minor*, JS 14, we find a winding, menacing theme from the first violin and a more chromatic second theme that anticipates the 'Great Hostility' section of the *Press Celebrations Music* of 1899. Later the hushed, restrained writing is reminiscent of Bach.

Among the larger-scale unfinished works from this period is a melodrama for recitation and string quartet, *Den lilla sjöjungfrun* (*The Little Mermaid*), JS 59, to a Swedish translation of the well-known tale (1836) by Hans Christian Andersen. Only a first violin part for the first four sections survives, with some indications of the associated text passages. Sibelius evidently planned to write the piece as a series of musical episodes. The violin part shows that the second and third sections were almost identical to quartet pieces that have survived in other manuscripts. A comparison of *Den lilla sjöjungfrun* with the 'source' works reveals a number of mostly small differences of tempo, dynamics, phrasing and pitch – some of them clearly designed to prevent the narration becoming inaudible over the instruments. The second section, a scherzo and trio, corresponds to the *Allegretto in A major* and *Più lento in F major* discussed above,[19] although the *Allegretto* is here marked *Vivace*. The text for this part of the work started with: 'All day long they played in the great halls of the castle, or among the living flowers that grew out of the walls...', and the music is admirably suited to depict the mermaids at play. Otherwise the music seems to have little direct connection with the narrative, which suggests that Sibelius reused the separate pieces in the melodrama rather than vice versa, although there is no documentary evidence to prove which came first. The third section of *Den lilla sjöjungfrun*, accompanying the text starting from: 'She was a strange child, quiet and thoughtful', was based on the *Andantino in C major*, JS 39, a work provisionally dated to 1887–88. In the first violin part for the first and fourth sections there are some surprisingly exotic moments, and we can observe some of Sibelius's rhythmic and melodic trademarks. The lack of lower parts, however, makes it impossible to form an overall opinion of these passages. The fourth section is quite short and, moreover, breaks off abruptly. The first four episodes alone would play for some ten minutes, and cover only the first few pages of the story. The tale in its entirety would thus have required a composition of vast length. Perhaps it was in recognition of this that Sibelius put it aside.

During his study years in Helsinki Sibelius seems to have been content to write separate movements, albeit substantial ones, rather than combining them to form a full-size, multi-movement quartet. Pride of place among these separate movements goes to the magnificent *Moderato–Allegro appassionato in C sharp minor* for string quartet, JS 131, from 1888–89. This sonata-form piece, complete with slow introduction, plays for more than ten minutes and has a breadth and integrity that rival the first movement of *Kullervo*; indeed, the vivid and intense main theme of the quartet piece seems to anticipate the first theme of *Kullervo* in rhythmic and melodic shape (long opening note, rapid rising motif, slowly descending melody towards the end of the phrase). The second thematic group, by contrast, is more lyrical. The *Moderato–Allegro appassionato* is full of Sibelius's trademarks: triplets, short–long–short syncopations and dotted rhythms on the last beat of the bar. There are also clear hints of his Symbolist music of the 1890s, for instance in the rising and falling motif of a fourth heard from the second violin at the start of the main theme – a detail that adds characteristic colour to later works such as *The Wood-Nymph* and *Lemminkäinen and the Maidens of the Island*.

If the *Moderato–Allegro appassionato* could have been the first movement of a full-scale quartet, the *Andante molto sostenuto in B minor*, JS 37 (1888–89), could well function as the slow movement of such a work. It is an expressive and sometimes extremely poignant piece in rondo form, rich in thematic inspiration. The *Andante–Allegro molto in D major*, JS 32 (1888–89) sounds like an attempt to write a rondo finale. The first motif of the five-bar long *Andante* introduction is taken up again as the main theme of the *Allegro molto*. Later the piece features a rhythmic idea to which Sibelius would return, in slightly modified form, both in the *Coronation Cantata* and, many years later, in the finale of the *Third Symphony*. The relationships between the keys of the quartet pieces, however, make it unlikely that they were planned for the same work.

An [*Allegro*] *in G minor* for string quartet from 1888–89[20] starts out boldly; Sibelius presents thematic material with great potential for development. After just a few bars of this sonata exposition, however, he seems to lose interest and rapidly writes a conclusion.

Solo instrument [and piano]

Student exercises: A [*Sonata Allegro Exposition*] *in B minor*, JS 90, for violin and piano is believed to date from the autumn term of 1887 and to be an exercise for Wegelius. Stylistically this dating is very plausible: the triplet sequences and certain cadences in the violin part call to mind works from a few months earlier such as the *Minuet and Allegro* for string trio and even the *'Korpo' Trio* itself. The writing is conspicuously elegant, although the thematic invention itself is not especially memorable.

A [*Menuetto*] *in E minor*, JS 67, for violin and piano, in rondo form, is more of a stylized concert piece than most of Sibelius's minuets from this period, with a rustic episode and a dreamy passage in 2/4. Although provisionally dated to 1886–87, it most probably comes from the latter part of that period, the autumn of 1887, as its manuscript source [21] also contains a 40-bar wordless sketch for an *a cappella* mixed choir setting of *Credo in unum Deum*. This is an early vocal counterpoint exercise; the majority of Sibelius's experiments in this genre probably date from 1888.

A manuscript from 1888 [22] contains pieces with a baroque flavour. Two of them are for violin and piano, framing a short sketch for solo piano. The *Moderato–Maestoso in E flat major*, JS 132, is memorable for its long-breathed, stately melody, and a similar dignified quality is shared by the [*Maestoso*] *in C minor*. In Timo Koivusalo's biographical film *Sibelius* (2003) this sketch was transcribed for string quartet and used as an illustration of Sibelius's student works that were performed in Helsinki. Attractive though it is, however, this baroque-style snippet is in no way representative of either the style or the quality of Sibelius's major compositions from this period.

The later phase of Sibelius's studies in Helsinki is well illustrated by the *Allegro in A minor* for violin and piano, JS 26 – a large-scale sonata exposition, most of the weight of which is concentrated in the first theme with its violent outbursts and frenetic energy. One might well regard this torso as a forerunner of the first movement of the *Sonata in F major*, JS 178, that was completed in the summer of 1889.

Souvenirs and sketches: As the violin was Sibelius's own instrument it comes as no surprise that he continued to compose music that was most likely intended for his own use throughout his student period. In the case of the two pieces preserved in a manuscript [23] from 1887–88, however, one suspects another purpose. 'Yesterday I finished the first movement of a cello concerto for Kitti (*à mon frère*). Kitti seems to think there are too few technical bravura passages and difficulties, but in my opinion they sound abominable on the cello whose strong point is precisely its cantilena', Sibelius wrote to uncle Pehr on 31st March 1888. For both the [*Lento*] *in E flat minor*, JS 76, and the *Allegretto in E flat* major, JS 22, cello parts (of earlier provenance) also exist. The pieces sound like fragments of a larger work; the violin versions may therefore be reused sketches for the cello concerto. The dignified solo part of the [*Lento*] is certainly well suited to the cello, as are the elegant Kreislerian flourishes of the *Allegretto*. These pieces are the first examples of Sibelius composing a work for alternative solo instruments; many years later, of course, he would make both the *Serious Melodies*, Op. 77, and the *Four Pieces*, Op. 78, available either for violin or for cello.

Three more cello fragments, all in B minor, can be dated to 1888–89 and may be related to the cello concerto project. The [*Andante*] *in B minor*, JS 91, is believed to be the earliest of these; the cello part is preserved in its entirety, but the beginning of the piano part is lost. The [*Andantino*] *in B minor*, JS 92, features warm, lyrical writing as well as some more march-like ideas; the cello's theme features an 'S-motif'. Unfortunately at least one page is missing from the end of this piece; the manuscript stops just after the introduction of a new, very expressive theme. This same theme occurs in the beautiful *Andante molto in B minor*, which also breaks off before the end (with the addition of one chord, however, it is fully performable). The rapid triplets are a characteristic Sibelian touch, though the rhythm and interval structure of the opening cello theme is reminiscent of *See, the conqu'ring hero comes* from Handel's oratorio *Judas Maccabaeus*, familiar to cellists (and thus presumably also to Christian Sibelius) from Beethoven's *Variations in G major on 'See, the Conqu'ring Hero Comes'*, WoO 45.

In addition, two manuscripts for solo cello have survived – a *Moderato in F major* and a very brief [*Mazurka*] *in G minor*. These were written during the period 1885–89, in all probability for Christian.

The opening of the *Allegretto in C major* for violin and piano, JS 19 (1888), offers the violinist good practice in double stopping, and later the melody soars gracefully aloft. Regular phrase-lengths lend the piece an easy-going atmosphere, whilst the piano has very much an accompanimental function. A stylish [*Tempo di valse*] *in A major* (1888) is probably too short to be a souvenir, and may simply be a thematic experiment.

Vocal and choral music

Student exercises: As part of his studies Sibelius produced a number of contrapuntal exercises and chorale arrangements for mixed choir *a cappella*. There are two settings of *Gloria Deo in excelsis* and one of *Kyrie eleison* as well as several Swedish texts: *Säll är den som fruktar Herren* (*Blessed is he who fears the Lord*), *Allt hvad anda hafver* (*All that has breath*; two versions), *Morgonens och aftonens portar* (*The Gates of Morning and Evening*) and *Svara mig Gud när jag ropar* (*Answer me, God, when I call*). All of these can be dated to 1888.

Souvenirs and sketches: The song with cello and piano *Då världar ännu skapade ej voro* (*When Worlds Still Uncreated Were*), JS 56, is sadly incomplete. We do not even know the name of the text author for this fragment, which is believed to date from 1888; in view of the presence of a cello part, it seems likely that it was written for friends or family, perhaps in Lovisa.

Among the more developed fragments of vocal music we find a 22-bar song sketch with the text *Solen slog himlen röd* (*The Sun Reddened the Sky*)[24] which dates from the academic year 1888/89, as the same manuscript contains a sketch for the slow movement of the *String Quartet in A minor*. Sibelius evidently made better progress with a setting of the Swedish poet Viktor Rydberg's *Höstkväll* (*Autumn Evening*), as sketches and part of a fair copy have survived. Intriguingly, this is musically totally different from the published song composed in 1903. Unfortunately the 1888/89 fragment, in F sharp minor, breaks off after 28 bars; neither the sketches nor the fair copy contain an ending. Either from 1889 or shortly afterwards there is a sketch in A major, some 20 bars long, with the text *Jag kysser dig ej* (*I Shall not Kiss You*).

Among the completed songs from this period we find *Orgier* (*Orgies*), to words by the priest and poet Lars Stenbäck; it is also believed to date from 1888/89 and is a relentless, energetic portrayal of Bacchic revelry. Might Sibelius's choice of text have been influenced by his own early experiences of student drinking bouts in Helsinki? The music is certainly manic enough to suggest that its creator had personal experience of inebriation. The song was first published in 2005 and, in his preface,[25] Jukka Tiilikainen has pointed out its similarity of topic, melody and rhythm with the aria *Finch' han dal vino* from Mozart's *Don Giovanni*.

It was around this time that Sibelius made his first setting of Rydberg's poem *Skogsrået* (*The Wood-Nymph*). One of the very longest of his songs with piano, the version from 1888–89 is musically unrelated to the later tone poem, melodrama and piano piece. The poem opens with a portrayal of the dashing hero, Björn, who is is led astray by evil forest dwarves. There follows a love scene in which Björn encounters and falls in love with the wood-nymph of the title: this is represented in the song with a coquettish waltz-like idea (though notated in 6/8). In the concluding section, where Björn realizes that he has lost any hope of mortal happiness, Sibelius returns to the musical material of the opening. Although it is to some extent episodic, the song is thematically more unified than the tone poem and moves within a narrower range of tempi.

Also from 1888/89 comes an arrangement of some verses from a long ballad from Pernaja, *Ack, hör du fröken Gyllenborg* (*Ah, Do You Hear, Miss Gyllenborg*, JS 10) for mixed choir *a cappella*. The original poem had been published in 1887 in *Nyländska folkvisor, ordnade och utgifna af Ernst Lagus* (*Folk-songs from Uusimaa, arranged and published by Ernst Lagus*).

In early 1888, having tried his hand at melodramas and also produced contrapuntal exercises, Sibelius was ready to try his hand at solo and choral songs. In January he completed his first song: a *Serenade* to a text by Johan Ludvig Runeberg, JS 167. The impulse may have been provided by Martin Wegelius, who was preparing a new edition of a song book entitled *Det sjungande Finland* (*Singing Finland*), volume 2. When it was issued by K. E. Holm's publishing firm in Helsinki in February 1888, it became the first of Sibelius's works to appear in print. The song has an intimate character and a lilting, barcarole-like metre except in the third strophe, where the simpler melodic line and largely chordal piano writing suggest a more devout atmosphere as the poet's beloved says her prayers.

In the spring of 1888 Wegelius paid his student a great honour: he invited him to help with the composition of incidental music to the 'dramatic runic sorcery' *Näcken* (*The Watersprite*) by Gunnar Wennerberg, premièred at the Music Institute on 9th April. Sibelius's contribution was the second of six musical numbers, a song and recitation in A flat major with piano trio accompaniment (JS 138). In a gently lilting 6/8-time, rather like a siciliano, this piece is much in the style of the souvenirs that he composed for friends and family, but it seems to have been put together with some care: the accompaniment is subtly varied in each verse. A separate fragment for piano trio ([*Allegretto*]) has survived which is stylistically very similar – in the same metre and key – and was very possibly a preliminary version of this piece. The *Näcken* song was favourably received by the critic Richard Faltin, although its effectiveness as a concert piece is undermined by an unexpected shift to D minor at the end – necessary because Wegelius's music continued in that key.

On 17th May Sibelius wrote a piano piece, the *Andantino in E major*,

JS 41, for his friend Adolf Paul, who was a capable player. It is very typical of Sibelius's souvenirs: short (just 41 bars), relaxed in mood, unpretentious and easy to listen to. On the back of the same sheet of paper we find two versions of a jaunty little scherzo-like idea, also for piano. These [*Two Sketches. Presto*] *in A minor*, JS 6, were probably written as exercises for Wegelius.

A few weeks later, on 31st May, Sibelius had another important work to present at the Music Institute: the *Theme and Variations in C sharp minor* for string quartet, JS 195. He regarded this work highly enough to include it in his first sequential list of works in 1896 and in his first opus list from 1897, in both of which it bore the number 1, a position that it retained until 1911. Sibelius played the viola at the première, and his brother Christian was the cellist; the violinists were Jean's teacher Hermann Csillag and his old friend from Hämeenlinna, Anna Tigerstedt. Jean wrote to his uncle Pehr: 'I was applauded and called back almost countless times. It was so unexpected for the large audience to hear a string quartet by a Finn, because no Finn has ever composed anything in this genre.'[26] Richard Faltin in *Nya Pressen* wrote that the piece exhibited 'fine technical ability and notable richness of imagination', and the work certainly consolidated Sibelius's reputation as a composer. Sadly the piece has not survived quite intact but, with some careful ordering of the manuscript pages[27] and the addition of five bars by Kalevi Aho (replacing five lost bars at the beginning of the third variation), it is fully performable – though we cannot discount the possibility that some complete variations have also gone missing. Despite its apparent simplicity, the theme has a brooding quality, a sense of latent energy that is instantly recognizable as Sibelius. It is less austere than a work by the mature composer, but no less eloquent. There are seven variations, centring on the tonic note C sharp/D flat, which display considerable rhythmic and tonal variety.

The performance of the *Theme and Variations* marked the end of term in Helsinki, and Sibelius set off for Lovisa for the summer. This was the first time for some years that the family had been able to use their Lovisa house. Since the death of the composer's grandmother Katarina Sibelius in 1879, aunt Evelina had been renting it out and staying with her brother Pehr in Turku, but now the tenants had moved out. During the summer Jean composed the last of his big trios, the *Piano Trio in C major 'Lovisa'*, JS 208, which has become one of the most frequently played of his chamber works – partly on account of its sparkling thematic invention and its manageable proportions, but more specifically because it was one of the first of his pieces from this period to be rediscovered. In later life Sibelius was notoriously reluctant to allow his early music to be played, but in the case of this piece he even sanctioned a performance at the opening of the

Sibelius Museum in Turku in 1952. Much of the weight of the 'Lovisa' Trio is concentrated in its sonata-form first movement, with its classically elegant main theme and more march-like second group. Despite the broad sweep of its melody, the slow movement is relatively concise; a brief fugal passage is perhaps a nod in the direction of academicism. As in the 'Korpo' Trio from the previous summer, Sibelius links the slow movement and finale of the 'Lovisa' Trio with a transitional passage. These link passages are early examples of the formal ambiguity and compression that would characterize much of Sibelius's later work, finding their ultimate manifestation in the Seventh Symphony. In the case of the 'Lovisa' Trio, the transition leads into an exhilarating concluding rondo.

From Sibelius's surviving sketches it is apparent that he worked on the 'Lovisa' Trio and the Suite in E major for violin and piano, JS 188, at the same time, and the suite likewise contains link passages between all four of its movements. The suite is one of the sunniest of his early works, with melodic invention that is of a consistently high quality throughout, and calls to mind the virtuoso pieces of composers such as Bériot and Vieuxtemps; by then Sibelius had already performed music by both. The first movement is lively and Mendelssohnian, and some of its thematic material is closely related to ideas from the previous year's 'Korpo' Trio. The transition at the end of the movement takes the form of a cadenza. Sibelius had already experimented with the use of a violin cadenza to link two movements in Ljunga Wirginia from 1885. After the bravura showmanship of the second movement, the wistful third movement has the character of a slow waltz. The finale is a dazzling polonaise, though not without more thoughtful passages. Although it would seem probable that Sibelius wrote the Suite in E major as a vehicle to display his own technical ability, we do not know whether or not he ever performed it.

Ellen Hackzell, who had presented Sibelius with flowers after a concert in Lovisa in 1885, liked to write poetry, and among her works was O, om du sett (Oh, If You Had Seen), which Sibelius turned into a melodrama for speaker and piano (JS 141). It is typical of his souvenirs from this era, civilized in style and modest in aspiration. As lines from the poem do not overlap but instead alternate with instrumental passages (with false endings in the first section and middle section), it is tempting to think that Sibelius merely adapted a piano piece that he had to hand as a gift for his friend.

The busy composing summer in Lovisa also brought forth a solo song, albeit a very brief one – just 22 bars long. With a text by Baeckman, En visa (A Song, JS 71) has the same 9/8 metre as the earlier Runeberg Serenade but its vocal line has a more declamatory character; the closing bars contain an anticipation of Valse triste. The manuscript is marked 'Minne af J. S.' ('Souvenir of J. S.') but the recipient's identity is unknown.

Back in Helsinki for the autumn term, Sibelius still had new musical genres to explore. Having tried his hand at contrapuntal exercises for choir, he was now ready to write independently for the medium. The Nordic countries have a strong choral tradition, and in Finland choral music was very much an up-and-coming genre in the 1880s. Predictably, a clear division emerged between Finnish and Swedish speakers, and Sibelius followed Wegelius's lead by composing pieces to Swedish texts. The earliest of his choral songs date from 1888, and are mostly for mixed choir *a cappella*. With its rocking 6/8 metre and a melody tinged with sadness, *Ensam i dunkla skogarnas famn* (*Alone in the Depths of the Forests*), JS 72, is a stylish setting of a poem by Emil von Qvanten. Its theme – a solitary wanderer in a nocturnal forest – is just the sort of topic that appealed to Sibelius.

Emphatic dotted rhythms characterize three Runeberg settings for mixed choir. The strophic song *När sig våren åter föder* (*When Spring Once More Comes to Life*), JS 139, and *Tanke, se hur fågeln svingar* (*Imagine, See how the Bird Swoops*), JS 191, have rather similar thematic material, but the latter has less homophonic choral writing. The third setting, *Hur blekt är allt* (*How Pale is All*), JS 96, is also strophic; one wishes that the last verse had a more effective ending. It is surprising that Sibelius did not respond with more sensitivity to Runeberg's atmospheric description of an autumn evening; he is far more responsive to the text in *Upp genom luften* (*Up through the Air*), JS 213 for mixed chorus with piano, which is found in the same manuscript source.[28] The words come from the fairy-tale play *Lycksalighetens ö* (*The Island of Happiness*; 1824) by Per Atterbom. Although no records of a performance there have survived, the piece may have been intended for use at the Music Institute.

During the autumn term Sibelius met Ferruccio Busoni, who had been engaged from the autumn of 1888 until 1890 as a teacher of piano at the Music Institute. Despite his pre-eminence as a rising star among international piano virtuosi, Busoni was in fact slightly younger than Sibelius, and the two became close friends, meeting up at Ericson's café or the Hotel Kämp. 'My acquaintance with Busoni was most stimulating to me. In one respect we were as unlike each other as possible. Busoni had grown up as an infant prodigy and had spent his youth in hotels in practically every town in Europe. He came into contact with nature for the first time in Finland. In the early stages of our acquaintance he was surprised by the great benefits I was able to draw from my communing with nature. Later he understood me better.' Together with other pupils at the Institute – such as Adolf Paul and Armas Järnefelt – Sibelius and Busoni formed a social group that frequented Helsinki's restaurants and was known as the Leskovites, named after Busoni's dog, Lesko.

1889

Sibelius also continued to play the violin, and in early 1889 even played as a soloist with the Academic Orchestra in Beethoven's *Romance in F major*. But his fledgling career as a concert violinist was already as good as over. In April 1889 he fell ill: ever the hypochondriac, he believed himself to be dying. As he convalesced at home, at the Kaivopuisto villa, he had an opportunity to take stock of his life so far, and felt unsatisfied with his achievements. In his heart of hearts he now realized that his ambition to become a virtuoso violinist was unrealistic. Nonetheless he did not withdraw entirely into himself. When Adolf Paul brought him an armful of yellow roses, Sibelius was not slow in returning the favour: on 22nd April he composed a piano suite, *Florestan*, JS 82, for his friend. The Schumannesque title does not imply, however, that this suite displays the forceful, extrovert side of the composer's character. In fact, apart from some passages in the inner movements, it is essentially meditative and lyrical – indeed, not far removed in mood and idiom from the *Andantino in E major* that Sibelius had composed for Paul eleven months previously. A degree of cyclical unity is achieved, as the last movement reuses melodic material from the first. Many years later Adolf Paul described *Florestan* as 'one of the most beautiful and most atmospheric works ever produced by the young Sibelius. And he dedicated it to me – for an armful of roses. And thereby he gave me the most precious of my youthful memories'. *Florestan* is among the best-known of Sibelius's early piano works; its first modern performance was given by Izumi Tateno during the Järvenpää Sibelius Weeks in December 1996.

Sibelius himself provided prose descriptions of the four movements:

    I. Florestan goes out into the forest. He is dejected and unhappy. Scents of wild moss and wet bark.

    II. Florestan comes to a cataract whose foaming waters are transformed before his eyes into water-nymphs. Scents of water-lilies.

    III. One of the water-nymphs has moist, black eyes and golden yellow hair. Florestan falls in love with her.

    IV. Florestan tries to entice her to him, but she disappears. Dejected and unhappy, Florestan returns through the forest.

In February 1889 Wegelius recommended Sibelius for a state scholarship, noting his 'formal skill... matched by a genuine musical impulse, a lively inventive capacity together with a rich and inventive fund of inspiration', and praising his string quartet writing in particular. It is extremely unlikely that Sibelius would have shown his teacher the *String Quartet in E flat major* that he had written before arriving in Helsinki. Wegelius's remark must therefore have been based on the separate movements that had been composed during the previous terms and what he had seen of the *String Quartet in A minor*, which would at that stage have been nearing completion. At any rate the recommendation had the desired effect: Sibelius was awarded 2,000 marks to pursue his composition and violin studies abroad.

The last two major works of Sibelius's study period in Helsinki were a *Suite in A major, for Violin, Viola and Cello*, and the above-mentioned *String Quartet in A minor*.

It is hard to summon up much enthusiasm for the *Suite in A major*, JS 186, which was written as an exercise for Wegelius and has elements of pastiche about it. Of its five original movements, only four are playable today: the violin part of the fourth movement, *Air*, is lost. The rapid first movement, *Prélude*, has an insipid texture and wan colour. At least, however, it contains recognizably Sibelian rhythmic patterns and, at the solemn rising scale figure in bars 49 and 57, a flash of true feeling. The concluding *Gigue* seems merely to be treading water and must be ranked as one of Sibelius's most forgettable movements. In between we find a considerably more elegant *Andante con moto* movement, and a heavy, uninspired *Menuetto* with a particularly clodhopping main motif (although, admittedly, the trio section is more sensitively written). The suite was premièred on 13th April by Hermann Csillag, Karl Fredrik Wasenius (for many years a feared critic with the pen name 'Bis') and Wilhelm Renck. Many years later Busoni called the suite 'far more than a student work', but he made this statement in an article for the Swiss press in 1916 and so an element of hyperbole concerning what was by then an unknown piece is to be expected. Karl Flodin was positive but also observed that it lacked melodic inspiration.

A separate *Andantino in A major* for string trio, JS 38, was probably intended as an alternative first movement for the *A major Suite*, as its manuscript bears the word 'Preludio' (later crossed out), and its proportions are very similar to those of the movements of the suite. If this was indeed the case, it is a pity that Sibelius changed his mind, as the *Andantino* has an easy-going charm with flowing sextuplets in the violin and viola above a drone bass from the cello.

The *String Quartet in A minor*, JS 183, on the other hand, does mark a significant milestone, combining the freshness and vigour of his summer compositions from the previous few years with technical advances that point clearly towards his mature style. The slow introduction to the first movement, for instance, although notated in 6/4-time, is liberated from the constraining influence of the bar-line to the extent that it becomes impossible for the listener to tell what metre it is in. The music has the mood of a pleasant daydream, from which one awakes abruptly at the start of the main *Allegro* with its energetic and thrusting main theme, propelled forward by insistent semiquaver runs and dotted rhythms. The idea that follows has one of Sibelius's favourite rhythmic patterns (short–long–short); Sibelius's characteristic triplets are often present in the background. Structurally the movement is in conventional sonata form. As in the 'Korpo' Trio the development contains a fugal passage – although, unlike in the trio, this constitutes only part of the development section rather than its entirety. The movement ends with ethereal chords that set the tone for the slow movement, one of Sibelius's beautiful, lilting, barcarole-like pieces reminiscent of the corresponding movement in the 'Hafträsk' Trio. The scherzo is also in the style of Sibelius's earlier music, a descendant of the scherzo in the *Piano Quartet in D minor* but with a more determined, Beethovenian cast. For the first time in a major work, Sibelius writes two trio sections, although he had previously written independent pieces with two trios, for instance the *Scherzo in E minor* for piano quartet. The second trio is another example of the rhythmic freedom found in the first movement's introduction. The finale begins with a lively fugal idea based on an anapaestic rhythm (and thus related to a subsidiary motif from the first movement), whilst its second theme – a sort of inverted form of the main theme of the slow movement of the *Fourth Symphony* – is more lyrical. The work gathers intensity and speed to an overwhelming final climax, the anapæsts becoming ever more dominant until they end the work in a defiant blaze.

The *String Quartet in A minor* almost had to make do with a much less suitable finale. For this purpose Sibelius originally wrote a loud and rather unremitting fugue based on a daring but ugly theme featuring a descending ninth, a rising scale figure and much syncopation. This charmless movement has plenty of physical excitement but sounds far too much like an academic exercise to serve as a convincing finale for the quartet. Indeed, it was once believed to be nothing more than an exercise, because Sibelius marked the manuscript 'Fuga för Martin W'; research by Kari Kilpeläinen has revealed its original objective. Nowadays, as a result of Sibelius's marking, the piece is now known as the *Fugue for Martin Wegelius*, JS 85.

The première of the *String Quartet in A minor* took place on 29th May and was given by the same players who had performed the *A major Suite* – Csillag, Wasenius and Renck – plus Wilhelm Santé as second violinist. This performance marked Sibelius's graduation from the Helsinki Music Institute, and fortunately it was very well received. This was the occasion that caused Flodin to make his often quoted claim that Sibelius had 'with one stroke placed himself foremost among those who have been entrusted with bearing the banner of Finnish music'. It was also apparently at this concert that Robert Kajanus became personally acquainted with Sibelius. Kajanus is supposed to have commented that there was no longer any reason for him to compose; thus the seeds of the jealousy that would never be far beneath the surface during their long friendship were sown already at their first meeting!

Around this time there seems to have been a cooling-off in Sibelius's relationship with Aino Järnefelt. In her memoirs *Min Värld* (*My World*), Alma Söderhjelm recalled that 'we were all in love with him'. He was by then regarded very much as an eligible bachelor. Söderhjelm also recounts an anecdote from that summer: Sibelius was supposed to join a group of ladies for coffee. When they were all sitting primly with their coffee and cakes he burst into the salon, went to the piano and began to improvise as though nobody else was present. When he joined his fellow-students and teachers from the Music Institute for an end-of-term visit to the Martin Wegelius's summer villa on Granholmen island (Kuusisaari) on 1st June 1889, Sibelius took a keen interest in a young lady named Alma Tavaststjerna, then aged 18. It was as a souvenir for her that he composed an elegant slow waltz for piano, the *Allegretto in E major*, JS 21.

Summer meant the traditional visit to Lovisa. Sibelius had begun a brief relationship with the daughter of a senator, the twenty-year-old Betsy Lerche. She was a friend of Walter von Konow but might also have have encountered Sibelius at the Music Institute, where she was one of Busoni's piano pupils. On 29th June Sibelius completed a piece for her, the flamboyant *Valse. À Betsy Lerche* in A flat major, JS 1, a Viennese-style waltz with clearly defined episodes.

The main work from this busy summer is the *Sonata in F major* for violin and piano, JS 178, on which Sibelius had started work before leaving Helsinki. This is one of the most substantial works from his early period and the culmination of his early output for violin and piano. In this piece he continues to develop the essentially elegant, classically influenced style found in his music from the early and mid-1880s, in the direction of a more adventurous, Romantic idiom.

In a letter from Sibelius to his uncle Pehr (6th July 1889) he describes the sonata in some detail, and even suggests a partial programme for it: 'the first movement, 2/4 in F major, is fresh and daring as well as gloomy with some brilliant episodes; the second movement, A minor, is Finnish and melancholy; it is an authentic Finnish girl who sings on the A string; then some peasant lads perform a Finnish dance and try to entice her to smile, but it doesn't work; she only sings with greater sadness and melancholy than before. The third movement, 3/8, F major, is fresh and spirited as well as romantic. There are people in a meadow singing and playing on Midsummer Night. Meanwhile, a meteor falls down among them. They are amazed, but even continue playing, but not as readily as before because everyone is more serious. At the end the mood becomes splendid but gloomy [the meteor!] and also playful and happy.'

The *Sonata in F major* anticipates Sibelius's major works in the Symbolist style of the 1890s while still retaining elements of the classical forms and folk-influenced character often found in his chamber works from the late 1880s. The melody of the 'Finnish girl who sings' in the slow movement is often said to resemble a theme from *En saga*, but in fact it is even more closely related to a motif from the later orchestral song *The Rapids-Rider's Brides*. Sibelius gave the sonata its successful first performance at a charity soirée in Lovisa on 16th July. The work's first modern performance took place at the Kuhmo Chamber Music Festival in July 1994.

In the summer of each year since 1886, Sibelius had composed a major work for piano trio. 1889 was to be the year in which this tradition was broken: he did begin such a piece, but abandoned it before reaching the end of the first movement. We do not know what caused him to abandon the trio, but it cannot have been the quality of the music, as the surviving torso – an [*Allegro*] *in D minor* – has impressive concentration and energy. In 2002 Kalevi Aho composed a concert ending for the movement.

A brief *Canon* in G minor for violin and cello, JS 50, saw the light of day on 13th June. This technically very straightforward minuet was presumably written for private use.

A more significant piece from the same period is the *Overture in F minor* for *torviseitsikko* (brass septet). Although small brass ensembles were not a new phenomenon, the *torviseitsikko* (E flat soprano cornet, two B flat cornets, E flat althorn, B flat tenorhorn, B flat euphonium, E flat bass and percussion) is a specifically Finnish instrumental combination that traces its immediate roots back to 1870, when such a group was founded as a military ensemble by a sergeant, Adolf Leander. Even if it drew inspiration from similar ensembles in Russia, Sweden and Germany, the *torviseitsikko* soon developed its own unique repertoire and gained popularity. Lovisa's volunteer fire brigade had an active *torviseitsikko* and it was almost certainly for this ensemble (directed by the German-born Christian Haupt, a personal friend of Sibelius's who also played the horn in the Philharmonic Society orchestra) that Sibelius composed the overture, which is his longest and most thoroughly worked-out work for brass ensemble. After an imposing *Lento* introduction Sibelius delights in writing sparkling, witty and often agile themes. Apart from ensuring that the writing does not exceed the instruments' practical capabilities, he does not adapt his compositional style when writing for brass rather than string instruments: indeed, some passages could easily and effectively be performed by a string ensemble.

While in Lovisa Sibelius composed several cello pieces for his brother Christian. Foremost among these was a large-scale *Fantasy* in five sections – his most extensive cello piece, running to more than 500 bars in length. The sections have clearly defined characters, including a slowish waltz, an *Alla polacca* and a march, and the themes are characterful and inventive; Christian performed the piece that August. It is most unfortunate that the piano part has been lost; from the surviving cello part we can gain only an imperfect impression of its qualities. At least the '*Lulu*' *Waltz* (or, more pedantically, *Tempo di valse in F sharp minor*, JS 194) from the same period has survived, although the identity of 'Lulu' herself has not. Sibelius wrote this on 19th August. Only 32 bars long, it is a delightfully spontaneous, unstudied miniature – maybe a sketch for the *Fantasy* that assumed an independent existence. Shorter still – a mere 16 bars – is the *Adagio in F sharp minor*, JS 15, which also has the character of a waltz, albeit a very slow one.

Jean also started work on a piano sonata, but the ambitious first movement remained incomplete. In 1999, for performance purposes, Kalevi Aho added a recapitulation to the surviving [*Sonata Allegro Exposition and Development Section*] *in D minor*, JS 179a, a work which has clear stylistic similarities with the *Violin Sonata in F major*.

No doubt spurred on by the success of the *String Quartet in A minor*, Sibelius started work on a new quartet – in B flat major – although he was not to finish it for more than a year. He also began to write a piano sonata in D minor, but abandoned this after composing just 58 bars of the first movement's exposition and development. This torso has the occasional hint of Grieg, and some of its thematic material is closely related to ideas in the *Violin Sonata in F minor*.

CHAPTER 3

BERLIN AND VIENNA: 1889–1891

The wider world beckoned and it was soon time for Sibelius to begin his studies abroad. His destination was Berlin: abandoning a plan to visit his uncle Pehr in Turku, he embarked on the steamer *Storfursten*, bound for Lübeck via Tallinn, on 7th September. Also on board and heading for Berlin was Werner Söderhjelm, later a distinguished professor of philology and literature, who was six years older than Sibelius and had been asked by Wegelius to watch out for him, and Ilmari Krohn, the future composer and musicologist. Söderhjelm was also planning to spend a year in Berlin on a scholarship but his situation was vastly different from that of Sibelius, as he had his wife and two small children with him. Sibelius had not met Söderhjelm before, but he made a good impression: Söderhjelm wrote to his mother that Sibelius was 'a very pleasant and talented young man'. Coincidentally Eero Järnefelt and Juhani Aho, who were en route to Paris, were on the same ship. Sibelius's family and friends gathered to see him off at Helsinki harbour, and a letter that he wrote to Pehr while on board radiates optimism: 'I am burning with desire to hear the most splendid orchestras one can imagine. I will do my utmost to be thrifty with my money.'

Berlin was Sibelius's first taste of life in a major metropolis, and he developed a liking for it that was to last throughout his career. He was to make countless visits to the city, often stopping off there en route to other destinations. He lost little time in making contact with other Nordic artists in Berlin. From Denmark there was the composer and violinist Fini Henriques and the violinist Frederik Schnedler-Petersen, and from Norway the author Gabriel Finne, the pianist Alf Klingenberg and the composer Christian Sinding – who was something of an elder statesman in the group, as he had been born in 1856, the same year as Robert Kajanus, and – like

Kajanus – had already undertaken composition studies in Leipzig under Salomon Jadassohn. Adolf Paul, who had been studying the piano under Busoni in Weimar, soon joined the group as well. From further afield there were also some Americans – the violinist Theodore Spiering and the brother and sister Paul and Geraldine Morgan, who played the cello and violin respectively. The friends performed chamber music together, but also socialized extensively. Student life in the German capital proved to be a decisive, character-forming influence – for better and for worse. Before leaving Finland Sibelius had not mended his relationship with Aino Järnefelt, and he was thus a free agent and so, ignoring his promise to be thrifty, he lived life to the full. In so doing he exhibited the carefree attitude to money that he had inherited from his father.

Once established in Berlin (he initially lodged at Marienstraße 4, but moved in mid-October to Magdeburger Straße 31, where he shared digs with his friends) Sibelius commenced his studies under the respected teacher Albert Becker at the Scharwenka Conservatory. Becker had studied counterpoint and composition under Siegfried Dehn in Berlin in the 1850s, and had taught composition in that city since 1869. He was also a prolific composer, especially of sacred choral music. Among his major works are a *Mass in B minor* (1878 – combining the Latin mass text with instrumental quotations from Protestant hymn tunes) and a *Reformation Cantata* (1883); while teaching Sibelius he was at work on the oratorio *Selig aus Gnade*. The position of respect he held in Berlin musical circles can be judged from the fact that, when he was offered the post of Thomaskantor in Leipzig in 1892, he declined at the wishes of the Kaiser himself; as compensation he was accepted into the Prussian Academy of Arts.

Berlin itself may have brought out new sides to Sibelius's personality, but in terms of his development as a composer it was a period of consolidation rather than advance. He felt that Becker's thorough but pedantic tuition was stifling his creativity and famously called his teacher 'a stuffed shirt from top to toe', but he undoubtedly benefited from the German's academic thoroughness.

An *Allegretto in B flat major* for string quartet, dated 20th September 1889, has a rococo dance character. The coincidence of key leads one to suspect that it may be an abandoned sketch for the *String Quartet in B flat major*.

Becker could not disguise his lack of enthusiasm for what he regarded as Sibelius's more undisciplined compositions, and set him countless contrapuntal exercises. Some of these exercises have survived: there is a group of chorale settings for mixed choir *a cappella*[1] and, more significantly, two chorale settings with orchestral accompaniment – *Herr du bist ein Fels* (*Lord, You are a Rock*) and *Herr erzeige uns deine Gnade* (*Lord,*

Show us your Mercy). These settings date from the autumn of 1889 and are the earliest surviving examples of Sibelius's orchestral writing. In the circumstances it almost goes without saying that the music does not sound much, if at all, like Sibelius. There are two manuscript copies of each chorale (and an unfinished version of *Herr du bist ein Fels* for mixed choir and piano). As there are various small differences between the two, it seems probable that one set was Sibelius's first attempt, and the other incorporates amendments suggested by Becker.

Four attempts at the first movement of a piano sonata (alongside no less than thirteen other, shorter sketches, several of which are related to the sonata attempts) have also survived, presumably from the autumn of 1889 and written for Becker (JS 179b–e). Three of these (in F minor, C major and C minor) are incomplete; of them, the one in F minor is of the greatest interest because it incorporates a theme Sibelius would use the following spring in his *Piano Quintet in G minor*. Another motif, more surprisingly, lay dormant for forty years before resurfacing in the piano piece *Talvikuva* (*Winter Scene*) from Op. 114. The C minor sketch further develops a theme from the unfinished sonata movement in D minor from his summer trip to Lovisa. The remaining sonata movement, in E major, is a virtuoso piece that uses various motifs from a piece for violin and piano, *Romance in B minor*, that he had composed earlier in the year.

One piece from that autumn that was not written for Becker was an *Allegro* for brass septet and triangle, JS 25, Sibelius's entry in a competition arranged by the Finnish Society for Popular Education (Kansanvalistusseura). The competition brief was to write a fantasy on (rather than an arrangement of) a Finnish folk-song, and Sibelius used two such melodies, *Hevonen kuin koirasteeri* and *Tuomi on virran reunalla*. The entry was submitted under the pseudonym '-n-l-s' but failed to secure a prize.

At this period Sibelius was still receiving violin tuition; his teacher in Berlin was Fritz Strauss, an associate of Becker's. By now there was no doubt that composition was his main focus, but his scholarship had been granted partly for violin studies, and he no doubt felt obliged to continue with his lessons.

If his composition lessons from Becker were less than inspirational, the concerts he attended proved something of a revelation. Among the works he heard were Mozart's *Don Giovanni*, Wagner's *Tannhäuser* and *Meistersinger*, Richard Strauss's *Don Juan*, string quartet concerts by the Joachim Quartet and piano recitals by Hans von Bülow. In February 1890 Robert Kajanus arrived from Helsinki to conduct one of his own works, the symphonic poem *Aino*, with the Berlin Philharmonic Orchestra. *Aino*, a fifteen-minute work for male chorus and orchestra, is widely regarded as Kajanus's masterpiece.[2] The first edition of the *Kalevala* had been published in 1835 by the physician Elias Lönnrot, and Kajanus wrote his symphonic poem in 1885 for an event marking its fiftieth anniversary, although curiously the sung text itself is anonymous. Stylistically, like many of Kajanus's works from this period, it owes much to Wagner, but for Sibelius its significance lay rather in the use of the *Kalevala* as inspiration for new Finnish music.

In an attempt to control their expenditure, Sibelius and his friends signed an agreement whereby Schnedler-Pedersen was appointed as guardian for all of their money, with the strict order not to release more than 10 marks at a time. As soon as this system had been set up, Sibelius requested 100 marks. Expensive meals and opera tickets strained his finances, and he soon began to send telegrams home to Finland, asking for more money – much to the consternation of his mother, brother and aunt Evelina. There was worse to come. Within a month of arriving in Berlin Sibelius had confessed in a letter to uncle Pehr: 'I have now already become a real Berliner, although I don't drink beer. The doctors have forbidden it,' and the following month he had to be admitted to hospital. It seems that, in the course of his extravagant social life, Sibelius had contracted some form of sexually transmitted disease, although fortunately he made a full recovery. Adolf Paul later remembered that in Sibelius's group of friends 'women were generously represented. I could never prevent myself from wondering if they were only studying how to flirt, rather than music, singing, violin playing or composition. I hope they all then managed to find a husband.'[3]

Sibelius stayed in Berlin for Christmas, no doubt all too aware that he had produced very little independent music over the past few months. This was the first time he had spent Christmas away from his family; on Christmas Eve he visited the Söderhjelms. Busoni came to Berlin too, and invited Sibelius and Paul to go to Leipzig, where Busoni and the Brodsky Quartet were to play Sinding's *Piano Quintet in E minor*, Op. 5 (1882–84) at the Gewandhaus on 19th January. Somehow Sibelius and Paul – whose financial situation was even more precarious – scraped together enough money for the trip, and Paul later related the almost surreal anecdote: 'It is a mystery to me how we made it to Leipzig and back. Neither of us had a penny to our names, but we managed to stay there for eight days. Throughout the journey the rain came down in torrents. Sibelius's only headgear was a splendid top hat that he had bought in Berlin in Sinding's honour. He wore it all the time. But such a fine top hat is not ideal for keeping the rain off. When we returned to Berlin it almost reminded me of a wet cat. I shall never forget the gentlemanly gesture with which Sibelius gave the battered top hat to the cab driver (second class) who brought us home.'[4]

1890

Shortly after returning to Berlin, Sibelius received bad news from home: his uncle Pehr had passed away in January. It must have saddened the composer profoundly that he could not return to Finland for the funeral of a close relative in whom he had confided so much – 'my Pappa's substitute here on the earth', as he had claimed in a letter some years earlier.

It seems highly probable that the experience of hearing Busoni play Sinding's quintet was the catalyst for Sibelius to start composing with more enthusiasm again, and his next work, which occupied him during the early spring of 1890, was to be the most important new work from his year in Berlin – the *Piano Quintet in G minor*, JS 159. In fact this is without doubt one of the most significant of all his chamber pieces in terms both of duration and of expressive content. It is cast in five movements rather than the traditional four, with an *Intermezzo* placed between the first and the slow movement. Right from the outset – a declamatory, slow introduction, based on an emphatic 'S-motif' – it is evident that Sibelius was aiming here for a tougher, more sombre atmosphere than in most of his earlier chamber music, and this mood is maintained throughout the sonata-form first movement with its characteristic 3/2 metre. Sibelius is quite lavish with his thematic material, and the various thematic ideas are shared between all five instruments with commendable even-handedness; the *tutti* sound is almost orchestral in its colour and richness. Special mention should be made of the whispering chromatic writing in the development section, which has something of the austerity of middle-period Sibelius.

The *Intermezzo* that follows is much more relaxed in mood, with songful melodies and more than a touch of Finnish melancholy. This vein is even more prominent in the hymn-like main theme of the slow movement, which both rhythmically and melodically typifies the folk-influenced themes so common in Sibelius's chamber music from this period. Curiously, this idea turns up again at the other end of Sibelius's career in the surviving sketches tentatively associated with the *Eighth Symphony*! The movement is formally a rondo, and the contrasting theme is another folk-like idea, a major-key march with effective dotted rhythms. Towards the end of the movement Sibelius attempts – not wholly convincingly – to combine the two principal themes.

The restless, mercurial scherzo (*Vivacissimo*) is placed fourth; its trio section in 12/8 time is dominated by a broad, lilting melody. In another context this melody could have made an effective berceuse, but Sibelius here scores it with great weight and intensity. A very fine alternative scherzo (*Vivace*) for the *Piano Quintet* has also survived. Musically this is wholly different from the movement that Sibelius eventually chose; it is a good-humoured, extrovert piece with memorable, attractive themes that are passed between the instruments with great skill. The warmth of the piano theme in the trio section, with its broken chords, belies the common perception of Sibelius as a 'cold' composer. (In his *Serenade for Strings* many years later (1937), the Swedish composer Dag Wirén – who could not possibly have known Sibelius's *Vivace* – produced an opening texture of astonishing similarity.) One can only assume that Sibelius chose not to use this delightful movement because its bright, buoyant character would have clashed with the intense, dramatic tone of the rest of the quintet.

The finale is again generous with its thematic material, and is often very exciting with *sul ponticello* effects, furious piano semiquaver runs and dramatic silences. Sibelius seems to be striving for even larger sonorities than a piano quintet can produce; the very weight of sound in the piano and melody instruments can easily obscure many fascinating details in the inner parts. Moreover, the joins between the various sections are far from invisible. Sibelius must have felt that he had not exhausted the potential of these ideas: the main theme of the movement was to turn up again in a *Rondo* for viola and piano three years later, and a later variant of it was re-used as the theme of the first of the six *Impromptus* for piano, Op. 5. The *Piano Quintet* has outgrown the melodic charm of Sibelius's earlier chamber music but not yet attained the mastery of form of his later work. Nonetheless, it is hard not to admire such an intense and heartfelt work.

Sibelius managed to complete his *Piano Quintet in G minor* in April 1890. Before sending it to Finland, where Wegelius planned to have it performed at one of the Music Institute's concerts, he showed it not only to Albert Becker but also to his friends. Schnedler-Petersen described Sibelius's compositional process that spring in terms that recall the Korpo summer of 1887: 'Sometimes he hid himself away for days on end, and when he came back he normally had a newly composed work to show us. In particular I remember the time he brought his new piano quintet, about which we were all very enthusiastic. We immediately set about playing it through...'[5] One would be curious to know which other works he produced for these gatherings, as nothing else can be dated with precision to the spring term of 1890. A fragment for violin and piano – a [*Largamente*] *in E minor* – might be one of them. This shares its 3/2 metre and some rhythmic features with the first movement of the *Piano Quintet* and the violin part's almost constant double stopping – often in octaves – also resembles the string writing in the quintet. Otherwise we must assume that they were either sketches for later pieces or works that Sibelius subsequently destroyed.

The quintet received its baptism of fire in a concert at the Helsinki

Music Institute on 5th May 1890, while its composer was still in Berlin.
The pianist was Busoni and the first violinist Johan Halvorsen; Karl
Fredrik Wasenius played second violin, Josef Schwartz viola and Otto
Hutschenreuter cello. A shortage of rehearsal time, however, meant that
only the first and third movements could be included, and the second
performance – at the Old Academy Hall in Turku on 11th October with
Adolf Paul as pianist – was also incomplete, as the last movement was
omitted. In fact the finale remained unperformed during the composer's
lifetime; it was first heard in public in 1965. In general the quintet seems
to have been well received, but there was one dissenting voice: Martin
Wegelius, who was especially critical of the first movement's piano writing
and the high register of the cello part, and regretted that all of Sibelius's
'curious whims and fancies' had obscured his 'real self'. But Busoni and
Halvorsen were impressed and, moreover, Sibelius had won the friendship
and trust of Becker, who wrote a sufficiently glowing testimonial to ensure
the renewal of Sibelius's 2,000-mark scholarship for a further year.

It is supposed that *Vi kysser du fader min fästmö här* (*Why Kiss You,
Father, My Sweetheart Here*), JS 218, a setting for female choir and piano
of Runeberg's *Sonens brud* (*The Son's Bride*), was composed in Berlin as
a result of a request from Martin Wegelius, who asked Sibelius for a vocal
piece for the Music Institute. After a bold opening piano flourish, the piece
settles down into a style resembling that of the *Piano Quintet.*

In June Sibelius suffered another bout of ill health, and his family again
sent him money along with the good news about his scholarship. Later that
month he was well enough to travel back to Finland. He arrived penniless,
having spent the last of his money on cigars in Stockholm, but could at
least be sure of a warm welcome in Lovisa, where he spent a week in bed
recovering his strength.

Sibelius may have paid no heed to Aino while he was in Berlin, but she
had certainly not forgotten him. In the summer of 1890 she grew increasingly impatient to see him, especially after they narrowly missed each
other in Helsinki: Sibelius had visited his mother, sister and uncle Otto in
Tampere and did not arrive in the capital until Aino was already on her
way to her family in Vaasa. Before long, in the company of her brother
Armas, Sibelius followed her there. It was on this visit that Aino made her
feelings towards him plain.

We do not know exactly when Sibelius wrote the *Romance in B minor,*
sometimes simply called *Grave,* for violin and piano, Op. 2a, a bolder piece
than most of his shorter violin works. A date of 1890 is probable, as it
reuses a theme from the E major *Sonata Allegro* that Sibelius had written
for Becker; Sibelius revised the *Romance* significantly in 1911. The piano's
dry chords at the beginning, accompanying the violin's sombre lament,

anticipate the end of the third movement of *Kullervo*, although the work ends with a conciliatory shift to the major. This was the piece that he chose to perform when he was taken by Wegelius to meet the distinguished author, journalist, lyric poet and historian Zachris Topelius, whom Sibelius admired greatly (and many of whose poems he was to set). It was Topelius who had written the libretto for Finland's first grand opera, Pacius's *Kung Karls jakt* (*The Hunt of King Charles*; 1852). Unfortunately the meeting did not go altogether smoothly. First of all Sibelius annoyed his host by excluding a number of inquisitive young ladies from the music room. When they went on to discuss literature things went from bad to worse: 'Mention was made of Strindberg, whose books Topelius despisingly called "mere dung", while I could not repress my admiration for *The Red Room*. The old man must have thought that I was tainted with the same disrespectful spirit as the despised Strindberg, for after this I saw clearly that he could not really get on with me.'

A [*Larghetto, Fragment*] *in D minor* for violin and piano may have been planned as an exercise or as an independent work, and has been dated to 1890–92. In view of its stylistic proximity to Sibelius's souvenirs from the late 1880s, I would be inclined to suggest that it was an unfinished example of this genre, perhaps from the summer of 1890.

On 12th June 1890, the Imperial Postal Manifesto transferred responsibility for the formerly independent Finnish postal system to the Russian Ministry of the Interior and, from January 1892, made it mandatory to use Russian stamps on letters to other parts of the Russian empire (the system imposed was complicated: Finnish stamps could still be used for domestic post, and until 1900 remained valid to other international destinations). This was to be one of many measures taken by the Russians to curtail Finland's autonomy during the 1890s and only served to increase the Finns' resentment. Resistance became fashionable, and patriotic soirées became popular social occasions, and in due course Sibelius would play an active part in such events.

For now, however, he had other things on his mind. For a start he decided that his second year of study abroad would be spent in Vienna rather than Berlin. In addition, he had come to realize that his feelings for Aino were as sincere as hers for him. Matters came to a head when Aino arrived in Helsinki from Tottesund later in the summer. After one of the Music Institute's concerts in Helsinki on 29th September Jean proposed, and Aino accepted. Although they decided to keep their engagement secret for the time being, Sibelius permitted himself at least one lavish romantic gesture: when the time came for Aino to leave Helsinki, he ordered her compartment on the train to be filled with flowers.

Sibelius also found time to compose during the summer. At this period of his career his music seemed to be progressing on a parallel but totally separate track from his personal life: the pieces completed in the summer continue the by now impressive series of chamber works from the previous decade, but (as far as one can ascertain) do not allude in any way to his love for Aino: there are no serenades, love songs or other such overt musical declarations of his feelings.

The *Adagio in D minor* for string quartet, JS 12, is essentially a set of variations and was written in Lovisa in the summer of 1890. Its measured main theme describes a tritone, and some of the variations contain a degree of harmonic expressivity that is more often found in Sibelius's mature music, such as the theatre scores for *Ödlan* (1909) and *Everyman* (1916). In characteristic 3/2 metre, the theme has something of the nobility and serenity found in the *Seventh Symphony*. The *Adagio* probably remained unperformed until 1994, when it was played by the Russo Quartet at the Kuhmo Chamber Music Festival. Kari Kilpeläinen has suggested that it may have been intended as a slow movement for the *String Quartet in B flat major* (Op. 4), and points out the lack of a final climax as well as traces of rondo and sonata form within the variation structure.

The *String Quartet in B flat major* was completed in Lovisa in September. It is often assumed that Sibelius thought more highly of this than of his other student works: after all, unlike the others, it bears an opus number. This may be true, but the presence of an opus number is in itself no guarantee of quality: many works from his first period were given opus numbers in provisional lists, only to lose them when the definitive catalogue was compiled.

The *String Quartet in B flat major* continues in the tradition of Sibelius's earlier chamber works rather than reflecting either the rigours of his student exercises for Becker or the wide range of music that he had heard in Berlin. In the first of the four movements, Sibelius separates the opening phrases from the rest of the movement, creating an impression of a 'slow introduction' without actually changing tempo – a result he would achieve again, by more refined means, in the *Sixth Symphony*. For the first time in such a work, Sibelius here dispenses with an exposition repeat (a feature which none of his symphonies has, nor indeed *Kullervo*). Curiously, the opening minutes of the piece are completely lacking Sibelius's trademark triplets, although they appear in abundance later on.

Elsewhere in the work Sibelius continues to consolidate and broaden his expressive range. In the slow movement, for instance, the use of rhythmically complex *pizzicati* in the supporting parts and sometimes very busy textures calls to mind orchestral sonority. The third movement, *Presto*, is often heard separately in Sibelius's later transcription for orchestral strings. The first violin's long note at the beginning is like an 'invitation to the dance', and the piece has an insistent rhythmic energy and virtuosity reminiscent of the earlier *Scherzo in E minor* for violin, cello and piano four hands, JS 165. The beginning of the finale sounds like a distant ancestor of the finale of the *Violin Concerto*, albeit in 4/4 rather than 3/4 time. Motivically, the quartet displays the composer's increasing interest in integration: the opening theme of the first movement contains the germ cell of an undulating motif that plays a crucial role in the finale and, indeed, leads the work to its exquisitely calm and beautiful conclusion.

The *String Quartet in B flat major* was first performed on 13th October at a concert in the Music Institute: the institute's quartet comprised Johan Halvorsen, Wilhelm Santé, Josef Schwartz and Otto Hutschenreuter.

According to a note on the score, the *Andantino and Minuet* for brass septet, JS 45, was composed in Lovisa. It must therefore have been written during the summer of 1890 even though it was not performed until the town's Runeberg festivities on 5th February (Runeberg Day) 1891. The *Andantino* is a gentle, melancholy piece in a flowing 3/4 time, whilst the *Minuet* is brighter, almost in the manner of a mazurka.

Compared with his sojourn in Berlin, Sibelius's study visit to Vienna was a relatively impromptu affair. He set off on 19th October 1890 with vague dreams of being taught by Brahms or Bruckner, but with no predetermined course of study. Busoni had written a letter of introduction to Brahms but it was hardly a glowing recommendation: 'In accordance with his Nordic origins, he has developed later than us.' In consequence Brahms refused even to meet Sibelius. The closing date for applications to the Conservatory had already passed. Private lessons were the only option.

On 12th November, armed with a letter of introduction from Wegelius, Sibelius persuaded Karl Goldmark to be his teacher. Goldmark's tuition was not, however, of the conventional type. Sibelius would present completed works to him for evaluation and comments. No doubt such an intuitive, inspirational method of teaching – more like a consultation than a formal lesson – appealed to a free spirit such as Sibelius, and it would certainly have come as a relief after the previous year of academic toil under Becker. On its own, though, it was not enough, and even Sibelius admitted: 'I need a teacher who is less of a genius.'

On the recommendation of Hans Richter, no less, Sibelius also managed to secure private lessons from Robert Fuchs, who also taught at the Conservatory, and conducted its orchestra. He was thus in good company: Fuchs also taught such diverse figures as Mahler, Korngold, Franz Schmidt, Wolf and Zemlinsky, not to mention the Finnish composer Erkki Melartin almost a decade after Sibelius. Few specific details are known of Sibelius's lessons with him, but it seems clear that Fuchs, both as a composer and a teacher, was primarily concerned with technical matters and craftsmanship, and thus formed a useful counterweight to Goldmark's less formal approach.

Sibelius was still active as a violinist, and played in the Conservatory orchestra, whose members he described as 'self-important and conceited, with long hair and shabby trousers'. Some of them soon became his friends, however, among them the Viennese pianist and composer Carl Frühling, the Hungarian pianist Árpád Lászlo and the Romanian cellist Dmitri Dinicu. Unlike in Berlin, he did not surround himself with Nordic companions. But the hustle and bustle of Vienna could not fail to provoke Sibelius to the same kind of riotous behaviour that had landed him in trouble in Berlin the previous year. He wrote home: 'Vienna is all laughter and waltzes.' Once again he was supposed to fend for himself; once again he could not resist spending money lavishly (not least in the wine bars that he and his student colleagues frequented), and once again he was forced to fall back on the generosity of his family back in Finland.

Sibelius also moved in more elevated social circles. From the Finnish baritone Filip Forstén he secured an introduction to the celebrated Viennese opera singer Pauline Lucca, and became a frequent guest at her prestigious social gatherings. In fact they had met before: while Sibelius was a pupil at the grammar school, Lucca had visited Hämeenlinna for a concert, and he had served as page-turner.

Jean's and Aino's clandestine engagement did not remain a secret for long, at least not from her family. At the end of November – without telling her husband-to-be – Aino revealed the truth to her father. Fortunately the General was well disposed towards Sibelius, although he agreed that there was no rush to make the news public.

At Christmas Sibelius read the story *Yksin* (*Alone*) by Juhani Aho. By the standards of Finnish literature of the time, the story – a tale of unfulfilled love – was controversially bold. The book had been a present from Aino, and Sibelius was horrified to discover that it was largely autobiographical: the first-person narrator was based on the author himself, and the character of Anna was clearly modelled on Aino. The initial feelings of anger and jealousy that the story provoked were soon forgotten, however, and in later life Aho and Sibelius were close friends as well as neighbours in Järvenpää. Sibelius's irritation may have been tempered by the realization that the life he was leading in Vienna was by no means whiter than white. 'I have all the propensities towards vice that most young men have and perhaps more than most', he admitted in a letter to his fiancée. He certainly had an eye for the young ladies of Vienna and was even still receiving gifts from admirers at home: shortly after his arrival in Vienna, Ellen Hackzell from Lovisa sent him roses.

1891

As a musician Sibelius was developing in leaps and bounds. He studied the works of Beethoven and Wagner; the latter's *Tristan und Isolde*, which he heard shortly after his arrival in Vienna, roused his enthusiasm, as did *Siegfried*, which he heard the following spring. Sibelius also attended the first performance of the revised version of Bruckner's *Third Symphony*, given in the presence of the composer, and the piece made a deep impression on him: Bruckner was 'the greatest of all living composers', according to a letter that Sibelius wrote to Aino. The influence of this particular symphony can be heard in the first movement of *Kullervo*. He never met Bruckner personally, although he did sit close to him at a chamber concert and described him as 'a kindly little old man, who seemed rather lost in the world', but he claimed to his biographer Kark Ekman that he did manage to make contact with Brahms, at a fashionable café. Further evidence that his sympathies then lay firmly with Bruckner and Wagner is found in a letter home, referring to Brahms's *String Quintet in F major* and his friend Busoni's *Violin Sonata in E minor* (No. 1): 'I do not understand how they manage to get these and works like them published.'

On 9th January Sibelius auditioned to become a violinist in the Vienna Philharmonic Orchestra, a position that would have brought him a welcome income, but failed owing to an attack of stage fright, a problem that had already affected him during his studies in Helsinki.

Sibelius had not yet settled into his Symbolist style, but the works he wrote in Vienna feature some surprisingly bold writing, in some ways more radical than his compositions from the following fifteen years. Not all of his experiments were successful: in November 1890 Sibelius used Runeberg's poem *Likhet* (*Resemblance*) as the basis for a song with piano (JS 120). It is a noisy and melodically undistinguished setting, which may explain why he did not include it in the selection of Runeberg songs that he published the following year (Op. 13).

The pieces from this time reveal a composer in search of his own individual style. This is evident in everything from orchestral works to piano music. Spurred on by the music he heard and by Goldmark's coaching, he decided to make his first attempt at a symphony. It is perhaps curious that he did not turn first to opera, bearing in mind the splendid opera performances he had heard and Wegelius's enthusiasm for Wagner. As is shown by his reaction to the previous year's *Piano Quintet*, however, Wegelius seems to have regarded his star pupil as more of a Finnish Mendelssohn than a bearer of the Wagnerian torch.

The most remarkable piano piece from this time is the demanding *Scherzo in F sharp minor*, JS 164, a violent and thrilling musical storm launched by insistently repeated notes (a device that prefigures the *Caprice* from Op. 24); its surging waves are on occasion interrupted by thematic fragments in the Finnish folk style. This is found in a major book of sketches, as are two versions of a *Minuet* – an incomplete sketch in F major for violin and cello, and a complete draft in B flat major for piano. Sibelius evidently liked this piece: in 1894 he reworked it for orchestra and, some years later still, he simplified it and included it in the music for Adolf Paul's play *King Christian II*. These pieces can be dated with certainty to early 1891, as the same sketchbook contains sketches for the orchestral *Scène de ballet* that was premièred in Helsinki in April; among the many other works that were already in draft form were long passages from *Kullervo* and the solo songs *Under strandens granar* and *Jägargossen*.

An almost complete *Waltz in D flat major* for piano has been provisionally dated to 1891–93 and may thus have been written in Vienna. It certainly has a Viennese flavour and it is tempting to see the piece as a sparkling tribute to high society in the Austrian capital. A comparable but shorter piano fragment is the [*Polka, Fragment*] *in E minor* (1890–92), which has a modal quality close to Finnish folk music.[6]

The extent to which the world of Finnish folk culture had started to fire Sibelius's imagination is evident in his setting for voice and piano of Runeberg's *Drömmen* (*The Dream*, Op. 13 No. 5). This dates from January 1891 and begins with a vocal melody which, though in fact in 3/4, hints at the 5/4 metre and character of a Finnish folk chant – a similarity that emerges with great force in the song's first recording, made by the great Finnish bass-baritone Abraham Ojanperä in 1906. It seems peculiar that such a vocal line is combined with Runeberg's noble Swedish text, which has nothing whatsoever to do with the *Kalevala* or its cultural sphere. The dream to which the title alludes is portrayed in a magically rapt middle section. A further Runeberg setting, *Hjärtats morgon* (*The Heart's Morning*, Op. 13 No. 3), is a dramatic song in which love's capacity to warm and enliven the heart is compared with the sun's ability to dispel night's darkness and mist. During the spring Sibelius composed one of his best-known songs, *Våren flyktar hastigt* (*Spring is Flying*, Op. 13 No. 4), again to words by Runeberg, this time from *Idyll och epigram*. This concise, lyrical song captures the moods of the poem to perfection: a girl laments the passing of the seasons and the transience of beauty – but, as her partner points out, memories will remain and youth is the time for loving and kissing. From the same period comes *Sov in!* (*Go to Sleep!*) Op. 17 No. 2, to a poem by Tavaststjerna, a lullaby for a sick child. The occasional touch of chromaticism in the piano part lends this berceuse an uneasy, slightly sinister atmosphere.

Not all the songs that Sibelius began at this time were completed, though in some cases significant fragments have survived. Among these is another Tavaststjerna setting, *Frihet* (*Freedom*), which is found immediately after the drafts for *Sov in!* in the manuscript[7] and was thus presumably planned as a companion piece. The same source contains *Drick, De förflyga de susande pärlorna* (*Drink, the Fizzling Pearls are Flying Away*), to a poem by Franzén about champagne, a subject with which Sibelius had by now gained considerable familiarity. He also jotted down and then abandoned several beginnings for a setting of Runeberg's *Flickans årstider* (*The Maiden's Seasons*), to which he was to return in 1911 in *Arioso*. The same author's poem *Löjet* (*The Smile*) provides the words for a rather longer song draft from the same period.

Early in the year Christian Sibelius asked his brother to write a short piece for Asis (the Anatomical Institute of Helsinki University), and Sibelius was happy to oblige. On 12th February, in a letter to Axel von Bonsdorff, Christian wrote: 'The greatest "event" for us medical students was a gathering at Kajsis [Kaisaniemi restaurant?]. For that is where the march that Janne composed was performed... It was encored three times and made a great impact; we drank a toast to Janne and a long telegram in French was sent off... as thanks for "la pompeuse marche d'asis". At first the march is deeply tragic in a slow, rocking rhythm; this turns into a wild, csárdás-like affair and a refrain where everybody can join in. Here and there howling can be heard, mostly from the cello (two-octave-long *glissandos*, or chromatic passages in octaves).' The piece – which has become known as *La pompeuse Marche d'Asis*, JS 116, was apparently for string quartet, and – in this form – is believed to be lost. Sibelius arranged the march for two violins, cello and piano that November, and it would seem that he also made a version for piano trio: at least, the only surviving work to fit the description (complete with a two-octave *glissando* in the cello) is scored for piano trio. In its way this remarkable little piece is as bizarre and original as anything he composed in Vienna. Its opening flourish calls to mind Saint-Saëns (*Carnival of the Animals*); the dactylic main theme itself is infectious and nonchalant, whilst the later 'wild, csárdás-like' idea has great vehemence.

Almost as startling, though less good-humoured, is a *Perpetuum mobile* for violin and piano, a spiky piece with a prominent tritone in its principal theme. Sibelius may have performed this piece together with Karl Ekman at a concert in Tammisaari in August 1891; in any case it was published that year in a Christmas supplement named *Nuori Suomi*. In 1911 Sibelius reworked the piece (as *Epilogue*, Op. 2b) and altered its character completely.

In February Sibelius sent a new piano work to Aino in Vaasa – the *Theme and Seven Variations in C minor*, JS 198, and in April he expanded it to produce the *Quartet in C minor* for two violins, cello and piano, JS 156. Unfortunately the original piano version has not survived, but we know that the monumental introduction was added in the revision (the introduction is in C major and many sources thus list the entire piece as being in the major). Its slow triple metre was by now an established Sibelian characteristic. This is followed by the theme, in C minor and with the character of a mazurka; there are similarities with the first movement of the previous year's *Piano Quintet*. The role of the piano is prominent, reflecting the work's origins as a solo piano piece. Overall the variations are impassioned and brooding, and it comes as a surprise when Sibelius ends the piece quietly and succinctly. There is no slackening of pace; the music merely becomes quieter and stops. In this respect it follows the example of the *'Hafträsk' Trio* and sets a precedent for the *Fourth Symphony*.

It was in Vienna that Sibelius took his first independent steps as a composer of orchestral music – and they were undeniably bold steps, as his intention was to compose a symphony. He started work on it in February 1891 and within a few weeks had two movements complete, but then abandoned the symphonic plan. The first two movements were instead named *Overture in E major*, JS 145, and *Scène de ballet*, JS 163.

The overture is in clear sonata form, and several of its themes explore the sound world of Finnish folk music without resorting to direct quotation. Sibelius even mentioned in a letter to Aino that a folk-song was a primary source of inspiration for his planned symphony. He had, in fact, used a similar theme some eighteen months earlier in the brass *Allegro* that he had submitted from Berlin for the Society for Popular Education competition. 'The second theme is you yourself,' Sibelius wrote to Aino on 10th February, 'tender and feminine but also passionate.' (This theme here sounds like a folk-song, but variants of it, in increasingly individual form, would crop up throughout Sibelius's career – the slow movement of the *First Symphony*, the piano piece *The Birch* and even the trombone solo in the *Seventh Symphony*.) Sibelius's inexperience in writing for full orchestra makes itself felt in matters of balance: if all the instruments play exactly the dynamics indicated in the score, many of the carefully wrought details will be quite inaudible. Overall, however, the piece has an infectious, youthful energy, and is full of ingenious ideas – such as the carefully notated broadening of tempo for the recapitulation (the music moves from 4/4 to 12/8). Some of the orchestral parts bear the subtitle *A Wolf Hunt in Siberia* which, if it originated with the composer, suggests a degree of programmatic motivation that is not unknown in Sibelius's large-scale chamber works from the 1880s, though he would soon renounce it in his symphonic output. In the *'Korpo' Trio* and *F major Violin Sonata* one suspects that

Sibelius alluded to programmes as a sort of defence mechanism in case the music was criticized on its own terms. Soon he would realize that his work could speak for itself.

The *Scène de ballet* is far more cosmopolitan; it is a whirlwind of a piece in which the orchestral greenhorn creates an intoxicating and exotic blend of musical impulses – a kind of Finnish precursor to Ravel's *La Valse*. In a letter to Adolf Paul the following year Sibelius suggested that his inspiration had come from a night 'in a whorehouse in Vienna, where the whores were dancing'. He was by no means reticent with his scoring, using piccolo, cor anglais, bass clarinet and a sizeable percussion section. A prominent role is played by the motif F sharp–G sharp–B–E, similar in contour to the opening idea of the *Fourth Symphony* but without the tritone. This is perhaps the most vivid example of Sibelius's many experiments with timbre and colour during his year in Vienna; at one point (*Molto vivace*, bar 303 ff.) it sounds astonishingly like the second movement of Nielsen's *Fifth Symphony*, which would not be written for another thirty years – although Nielsen could not have been familiar with Sibelius's piece, which did not maintain its place in the repertoire.

By comparison with the *Overture* and *Scène de ballet* the song *Fågellek* (*Play of the Birds*), Op. 17 No. 3, is a conventional piece, albeit a very agreeable one, to words by Tavaststjerna. The poem's nature imagery is here viewed with the decorum of the salon rather than the immediacy of personal experience. The song is in ABA form; the outer sections have an undulating chordal accompaniment, while the sparkling figurations of the middle section create a certain ambivalence of mood. Sibelius admitted in a letter to Aino that he 'may have misunderstood the poet a little'.

The *Overture* and *Scène de ballet* were sent home to Helsinki, where Robert Kajanus conducted them at one of his 'popular concerts' in April. In many ways these concerts represented Sibelius's baptism of fire as a composer. True, some of his chamber music had been performed both privately and at the Music Institute's concerts, but to some extent those performances were given to a captive audience. Now the works on which he cut his orchestral teeth were subject to wider scrutiny, and had to measure up to established popular classics. Moreover, with the composer safely ensconced in the watering holes of a city so many miles away, the critics did not need to pull any punches. Kajanus himself was quite fond of the pieces, but they proved too radical for the Helsinki audience.

At much the same time Sibelius was busy composing two pieces that have sadly not survived: both the orchestral *Zirkusmarsch* (*Circus March*), JS 223, and *Fäktmusik* (*Fencing Music*), JS 80, have been dated to March 1891. The *Fäktmusik* was an unsuccessful entry in a composition contest organized by a Viennese fencer named Hartl, but it was regarded as 'serious' and 'not Viennese'. Sibelius was, however, asked to orchestrate a potpourri drawn from the winning entry!

He was by now working on a project that would in time to develop into his largest and most important work so far: *Kullervo*, Op. 7. In April he wrote to Aino about this, and he also showed sketches to Robert Fuchs. The outline of the first movement's main theme was certainly clear by this time, although its rhythmic pattern was still uncertain (he experimented with a variant of the theme in 6/4 time, for instance).

In the late spring of 1891 Sibelius's health gave cause for concern. He spent some time at one of Vienna's most exclusive and expensive private hospitals – Dr Eder's sanatorium at Schmidgasse 14, where he had an operation. Exact details of his condition are unknown, although he wrote to Aino after the event: 'I had the beginnings of a stone. Professor Neumann thinks I may have had it for several years.' But he could not pay his bill, and once again was forced to turn to his family in Lovisa for help. He was finally discharged in early June, and set off homewards without delay. Stopping off in Berlin, he met up with his friends, including Adolf Paul, and promptly drank away all of the funds that his brother Christian had gone to such trouble to secure. He was forced to ask his family for even more money, and even so had to sell some of his clothes to pay the fare home. But eventually he did set sail from Lübeck on the M/S *Storfursten*, still wearing his evening dress and no doubt anticipating a fully deserved reprimand from Christian and Evelina when he arrived.

In June 1891 Sibelius returned to his grandmother's house in Lovisa, where work on *Kullervo* continued. The final form of the piece was not yet determined: as late as November 1891 he had not decided if the choir should be mixed or only male voices, or whether to include a narrator. Moreover, after the disgrace of his return from Vienna, he needed to prove his capacity to earn money if he wished to stand any chance of being allowed to marry Aino, and he gave some private lessons in 'violin playing, ensemble playing and musical theory', to quote from the advertisement he placed in the Lovisa newspaper. It may well have been in this context that he wrote a *Duo for violin and viola in C major*, JS 66. It is assumed that Sibelius himself played the viola (for which the writing is surprisingly uncomfortable) while his unknown pupil took the violin part in this modest piece, which only rarely betrays the identity of its composer.

The *Prelude* for brass septet, JS 83, is perhaps best seen as an experiment. In all probability this piece is a product of the summer visit to Lovisa. The only manuscript source for the piece[8] is a major book of sketches that starts with drafts for the *Scène de ballet* and contains much that was destined for *Kullervo*, and so we cannot rule out the possibility that the *Prelude* was composed in Vienna in the spring. It is much more likely, however, that Sibelius simply carried on working with the book of sketches after he left Vienna; after all, he would hardly have left behind a document that contained many of his ideas for a work of the stature of *Kullervo*. The brass piece is based on fanfare-like themes, insistent triplet rhythms and a more lyrical, slow-moving idea. The disparate elements are combined skilfully, but the invention is not distinctive enough for the piece to make a lasting impression.

Just before the *Prelude* in the sketchbook there is an [*Allegretto*] *in E flat major* for piano trio. The easy-going character of this fragment suggests that it was intended for use among family or friends, but the piece breaks off after just sixteen bars. In 2002 Jaakko Kuusisto added an ending to make a performable version of this delightful miniature.

From his base in Lovisa, Sibelius made various trips during the summer and autumn. During the summer he made the long train journey up to Tottesund to visit the Järnefelts, especially Aino, at their summer home. According to Aino's mother Elisabeth, Jean spent a considerable time playing music together with Armas.

From Tottesund Sibelius headed south to the small town of Tammisaari, where he had promised to be a judge at a Swedish-language choral competition, even though his own output for mixed choir was still modest and he had not yet written his finest works in the genre. The brass septet from Lovisa was present, and performed the *Andantino* previously heard at Runeberg's birthday celebrations that February. In August, he paid a visit to Martin Wegelius at his summer house in Pohja; here Sibelius wrote another Runeberg setting, the Schubertian *Jägargossen* (*The Young Huntsman*, Op. 13 No. 7). It is written for voice and piano, although surviving sketches indicate that he also considered making a version with orchestra.

Sibelius spent some time in Helsinki during the autumn. He was suffering from a rushing sound in his ears, which him forced to consult a doctor in November. The doctor, fearing that Sibelius's hearing would grow worse and that he would ultimately become deaf, forbade alcohol, cigars and bathing in cold water – advice that the composer ignored. On 24th November he made his first public appearance as a conductor, performing his *Overture* and *Scène de ballet* with Kajanus's orchestra at a popular concert. Aino had by now returned to Helsinki and was in the audience. By now Sibelius had become so embroiled in the composition of *Kullervo* that he was prepared to be less than complimentary about his earlier orchestral pieces. He wrote to Adolf Paul: 'It was marvellous to conduct. I wasn't nervous at all… If only the compositions were less awful.'

Around a week later he set out in the company of a young friend named Yrjö Hirn – later professor of æsthetics and contemporary literature at

Helsinki University – from Lovisa to the small town of Borgå (Porvoo) with
the aim of meeting and listening to a remarkable old lady: the runic singer
Larin Paraske from Ingermanland (Inkerinmaa), whose vast repertoire
– rumoured to include no less than 32,000 verses – had made her something
of a celebrity. She was in Borgå to visit one of her foremost supporters, a
pastor named Adolf Neuvius, who wished to note down some of her chants
for posterity. Hirn later wrote: 'I found myself with Jean Sibelius on a
journey from Lovisa ... at the time his head was full of ideas that were to
culminate the following year in *Kullervo* and was anxious to hear what the
Karelian runic melodies were like when they were sung in an authentic way.
I was naturally glad to be present when they met... he listened to her with
great attention and made notes on her inflections and rhythm.'

Cultural life in Finland at this time was assuming an increasingly
political dimension, and Sibelius found himself increasingly drawn towards
the so-called '*Päivälehti* circle'. Sibelius already knew from his contacts
with the Järnefelt family that a Finnish-language newspaper was being
planned. *Päivälehti* aimed to stand up for social justice and humanity,
and was the forerunner of today's *Helsingin Sanomat*. It was founded in
1889 by a group of 'Young Finns', a group of cultural figures of liberal
and democratic inclination with a profound dislike of the Russificiation
to which Finland was being subjected. Prominent members of this circle
incuded Arvid and Eero Järnefelt, Juhani Aho, Eero Erkko, Robert
Kajanus, the authors Eino Leino and Minna Canth, the composer and
critic Oskar Merikanto, and Kaarlo Ståhlberg, who would become the
first President of Finland. The group was not rigidly organized, but served
rather as a focus and stimulus for the participants' creative powers. Starting
in 1891, *Päivälehti* produced a Christmas supplement, *Nuori Suomi* (*Young
Finland*), which served as an outlet for some of the group's work; the first
issue contained an article in which Sibelius was placed alongside Kajanus,
Oskar Merikanto and Emil Sivori (an influential figure in the musical life
of Viipuri) as one of Finland's foremost composers.

That year Adolf Paul published his first novel, and dedicated it to
Sibelius. There was, however, a sting in the tail: *En bok om en människa*
(*A Book about a Man*) is an autobiographical work that tells of Paul's
student days in Helsinki and Berlin. Paul (who appears in the novel as
Hans) is a close friend of a composer (in the novel called Sillén) and does
not hesitate to go into details of the latter's wild and dissolute lifestyle.
Aino read the book and, understandably, was less than delighted. Sibelius
himself feared that the book would ruin his reputation – although he made
no secret of the extravagant lifestyle that he was then leading in Helsinki.
At any rate, the book did not lead to a rift between the two friends and
did not materially affect Sibelius's stature.

CHAPTER 4

KULLERVO: 1892–1893

1892

Spending the New Year of 1892 in Lovisa, Sibelius could have had little idea how decisive the coming twelve months would prove to be.

The final stages of work on *Kullervo* were accomplished in some haste, and in a rather unusual environment. In late January he left Lovisa and took lodgings at the Ullanlinna spa in Helsinki, by the waterfront at Kaivopuisto. The spa had been established in 1834 and the building in which Sibelius lived (sadly destroyed during the Continuation War, in 1944) was a distinguished structure built to plans by Carl Ludvig Engel, who had also designed Helsinki's Senate Square. According to Juhani Aho, who visited him there, 'he had found a calm and remote place to work ... he had a table, a piano, a bed, a few chairs and a lot of tobacco smoke. During his best working days he did not give a thought to eating or drinking; a strong cigar was enough to maintain his strength.' Not every day was consumed by work, however: he spent much of his time socializing and drinking with Robert Kajanus and other supporters of the Finnish cause, even though this meant that his relationship with his mentor Martin Wegelius, whose orientation was towards the Swedish language and culture, grew somewhat cooler. Wegelius was, however, willing to find Sibelius some teaching work at the Music Institute; any extra income was welcome. Kajanus's popular concerts were also a regular feature of Sibelius's schedule, and he secured promises of teaching work from both Wegelius and Kajanus, which at least provided some hope of the financial security that he would need if he wished to marry Aino.

Sibelius wrote frequently to Aino about his progress with *Kullervo*, but, of course, the young couple also had other plans for the future. Jean was already dreaming of having a son whom they would name Edvard. In early March Sibelius decided to make the choral sections of *Kullervo* for male instead of mixed chorus, perhaps as the result of a conversation with Wegelius where the older man pointed out that the ladies in the choir might be too embarrassed to sing such an explicit text. In the weeks before the première, the copyists worked tirelessly to copy out the parts. According to Jukka Rautio, a member of the chorus at the first performance: 'There were only a few days left before the concert. We doubted that we could learn our parts. But our chorus-master reassured us, saying that the young composer himself would come and hold special rehearsals with us. This raised our self-esteem. And he came. His eyes were ablaze! It was that inspirational fire of which the poets speak. And he spoke Finnish! He was polite; he called us "gentlemen" even though we were just training to be parish clerks.' Sibelius needed to speak several languages at the rehearsals: Finnish and Swedish to the choir, and German to the orchestra, as many of the orchestral players were from Germany.

As his first major orchestral work, *Kullervo* plainly marks a crucial turning point in Sibelius's career. After this point, orchestral music became his primary focus, or at least *primus inter pares* alongside his work in other genres. *Kullervo* marks a major step forward. Compared with the *Overture* and *Scène de ballet*, the orchestral writing is much more confident and the thematic material is more memorable and coherent. Indeed, the way he relates themes and motifs within and between movements clearly points towards the tightly woven inner relationships and interdependencies of his mature style.

As well as providing the orchestral score, Sibelius prepared versions of the third and fifth movements with piano accompaniment, completing the third at the end of February and the fifth by the middle of April. Even though the piano writing is very demanding, these were probably made for rehearsal purposes. Slight differences in the choral parts reflect Sibelius's constant refinement of his material before the première.

In the *Kalevala*, Kullervo is a tragic and most unfortunate figure. Even before he is born his uncle Untamo attacks his clan. Believing that Untamo has killed everyone except his mother, the young Kullervo grows up desiring revenge, but his attempts to frustrate Untamo only result in his being sold as a slave to the smith Ilmarinen. He is set to work as a herdsman but, after becoming involved in the death of Ilmarinen's wife, he escapes and is reunited with his parents. Kullervo's attempts to work for his parents fail, and so he is sent to deliver the family's taxes. On his way home he meets and ravishes a girl who turns out to be his long-lost sister. His mother persuades him not to kill himself; instead, he goes to war against his uncle and, with a splendid new sword granted him by

Ukko, chief of the gods, he slaughters Untamo's entire tribe. By the time he returns home, however, his family is dead. Wandering in the forest, he chances upon the place where he ravished his sister; consumed by guilt, he throws himself on his sword.

Sibelius's *Kullervo* begins with a purely orchestral *Introduction* in sonata form. The opening theme, which returns at the end of the finale, has a Brucknerian sweep (Sibelius had, after all, heard Bruckner's *Third Symphony* in Vienna), although it also has a kinship with Finnish folk music. On the whole the orchestral writing is typical of Sibelius's orchestral music from the early 1890s; his characteristic triplet rhythms and *pizzicato* figures are used extensively. Only occasionally – such as in the daringly exposed oboe sextuplets in the development section – does one suspect that Sibelius's musical imagination exceeded what his players could probably deliver.

Neither in the first nor in the slow second movement, *Kullervo's Youth*, does Sibelius attempt to follow the narrative of the *Kalevala* story. Indeed, according to Tawaststjerna, the composer referred to this rondo-form movement as a lullaby with variations which increase in emotional intensity. Several of the thematic ideas are strikingly reminiscent of runic style, and these are contrasted with music of a more pastoral character.

In the huge third movement, *Kullervo and his Sister*, Sibelius brings in the two soloists and male chorus. The first part of the movement is in the 5/4 metre frequently encountered in traditional runic singing. After an orchestral introduction, the choir, often in unison, describes Kullervo's journey by sledge. The orchestra plays a prominent part both in the presentation of themes and in maintaining the rhythmic impetus. The baritone and mezzo-soprano soloists act out a series of brief dialogues between Kullervo and the maidens he meets and attempts to seduce on his travels. With the third maiden he eventually succeeds, and entices her into his sledge, after which the orchestra portrays the actual seduction. Then the truth is revealed: the maiden is Kullervo's long-lost sister. She sings an impassioned *scena*, telling of the vicissitudes of her life since, years earlier, she had become lost while gathering berries (in the *Kalevala* she then drowns herself, though this is not portrayed in the music). Kullervo, consumed by remorse, rounds off the movement by singing a monologue, accompanied by violent hammer-blow chords from the orchestra – a distant ancestor of the widely spaced chords that end the *Fifth Symphony*. The bold concluding section of this movement soon took on an independent existence: either in 1892 or early 1893 Sibelius turned it into a song with piano accompaniment, using a German translation by Franz Anton von Schiefner, and he returned to it several times later in his career.

The fourth movement, again for orchestra alone, is a vigorous scherzo entitled *Kullervo Goes to War*. As with the first two movements, Sibelius makes no attempt to follow the *Kalevala* story in detail, although some warlike fanfares are woven into the fabric of the music and the final bars could be interpreted as depicting Kullervo's victory over Untamo's clan. Despite the indication *Alla marcia* this exuberant, colourfully scored movement is full of complicated rhythmic patterns and syncopations.

The fifth movement, *Kullervo's Death*, is for choir and orchestra, and it is here that the thematic echoes from earlier in the work, especially from the first movement, are at their most pronounced. This movement has an inexorable tread and cumulative power that are without equal in Sibelius's work and make an overwhelming impact in performance. Sibelius separates the final scene (in which Kullervo places his sword on the ground and impales himself upon it) from the rest of the movement by a long pause. This marks the moment when Kullervo's decision to kill himself becomes irrevocable. After it, the choir relates the actual suicide in music of great intensity, followed by a calmer, purely orchestral interlude of a retrospective, almost nostalgic character before the fateful yet majestic final coda.

The soloists at the première were Emmy Achté and Abraham Ojanperä. The Helsinki orchestra numbered only 38 permanent members at that time, and needed to hire extra musicians for the performance. The male choir, around forty strong, was drawn from the Helsinki Parish Clerk and Organ School's student choir and the University Chorus.

The concert on 28th April was a huge success; the hall was full and the performance was described by the composer and pedagogue Axel Törnudd as 'like a volcanic eruption'. Advance information about the work had been circulating in the newspapers all month and, on the day of the concert, Oskar Merikanto wrote in *Päivälehti*: 'We knew [these melodies] as our own, although we had never heard them', a view echoed by Juho Ranta, one of the choir members at the première: 'Although, at least at a conscious level, I did not hear in the music any fragments of familiar pieces, it was still like something that I had known for a long time and heard before. It was *Finnish* music.' All the same, the première of such a long, bold and complicated work as *Kullervo* must have startled as many people as it impressed. Even some critics – including Leonard Salin in *Hufvudstadsbladet* – were taken aback. The musicians themselves also seem to have harboured doubts. In the words of Emmy Achté: 'I shall never forget the first orchestral rehearsal, when, after I had sung my first recitative, members of the orchestra burst out into uncontrollable laughter to the extent that they were bent double. Indeed, since then, understanding of Sibelius's music has progressed by huge degrees, even though he has perhaps not composed anything so wholly realistic as this recitative.'

Kullervo was heard again in full the following day and, the day after that, Robert Kajanus included the fourth movement in a popular concert.

There can be no doubt that the performance of *Kullervo* raised Sibelius's profile enormously and, according to Aino, its success persuaded her parents to consent to their marriage. Once consent had been obtained, no time was lost in making the arrangements, and the wedding took place at the Järnefelts' summer residence at Tottesund on 10th June 1892. Sibelius's mother was ill and could not attend, but both Linda and Christian were present.

For their honeymoon, Jean and Aino travelled deep into the countryside, to Karelia. By way of Imatra they headed for Joensuu, where they hired a piano, and from there they took a boat northwards to Lieksa, staying by the shore of Lake Pielinen at Monola. No doubt the rented piano and the boat journey reminded Sibelius of his family holiday visits to Korpo in 1886 and 1887. While they were at Monola (a period of roughly a month starting in mid-June) Jean composed three songs, all to words by Runeberg: *Under strandens granar* (*Under the Fir-Trees*), Op. 13 No. 1 – the realization of sketches made in Vienna, *Kyssens hopp* (*The Kiss's Hope*), Op. 13 No. 2 and *Till Frigga* (*To Frigga*), Op. 13 No. 6. *Under strandens granar* is an extended narrative song, which contains a foretaste of the nature imagery that was to become an essential feature of later vocal pieces such as *Höstkväll*, *På verandan vid havet* and *Luonnotar*. Here this is effectively combined with a story of a nymph abducting first a child, then the child's mother – there are some similarities with Goethe's *Erlkönig*, though Runeberg's poem (based on a Serbian folk-song) is less sinister. *Kyssens hopp* is a charming song in which kisses whisper to each other in the poet's daydreams. *Till Frigga* is an ambitious love song. In earlier pieces, such as the slow movement of the 'Hafträsk' Trio, Sibelius had used a nine-beat metre to convey a gentle, barcarole-like character; here, however, a similar metre is used in the context of a sinister, dark-hued mood-painting with melodies and rhythms that anticipate the *Second Symphony* and *Valse triste*. Orchestral music was not forgotten either. Kajanus had already asked him to write a short 'da capo' piece, but Sibelius had other ideas. He had set his sights on a more ambitious work – the tone poem *En saga*.

In Lieksa Sibelius noted down some 15–20 folk melodies, marking the manuscript both with the place and with the singer's name: '(Lieksa) Mikko Tolvanen'. A small arrangement for voice and piano of the folk-song *Tule, tule, kultani* (*Come, Come, My Sweetheart*), JS 211, is found in the same manuscript.

Sibelius had been granted a scholarship from Helsinki University to study Karelian runic song and *kantele* playing. To this end he now travelled eastwards into the Ilomantsi, Korpiselkä and Suojärvi region, where he heard folk artists such as Mikko Tolvanen, Stepnaii Kokkonen, Mikhail Wornanen and Pedri Shemeikka. Ancient Finnish runic singing was still well-preserved in Karelia and, around sixty years earlier, Elias Lönnrot had made pioneering journeys in the region to gather material for the *Kalevala*. 'Karelianism', a movement that favoured folk culture from Karelia, became a force to be reckoned with in Finnish cultural circles in the late nineteenth century, not least as a consequence of the increasing Russian interference in the running of the Grand Duchy. Although Sibelius's research was by no means exhaustive or definitive, he duly noted down a number of the runic melodies as part of his submission to the University, and one of them – an antiphonal 5/4 melody – even found its way into the first tableau of his *Karelia* music the following year. This was very much an exception; in general, Sibelius did not need to resort to direct quotation to capture the spirit of folk music. There can be little doubt, however, that the trip helped to ingrain the rhythms and motifs of Karelian music in him, and to align him with the supporters of Karelianism.

Aino did not accompany Sibelius on his expedition, which was probably a wise choice as it turned out that Jean had wasted no time in making his new wife pregnant. She set off instead to visit her aunt Aurora Gräsbeck in Kuopio, where he later joined her. In Kuopio they mixed with the literary circle of the dramatist Minna Canth and the poet Karl August Tavaststjerna.

Back in Helsinki, Jean and Aino rented a large four-roomed flat at Wladimirinkatu 45 (nowadays Kalevankatu) in central Helsinki. The rent demanded by their landlord, John Rikström, was considerable, but Christian Sibelius – as always, more financially astute than his brother – moved in with them and made his own contribution. To earn a living Sibelius taught theory and violin playing – for up to thirty hours per week – at Kajanus's Orchestral School and Wegelius's Music Institute. He also returned to his post as second violin in the Music Institute's string quartet, though only for one season. His main work in progress at this stage was still *En saga*.

The four Runeberg songs that Sibelius had written on his honeymoon were now gathered together with three other settings of the same poet from Sibelius's Vienna year (*Hjärtats morgon*, *Våren flyktar hastigt* and *Drömmen*) and issued in December 1892 as his Op. 13 by the Finnish publisher Otava.

Other songs from 1891/92 include the glorious *Se'n har jag ej frågat mera* (*Since Then I have Questioned no Further*), Op. 17 No. 1, to words by Runeberg. Here Sibelius shows how much intensity of expression can be wrung from a slow, simple melodic line with a chordal accompaniment. As so often in his music, the piece has a modal, in this case Dorian inflection. We do not know when this song was first performed, but in 1895 Ida Morduch (later Ekman), accompanied by Hanslick, sang it to Brahms in Vienna. Brahms asked her to sing it again, and this time he himself played the piano part. According to the singer's later recollection, Brahms was unusually complimentary about Sibelius's song: he uttered the laconic but prophetic words: 'He'll be something special', kissed her on the forehead and expressed the wish that: 'When we next meet you must sing more Sibelius than Brahms.'

A further Runeberg setting from this period remained incomplete: *Den första kyssen* (*The First Kiss*), though several sketches and drafts have survived. Almost a decade later Sibelius would return to this poem and use it as the basis of one of his best-known songs, but nothing from the 1891/92 sketches was retained in the later song.

It was probably during that autumn that Sibelius befriended the painter Axel Gallén (later known by the Finnish form of his name, Akseli Gallen-Kallela). Gallén – who also had a keen interest in Karelianism – was only a few months older than Sibelius and, like him, had been born in the provinces: he grew up on a farm in Tyrvää, 30 miles west of Pori on the west coast. Like Sibelius, Gallén came from a middle-class family (his father was a bank official, and later a police superintendent and lawyer) and spoke Swedish at home, although he learned Finnish from the farm workers on the family estate. Gallén had been sent to school in Helsinki when he was only eleven; he had married in 1890 and, like Sibelius, had spent his honeymoon in Karelia.

It was, of course, important for an up-and-coming personality such as Sibelius to spend time with other cultural figures of similar standing. It is to Aino's great credit that she did not try to force him to place his new responsibilities as a husband and father-to-be in front of such 'networking'. On the other hand, she could not have been pleased that the primary forum for such encounters was the Hotel Kämp, where Jean and his friends would talk and drink for days on end. This was the period of the notorious 'Symposium' gatherings, with their core group of Sibelius, Kajanus, Armas Järnefelt, Adolf Paul and Axel Gallén. Naturally, the participants' wives were excluded from these well-lubricated gatherings. By all accounts their discussions on topics concerning life, art and philosophy were wide-ranging and lively – at least until the after-effects of the alcohol kicked in – and served as a valuable creative stimulus for all involved. For Sibelius there was a practical benefit, too: by thus consolidating his relationship with Kajanus, he gained privileged access to the Philharmonic Society orchestra as well.

The closing months of the year brought one further change in Sibelius's personal life. On 4th December his grandmother Juliana Borg died in Hämeenlinna. He attended the funeral – but that was to be his last visit to the house in which he had grown up, which was subsequently sold. Sibelius's former teacher Eva Savonius later gave an account which offers us a fascinating glimpse of him at his most vulnerable: 'I had not seen Janne for a long time... but I did not dare disturb him, for he appeared to be very upset... Apart from deeply missing the departed, we also realized, with great melancholy, that this dear old house, so rich in memories for us all, would soon be just a memory... We ate dinner almost in silence, after which Janne went into the next room, all eyes following him. He stood gazing at the things there. Then he went up to one thing after another, touching them all as if to say farewell and brushing his fingers over the leather spines of the books on the shelves... Then Janne sat down at the harmonium, his fingers began to touch the keys, and the ancient family instrument began to give out amazing melodies. We all knew Janne, and that he was "giving a speech" in music. And certainly no words would have been able to express what those notes did... I can swear that there was not a single dry eye in the room. Then Janne stopped, glanced at his watch, got up suddenly from the chair, bowed and left the house. We knew that he was hurrying to catch the train, and none of us was surprised that he did not say goodbye. We went on crying after he had left, for we knew that this son of Hämeenlinna, Janne Sibelius, would no longer belong to us; we already knew that he belonged to the whole of Finland.'

As the year drew to a close, Sibelius made a chamber arrangement ('piccolo, violin, viola and a couple of other instruments'; JS 151) of the well-known *Porilaisten marssi* (*March of the Pori Regiment*) for the unveiling of a painting of the same name by Albert Edelfelt. Based on an old melody used in an eighteenth-century ballet in Stockholm and also found in a song by Carl Michael Bellman, the tune was popularized in Finland by a certain Christian Kress. Its final form was provided by Conrad Greve, who arranged it for wind orchestra and gave it its title. The march was sung to words by Topelius (1858) and later to a more patriotic text by Runeberg (1860); Fredrik Pacius arranged it for male choir. *Porilaisten marssi* became the honorary and parade march of the Finnish armed forces in 1918 and is nowadays played at official ceremonies involving the President of Finland. Sadly this arrangement by Sibelius has not survived.

1893

Back in Helsinki, Sibelius once more felt a pressing need to raise funds. To this end he went to Lovisa on New Year's Day and, within a few days, managed to secure a loan from the bank manager there. This may well have been his final visit to Lovisa; the ties with his childhood were gradually being severed.

On 5th February 1893 another Runeberg setting saw the light of day at the Runeberg birthday festivities organized by the Helsinki Music Institute. This was the *Melodrama from 'Svartsjukans nätter'* (*'Nights of Jealousy'*), JS 125; Sibelius later stated that he had composed the piece at the request of Martin Wegelius. It is quite possible that Sibelius himself played the violin part at the première. The forces required – narrator, soprano and piano trio – are identical to those used in *Näcken* (1888), his earlier collaboration with Wegelius. The new melodrama is a far more extensive piece than any previous Runeberg setting by Sibelius, playing for some fifteen minutes; its overall shape is determined by the shifting moods of the poem. *Svartsjukans nätter* is a fervent yet intimate piece with passages of remarkable intensity, as befits a text that is highly charged, even erotic. It begins with a lengthy instrumental introduction, after which the narrator begins to recite Runeberg's poem about a dream in which the poet regains the happiness he knew with a former lover. At the moment when his joy seems complete, he suddenly awakes. Musically the piece is wide-ranging: the instrumental introduction is followed by atmospheric episodes of varying character in which the instruments lend colour and support to the narration. The soprano appears only briefly with a vocalise, representing the poet's lost love. Sibelius presumably regarded the work as an occasional piece, as he re-used some of its the thematic material in the fifth and sixth *Impromptus* for piano a few months later.

Sibelius had by now completed his symphonic poem *En saga*, Op. 9, in readiness for its first performance in Helsinki on 16th February 1893 – which nearly did not take place at all, as some of the orchestral players took a dislike to the new piece at rehearsal and Kajanus was forced to intervene. Once again Sibelius's challenging new work was juxtaposed with established classics – Grieg's *Peer Gynt Suite No. 2*, Schumann's *Manfred* overture and some opera arias. *En saga* was heard under the composer's baton, whilst Kajanus conducted the rest of the programme.

In its original form *En saga* is twice as long as the *Overture in E major* but shares some of the overture's immediacy and rugged resilience. In this work Sibelius further refined the orchestral style that he had already explored in the *Overture*, *Scène de ballet* and *Kullervo*, adding innovations that would become characteristic traits, such as the strings' *spiccato* arpeggios at the very beginning. The orchestration of the work was elegantly described by Michael Heenan in an article first published in the magazine *Gramophone* in 1950: 'the pages of *tremolando* for the strings, the held notes appearing out of a foggy dissonance and resolving themselves into the anacruses of irregularly dancing tunes, the chromatic and startling harmony based firmly on incredibly long internal pedal-points scored with great ingenuity and a highly developed sense of balance and timbre: these are the factors which, welded together in a most masterly manner, inform the whole work with that sense of gloomy spaciousness set in the baleful opening bars and echoed in the long clarinet solo at the end.' Sibelius's boldness – or inexperience – did, however, lead him to incorporate a number of abrupt key changes, which frequently result in startling discords and themes being presented in a register where they do not sound entirely comfortable. Aino certainly approved of what she called the 'wild passages' in the piece, but the critics were less appreciative. Karl Flodin wrote in *Nya Pressen*: 'If only he could contain his inspiration a little more' and Oskar Merikanto, though in general favourably disposed towards the piece, wrote that it could benefit from the excision of some superfluous passages.

It has been suggested that some of the thematic material of *En saga* derives from earlier sketches for a septet or octet for strings, flute and clarinet, but little is known with certainty about the origin of the themes and motifs. It is safe to say that, unlike *Kullervo*, this tone poem has no direct connection with the *Kalevala*. *En saga* is often claimed to be based on sonata form – although here, as in his later music, Sibelius lets the themes themselves determine the overall shape of the music. In his commentary for the first recording of the original version,[1] Kari Kilpeläinen summarized Sibelius's structural approach as follows: 'we can observe a very free application of formal principles, although the music remains based on sonata form. The exposition, development and recapitulation sections are discernible, though the divisions between them are blurred. Behind this type of sonata form expansion lies a characteristic striving to unite all the musical elements.' The (Swedish) title *En saga* might be translated as 'A Fairy-Tale', but Sibelius made it plain that it did not have an explicit programme: '*En saga* is [only] an expression of a state of mind... In none of my other works have I revealed myself as completely as in *En saga*.'

On 6th, 8th and 12th March 1893 Sibelius conducted three further complete performances of *Kullervo*. After the performances the previous year Adolf Paul had taken the score to Vienna, where he showed it to Felix Weingartner; it was not returned until February 1893, dangerously close to the date of the new concerts. These were to be the last complete performances of *Kullervo* in the composer's lifetime and, strangely enough, they were received far less enthusiastically than the previous ones. Sibelius, however, had other things on his mind: Aino was due to give birth to their first child any day.

On 19th March Sibelius became a father; Jean and Aino's plan to name

their first child Edvard was rather scuppered by the fact that the baby
turned out to be girl, and so they settled on Eva, in honour of Sibelius's
aunt Evelina in Lovisa.

The *String Trio in G minor*, JS 210, is a special case within Sibelius's
chamber music. Although it was written after *Kullervo*, it is (as far as
we know) a purely abstract piece that neither inhabits a world of Finnish
mythology not betrays any particular sign of influence from folk music. Its
first movement is big, intense and concentrated. The form of the music is
hard to determine; in the preface to the published edition Kari Kilpeläinen
has described it as 'an attempt to combine Lied form with sonata form
and continuous development of the material, thereby forming a grand
symphonic arch'. The music's serious intent is evident from the very first
bars, with swelling chords that anticipate the patriotic music of the end
of the decade – *Finlandia* and *Islossningen*. Among the other important
thematic ideas we find a descending scale-based idea that spans a tritone.
The swelling chords contain the outlines of a theme that, when it recurs
later, will display a prominent 'S-motif' – in a form that is moreover very
similar to its occurrence in the cello fantasy *Malinconia*.

Only fragments of the second and third movements have survived – in
all likelihood these movements were never completed. For the second
movement Sibelius sketched a dance-like idea (related to a subsidiary motif
in the first movement) later used in the *Impromptu* for women's voices and
orchestra, Op. 19. In the third movement he returned to the grandiloquence
and to the musical material of the first movement, combining it with more
lyrical music in a siciliano rhythm from the same mould as the finale of
the *Piano Quintet* and, towards the end, anticipating the choral song *Oi
Lempi, sun valtas ääretön on* (*O Love, Your Realm is Limitless*) from the
university cantata of 1897.

We cannot say exactly when the *String Trio in G minor* was written.
It was certainly not in 1885, as the composer himself later claimed. The
manuscript has been dated to 1893–94, which makes it the last of Sibelius's
major youth chamber pieces, but beyond that we can only speculate. If we
assume that Sibelius would not have started work on such an ambitious score
when he was frantically busy with other projects, we must rule out much of
the latter part of 1893 (*Karelia*, the *Piano Sonata* and *Impromptus*) as well
as the spring of 1894 (*Rakastava, Promotional Cantata, Improvisation/
Spring Song*). Despite its anticipations of later music, the *String Trio* is
stylistically closer to the series of big chamber pieces that started in the mid-
1880s than to the works in a national Romantic or Wagnerian idiom that
would have consumed his creative energies later in 1894. It would therefore
seem likely that the *String Trio* dates from the first months of 1893 (*En
saga* had been finished in December, though the rehearsals and concerts

would of course have kept the piece at the forefront of the composer's mind). If this is indeed the case, then perhaps the upheavals in his family life caused by the birth of his daughter Eva would account for the work remaining incomplete; by the time Sibelius could once more concentrate on composition, new challenges awaited.

In addition to being a prominent author, educator, theatre director and translator, Jalmari Hahl was, during the years 1892–97, also conductor of YL (Ylioppilaskunnan Laulajat – the Helsinki University Male-Voice Choir). Sibelius responded to a request from Hahl to write a piece for the choir's tenth anniversary concert – one of nine pieces by various composers written specially for this event. He produced *Venematka* (*The Boat Journey*), Op. 18 No. 3, a short choral song on a text about 'old and steadfast Väinämöinen' from the *Kalevala* – his first work for male choir *a cappella*, first performed on 4th April 1893. This lively piece, with its regular, short phrases in 5/4, immediately made a good impression. Oskar Merikanto wrote: 'The song is brief, but a delicacy. As with all Sibelius's compositions, it is thoroughly grounded in Finnish runic singing and immediately identifiable as his work. His depiction of the sailing, of the joy on the waters and the maidens on the capes in particular is masterly.' *Venematka* marked the beginning of a long-standing association between the YL choir and Sibelius's music; to this day the choir is the foremost interpreter of his *a cappella* compositions for male choir.

If *En saga* had been less of a crowd-pleaser than Kajanus had hoped for, ample recompense was to come with the *Karelia* music. During the spring the Viipuri Student Association at Helsinki University had announced its intention to organize a pageant – nominally in support of popular education in the Viipuri district, but in reality a nationalist rally. The event was to comprise an overture and a series of tableaux depicting moments in Karelian history; music was to be played during and between the tableaux. The impact that *Kullervo* had made was so significant that Sibelius was an obvious choice as composer, and he worked on the score during the summer which, that year, he spent with Aino and the baby at Ruovesi, north of Tampere; they rented accommodation at Pekkala Primary School for some weeks in June.

Work on the *Karelia* score proceeded in parallel with several other projects, one of which was a piano sonata. Sibelius had of course already completed two violin sonatas, but all his earlier attempts at a piano sonata (such as the movements he composed in Berlin for Becker) had run into the sand. The *Piano Sonata in F major*, Op. 12, was probably written mostly in Ruovesi. The work shares not only its key with the second of his violin sonatas, written four years earlier, but also its down-to-earth character with more than a hint of the Finnish folk style; the two sonatas also show

Sibelius's debt to Grieg. The outer movements are melodically appealing, well proportioned and structurally self-evident, even if critics have attacked its 'unpianistic layout' (Tawaststjerna). The main theme of the rondo-form slow movement was adapted from an unfinished choral song on a *Kalevala* text, *Heitä, koski, kuohuminen* (*Rapids, Cease Your Foaming*), JS 94, on which Sibelius had also been working during the summer, although in the piano version the five-beat incantations of the vocal line are simplified into a four-beat melody. The sketches for *Heitä, koski, kuohuminen* are on the same manuscript as a draft for *Venematka* and, as the texts also belong together,[2] it is reasonable to assume that Sibelius was planning *Heitä, koski, kuohuminen* as a continuation of the earlier song. After Sibelius's death the composer Erik Bergman completed the fragment of *Heitä, koski, kuohuminen* in collaboration with Sibelius's son-in-law Jussi Jalas and Erik Tawaststjerna, and this version was first performed by the Muntra Musikanter choir in Helsinki on 18th March 1961.

The third major musical undertaking during the summer was the first significant phase of work on an opera, *Veneen luominen* (*The Building of the Boat*), based on stories from the *Kalevala*. The opera was to be Sibelius's attempt to create a Wagnerian music drama, and he himself made a draft plot summary (most of this was rediscovered by the Sibelius scholar Markku Hartikainen in 1998).

The fashioning of the libretto itself was initially entrusted to the poet J. H. Erkko, another member of the *Päivälehti* circle, and in August Sibelius travelled north to Kuopio to discuss the plan with him. Erkko, born in Orimattila (a few miles south of Lahti) in 1849, was an experienced poet but, at this stage in his career, was still working as a teacher and administrator as well; he did not devote himself entirely to writing until 1896. While there, Sibelius composed an overture for the opera – the piece now known as *The Swan of Tuonela*, although it is impossible to say to what extent he revised the score when he later included it in the *Lemminkäinen Suite*. Sibelius and Erkko took time off from their operatic discussions to produce a song, *Työkansan marssi* (*Workers' March*), JS 212, for the Finnish workers' movement. Neither Erkko's text – in exaltation of work – nor Sibelius's rather conventional march setting suggest that they wasted too much time on the project. The piece should certainly not be taken as indicative of a genuine interest in socialism – a cause which, admittedly, the Finnish workers' movement had not yet espoused in a radical form. In fact Sibelius's true attitude to the working class was probably less sympathetic; a few years later he noted: 'Flirting with the workers [is] worse than currying favour with the upper class. One has to crush so much of one's own personality'. Plainly, however, Erkko's words have a nationalist message: 'In us lies the greatness which is Finland's, likewise her people's strength, so let us rise!' which would presumably have been appealed to the composer.

While he was in Kuopio Sibelius met up with Richard Faltin. He showed him the newly completed piano sonata (in fact he may have waited until he reached Kuopio to put the finishing touches to the work) and Faltin promptly sight-read the entire piece in his 'staccato-like style'. The sonata was not performed in public, however, until 1895.

On 20th August aunt Evelina died. The house in Lovisa was sold and another link to Sibelius's youth was broken. This building has, at least, met a kinder fate than his childhood home in Hämeenlinna: the Lovisa house is now a museum devoted to Sibelius.

During the summer or autumn of 1893 Sibelius assembled a set of six *Impromptus* for piano, Op. 5. Some of these pieces clearly bear the traces of Sibelius's contacts with Finnish folk music; Erik Tawaststjerna aptly characterizes the second impromptu as a 'Karelian trepak', whilst the march-like third includes a motif very similar to folk-like ideas in the *F major Violin Sonata* or, indeed, in *En saga*. The fourth impromptu has a melancholy, quasi-runic melody, and the broken chords in the initial statement of the theme call to mind the sound of the *kantele*. Framing these three folk-inspired pieces are three others that can perhaps be seen as a 'rescue attempt' on Sibelius's part for music that he regarded as too good to waste. The first of the set employs a theme from the finale of the *Piano Quintet in G minor* from 1890 – a movement that had not been played and which Sibelius may well have regarded as a lost cause. Meanwhile the fifth and sixth recycle material from the *Svartsjukans nätter* melodrama, a piece that Sibelius might have expected to sink without trace after its performance that February at the Runeberg jubilee. So reluctant was Sibelius to abandon the material of these two movements that he arranged them for string orchestra some months later. Whilst Sibelius does not truly attempt to link the six impromptus thematically as a cycle, they do form a highly effective suite, and – perhaps by coincidence – the march theme from the third impromptu is a variant of the main theme of the fifth piece.

While rescuing material from the *Piano Quintet*, presumably in the autumn of 1893, Sibelius composed his only surviving work for viola and piano: the *Rondo in D minor*, JS 162, which, like the first of the piano *Impromptus*, is based on a theme from the quintet's finale. The piece was dedicated to Arvid Järnefelt and was premièred a few months later – on 10th March 1894 – by Knut Heikel and Oskar Merikanto at a popular concert in Helsinki's Seurahuone (Societetshuset – now the Town Hall).

Back in Helsinki, the Sibelius family needed to find a new apartment, as they had given up their previous home in Wladimirinkatu before the summer – partly to save money, but also because their landlord had been declared bankrupt and the property was to be sold. In due course they moved into premises in Puistokatu 9, in the southern part of the city but still within easy walking distance of the fashionable restaurants in the centre.

The music for *Karelia*, JS 115, was completed in time for the Viipuri Student Association's soirée at the Seurahuone on 13th November 1893. The organizers had done their utmost to make the pageant an evening to remember. If the organizers had seen Sibelius as the foremost Karelianist composer, they saw Axel Gallén as his counterpart in pictorial art – and so Gallén, along with the sculptor Emil Wikström and the architect and author Jac Ahrenberg, had been commissioned to provide the stage sets. The *Karelia* project was in fact the only artistic occasion on which Sibelius and Gallén collaborated; otherwise their creative paths proceeded without intersection. The great runic singer Larin Paraske herself made an appearance on stage in the role of a farmer's wife, and the music was performed by the Philharmonic Society orchestra under Sibelius's own baton. There was also an introductory speech by Gabriel Lagus, an expert on the history of Viipuri. The lottery offered generous prizes – including paintings by leading artists, and suites of furniture – and the evening was sold out.

Sibelius was only one of many prominent contributors to *Karelia*, and the audience was drawn from a wider pool than the normal circle of Helsinki concert-goers; there was thus a risk that the music would be overlooked – and so it turned out. So enthusiastically talkative was the audience that only the *Ballade*, with a Mr Kruskopf as baritone soloist, was granted any sort of respectful silence. This must have come as an irritation for Sibelius, but he seems to have planned for such an eventuality. The complete pageant was given its second – and final – stage performance on 18th November, and the very next day he included an extended suite from the score at a 'composer's portrait' concert in Helsinki, again with the Philharmonic Society orchestra. Over the coming seasons he conducted various different selections from the score, billed as 'Suite for Orchestra' or 'Suite on Historical Motifs'. It is quite possible that Sibelius was advised by Robert Kajanus (who was, after all, still waiting for his 'short "da capo" piece') when choosing the most effective pieces for concert use. At any rate, in one of the earliest of these concerts, on 23rd November 1893, he chanced upon the four movements that he would eventually choose to publish – the *Overture*, *Alla marcia* (from tableau III), *Ballade* (already now with cor anglais replacing the baritone solo) and *Intermezzo* (from tableau V). It should be noted that the titles of the *Alla marcia* and *Intermezzo* eventually changed places; at the concert on 23rd November, the pieces were played in the order of the published suite!

Robert Kajanus kept the original manuscript of the *Karelia* music, and it was only returned to Sibelius in 1936, three years after Kajanus's death. During the 1940s Sibelius burned much of the only existing score, although many of the original parts survived and these formed the basis of a score assembled by Kalevi Kuosa in 1965. This was still unperformable, however, as Kuosa had to leave blank spaces where various parts (often for the lower strings) were missing. In the 1990s two different – and very skilful – reconstructions were made by the composers Kalevi Aho and Jouni Kaipainen, permitting us to hear the *Karelia* score in something close to its original form.

At least parts of the *Karelia* score were written in some haste, and this may help to explain the uneven musical quality. Some of the movements offer little more than background atmosphere, whilst others – even in their original form – are exquisitely crafted concert items. Several themes appear in more than one movement, but they are not used with consistent representative purpose and thus cannot be seen as leitmotifs in the Wagnerian sense. The overture (to which Sibelius made only the tiniest of modifications before publication in 1906) contains several of these ideas: its second theme is a melancholy melody in the folk style which is heard again in tableaux III and VI, and later on there are fanfares and a march theme in the woodwind that recur most promi-nently in the first intermezzo. The main theme is festive and exuberant, with telling use of Sibelius's trademark triplet rhythms. The opening bars bear a close resemblance to a string quartet piece written some five years earlier, the *Andantino in C major*, JS 39, and this may be one of the reasons why Sibelius later told his publisher Breitkopf & Härtel that the piece sounded 'almost too "youthful"' and insisted that the date of composition be printed on the score. An extensive sketch for the overture[3] contains a programmatic explanation by Sibelius: 'A soul searching for peace [corrected to: happiness] / Searches but cannot find. Mood grows impatient. / Surrenders and tries to kill joy. / Bacchanalia. / I retreat to solitude by a distant forest lake. It is evening. / A lonely water bird is singing sorrowfully.'

The first tableau depicts a Karelian home in the year 1293. After an atmospheric introduction, two singers perform a genuine 5/4 runic melody antiphonally; the text comes from Runo 14 of the *Kalevala*. The tune is a souvenir of Sibelius's Karelian expedition the previous year, whilst the *pizzicato* accompaniment resembles the sound of the *kantele*. The timeless folk melody is interrupted with frightening abruptness by a *fff* outburst and, at the end of the tableau, a messenger announces the outbreak of war. Here the horn calls and *tremolo* background create a magical atmosphere comparable to that of the closing bars of the prelude to Shakespeare's

Tempest, written more than three decades later. When Sibelius burned parts of the score in his old age, this was the only unpublished movement that he spared.

In the musically less original second tableau, again set in 1293, the foundations of Viipuri castle were laid. The opening fugue, based on a single theme in *Moderato assai* tempo, survived intact in the parts, but the original viola, cello and double bass lines at the end of the movement were lost. Kalevi Aho calls this part of the movement 'a chorale with a Gregorian atmosphere'.

The music for the third tableau falls into two parts. The first is based on the second theme of the overture, later combined with a derivation of the overture's fanfare motif (here, too, the lower string parts required completion). This leads directly into the first *Intermezzo*, where the fanfares and associated march theme accompany a Lithuanian Duke, Narimont, as he gathers tax tributes in the Käkisalmi district (near Lake Ladoga, now in Russia) in the winter of 1333. This *Intermezzo*, with small revisions – most noticeably a less prominent tambourine part – became the first movement of the published suite, and Sibelius also transcribed it for solo piano, at the latest in 1897.

The fourth tableau became the second movement of the published suite, the *Ballade*. The year is 1446, and the scene is a room in Viipuri castle, at the court of Karl Knutsson Bonde, who later became King of Sweden. A singer entertains the nobleman and his retinue with a gentle ballad (heard at the end of the tableau). The text comes from the Swedish folk ballad *Dansen i rosenlund (The Dance in the Flowering Grove)*, and tells how a page boy rides his grey horse to a flowering grove, where he encounters dancing women and maids. The music certainly reflects the melancholy refrain 'I biden mig väl!' ('You wait for me then!') rather than the joy of the dance. For concert use the baritone soloist was replaced by a cor anglais, and the original three verses were reduced to one. This movement, too, appeared in a piano transcription.

The fifth tableau takes us to 1580, and the conquest of the town of Käkisalmi by the French-born Swedish commander Pontus De la Gardie. At the original pageant there were fireworks on stage to depict the firing of De la Gardie's guns. Unfortunately this movement also lacks its original lower string parts, and here it is plain that the lower strings were essential to the musical argument. This is followed by another intermezzo, referred to variously as 'Tableau 5 1/2', 'Pontus De la Gardie's March' and 'Marsch nach einem alten Motiv'. This vibrant, exuberant march, with very tiny amendments, became the last movement of the published suite, *Alla marcia*.

The siege of Viipuri castle in 1710 provided the setting for the sixth tableau, although the castle itself was not depicted on stage. Like the second tableau, this movement is based on a fugue – this time at a rather quicker tempo – but unfortunately, as in the fifth tableau, the original cello and bass parts, as well as some of the viola part, are lost. After some imposing brass fanfares, the woodwind weave the second theme of the overture into the texture.

The last two tableaux are played without a break and depict the reunion of Old Finland [Karelia] with the rest of Finland in 1811. Two versions of the seventh tableau have survived intact, one considerably simpler than the other. In the eighth tableau, however, the flute and cello parts are incomplete. The newspaper *Nya Pressen* described the stage production as follows: 'The curtain rises to reveal Finland, a maiden, one arm bearing a shield depicting the lion, the other arm embracing a young Karelian woman who is snuggling up to her. To the right and left are peasants from the Häme region, a man and a woman, carrying spade and distaff.' Sibelius's music in the seventh tableau has impressive cumulative power and creates a genuine feeling of anticipation; in the eighth tableau the tension is released with a rousing arrangement of Pacius's patriotic song *Vårt land* (*Maamme* / *Our Country*). This song, written in 1848 and with words by Runeberg, was by then so well-known that the audience spontaneously joined in; when Finland gained independence, it became the national anthem. It brought the pageant to a close amid intense feelings of patriotic fervour.

The favourable reception of *Karelia* came at a time when Sibelius was badly in need of another success as an orchestral composer; previously, his only great triumph had been the 1892 performance of *Kullervo*, and even that had bewildered some of its listeners. His thoughts were still very much occupied with *The Building of the Boat*, however, and he showed the draft libretto to the influential and highly respected theatre director Kaarlo Bergbom. In addition to founding the Finnish Theatre, Bergbom also supervised Finnish-language opera productions, and the opening of the new Finnish National Theatre building in 1902 was to crown his distinguished career. In Bergbom's view the text was too lyrical, and Sibelius had to admit that he was right, although this was by no means the final nail in the opera's coffin.

CHAPTER 5

THE TONE PAINTER AND POET:
1894–1898

1894

The Symposium gatherings at the Hotel Kämp were still going strong, sometimes for days on end, and the presence of Adolf Paul – on a visit from Berlin – gave further cause to celebrate the new year. Perhaps it was a consequence of such distractions that Sibelius's compositions from the first few months of 1894 are smaller-scale works. On 17th February 1894, he conducted a concert in Turku that included *En saga*, an extended selection from *Karelia* (again with cor anglais in the *Ballade*) and two 'new' works for strings, a *Presto* and an *Impromptu*.[1] In fact both of the novelties were arrangements rather than new compositions: the *Presto* was the scherzo from the *String Quartet in B flat major*, whilst the *Impromptu* was a combination of the fifth and sixth piano *Impromptus* from the previous year (themselves a reworking of material from the *Melodrama from 'Svartsjukans nätter'*). A different arrangement for strings of just the fifth piano *Impromptu* has also survived in in the collection of the National Library of Finland.

During the spring, the YL choir declared the result of a composition competition that had been announced the previous year. Sibelius's entry was *Rakastava (The Lover)*, JS 160a, one of his most challenging choral works, with texts from the *Kanteletar* – a major collection of ballads and lyrics published in 1840–41 which can be regarded as lyric poetry's counterpart to the *Kalevala*. Like the *Kalevala*, it was based on ancient poems passed on by word of mouth, and was assembled by Elias Lönnrot, who proudly boasted in his preface that 'in literary poetry Finland lags far behind many other nations; but this need not greatly trouble us, for in folk poetry it is among the leaders'.

Sibelius's piece, a choral suite in all but name, falls into three main parts, and the long final section can itself be divided into two; the concluding section requires a tenor solo. The robust opening section, *Miss' on kussa minun hyväni* (*Where is my beloved?*) gives little hint of the technical challenges to come, but the second, *Eilaa, eilaa*, contains elements that were unheard of in Finnish choral music of the 1890s, such as falsetto tenors, an incessant quasi-vocalise on the untranslatable word 'eilaa' and the presentation of the text (often enunciated very quickly) in a manner close to *Sprechgesang*. The first part of the final section, *Hyvää iltaa, lintuseni* (*Good evening, my little bird*) returns to the more straightforward style of the opening, but before long the solo tenor enters; the rest of the choir returns to the repeated intonation of the word 'eilaa', now more slowly and elegiacally, while the soloist has an eloquent and sometimes dissonant line (the music's metre here closely follows the requirements of the text; the time signature varies between 5/2, 7/2 and 3/2). The overall structure of the piece thus alternates between relatively vigorous, essentially homophonic passages and atmospheric sections that are freer in both rhythm and texture.

Rakastava was awarded second prize; the winning entry was *Hakkapeliitta*, a patriotic piece by one of Sibelius's former schoolteachers in Hämeenlinna, Emil Genetz – the name (from the war cry 'hakkaa päälle') refers to an élite troupe of Finnish cavalrymen. The winning entries were performed on 28th April. Because Genetz's song involved the participation of a string orchestra, Sibelius – mindful of the technical difficulties inherent in his work – decided to add a discreet string backing to *Rakastava* as well (JS 160b). But if his intention had been to make life easier for the singers by adding an accompaniment, Sibelius failed: there were such severe problems of intonation that the conductor Jalmari Hahl decided to perform it *a cappella* anyway. In his later choral music Sibelius did not follow up on the innovations he had tried in *Rakastava*. Perhaps he was discouraged by the problems encountered at its first performance.

It was most probably around this time that Sibelius wrote another song for tenor and choir on a *Kanteletar* text: *Soitapas sorea neito* (*Play, Pretty Maiden*), JS 176 (a precise dating within the 1893–94 period is impossible). There are clear similarities between the tenor solos in the two works; here too the metre changes to suit the text, and here too the word 'eilaa' is used a colouristic element. Unlike the first version of *Rakastava*, however, this short piece is for mixed choir.

Three other fragments can be dated to no later than 1894, although we know very little about their origins and they may have been written up to three years earlier. A [*Mazurka, Sketch*] *in D minor* for piano is reminiscent of the chordal theme in the finale of the *'Hafträsk' Trio*. An *[Allegretto] in A major* for solo violin is an effective display piece in a virtuosic style. More interesting – and certainly more characteristic – is the *[Grave, Fragment] in D minor* for violin and piano, which not only opens with a bar virtually stolen from the introduction to the *Svartsjukans nätter* melodrama (and which subsequently found its way into the revised 1895 version of *Spring Song*) but goes on to develop an anguished, at times chromatic theme in slow 3/2 time that is a forerunner of the *Great Hostility* movement from the *Press Celebrations Music* of 1899.

In 1894 Axel Gallén was inspired by the tone poem *En saga* to paint a small diptych including a portrait of Sibelius on the right, and a landscape inspired by the music on the left, with a space beneath for a quotation from *En saga*. The painting found its way into Sibelius's possession, but he never filled in the blank space. Had he done so, this would probably have been seen as a confirmation that the mood of the painting corresponded to Sibelius's 'expression of a state of mind' – and it comes as no surprise that he was unwilling to provide such an endorsement.

During the spring Richard Faltin secured for Sibelius a temporary lecturing position at Helsinki University. Sibelius might not have been overjoyed at the prospect of teaching, but at least it was paid employment and an incentive not to spend too many of his waking hours at the Kämp. One of the duties he had to perform was to compose a cantata – the *Promotional Cantata* – or, more exactly, *Cantata for the University Graduation Ceremonies of 1894*, JS 105 – his first piece in this genre and one of three such pieces that he produced for specific occasions in Helsinki in the 1890s.

Thus Sibelius did not write the piece from any particular inner compulsion, but rather because it was expected of him, and apparently he left it until the last moment. The at times rather inelegant text is by Kasimir Lönnbohm, elder brother of Eino Leino, and it is reported that the relationship between author and composer was not without strain. After its first performance on 31st May 1894, the piece was soon forgotten, except for an *a cappella* arrangement of the march section at the end of the second movement that was published separately under the title of *Juhlamarssi (Festive March)* in 1896. The soloists at the première were Aino Ackté (daughter of Emmy Achté who had sung in the première of *Kullervo*) and Abraham Ojanperä.

If the fires of Sibelius's inspiration burn rather less brightly in the *Promotional Cantata* than in some of his other works from the 1890s, the piece does not quite deserve the invective that has been poured upon it; even Erik Tawaststjerna dismissed it as 'banal'. Much of the weight of the first movement is concentrated in the chorale-like theme heard from the choir at the beginning. The choir theme remains essentially unchanged during the course of its four appearances, though the orchestral writing is more varied, incorporating a fugue and culminating in a furious *tutti*. Sibelius had used the same procedure – varying the texture of the accompaniment rather than developing the theme itself – the previous year in the slow movement of his *Piano Sonata in F major*.

The long second movement features soprano and baritone soloists as well as choir and orchestra. Only two years had elapsed since *Kullervo*, with its even longer central movement for soloists, choir and orchestra – and, like *Kullervo*, the cantata movement gives some idea of what an opera by Sibelius might have sounded like. The movement opens with a characteristic Sibelian theme that bears the imprint of folk music without resorting to direct quotation. Later the music betrays that this was a period during which Wagner loomed large in Sibelius's musical consciousness. Might Sibelius, in his haste to complete the university project, also have borrowed some ideas from the projected *Building of the Boat* opera for his cantata? As with folk music, so too with Wagner: Sibelius never attempts to copy the style directly, but assimilates elements of the original into his own unmistakable idiom.

Unlike the central movement of *Kullervo* which begins very effectively in 5/4 time, the cantata movement remains in a steady four crotchets to the bar throughout. In both works the solo passages by and large alternate with choral sections. The soloists and choir do, however, join forces in the splendidly bombastic march with which the cantata movement ends. Naturally the cantata lacks the vivid narrative and dramatic story-line of *Kullervo*. We also search Lönnbohm's text in vain for the hypnotic metrical regularity and linguistic resourcefulness of the *Kalevala* text used in *Kullervo*, even if there is a passing reference to the old magician in the *Kalevala*, Väinämöinen.

The third movement of the *Promotional Cantata* was originally performed separately in the degree ceremony, and can thus be seen almost as an appendix. There is no choir in this movement and, unfortunately, in modern performances, there is no soloist either. Originally there had been a soprano solo in the brief central trio section, but the solo part is now lost. Its absence does not, however, render the piece unperformable. The main section of the piece is a stylish minuet featuring two themes that, many years later, Sibelius incorporated into *At the Draw-Bridge*, the last piece in the second set of *Scènes historiques* (1912). For Sibelius, whose interest in dance forms of various kinds is often underestimated, minuets were evidently of great interest at this period: for instance, the well-known *Ballade* from the *Karelia* music had been written just a few months earlier. The orchestral accompaniment in the trio section of the cantata movement

– rising cello *pizzicato* figures, beneath ethereal chords from the upper strings – has a clear affinity to the orchestral writing at the beginning of the *Serenade* for baritone and orchestra (1894–95) to words by Stagnelius. There is, it should be noted, a vast difference between the stately, gracious minuets that Sibelius composed in the 1890s and the bolder, more stylized attempts at the same dance form from later in his career.

In June Sibelius and Aino visited Vaasa to present a new work at a choral festival arranged by the Society for Popular Education. That summer the family were the guests of Edvard Björkenheim at Orismala, to the south-east of the city. At an open-air concert on 21st June 1894 – with General Järnefelt in the audience – the premières were given both of the tone poem *Korsholm* by Armas Järnefelt and of an *Improvisation* in D major for orchestra by Sibelius. The event was prestigious enough to have attracted many orchestral players from Helsinki's Philharmonic Society orchestra, and the leading figures in Finnish music conducted their own music – Faltin, Wegelius and Kajanus as well as Sibelius and Järnefelt. Järnefelt's *Korsholm*, a grand, rhapsodic, patriotic tone poem, was received with greater enthusiasm than Sibelius's relatively unassuming and predominantly lyrical work.

The *Improvisation* was soon withdrawn from circulation, but Sibelius revised it the following spring and named it *Spring Song*. It was formerly assumed that the 1894 *Improvisation*/*Spring Song* was lost. Much credence was attached to contemporary reports that mentioned a concluding *Allegro* section: 'The musical idea of the movement evolves to a gradually continuing *crescendo*, yet not dependent on the growing mass effect of tones, but on a wonderful inner heightening, which reaches its culmination, suddenly changes and moves on to a conclusion in the rhythm of a Spanish dance with brisk flicks of tambourines' (*Nya Pressen*, 23rd June 1894). A set of parts (without a score) for a D major version that turned up in the 1930s contained no such dance section – and no tambourine part – and these parts were thus assumed to represent the revised version of 1895. Between 1895 and its publication in 1903, *Spring Song* was frequently performed. It was believed that a further extensive revision (and a change of key from D major to F major) took place shortly before publication.

The research undertaken by Tuija Wicklund in preparation for the critical edition of the work (2006), however, makes a persuasive case for a different scenario. For a start, reviews indicate that the 1895 version was already in F major, and suggest that it contained an appreciable amount of *tremolo* writing (which is much more noticeable in the published score than in the earlier version). In addition, the orchestral parts for the D major version are hardly used, whilst two surviving hand-copied parts for the F major version exhibit extensive wear and tear – which would not

be the case if the F major version had been published immediately after
its composition. The inescapable conclusion is that the piece was revised
only once, for the performance in 1895. It would thus seem likely that the
tambourine part was simply mislaid and that the mere inclusion of the
instrument in the 1894 performance was enough to cause the reviewer to
write of 'the rhythm of a Spanish dance'.

Though it may have paled alongside the patriotic bombast of Järnefelt's
Korsholm, the 1894 *Improvisation/Spring Song* was probably Sibelius's
most easy-going and accessible orchestral work to date. For this work the
composer put aside any dreams of Wagnerian opera. There are no apparent
links with the *Kalevala* or indeed with any other literary programme; just
like *En saga*, it is an 'expression of a state of mind'. Although trademarks
such as triplet fanfares are present, Sibelius focuses unashamedly on
melody, and endows the piece with thematic invention that is as fresh as
it is sumptuous. As his friend and patron Axel Carpelan later observed,
the piece portrays 'the slow, laborious arrival of the Nordic spring and
wistful melancholy'.[2]

During the summer it was time to come to grips with *The Building of
the Boat* – and with his attitude to Wagner – once and for all. The opera
project was then in abeyance, as Sibelius had decided that Erkko was
not after all a suitable librettist. The poet and university lecturer Paavo
Cajander seemed a suitable replacement, and in early July Sibelius met
up with him near Hämeenlinna and persuaded him to participate in the
enterprise. After that, Sibelius set off for Bayreuth. He had inherited some
money when Aunt Evelina had died, and some of this was used to fund the
journey. He travelled alone: Aino was advised against travelling as she was
pregnant. Sibelius took the boat down the Rhine from Hamburg to Mainz,
equipped with scores for *Lohengrin* and *Tannhäuser*. On the very day he
arrived in Bayreuth he went to see *Parsifal*, which made an overwhelming
impression on him. 'Nothing on earth has made such an impression on me,'
he wrote to Aino. 'All my innermost heartstrings throbbed... I can't begin
to tell you how *Parsifal* has transported me.' He was to be less impressed
by either *Lohengrin* or *Tannhäuser* over the next few days, and he soon
moved on to Munich, where he planned to study Wagner's scores in peace
and make progress with *The Building of the Boat*. As soon as he left the
epicentre of Wagner-veneration, he was able to take a more balanced view,
and to set Wagner's work in the context of the broader German cultural
tradition. He wrote to Aino: 'There are large collections here. The other
arts fascinate me more than does other people's music... Wagner's music
does not have an overwhelming effect on me. In my view it is altogether
too well calculated... Besides, his musical ideas themselves strike me as
manufactured (not fresh).' In the same letter he mentions the idea of

writing another, more traditional opera about an unfaithful student. Very possibly this new opera plan was never a serious proposal; if Sibelius did ever start work on it, he either discarded the material or used it in other compositions.

Sibelius was thus already entertaining doubts about whether or not he should follow a Wagnerian path when he met up with Armas Järnefelt in Munich. Järnefelt was accompanied by his wife Maikki, whom he had married the previous year. Maikki Järnefelt was one of Finland's leading singers of her generation, who appeared regularly in Wagnerian roles and later became a distinguished recitalist and singing teacher. Armas accompanied Sibelius on his visits to Munich's art galleries and will have witnessed his enthusiastic response to the Symbolist painters, especially Böcklin. The composer's increasingly sceptical feelings towards Wagner were thus not mirrored by his attitude to Symbolism in pictorial art.

Armas and Maikki shared an enthusiasm for Wagner, and they persuaded Sibelius to return to Bayreuth for another performance of *Parsifal*. Before he left Germany, he also heard *Tristan*, *Die Walküre*, *Siegfried* and *Götterdämmerung*. Sibelius was impressed – especially by *Parsifal* and *Tristan* – but these performances served only to strengthen his conviction that his own path lay in a different direction. He wrote to Aino on 17th August: 'It [*Götterdämmerung*] is marvellous but only in places. I am not so confirmed a Wagnerite as the others.' Within days he came to the conclusion: 'I believe that I am above all a tone painter and poet. Liszt's view of music is the one to which I am closest. That is, the symphonic poem. I'm working on a theme that I'm very pleased with.' It is probable that the theme Sibelius mentions here was either from *The Wood-Nymph* or the *Lemminkäinen Suite*. On 21st August he heard *Die Meistersinger*, a work he very much liked, but it was too late; his mind was made up. 'I am no longer an Wagnerite', he wrote to Aino the following day.

Of course the stylistic difference between Wagner and Liszt does not represent an unbreachable gulf. It is, however, significant that Sibelius was already thinking in terms of symphonic poems. His operatic plans – both *The Building of the Boat* and the unnamed opera about the errant student – faded from the picture. The effort Sibelius had put into his abandoned opera was not wholly wasted, as many of the musical ideas were transferred to the *Lemminkäinen Suite*, also based on themes from the *Kalevala*. The likelihood that *The Wood-Nymph* – his other major symphonic poem from the next few years – also drew some of its thematic material from the operatic sketches is fairly high. And thus, even after his Wagner crisis, the words that he had written to Erkko in July 1893, when his enthusiasm for *The Building of the Boat* was at its height, still held partly true: 'I believe that music alone, that is to say absolute music, is in itself not enough...

Music attains its fullest power only when it is motivated by poetic impulse. In other words when words and music blend.'

Having confronted his Wagnerian demons, Sibelius took a brief but enjoyable holiday in Venice – his first visit to Italy – before heading for Berlin, where he visited his old friends Busoni and Paul, and immersed himself in the score of Liszt's *Faust Symphony* ('it is magnificent and I am learning much from it', he wrote to Aino on 7th September). He did not arrive back in Helsinki until the middle of September.

Sibelius may have been impressed with the Symbolist paintings he saw in Germany, but one work in that style that was exhibited in Helsinki that autumn had a more immediate relevance. The picture in question was Axel Gallén's *The Problem* (a new version of his painting *Symposium* from the previous year), depicting Sibelius, Kajanus and the artist himself at a restaurant, clearly the worse for wear and deeply absorbed in conversation. In its day this painting was as 'sensational' as some of today's paparazzi photographs, but none of the participants could deny its veracity.

Even as a child Sibelius had not been especially close to his mother, but from now on she seems almost to vanish from his life. There is nothing to suggest any particular rift between them, but nor do we find evidence that the deeply religious and aloof Maria Sibelius made any attempt to become intimate with his new circle of friends, or even with the Järnefelts. Presumably she was pleased to become a grandmother. Unlike the Järnefelts, she did not attend any of Jean's important concerts. In the autumn of 1894 she moved to the industrial city of Tampere, where she set up house with the composer's sister Linda, who had moved there the previous year and was working as a teacher. Maria's youngest brother Otto also lived in Tampere and was in the same profession. Tampere was only about a hundred miles from Helsinki and the railways made it easily accessible. In the 1890s the city already had a thriving interest in theatre,[3] but was not yet an established venue for orchestral music; its orchestra (now the Tampere Philharmonic Orchestra) was not founded until 1930.

At a popular concert at Helsinki's Seurahuone on 23rd October Robert Kajanus conducted the first performance of a *Menuetto* for orchestra, JS 127, that Sibelius had concocted from the minuet he had written for solo piano in Vienna, and had also sketched for violin and cello; this material would later end up in the incidental music to *King Christian II*. It is possible, or even probable, that the orchestral minuet was written at Kajanus's suggestion.

The last months of 1894 were a period of some stress for Sibelius and his family. After his extended trip abroad, he was forced to take temporary lodgings while looking for accommodation for the season. The flat he eventually found, in Itäinen Kaivopuisto, was conveniently located but rather small. After they moved in, Eva contracted typhoid and Aino, who was by now heavily pregnant, had to turn to her mother for help in nursing her (Alexander and Elisabeth Järnefelt had just moved to Helsinki, where the General had been awarded a ministerial position). On 23rd November Aino gave birth to another daughter, Ruth. With all of these distractions it is no surprise that this period brought forth little in the way of new compositions. At least Sibelius managed to persuade Wegelius to grant him leave of absence from the Music Institute; one obstacle to the production of new works was thus removed. And Aino must have breathed a sigh of relief when Axel Gallén left for Ruovesi (and subsequently Berlin), thereby depriving her husband of a further distraction.

Meanwhile the death of Tsar Alexander III at the Livadia Palace in the Crimea on 1st November 1894 heralded a new and threatening chapter of Finnish history. He was succeeded by his eldest son, who became Tsar Nicholas II.

1895

On 9th March 1895 a fundraising lottery was arranged by the Finnish Theatre at the Seurahuone in Helsinki, and Sibelius contributed a vivid and colourful new melodrama: *The Wood-Nymph*, Op. 15, the same text by Rydberg that he had set as a solo song some years earlier. Just over a month later, on 17th April, he produced a major tone poem for full orchestra, Op. 16, based on the same material. Oskar Merikanto in *Päivälehti* opined that the melodrama was 'the most beautifully coloured of all Sibelius's small tone paintings', and that 'the final section is some of the most attractive music that Sibelius has written'. Quite when Sibelius started work on this project is unclear, but it may well have been during his time in Germany the previous autumn. In any case it is highly unlikely that he could have written this melodrama unless he was already well advanced with the orchestral tone poem. The weeks that elapsed between the first performance of the melodrama version and the première of the orchestral tone poem would clearly have been insufficient for him to have expanded the melodrama, which is roughly ten minutes long, into the tone poem, which plays for more than twenty. The relatively small forces required by the melodrama – narrator, two horns, strings and piano, with the piano replacing many of the woodwind and brass parts of the tone poem version – strongly suggest that he simply abbreviated the almost complete tone poem to produce a work suitable for the lottery event.

The music is episodic in nature, and follows the narrative closely. The hero, Björn, is imposingly depicted in the first part of the work with a noble march theme in C major, heard above a groundswell of string triplets.

In the second section, when the dwarves tempt him, the music portrays their wild dancing with a long, gradual build-up that remains resolutely anchored in A minor. In the scene where Björn falls in love with the wood-nymph, Sibelius interprets the poem in a wholly different way from the earlier song version: this time he writes a tranquil passage for horn and solo cello; in the tone poem the mood is shattered at one point by a wild, exotic outburst. The concluding section, Björn's realization of his fate, has the atmosphere of a funeral march and makes constant use of Sibelius's much favoured rhythmic pattern of 'short–long–short' notes. The mood is intensely sombre, with sonorous orchestral writing.

Wagner certainly looms large in the *The Wood-Nymph* although, as always, Sibelius is no mere imitator. Rydberg's poem has nothing to do with the *Kalevala*, but stylistically some aspects of *The Wood-Nymph* are related to Symbolist works such as the *Lemminkäinen Suite*. For many years the melodrama and tone poem versions of this glorious work were known to Sibelius enthusiasts only as entries in his catalogue of works. They remained unpublished and virtually unplayed until they were triumphantly reintroduced to the repertoire by Osmo Vänskä and the Lahti Symphony Orchestra in 1996.

The concert at the University Hall on 17th April gave the Helsinki public an opportunity to become acquainted with a number of Sibelius's recent orchestral works under the composer's own baton. The programme comprised a selection of movements from *Karelia*, the *Piano Sonata in F major* (played by Oskar Merikanto), *Spring Song*, the *Serenade* for baritone and orchestra and the tone poem version of *The Wood-Nymph*. The orchestral items were repeated two days later.

Spring Song was now heard in its more or less definitive F major form. It was described by Oskar Merikanto as 'the fairest flower among Sibelius's orchestral pieces', and Karl Flodin felt that the piece now had 'a tone that is just as fresh and appealingly Nordic as in the works of Grieg and Sinding'. As with the original version, much of the work's appeal resides in the breadth and eloquence of its themes, but these are now treated with greater concision and elegance. The F major version is 67 bars shorter than the one in D major and rises to an imposing climax at which the bells ring out imposingly (the two handwritten parts show that Sibelius once envisaged a shorter ending for the piece, but changed his mind – perhaps even before the first performance of this version).

If *Spring Song* focuses on melody, the *Serenade* for baritone and orchestra, a setting of a rather intense poem by Erik Johan Stagnelius, is more concerned with atmosphere. We do not know exactly when the song was composed; it may have been written especially for this concert, where it was sung by Abraham Ojanperä. Over a backdrop of shimmering violins and *pizzicato* cellos, the baritone sings a nocturnal lament for his lost love. The vocal line has elements of chromaticism that again reflect Sibelius's dalliance with Wagner. A planned revision of this song in 1910 never came about, but Sibelius transferred elements of its vocal line to a new song, *Långsamt som kvällskyn* (*Slowly as the Evening Sky*), to a poem by Tavaststjerna.

In May Busoni came to Helsinki for a series of concerts, and came up with the idea that Sibelius should try to have his music issued by Mitrofan Belyayev's publishing house in St Petersburg. Belyayev, who started his career as a timber merchant, was an unusually generous musical patron but, when he turned to music publishing in 1885, decided to limit the repertoire of his company to the work of Russian composers. His catalogue featured works by the foremost homegrown talents, for instance Balakirev, Borodin, Glazunov, Rimsky-Korsakov and Mussorgsky. As Finland was still officially a Russian grand duchy, Sibelius could have been considered eligible. Busoni's idea was a good one and prompted Sibelius to write to Belyayev, but nothing more came of the initiative. It is interesting to speculate as to whether Sibelius's music might have developed differently if he had been accepted into the Russian musical establishment. As things were, however, he pursued the western European course that had been virtually predetermined by his studies in Helsinki, Berlin and Vienna.

Moving out of their lodgings in Itäinen Kaivopuisto, Sibelius and his family headed for Vaania, by Lake Vesijärvi north of Lahti, for the summer of 1895. It was a happy time. Despite almost constant rain and the stress of looking after two young daughters, Aino managed to relax by picking berries and going fishing with her husband. When not spending time with his family Sibelius retired to his room and composed. One result of his labours was the elegant male choir song *Saarella palaa* (*Fire on the Island*), Op. 18 No. 4, a setting of a shepherd's song – No. 186 in the *Kanteletar*, where it is named *Työnsä kumpasellaki* (*To Each his Work*) – that tells of the preparations for a country wedding. The main theme is introduced as a vocalise above a bass pedal point on the words 'Saarella palaa', which leads one to suspect that Sibelius was already well advanced with his plans for *Lemminkäinen and the Maidens of the Island*, where a similar effect is created at the first appearance of the dance-like main theme.

Even though there was no piano in the rented cottage, it was here that he wrote one of the most impressive of his single-movement piano works, the *Romance in A major*, Op. 24 No. 2. This piece, which has the scale and emotional range of a tone poem, begins with the character of a sinister barcarole but later evolves into an intensely dramatic mood painting. With its broadly arching melodies and its characteristic use of descending fourths and fifths, the work bears the hallmarks of Sibelius's

COLORADO COLLEGE LIBRARY
COLORADO SPRINGS, COLORADO

musical Symbolism and of the forthcoming *Lemminkäinen Suite*. The rhythm of the opening right-hand motif certainly suggests *Lemminkäinen in Tuonela*. Later, however, the phrase structure in 6/4-time (notably the positioning of ascending quaver groups within the phrase) brings to mind *Lemminkäinen and the Maidens of the Island*; the lengthy build-up to an impressive climax and subsequent fall back to a serene coda are also reminiscent of that work. One thus wonders if the expressive world or even the thematic material of this *Romance* might likewise derive in some way from the shattered fragments of Sibelius's operatic boat.

The *Romance in A major* was published by Lindgren in Helsinki later that year together with two other piano pieces. One was the G minor *Impromptu*, Op. 24 No. 1.[4] The *Impromptu*, also composed in Vaania, opens in a tumultuous, scherzo-like mood, but this soon slows down and turns into a brooding waltz. Both the waltz theme itself and the *Vivace* middle section anticipate *Valse triste*. The third piece in Lindgren's edition was a transcription of the final peroration from *The Wood-Nymph*. The manuscript is lost but it is likely that the transcription was also made in Vaania with the forthcoming publication in mind.

It was probably in Vaania that Sibelius wrote a demonic dance for piano with the title *Caprizzio*. Stylistically close to the *Impromptu*, the *Caprizzio* features a theme that sounds like a macabre variant of the second group in the first movement of Tchaikovsky's *Fifth Symphony*. The manuscript is virtually complete but in poor condition, and the piece was rescued from oblivion only when Folke Gräsbeck gave it its first performance in 2002. The manuscript of the *Caprizzio* is dated 26th August 1895, which is roughly when the Sibelius family ended their holiday, visiting the von Konows and Sibelius's mother on the way back to Helsinki. By mid-September they had found a new home near the city centre, Kasarminkatu 22, which they were to occupy until the spring of 1898 – a break from their normal practice of moving house each season.

The principal musical undertaking for Sibelius at this time was the conversion of his operatic wreckage into a series of tone poems for orchestra, the *Lemminkäinen Suite*, and he took some time off from his teaching duties to concentrate on this project. In addition, however, he collaborated with A. A. Borenius on a series of runic song arrangements that were published in 1895 as part of the commentary to a new edition of the *Kalevala* by Suomen kirjallisuuden seura (the Finnish Literature Society). Seventeen melodies are included, five of them wedding tunes, and the majority had been collected by Borenius. Sibelius's involvement with runic melodies was nothing new: he had, after all, listened intently to Larin Paraske's incantations while composing *Kullervo*, and had spent time on his honeymoon trip exploring Karelian folk-songs. It is presumably purely coincidental that the runic song project came along while he was developing his own ideas for the *Lemminkäinen Suite*.

At a concert in the University Hall on 7th December – the day before Sibelius's 30th birthday – YL and Jalmari Hahl not only gave the first performance of *Saarella palaa* but also presented an *a cappella* arrangement that Sibelius had made of a ballad by the Latvian conductor, writer and composer Jāzeps Vītols. Vītols later achieved distinction as professor of composition at the St Petersburg Conservatory and became the first rector of the Latvian Conservatory in Riga when it was founded in 1919; the institute is now known as the Jāzeps Vītols Latvian Academy of Music. In 1891 Vītols made a setting of words by Auseklis (pseudonym of the poet Mikus Krogzemis), *Beverinas dziedonis*, for mixed choir and orchestra, and this formed the basis of Sibelius's arrangement for male voices, *Laulun mahti* (*The Power of Song*), JS 118, to a Finnish translation of the text by Jooseppi Julius Mikkola. The text describes a struggle between the Latvians and their jealous Estonian neighbours which is quelled by an 'old, grey-haired man with a *kantele*'. Clearly this figure resembles the *Kalevala*'s Väinämöinen, and the similarity between the conflict described in the song and the Finns' relationship with the Russians cannot have gone unnoticed.

1896

For Sibelius, 1896 was a year that started uneventfully. During its opening months he busied himself with the transformation of material from his sketches for the opera *The Building of the Boat* into the *Lemminkäinen Suite*, Op. 22. The suite focuses on the story of the daredevil young Lemminkäinen from the *Kalevala* – who has been compared to such heroes as Don Juan, Siegfried or Achilles. In the suite, unlike in *The Wood-Nymph*, Sibelius does not adhere strictly to the sequence of events in the narrative, concentrating instead upon evoking the general mood of the story; this scarcely comes as a surprise when we remember where much of the material had originated. Sketches preserved in the National Library of Finland (formerly known as the Helsinki University Library) confirm the close link between the *Lemminkäinen Suite* and the unfinished opera. Sibelius's work should also be seen against the background of the artistic climate of Helsinki, where Symbolism – for instance the paintings of such artists as Arnold Böcklin and Magnus Enckell, with their images of swans, water and death, desolate moods and other-worldly colourings – was very much in fashion.

We can only speculate about Martin Wegelius's attitude to Sibelius's decision to abandon *The Building of the Boat*. He must have been disappointed that his protégé had turned his back on the Wagnerian ideal. But by this time Sibelius and Wegelius were no longer the close confidants that they had been five years earlier. Ever since the time of *Kullervo* they had drifted apart; Wegelius's loyalties remained first and foremost with the Swedish-speaking faction, while Sibelius was increasingly drawn towards the Finnish speakers.

The *Lemminkäinen Suite* of 1896 was to undergo numerous changes before it reached the form that is normally played today. In 1897 Sibelius presented a revised version, and in 1900 *The Swan of Tuonela* and *Lemminkäinen's Return* were revised again in readiness for publication as separate pieces in 1901. The other two pieces remained unpublished and untouched for nearly forty years – apparently (according to Aino Sibelius) because Robert Kajanus was less than enthusiastic about them. With the *Karelia* music three years earlier Kajanus had proved to be a shrewd judge of which movements would be best suited to concert use – and at this stage Sibelius would have had no reason to question his friend's judgement.

Lemminkäinen and the Maidens of the Island is based on events related in Runo 29 of the *Kalevala*. Lemminkäinen sails his boat to an island where the menfolk are all away. He enjoys various amorous adventures with the women before being forced to flee when the men return and seek vengeance. Some critics have identified a sonata form structure in the piece, but – as so often – Sibelius handles his material with great freedom, and so formal analysis is of limited value. The movement, which lasts a quarter of an hour in performance, is thematically rich and diverse. The original version is even more colourfully scored than the final revision, made in 1939: it requires both tambourine and glockenspiel. A listener familiar with the revised version will notice innumerable small adjustments in the first part of the piece; the middle section, however, was virtually recomposed in 1939, to the extent that some passages are virtually unrecognizable even though the thematic material itself is basically unchanged. As with *En saga*, the original version sounds less integrated and rougher than the revised score. In the latter part of the movement the changes are much less drastic, although the original contained two successive wave-like *crescendos* (a device that he would later employ in *The Oceanides*) instead of a single, sustained climax.

The original second movement, *Lemminkäinen in Tuonela*, is dramatic, and rich in contrasts of dynamics and tempo. The *Kalevala* episodes upon which the movement is based (Runos 14–15) describe how Lemminkäinen, on a mission to kill the Swan of Tuonela and win the hand of the Daughter of the Northland, is ambushed and killed alongside the sacred river of Tuonela. His body is cut into pieces and thrown into the river, but he is rescued and brought back to life by his mother's magic. The outer sections feature extensive string *tremoli* – creating a relentless, wave-like effect anticipating the prelude to *The Tempest* (1925), and great thematic importance is attached to a four-note motif and its derivatives. A magical atmosphere is created by the middle section in A minor, *Molto lento*, with divided strings playing *ppp* above an almost imperceptible side-drum roll. The composer labelled his sketches for this passage with the words 'Tuonen tytti' ('The Maiden of Tuoni [Death]'). This is an allusion to the passage in the *Kalevala* where the maiden rows Väinämöinen, the minstrel and magician, across the river to Tuonela, the kingdom of the dead. Sibelius had planned a scene in *The Building of the Boat* in which Väinämöinen descends to Tuonela, which presumably served as the source for this passage.

In the case of *Lemminkäinen in Tuonela*, Sibelius's revisions have proved confusing, as the surviving orchestral parts are not always consistent with the manuscript. Clearly some passages were cut and the corresponding pages have been removed from the manuscript; in the parts these passages are crossed out but are still – just – decipherable. Whether the cuts were made during the rehearsals for the 1896 première, or for the revised 1897 performance, must remain a matter of conjecture. Moreover, the manuscript score contains a dramatic four-bar chord of A minor (a sonority that unmistakably alludes to *The Swan of Tuonela*) before the magical central *Molto lento* section; this chord is absent from the parts. In 2004, by comparing the available sources, Colin Davis at the University of North Texas was able make a reconstruction of the original form of the piece. Most importantly, he has been able to reinstate a 32-bar chordal introduction for woodwind and horns, and a 76-bar passage in the *Molto lento* section. Davis has pointed out that this second episode plays 'an important role... by eliciting further programmatic implications. In this section two motifs, derived from the introduction, are woven together throughout individual wind instruments, echoing the sewing together of the pieces of Lemminkäinen's body',[5] but in performance this passage is singularly monotonous and lacking in direction, and it is no surprise that Sibelius chose to remove it.

A previously noted, the overture to *The Building of the Boat* was revised to form the suite's most famous movement, *The Swan of Tuonela*. A special aspect of Sibelius's interest in nature was the particular fascination he felt for big migrating birds such as swans and cranes. They are a frequent theme in his music and often inspired him to produce works of great intensity. The first edition of the score of *The Swan of Tuonela* contained the following evocative description: 'Tuonela, the land of Death, the hell of Finnish mythology, is surrounded by a large river with black waters and a rapid current, on which the Swan of Tuonela floats majestically, singing.'

The piece features a solo cor anglais which – uniquely among Sibelius's tone poems – is treated almost like a concerto soloist. The orchestration is predominantly dark – Sibelius omits flutes, clarinets (except bass clarinet) and trumpets, and the oboe plays only twice, its function being merely to strengthen the cor anglais line. Remarkably, the double basses play in only 24 bars. Additional colour is provided by the harp which, when set against the full string sections playing *col legno* and *ppp*, creates an eerie sonority. An extraordinary and highly original example of orchestral tone-painting, *The Swan of Tuonela* has become the most popular movement in the *Lemminkäinen Suite*, and is frequently played as an independent concert piece.

Lemminkäinen's Return takes up not only the story but also the four-note motif from *Lemminkäinen in Tuonela*. Sibelius constantly modifies, varies and develops his material at a never-slackening pace. The storyline given in the score explains: 'Exhausted after a long series of wars and battles, Lemminkäinen decides to return home. He transforms his cares and worries into war-horses and sets off. After a voyage that is rich in adventure, he finally arrives in his native land, where he rediscovers the places that are so full of childhood memories.' In 1921 Sibelius spoke of the character of the piece as follows: 'I think we Finns ought not to be ashamed to show more pride in ourselves. Let us wear our caps at an angle! Why should we be ashamed of ourselves? That is the underlying sentiment throughout *Lemminkäinen's Return*. Lemminkäinen is just as good as the noblest of earls. He is an aristocrat, without question an aristocrat!'[6]

The *Lemminkäinen's Return* that was performed in 1896 was considerably longer than the version we know today; it contained two lengthy passages which Sibelius later cut. The first of these (at the place equivalent to eight bars before D in the published score) introduces – in extended and slightly different form – material Sibelius eventually decided to withhold until much later in the piece. At times the orchestral colour in this passage is strikingly reminiscent of the *Karelia* music. The section that follows is longer in the original version, where some motifs are repeated more frequently. The other major difference occurs at the end of the movement. Here the original score has a trombone fanfare, heralding an entirely new thematic section and the first change of tempo in the entire piece, to *Molto vivace*. Both the theme of this section and the fanfares are also found in a song for male chorus and orchestra, *Laulu Lemminkäiselle* (*A Song for Lemminkäinen*) that was premièred some eight months later. It is not known exactly when Sibelius decided to transplant the final section of the movement into the song. A chordal passage then leads to a *fermata* followed by an 'amen' cadence, dying away to *piano*.

Sibelius conducted the first performance of the suite with the Philharmonic

Society orchestra in Helsinki on 13th April 1896. Despite the composer's nervousness, which apparently caused some resentment at rehearsals, the work was extremely well received by the public. The reactions of the critics were to some extent determined by the factions they represented. The pro-Swedish Karl Flodin, writing in *Nya Pressen*, thought highly of *Lemminkäinen and the Maidens of the Island*, though the specifically Finnish aspects of the music eluded him: 'the composer builds entirely on modern, cosmopolitan groundwork. His thematic structures are more closely related to the Lisztian style while the influence both of Wagner and Tchaikovsky can be discerned.' Flodin was less positive about the other movements; he even dismissed the cor anglais solo in *The Swan of Tuonela* as 'colossally long and tedious'. It would be wrong to assume, however, that Flodin's opinions were shaped only by the question of language; his was an authoritative voice to which Sibelius paid careful attention. Given the composer's support of the Finnish cause and his friendship with the members of the *Päivälehti* circle, it is no surprise that Oskar Merikanto, in that very newspaper, not only discerned a Finnish quality in the suite but also judged its creator to be 'in every respect a mature artist'.

The great public success of the *Lemminkäinen Suite* had to be set against bad news of a more personal nature. On 15th April, aged just 63, General Alexander Järnefelt died, having suffered a stroke. He was buried at the Hietaniemi cemetery in Helsinki a week later; Sibelius was one of the pall-bearers.

For some members of the Järnefelt family, the impact of the General's death was not entirely negative. In 1891 Arvid, who had inherited an interest in Tolstoy from his mother, became so overwhelmed by the Russian author's work that he abandoned his legal career in order to become a full-time writer. A few years later he went to Moscow to meet Tolstoy, and subsequently translated some of his works into Finnish. General Järnefelt had been opposed to his son's pacifism and liberal views, but after his father's death Arvid could openly display his preference for a simple life: he moved to a farm, Rantala, near his mother's property (named Vieremä) in Lohja, to the west of Helsinki.

One more upheaval would affect the Järnefelts in 1896. Aili Järnefelt, then aged 26 and engaged to be married, was involved in a serious railway incident at Antrea, north of Viipuri. She survived, but lost both her legs in the accident. Aili was a *kantele* player and it was as a present for her during her convalescence – rather than as a direct result of his interest in the Finnish folk-music heritage – that Sibelius composed two pieces for the instrument, *Moderato*, JS 130, and *Dolcissimo*, JS 63. These two pieces remained unknown until as recently as 1989, when the manuscripts were donated to the Sibelius Museum in Turku.

At this time Sibelius's renown as a composer was growing but had not yet spread beyond Finland's borders; for the moment his musical activities were very much concentrated in the Helsinki area. His dreams of becoming a violin virtuoso were long gone, but he had been making the occasional appearance as a rank-and-file player in the Philharmonic Society orchestra under Kajanus's baton. The last time he did this was at a series of Beethoven concerts in late April.

On 25th May 1896 a memorial was unveiled to Josef Pippingsköld, professor of obstetrics at Helsinki University. For this occasion Sibelius composed and conducted a new work for male choir *a cappella*, the *Hymn* (*Natus in curas*), Op. 21. With its steady, dignified 3/2 pulse the song anticipates the *Seventh Symphony*. Fridolf Gustafsson's text is in Latin and – strangely for such a commemoration – not only praises man's diligent labours but also points out how future generations belittle his achievements!

After the death of General Järnefelt, Aino had inherited a certain amount of money in compensation for the fact that, unlike her brothers, she had not enjoyed the benefits of a university education. Making use of these funds, Jean and Aino now set off for a visit to Berlin. Very little is known of their trip; they must have set off in the last days of May, after the unveiling of the Pippingsköld memorial, and the trip lasted no more than a couple of weeks. While in Berlin they met up with Busoni. This was Aino's first journey abroad and no doubt Sibelius was keen to show her the sights of the city where he had studied and to which he was always keen to return.

After the Berlin trip the Sibelius family once more spent a summer holiday in Vaania. At this time he started to incorporate a sort of diary into his musical sketchbooks. Many of the entries are confined to a word or two – some in Latin and Greek – and, especially after the autumn of 1896, many are undated. From these jottings, however, it is clear that Sibelius's moods could vary dramatically from day to day, from 'It is remarkable how my life often feels empty' (22nd August 1896) to 'Life feels so rich again' (23rd). It is also apparent that he already acknowledged the negative effect that his drinking had both on his state of mind and on his capacity for work.

In total contrast to the earnestness of the *Hymn* and the expansive Symbolist landscapes of the *Lemminkäinen Suite*, is the *Allegretto in F major* for piano, JS 23 – an easy-going, lyrical minuet. It has been dated to 1895–96, but no further details of its origin or purpose are known. Might it have served as a soothing lullaby for the young Eva and Ruth?

One wonders if Sibelius was tempted to include the *Lento in E major*, JS 119 (1896–97) in his Op. 24 collection of piano pieces; its proportions and style would seem to qualify it for such a position. The piece traverses a wide range of emotions. As in the *Romance in A major*, the rapt main theme emerges almost unnoticed from the tranquil opening in 6/4 time. The piece is in ABA form, and the much more agitated B section builds up – via a few *quasi ostinato* bars that hint at the first movement of the *Violin Concerto* – to a climax that clearly anticipates the *Serenade* from the music to *King Christian II* before the return of the A section takes us back to the world of dreams.

During 1896 the *Juhlamarssi* (*Festive March*) from the *Promotional Cantata* of 1894 was extracted and published in a version for mixed choir *a cappella*. In this form it was first heard at a song festival in Mikkeli the following June. But 1896 also saw the composition of a completely new cantata: the two-movement *Cantata for the Coronation of Nicholas II*, JS 104, for mixed chorus and orchestra, setting words by Paavo Cajander. The coronation of Nicholas II had taken place in Moscow some eighteen months after he had acceded to the throne, on 26th May 1896. It was not until November, however, that the event was commemorated in the Great Hall of Helsinki University – of which the Tsar was by tradition the Chancellor. He was not present at the occasion; he and his wife, Empress Alexandra, were represented by plaster effigies.

Following the retirement of Richard Faltin, Sibelius had taken on some teaching work at the university, which he started rather grudgingly on 14th September, describing it as 'servitude'. Somehow he also managed to find time to work on the cantata during the autumn. He conducted its first performance on 2nd November, with a 'Symphony Chorus' and the Philharmonic Society orchestra, but it was not a success. Sibelius later blamed this on the tuba player, who 'arrived very drunk and could not be sobered in any way. He started to improvise in the middle of a fugued movement and spoilt the whole impression completely' – even though there is no tuba in the orchestra for this cantata! After its first performance, the *Coronation Cantata* was soon forgotten and remained unperformed until the 1990s, even though two passages from the first movement were extracted for separate use: the purely orchestral *Coronation March*, probably for a popular concert in Helsinki, and the section *Terve ruhtinatar*, arranged around 1913 for children's choir *a cappella*.

It is probably safe to assume that both Sibelius and Cajander, as patriotic Finns, would have worked on the piece more from duty than from inspiration. That is not to say, however, that the piece lacks merit. Despite some march-like fanfares, the mood of the first movement is lyrical and relaxed. Two motifs have antecedents in Sibelius's music for string quartet: one is clearly related to the scherzo of the *String Quartet in A minor*, whilst another develops a rhythmic pattern from the *Andante–Allegro molto* in D major, JS 32 – an idea that would later dominate the finale of the *Third Symphony*. The second movement not only contains some capable fugal writing but also shows how the composer was capable of gradually increasing the musical tension towards a climax, anticipating similar writing in the finale of the *Second Symphony*.

It was at precisely this moment that Sibelius finally produced an opera; indeed, the composition of the *Coronation Cantata* must have come as an unwelcome distraction. The opera – *Jungfrun i tornet* (*The Maiden in the Tower*), JS 101 – has nothing to do with the *The Building of the Boat*, but is a concise one-act piece with words by the poet and novelist Rafael Hertzberg. It is generally agreed that the effectiveness of the piece is severely compromised by the weakness of the libretto.

The immediate impulse to compose *The Maiden in the Tower* was a commission in the spring of 1896 to write a piece for a lottery evening in support of the Philharmonic Society orchestra. The first performance took place on 7th November, and the work was only just ready in time: the mezzo-soprano Emmy Achté, who sang the role of the Chatelaine at the première, wrote to her daughter Aino: 'As you can imagine, we have not yet received the finale for Sibelius's opera... and there are only two weeks and three days before the performance. The music is dramatically impressive and would work very well if only we had the time... I must continually visit Sibelius and give him the very necessary reminder that we cannot guess what his music should be; we do actually need the parts.'

The plot of *The Maiden in the Tower* is a simple tale of chivalry. After a brief overture, which contains some of the work's principal themes, the first scene is a duet in which the Maiden, picking flowers by the shore, is accosted by the Bailiff; when she rejects his professions of love, he abducts her and imprisons her in his castle. An interlude leads to the second scene, an aria in which the Maiden prays for help. In the third scene, help approaches in the form of an off-stage choir in which the Maiden recognizes her father's voice; the music at this point resembles the fourth movement of *Kullervo*. But the choir misinterprets the situation: the Maiden's protestations of innocence are ignored, and the choir retreats. After another interlude, the Lover arrives (Scene 4) for an assignation with the Maiden. In the fifth scene, a duet for the Maiden and the Lover, she calls down from the tower and explains her predicament; they declare their love and he reassures her. The Bailiff arrives in Scene 6 and argues with the Lover. A duel seems imminent, but in Scene 7 the Chatelaine arrives; she orders the Maiden's release and has the Bailiff arrested. In the jubilant final scene the Maiden and Lover, joined by the chorus, sing the praises of the Chatelaine.

Given the cultural and political climate of Finland in the 1890s, the storyline of *The Maiden in the Tower* could easily bear an allegorical interpretation: the virtuous Maiden could represent Finland, the villainous Bailiff could be Russia, and the Lover and Chatelaine could stand for the Finnish patriots. Indeed, a strikingly similar tale – a queen, imprisoned by a tyrant in a castle and liberated by a hero – is told in Cajander's poem *Vapautettu kuningatar* (*The Captive Queen*), c. 1881, which Sibelius later used in a patriotic cantata. It seems improbable that Sibelius did not recognize the story's potential for bearing a patriotic message but, remarkably, he seems to have taken the opera plot at face value. His aim may have been to preserve something of the simplicity of Hertzberg's Swedish-language text, based on a folk ballad, or he may simply have regarded the libretto as too naïve to support a second level of meaning.

The opera is modest in scale: there are only four solo singers, and the orchestra is smaller than in most of Sibelius's major symphonic works. Stylistically there is much that is characteristic of his work in the 1890s: the orchestral sonority has often been compared to that of the *Karelia* music, and the ghost of Wagner occasionally hovers in the background. At its finest, the vocal writing anticipates such songs as *Höstkväll* and *Jubal* from the 1900s. Erik Tawaststjerna suggested that Mascagni's *Cavalleria rusticana*, which Sibelius had heard in Vienna in 1891, may also have served as a model. After conducting three performances in Helsinki in 1896, Sibelius refused a request for the opera to be performed in Mikkeli, claiming that he wished to revise it. No revision was forthcoming, however and, as he himself put it, 'the maiden may remain in the tower'. And so she did until 1981, when Jussi Jalas conducted a radio performance. *The Maiden in the Tower* has yet to become established as a stage work, although numerous concert performances have taken place in recent years.

Whatever misgivings Sibelius had about his teaching work, he nevertheless decided to apply for a permanent position at Helsinki University as successor to Richard Faltin. In doing so he chose to lock horns with some powerful and influential rivals: Robert Kajanus, and the budding musicologist Ilmari Krohn. The less than glorious première of the *Coronation Cantata* counted against Sibelius, at least in the eyes of his rivals, especially as much of Sibelius's case rested on his artistic achievements rather than specifically academic accomplishments. As part of his application he delivered a paper on 25th November on the subject of folk music's influence on art music. By all accounts the lecture was delivered with great spontaneity – as a public speaker Sibelius clearly spoke in the same 'paradoxes and metaphors' that Karl Flodin found characteristic of his everyday speech. No doubt the runic song edition he had prepared the previous year helped to shape the opinions that he expressed in his talk, but he did not confine himself to empirical observation. Indeed, he ranged over a wide variety of topics related to the fate of tonality and harmony in art music, and the need for a composer to establish a genuine artistic personality. 'We see how fruitful an influence folk music is on a composer's upbringing ... In his work, however, he must free himself... from any suggestion of the parochial. He will achieve that in proportion to the stature of his personality.' His words may have been spoken with little regard to rhetorical convention, but the opinions he expressed were deeply felt. There is a striking congruity between the artistic standpoint expressed here and his words almost three decades later in an interview with the Italian journalist Alberto Gasco: 'I have composed much that is in the style of folk melodies, but the notes themselves have always come from my own imagination, or rather from my ardent Finnish heart.'

His competitor Kajanus's chosen topic was the music of Bernhard Henrik Crusell, and he relied heavily on direct quotations from a biography of Crusell by Henrik August Reinholm. The candidates were kept waiting for some months for a decision.

One more novelty saw the light of day in 1896: on 10th December Jalmari Hahl conducted the YL choir and the Philharmonic Society orchestra in *Laulu Lemminkäiselle* (*A Song for Lemminkäinen*), Op. 31 No. 1; at the première it was billed as *Lemminkäisen laulu* (*Lemminkäinen's Song*). Despite its title, this song does not have a *Kalevala* text; it is a setting of a youthful poem by the prolific author, translator and publisher Yrjö Weijola. The opening fanfares and main theme come straight from the end of *Lemminkäinen's Return* (original version). This is surprising: Sibelius was normally careful to avoid direct quotations from his own works when the 'source' was fresh in the listeners' memories. Perhaps on this occasion his other commitments – the *Coronation Cantata, The Maiden in the Tower*, his university lecture and teaching work – simply left him insufficient time to compose a wholly new work, and he may well have predicted (correctly, as it turned out) that the choral work would not achieve widespread exposure. Stylistically, *Laulu Lemminkäiselle* might be compared to a hunting chorus from a Romantic opera. Such choruses are not especially characteristic of Sibelius, but in *The Maiden in the Tower* there is a choral passage of strikingly similar tone (*Nu i skogen vårens vindar susa...* in Scene 3).

Nonetheless, the use of thematic material from the *Lemminkäinen Suite* has led some scholars to speculate that the suite and choral piece might indeed be related at a deeper level – even that *Laulu Lemminkäiselle* might be some sort of unused fifth movement for the suite. This is highly improbable: the use of a contemporary text in the context of work on *Kalevala* motifs would seem incongruous, and moreover the purely practical considerations of hiring and rehearsing a choir for such a brief movement would be a significant disincentive. It is much more credible, however, that the song and the suite could have shared a common ancestor in the sketches for *The Building of the Boat.*

1897

It must have been with some trepidation that Sibelius, in early 1897, started to compose a new cantata for the university's forthcoming degree ceremonies. After the *Coronation Cantata*, a further sub-standard performance at this point would be catastrophic for his job application. This time he chose to write a piece with soprano and baritone soloists as well as a choir and orchestra. The text, which Sibelius treated with some freedom, was by August Valdemar Forsman, and assigned to the soloists the roles of Kalevatar and Väinämöinen. It does not, however, attempt to mimic the verse style of the *Kalevala.* Sadly the complete score for this work has not survived, although a handful of orchestral parts still exist and a rehearsal score with piano accompaniment has been preserved almost intact. From those orchestral parts it has been deduced that the *Cantata for the University Graduation Ceremonies of 1897* was never performed in its entirety. After the performance on 30th May the critic of *Päivälehti* – probably Oskar Merikanto – found the music to be commendably approachable: 'Nobody could claim, as was formerly the case, that he could not understand this music! It is as readily comprehensible as a Finnish folk-song.' Sibelius subsequently arranged ten of the musical numbers for mixed choir as his Op. 23; some retain the soloists, and there is added percussion in the penultimate song. It would seem that he made few changes to the movements of the original cantata that were originally scored for choir, although in the sections that originally had orchestral accompaniment he reworked the orchestral part for chorus.

By far the most famous of these songs – and understandably so – is the sixth, *Soi kiitokseksi Luojan* (*We praise Thee, our Creator*), which has become a popular hymn in Finland, with a melody that is genuinely attractive and memorable. The remaining songs all exhibit Sibelian features even if they are not among his most distinctive compositions. *Me nuoriso Suomen* (*We the Youth of Finland*), No. 1, for instance, is a sturdy march. *Tuuli tuudittele* (*The Wind Rocks*), No. 2, is a pliable piece in a 5/2 time redolent of folk music, whilst *Oi toivo, toivo, sä lietomieli* (*Oh Hope, Hope, You Dreamer*), No. 3, has a gently rocking 6/4 pulse. In *Montapa elon merellä* (*Many on the Sea of Life*), No. 4, the interest is focused more in the harmonies. *Sammuva sainio maan* (*The Fading Thoughts of the Earth*), No. 5, develops the material from the previous song in an expressive mezzo-soprano solo. After *Soi kiitokseksi Luojan* comes *Tuule, tuuli, leppeämmin* (*Blow, Wind, More Gently*), No. 6b, in which the opening melody anticipates the music to *Everyman* of 1916, especially as its opening bars are in unison (in *Everyman* the corresponding idea, to the text *Maat ja metsät viheriöivät*, is given to a solo voice, and a solo mezzo-soprano appears here too, albeit later in the piece). The outer sections of *Oi Lempi, sun valtas ääretön on* (*O Love, Your Realm is Limitless*), No. 7, feature siciliano rhythms, framing a more relaxed, tender middle section. In *Kun virta vuolas* (*As the Swift Current*), No. 9, the colourful percussion emphasizes the march rhythm – an anticipation of the *Oriental Procession* from *Belshazzar's Feast*, but without the eastern harmonies. Finally, as at the end of Bach's church cantatas, there is a simple chorale, *Oi kallis Suomi, äiti verraton* (*O Precious Finland, Mother Beyond Compare*), No. 10 – although with a text that was patriotic enough to risk provoking the ire of the Russians.

Finally news came through about the teaching post at the University. The choice initially fell upon Sibelius, by an overwhelming majority. Kajanus appealed, citing the *Coronation Cantata*'s unsuccessful performance as part of his case, and managed to have the decision reversed. Although Sibelius perhaps did not possess the ideal temperament for a teacher, and his application was motivated as much by his need for financial security as by the prestige of the job itself, his pride was wounded. The dispute caused a rift between the two friends that was never wholly to be repaired: their mutual trust was undermined and Sibelius was quick to find a sub-plot, motivated by jealousy, in all that Kajanus said or did. In the short term, their feuding marked the end of the Symposium group. Nonetheless, Kajanus could not afford to ignore Sibelius's music, and Sibelius could not risk losing access to Kajanus's orchestra – and so they were wise enough to continue their collaboration.

In June, while waiting for a final decision about the university appointment, Sibelius headed south in the company of his friend Walter von Konow. They took the boat across the Baltic to Stettin and then continued by train to Italy for a holiday taking in Berlin, Dresden and Vienna on the way. It may have been during this trip to Italy that Sibelius, following a visit to the Uffizi gallery in Florence, improvised a waltz that, in the opinion of von Konow, surpassed even Strauss's *An der schönen blauen Donau*. 'Do you see, Walter, how the diamonds glitter in Princess Medici's crown?' asked Sibelius as he played – but he refused categorically to publish the waltz. He was back in Finland in early July, where he headed for Lohja to join Aino, Eva and Ruth who were staying there with Aino's mother.

Two oddities from this period are *Ohi, 'Caroli'* and *Trippole Trappole*, arrangements for accompanied mixed choir of Italian folk-songs (JS 99).

Their precise date cannot be determined but it seems logical that they would have been written during or shortly after Sibelius's trip to Italy. Unfortunately only a draft choir score has survived.

He now turned his attention to a bigger and more dramatic piece: the orchestral song *Koskenlaskijan morsiamet* (*The Rapids-Rider's Brides*), Op. 33, a free setting of a text by A.Oksanen, a colourful figure who was born in Kuopio, the illegitimate son of a distinguished soldier, and rose to become the first professor of Finnish at Helsinki University. A keen proponent of European literary traditions, he wrote novels as well as poetry, and was a fierce critic of the writings of Aleksis Kivi, whose work he found to be too down-to-earth. *The Rapids-Rider's Brides* tells how a water maiden, the daughter of Vellamo, is so consumed by envy that she destroys the boat in which her beloved Vilhelmi and his mortal bride Anna are travelling, killing them both. The poem can lay claim to being the first poetic ballad in Finnish.

Sibelius's setting of *The Rapids-Rider's Brides* is a typical example of his work in the late 1890s with vivid colours and great immediacy of expression. The opening four-note motif is instantly recognizable from *Lemminkäinen's Return*, and the orchestral writing often betrays Sibelius's interest in Wagner as well as his own established fingerprints of triplets, descending fifths, 'S-motifs' and the like. When Anna is deep in melancholy reflection ('Oi kuinka kirkas on illan kuu...' ['Oh, how bright is the evening moon...']) the vocal line is almost a direct quotation from the slow movement of the *Violin Sonata in F major* of 1889, which Sibelius had specifically described as 'Finnish and melancholy; it is an authentic Finnish girl who sings on the A string'. The song is generally performed by a baritone but is also suitable for a mezzo-soprano voice. A version for voice and piano probably dates from the same time and is notable for the virtuosic nature of its piano writing. As so often with Sibelius's piano transcriptions, this is no mere rehearsal score but a performing version in its own right.

For a while Sibelius's career had seemed to be lacking in direction, as he recovered from his encounters with Wagner and with academic life. But on 20th October 1897 an event occurred that crystallized the direction his music was to take: Kajanus conducted the first performance of a *Symphony in F minor* by a very young composer named Ernst Mielck at the University Hall. Mielck was born in Viipuri on 24th October 1877. Although his health was poor even as a child, his musical talent was soon recognized and he was sent to Berlin in 1891, where he studied at the Sternsches Konservatorium under Heinrich Ehrlich (piano), Robert Radecke (theory), Ludwig Bußler (counterpoint) and Arno Kleffel (composition). Returning to Finland, he became known as an accomplished pianist and also made some impression as a composer, before returning to Berlin in 1895 to study under Max Bruch. Mielck's symphony was not the first Finnish work in this genre – Axel Ingelius, for instance, had composed one in 1847 – but the emergence of such a work from a talented young composer in the musical climate of the 1890s attracted attention. Karl Flodin in *Nya Pressen* wrote a positive review of Mielck's symphony, but his article was also a thinly veiled challenge to Sibelius: 'This 19-year-old youth [Mielck] is a brilliant new composing talent and his skill in handling form is quite remarkable. These days young composers are justly criticized for their lack of a sense of form. Everybody turns out rhapsodies, symphonic poems, and suites, but only a select band dares to attempt the majestic edifice of the symphony. This stems from the fact that very few have grasped the art of logically and comprehensively thinking through a musical idea to the end, the skill of nurturing this idea to reveal a universal meaning and to realize spiritually a chosen goal.' Sadly Mielck had no opportunity to develop his symphonic skills, as he died of tuberculosis in Switzerland in 1899. What would have become of him had he lived longer can only be guessed. As a composer of orchestral works he started at a much earlier age than Sibelius, and it is no surprise that his music was closely modelled on the European – especially German – Romantics, although he did not shy away from using Finnish folk melodies. There is no question that the nineteen-year-old Mielck's *Symphony in F minor* is a more ambitious and prestigious work than the nineteen-year-old Sibelius's *String Quartet in E flat major*. Whether or nor Mielck would have developed the interest in *Kalevala* themes that helped to make Sibelius's music so topical, or indeed the blend of concentration and innovation that made it unique, is open to question.

For Sibelius, however, the challenge of the symphony was still in the future; he was still not satisfied with the *Lemminkäinen Suite*. On 1st November he conducted the Philharmonic Society orchestra in a concert that included a revised version of the suite as well as the first performance of *The Rapids-Rider's Brides* (with Abraham Ojanperä as soloist). The full extent and nature of the revisions he made for the 1897 performance of the *Lemminkäinen Suite* cannot be determined with accuracy. To judge from the cuts marked in the orchestral parts, he may now have removed the introduction from *Lemminkäinen in Tuonela* along with the meandering 76-bar passage from its *Molto lento* section. It was presumably also for this occasion that Sibelius reworked the relatively unassuming ending of *Lemminkäinen's Return*, retaining the passage that shared its themes with *Laulu Lemminkäiselle* but following it with a dashing coda that is very similar to that found in the final version.

Both the audience and the Finnish-language reviews were more than content with the *Lemminkäinen Suite*, but Karl Flodin in *Nya Pressen* was again a dissenting voice – this time a more determined and candid one than the previous year. 'This sort of music seems absolutely pathological, and leaves impressions that are so mixed, painful and by their very nature indefinable that they have very little in common with the æsthetic feeling of pleasure that all fine art, above all music, should engender... The *Lemminkäinen* pictures depress me, make me unhappy, worn down and apathetic. Should music kindle such feelings?' Flodin's words are in stark contrast to his recent praise for Ernst Mielck. Plainly he felt that Sibelius's talent was in danger of being squandered.

After several months of manœuvring, and with the support of the Fennoman historian and senator Georg Yrjö-Koskinen, Sibelius was granted official recognition in the form of a state artistic scholarship at the end of November. This was his 'compensation' for not having been awarded the university position, and the behind-the-scenes involvement of Sibelius's victorious rival Robert Kajanus in securing the scholarship for him cannot be discounted. The new source of funds permitted him to reduce his teaching commitments – which was beneficial not only because it freed up more time for composition, but also because teaching was for Sibelius little more than a duty that he performed to earn money; his heart was not in it. One of the most persistent misconceptions about Sibelius's life is that his state pension gave him total financial security. Nothing could be further from the truth. Even though the sum involved (3,000 marks per year) was roughly half of a professor's salary, it was by no means enough to fund Sibelius's extravagant lifestyle. Moreover, the initial award was only for a ten-year period. Not until the end of that time – by which time Sibelius's iconic stature as a national composer was well established – was the scholarship converted into a life pension.

On 19th December Sibelius produced a piece of decidedly non-symphonic aspirations – a piano solo, the *Allegretto in G minor*, JS 225. To judge from its style this was written as a souvenir; its character is roguish – slightly march-like but not unequivocally so. The only certain fact is its date of completion, helpfully noted by the composer at the top of the manuscript. It may have been around this time that he also produced a strophic Christmas song, *Det mörknar ute* (*Outside it is Growing Dark*) to words by Topelius. Later published as the third in a group of *Five Christmas Songs* with the very misleading opus number of 1, this was the first of the set to be written.

As a Christmas present for Eero Järnefelt, Sibelius composed an *Andantino* for piano, a gentle, berceuse-like melody in 6/8, a preliminary version of the *Idyll* that was later included in the Op. 24 collection. The beginning of its theme resembles a song by Robert Kajanus, *Flyg ej undan!* (*Do not Flee!*) from his Op. 4 collection (1880–81).

On Christmas Day Sibelius's mother came down with a serious lung inflammation, and in the evening of 29th December she passed away, aged only 56. Christian and Linda were at her bedside, but Jean stayed away.

1898

Sibelius's first major contribution to the genre of incidental music for the theatre was his score for his friend Adolf Paul's five-act historical drama *King Christian II*, Op. 27. The play is set in the sixteenth century, and centres around the love of King Christian II of Denmark, Norway and Sweden (1481–1559) for his mistress Dyveke ('little dove'), a Dutch girl of bourgeois birth. Paul finished writing the play on 20th March 1897, and Sibelius produced four musical numbers – *Elegy, Musette, Minuet* and *Fool's Song* – for its première at the Swedish Theatre in Helsinki on 24th February 1898. If Paul's own later account is to be believed, the music was composed very quickly; for the *Minuet*, indeed, Sibelius merely wrote out a simplified version of the orchestral *Menuetto* of 1894, itself an arrangement of a piano piece from his student period in Vienna.

A separate *Minuet in B flat major* – a piano piece from around this time – has survived, and Folke Gräsbeck has suggested that it was a rejected proposal for *King Christian*, given the coincidence of key and style. This would, however, imply that the piece was drafted in the first instance for the piano, before an orchestral version saw (or in this case not did not see) the light of day. Such a *modus operandi* is not unheard of for Sibelius but would have been contrary to his normal practice. The delightful naïvety of the *Minuet* works excellently on the piano but would be less effective if scored for *pizzicato* strings, the effect Sibelius specifies in the minuet from the theatre score.

Sibelius himself conducted the première of *King Christian II* with an ensemble drawn from the Philharmonic Society orchestra. The four movements are scored for small orchestra – strings, two flutes, two clarinets, two bassoons, harp and triangle. The production was well received, and the play was given no less than 24 times during the spring of 1898. The four original pieces are barely more ambitious or longer than the many independent souvenirs that Sibelius had written for various chamber ensembles from the 1880s onwards and, like many of his movements for the theatre, can be seen as a logical continuation of that genre. The music was published without delay by Karl Fredrik Wasenius, and Sibelius wasted no time in preparing a piano transcription of all four pieces.

The *Elegy*, for strings alone, was performed behind the curtain as an overture to the play; its sustained main theme is contrasted with a more improvisatory idea from the cellos. The *Musette* is played by street musicians under Dyveke's window during the second act. Adolf Paul here specified an 'old dance' played by bagpipes and chalumeau, an effect Sibelius created with bassoons and clarinets. The piece soon became a great public favourite, and the words 'Minä menen Kämppiin takaisin' ('Now I'm off to the Kämp again') – a reference to Sibelius's notorious drinking sessions at the Helsinki's Hotel Kämp – came to be associated with its melody. The *Minuet* was played behind the curtain to introduce Act III; the stage directions call for 'festive dance music' at this point. The *Sången om korsspindeln* (*Fool's Song of the Spider*) opens the final scene of the play, set in 1549 in Sønderborg Castle, where the king has been imprisoned for many years. The text, about an insidious spider whose web captures anyone who passes by but is unable to imprison his soul, is a clear allegorical reference to the political relationship between Russia and Finland. Two of the *King Christian* movements were among the earliest of Sibelius's works to be recorded. The *Musette* was set down by a brass band in Helsinki in 1904 and, the same year, the *Fool's Song* was recorded both by Alarik Uggla in Helsinki and by William Hammar in Berlin. Both have remained very popular ever since.

Around this time Sibelius was approached by an old schoolfriend, the photographer Into Inha, with a request to set a poem by 'Aino Suonio', a pseudonym for Aino Krohn. At the time Inha was courting Aino Krohn, and the resultant song for male choir *a cappella*, *Kuutamolla* (*In the Moonlight*), JS 114, was sung in April and July as a serenade at her window. As so often in works of this character during the 1890s, Sibelius chose a relaxed 9/4 metre. Motivically, too, the song betrays its period of composition: its first four notes, for instance, anticipate the second group of the first movement of the *First Symphony*.

Shortly after the première of *King Christian II*, Sibelius and Aino went to Berlin, where they found lodgings with a Frau Dierk in the Potsdamerstraße. On a personal level the visit was enjoyable: he consorted with his friends Paul, Gallén and Busoni – and also with his brother Christian, who was in Berlin as a student of pathology. After a while, however, city life proved too much for Aino, who was once again pregnant, and she returned to Finland. Commercially the trip was promising: Paul took him to Leipzig to meet Oskar von Hase, publishing manager of the prestigious publisher Breitkopf & Härtel. For the German firm Sibelius was not an entirely unknown quantity. It was not unusual for large publishers to organize the production of scores for smaller firms, and Breitkopf had done this for Wasenius in the case of the *King Christian II* music. Now Breitkopf bought the German rights to *King Christian II*, thereby launching a long collaboration with Sibelius. Indeed, in the long term no publisher has done more for him; many years after his death it was Breitkopf & Härtel who launched the critical JSW edition of his entire œuvre. At the time of writing this edition is making good progress and is proving a goldmine of information for scholars and performers alike.

While in Berlin, Sibelius set a group of three school songs – *Ecce novum gaudium*, *Angelus emittitur* and *In stadio laboris* – under the common title of *Carminalia*, JS 51. These had recently been rediscovered in Lovisa by a family friend, Elise Stenbäck, a teacher at a Swedish-language school in Helsinki. Stenbäck had sung the songs to Sibelius before he left for Berlin, and he had noted them down; as far as we know, neither Stenbäck nor Sibelius knew that these were among the items included in the *Piæ Cantiones* collection, published in Greifswald in 1582. Sibelius made three separate versions of this miniature suite, one for three-part choir *a cappella*, one for female voices and harmonium, and one for female voices and piano, but did not regard the set very highly. In 1910, when Breitkopf & Härtel acquired the rights to this and other works, he described *Carminalia* as 'a weak piece... Preferably they should not be published. Or at least I should rework them at some point.'

In January 1898 the Muntra Musikanter male-voice choir had announced a composition competition, and Sibelius spent some of his time in Berlin working on his own entry. He completed it in time for the deadline of 20th April, and submitted it under the (nowadays rather suggestive) pseudonym of 'HOMO'. The piece in question was *Sandels*, Op. 28, a ten-minute work for male choir and orchestra (Sibelius also made a version for choir and piano) based on the eleventh poem in Runeberg's collection *Fänrik Ståls sägner* (*The Tales of Ensign Stål*). The poem is based on the true story of a Swedish army commander, General Johan Sandels who, during the Russo-Finnish war of 1808–09, defeated a much larger Russian army at Koljonvirta (the battle of Virta Bro – north of Iisalmi in the province of Northern Savonia) on 27th October 1808. In the poem, Sandels is enjoying a meal in the village of Partala with his regimental pastor and refuses to believe a messenger's news that the Russians have attacked. Only when the messenger suggests that Sandels is a coward does he go forth into battle, leading his men from the jaws of defeat to a glorious victory.

In *Sandels* Sibelius seems consciously to avoid the Symbolism that had characterized his major works of the previous years, and aims instead for a more generalized style, although his fingerprints are clear enough – for instance the lilting, syncopated accompaniment at the outset, or the fanfare-like brass outbursts with a triplet up-beat. He is certainly responsive to the moods of the poem: Sandels relaxes at the meal table, for example, accompanied by elegant melodies and decorous scale figures. By contrast the messenger's increasingly exasperated entreaties are set to urgent vocal lines with a restricted compass, often in dactylic rhythms (to some extent these are required by the text, but Sibelius uses them as a pretext for pugnacious characterization) and a melodic line that rises in pitch as it accelerates. The 'battle scene' features chromatic scales in 6/4 metre that are unmistakably related to the development section of the *First Symphony*'s first movement. Sibelius's piece was awarded first prize on 26th May but for the time being no public performance ensued.

After completing *Sandels*, Sibelius started to compose his *First Symphony*, although the distractions of Berlin prevented him from making significant progress with it at this stage. After returning to Finland in late May he stayed at his mother-in-law's house in Lohja where, during the summer, he added three longer and more ambitious movements to the *King Christian II* score: *Nocturne*, *Serenade* and *Ballade*, scored for large orchestra. Apparently the extra pieces were composed at Adolf Paul's request. The *Nocturne* – subtitled 'Interlude No. 1' in the score, and to be played between the first and second acts – is warm and sunny in character, characterized by broad, *cantabile* melodies. At the climax, the tambourine adds a slightly Mediterranean colour – an effect surprisingly common in early- and middle-period Sibelius, especially in music of a programmatic or descriptive character, such the third tableau of the *Press Celebrations Music*, *The Wood-Nymph* and *The Dryad*. The *Serenade* is the prelude to Act III, as an alternative to the shorter *Minuet*. It starts out as a festive minuet; brass fanfares then herald a middle section in 9/4 time, the principal element of which is a *cantabile* string melody. At the end of the movement, as the curtain rises, there is a brief recapitulation of the minuet material. The *Ballade*, subtitled 'Interlude No. 3' in the score, portrays the Stockholm blood bath of 1520, and can be seen as a musical substitute for the fourth act of the play, which was omitted in the stage production. Its energy and, to some extent, its motivic material are reminiscent of the finale of the *First Symphony*, or of *Lemminkäinen's Return*.

Of the seven musical numbers for *King Christian II*, five were extracted (and arranged in a different playing order) to form an independent concert suite: *Nocturne*, *Elegy*, *Musette*, *Serenade* and *Ballade*. The published suite, which was first performed in Helsinki on 5th December under Kajanus's baton, is symphonic both in proportions and in lay-out, which perhaps comes as no surprise given that Sibelius had started work on his *First Symphony* by the time he composed the three larger-scale movements. Few musical changes were made in the preparation of the concert suite; the most significant was the addition of string accompaniment to the clarinets and bassoons in the *Musette*. In the published version of the *Ballade*, a fugal passage is significantly shorter than in the original, but, as the three new movements were not played in the theatre until 7th December, two days after their concert première, it would seem that the passage in question was not cut for concert use, but rather in preparation for publication by Wasenius just a few weeks later, in February 1899. Perhaps Sibelius simply found the fugal section too long (it would be easy to concur with such a judgement). With performances in Stockholm and Leipzig in 1899 and London at the 1901 Proms (conducted by Henry Wood), the music to *King Christian II* was among the first of Sibelius's orchestral works to be played internationally.

In the autumn of 1898 the Sibelius family had moved to a large apartment in Liisankatu 21, on the corner of Snellmaninkatu. Once again, Christian joined them and paid a share of the rent. It was in this house, while Aino was heavily pregnant, that Sibelius wrote *Sydämeni laulu* (*Song of my Heart*), Op. 18 No. 6, a setting of words from Aleksis Kivi's *Seitsemän veljestä* (*Seven Brothers*) that deals with the death of a child. This was to prove eerily prophetic. Sibelius later claimed that he found it 'time-consuming and difficult' to set Kivi's words, but *Sydämeni laulu* is one of his most poignant and best-loved songs for male choir *a cappella* – a work that captures the understated eloquence of the poem from the very first chord. It was first performed by YL conducted by Heikki Klemetti on 1st December. Here, as in the opening bars of *The Swan of Tuonela*, long-held chords with gentle *crescendos* are used in a work that has death as its subject, though the choral piece eschews *The Swan*'s seamless flow in favour of a regular pulse that is better suited to its more intimate character.

During the autumn Sibelius wrote one of his rare Finnish-language solo songs, *Illalle* (*To Evening*), Op. 17 No. 6, to a newly written sonnet by A.V. Forsman. The title conceals a double meaning: the poet's wife was named Ilta and thus it can be understood as either 'To Evening' or 'To Ilta'. Consisting of variations on a single phrase, this song is widely regarded as one of Sibelius's most perfect miniatures.

Around the same time, in preparation for publication, Sibelius reworked the *Hymn* (*Natus in curas*) for male choir that he had written two years earlier. The changes are generally very modest – a few chords are differently voiced and he added several tempo markings. The only obvious difference is a new, slightly longer ending; buried in the texture of the final cadence is an 'S-motif' in the second tenors and first basses.

On 14th November Jean and Aino celebrated the birth of their third daughter, Kirsti. The demands of raising a growing family in the city centre, however, were taking their toll on Sibelius's creative energies and stifling progress on the *First Symphony*. Moreover, the rent for the house in Liisankatu was expensive.

OTHER WORKS FROM 1898

These include a *Caprice* for piano, later numbered as the third piece in the Op. 24 collection. In fact two versions of this piece have survived. The first of these opens with a rhetorical, declamatory passage that was omitted from the definitive version. Ultimately the music becomes more lyrical, a mood that is maintained for the rest of the piece. The published edition is quite different: it opens and closes with a vigorous display passage full of repeated notes and virtuoso flourishes. The middle section is recognizable from the original version but it is now in E minor, a fifth lower than the original.

Several other piano pieces can be provisionally but not definitively dated to 1898. Two of them were published that year by Lindgren in Helsinki (originally issued as *Two Miniatures*, and later included as Nos 4 and 5 of Op. 24). The first is a *Romance in D minor*, the earliest sketches for which come from 1896. Its slow, reflective main theme is like a minuet, and the descending fourth at the end of the phrase lends it a very characteristic Sibelian outline. This theme is liberally elaborated and ornamented before a chordal *stretto* leads to a climax. The lugubrious closing bars offer an anticipation of *Valse triste*. The second piece is a *Waltz in E major*, a mercurial little piece that maintains the tradition of writing waltzes that Sibelius had established during his student years. The second theme again anticipates *Valse triste*, though at a much livelier tempo.

Also included in Op. 24 piano pieces was an *Idyll* (No. 6 of the set), for which Sibelius signed a publication contract with Helsingfors Nya Musikhandel on 25th October 1898. This piece is a reworking of the *Andantino* written the previous Christmas for Eero Järnefelt; its placid melody in 6/8 now gains a lavishly embellished central section before the theme returns unadorned in the last four bars.

The significance of three piano sketches in a manuscript from the same period – in B flat minor, D flat major and C major respectively – lies in the first of the group, a solemn and dignified idea for which Sibelius later found a home in the orchestral *Cassazione* and, many years afterwards, in the *Epilogue* from *The Tempest*. The second of them is a contrapuntal exercise, whilst the third, with dance-like character, is obviously incomplete. A separate fragment, a *Largamente* in D minor, exhibits a sonority and pathos redolent of several of the Op. 24 pieces; indeed, the manuscript also contains sketches for the Idyll.

Vilse (*Astray*), Op. 17 No. 4, again shows how effectively Sibelius could create a mood even in the shortest of miniatures. It is a playful, rather Schubertian song, a declaration of love, to words by Tavaststjerna. The composer made some changes four years later and it was first performed in September 1903.

Finally there was a collection of pieces for mixed choir, published by
K. E. Holm in the collection *Sävelistö*. Sibelius's contributions are believed
to have been made especially for this publication and consisted of arrangements of works originally for male voices (*Rakastava, Saarella palaa*) as
well as three new pieces. One of these is *Aamusumussa* (*In the Morning
Mist*), JS 9a, a setting of J. H. Erkko in which the strong patriotic message
of the poem ('A heartfelt hope burns in our souls: our sun will shine at
last!... let Finland fight with toil and sweat of brow... The power to expel
the murky dark rests firmly in our will.') is disguised by the music's calm,
amiable character in the manner of a folk-song. The second has no such
concealed message: *Min rastas raataa* (*Busy as a Thrush*), JS 129, has
alliterative words from the *Kanteletar*, and Sibelius's flexible setting is full
of life. Finally there was *Sortunut ääni* (*The Broken Voice*), Op. 18 No. 1,
which also exists in a version for male choir, and was first performed in
that form by YL under Heikki Klemetti on 21st April of the following
year. Its text is likewise from the *Kanteletar* and is set in a supple 5/4 time.
The text speaks of a powerful voice that is silenced by sorrow, perhaps an
allusion to the suppression of Finnish people's freedom of expression.

CHAPTER 6

A SYMPHONY AND THE DEATH
OF A CHILD: 1899–1900

1899

'Life here [in Helsinki] is terrible; I would rather go and work in the country,' Sibelius wrote to Adolf Paul in December 1898. A few weeks later he acted on his instincts: leaving his family in the Liisankatu apartment, he took a room in the Old Vicarage, a villa near the railway station in Kerava, a few miles north of the city. Here he found the peace and quiet he needed to complete his *First Symphony*, while Aino and the girls remained in Helsinki.

On 15th February Tsar Nicholas II revealed the 'February Manifesto', making it possible for the Tsarist government to administer Finland without the consent of the Finnish Senate or the Diet, which were reduced to mere forums for discussion. The Finnish army was to be placed under Russian control. In effect, the February Manifesto ended Finland's autonomy. More than 500,000 Finns signed petitions of protest – the so-called 'Great Address' – although Nicholas II chose to ignore them.

The February Manifesto was a significant political development with wide social implications, but it did not stifle the cultural contacts between Finland and Russia. It was no coincidence that now was the time that Arvid Järnefelt chose to visit his hero Tolstoy in Moscow, finding him far from unsympathetic to the Finnish cause insofar as it promoted individual freedom. Meanwhile Russian composers remained welcome visitors to Helsinki. Kajanus was a great admirer of Glazunov, who visited Finland on numerous occasions; other Russian composers whose music was played in Helsinki included Anton Rubinstein, Kalinnikov, Arensky and Rimsky-Korsakov. Tchaikovsky's *Symphonie pathétique*, written as recently as 1893, had been performed in Helsinki in 1894 and 1897.

Might it have been in direct response to the February Manifesto that Sibelius made a setting of Cajander's *Isänmaalle* (*To the Fatherland*), JS 98? The earliest version of this song is for male choir *a cappella* and dates from 1899. This version has greater rhythmic variety than the later arrangements (for mixed choir in 1900 and again for male choir in 1908 – although the most commonly performed male-choir version is an arrangement by Selim Palmgren made around 1902).

A spirit of protest can be discerned in *Athenarnes sång* (*Song of the Athenians*), Op. 31 No. 3. Here, as earlier in *Sandels*, Sibelius makes no attempt to mitigate the dactylic rhythms of the text but instead exploits them to lend a militaristic quality to the music, further emphasized by the unison choral writing. Rydberg's text, from the poem *Dexippos*, is set in Athens in AD 267. From a Finnish perspective the Athenians, with their glorification of death in a noble patriotic cause, were an obvious symbol of the Finns themselves. The symbolic use of geographically and temporally remote cultures follows a precedent set almost sixty years earlier by Verdi with the chorus of Hebrew slaves in *Nabucco*, which used the plight of the Israelites in Egypt to represent that of the Italians under Austrian rule. Indeed, Sibelius was well on the way to becoming a musical symbol of Finland's struggle for the independence in much the same way that Verdi became associated with the *Risorgimento* in Italy. Within a few months of its première, as Russian censorship tightened, *Song of the Athenians* was widely performed in various arrangements. Sibelius himself made several of these: for piano solo, for boys' and mens' voices with piano (both in E major, with harmonium *ad libitum*), for boys' and mens' voices, brass septet and percussion (the published edition, in E flat major), and for boys' and men's voices *a cappella* (this is the only authentic setting that is not in unison). The original E major version, composed in early March, is for boys' and mens' voices, double woodwind, full orchestral brass, percussion and double bass. In letters to Breitkopf & Härtel Sibelius described this version as more 'konzertfähig' ('suited to concert performance') than the brass version.

Both the *First Symphony* and *Song of the Athenians* were heard for the first time on 26th April, at the University Hall in Helsinki; the concert opened with the tone poem version of *The Wood-Nymph*. The straightforward *Song of the Athenians* was an immediate hit with the audience but the critics were not slow to realize the importance of the symphony either. Oskar Merikanto in *Päivälehti* called it 'the greatest work that Finnish music has hitherto brought forth', whilst Richard Faltin in *Nya Pressen* declared that 'the composer speaks the language of all mankind, yet a tongue that is nonetheless his own.'

Sibelius's *Symphony No. 1 in E minor*, Op. 39, is in four movements in accordance with classical tradition, and is scored for full orchestra including tuba and harp. Stylistically it is often compared to the Russian Romantics that were at that time a regular part of Helsinki's musical diet. The thematic material of the symphony is highly unified, though in a very subtle way. The work opens with a broad clarinet solo (incorporating an 'S-motif') accompanied only by timpani (*Andante, ma non troppo*); this idea, often called the work's 'motto theme', contains the symphony's most important motivic material. The following *Allegro energico*'s assertive main theme has a rhythmic tautness reminiscent of the first movements of Tchaikovsky's *Fifth Symphony* and of Beethoven's *Seventh*, although this becomes fully apparent only if it is played with some vigour. In 1943 Sibelius suggested a metronome marking of dotted minim = 108 for this movement, an urgent rather than a stately tempo. Even if it is unwise to treat his metronome markings here and in other works as sacrosanct, they do offer a broad indication of how the music should sound. Tonally this thematic group is ambiguous, hovering between G major and E minor. There is a noticeable similarity between the main theme of the first movement of Borodin's *First Symphony* (1862–67), which had been played in Helsinki in October 1896, and the corresponding place in the Sibelius, although Sibelius denied having heard Borodin's symphony. A more surprising (though presumably also coincidental) similarity exists between Sibelius's theme and an idea from *Viva il vino spumeggiante* from Mascagni's *Cavalleria rusticana* of 1890. The second group begins with a chirpy flute motif related to the opening clarinet solo. In the development, the interwoven descending chromatic scales from the woodwind echo the battle music from the choral piece *Sandels*, but in the symphony they are given an added sense of direction by being combined with *ascending* chromatic scales in the cellos and basses. The movement pays lip service to the principles of sonata form, but the way Sibelius dovetails the end of the development into the beginning of the recapitulation is just one example of the formal compression which was already becoming a hallmark of his work. The movement ends with two sombre *pizzicato* chords.

The second movement is a sort of rondo, although this term gives little idea of its emotional range or stylistic cohesion. It opens with a soothing, song-like theme on muted violins and cellos. A free adaptation of this passage also exists in a piano arrangement, though this can hardly have been intended for concert use. After a quasi-fugal interlude in which the bassoon alludes to the clarinet solo from the beginning of the symphony we hear a descending variant of the main theme: this approximates both in rhythm and in melodic shape to one of the folk-like themes of the *Overture in E major* of 1891, although here it has lost any trace of folk character.

The movement rises to an impassioned climax before dying away with a serene restatement of the opening material, *espressivo semplice*.

The scherzo begins with a robust, Brucknerian rhythmic pulse. Within Sibelius's own output its closest antecedent is the scherzo of the *'Hafträsk' Trio* from 1886. As the music progresses, it becomes increasingly mercurial, the woodwind and string lines dovetailing together with whirlwind velocity. The trio is calmer, echoing the mood of pastoral interlude in the slow movement, and the movement ends with an abbreviated reprise of the scherzo section.

The finale is introduced by a weighty string restatement of the clarinet theme with its 'S-motif' from the first movement, echoed more gently by the woodwind – although this theme is to play no further direct part in the movement. The main theme is frenzied and rises to a climax with explosive chords from the orchestra. The style and even the substance of this fast music recalls the *Ballade* from the previous year's music to *King Christian II*, but in the symphony it is effectively integrated into a longer musical span. Contrasted with this tempestuous activity is a broad, fervent subsidiary idea, not dissimilar to the principal theme of the slow movement; this is first heard *cantabile ed espressivo* from the violins. The *Allegro molto* returns, again culminating in emphatic chords, and the impassioned subsidiary theme then leads the symphony on to a climax of great Romantic splendour. Unlike Tchaikovsky, Sibelius resists the temptation to end his symphony triumphantly with a major-key version of the 'motto' theme: the overwhelming, tragic coda is snuffed out by two *pizzicato* chords, similar to those that ended the first movement.

Sibelius's friendship with Kajanus was by now restored to the extent that they could collaborate as judges at a choral festival in Jyväskylä in June, from where they continued to Axel Gallén's studio in Ruovesi to celebrate the christening of Gallén's children Kirsti, then aged almost 3, and the ten-month-old Jorma. Sibelius played the piano at the service and later improvised at the piano: 'Now you shall hear what impression Kalela [Gallén's home] and its moods make on me,' he said, and played a theme that later found its way into the finale of the *Second Symphony* – according to Kirsti Gallen-Kallela, who was too young to remember the event itself but later came across a note by Gallén's brother-in-law, Mikko Slöör, describing the occasion.

In a list of works from 1915, Sibelius claimed that *Metsämiehen laulu (The Woodsman's Song)*, Op. 18 No. 5, for male choir *a cappella* was written in Vaania near Lahti, but this is must be wrong, as he did not visit Vaania in 1899. Like *Sydämeni laulu* from the previous year, it has words by Aleksis Kivi, and was probably written for YL, at the instigation of Heikki Klemetti. In character, however, it differs radically from *Sydämeni laulu*: *Metsämiehen laulu* is a vigorous piece in march time – almost a 2/4 counterpart to *Venematka* of 1893.

In June 1899 Aino and the children joined Sibelius in Kerava. They rented a recently constructed and well-proportioned house, Mattila, for which they paid a fraction of the rent that they had been paying in Helsinki. Even though the family spent lengthy periods away from Mattila, they rented it for more than three years and thereby proved to themselves that it was possible to live without the temptations of the city.

On 11th September Sibelius visited the home of the painter Pekka Halonen on the shores of Lake Tuusula, not far from the plot of land where the composer's own villa would be built a few years later. The purpose of the visit was to celebrate the birthday of their mutual friend Juhani Aho. Halonen could play the *kantele*, having been taught to do so by his mother, and he performed a Finnish folk tune for which Sibelius jotted down a complementary violin part, thereby creating the *Lullaby* (or *Waltz*) for violin and *kantele*, JS 222.

In his solo vocal works from this period Sibelius was able to distance himself from the political despondency of the era. It is almost as if his use of Swedish-language texts allowed him to retreat from the intense national sentiments that he was expected to express in music. A distinguished example of this is the Runeberg setting *Men min fågel märks dock icke* (*But my Bird is Long in Homing*), Op. 36 No. 2, first performed by Ida Ekman on 21st September. In the poem the richness of nature as springtime approaches is contrasted with the sadness of a girl who waits in vain for her beloved. Such imagery was tailor-made for Sibelius – there is even a reference to his beloved swans – and he responded with a taut, concentrated song that exudes an air of powerful melancholy.

The same concert included the première of what is probably Sibelius's most popular song: *Svarta rosor* (*Black Roses*), Op. 36 No. 1. This setting of words by the Swedish poet Ernst Josephson was sketched in Helsinki in April but seems to have been completed in Kerava a few months later. Far more than in *Men min fågel...*, Sibelius here plays to the gallery, and the song's appeal to singers and audiences alike is easy to understand. Although its proportions are compact, it has a broadly arching vocal line and a climax full of operatic intensity. The poem tells of a rose tree that grows within the human heart, its thorns a constant source of torment. It seems churlish to observe that neither the melodic line nor the accompaniment is especially characteristic of Sibelius, despite the expressive harmonies at the words 'Ty sorgen har nattsvarta rosor' ('For sorrow has roses as black as night').

Bollspelet vid Trianon (*Tennis at Trianon*), Op. 36 No. 3, to a text by another Swedish poet, Gustaf Fröding, occupies a totally different world again: it is a bright and lyrical song portraying the frivolity and grace of the eighteenth-century French court. Only the last lines of the poem, when an urchin sneaks away from the aristocrats' tennis game, remind us of the superficiality of such a way of life.

Svarta rosor, Men min fågel... and *Bollspelet vid Trianon* were all published by Helsingfors Nya Musikhandel, and the edition contained German translations by the man of letters and critic Johannes Öhquist. The same Öhquist wrote a poem in German entitled *Segelfahrt* (*Sailing*), JS 166, which Sibelius set to music; one suspects that this was the composer's way of thanking Öhquist for the translations. It is a rather simple song: most of the time the piano accompaniment is a *tremolo*-like rumble of semiquavers, and only in the third verse – where the vocal line is at its most varied – and at the very end does the accompaniment break into characteristic short–long–short syncopations and scale runs. *Segelfahrt*'s greatest claim to fame is probably that it contains the germ of Sibelius's popular Christmas song *Giv mig ej glans...* (1909): the first two bars of their themes are virtually identical.

One more solo song dates from the autumn of 1899, and unusually it has Finnish words. The poet A. V. Forsman, who had written the texts for the university cantata of 1897, visited Sibelius in Kerava and showed him a newly written poem, *Souda, souda, sinisorsa* (*Swim, Duck, Swim*). The composer immediately set to work and, a few weeks later, sent Forsman the completed setting, JS 180. Although it remained unpublished until a facsimile edition was released in 1925, this little strophic song, almost childlike in its simplicity, has become very popular.

Islossningen i Uleå älv (*The Breaking of the Ice on the Oulu River*), Op. 30, for narrator, male choir and orchestra, was first performed at a lottery soirée arranged by the Savo-Karelian Students' Association in Helsinki on 21st October 1899; Sibelius himself conducted the Philharmonic Society orchestra, and the narrator was Axel Ahlberg. As so often, Sibelius had completed the score at the last moment, and neither the narrator nor the choir had much opportunity to learn the piece. *Islossningen* is a setting of a Swedish-language poem by Topelius; the poem dates from 1856 and, as it had originally been written in honour of Tsar Alexander II, did not attract the attention of the Russian censor. Nevertheless, in the political climate of 1899, there can have been little doubt as to its intended patriotic message – especially as the first performance was followed by a performance of *Song of the Athenians*, given in classical costume.

Stylistically, *Islossningen* is closely related to *Finlandia*, and it is reasonable to assume that Sibelius worked on the two scores simultaneously: one might even speculate that he used *Islossningen* as a testing-ground for some of the motifs and sonorities in *Finlandia*. The narrator appears at the beginning and end, his words sometimes separated by dramatic chords, sometimes supported by the merest whisper from the orchestra. The choral writing is often in unison, while the orchestral writing contains characteristic brass fanfares, a brief but expressive cello solo, murmuring string tremolos and syncopated accompaniment figures. Sibelius marked the fair copy of the score 'To be revised' – but never found time to do so.

During this politically volatile year Sibelius wrote a dramatic piano piece that he named *Marche triste*, JS 124. It is in ABA form, with outer sections that are dark-hued, astringent and defiant. By contrast the middle section, in 12/8, is sweet and idyllic, like a memory of lost happiness. For some reason, *Marche triste* was never published. Folke Gräsbeck has speculated that its title and mood would have attracted the unwelcome attention of the Russian censors. The beautiful middle section, however, was transplanted into the *Andantino in F major*, Op. 24 No. 7, a calmer and less belligerent piece. This, too, is in ABA form, but here the A and B sections are closely related both rhythmically and melodically. The original version of the *Andantino* was immediately published by Wasenius in Helsinki but Sibelius soon produced a revised version that Wasenius issued the following year and which has become better known. The principal difference comes in bar 7 (and the corresponding place towards the end of the piece), where two bars of 9/4 replaced four bars of 6/4; this change has the effect of avoiding disruption to the steady flow of the melody. So seamlessly integrated are the A and B sections of the *Andantino* that one easily forgets that the B section was originally conceived in a wholly different context. Admittedly we cannot be absolutely certain that the *Marche triste* came first, but it would be most uncharacteristic if Sibelius borrowed a passage from a work that had already been published.[1]

If the *Marche triste* was indeed withdrawn to avoid irritating the censors, Sibelius's nervousness was undeniably well-founded. September 1899 brought another attack on Finnish freedom of expression: *Päivälehti* was banned, a state of affairs which persisted for several months. A pageant was arranged in Helsinki on 3rd–5th November 1899, ostensibly to raise money for the Press Pension Fund, but this was a thin disguise for its true purpose: to rally support for the freedom of the press. The three days of public events included a fund-raising gala (4th November) at the Swedish Theatre in Helsinki, with tableaux depicting scenes from Finnish history, directed by Kaarlo Bergbom. Sibelius was asked to write music for the event; he provided a prelude, music to introduce each of the six tableaux, and some bars to be played during the fifth tableau.

At the gala evening, speeches in both Finnish and Swedish opened the proceedings. Verses to accompany the tableaux had been specially commissioned from Eino Leino – a surprising choice, since Leino, though a member of Sibelius's artistic circle, was not on good terms with Bergbom. Leino did not finish the texts in time, and they were completed by Jalmari Finne, a versatile cultural figure whose talents included writing, dramaturgy, translating and composing. The original texts are preserved in the Finnish State Archives.

Like the première of the *Karelia* music six years earlier, the gala evening at which the *Press Celebrations Music*, JS 137, was first heard was a highlight of Helsinki's social calendar. Sibelius himself conducted the Philharmonic Society orchestra, and – for the benefit of those who had failed to gain admission on 4th November – a repeat performance was held two days later.

Unlike the *Karelia* score, the *Press Celebrations Music* is purely instrumental. It begins with a ceremonial *Preludio*, complete with fanfares, scored for wind and brass alone. If this was intended to quieten the audience at the gala evening, it apparently failed. The first tableau depicts how 'Väinämöinen [the venerable magician in the *Kalevala*] is discovered seated on a rock playing the kantele. Not only do the inhabitants of Kaleva and Pohjola listen entranced but so do the powers of nature' (from a review of the tableaux on 5th November in *Hufvudstadsbladet*). Sibelius makes no attempt to mimic the sound of Väinämöinen's kantele or of runic singing, however, and – although Väinämöinen is traditionally depicted as an old man – Sibelius's music is bright and sprightly in character.

In the second tableau 'Bishop Henrik baptizes a young Finnish chieftain and others await baptism' (*Hufvudstadsbladet*). Bishop Henrik took part in the so-called 'First Crusade to Finland' in 1155 along with the Swedish King Erik; both men were later canonized as St Henrik (patron saint of Finland) and St Erik (patron saint of Sweden) respectively. According to legend, Henrik was murdered the following year by a peasant named Lalli on the frozen surface of Lake Köyliö. Also in the tableau, three angels symbolically give the Finnish people a cross, palm and Bible. The sonorities are predominantly rich and heavy, almost Elgarian, and a tolling bell – heard four times in the first half of the piece – contributes to the atmosphere of religious solemnity. The movement ends with a grand plagal ('amen') cadence.

The third tableau is much lighter in mood. It is set in the 1550s and depicts a 'Scene from Duke Johan's Court' at Turku Castle (Turku remained the capital of Finland until 1812). Johan (1537–92), second son of the Swedish king Gustavus Vasa, was at that time Duke of Finland; in 1568 he became King Johan III of Sweden. Although Johan's wife, Katarina Jagellonica, was the sister of Sigismund II Augustus of Poland, Sibelius's music – *Quasi tempo di menuetto* – has more of a Spanish flavour. During the festivities presented in this tableau, Duke Johan affirms his love for Finland and his desire to make the country a place of happiness.

The fourth tableau depicted the Finns in the Thirty Years War (1618–48). 'From a height young Finnish peasants hurry to the struggle. The arbiter of battle hands them the key to the war, the banner of freedom' (*Hufvudstadsbladet*). The music begins with a melancholy minuet, abruptly interrupted by fanfares (this theme is also found in an unfinished set of *Piano Works for Children*). Both here and in the passage that follows, the melodic shapes and rhythms anticipate the first movement of the *Third Symphony*, though the harmonies and musical character are very different. The movement ends with a bright, festive march.

In 1700, while Finland was under Swedish rule, the Great Northern War broke out: the Russians invaded, taking Viipuri in 1710 and occupying all of Finland in 1713. This occupation, called the Great Hostility, lasted until 1721, and was characterized by violence and destruction: not only did the Russians terrorize the local population, but also the retreating Swedish army caused considerable damage. The peace treaty of Uusikaupunki, by which Sweden lost the south-eastern part of Finland, was dictated by Russians and signed in 1721. This period in Finnish history was the subject of the fifth tableau. 'Mother Finland is seated among snowdrifts surrounded by her frozen children. War, starvation, the cold, and death threaten them all with disaster' (*Hufvudstadsbladet*). The thematic material of this movement shows Sibelius at his most lugubrious, and generates great intensity. The motif first heard on muted horns in this movement originates from a fragment for violin and piano dating back to the early 1890s ([*Grave*] in D minor). In addition to composing an introduction to this scene, Sibelius also provided a brief piece of music – four atmospheric string chords, played *pianissimo* – to be performed during the tableau.

'Finland Awakes' – the original incarnation of *Finlandia* – was the grand finale to the gala evening. According to *Hufvudstadsbladet*: 'The powers of darkness menacing Finland have not succeeded in their terrible threats. Finland awakes. Among the great men of the time that adorn the pages of history, one tells the story of Alexander II, and other memories of Finland's renaissance stir: Runeberg listens to his muse, Snellman inspires his students, Lönnrot transcribes the runes; four speakers of the first Diet, the beginning of elementary education and the first steam locomotive are all recorded.' The title *Finland Awakes* (*Suomi herää*) alludes to the name of the choral song *Herää Suomi* (*Awaken, Finland*) by Emil Genetz, the middle section of which bears a resemblance to the opening of the 'hymn' theme in Sibelius's piece. Genetz's song had been published in 1882 and was often performed by the YL choir. This musical resemblance is unlikely to have been a total coincidence. Sibelius would have had no reason to

avoid hinting at a popular patriotic song in this context (arguably quite
the reverse). In the grand finale of the *Karelia* music, he had made a
far more overt reference to Pacius's patriotic song *Vårt land*, the future
national anthem.

Finland Awakes/Finlandia contains plenty of Sibelian fingerprints,
but no single element would seem to explain its immediate and lasting
popularity. It goes without saying (but is worth repeating, if only to
repudiate a lasting misconception) that Sibelius did not draw on traditional melodies or folk music for any of the themes. The swelling, snarling
chords at the outset, which he had so recently tested out in *Islossningen*,
can trace their roots back at least as far as the *String Trio in G minor*
of 1893, and other thematic elements of the opening *Andante sostenuto*
section have an ancestor in the *Theme and Variations in C sharp minor*
for string quartet (1888). The fanfare-like brass motif on a single note
in the *Allegro* is a 4/4 variant of a device Sibelius had formerly used in
No. 32 of the [*33 Small Pieces*] for string quartet and in the unfinished
second movement of the *G minor String Trio*, and even the famous 'hymn',
despite its links with Genetz's choral song, is quintessentially Sibelian in
its use of an 'S-motif' and a dotted rhythm on the penultimate beat of
each phrase. In *Finlandia* the 'S-motif' functions as a unifying factor:
though heard most prominently at the start of the hymn section, it is also
clearly discernible in almost every other part of the work. It seems to have
been fortuitous that Sibelius combined these elements in a manner that
found public favour and, moreover, suited the political mood. Evidently
the composer himself was surprised by the immense acclaim enjoyed by
Finlandia: in 1911 he even called it 'a relatively insignificant piece'.

Kari Kilpeläinen has suggested that a further piece of music – the 'tone
picture for brass and percussion' *Tiera*, JS 200 – was once planned to form
part of the *Press Celebrations Music*. *Tiera* is named after a character from
the *Kalevala*, a comrade-in-arms of Lemminkäinen, and consists of a slow,
chromatic introduction followed by an easy-going march.

Sibelius conducted various combinations of movements from the
Press Celebrations Music in concert, but it was at a symphony concert
conducted by Robert Kajanus on 14th December 1899 that a more
recognizable selection began to emerge: he played the *Preludio* followed
by tableaux 1 (now named *All'Overtura*), 4 (*Scena*), 3 (*Quasi Bolero*)
and 6 (*Finale*). Here, as with *Karelia*, Sibelius may have been guided
by Kajanus's instincts about which sections would work well in concert.
It was presumably for these early concerts that Sibelius discarded the
rather brash original ending of *Finland Awakes* and replaced it with a
restatement of the famous 'hymn' tune in its entirety, this time played
with full splendour by the brass.

Meanwhile, on 25th November, Kajanus had conducted Sibelius's earlier 'Historical Suite' – the *Overture, Intermezzo, Ballade* and *Alla marcia* from the pageant score of 1893 – under a new title, 'Carelia-Suite', to distinguish it from the *Press Celebrations* music. The following October he performed the last three movements without the overture, and the *Karelia Suite* in its familiar form was born.

On 20th December Sibelius signed a contract with Helsingfors Nya Musikhandel to produce a set of *Pianokompositioner för barn* (*Piano Works for Children*, JS 148). Even though the publisher paid him an advance, the composer never went beyond the stage of sketching the 21 pieces. He did, however, re-use many of the motifs elsewhere. The themes of *Rosenlied* (Op. 50 No. 6), the last movement of *Kyllikki* (Op. 41), the *Scout March* (Op. 91b), the first version of *Har du mod?* (JS 93), the *Souvenir* (Op. 79 No. 1), the fanfare from the tableau depicting the Finns in the Thirty Years War from *Press Celebrations Music* and even the stepwise descending theme that is a central element in the first movement of the *Second Symphony* are all found in this unassuming project! The theme later used in the *Scout March* is also found in a sketch for torviseitsikko and percussion from 1897–99 (the percussion line is not fully written out); one might surmise that this was written around the same time as the *Pianokompositioner för barn.*

At the turn of the century Sibelius's star was still very much in the ascendant. Not only had he achieved undisputed prominence in Helsinki, but his music had at last started to be published and performed abroad. He had launched himself as a symphonist, though at this stage nobody could have foreseen how the symphony would come to dominate his creative output. But the social climate in which he lived was still under threat, and in that respect things would get worse before they got better. Sibelius wrote to Aino on New Year's Day: 'We shall see what the new century brings for Finland and the Finns. At least the judgement of history will not be in the Finns' disfavour. And the fact that our cause is just gives us dignity and peace of mind.' He needed to write to his wife because they spent the New Year apart, for the saddest of reasons: Aino needed to go to Lohja to visit her brother Arvid, whose small daughter Anna had just died of typhus.

1900

It was not just in the Lohja area that typhus was a threat: in early 1900 a typhus epidemic broke out in Kerava. Sibelius's youngest daughter Kirsti, who was only fifteen months old, contracted the disease and, on 13th February, she died. Aino suspected that she herself might have carried the disease home from her recent visit to Arvid's family. The effects of Kirsti's death on the entire family were, naturally enough, devastating: according to Aino, Jean had been especially fond of her. She was buried at the Järnefelt family grave in Helsinki's Hietaniemi cemetery four days later. Fearful that the other girls might also contract the disease, Aino took Eva and Ruth to her mother's house in Lohja. Sibelius himself increasingly sought refuge in drink.

In the aftermath of Kirsti's death Sibelius composed his longest surviving piece for cello and piano: *Malinconia*, Op. 20. Allegedly written in the space of just three hours, *Malinconia* was dedicated to the Finnish conductor and cellist Georg Schnéevoigt, who gave its first performance in Helsinki on 12th March 1900 (under the title 'Fantasia') with his wife Sigrid at the piano, at a concert to raise funds for the Philharmonic Society orchestra. *Malinconia* contains intense, impassioned music and highly virtuosic writing for both instruments (although these qualities have not always protected it from the vitriol of the critics). On occasion it betrays a stylistic affinity with the forthcoming *Second Symphony*, and the themes include one with an unmistakable 'S-motif'. In 1914, when asked by the American cellist Laura Tappen whether he had composed any cello music, Sibelius replied that *Malinconia* was not suited to young ladies, but rather to dissolute old men!

Four days after the première of *Malinconia*, on 16th March, Gösta Sohlström conducted the Muntra Musikanter male choir and Philharmonic Society orchestra in the first performance of *Sandels*, written almost two years previously. The numerous changes of tempo, at times frenetic choral writing and the often dense textures at climaxes mean that *Sandels* is not an easy work to perform effectively, and the piece did not win particular acclaim at its première (Oscar Merikanto wrote that it was 'far from being one of Sibelius's best works'). Nowadays it receives occasional airings but has not won a place in the repertoire.

Even at this time of personal tragedy, opportunities were to arise that Sibelius could not afford to ignore. One such opening was offered by the Paris World Exhibition of 1900. The Russians were still tightening their grip on Finland: on 6th February the so-called 'Language Manifesto' had made Russian the language of official correspondence and some public bodies, and attempted to curtail freedom of public assembly. The World Exhibition gave the Finns the opportunity to make an unmistakable gesture of defiance; they refused to be regarded merely as part of Russia and proudly designed their own pavilion – calling on some of the foremost Finnish architects of the time, Eliel Saarinen, Armas Lindgren and Herman Gesellius. To coincide with the exhibition, plans were being laid for a major European tour for Kajanus and the Philharmonic Society orchestra. A total of 19 concerts were planned in thirteen different cities, culminating in two performances in Paris.

The World Exhibition and orchestral concerts were widely regarded as a demonstration of national identity and a showcase for the Finnish cause, but at least one man – viewing the situation from a certain distance – recognized that a high-profile international tour offered the potential to combine such sentiments with Sibelius's development as a creative artist. In March an anonymous letter arrived, encouraging Sibelius to write an overture for the tour, with the inspired proposal that it should be named 'Finlandia'.

The orchestra's tour's repertoire naturally centred on Finnish music. The major work was to be the *Symphony in F minor* by Ernst Mielck; compositions by both Kajanus and Armas Järnefelt were to be included, and Sibelius was to be represented with *Finlandia* (though this name was not used in the programmes), *Lemminkäinen's Return*, *The Swan of Tuonela* and movements from *King Christian II*.

On 7th June the anonymous letter-writer sent another missive. This time he recommended that Sibelius should undertake a journey to Italy, 'where one learns *cantabile*, moderation and harmony, plasticity and symmetry of line, where everything is beautiful – even the ugly. Remember what Italy meant for Tchaikovsky's development – and that of Richard Strauss.' To finance this journey the writer would eventually raise no less than 5,000 marks – 3,000 from Axel Tamm in Stockholm, and 2,000 from Magnus Dahlström in Turku.

The forthcoming tour served as something of a catalyst for Sibelius. During the spring he reworked his *First Symphony* – allegedly in just three days and two nights, and in its revised form it replaced Mielck's symphony on the tour programmes. The surviving materials[2] do not allow us to reconstruct the complete symphony in its original form but do offer a tantalizing glimpse of what it must have been like. We can be fairly certain that he either added or exchanged the slow introduction to the first movement at this stage, and changed the corresponding passage in the finale accordingly. There are indications that the first movement originally contained parts for side drum and, surprisingly, castanets. In the slow movement there was originally a restatement of the opening theme, the melody now scored for clarinets and violas (at letter B in the published score). The scherzo would at first glance appear to have been much longer, the formal plan of the movement following the scheme AABA, but it cannot be said with certainty that this was Sibelius's intention. In the finale the restatement of the 'big tune' is differently scored (starting at the *Andante (ma non troppo)* after letter S), and the coda was originally slightly shorter.

No later than June Sibelius made some further revisions to *Finlandia*, now tautening up the coda by once more removing the third appearance of the 'hymn' tune in the brass. He probably made the piano version of the work at the same time – the most virtuosic of all Sibelius's piano transcriptions, attempting with massive chords and sparkling, wide-ranging *bravura* writing to emulate both the sustaining power and the exuberance of a symphony orchestra in full flow. At this stage the name *Finlandia* was still something of a problem for the Russian authorities. At a concert at the Volunteeer Fire Brigade Hall on 2nd July, the day before the orchestra's departure, the work was heard in its definitive form for the first time – but was called simply *Suomi* (*Finland*). During the tour itself the piece was billed as *Vaterland* or *La Patrie*. In the years that followed, Georg Schnéevoigt conducted it under the title *Impromptu*. On the other hand, the piano transcription was published in November 1900 as *Finlandia*, and this title was also used at one of Kajanus's popular concerts in Helsinki the following February.

The 'S-motif' that is so prominent in *Finlandia* is also clearly evident in the *Nocturno* for piano, Op. 24 No. 8, from 1900. Though it is not one of the more assertive of the Op. 24 set, this piece with its almost constant syncopations and songful melodic line exudes an air of National Romanticism typical of Sibelius's music from this period.

In June 1900 a choral festival was arranged by the Society for Popular Education in Helsinki – the first such event since the publication of the February Manifesto. The festival included several Sibelius premières. Kajanus conducted the brass piece *Tiera*, written the previous autumn, and Oskar Merikanto directed a new arrangement for mixed choir that Sibelius had made of his song *Isänmaalle* (*To the Fatherland*). Compared with the original male-choir version from the previous year, he made numerous rhythmic changes which, although insignificant when taken in isolation, combine to impart a much smoother and more integrated character. The song was soon in wide circulation, often in unauthorized editions, and was one of the first of Sibelius's works to be recorded – as early as 1901, by the Finnish Choral Society of St Petersburg, conducted by Mooses Putro.

The time had arrived for the Philharmonic Society orchestra to begin its tour. Sibelius – who, on account both of his compositions and of his friendship with Kajanus, had assumed a role that might nowadays be described as 'composer-in-residence' – accompanied the orchestra on its travels, although Kajanus conducted all of the concerts. The anonymous figure who had suggested the title *Finlandia* waved them off at the quayside as the ship *Wellamo* set off on its short voyage to Stockholm. On board, on 3rd July, Sibelius set about providing the orchestra with an encore for its coming concerts. He made an arrangement of *Porilaisten marssi* (*March of the Pori Regiment*); unlike his earlier chamber version of December 1892, the orchestral one has survived, although it is rarely heard. Four years later Kajanus too made an orchestral arrangement, and it is Kajanus's version that is more usually played today.

The orchestra played first in the Olympia circus hall in Stockholm and the concert was a great success despite the poor acoustic; it also offered an opportunity for Sibelius to meet the prominent Swedish composers Hugo Alfvén, Wilhelm Stenhammar and Emil Sjögren, with whom he consumed an immoderate quantity of absinthe. The Tchaikovskian aspects of the *First Symphony* did not go unnoticed by the three Swedes and, when reporting their opinions in a letter home to Aino, Sibelius made the oft quoted remark: 'I know that I have much in common with that man [Tchaikovsky] – but nothing can be done about that.' A second concert at Stockholm's open-air Hasselbacken Theatre was also rapturously received.

Sibelius had made useful contacts in Stockholm, but that city was also home to one of his fiercest adversaries – Wilhelm Peterson-Berger. Some fifteen months younger than Sibelius and an enthusiastic champion of Wagner and Grieg, 'P.-B' was a critic who wrote fearlessly and from the heart in the newspaper *Dagens Nyheter*. He was hugely influential on the Swedish musical scene, but his judgements were often wide of the mark. Over the coming years he rarely found anything positive to say about Sibelius's music; Sibelius for his part found P.-B's antagonistic tone exasperating. The situation was hot helped by the fact that Peterson-Berger was also a composer: between 1900 and 1933 he wrote five symphonies and four operas. By and large, however, his larger works were regarded by his Swedish colleagues with considerable disdain, although some smaller piecs (such as the *Frösöblomster* [*Frösö Flowers*] for piano) achieved some popularity. The inappropriateness of such an untalented composer finding fault with works that were otherwise widely acclaimed was evidently lost on Peterson-Berger.

The orchestra, with Sibelius in tow, then took the train to Norway for a concert in Kristiania (Oslo). Sibelius missed the orchestra's concerts in Gothenburg and Malmö, meeting up with them at their next port of call, Copenhagen, where Charles Kjerulf wrote in *Politiken* that 'Sibelius's composing talent is of a quite uncommon quality; only the very finest contemporary figures write such ruthlessly courageous and thoroughly independent music.'

From Denmark the tour continued to Germany, with concerts in Lübeck, Hamburg and Berlin. Of these venues, there can be no doubt that the most important was Berlin, where the critics would be certain to judge both the orchestra and the music itself according to the most exacting standards of a city that took immense pride in its musical heritage. On the whole Sibelius did not fare badly: the Berlin critics were not bowled over by Sibelius's music, but nor were they hostile. Otto Taubmann (*Berliner Börsen-Courier*) wrote for instance of its 'fine craftsmanship and seriousness of tone' and of Sibelius's 'new and unusual' musical style. Other reviews welcomed Sibelius as a fresh new voice even if they were shocked by the immediacy and power of his expressive means.

From Berlin the orchestra moved on through the Netherlands and Belgium, with concerts in Amsterdam, The Hague, Rotterdam and Brussels, although a heatwave kept audience numbers small. The ultimate destination, Paris, was reached on 25th July, but by then the concert season was well and truly over, and the concerts – despite generally positive reviews – failed to attract widespread attention.

Sibelius returned to Finland in early August and was surprised to discover that Aino and the girls were still away in Kuopio, vising her brother Kasper and his family. He had never received Aino's letter informing him that she would return to Kerava later than planned, and his idea of arriving home unannounced thus fell flat. When Aino did arrive home she did, at least, find her husband in the best of humours.

Overall the concert trip was a significant milestone in Sibelius's career. 'Without him the orchestra's so-called Paris trip would not have come to anything, because we would not have had any reason to undertake the tour', Kajanus recalled. By and large Kajanus and the orchestra had acquitted themselves honourably, and in so doing had made a persuasive case for Sibelius's music. He was now known internationally as a symphonic composer and had made many valuable new contacts, some of whom – such as the pianist and composer Wilhelm Stenhammar – would later become close friends. The acclaim he had received in the Scandinavian countries is perhaps unsurprising, but in Germany (if not in France) he had made genuine progress.

After the tour, Sibelius discovered that the sender of the anonymous but inspirational letters was Baron Axel Carpelan, a curious and eccentric figure who hailed from Odensaari near Turku but in 1903 moved to Tampere, well away from the mainstream of the Finnish musical scene. He was seven years older than Sibelius and, like him, had dreamed in his youth of becoming a violinist. Unlike Sibelius, however, he could not persuade his family to support him in his musical studies. He reacted by abandoning any hopes of a professional career of any kind and devoting himself on an amateur basis to music and literature. Carpelan was an idealist, a hypochondriac who could not reconcile himself with some of life's more mundane aspects. He never married, and his lack of a job meant that he lived in poverty, even though he maintained contacts with wealthy music lovers such as the Swedish patron of the arts Axel Tamm. He exchanged letters with Viktor Rydberg, and also offered advice to Robert Kajanus.

Carpelan may have lived in a world of his own but he did appreciate that money was necessary to provide the conditions in which art could flower. Accordingly, over the years he unselfishly used his own contacts to raise funds for Sibelius, and supplemented this very tangible support with a virtually constant flow of suggestions and advice. Perhaps because Carpelan was an outsider, he saw Sibelius's talent from a wholly different, more visionary perspective. Moreover, his opinions were clearly attuned to the imaginative side of Sibelius's own character. As time went by, Sibelius and Carpelan became close confidants and remained so until Carpelan's death in 1919. When speaking with pupils, interviewers and biographers Sibelius was eloquent on a wide variety of topics but notoriously reticent on the subject of his own music. With Carpelan he showed no such diffidence: he repaid Carpelan's enthusiasm by giving him unique insights into his creative process.

In November 1899 Sibelius had signed a contract with Karl Fredrik Wasenius to publish *The Swan of Tuonela* and *Lemminkäinen's Return*, and in 1900 he overhauled the pieces once again (the actual production of the scores was undertaken by Breitkopf & Härtel in Germany). In the case of *The Swan*, neither the original autograph nor any of the earlier versions have survived, and so we can only speculate as to the extent and nature of the revisions. In *Lemminkäinen's Return* the changes were extensive, although it is impossible to determine which were made for the 1897 performance and which date from the 1900 revision. There are many small adjustments to the scoring, phrasing and dynamics and various cuts both large and small; the large cuts were a two-and-a-half-minute passage from the middle of the movement and the entire 'song' section near the end.

The shadow of Kirsti's death was still hanging over the Sibelius family's home in Kerava, and Carpelan's suggested trip to Italy must have struck him as an excellent idea. Before he could set off, however, there was a new piece to compose for a fund-raising soirée arranged by the Philharmonic Society orchestra to replenish its coffers following the European tour. The work in question was *Snöfrid* and it was shortly after this piece's first performance, which Sibelius conducted on 20th October 1900, that he finally met Axel Carpelan for the first time. Carpelan could not attend the concert, but Sibelius sought him out three days later in Helsinki's Kruunuhaka district, where the Baron was staying with relatives.

Snöfrid, an 'improvisation' for speaker, mixed chorus and orchestra, is a setting of words by Viktor Rydberg. Unlike Stenhammar, who had set this poem to music in 1891, Sibelius selected only extracts from the poem. The composer told Jussi Jalas in 1943 that he had written the piece very rapidly: 'I composed *Snöfrid* more or less in one sitting, after coming home from a three-day binge.'

The anonymous reviewer in *Päivälehti* assessed the work very positively: 'The highlight of the evening, however, was the last item on the programme, Sibelius's newest composition, the melodrama *Snöfrid*... The work as a whole makes an impression of great feeling and warmth; it seems so clear and inspired that it is undeniably to be numbered among Sibelius's masterpieces... The piece had to be encored immediately, and heartfelt was the appreciation with which our country's most eminent composer was thanked for this estimable composition, which lent musical dignity and cachet to the lottery event.'

Especially after the popular success of the patriotic *Song of the Athenians* a year earlier, also with words by Rydberg, the obvious provocative and political associations of *Snöfrid* could not be overlooked ('Draw your sword against vile giants, bleed valiantly for the weak'), but whereas the nationalist element is the raison d'être of *Song of the Athenians*, in *Snöfrid* it is merely one aspect of a far more wide-ranging and imaginative composition. In fact, among Sibelius's Rydberg settings, it is far more worthwhile to compare *Snöfrid* with *The Wood-Nymph*, with which it reveals clear parallels in both structure and narrative. Like *The Wood-Nymph*, *Snöfrid* is episodic in construction, and tells of a young man's encounter with a mysterious and magical female being. A stormy orchestral introduction sets the scene; then the choir, serenely and idealistically, tells of the sylph Snöfrid's beauty. This is followed by a fast, dramatic passage in which trolls offer Gunnar (the hero) gold and treasures in exchange for his soul – a passage reminiscent of Mussorgsky's *Night on a Bare Mountain* (1867). Next comes a moving love scene in which Gunnar is offered a choice between good or evil. Above atmospheric brass chords, the narrator then recites Snöfrid's words, encouraging the hero to be valiant and selfless. In the concluding section the music radiates a calm confidence that the hero will make a wise choice. *Snöfrid* is a vastly underrated composition in which Sibelius not only added a new dimension to Rydberg's words but also composed music that is colourful, stirring and often very poignant.

In a more pensive mood, Sibelius also wrote some songs during the autumn, including several of his most popular. Just months after Kirsti had passed away he turned his attention to a group of poems that all in some way touch on the theme of death, either within an environment peopled by humans or gods, or within the realm of nature. *Den första kyssen* (*The First Kiss*), Op. 37 No. 1, one of Sibelius's most popular songs, was probably composed at Lohja in the autumn of 1900, though it draws on material sketched in 1891/92; at any rate it was premièred at the University Hall on 22nd November by Adée Leander-Flodin, who recorded it just four years later. This Runeberg setting finds Sibelius in a Romantic, almost Wagnerian mood: the heavens rejoice when a maiden is kissed for the first time, but Death turns aside and weeps.

Säv, säv, susa (*Sigh, Sigh, Sedges*), Op. 36 No. 4, is a setting of Fröding and tells of the suicide by drowning of a girl named Ingalill. The song's popularity is easily explained by its mellifluous vocal line and a piano part that gently imitates the swaying reeds on the lake. *Säv, säv, susa* was also among the earliest Sibelius songs to be recorded, by Alexandra Ahnger accompanied by Oskar Merikanto in Helsinki in 1904 and then by Maikki and Armas Järnefelt two years later. A 28-bar *Andantino in E flat minor* for voice and piano, JS 42, probably from 1900, is believed to be an earlier attempt to set the same text, although musically the two versions are wholly independent and no text is actually included in the manuscript of the *Andantino*.

Less well known is *Marssnön* (*The March Snow*), Op. 36 No. 5, to a text by Josef Julius Wecksell. Despite its 5/4 time signature, this song is far removed from the world of the *Kalevala*; its nobility of line and restrained accompaniment make this one of the most personal and intimate of Sibelius's shorter songs. The poem appeals to spring to remain within winter's clutches: 'sleep soundly in the gentle, friendly snow – you will blossom more strongly, and then die richer'. The text of *Demanten på marssnön* (*The Diamond on the March Snow*), Op. 36 No. 6, another Wecksell setting, carries quite the opposite message: the ice crystals are in love with the sun, although they are melted by its heat. Although in many ways it is a conventional song, its uncomplicated and easily memorable vocal line accounts for its popularity. Once again Alexandra Ahnger and Oskar Merikanto made a recording of this song in 1904, but this time they had also given the première, in Helsinki on 8th February 1901. Although the two Wecksell poems are not pantheistic in a conventional sense, we find in them a clear suggestion that nature is symbolic of the human condition.

Although his songs show that Sibelius could set words with great sensitivity, he himself was apparently not endowed with a good singing voice. A few months earlier, his friend Wenzel Hagelstam had recounted in a letter to Axel Gallén that Sibelius, rather the worse for wear, had been playing the piano, 'which was not as shocking as the fact that his musical delirium caused singing, which was more violent than pleasant'.

A week after the première of *Snöfrid*, on 27th October, Sibelius and his family left Finland, and their first stop was Berlin, where they were to stay for several months, living in an expensive hotel and rapidly consuming the money set aside for their Italian journey. Sibelius himself regarded it as a high priority to consolidate his position in Germany by making his presence felt in Berlin, and he also paid a visit to Arthur Nikisch in Leipzig, though he found time to compose a few small works as well, among them *Kavaljeren* (*The Cavalier*), JS 109, a bright and lively march for piano that was written for the humorous monthly journal *Fyren*. The Sibelius family spent Christmas as guests of Adolf Paul.

Sibelius's activities – and expenditure – in Berlin were regarded with some dismay by Axel Carpelan, who had after all raised funds so that Sibelius could go to Italy. Luckily Sibelius managed to procure the extra resources he needed from Finland through his own channels.

CHAPTER 7

FINLAND'S OWN BEETHOVEN –
THE SECOND SYMPHONY: 1901–1903

1901

Before leaving Berlin, Sibelius wrote *Flickan kom ifrån sin älsklings möte* (*The Tryst*), Op. 37 No. 5, a song that has won widespread popularity for its unashamed, full-blooded tunefulness and direct though unhackneyed expressivity. The poem is by Runeberg and tells how a girl conceals her romantic assignations from her mother, only to confess all when her lover proves unfaithful. Ida Ekman gave the song's first performance at a soirée in Berlin in late January.

After that the family finally headed for Italy, and chose to stay in Rapallo, a small coastal town not far from Genoa. Aino and the girls stayed in a guest house, but Sibelius himself rented a study in the mountain villa of a Signor Molfino, surrounded by a garden full of 'roses in bloom, camellias, almond trees, cactus..., magnolia, cypresses, vine, palm trees and a manifold variety of flowers', as he wrote to Axel Carpelan. Stimulated not only by these idyllic surroundings but also by the books he had brought with him on his journey, among them Adolph Törneros's *Bref och dagboksanteckningar* (*Letters and Diaries*) and Henri-Frédéric Amiel's *Journal intime* (*Diary of a Dreamer*), he sketched many musical ideas. On 11th February he compared in his own mind the mountain villa with Don Juan's palace surrounded by an enchanted garden, and wrote the following lines: 'Don Juan. Sit in the twilight in my palace, a guest [the Stone Guest] comes in. I ask more than once who he is. – No answer. I try to amuse him. He remains silent. Finally the stranger starts to sing. Then Don Juan recognizes who he is: Death', along with the main theme of the slow movement of the *Second Symphony*. At this stage, of course, he did not know that it would end up in a symphony; instead he envisaged it as part of a projected work based on the Don Juan theme entitled *Festival: Four Tone-Poems for Orchestra*.

Axel Carpelan had been right to believe that Italy would be an effective creative stimulus to Sibelius, but the trip was not without its share of drama. The rapid depletion of the family's reserves of money was a familiar enough scenario, but the whole family must have been panic-stricken when Ruth fell seriously ill with what appeared to be typhus but was probably a form of gastric fever. Fortunately she recovered – but her illness placed additional strain on Jean's relationship with Aino. Sibelius's reaction was as unexpected as it was selfish: in March, as soon as Ruth was on the road to recovery, he left his family in Rapallo and set off without warning for Rome, where he rented a room and continued to compose, as well as visiting the Colosseum and the opera. Almost immediately he was beset by wholly justified pangs of conscience and wrote to Aino: 'It is because of my thoughtlessness and insincerity that I have been unable to make you happy. Besides this, my nature is so volatile.' It says something for Aino's reserves of love and patience that she forgave him for this lapse. The Sibelius family's return journey to Finland took them first to Florence (where the composer considered making a setting of part of Dante's *Divina Commedia*; he sketched what would become the second theme of the symphony's slow movement [*Andante sostenuto*, divided strings, *ppp*], labelling it 'Christus'), and then to Vienna and Prague. Here Sibelius briefly met Antonín Dvořák, whom he later described as 'naturalness and modesty personified'.

Back in Kerava in May, Sibelius set about writing a choral piece for Heikki Klemetti and the Suomen Laulu Choir, who were planning a concert tour to central Europe. Suomen Laulu was an élite male-voice choir, founded in 1900 and drawn initially from the singers of YL. In 1907 it became a mixed choir, in which form it is still active today. In 1901 the choir boasted an especially fine low bass singer named Enckell, and Klemetti was keen to have a piece to show off his voice. Sibelius responded with *Terve, kuu* (*Hail, Moon*), Op. 18 No. 2, a challenging song – more polyphonic than much of his choral music – in which, towards the end, the basses descend to the very bottom of the register. Sibelius marks this passage *ff* for the second basses and *ppp* for the rest of the choir. The text comes from the *Kalevala* and is a greeting from Väinämöinen to the sun and moon. Klemetti premièred the piece on 30th May before setting off on his concert tour.

Sibelius did not attend Klemetti's concert because by then he had already packed his bags and headed southwards again. His destination was Germany, where he had been invited to conduct *The Swan of Tuonela* and *Lemminkäinen's Return* (in their definitive published versions) at the Festival of the Allgemeiner deutscher Musikverein in Heidelberg. The festival was devoted to new music, and its artistic director was Richard Strauss, with whom Sibelius established a positive relationship. Although the rehearsals were less than promising, the concert itself went well and consolidated Sibelius's reputation in the eyes of the German critics.

Back in Finland the political situation worsened yet again in July. In the wake of the February Manifesto of 1899, the Tsar now did away with the independent Finnish army, incorporating it into the Russian army. Another petition of complaint was arranged, but this proved no more successful than the earlier one. The all too predictable result of such heavy-handed government was that the Finns began a campaign of passive resistance – with Sibelius playing his role as a figurehead for the Finnish cause.

During the summer Sibelius visited the Järnefelt villa in Lohja, worked on his Dante project and also started to concentrate on his *Second Symphony*, which he hoped to present before the end of the year. He was encouraged all the while by Axel Carpelan, who was also doing his best to raise money on Sibelius's behalf and was able to send him 500 marks at three-monthly intervals. It soon became apparent that the Dante plans would come to nothing, and he transferred his creative energies to the symphony, which he proposed to dedicate to Carpelan. In early October he told Carpelan that he envisaged the symphony as a 'great five-movement work', though his plans would soon change: the completed symphony has only four movements. Composition was now occupying so much of Sibelius's time that he gave up his teaching commitments at the Music Institute, thereby placing further strain on his already precarious finances.

In total contrast to his work on the symphony, Sibelius wrote a tiny strophic Christmas song to words by Wilkku Joukahainen, *On hanget korkeat, nietokset (High are the Snowdrifts)*, later incorporated as the fifth song in Op. 1, probably at the request of a Helsinki publisher. Along with the later *Giv mig ej glans...*, this unassuming little piece has won an unassailable place in the repertoire of Finnish Christmas songs.

While in the festive spirit, Sibelius wrote the *Romance in D flat major*, Op. 24 No. 9, as a Christmas present for Axel Carpelan. This piece occupies a similar position within Sibelius's œuvre for solo piano as *Flickan kom ifrån sin älsklings möte* does among his songs, or the *Violin Concerto* among his orchestral works: a vibrant expression of lush Romanticism that flows with majesty and inevitability. This is no doubt the principal reason why it has assumed a position of pre-eminence among Sibelius's shorter piano pieces. The atmosphere of the piece may be Tchaikovskian, but the thematic material exhibits clear Sibelian fingerprints: the principal idea is clearly based on an 'S-motif' and also features the interval of a descending fifth.

1902

Sibelius did not manage to complete the *Symphony No. 2 in D major*, Op. 43, in time to perform it in the autumn of 1901, but in the new year he could deliver it to the copyist and, on 8th March, he finally raised his baton to conduct its first performance in the University Hall in Helsinki. It was a triumphant success: repeat concerts were held on 10th, 14th and 16th March (the last of them in the Volunteer Fire Brigade Hall), and all were sold out – an unprecedented success for a new orchestral work in Finland. The reviewers were ecstatic, and Karl Flodin described the symphony as 'a definitive masterpiece, one of the few symphonic creations of our time that points in the same direction as Beethoven's symphonies'.

After the première, Robert Kajanus wrote a highly misleading article in *Hufvudstadsbladet* in which he interpreted the work as a portrayal of the Finnish people's resistance to their increasingly dominant Russian overlords. This viewpoint was maintained by such influential figures as the conductor Georg Schnéevoigt and the musicologist Ilmari Krohn, who in the mid-1940s even called the work the 'Liberation Symphony'. Such a nationalistic interpretation – which stemmed more from the writers' eagerness to inflate the nationalist credentials of the composer of *Finlandia* than from the intrinsic qualities of the symphony – was emphatically rejected by the composer.

In the *Second Symphony*, the Russian influences that had been discernible in the *First* are less strongly felt. Although its duration and emotional range are fully compatible with the demands of late Romanticism, the nature of the themes themselves shifts perceptibly towards lightness and Classicism – especially in the first movement. The symphony is in the bright key of D major, which the composer associated with the colour yellow, and many commentators have shared Flodin's view that the work is in the same spirit as Beethoven's symphonies, not least Axel Carpelan, who in 1900 had remarked that 'Finland is gaining its own Beethoven in Sibelius, having lost its own Mozart in Mielck'.

Much praise has been lavished on the taut construction of the first movement, but although most critics regard it as being in sonata form, their analyses of its structure vary widely. Two principal thematic types may be discerned, and these also recur in later movements. One is a three-note figure, rising or falling stepwise: the opening string idea and subsequent woodwind theme are examples of this. The other, contrasting type features a long opening note, often followed by a slow (notated) turn or trill and a descending interval of a fifth.

As usual with Sibelius's symphonies, the version heard at the première differed slightly from the published edition. In the autograph score, used at the first performance, the bar lines at the beginning of the symphony were placed differently and the phrase endings were of a more regular construction. In addition, cæsuras were placed at the end of the horn motifs that precede each appearance of the stepwise theme (comparison with other manuscripts suggests that Sibelius used the cæsura simply to ensure clear articulation; he presumably removed them so that conductors would not be tempted to interpret them as long pauses). Numerous other small changes can be found throughout the symphony. Among them was a slight increase in the tempo of the first movement, changing the marking from *Allegretto moderato* to *Allegretto*. In later life Sibelius complained to the conductors Tor Mann and Jussi Jalas: 'This theme is the most joyful I have ever written. I don't understand why it is often played too slowly.'

The more rhapsodic slow movement begins with an extraordinary passage for double basses and cellos, playing *pizzicato*, which Sir Thomas Beecham once described as 'meandering through the lower reaches of the orchestra like an amiable tapeworm'. Sibelius delays the appearance of the main theme ('Death'), which is finally heard from the bassoons in octaves. As the tempo increases to *Poco Allegro*, the violins present a jagged motif which will later assume great significance. The music builds up to a thundering, brassy climax, after which the jagged violin motif is suddenly and magically transformed into the ethereal second theme, first heard in F sharp major – the idea which Sibelius had labelled 'Christus' while he was in Italy (at the first performance this theme appeared in a different, slightly longer form at this point). The two principal themes do battle for the rest of the movement, with the 'Death' theme apparently emerging triumphant.

The Romantic cobwebs of the slow movement are blown away by the fresh storm winds of the scherzo, *Vivacissimo*; here, in the rushing quavers, we find an 'S-motif' as one of the music's principal building blocks. The vigorous flow of this highly virtuosic movement is interrupted by five isolated timpani strokes which usher in the pastoral trio, *Lento e suave*. This opens with an oboe solo that is highly characteristic of the composer: the repeated opening note, the descending fifth and the triplet towards the end of the phrase identify this theme as belonging to the second of the two basic types indicated above. The scherzo and trio are both repeated; a bridge passage then grows out of the trio and leads without a break into the last movement.

The main theme of the sonata-form finale has all of the qualities required for popularity: it is simple and readily memorable, heroic in bearing and glowingly orchestrated with ardent strings, radiant trumpets, sonorous horns and, insistently in the background, a threatening rhythmic motif from the trombones. The second theme is more subdued: over ostinato scale passages from the strings we hear a lamenting theme which suggests Finnish folk-music. According to the composer's wife Aino, this theme was originally composed in memory of Sibelius's sister-in-law, Elli Järnefelt, who had committed suicide. The development section is strictly contrapuntal, and the recapitulation builds inexorably towards the fervent final climax and triumphant coda; this is apparently the theme that had been improvised in June 1899 at Axel Gallén's exotic home in Ruovesi.

Two further works were composed to fill out the programme for the the concert at which the *Second Symphony* was premièred. One is the rarely heard *Overture in A minor*, JS 144. The piece opens with unaccompanied trumpet fanfares, joined after a while by the timpani, strings and trombones. The main part of the work, however, is an *Allegro* in a much lighter, more relaxed mood; here Sibelius uses a theme to which he would later return in the finale of his *Voces intimae* string quartet. Eventually the fanfares return, more luxuriantly scored. A typical example of Sibelius's occasional pieces, the overture is said to have been composed in a single night in a Helsinki hotel room.

Stylistically the overture looks both backwards and forwards. The slow brass fanfares at the beginning and the lighter, faster music that follows might be compared with the brass piece *Tiera*, composed three years earlier. On the other hand, the *Voces intimae* 'quotation' and also the musical character of the piece anticipate Sibelius's more 'classical' music from the years 1906–10. This aspect is perhaps disguised by the work's underlying bonhomie but, as the musicologist Veijo Murtomäki has pointed out, 'it is the first, exploratory piece of a new classical – one might even say neo-classical – style in Sibelius's œuvre. In it we find Sibelius at his most uninhibited, in the process of discovering the keys to the future.'

The classical allusions are even more pronounced in the third work in the concert, the *Impromptu* for women's voices and orchestra, Op. 19, to words from Rydberg's *Livslust och livsleda*. This piece too mixes forward-looking and retrospective elements. The undulating accompanimental figure at the outset, in the manner of a slow waltz, anticipates the song *Hertig Magnus* from 1909, and the flute pendant to the first phrase of the main theme has a clear resemblance to a motif heard near the beginning of the *Third Symphony*'s finale. On the other hand one of the later themes comes from the fragmentary second movement of the *String Trio in G minor* from 1893 which is in turn a derivation of No. 32 from the [*33 Small Pieces*] for string quartet of 1888–89; this idea could well have been inspired by the minuet from Schubert's *Piano Sonata in G major*, Op. 78. The latter part of the piece is more reminiscent of Tchaikovsky's ballet music. The classical feeling is reinforced by the text, which could also be said to have nationalist overtones. In the earlier Rydberg setting *Song of the*

Athenians (1899), the enlightened Greeks were used to symbolize the Finns in their long-running feud with their Russian rulers, and in the *Impromptu* the 'young Hellenics' in the poem might be interpreted as representing the Finnish people. The music itself, however, makes little attempt to probe such symbolic meanings. This modest piece is scored quite lavishly, requiring a harp and a fairly large percussion section (timpani, bass drum, tambourine, cymbals, triangle and castanets), although the heavy brass instruments are omitted. Sibelius also made a version with piano accompaniment.

With the *Second Symphony* out of the way, Sibelius could devote some time to a cantata that he had agreed to compose for the opening of the National Theatre in Helsinki, which was only a month away. The new piece was based on a *Kalevala* text and was named *Tulen synty* (*The Origin of Fire*), Op. 32. Sibelius conducted the première at the theatre's opening ceremony on 9th April with the Philharmonic Society orchestra and a choir of no less than 350 singers; the baritone soloist (it almost goes without saying) was Abraham Ojanperä. As part of a long programme, the cantata did not attract any particular attention.

The Origin of Fire is in two sections, in the first of which the orchestra is joined by the solo baritone. An orchestral introduction establishes a mood of gloom before the soloist narrates the first part of the story. Kalevala is in darkness because Louhi, the Mistress of Pohjola, has captured the sun and the moon and stolen fire from Kalevala's homes. Even Ukko, chief of the gods, is unable to find them. During this overtly operatic passage the orchestra remains on the whole subdued, despite one glorious Wagnerian outburst after the words 'ikävä itse Ukonki' ('Miserable even for Ukko himself'). In the second part of the cantata the soloist falls silent and the male chorus enters. Here the pace increases: Ukko creates new fire with his sword and entrusts it to the Maiden of the Air, who drops it. Despite the simplicity of the choral writing, the piece builds up to a climax of impressive breadth and grandeur.

The *Kalevala* text lent itself well to an allegorical interpretation. Finland during the years of Russian oppression could be said to be experiencing an endless night, without sunlight or fire – a situation that would provoke the Finnish people, like Ukko, to forge new light. The musical material of the cantata can be traced back to sketches from 1893–94, which perhaps accounts for the hints of Wagner in the piece.

In May, Sibelius worked on two new songs for Ida Ekman, both of which were later included in his Op. 37 collection. Topelius's poem *Lasse liten* (*Little Lasse*), Op. 37 No. 2, comes from his collection of children's poetry *Läsning för barn* (*Reading for Children*), but in Sibelius's setting a lean, moody piano part meanders chromatically, often in triplets or quintuplets, lending a restless, almost nightmarish ambience to the naïve vocal line. The sudden change to the major key in the last two bars comes as a complete surprise.

Its companion piece is *Soluppgång* (*Sunrise*), Op. 37 No. 3, to words by Tor Hedberg. Sibelius first drafted the entire piece in preliminary form (JS 87 – although the manuscript[1] lacks both title and text). Before long he returned to the piece, making relatively small changes to the piano part but completely reworking the vocal line, especially in the outer sections. The poem starts with an intimate description of the natural world at dawn, to which Sibelius responds with his usual sensitivity. In the middle section a knight observes the scene expectantly; his horn call is clearly depicted in the music. The revised version uses a rising vocal line and accompaniment to portray the calm sunrise with great beauty. To judge from a letter from Axel Carpelan to his cousin Lydia Rosengren a few months later, however, he did not complete either *Lasse liten* or *Soluppgång* before his summer holiday.

Although Sibelius continued to rent the Mattila house in Kerava until September, the family did not really use it during the summer. In June the composer paid a brief visit to Berlin, where he spent time with his brother and sister as well as his old friend Adolf Paul. He met up with the conductors Arthur Nikisch and Felix Weingartner; the latter promised to study the manuscript of the *Second Symphony* before forwarding it to Breitkopf & Härtel for publication. The best news, however, came in a letter from Busoni, inviting Sibelius to conduct *En saga* that November with the Berlin Philharmonic Orchestra.

Meanwhile Aino – who was again pregnant – and the girls had gone to stay with her mother in Lohja, and Sibelius, on his return from Berlin, could pass the time at leisure by the sea at Tvärminne, not far from Hanko, where his sister was also staying. Nearly five years after the death of her mother, Linda was increasingly prone to depression, and was already sliding remorselessly towards mental illness. In Tvärminne Sibelius indulged in some heavy drinking – thereby proving that he was perfectly capable of succumbing to temptation even without the bright lights of the city. He arranged for a piano to be delivered, and busied himself with yet another song for Ida Ekman. This time his choice fell upon the poem *Var det en dröm?* (*Was it a Dream?*) by Wecksell. The poem is a recollection of lost love, so magical that it seems like a dream. Sibelius was clearly keen to make the most of Ekman's voice, writing a powerful, broadly arching melody of great dramatic intensity (Op. 37 No. 4), not dissimilar in character to the 'big tune' in the finale of the *First Symphony*.

While in Tvärminne he received a visit from Axel Carpelan, who reported enthusiastically to his cousin Lydia about the composer's work:

'Four new songs are in progress: *Vilse* (Tavaststjerna),[2] *Soluppgång* (Tor Hedberg), *Lasse liten* (Topelius) and *Var det en dröm?* (Wecksell). I believe that these songs represent a great step forward compared to the earlier ones; Wecksell's marvellous poem in particular has been made into music in a way that ought to be hugely influential.' Carpelan also mentioned a number of other forthcoming works: a *Kanteletar* ballad for soprano and large orchestra (for Ida Ekman), twenty musical numbers for a ballet without text, a violin concerto, a large-scale orchestral fantasy, a book of piano pieces and a string quartet. What came of some of these ideas is unclear, but among the earliest sketches for the string quartet *Voces intimae* (from the years 1899–1903) is one for its first movement[3] (which must date from before the summer of 1902, as it includes material used in the *Second Symphony*) that also includes material for the *Violin Concerto*. It is thus quite plausible that Sibelius discussed these two works with Carpelan. The *Violin Concerto* at least was becoming a rather more definite plan. At least one of the surviving early sketches was identifiably written in Tvärminne,[4] and on 18th September, just before the family moved to Helsinki, Sibelius wrote to Aino: 'I have found some splendid themes for the violin concerto.'

The prospect of conducting the Berlin Philharmonic Orchestra prompted Sibelius to set about overhauling *En saga*. Almost a decade had passed since he had written the piece, and he was no doubt keen to make sure that he was represented at such a prestigious event by a work that was thoroughly up to date in its craftsmanship and style. The revision certainly made *En saga* more integrated, more refined in sonority and more cohesive, but in the process a considerable amount of some fine and very characteristic music was removed. In its revised form the work is almost 150 bars shorter than the first version; Sibelius discarded some of the original's thematic material, reduced the number of changes of tempo and key, and made numerous changes in the orchestration. Fortunately some of the most striking features of the original survived, for example the long clarinet solo at the end.

From his base on the coast Sibelius paid a visit to Pohja, where he was the guest of his former mentor Martin Wegelius, and went to see Walter von Konow in Sääksmäki. At the time of his visit, Eino Levón – a former teacher of both Sibelius and von Konow – was staying at one of Walter's holiday homes in the area. On one occasion Levón's daughters Anna, Elli and Karin sang a Finnish folk-song for Sibelius. To thank the young ladies, the composer set to music von Konow's occasional poem *Kotikaipaus* (*Homesickness*), JS 111.

As the summer drew to a close, Sibelius – who had already decided to give up the rented property in Kerava – experienced some difficulty finding a suitable apartment for his family in Helsinki. He had become accustomed to the lower rent costs of Kerava and now rejected properties in Kruunuhaka, Tehtaankatu and Seurasaarentie. Eero Järnefelt managed to locate a potential flat in Eerikinkatu, but its second floor location ruled it out as Aino's pregnancy ran its course. Eventually the family managed to rent the single-storey house next door – but as soon as they moved in at the beginning of October it became apparent that Sibelius was drawn as if by an invisible magnet towards his friends' gatherings at the city's restaurants.

On 25th October, Thérèse Hahl celebrated her sixtieth bithday. Together with her husband Taavi, Thérèse was a leading figure in Finnish choral music at the turn of the century. She had formerly been much in demand as an oratorio soloist and had rehearsed the chorus for the premières of several of Sibelius's works for chorus and orchestra. She was also a co-editor (with her husband and with the choral conductor Emil Forsström) of the *Sävelistö* volumes in which some of Sibelius's *a cappella* works had been published. For her birthday celebrations Sibelius composed and conducted a new song for mixed choir with a text by Nils Wasastjerna, now known by the functional rather than inspired title of *Den 25 oktober 1902. Till Thérèse Hahl* (*25th October 1902. To Thérèse Hahl*), JS 60. Presumably Wasastjerna was not keen on this equable, elegantly flowing composition (which incidentally begins with an 'S-motif'), as a short while later Sibelius made a second attempt, JS 61; at the end of the manuscript he noted: 'I preferred the first setting of Wasast[jerna]'s song. But I wanted to revise it. Perhaps the poet will like this one better.' The second song, in a characteristically Sibelian measured 3/2 time, has a wider expressive range, although the themes themselves are less memorable.

On 2nd November Sibelius signed a contract with Helsingfors Nya Musikhandel to publish *Spring Song*, and the printed edition appeared a year later. The following day Kajanus conducted the first performance of the revised *En saga* at the University Hall in Helsinki. From now on this became the 'standard' version of the piece, and this is the form in which it was published the following year. Unusually, though, the original did not entirely disappear: during Sibelius's lifetime it was heard at least three more times, twice in 1935 and once in 1944. On the last occasion both versions were played in succession.

Sibelius then took the train via St. Petersburg to Berlin, where his concert was scheduled for 15th November. *En saga* was part of an eclectic programme of recent compositions, among them *The Death of Pan* by the Hungarian composer Ödön von Mihalovich, a piano concerto by Théophile Ysaÿe and the original version of Delius's *Paris*. *En saga* was regarded as the most successful of the four, and Sibelius was proud to have acquitted himself well with such a prestigious orchestra. He also took the opportunity to socialize liberally with Busoni and his friends, and lived in luxury at the Grand Hotel Bellevue. While in Berlin he may have met the violin virtuoso Willy Burmester, who already had strong ties to Finland as he had been leader of Kajanus's orchestra until 1895 and had married Naëma Fazer, sister of the music publisher Konrad Fazer. This was not to be an extended visit, however, and Sibelius was back in Finland in time to conduct the *First Symphony* in Turku in December.

The only claim we can make with reasonable certainty about the origins of the [*Allegro*] *in G minor* for piano is that it comes from the period 1899–1903. Within this time frame, however, it would seem reasonable to date it in some proximity to the revision of *En saga*, as it shows thematic and, especially, rhythmic similarities with the tone poem. It is a hectic, richly sonorous piece that proceeds in a single burst of energy from the first bar to the last. From much the same period (1902–05) comes another piano piece, a [*Polka*] *in C minor*, a sturdy folk-like snippet that lasts a mere twenty seconds. The manuscript is inscribed 'Aino' – perhaps signifying that it was a small gift or token of affection.

Before the year was out, Sibelius wrote a short Finnish-language song. Though it was originally intended for use in primary schools, *Lastu lainehilla* (*Driftwood*) was included as the seventh and last of his Op. 17 collection. The text is an occasional poem written by Ilmari Calamnius that year for the Christmas publication *Joulupukki* (*Father Christmas*). In the phrase structure and melodic shape of the vocal line, and also in the calmly pulsating syncopated accompaniment, this song is closely related to the Forsman setting *Souda, souda, sinisorsa* from 1899.

1903

Towards the end of his studies in Helsinki Sibelius had eagerly participated in the meetings of the Leskovites, in the 1890s it was the turn of the Symposium gatherings, and in the beginning of the new century a new circle formed: the Euterpists. This group, which was closely associated with the Swedish Theatre, was named after the journal *Euterpe*, a Swedish-language literary magazine edited by Sibelius's friend Werner Söderhjelm. The group was not confined to the theatrical world, however: it included for example playwrights, musicians and architects. The group may have had lofty cultural ambitions, but the meetings themselves had conspicuous similarities to those of the Symposium period: all-night drinking sessions at the Kämp or the König restaurants and a consequent neglect of spouse and family. Sibelius's absences at this time were especially reprehensible, as the family had just increased in size again with the birth of his fourth daughter, Katarina, on 12th January and Aino was not at her strongest.

Moreover, keeping his creative muse well lubricated involved spending money that Sibelius simply did not have. At least he was in some demand as a conductor, even though the concerts did not always generate much income. That spring he performed his works not only in Helsinki but also in Tampere, and in May – at the invitation of Georg Schnéevoigt – made his first visit to Estonia, where he conducted the *First Symphony* and *Finlandia* (billed on this occasion as *Impromptu* to avoid irritating the Russians) in the seaside resort of Kadriorg near Tallinn. 'There is much in my make-up that is weak. Take only one instance: when I am standing in front of a grand orchestra and have drunk half a bottle of champagne, then I conduct like a young god. Otherwise I am nervous and tremble, feel unsure of myself, and then everything is lost. The same is true of my visits to the bank manager', he confided to his brother Christian.

When Sibelius could tear himself away from the Kämp and the König restaurants, he worked on his violin concerto. It is possible that he also composed a piano piece, *Barcarole*, Op. 24 No. 10, during the spring, although he had signed a contract relating to the piece as early as the beginning of January (it appeared in print in September). It is a much darker piece than the barcarole-like slow movement of the *'Hafträsk' Trio*; indeed, although we do not know of any specific programme associated with the piece, it sounds steeped in the Symbolist world of the *Lemminkäinen Suite*.

In early June Sibelius signed a contract for the publication of *Six Finnish Folk-Songs*, JS 81, in new piano arrangements. The original impetus probably came from Axel Carpelan, who had suggested in May of the previous year that Sibelius should arrange some Finnish folk tunes for strings. If he had in mind the kind of popular folk suite that would present familiar melodies in an easily accessible and crowd-pleasing format, he would be disappointed. Instead Sibelius made a set of concise and decidedly un-romantic transcriptions in a style that has often been compared to Bartók. The first folk-song in the published collection is *Minun kultani kaunis on, sen suu kuin auran kukka* (*My beloved is beautiful, her mouth like a corn-cockle*). This should not be confused with the similarly named *Minun kultani kaunis on, vaikk' on kaitulainen* (*My beloved is beautiful, even though her frame is slender*), which uses a different melody. In fact Sibelius transcribed that song as well, but did not include it in the published edition, perhaps because it differs stylistically from the others, with a cadenza-like central flourish. That version, a performable (though probably not final) draft, has survived in a manuscript in the National Library of Finland collection.[5] The remaining five published folk-songs are *Sydämestäni rakastan* (*I love you with all my heart*), *Ilta tulee, ehtoo joutuu* (*Evening is coming*), *Tuopa tyttö*, *kaunis tyttö* (*That beautiful girl*), *Velisuurmaaja* (*The Fratricide*) and *Häämuistelma* (*Wedding memory*).

Axel Carpelan agreed with Aino that it would be best to keep Sibelius away from the temptations of the capital. Sibelius was quite ready to be persuaded by his friend's reasoning, and in the summer the family went to Lohja. Here he could work on the *Violin Concerto* with the aim of having it premièred in the autumn. While he was there, in July, there came news that his uncle Axel Borg had passed away. As his uncle had been a wealthy bachelor, Sibelius stood to inherit some money – and this time Aino would not let him squander it. Her brother Eero Järnefelt was already living near the village of Järvenpää, and the opportunity arose to purchase a plot of land there. Aino wrote to Eero's wife Saimi: 'Now, in July, we are supposed to go to Järvenpää to examine things in greater detail and reach a decision... At first I found it quite impossible to think of living there in isolation, because even the road is so far away – but, when I now think about it, perhaps it wouldn't be so difficult after all. After he came to see you, Janne was so enthusiastic that he was jumping up and down and demanding that I should take the train on my own to Järvenpää and decide.' Friends promised to secure labour and materials at advantageous rates, and the eminent architect Lars Sonck agreed to draw up plans for a house. Although nothing was finalized during the summer, the train of events that would lead to Sibelius leaving Helsinki for good was now set in motion.

As the holiday season drew to a close, Aino and the girls remained in Lohja while Jean returned to Helsinki to find a new place to live. At the end of August he moved into a rented house on Antinkatu. Initially he had only the maid, Mari, for company; not until the end of September did Aino and the children join him. In August he wrote one of his most impressive solo songs, the 'mighty autumnal lament' *Höstkväll* (*Autumn Evening*), Op. 38 No. 1, to a text by Rydberg. Sibelius was clearly attracted by the poem's pantheism and vivid depictions of the natural world, and by the image of a solitary wanderer contemplating nature in all its brooding majesty. The music fits the words like a glove, from the bold, descending motif at the outset that describes the setting sun to the whispering patter of falling raindrops, and the song has an almost operatic sweep and grandeur. However much we might nowadays admire the song's artistic vision, its first publisher, Konrad Fazer of Helsingfors Nya Musikhandel, was more concerned with practical difficulties, writing to Sibelius on 3rd September: 'It is, of course, too late to change the key. I would have liked it to be *lower*, as I'm afraid that otherwise only a very few singers will manage it. Perhaps we shall have to issue a version for middle voice later on.'

In September, while waiting for his family to arrive, Sibelius set two more poems by Rydberg, *På verandan vid havet* (*On a Balcony by the Sea*), Op. 38 No. 2, and *I natten* (*In the Night*), Op. 38 No. 3. *På verandan* is a masterpiece; it takes up the pantheistic moods of *Höstkväll* and rises to a mighty climax on the final words: 'Allt som i aning om Gud' ('as if awaiting God'). As well as containing some chromatic writing, the song makes prominent thematic use of the tritone. Although *I natten* is a more conventional, strophic song, it conjures up a mysterious, often lugubrious atmosphere in the first and third verses that is effectively lightened in the second and fourth. Both were premièred by Ida Edman at the University Hall on 16th October.

Ekman must have liked the two Rydberg settings, for she also included them – along with *Se'n har jag ej frågat mera* from Op. 17 – in an orchestral concert conducted by Kajanus at the National Theatre a few weeks later (10th November) to raise funds for the Philharmonic Society orchestra. Sibelius himself made the orchestrations of the two new songs, and in all probability *Se'n har jag ej frågat mera* was also orchestrated for this occasion.

On 18th November Sibelius finally signed a purchase contract for the plot of land near Järvenpää. In a year when his outgoings already vastly exceeded his income, it was a bold decision – so bold, indeed, that one wonders if Sibelius's naïvety in pecuniary matters blinded him to the risks involved. Lars Sonck was soon ready with the plans, and work on the footings began almost immediately.

In the autumn Sibelius announced that the *Violin Concerto* would be dedicated to Willy Burmester, but this did not mean that the piece was ready; far from it. Indeed, towards the end of 1903 his musical energies were to be directed in a wholly different direction.

Sibelius and his friends had been interested in Symbolism at least since the 1890s (perhaps earlier if Wegelius had managed to impart much of his Wagner worship to his students). Sibelius's interest can be seen as a manifestation of the dreamy, imaginative and spiritual side of his personality that had been evident since his childhood in Hämeenlinna, and (notwithstanding the difficulties of defining Symbolism in music) a strong case could be made for regarding the tone poems from the 1890s, especially those written after his Wagner crisis of 1894, as Symbolist works. Symbolism was a favoured discussion topic at meetings of the Euterpist circle. Finnish painters such as Magnus Enckell and Axel Gallén were prominent exponents of Symbolism – not least in Gallén's painting *The Problem*. In the first decade of the twentieth century Symbolist playwrights such as Mæterlinck were very much in vogue in Helsinki, and it was only natural that Finnish authors should also follow the current. It was against this backdrop that Arvid Järnefelt wrote the play *Kuolema* (*Death*) in 1903. That Sibelius should compose the music was a foregone conclusion.

Writing an independent piece of music that attracts the epithet 'Symbolist' is quite different from composing incidental music to a Symbolist play. For the purposes of writing incidental music it is of little practical consideration whether the play is Symbolist or not. In his music for *Kuolema* and the other Symbolist plays for which he supplied scores in the first decade of the twentieth century, Sibelius concentrated on colour and characterization no more and no less than in his scores for other theatrical works. Naturally the music tries to reflect the underlying character of the play, but its Symbolist character was the playwright's choice, not the composer's. In many of Sibelius's theatre scores the music contains brief sketches of characters or events, and in writing such pieces he drew on the experience he had gained in the 1880s of writing character pieces and souvenirs for friends and family. In those works we can assume that Sibelius pandered to the taste of the dedicatee, and thus the *Andante cantabile in G major*, JS 33, ought to depict Ruth Ringbom, and the *Valse. À Betsy Lerche*, JS 1, ought to reflect Betsy's character[6] with no less accuracy than the portrayals of Mélisande, Khadra, Swanwhite and the Prince, Prospero, Caliban and Miranda in the later theatre scores.

Sibelius worked on the *Kuolema* score, JS 113, in October and November 1903. In all he wrote six musical numbers for string orchestra of which the first, *Tempo di valse lente*, was to be capture the public's imagination to an astonishing degree under its eventual title: *Valse triste*. Arvid Järnefelt's son Eero later recalled: 'Once my father said to him [Sibelius]: "I've written a play; will you write music for it?" – "I'll think about it," Sibelius replied. So one sunny morning he came to see us and sat down by the piano. My father sat beside him and explained the play to him. Sibelius began to play. Suddenly he exclaimed: "Good Lord, what bright sunshine! I should be wearing tails, then I'd be able to play better!" And he carried on playing. Then the melody of *Valse triste* rang out for the first time. I was present to hear its birth.' The melody was evidently not committed to paper at that time, as is shown by a recollection by Sibelius's eccentric friend, the sculptor, painter, writer and linguistic theorist Sigurd Wettenhovi-Aspa: 'I met the maestro one evening at around 8 p.m., and he told me he had promised Arvid Järnefelt he would write at least a piano arrangement of a "death waltz"... for a new play of Arvid's to be called *Kuolema*. In it... a dying woman delirious with fever is lying in bed and rises up to dance a final waltz with an imaginary, non-existent partner. But in the midst of the waltz a new man enters unexpectedly to take over the dance. The gate-crasher is Death himself, and when the woman's son awakes (he has been keeping vigil by her bed and has fallen asleep) he finds his mother dead. Sibelius confessed somewhat sheepishly that he had not written a single note for the work. At this I asked him if it would not then be best if I were to accompany him to his house in Antinkatu, where he lived in those days; but no! He was adamant. Sibelius had no wish to go home, even though he clearly had a nasty chill. The only alternative course was to step out to Stigzelius's, the court pharmacist's, and buy for him six one-gramme bags of quinine powder... We sailed into the Kämp and headed upstairs, to the top floor, and into a private piano room. We immediately ordered some soda water, and the maestro promptly swallowed two whole one-gramme doses of quinine with death-defying fortitude, showing not the slightest revulsion at the unpleasant taste of the medicine, which he washed down with soda water... Gradually we began to think and to speak in a waltz measure. Janne dived back into the memories of his youth; how he had been at a grand Imperial court ball in Vienna... summoning up before my eyes the picture of the uncrowned queen of the ball, the superlative Austrian soprano Pauline Lucca herself, who had been a great favourite of both Sibelius and Emperor Franz Joseph... The maestro moved to the piano, toyed with the dampers, and began to play softly. I sat on the divan and closed my eyes. In this way I heard for the first time the waltz of death – which has since travelled around the world as *Valse triste*. Sibelius played for a long while, playing in the same mysterious, half-hypnotic waltz-time that our conversation had somehow invoked.'[7] Even though Wettenhovi-Aspa's account does not quite contradict Eero Järnefelt's version, we can assume that for both men the urge to claim that they were present at the conception of *Valse triste* was irresistible!

The next three numbers all come from the second act of the play. No. 2 is a song, *Pakkanen puhurin poika* (*Jack Frost, Son of the Icy North Wind*): in the stage production this was sung by Paavali, the dead woman's son, who has now grown up and is performing charitable acts at the cottage of a sick witch amid a winter storm. Its three verses, each preceded by an atmospheric introduction, were interspersed with dialogue. The third musical number, *Moderato assai – Moderato – Poco adagio*, has thematic material that is without affectation and very sensitive; the mood is tranquil throughout. In it we return to the seamless, free-flowing texture of the previous song's introduction, although the music itself is different. The middle part of this number features a solo soprano as Elsa, Paavali's future wife, whom he meets in the forest in summertime; she sings the same quasi-vocalise on the word 'eilaa' that Sibelius had used in the choral suite *Rakastava*. The final section is to some extent a reprise of the first, but there are also some new musical elements, among them a few wispy motifs from the solo violin. The fourth number is little more than a sound effect: the violins imitate the call of cranes. In the play, as Paavali and Elsa sleep in the forest, a flock of cranes passes and one bird, detaching itself from the flock, brings them a baby. As Sibelius was so fond of swans and cranes, he must have been pleased that they were featured (in his later revision of the play, Järnefelt used a solitary crane as a symbol of Paavali's dead mother).

The third act is set many years later, when Paavali and Elsa have a growing family and Paavali lives by virtuous, idealistic principles. Their house catches fire and Paavali remains in the burning building, which finally comes crashing down. This is the scene depicted in the fifth musical number, where the melody of Paavali's song is heard against insistent sextuplets that constantly increase in intensity – an effect that anticipates on a modest scale the shipwreck scene from *The Tempest*. The sixth movement is again purely descriptive: the dust settles (*spiccato* arpeggios reminiscent of the opening of *En saga*, though harmonically they are quite different) and a church bell is heard. Paavali is dead but will live on in the hearts of the people whose lives he touched.

The first performance of *Kuolema* was planned for November, but had to be postponed because the music was not ready in time. It was finally premièred at the National Theatre on 2nd December, the first of a run of just six performances. On the first night Sibelius himself conducted members of the Philharmonic Society orchestra. Abraham Ojanperä sang Paavali's song, although on stage the adult Paavali was played by Knut Weckman; Elsa's song was performed by the actress who played the role, Hanna Granfelt. The reviews mentioned the play's fairy-tale character but did not focus on the music as such, even though Sibelius's name had been a major attraction: 'and that was why musical Helsinki, together with the friends of Finnish theatre, gathered yesterday in such numbers in the light, beautiful auditorium of the National Theatre', wrote the theatre critic Hjalmar Lenning in *Hufvudstadsbladet* the following day.

CHAPTER 8

THE VIOLIN CONCERTO AND FIRST YEARS AT AINOLA: 1904–1906

1904

The beginning of 1904 saw the completion of the *Violin Concerto in D minor*, Op. 47, in its original form. Burmester suggested performing it in March, but Sibelius's need for cash was too urgent for this to be an option: the materials for the construction of his new house were now on site and a team of thirteen carpenters was to commence building work in earnest on 10th February. He was thus compelled to agree to a far less prestigious première, in Helsinki on 8th February (repeated on 10th and 14th). Sibelius himself conducted a programme consisting of three new pieces, *Cassazione*, the choral song *Har du mod? (Have You Courage?)* and the concerto, concluding with the cantata *The Origin of Fire*, at that time still in its original, longer form.

Clearly Sibelius's own abilities as a violinist would have been insufficient to play the *Violin Concerto* convincingly himself, but his experience as a violinist allowed him to write for the instrument in a manner that is idiomatic despite all of its complexities. In Burmester's absence the solo part was entrusted to a young Helsinki violin teacher named Viktor Nováček. Unfortunately Nováček was a far less distinguished player than Burmester, and failed to rise to the formidable technical challenges of Sibelius's piece. Karl Flodin – whose negative opinions had been a contributory factor in the withdrawal of two movements of the *Lemminkäinen Suiite* a few years previously – was blunt about Nováček's playing, writing that it 'offered up a mass of joyless things. From time to time there were terrible sounds...' but was equally scathing about the music itself, describing the work as 'boring' and 'a mistake'; 'the new *Violin Concerto* will not form a link in the chain of genuinely significant modern creations in this artistic form'.

Sibelius thus turned down Burmester's offer to play the concerto that October in Helsinki ('I shall play the concerto in Helsinki in such a way that the city will be at your feet') and undertook to revise the piece.

The *Violin Concerto* might be regarded as Sibelius's last major orchestral work in the national romantic style. Both thematically and in atmosphere it has less in common with Sibelius's Symbolist-inspired tone poems of the 1890s than with his warmly romantic chamber music from the late 1880s. It has something of the breadth and humanity of Tchaikovsky's concerto and the lyricism of Mendelssohn's, and – especially in this original version – does not try to integrate soloist and orchestra in the manner of Brahms. The first movement is on the broadest of scales: in its original version it plays for almost twenty minutes. The solo part is full of fearsome virtuosic writing and features two lengthy solo cadenzas, one that replaces the development section and was retained in the final version of the concerto, and a second one that was later omitted. Much of the lyrical music before and during this second cadenza can trace its roots back to the slow movement of the *'Korpo' Trio* of 1887, though stylistically the cadenza also has much in common with Bach's solo violin music.

The slow movement is an expressive, pensive romance with a rich and noble melody.[1] Characteristic Sibelian devices such as short–long–short syncopations (which often drive the music remorselessly forwards) and triplets (for instance in the soloist's virtuosic ornamentation of the melody) serve to personalize the movement without robbing it of its highly charged, romantic immediacy. At the end of this movement in the original version, the tranquillity is disturbed by a ghostly, cadenza-like *spiccato* flourish.

The finale's polonaise-like character harks back to such works as the *String Quartet in E flat major* from 1885 and *E major Suite* from 1888, but here has an added earthiness that led Donald Tovey to describe the revised version colourfully as 'a polonaise for polar bears'. The movement – especially in its original incarnation – requires the soloist to display his virtuosity to the full. It demands a consummate mastery of the instrument and is cruelly unforgiving of technical deficiencies. When asked how the movement should be played, Sibelius replied that it should be 'played with absolute mastery. Fast, of course, but no faster than it can be played perfectly *von oben*.'

Of the other new works on the programme at the concerto's première, *Cassazione*, Op. 6, had been composed in some haste during the previous few weeks. The work is in a single movement, although it is clearly episodic. With its colourful orchestration and its abundance of rich melodic invention (including a hymn-like string theme later re-used in the epilogue to *The Tempest*, and a theme closely related to the first movement of the *Violin Concerto*), and with an exciting final section that anticipates the

finale of the *Third Symphony*, *Cassazione* is one of the most impressive
of Sibelius's *pièces d'occasion*, even if Oskar Merikanto in *Helsingin
Sanomat* dismissed it somewhat unkindly as 'rather insignificant'.

That description might more justifiably have been applied to *Har du
mod?* Op. 31 No. 2, a simple and bombastic patriotic march for male
voices and orchestra which, like *Sandels* and *Song of the Athenians*, makes
much of the dactylic rhythms of Wecksell's text (Sibelius also made an
arrangement for male voices and piano). Perhaps Sibelius tacitly acknowledged that the accompaniment to *Har du mod?* was neither imaginative
nor subtle, but he must have had some fondness for the theme itself. Some
years later he tried out an assortment of widely divergent accompaniments
for it. But the version heard in February 1904 was not his first attempt
to set this poem. In the preceding months he had composed a version for
male choir *a cappella* that is based on wholly different musical material
(JS 93). Presumably it was intended as a preliminary study for the piece
performed in February, even though there is no trace of an accompaniment
for JS 93.

Sibelius, no doubt downhearted after the failure of the *Violin Concerto*,
managed to spend on drink much of the money that should have been
used to pay the builders in Järvenpää. Aino and Christian Sibelius used
every means at their disposal to encourage him to stop, and eventually the
financial situation was eased by a series of concerts not only in Helsinki,
Turku and Vaasa but also in Estonia and Latvia. Nonetheless, the building
of the house was expensive: Sibelius's debts, which had in any case been
racing ahead of his income, suddenly quadrupled at this time.

Among the orchestral novelties first performed during the spring of 1904
was *Musik zu einer Scène*. Sibelius conducted this piece (with the motto
Ein Fichtenbaum – träumt von einer Palme [Heine]) at a fundraising
evening in Helsinki on 5th March. Originally this six-minute piece served
as the accompaniment to a tableau. Much of its musical weight is concentrated in an intense, dramatic introduction, which gradually yields to a
much lighter mood. An infectious, dance-like idea in B flat major then
emerges, and dominates the second half of the piece.

Shortly afterwards, Sibelius made a piano version of *Musik zu einer
Scène*. In this case the piano piece differed radically from the original: it
is much shorter, as most of the weighty opening section is missing, and
the dance section is also modified and provided with a more suitable
concert ending. The result, renamed *Dance-Intermezzo*, Op. 45 No. 2, is
a work with a much lighter tone, almost trivial by comparison with the
original. The modifications would not filter down into the orchestral score
for several years.

Of similar duration is the heartfelt *Romance in C major* for strings,

Op. 42, originally called simply *Andante*. Much of this piece is written in an easily flowing, melodious style reminiscent of Grieg or Tchaikovsky, but the harmonic ambiguity of the first theme (E minor/C major) is characteristic of the mature Sibelius. The *Romance* was written in a few days in late March 1904 and first performed in Turku on 26th of that month at an all-Sibelius concert that also included the *Violin Concerto, Cassazione, En saga* and the finale of the *Second Symphony*. One of the manuscript sketches for the *Romance* also contains a fragment for piano, an [*Adagio*] *in C major* in a style strongly reminiscent of Finnish folk music.

Almost exactly a month later, on 25th April, Sibelius conducted the *Romance* with the Philharmonic Society orchestra at the University Hall in Helsinki, a concert that also included the first performance of a revised concert version of *Valse triste*, Op. 44 No. 1. Sibelius had already been working on a provisional piano arrangement in which he made refinements throughout the piece; the melody retained the contours of the original theatre waltz but its abrupt ending was replaced by a much more effective conclusion – though played a semitone lower than in the final version, after an unexpected and disconcerting change of key. The definitive orchestral score incorporates most of these changes but also makes small but telling alterations to the melodic line and abandons the sudden key-change in the second half of the piece; parts for flute, clarinet, two horns and timpani are added. The published piano transcription is mostly (though not exclusively) based on the revised orchestral score.

With hindsight Sibelius's decision to sell the rights to *Valse triste* to Helsingfors Nya Musikhandel for a very modest sum – 300 marks – was a serious mistake. At that time, however, he had no way of knowing that the piece would become an instant hit and would soon be heard in innumerable arrangements from salon orchestras and in restaurants all over the world.

In June Sibelius conducted in Estonia for the second (and last) time, once again invited by Schnéevoigt to perform at Kadriorg. This time the *Second Symphony* was on the programme.

On 16th June a young Finnish patriot named Eugen Schauman secured himself a place in history by shooting the despised Russian Governor-General Nikolai Bobrikov as he arrived at the Senate House at eleven in the morning. Schauman, who was actually born in Kharkiv [Kharkov], Ukraine, to Swedish-speaking Finnish parents in 1875, worked as a clerk at the Senate House and his interest in shooting had previously led him to organize marksmanship classes for Helsinki students. His was not the first attempt to assassinate the Governor-General, but it was the decisive one. Schauman descended from an upper floor and, after firing three shots at Bobrikov, one of which wounded him fatally in the stomach, turned the gun on himself. For Schauman death was instantaneous, but Bobrikov clung on to life for some hours. For the Finns, joy at the demise of their hated leader was mixed with a sense of foreboding about what the Russians would do next. In fact the Tsar himself was relatively unconcerned, writing in his diary the next day: 'In the morning I got to know, to my sorrow, that Bobrikov died from his wounds at one o'clock in the night. The weather was warm. After the presentation I received 86 officers of the Nikolayev General Staff Academy in the halls, and after the breakfast, the Spanish emissary. Uncle Vladimir drank tea with us. I read a lot. I bicycled, and I shot two ravens, one yesterday. We ate dinner at the terrace. In the evening it was cooler.'[2]

Unsurprisingly Sibelius and his friends were jubilant. Indeed, so eagerly did they celebrate that they were arrested for displaying 'unmotivated joy'.

In July Sibelius received a letter from the publisher Fazer concerning a piano piece he had written some years earlier: 'Some years ago, B&H made the mistake of not registering the copyright for the *Idyll* [Op. 24 No. 6]. Now I can imagine a new edition to put right this omission. This cannot happen, however, without some changes being made to the composition – performance markings and so on. Then the new edition can be labelled "Revised by (J.S.)".' Sibelius duly made some small changes and the 'revised' version was published in September.

In August Sibelius went to conduct in Latvia. He gave two concerts at the coastal resort of Dubbeln (Dubulti), near Rīga, in between which he visited Libau (Liepāja) before returning home overland via St Petersburg. The programme for this visit offered a generous selection of Sibelius's most important works to date, including the *Second Symphony*, *En saga*, *The Swan of Tuonela* and *Lemminkäinen's Return*, *Spring Song*, the *Romance in C major*, movements from *King Christian II*, *Valse triste* and *Finlandia* (still billed neutrally as *Impromptu*).

By the late summer the building work in Järvenpää was complete, and on 24th September the family – who had been living nearby at Kylänpää in Tuusula during the summer – moved in. The villa was named Ainola as a tribute to Aino Sibelius. Among the family's new neighbours were the painter Pekka Halonen and the author Juhani Aho, not to mention Sibelius's brother-in-law Eero Järnefelt. Ainola in 1904 was very different from the house as we know it today. In most ways it reflected a simpler, more self-reliant way of life than would nowadays be expected, although a small room – large enough for just one servant – was provided next to the kitchen. All of the living accommodation was on a single floor, although there was a large attic space, and the outside surface was unpainted, unclad natural timber. Sibelius's study (which later became a sitting room and housed the piano that the composer was given for his fiftieth birthday) was adjacent to the dining room but was still separated from it by a solid wall. Jean and Aino slept in the room that later became his downstairs study, and the children's room was the future library. There was neither electricity nor running water; indeed, the house was not connected to a mains water supply until after Sibelius's death. Right from the start, however, there was a telephone, located in the lobby next to the dining room. An outbuilding housed the outside toilet and provided additional storage. The modern town of Järvenpää had yet to be built; apart from the railway station there was just a grocer's shop, bakery, inn and post office.

Sibelius wrote to Axel Carpelan on 21st September 1904: 'I'm working hard on a three-movement piano work. I'm sure I'll have it ready the day after tomorrow.' This suite was *Kyllikki*, Op. 41, the completion of which thus coincided more or less exactly with the family's move to Ainola. As with the *Violin Concerto*, the *Kyllikki* suite marks the end of a stylistic era: it is the last significant example of *Kalevala* romanticism in Sibelius's piano music (surviving sketches show that several of the melodies were originally conceived in a form which gave far more prominence to their folk-like character). It is hard to believe Sibelius's assertion that the music was unrelated to the *Kalevala* story of Lemminkäinen and Kyllikki. The hero's abduction of the maiden could well be portrayed in the first movement, whilst the second movement sounds very much like the melancholy runic chants sung by Kyllikki while Lemminkäinen is away waging war (in the distance we even hear warlike fanfares). In the last movement, if this interpretation is indeed true, Kyllikki is swept away by the whirl of the dance.

The same letter to Carpelan also mentions two recently completed songs, *Harpolekaren och hans son* (*The Harper and his Son*), Op. 38 No. 4, and *Jag ville, jag vore i Indialand* (*I wish I were in India*), Op. 38 No. 5, to texts by Rydberg and Fröding respectively. Both songs had recently been premièred in Helsinki – the former by Maikki Järnefelt on 9th September, and the latter three days later by Ida Ekman. Despite the piano's valiant attempt to imitate the harp with arpeggiated chords in *Harpolekaren*, neither this song nor *Jag ville, jag vore* plumbs any great psychological depths, and they are thus something of a disappointment by comparison with their companions in Op. 38.

Sibelius started work on incidental music for Mæterlinck's *Pelléas et Mélisande*, JS 147, in preparation for a production (in a Swedish translation by Bertel Gripenberg) at the Swedish Theatre in Helsinki, but made little headway; nor was there much progress with his *Third Symphony*, which was at an embryonic stage. A few weeks after moving into Ainola, he set off on a conducting tour to Pori and Oulu on the west coast of Finland.

The possibilities for overindulgence offered by this trip outweighed any musical merit that the concerts might have possessed, a fact that was not lost on Aino as she waited patiently at home. 'I am afraid and I suspect that things are close to breaking point... Dear Janne, you are still young, don't allow your life and your talents to be wrecked', she wrote to him while he was in Oulu. Throughout the autumn Sibelius had complained of ill health: poor hearing, colds and rheumatism; he even suspected that he had diabetes. Even if many of these problems were psychosomatic, he could not drink his way out of them, and the weeks before Christmas were a stressful period in Jean and Aino's marriage.

On 10th November, Adée Leander-Flodin gave the first performance of a new Sibelius song: *En slända* (*A Dragonfly*), Op. 17 No. 5, to words by Oscar Levertin. The naturalistic touches in this lengthy song (the trills in the voice imitate the hovering of the dragonfly) tend to obscure the many characteristic Sibelian rhythms and melodic patterns. Tonally it also mirrors the dragonfly's flight by refusing to settle. Its recitative style, and the spare piano writing which often seems merely to comment on the vocal line rather than offer an effective partnership, hint at the song *Jubal* of 1908.

On 2nd December the YL choir under Heikki Klemetti performed a new song composed as an acknowledgement that an increasing number of Finns were choosing to emigrate rather than suffer the indignities of Russian rule: *Veljeni vierailla mailla* (*My Brothers Abroad*), JS 217, to a text by Juhani Aho. This long and wide-ranging song is divided into three sections in different keys (the second and third are thematically quite closely related), unified by the emphatic descending motif at the end of each.

Other projects that came to fruition during 1904 included an arrangement for mixed chorus *a cappella* of *Sydämeni laulu*, probably made at the request of the Society for Popular Education. Two very effective orchestral versions of the song *Höstkväll* saw the light of day, one with full orchestra that was premièred in Paris on 14th January 1905 by the American soprano Minnie Tracey, conducted by Alfred Cortot, and one with string orchestra that had to wait a century for its first performance, sung by Helena Juntunen with the Lahti Symphony Orchestra under Osmo Vänskä on 8th September 2005. An arrangement of the Christmas song *On hanget korkeat, nietokset* for two voices and piano can be dated to the period 1903–05. It is believed to have been written for private use in the Sibelius family and, as Sibelius was to spend the Christmas of 1905 abroad, it seems probable that it was written no later than 1904 – maybe to celebrate their first Christmas in their new home.

1905

On New Year's Day of 1905 Jean and Aino visited Eero Järnefelt at his home, Suviranta, and Sibelius revealed that he was planning a requiem for Eugen Schauman. But in the immediate future his energies were channelled in other directions, as he had accepted an invitation from Busoni to go to Berlin. He arrived there on 5th January and, as well as socializing with Busoni, Burmester, Adolf Paul and Sinding, met Pfitzner and Magnard; he also heard major works including Mahler's *Fifth Symphony*, Debussy's *Nocturnes*, and Richard Strauss's *Ein Heldenleben* and *Sinfonia domestica*. The main reason for the trip, however, was a performance of the *Second Symphony*, which was a great success at the concert on 12th January. Sibelius also signed a new contract with the publisher Robert Lienau, which committed him to deliver four major works per year. He would soon discover that works of the size and calibre that Lienau expected could not be composed to such a rigid timetable, but for now at least the contract promised some degree of financial security. He wrote to Aino: 'I have been in such a state because of these "affairs" [i.e. business matters] at home. Now I can relax to some extent. The main thing is that we don't speak of such things! Remember that! We have had such sorrowful years over the past decade. Now at least things are more certain!' He stayed in Berlin for some weeks and, although his rented room had no piano, he busied himself with the score for *Pelléas et Mélisande*, making a piano reduction as he went along. He also took English lessons, as he had been invited by Granville Bantock to conduct a concert of his own music in Liverpool on 18th March. In the end, however, he cancelled his trip to England and returned to Helsinki; he was thus able to conduct the first performance of *Pelléas et Mélisande* himself on 17th March.

Pelléas et Mélisande was the highlight of the Helsinki theatre season, and Sibelius's music was well received. 'The theatre's production of *Pelléas et Mélisande* received the most valuable support from the exquisitely atmospheric, melodious music with which Jean Sibelius illustrated Mæterlinck's dream poem', wrote Hjalmar Lenning in *Hufvudstadsbladet*. Of the various musical adaptations of Mæterlinck's Symbolist play of 1892, Sibelius's music has more in common with Fauré's incidental music than with Debussy's opera or Schoenberg's symphonic poem: he composed ten numbers – mostly brief preludes or entr'actes – for a modestly proportioned orchestra. Only one movement – *The Three Blind Sisters* – calls for a vocal soloist. In his music for *Pelléas*, Sibelius again put to good use his ability to describe a personality or evoke a specific mood both colourfully and economically. So effective was the theatre score that he omitted only one number, made the occasional tiny adjustment to scoring and changed the order slightly to make a concert suite that is frequently performed to this day.

The story of *Pelléas et Mélisande* revolves around a love triangle set at the court of the ageing King Arkel. It is at the gate of Arkel's castle that the first scene of the play is set and Sibelius's *Prelude* (renamed *At the Castle Gate* in the suite), suggests the grandeur and strength of a medieval fortress; at the end of the piece the gate opens and the sun rises. Golaud encounters the mysterious Mélisande sitting and weeping by a spring in the forest and persuades her to marry him. As it is a slow waltz with a prominent part for the cor anglais, one might expect Sibelius's music for this scene (named *Mélisande* in the suite) to sound like a cross between *Valse triste* and *The Swan of Tuonela*, but in fact it has a restrained allure that resembles neither. This is followed by an *Adagio* (*By the Sea*), a sombre mood painting (one might almost call it a miniature *Lemminkäinen in Tuonela*) that many conductors omit in concert performances, perhaps because it does not offer the ready melodic appeal of the other movements. In the play this music accompanied a scene where Pelléas (Golaud's brother, who falls in love with Mélisande) and Mélisande observe a departing ship in the distance; it was on this ship that Mélisande had arrived in Arkel's kingdom.

At the beginning of Act II, Pelléas and Mélisande visit a fountain in the park. Mélisande accidentally drops a ring that Golaud had given her into the water. Sibelius's music (*By a Spring in the Park* in the suite) is an elegant waltz that acquires an unexpected, slightly macabre quality because, at nine bars, the main theme is perceived to be one bar too long. A mechanical viola motif heard throughout the rather sinister prelude to Act III depicts a spinning wheel at which Mélisande is busily working in the castle. This piece (renamed *Mélisande at the Spinning Wheel*) was moved to a later position in the concert suite, presumably to make a more satisfactory sequence of movements. In the second scene of Act III Pelléas listens to Mélisande singing a tranquil ballad, *The Three Blind Sisters*, as she combs her hair. The melody is doubled by clarinets and so the vocal part was omitted from the concert suite. A separate arrangement of this movement was also published as a song with piano, in which form its similarity with *Der Wegweiser* from Schubert's *Winterreise* is readily apparent.

A surviving sketch[3] shows that in the case of the seventh movement (the *Pastorale* in the suite) Sibelius used thematic material that he had conceived a few years earlier, around 1899–1901. This relaxed, summery music is heard just after the scene in which, as they emerge from a subterranean passage into bright daylight, Golaud asks Pelléas to stay away from Mélisande, who is pregnant. The next movement, the brightest and most optimistic in the score, is the prelude to Act IV (*Entr'acte* in the suite) and has the character of a gavotte. In the play, Pelléas and Mélisande agree to a secret assignation in the park. The ninth movement is a sombre dialogue between King Arkel and Mélisande – here cello and cor anglais – over a gently syncopated string accompaniment; this was the movement omitted from the concert suite. Sibelius did not write music to accompany the dramatic events that follow – when Golaud accuses Mélisande of infidelity, or when he meets the lovers in the park and kills Pelléas; the last musical number is a touching portrayal of Mélisande lying in her sickbed (*The Death of Mélisande* in the suite); Golaud never discovers whether or not she was unfaithful to him. For this scene Sibelius wrote an elegiac piece dominated by the strings, freer and metrically less predictable than the *Elegy* from *King Christian II* but every bit as deeply felt.

An attempt to set Tavaststjerna's poem *Romans* (*Romance*), from the poet's late epic *Laureatus*, came to nothing, although an incomplete draft for it has survived along with some sketches for *Pelléas et Mélisande*. Sibelius was to return to this text five years later, when composing his Op. 61 songs.

The Sibelius family continued to settle in at Ainola. Emboldened by his new contract with Lienau, Sibelius suggested building a sauna in the grounds and that summer, under the watchful eye of Aino, the builders set to work. In Finland a sauna is not an indulgence but an integral part of any self-respecting home, and the one at Ainola is not only large but also very robustly constructed.

Otherwise the spring of 1905 brought Sibelius some more conducting engagements, including a visit to Viipuri, and he also started seriously to consider writing an oratorio, *Marjatta*. The poet Jalmari Finne had proposed this as early as 1902 and had discussed it with Sibelius during 1904. The work is mentioned in Sibelius's correspondence, but only two sketch fragments for it have been positively identified. Had it been completed as planned, this would have been one of the largest and potentially most significant of Sibelius's works from this period. In June Finne provided a 265-strophe libretto in Finnish and German, and the oratorio was to have comprised three movements: *Birth*, *Funeral* and *Resurrection*. The story itself reflects events in the life of Jesus Christ. The first part, *Birth*, was adapted by Finne from the last runo of the *Kalevala*: the shepherd girl Marjatta, who correponds to the Virgin Mary, is a 'lowly maiden' who becomes pregnant from eating a cowberry in the forest and gives birth to a son, called Kiesus or Jeesus. A wise old man hails the boy as King of Karelia.

The remaining movements were to have used ideas from folk poetry, and some information about their disposition is known. *Funeral* was to have been in ABA' form, starting with a vast processional, no less than 55 strophes in length, depicting how the body of the young Kiesus was carried 'under cover of the spring rain' to be buried 'beneath the flowering canopy of the spruces'. Might Sibelius here have employed some of the material he had been planning for his requiem for Eugen Schauman? The burial scene was set at nightfall, followed by a lamentation from Marjatta, asking God to awaken Kiesus from death, and a return to the opening material.

The *Resurrection* movement fell into two sections. First Kiesus's passing was remembered and mourned, after which Marjatta repeated her prayer to God. This was followed by the second part, a sunrise, whereupon Kiesus rose again. The oratorio was to conclude with a general hymn of celebration, 'The Creator has arisen from the dead'.

On 30th April 1905 a farewell event was held at the Finnish National Theatre for Kaarlo Bergbom – for 33 years the dynamic director of the theatre as well as a playwright, literary critic and dramaturgist – and his older sister Emilie, Kaarlo's colleague at the theatre. The programme included Weber's *Freischütz* overture conducted by Robert Kajanus, and Act V of Shakespeare's *Tempest*. Sibelius was represented by the song *Höstkväll*, sung by Aino Ackté, and by a sparkling, good-humoured new orchestral piece, *Cortège*, JS 54. As the new piece played, a procession of actors dressed as characters from the Bergboms' most successful productions – including Kullervo, Daniel Hjort, Gustavus Adolphus II, Antigone and Ariel – paraded before the guests of honour.

During the spring Sibelius undertook some revisions to *Cassazione*: he reduced the size of orchestra required, rearranged the order of some musical elements and expanded what was originally a rather brief final section. Structurally the revisions were a success, but the revised version lacks the range of orchestral colour and sonority found in the original. Sibelius planned to make further changes to the piece; he marked the manuscript 'Should be reworked', and it remained unpublished during his lifetime.

In July Sibelius's major Finnish publisher, Helsingfors Nya Musikhandel, who owned the rights to most of Sibelius's major works including the first two symphonies, *Valse triste* and *Finlandia*, sold its entire Sibelius catalogue to Breitkopf & Härtel. Now the composer was represented by two major – and competing – German publishers. For now, at least, this was a positive development. Such big firms were well placed to promote his work aggressively, and his profile in Germany was high enough for it to be worthwhile for them to do so. Internationally, too, the German firms had far more influence than a relatively small Helsinki company.

In the summer of 1905 Sibelius finally made headway with the promised revisions to his *Violin Concerto*. He followed the same procedure as with *En saga*: abbreviation, simplification and purification, but at the cost of some fine and characteristic music. In the first movement he removed the Bach-like cadenza entirely. The remaining cadenza's function as a replacement for the development section – an example of Sibelius's characteristic formal compression – thus became far more readily discernible. A single viola's occasional echo of the solo violin line in this movement usually sounds as if the viola player has suddenly assumed delusions of soloistic grandeur. Might this be Sibelius's secret jibe at this often maligned instrument – his very own 'viola joke'? Perhaps not: in a sensitive performance, the soloist and viola player interact in a manner akin to chamber music, to much more satisfying effect.

The changes to the slow movement were relatively modest (it cannot have been a hard decision to remove the bizarre cadenza-like flourish in the closing bars of the original version), but in the finale Sibelius made extensive cuts. Many of the most extreme technical difficulties were removed from the solo part (although it remains a daunting challenge even for the finest virtuosos) and the orchestral sonorities became smoother and more integrated.

On 18th August the distinguished painter Albert Edelfelt died, shortly after his fifty-first birthday. Born in Porvoo, the son of an architect, Edelfelt had studied in Antwerp, Paris and St Petersburg and had become one of Finland's most eminent artists, known not least for his landscapes and portraits. He was also a friend of Sibelius, with whom he shared an admiration for the poetry of Runeberg. And it was to Runeberg's poetry – the concluding lines of *Molnets broder* (*The Cloud's Brother*) – that Sibelius turned in a short piece for mixed choir *a cappella* performed at Edelfelt's funeral on 24th August: *Ej med klagan* (*Not with Lamentation*), JS 69. When required to produce a commemorative piece at short notice, Sibelius often turned to ideas that he had already conceived for other works, and there is evidence to suggest that this happened here. A later, hitherto unidentified sketch returns to the essential thematic material of *Ej med klagan*, with its characteristic Sibelian progressions, scored for full symphony orchestra. It is tempting to think that this music might have originated in the *Marjatta* oratorio, which also dealt with death and burial.[4]

Politically, 1905 was a portentous year. Following the death of Bobrikov the Russians had moderated their policy in matters of Finnish government, but by now the Tsar was preoccupied with troubles elsewhere. For a start the military defeats of the Russo-Japanese war (1904–05) were a serious economic blow as well as causing a significant erosion of Russian self-confidence. In January 1905, unarmed and peaceful protestors in St Petersburg were shot *en masse* by the Tsarist secret police (Okhranka) on their way to deliver a petition to Nicholas II, in the incident known subsequently as Bloody Sunday. Turmoil spread through many strata of

Russian society. Rimsky-Korsakov, who supported the revolutionary cause, was dismissed from his post as professor at the St Petersburg Conservatory. In October there was a general strike, which soon spread to Finland as well. The political reforms that the Revolution of 1905 engendered within Russia were soon reflected in Finland: parts of the February Manifesto were abandoned and the following year a new Parliament was established to replace the Diet.

Sibelius was not present in Berlin on 19th October 1905, when the revised version of the *Violin Concerto* was first performed; Richard Strauss – no less – conducted the Berlin Philharmonic Orchestra. The soloist was not Burmester, whose schedule was already full, but Karel Halíř, the orchestra's leader. It is scarcely surprising that Burmester took offence; he never played Sibelius's concerto, and the work was eventually dedicated to a young Hungarian violinist named Ferenc von Vecsey. Nowadays the concerto is so firmly established in the repertoire (even of orchestras and conductors otherwise antipathetic to Sibelius) that it ranks as one of the few works by Sibelius to be in serious danger of over-exposure. This was not always the case, however: even the revised version of the concerto was not an immediate success, and took many years to become firmly established in the repertoire. The pioneering 1935 recording by Jascha Heifetz, conducted by Sir Thomas Beecham, seems to have won the concerto many friends. Since then it has been recorded countless times, but its challenges – stylistic and technical – can still catch out even the most respected soloists.

Was Sibelius right to revise his *Violin Concerto*? It is undeniably true that the process of revision made the work more concentrated and refined. Perhaps, though, he was so scared by the fate of the original version in Nováček's hands that he went too far in simplifying the work. Aino took a similar attitude to the concerto as she had done to *En saga*: after her husband's death she claimed that 'I like and have always liked the original version. "Papa" took away a number of wild passages. Now *En saga* is more civilized, more polished. Similarly I like the first version of the *Violin Concerto*. "Papa" changed it when it was criticized severely... He left out many of the most virtuosic passages. The concerto is now easier.'

Towards the end of the year, Sibelius set aside his *Marjatta* oratorio – possibly as a result of waning enthusiasm for Finne's text – and began work on another project that was destined never to materialize: an orchestral tone poem on the theme of Luonnotar, the spirit of nature from the *Kalevala* (a variant on the biblical Creation story). In fact we can regard this not so much as a separate project but as a continuation of *Marjatta*; the story itself was wholly different but much of the musical material seems to have been transferred from the oratorio to the tone poem. 'I have great hopes for this piece', Sibelius wrote to Axel Carpelan in late October. A surviving manuscript draft from the spring of 1906 moreover reveals that *Luonnotar* not only provided the raw materials for the following year's symphonic fantasia *Pohjola's Daughter* but also contained motifs that would, over the next few years, find their way into the slow movement of the *Third Symphony* and the *Love Song* from the second set of *Scènes historiques*. Sibelius was still toying with the idea of writing a requiem for Eugen Schauman in September, and one might speculate that he planned to use some of the ideas from the funeral movement of *Marjatta* in such a project.

In November Sibelius travelled to Copenhagen and Berlin, although a planned concert in Heidelberg had to be cancelled because the new work – *Luonnotar* – was not ready. The trip was, however, musically profitable. Sibelius now made his first visit to England: he landed in Dover on 29th November, travelling first to London, where he put up at the luxurious Langham Hotel near Regent's Park, and then onwards to Birmingham. Coincidentally his old ally Busoni was in Birmingham at the time, but Sibelius also found many new friends. He soon established a close rapport with his host, Granville Bantock, and also became acquainted with the conductor Henry Wood, the critic Ernest Newman and an influential lady named Rosa Newmarch, who were to prove persuasive advocates for Sibelius's music in Britain. The composer's interpretations of *Finlandia* and the *First Symphony*, which he conducted in Liverpool on 2nd December, were received with great acclaim.

It would seem logical that Sibelius's first attempt to set an English text to music was made at the time of his first visit to England. A fragment has survived of a projected song for mixed choir *a cappella*, JS 122, based on the youthful poem *Listen to the Water Mill* by Sarah Doudney; we do not know the precise circumstances of its composition, though Kari Kilpeläinen has dated the manuscript to 1905–06.[5] It cannot be a coincidence that the melodic line was re-used in a solo song on a similar topic: *Kvarnhjulet* (*The Mill Wheel*) of 1909.

He travelled onwards almost immediately to Paris, arriving in time to celebrate his fortieth birthday. He continued to work on *Luonnotar*, and even toyed with the idea of developing it into a symphony. Sibelius evidently liked Paris; on 11th December he wrote to Aino: 'Paris is indeed the city of cities, where one can absorb ideas.' Despite some performances of his music there, however, his reception was not sufficiently enthusiastic to guarantee him a place in the French repertoire. Indeed, Sibelius was to remain something of a curiosity on the French concert scene until the 1970s. The Finnish community in the French capital, however, welcomed him warmly, and he developed a particular friendship with the young painter Oscar Parviainen, no doubt nurtured by celebrations of a more enthusiastic kind than Aino would have liked. On one occasion Parviainen came across Sibelius, still in his party attire, some four days after a particularly lavish binge, and the two men went to Sibelius's hotel room, where Sibelius improvised at the piano while Parviainen sketched him, apparently improvising on themes from the now defunct *Marjatta* project (the sketch is now at the Joensuu Art Museum). Parviainen later wrote: 'I can't get "your funeral march" out of my head, and I am making one sketch after another... The "Prayer to God" is beautiful, I hear it often, but in the splendour of the most vivid red and the darkest black; now they are mine and I am taking them as my subject. I sometimes play "your great celebration" to myself when I need inner strength.' Sibelius later told Parviainen that the 'Prayer to God' theme was used in the second half of the finale of the *Third Symphony*. The 'funeral march', on the other hand, may have been associated in Sibelius's mind with Eugen Schauman and was thus quite possibly a staging post on the long road that would lead to *In memoriam* four years later.

Over the coming years Parviainen completed two paintings – *The Spanish Commander's Funeral Procession* and *Prayer to God* – which now hang at Ainola and of which Sibelius is said to have been especially fond. Parviainen developed ideas that were inspired by Sibelius's music and placed them in a new context. In the case of *The Spanish Commander's Funeral Procession*, the painting grew away from Sibelius's 'funeral march' concept, acquiring local colour and telling its own independent story. *Prayer to God*, on the other hand, dealt with a topic that was especially sensitive for Sibelius. It depicts a sick girl, her spirit flying skywards and her mother watching helplessly by candlelight. The parallels with the death of Sibelius's daughter Kirsti in 1900 are unmistakable, and at Ainola the painting was referred to as 'The Death of a Child'.

1906

From Paris Sibelius travelled to Berlin, where he met with Breitkopf & Härtel, and he finally returned home at the beginning of February 1906. By then his eldest daughter, Eva, had started secondary school at the Suomalainen Yhteiskoulu in Helsinki, which meant that she had to stay with a family friend, Martha Tornell, during the week, returning to Ainola at weekends and for holidays.

In Helsinki Sibelius found that his friends – not least Axel Gallén – were eagerly supporting the Russian revolutionaries. At a dinner party given by Eero Järnefelt in Järvenpää, Jean and Aino met Maxim Gorky, who was temporarily in hiding in Finland, but Sibelius himself did not play an active part in the political manœuvrings of the time. Even if he had wished to participate, he had commitments to fulfil. In a letter to Carpelan on 1st March he alluded to a new symphony that was in progress. As the *Third Symphony* was still far from ready, it is possible that he was still considering turning the *Luonnotar* tone poem into a symphony; at any rate, *Luonnotar* was still very much on his mind. More urgently, he needed to complete the 'dance intermezzo' *Pan and Echo*, Op. 53, an orchestral piece to accompany a tableau in which 'Pan and Echo are seen on a hill, looking at the nymphs dancing in the valley'. The tableau was part of a lottery evening at Helsinki's Seurahuone on 24th March, where Sibelius conducted the Philharmonic Society orchestra. The aim was to raise funds for a concert hall in Helsinki, a plan that was later abandoned. Though clearly an occasional piece, *Pan and Echo* is poetic, full of feeling and scored with great sensitivity. It opens with a reflective portrayal of Pan and Echo on the hill and continues with the nymphs' increasingly demonic dance. Luckily Sibelius was in a mood to work effectively; Aino wrote that 'at such times my husband could sit for up to two days without getting up from his desk'.

On 12th March the Finnish première of the *Violin Concerto* in its definitive form took place, with a Latvian soloist named Grevesmühl under the baton of Robert Kajanus; it received mixed reviews. Sibelius himself did not conduct the revised version of the concerto for many years.

Three weeks later, on 22nd March, Martin Wegelius died. The relationship between Sibelius and his former mentor was no longer close, and they had hardly been in direct contact at all for more than a decade. Wegelius never abandoned his strong Wagnerian leanings, and was also keen to praise Mahler and Richard Strauss. Perhaps Wegelius was disappointed that his former pupil did not share his tastes and had decided against following the operatic path. Sibelius hated funerals but in Wegelius's case he attended, and even conducted the *Elegy* from *King Christian II*.

Sibelius was then working on a cantata for the lavish celebrations to mark the centenary of the birth of the Finnish nationalist statesman and Hegelian philosopher Johan Snellman, an influential champion of the Finnish language who played a major role in the establishment of a Finnish cultural identity. Even after the death of Bobrikov and the repeal of his most extreme measures, the Finnish people was evidently prepared to take every opportunity to demonstrate its independence of spirit.

The new piece was *Vapautettu kuningatar* (*The Captive Queen*), Op. 48, freely based on a ballad by Paavo Cajander. The composer himself conducted the first performance of *The Captive Queen* with a 'symphony chorus' and the Philharmonic Society orchestra in Helsinki on the centenary itself, 12th May 1906. Cajander's ballad, which had originally been published to celebrate Snellman's 75th birthday in 1881, tells of a queen, imprisoned in a castle, who is liberated by a young hero (a more accurate translation of the title is 'The Liberated Queen'). So evident was the allegory of this tale that the piece had to be performed under a more neutral name, *Siell' laulavi kuningatar* (*There Sings the Queen*). Characteristic Sibelian features abound in this work, from *spiccato* string arpeggios – similar to the opening of *En saga* – to thematic motifs that melodically and rhythmically resemble the finale of the *Second Symphony*. Might this be a neat musical sleight of hand on Sibelius's part? Given the widespread belief that this symphony bore a patriotic message, one could almost imagine that his choice of thematic material was designed to exploit this misconception. In the second half of the piece a march theme is introduced that bears a conspicuous resemblance to his favourite Wagner opera, *Die Meistersinger*.

At this point something very strange happened to the projected *Luonnotar* tone poem, which by that time must have been almost ready. As the musicologist Timo Virtanen has observed, Sibelius chose to 'recompose the nearly complete composition, change the order of its elements, rearrange the formal and tonal design, and omit material which he seems to have regarded as intrinsically valuable'.[6] On 26th June, Sibelius wrote to Robert Lienau about a 'symphonic fantasia' on a completely new *Kalevala* theme: Väinämöinen and Pohjola's daughter. Sibelius sent the new tone poem to Lienau with a programmatic explanation – but without a title. Several months of wrangling followed. Lienau wrote to Sibelius (4th July): 'From your translation one can understand the content of your "symphonic poem" very well. I shall, however, shorten it and make it slightly more poetic. I am also in favour of giving the work a specific title. Doesn't the daughter of Pojala [sic!] have a name? Perhaps we could use that.' For his part, Sibelius favoured 'Wäinämöinen', but Lienau (probably wisely) found it unsuitable; he also took issue with Sibelius's second suggestion, 'L'aventure d'un héros' – and so, almost by default, a title of Lienau's invention came to be used: *Pohjola's Daughter*.

It was once believed that Sibelius wrote his 'symphonic fantasia' *Pohjola's Daughter*, Op. 49, in some haste in the summer of 1906. If that had been the case, the close integration of the thematic material and the lack of 'rough edges' in the work's construction would have signified an amazing achievement, even by Sibelius's elevated standards. In fact, however, the large number of surviving sketches and manuscript sources show that the 'new' work grew out of *Luonnotar*, and that 'these two pieces are essentially one and the same piece' (Virtanen). The motivic material is quintessentially Sibelian throughout and the 'S-motif' appears prominently: just after the introductory cello solo it is heard in passing from the bassoon and bass clarinet, and then more clearly from the cor anglais, in which guise it forms part of one of the work's principal thematic strands.

The new programme tells how Väinämöinen, travelling home from Pohjola (the Northland) in his sledge, meets and falls in love with Pohjola's daughter. She sets him an impossible challenge: to create a boat from her spindle. In the circumstances it is scarcely surprising that the music does not follow the story with precision but instead paints the characters and events with broader brushstrokes. By now, in any case, Sibelius's style in his major orchestral works had developed to the extent that it was sufficient for the music to follow its own inner logic: his tone poems were becoming more abstract and less immediately dependent upon the details of the narrative. *Pohjola's Daughter*, with its wide range of orchestral colour – from powerfully atmospheric writing for darker-hued instruments such as the cello and cor anglais to overwhelming yet perfectly judged brass climaxes – is rightly hailed as one of Sibelius's finest middle-period works.

Four years earlier, when Sibelius was holidaying in Tvärminne, he had been concerned about the mental health of his sister Linda. In June 1906 his worries proved well founded, as her condition took a turn for the worse. From then on, with the exception of brief visits to the outside world, she remained in an asylum for the rest of her life. Her illness blighted what would otherwise have been an idyllic summer during which the Sibelius family relaxed at Virolahti, a coastal town some 100 miles east of Helsinki.

By the time Sibelius sent *Pohjola's Daughter* to Lienau, he had already started work on a set of six songs that would be published as Op. 50. In this set Sibelius deserted his favourite Swedish-language poets and chose texts of decidedly variable quality by German writers. It seems probable that Lienau suggested the use of German lyrics; certainly songs in German would have been more readily accessible to European performers than works in Swedish or Finnish. Following his studies in Berlin and Vienna, Sibelius was a competent German speaker, fully capable of setting poetry in that language. Unlike any of Sibelius's earlier opus groups of songs, Op. 50 was conceived at one fell swoop; the songs were composed in August while he was still in Virolahti. Nonetheless, they do not constitute a 'song cycle' in the traditional sense; their themes are too diverse, and the literary styles of their poets too disparate.

Some of the poems used in Op. 50 treat subjects which rarely attracted Sibelius. An example is No. 1, *Lenzgesang* (*Spring Song*), to a poem by Arthur Fitger), in which the arrival of spring is described in effusive and spirited but rather conventional terms. Especially in the fourth strophe, the poem implies that nature can be subjugated by human will, an attitude far removed from the pantheism expressed in Sibelius's finest nature songs. Similarly, the platitudes of Emil Rudolf Weiss's *Sehnsucht* (*Longing*; No. 2) do not stimulate Sibelius beyond obvious gestures (it would be possible to interpret this song as a self-parody). The next three texts clearly held far greater appeal for the composer. In the third, *Im Feld ein Mädchen singt* (*In the Field a Maid Sings*) to a poem by Margareta Susman, the themes of death and solitude are combined with an empathy for the peaceful beauty of nature. The syncopated piano accompaniment creates a feeling of timelessness which anticipates the slow movement of the *Fourth Symphony*. The passions expressed in Richard Dehmel's *Aus banger Brust* (*From Anxious Heart*, No. 4) are as ardent and sensual as Weiss's are trivial and predictable. At one point the restless melodic line anticipates the third of the *Humoresques* for violin and orchestra (1917). Perhaps the most distinguished of the set, and certainly the most serene, is the fifth, *Die stille Stadt* (*The Silent City*), again with words by Dehmel, in which the simplicity of both the vocal line and the piano part produces a setting of great refinement. The Op. 50 group concludes with a rather Schubertian setting of Anna Ritter's *Rosenlied* (*Song of the Roses*) – a bright and pleasant song although Sibelius's own voice does not fully come through until the abrupt closing bars, '[Der Tag] senkt unsre Schönheit verwelkt in die Gruft' ('[The day] places our faded beauty into the grave'). Its melody derives from the *Pianokompositioner för barn* that Sibelius had sketched some years earlier.

In October Sibelius occupied himself with another German text – *Erloschen* (*Extinguished*) by Georg Busse-Palma, which he set as an expressive through-composed solo song for Ida Ekman (JS 74). The Wagnerian harmonies at the end of the first and last stanzas of the poem recall *Den första kyssen*, written six years previously.

During the autumn Sibelius worked on a new commission from the Swedish Theatre: music for Hjalmar Procopé's play *Belshazzar's Feast*, freely adapted from Chapter 5 of the Book of Daniel. Sibelius wrote a highly atmospheric score for small orchestra (JS 48), ten numbers in all, that demonstrates that he could produce *faux* orientalisms with just as much fluency as Nielsen did in his music to *Aladdin* just over a decade later.

A humble Jewish woman, Leschanah, is sent to Belshazzar's court in Babylon to assassinate him. The first musical number is set next to an idol in the city square where the king arrives in a procession. Leschanah is waiting with a dagger but Belshazzar falls in love with her and takes her to his palace. The oriental imagery in the music is clear in this overtly pictorial piece with its large percussion section including bass drum, cymbals, triangle and tambourine. Next comes a *Nocturne* (No. 2a) that depicts Leschanah in the King's palace at night – an anguished flute melody, full of the composer's fingerprints, above an atmospheric string accompaniment featuring Sibelius's characteristic short–long–short syncopations. Leschanah hears the distant, melancholy song of a Jewish girl who longs to return to Jerusalem (*The Jewish Girl's Song*, No. 2b). Belshazzar is keen to govern more fairly but Leschanah, in her quest to usurp the King's previous favourite, the slave girl Khadra, persuades him that Khadra must die. A great feast is arranged where Khadra will dance for the last time. To depict the bustle of the feast itself Sibelius provided music of a brisk, martial character, an eight-bar fragment (plus a bar of introduction) that is repeated as often as the stage production requires (No. 3). This breaks off abruptly when Leschanah arrives, and in due course Khadra begins to dance – first a *Dance of Life* (No. 4, a dialogue between flute and clarinets), then a macabre *Dance of Death* (No. 5, the clarinet in a low register) during which she receives a fatal snakebite. Sibelius also made piano transcriptions of these two dances.

At this point the Biblical story reasserts itself, and the words 'Mene, Mene, Tekel, Upharsin' appear on the wall. Khadra's strength is waning and she collapses as she tries to perform the *Dance of Life* once more (the sixth number is an extract from the fourth, but played more slowly). The prophet Daniel interprets the writing on the wall and explains that Belshazzar will die during the coming night. Leschanah has by now come to love the King and is unwilling to slay him. In the seventh musical number, a night scene, she contemplates her dilemma with slow-moving music, impassioned and darkly intense. Belshazzar, meanwhile, is anxiously awaiting his demise, and Sibelius provided a subtle accompaniment to the King's dialogue with his adviser, Aspenasi. The whispering strings and sighing clarinets play music loosely derived from the *Dance of Life*. Finally Leschanah arrives to discharge her duty. An abbreviated *Dance of Life* (No. 9) reminds the King of Khadra, but the music proceeds to the *Dance of Death* (No. 10) and Leschanah kills him with her dagger – and is herself killed by Belshazzar's Jewish advisor, Elieser.

The play's first performance at the Swedish Theatre was given on 7th November. Sibelius himself conducted the music, which was praised within the context of a less than overwhelming welcome for the play itself, which had been eagerly awaited. The première was sold out and the Oopperakellari restaurant offered a special menu including 'Tournedos à la Belsazar'!

Sibelius now left for a series of concerts in the Finnish cities of Oulu, Vaasa and Viipuri. The Vaasa concert, with the local orchestra, included a new arrangement of extracts from the incidental music to *Kuolema*, which Sibelius revised and combined into a single concert item, *Scene with*

Cranes, Op. 44 No. 2. Here he used the outer sections of the third musical number, but replaced the central vocalise with the calls of the cranes from the original fourth movement, now played by clarinets.

Before he left Vaasa Sibelius composed a short melodrama, *Grevinnans konterfej* (*The Countess's Portrait*), JS 88, at the behest of a Swedish-language Ladies' Association, for a lottery soirée in aid of the Kronoby adult education centre to be held the following month. The original poem, *Porträtterna* (*The Portraits*) was by the Swedish poet Anna Maria Lenngren and it was subsequently extended by Zachris Topelius, who noted that it should be accompanied by 'quiet music' – a direction with which Sibelius complied, writing a piece of undisturbed tranquillity and exquisite beauty.

Immediately after these provincial concerts came a much more prestigious event – a trip across the Russian border to St Petersburg, where he was to conduct *Lemminkäinen's Return* and the first performance of *Pohjola's Daughter* with the orchestra of the Mariinsky Theatre on 29th December. The concert formed part of the renowned series of concerts that Alexander Siloti arranged, financed, and usually also conducted, in St Petersburg between 1903 and 1917. On this occasion Sibelius shared the programme with Eugène Ysaÿe. Siloti, just two years older than Sibelius, had gained a reputation as an advocate of modern music; he was not only a trailblazing conductor but also a composer and pianist of considerable stature, who had lived in Europe for some years and also visited America. Axel Carpelan expressed reservations about the wisdom of going to St Petersburg, but the political tensions between Finland and Russia were no obstruction to cultural contacts, and even the composer of *Finlandia* was warmly welcomed. Both in size and in technical proficiency the Mariinsky Theatre orchestra was in a different league from those in the smaller Finnish cities, and *Pohjola's Daughter* thus received its première in favourable circumstances. The press reactions were positive, and the critic of *Russ* found its composer 'exceptionally talented and imaginative'.

CHAPTER 9

YOUNG CLASSICISM –
THE THIRD SYMPHONY: 1907–1909

1907

In December 1906 and January 1907 Sibelius returned to his theatre score to *Belshazzar's Feast* and prepared a selection for concert use (Op. 51). Some changes were made to the scoring but the music otherwise remained close to the original. The suite includes the opening march (now with the title *Oriental Procession*), the song (now purely instrumental, and named *Solitude*), the *Nocturne*, and an ABA-form conflation of the *Dance of Life* and *Dance of Death* (now named *Khadra's Dance*). During the spring he also made a piano arrangement of the concert suite and, presumably at the same time, made a version of *The Jewish Girl's Song* for voice and piano.

It was probably in January 1907 that Sibelius returned to the *Dance-Intermezzo* that he had arranged for piano from the orchestral *Musik zu einer Scène* of 1904, and made a new orchestral version based on the piano piece. Breitkopf & Härtel had asked for an orchestral version the previous year, after acquiring the rights to the piano score, but Sibelius had replied that 'the original form for orchestra is much too long and does not correspond to the piano reduction... Naturally I shall do my best to send you the score at the earliest opportunity.'

A hitherto unpublished *Adagio in E major* for piano, JS 13, dated 3rd February, anticipates by more than two years the main theme of the slow movement of the *Voces intimae* string quartet. It lasts for just 25 bars and can hardly have been intended for concert use.

The Sibelius family had now been living in Järvenpää for several years, but sometimes Aino must have wished that they had moved further away from Helsinki. During the early part of 1907 Sibelius – who had accepted an invitation from the Royal Philharmonic Society in London to conduct his forthcoming *Third Symphony* in the spring, and ought to have been hard at work – was often to be found in the capital's restaurants, whilst an exhausted Aino had to spend some time in hospital. In a letter to his friend Mikko Slöör the composer admitted that 'this boozing – in itself an exceptionally pleasant occupation – has gone much too far ... I have more ideas than ever. Also the capacity to work. And the desire to get on with my work. But time – time!! It is running away.' In the end time ran too fast: the new symphony was not ready, and Sibelius had to cancel the London appearance.

Sibelius rejected two piano transcriptions of the previous year's tableau music, *Pan and Echo*, made at Lienau's request, one by Paul Juon and the other (probably) by Alfredo Cairati. He wrote to the publisher: 'To be honest, I did not greatly care for the piano transcriptions. I shall arrange the things [*sic*] myself and send them to you. Of course it's very important that they are of good quality.' And so, in the late spring, he made his own – very effective – piano transcription of *Pan and Echo*.

In August Jean and Aino took a trip to Berlin. When they were not attending concerts or visiting museums, Sibelius tried to work on the symphony, but it was not completed until after their return to Finland; indeed, the orchestra received the concluding pages of the finale only at the last rehearsal. It was premièred in Helsinki on 25th September, sharing the programme with *Pohjola's Daughter* and the *Belshazzar's Feast* suite.

Even though the *Symphony No. 3 in C major*, Op. 52, had occupied Sibelius ever since his move to Järvenpää and even though its origins were inextricably intertwined with *Pohjola's Daughter* and the abandoned *Marjatta* project, it still marks a significant change of direction. In it he turns his back on the national Romanticism of the *First* and *Second Symphonies*, but has not yet adopted the bold modernism of the *Fourth*. Despite the apparent simplicity of musical style, however, the expressive message of the symphony – especially its second and third movements – is far from explicit. Over the years many great Sibelius conductors have failed to meet its interpretative challenges; some have refused to conduct the work at all. The *Third Symphony*'s reception must have come as something of a surprise and disappointment to Sibelius: six months before its première he had described it in a letter to Aino as 'one of the best things I have done. You know, it will be more brilliant... than my other [works].'

The concise, regular, rhythmically disciplined theme from the cellos and double basses which opens the symphony has often been referred to as 'Classical'. It is not of the neo-classical, pastiche variety, however, but closer to the concept of 'junge Klassizität' (young Classicism – a move away from the programmatic tendencies of the nineteenth century in favour of the melody and absolute music of Bach and Mozart) advocated by Busoni. The movement is in sonata form and scored for an orchestra that contains neither tuba nor harp. Throughout the work, the brass instruments are used much more sparingly than in the first two symphonies.

Sibelius himself remarked that: 'To my mind a Mozart *Allegro* is the most perfect model for a symphonic movement. Think of its wonderful unity and homogeneity! It is like an uninterrupted flowing, where nothing stands out and nothing encroaches upon the rest.' This description also suits the first movement of his own *Third Symphony* very well. The opening theme, with its insistent semiquaver motion, builds to a climax from the horns featuring Sibelius's trademark short–long–short syncopations. The second theme, like the first, is initially given to the cellos; derived to some extent from the horn climax, it is broader and more *cantabile*, although it retains a steady rhythmic pulse in the background. Only at the very end of the exposition is there any change to the underlying tempo (a mysterious *Tranquillo* passage, *ppp*). Motoric semiquavers from the strings dominate the development section. As the recapitulation approaches, the woodwind take up phrases from the second theme – most notably an extended bassoon solo which to some extent anticipates the bassoon lament in the development of the first movement of the *Fifth Symphony*. The recapitulation is forthright and energetic, and there is an imposing coda.

Axel Carpelan described the slow second movement as 'wonderful, like a child's prayer', but behind the façade of this apparently simple movement we find great subtlety and warmth. The tempo of the movement has long been a controversial point, as the indication in the score – *Andantino con moto, quasi allegretto* – is far from unambiguous. This marking has led many conductors to play it too quickly, thereby greatly diminishing its impact and stature. Through the metronome marking he provided in 1943 (crotchet = 116) and conversations with Jussi Jalas, Sibelius left no doubt that he intended a slower tempo, as favoured indeed by almost all Finnish conductors. In the 1980s Jalas also confirmed to me that Sibelius himself conducted the piece in six, not in two. Formally it is a rondo (though some prefer to see it as a theme with variations, or as one of a number of other formal types), and it cleverly exploits the rhythmic interaction between the parallel time signatures of 6/4 and 3/2. The gentle, pensive main theme is presented first by the flutes in thirds, then taken up by the clarinets and finally by the first violins. The first episode, intense and poignant, is scored for divided cellos, answered by the woodwind. When the main theme returns it is accompanied by string *pizzicati* which prepare the way for the slightly faster second episode, the restless character of which is relieved only by the final return of the main theme, now more confident and with a heavier tread. A brief recollection of the first episode firmly snuffs the movement out.

An early complete version of the slow movement has survived and is now in the National Library of Finland.[1] It must date from a late stage of work on the symphony, as the manuscript is a fair copy and even contains some copyist's markings, but Sibelius evidently decided to rework the movement before the first performance: the manuscript contains sketched additions that found their way into the final version. The differences are not vast, but the preliminary version is rather simpler and less ornamented. The introductory bars are foreshortened, for instance; the phrase structure of the first episode (here without its *Tranquillo* marking) is different, as is the scoring of the second episode; and the movement's final woodwind phrase is heard just once, rather than twice as in the published edition.

The finale combines elements of the traditional scherzo and finale into a single entity. Such a formal solution is typically Sibelian, and is not confined only to the symphonies: a similar structure is found in the following year's tone poem *Night Ride and Sunrise*. The composer himself described this movement as 'the crystallization of thought from chaos'. At first a number of motifs are introduced; there is a brief recollection of the main theme of the slow movement; then the thematic fragments are thrown about and woven together, rising to a vigorous climax. But this attempt to 'crystallize thought' fails, and the music falls back into unease and turbulence. Eventually the mists clear and a broad march theme emerges, tentatively at first and then confidently, *a tempo, con energia*, from the cellos. This theme, developed from a tiny descending motif first heard unobtrusively much earlier in the movement, dominates the remainder of the symphony, increasing in intensity all the while and eventually attaining a tremendous yet seemingly inevitable C major culmination.

The hymn-like, almost religious elements of the *Third Symphony* are often overlooked, but are an important component in its construction. No actual hymn tunes are quoted, but the coda of the first movement, various phrases in the slow movement and the entire second half of the finale all have a hymn-like character. Moreover, a horn motif heard earlier in the finale (between figures 5 and 6) closely resembles an idea from the hymn *Soi kittokseksi Luojan* from the university cantata of 1897. In his doctoral thesis on the *Third Symphony*, Timo Virtanen has suggested that the presence of such thematic material may reflect the work's origins in the *Marjatta* project, as may the symphony's three-movement structure, a theory that is very plausible, even though Virtanen admits that there is no firm evidence to support it. It would be wrong, however, to infer that the symphony is programmatic: as always the thoroughness of Sibelius's compositional technique distanced the finished product from its original source of inspiration.

'The *Third Symphony* was a disappointment for the audience, because everybody expected it to be like the *Second*', Sibelius told Jussi Jalas in 1943, and the reviews confirm this judgement – although Flodin hailed the composer as 'a classical master ... the new work fulfils all the requirements of a symphonic work of art in the modern sense, but its inner essence [is] simultaneously new and revolutionary, yet thoroughly Sibelian.' Sibelius dedicated his *Third Symphony* to his English champion Granville Bantock.

A month after the première of the *Third Symphony*, Gustav Mahler paid a brief visit to Helsinki. He was unimpressed by *Spring Song* and *Valse triste* at one of Kajanus's popular concerts, but after the two composers met the following day Mahler described Sibelius as 'a particularly sympathetic individual'. Sibelius too seems to have liked Mahler as a person, although their musical opinions were very different. 'When our conversation touched on the essence of the symphony,' Sibelius later told Karl Ekman, 'I maintained that I admired its strictness and the profound logic that creates an inner connection between all the motifs. This was my conviction, based on my creative work. Mahler had a wholly opposite opinion: "Nein, die Symphonie muss sein wie die Welt. Sie muss alles umfassen" ["No, the symphony must be like the world. It must contain everything"].' As one of the world's foremost conductors, Mahler assumed that Sibelius would want to propose some of his own music for performance, but this was not the case. It was not until March 1911 that an ailing Mahler programmed a work by Sibelius – the *Violin Concerto* in New York – but illness prevented him from conducting the concert.

A week or so after his meeting with Mahler, Sibelius conducted twice in Turku and then went to St Petersburg to conduct the *Third Symphony*. Aino joined him there in time for the concert, given at Siloti's invitation, but the symphony met with a generally unsympathetic response.

Sibelius's work on the symphony and his foreign travels had led him to neglect Axel Carpelan. While the composer was in St Petersburg Carpelan, ever the hypochondriac, wrote a 'last farewell' to Aino, convinced that he was about to die. But if Carpelan's health complaints were illusory, Sibelius himself was on the brink of a genuine crisis. Before Aino travelled to St Petersburg, Jean wrote to her complaining of a hoarseness of voice; his condition would deteriorate over the coming months.

In November 1907 Jean and Aino employed a young woman named Helmi Vainikainen, who had previously worked for Pekka Halonen, as a nurse and cook. She was to become an indispensable part of the family and remained at Ainola until the 1960s.

Sibelius made a second trip to Russia a few weeks later, this time conducting the symphony, *Pohjola's Daughter* and a selection of shorter works in Moscow. He had to forego the opportunity to perform the *Violin Concerto* – which he had still not conducted in its revised form – because the soloist was not equal to its demands. Nonetheless, Sibelius's only trip to Moscow can be regarded as a success and, even if his music was not received with rapturous acclaim, it met with greater understanding than it had found in St Petersburg.

The only other work that we can date to 1907 is a song, *Hundra vägar* (*A Hundred Ways*), Op. 72 No. 6, to words by Runeberg. Here, as in the earlier song *Drömmen* (1891), Sibelius does not hesitate to combine Runeberg's Swedish text with a melody that has contours and rhythms redolent of runic singing, though the harmonic context and subsequent development of the material are quite different. The song was published by the local firm of K. E. Holm in Helsinki in 1907.

1908

The hoarseness of which Sibelius had complained in St Petersburg continued to trouble him in the new year, and he spent several weeks in the Deaconess Hospital in Helsinki. At least, while recuperating, he found time to resume his correspondence with Carpelan, but the Baron's concern for Sibelius's health was mingled with the certainty that his problems were of his own making. On 26th January Carpelan wrote to Robert Kajanus: 'When you see Sibbe, send my regards and tell him that I have had a dream that he will soon be dead unless, after this severe illness, he stops smoking and consuming spirits. This illness was surely his last warning.'

For some weeks Sibelius was too ill to pursue the lifestyle of a globe-trotting composer-conductor, and planned visits to Rome, Warsaw and Berlin had to be cancelled. By the end of February, however, he was well enough to make the long journey to England. Once again he stayed at the Langham Hotel in London, and on 27th February he made his London début under the auspices of the Royal Philharmonic Society at the Queen's Hall. The composer was pleased with the performance, and the *Third Symphony* was received politely. Sibelius's English friends – Granville Bantock, Rosa Newmarch and Henry Wood – were as supportive as ever, but Mrs Newmarch noted that 'he was suffering from a painful throat condition'. On his way back to Finland he stopped off briefly in Berlin and Stockholm, where a correspondent for the newspaper *Svenska Dagbladet* noted that he now appeared much older than before, though retaining his characteristic nervousness, impatience and intensity.

At a guest appearance as Mélisande at the Swedish Theatre two years earlier, the young Norwegian actress Harriet Bosse had been sufficiently impressed by Sibelius's incidental music to *Pelléas et Mélisande* that she recommended him to her former husband August Strindberg to write the music for his play *Swanwhite (Swanevit)*. In 1901 Strindberg had written this play, a symbolist fairy-tale on the theme of love, as an engagement present for Bosse, who was to become his third wife but, by the time of their divorce in 1904, it remained unperformed.

However close his ties with the Finnish nationalist cause had become, Sibelius was keen to collaborate with such a prominent and highly regarded playwright as Strindberg, even if he did not share the Swede's preoccupation with moral values and social hypocrisy – or his Socialist political leanings. Strindberg had nothing against the choice of Sibelius to write music for *Swanwhite* but – to the composer's disappointment – their relationship never progressed beyond the level of businesslike formality. They never met in person, and this first collaboration was also to be their last.

Swanwhite is not one of Strindberg's major works; it is influenced by Mæterlinck's *Princess Maleine* and Rudyard Kipling's story *The Brushwood Boy*. The characters – kings, princes and princesses, wicked stepmothers, with fantasy animals such as a peacock – inhabit a world that seems curiously pallid by comparison with that of *Pelléas et Mélisande*. Much the same can be said of Sibelius's music (JS 189): it is sensitive, charming, poetic and admirably suited for its purpose, but it lacks either the strong characterization of the *Pelléas* score or the vivid local colour of *Belshazzar's Feast*. Nonetheless, there are a number of unifying elements: horn calls, *pizzicati* imitating a harp, scale-based themes and a preponderance of 3/2 or 6/4 rhythms. Sibelius later reworked the *Swanwhite* music into a seven-movement concert suite (Op. 54). He followed his usual practice of refining and combining the original movements, and on this occasion also expanded the orchestra, adding extra wind players, two more horns, castanets and harp (though removing the organ).

The play is set in the middle ages and centres around the 15-year-old Princess Swanwhite, who lives in a castle with her father (the Duke, who for much of the play is away at war) and wicked Stepmother. Though promised to the young king of the neighbouring principality, Swanwhite falls in love instead with his ambassador, a Prince who has been sent to teach her etiquette. The relationship is favoured by the spirits of the lovers' dead mothers, represented by swan figures, but Swanwhite's wicked stepmother tries to obstruct it, and the lovers quarrel. Later the Prince marries Swanwhite's step-sister, but Swanwhite – disguised by a veil – takes her place at the ceremony. As the newly-weds lie in bed, the stepmother surprises them and tries to separate them by force, whereupon the prince goes into hiding. As things turn out, when the neighbouring king arrives he rejects Swanwhite as a bride anyway. Seeing how happy she is, he threatens to burn down the castle and kill the prince who, having emerged from his concealment, promptly runs away. The duke returns and rules in favour of Swanwhite and the prince but, on his way back to her, the prince drowns. She succeeds in bringing him back to life, the stepmother abandons her evil ways, and they all live happily ever after.

It must be conceded that the prince is an unlikely hero. He argues with his beloved, marries the wrong girl, hides from his future mother-in-law, flees when threatened with death, and manages to drown while swimming back to his true love – hardly the epitome of valiant chivalry.

Some of the effects Sibelius employs are simple in the extreme: the first number is just a two-note horn call, summoning the duke to war, and the third and fifth consist of just one chord accompanying a swan (a symbol for Swanwhite's late mother) that flies past. Others are clearly descriptive: the cries of the peacock in the scene when the Prince first arrives are portrayed by a repeated E from the flute and clarinet (No. 2), and the sound of the harp is imitated by string *pizzicati* (No. 4). The smallish ensemble that played at the first performances did not include a harp, although when he later adapted the music for concert use Sibelius added a part for the instrument.

The sixth and seventh numbers accompanied scenes without dialogue. In the extended sixth movement, heard just after the visit of the dead mothers in the guise of swans, much of the musical material is strictly dictated by the requirements of the play, such as the chiming of a clock (triangle) or the song of a robin (flute). The dreamy seventh movement, scored for muted strings, accompanies an imagined dialogue between Swanwhite and the Prince; its melody progresses coyly and hesitantly.

To depict the Prince alone, after his quarrel with Swanwhite, Sibelius writes heavy, solemn music (No. 8) which, with its insistent double-dotted rhythms, sombrely foreshadows *Night Ride and Sunrise*. A slow waltz in E flat minor accompanies the 'trick' wedding of Swanwhite and the prince; a surviving manuscript fragment[2] shows that Sibelius also experimented with this music in a much more impassioned guise, in common time and C sharp minor. The scene where Swanwhite and the Prince are asleep – just before the stepmother bursts in and the Prince hides himself away – is depicted in one of the score's most attractive movements (No. 10), framed by gentle horn signals, in which a graceful violin melody is accompanied by celli *pizzicati*. Stylistically this movement is close to the souvenirs that Sibelius had composed in the 1880s.

The eleventh number, for the scene where the Prince emerges from hiding to be happily reunited with Swanwhite, includes an unmistakable premonition of the slow movement of the *Fifth Symphony*; this movement is entitled 'Swanwhite' in the original score. The twelfth movement is too extended to be a mere sound effect, but too short to have been included in the later concert suite. Faced with the king's threats, Swanwhite summons her father home with a horn call, which is answered as though from afar.

The final two numbers are similar in mood and tone colour – so much so that they were combined into a single movement in the later concert suite. No. 13, for the scene where the dead Prince is brought to Swanwhite, features rising motifs that foreshadow the slow movement of the *Fourth Symphony*, whilst its rhythms anticipate *Tapiola*. The last number is based on a simple, chorale-like idea – an acknowledgement of the play's devout conclusion, where the prince is resurrected and all the characters praise God. Shortly after the first performance, Sibelius (or his copyist Gottfried Bjurha) added an organ/harmonium part to the last two numbers.

Strindberg's *Swanwhite* and Sibelius's score both received their premières at the Swedish Theatre on 8th April, with the Swedish actress Lisa Håkansson in the title role, and won considerable acclaim. With reference to the section depicting the prince alone, 'Bis' Wasenius wrote in *Hufvudstadsbladet* that 'nothing is affected, nothing is over-refined, everything is truly felt, expressed in tones so simple and vibrant that a child would be moved by them, and yet... Sibelius's music is high art'. The favour it found was enduring: 'A circumstance that has moreover contributed greatly to making *Swanwhite* popular in Finland is that Jean Sibelius wrote stylish and beautiful music for the play that further supports and emphasizes the atmosphere of the poetry', wrote Hjalmar Lenning after a performance in 1921.

On 8th May Sibelius made a new arrangement of the patriotic choral song *Isänmaalle* (*To the Fatherland*) for the Turku Working Men's Choir and its conductor Anders Koskinen, who performed it at a song festival in Viipuri the following month. In his haste to deliver the piece Sibelius omitted most of the text and dynamic markings from the manuscript, asking the conductor to fill them in. This arrangement does not differ radically from the very effective male-choir version that Selim Palmgren had produced in 1902, but at least it has the distinction of being by Sibelius himself!

Sibelius's contract with Lienau had promised an improvement in his financial position, but so far the composer had struggled to deliver a sufficient quantity of new music and so, in real terms, his situation was little improved. Therefore a little teaching work during the spring of 1908 was not unwelcome. Of the two pupils that he accepted, one was the young and talented Toivo Kuula, who had already studied the violin (under Viktor Nováček) as well as theory and composition (under Wegelius) at the

Helsinki Music Institute in the years 1900–03 and was now in the middle of a second period of study there, under the guidance of Armas Järnefelt. At the time of his studies under Sibelius, Kuula was on the point of making his breakthrough with two major chamber pieces, the *Violin Sonata in E minor* (1907) and the *Piano Trio in A major* (1908). The trio was premièred on 27th March, and Kuula is known to have discussed the work with Sibelius, who after all had considerable experience of writing such pieces. Like those of Sibelius, Kuula's early chamber works are ambitious and full of promise, with a Romantic style and dark pathos that are close to Sibelius's own early music. The two composers also shared an interest in Finnish folk music, although Kuula went further than Sibelius and did on occasion quote genuine folk material. He produced some impressive vocal and choral pieces, although he never completed a symphony. He might have become a figure of immense stature in Finnish music, but was shot dead in an argument in Viipuri in 1918.

In the autumn Sibelius took on a second pupil, Leevi Madetoja, whose other teachers at the Music Institute were Armas Järnefelt and Erik Furuhjelm. Madetoja hailed from Oulu and much of his music is in the spirit of national Romanticism, with elements of the Finnish folk style and influences from French music as well. He became especially well-known for his choral music, and composed several operas as well as three symphonies (the score of a fourth was apparently stolen from his luggage at a railway station in Paris). Sibelius and Madetoja evidently got on well. Despite the older man's protestations that he was a poor teacher – which in a technical sense he probably was – Madetoja came away feeling greatly enriched by their discussions of general musical and æsthetic matters. 'Don't write any dead notes', Sibelius told him. 'Every note must live.' The resumption of teaching work serves to confirm how well established Sibelius had become in the firmament of Finnish music: in his early forties he was no longer seen as an up-and-coming talent but was himself expected to serve as a mentor to the new rising stars among Finnish composers.

Meanwhile Sibelius was still being troubled by throat pains. The composer's eagerness to consult doctors throughout his life may be put down in part to hypochondria, but in May 1908 his expeditiousness in seeking expert advice probably saved his life. A throat tumour was diagnosed and, on 12th May, he had a preliminary operation in Helsinki, in consequence of which he was advised to go to Berlin and see a leading specialist named Fränkel. A further foreign trip was an unwelcome prospect: for one thing Aino was pregnant, and in any case Sibelius simply could not afford to go. On the other hand he could hardly ignore his doctor's advice and so desperate efforts were made to borrow money. One can understand the lenders' reluctance: a man who was already in debt and who might be dying of cancer scarcely qualified as a low-risk borrower. In the end, however, funds were secured. Before the end of the month Jean and Aino set off for Berlin.

In Berlin, Professor Fränkel examined Sibelius and booked him in for surgery. Sibelius later told Karl Ekman: 'For a couple of weeks in June 1908 I underwent treatment from him that was both trying to my patience and painful. The professor was already an old man, yet he was, nevertheless, determined to remove the cause of the trouble with his own hand. I was obliged to submit to thirteen operations on my throat without any result. Finally the old man gave it up and handed the operation over to his young assistant... He lowered his instrument into my throat and found the bad place. A strong jerk, a shout of triumph: "Jetzt hab' ich's" ("Now I've got it!") – and he pulled out the instrument. I was released from torture.'

For some weeks after the operation Sibelius was unable to speak. The possibility of a recurrence of the tumour could not be excluded, and even he was forced to realize that it would be prudent to give up both alcohol and tobacco. His resolve lasted for almost seven years, a period that Aino later described as the happiest years of her life.

While convalescing in July, and encouraged by Lienau, Sibelius set to work on the concert suite from *Swanwhite*. He did not supply a piano transcription; Lienau suggested that Selim Palmgren should be commissioned to do so, but in the end published four movements in an arrangement by Johannes Doebber.

During the summer Sibelius worked on two songs that must be numbered among the strangest that he ever wrote: *Jubal* and *Teodora*, Op. 35 Nos 1 and 2. In the wake of his throat surgery he turned to a style that, in its expressionist fervour, was as far removed from the 'young Classicism' of the *Third Symphony* as it was from the lush Romanticism of *Svarta rosor* and *Flickan kom ifrån sin älsklings möte*. Everything is reduced to the bare essentials and, as Sibelius himself might have put it, there is not one superfluous note. For now this extreme concentration remained the exception rather than the rule, although within a few years it would become a dominant characteristic of his major works. A setting of Josephson, *Jubal* touches upon many themes that were close to Sibelius's heart: a solitary man amid the beauty of nature, and a swan that even in death has the power to bestow the gift of song and arouse pantheistic wonder. In the wide-ranging, free character of its writing for the voice, *Jubal* can be said to anticipate the later orchestral song *Luonnotar*,[3] although their thematic material is not directly related. Were the vocal line less lyrical, it could easily sound emaciated. Although the piano part is often reduced to a bare minimum, it continually hints at orchestral colour: one can easily imagine a whispering violin tremolo or, in the final stanza, the sigh of violas. Several orchestral arrangements have indeed been made – not by Sibelius himself but, for instance, by Simon Parmet and Ernest Pingoud.

Teodora has much of the orientalism of *Belshazzar's Feast* but is more sinister. Bertel Gripenberg's poem is a feverish declaration of passion for a *femme fatale*, a deceitful oriental empress, and the text is rich in colourful allusions: rustling silk, shining rubies, the full moon's shimmering light, a pleasure garden filled with Eastern roses, and a statue of Astaroth. Threatening, *ostinato* rumblings in the piano part are set against a tonally ambivalent vocal line that at times comes close to the character of *Sprechgesang*. Five years earlier Sibelius had improvised at the piano while the Norwegian actress Johanne Dybwad had recited this poem at a private gathering in Helsinki, and maybe the song captures some of the spirit of that occasion.

Among the surviving sketches for songs from this period, one of the more complete drafts has the text *Och skulle ditt hjärta jag fångat* (*And if I had captured your heart*). This survives in two different drafts,[4] each some twenty bars long. Its precise date and purpose remain unknown.

After the worries associated with Sibelius's throat operations in June, the family must have been pleased to celebrate the birth of another daughter, Margareta, on 10th September.

In the latter part of 1908 Sibelius busied himself with two major musical projects: first the tone poem *Night Ride and Sunrise*, Op. 55, and then the *String Quartet in D minor, 'Voces intimae'*, Op. 56, the opening of which he quoted in a letter to Carpelan on 15th December.

In one sense *Night Ride and Sunrise* stands apart from Sibelius's other tone poems. In these works, from *En saga* to *Pohjola's Daughter* – and even to some extent in the *Lemminkäinen Suite* – he tended to present his musical argument in broad brushstrokes. Here, however, he writes in a manner that is demonstrably pictorial and as episodic as *The Wood-Nymph*, though without the earlier work's literary basis. *Night Ride and Sunrise* was completed in November 1908. On various occasions the composer hinted that the work might have been inspired by trips he had made in Finland. Years later he told his secretary, Santeri Levas, that it was inspired by a sunrise he witnessed during a journey by sledge from Helsinki to Kerava around the turn of the century: 'The whole heavens were a sea of colours that shifted and flowed, producing the most inspiring sight, until it all ended in a growing light.' He said to Jussi Jalas that the impulse came from 'riding from Suojärvi to Värtsilä in the moonlight, through a nocturnal wilderness'. He also mentioned that part of the inspiration came to him just after his honeymoon, in August 1892 in Kuopio. On the other hand, he indicated to Karl Ekman that 'the principal idea of *Night Ride* was conceived during the spring of 1901 in Italy, when I made a trip to Rome in April' – and saw the Colosseum by moonlight (and in a list of works from 1915 he noted 'The motif 1901 – Rome'). He told Rosa Newmarch that the music was 'concerned ... with the inner experiences of an average man riding solitary through the forest gloom; sometimes glad to be alone with Nature; occasionally awe-stricken by the stillness or the strange sounds which break it; but thankful and rejoicing in the daybreak.'

Night Ride and Sunrise falls into two clear sections. The 'night ride' is dominated by an unusually insistent trochaic rhythm, which is eventually combined with a plaintive theme introduced by the woodwind. A transition – in which the latter idea is played with great eloquence by the strings – then leads to the 'sunrise' section, one of Sibelius's most overt portrayals of nature, in which obvious pictorial elements are combined with a calm grandeur that anticipates the *Fifth* and *Seventh Symphonies*. Structurally the work can be said to mirror the finale of the *Third Symphony*: the 'night ride' serves as an extended scherzo section whilst the 'sunrise' corresponds to the hymn-like idea in the symphony.

1909

Sibelius did not conduct the first performance of *Night Ride and Sunrise*: it was given by Alexander Siloti in St Petersburg on 23rd January 1909. The city was no more receptive to Sibelius's music then than it had been when Sibelius himself conducted the *Third Symphony* there just over a year earlier. Critical reaction was hostile, and Siloti later admitted to having made cuts in the score. But Alexander Glazunov, who was present at a rehearsal, told Sibelius that he had liked the piece. In 1894 Glazunov had himself explored a similar theme in a ten-minute orchestral fantasy entitled *Ot mraka ka svetu (From Darkness to Light)*.

In early 1909 Sibelius paid another visit to England, this time staying for a longer period in London where, on 13th February, he conducted *En saga* and *Finlandia* at an afternoon concert in the Queen's Hall with great success. The friends he had made on previous visits now worked hard to pamper him; he attended receptions in his honour where he consorted not only with Henry Wood, Granville Bantock and Rosa Newmarch but was also introduced to various members of the British aristocracy. No doubt the pomp and finery of London's social élite will have prompted comparisons in Sibelius's mind with the gatherings of Pauline Lucca in Vienna back in 1891, although this time he could not risk drinking any alcohol. In an otherwise enthusiastic letter to Aino it is possible to detect a hint of envy: 'Bantock ... has an important [academic] position here. Everyone else gets positions; only I compose and live in my moods and dreams', although, as events in Helsinki more than a decade earlier had shown, Sibelius was not temperamentally suited to the discharge of academic duties. Nonetheless, he was so encouraged by his welcome, both musically and socially, that he decided to stay in London for a while to compose. He checked out of the Langham Hotel and rented a room from a Mrs Dodd at 15, Gloucester Walk in Kensington, but was disturbed by the sounds of an amateur pianist practising in the adjoining house, and moved on to a room a couple of streets away at 15, Gordon Place. There he worked hard on *Voces intimae*.

Two particular encounters during Sibelius's stay in London deserve mention. On 27th February he attended a concert at the Queen's Hall to hear Debussy conduct his *Nocturnes* and *Prélude à l'après-midi d'un faune*, and the two composers exchanged compliments. Sibelius certainly had great respect for Debussy's work, although it is unlikely that Debussy had the opportunity to hear much Sibelius.

Less stimulating was an invitation to the Music Club, where a selection of his smaller pieces was performed and then a dinner was held in his honour. Evidently the music (some songs performed by the Danish soprano Ellen Beck) failed to make much of an impression on the rather fuddy-duddy members of the club, and – to judge from an account of the occasion by Sir Arnold Bax [5] – Sibelius's customary bonhomie for once deserted him: he 'gave one the notion that he had never laughed in his life, and never could... insensible to scruple, tenderness or humour of any sort'.

It was during his stay in London that Sibelius began once more to keep a diary – which he maintained from early 1909 until late 1913, and again from August 1914 until the 1940s (although the last decade or so is sparsely represented). Compared with the often laconic diary entries he had made in his sketchbooks in the last years of the nineteenth century, the new diary is rather more systematic, although it is far from a complete record of his life. He wrote in Swedish, with a few words in other languages when circumstances demanded. We thus have a first-hand account of Sibelius's state of mind when he wrote many of his greatest masterpieces, as well as an accurate means of dating many of his later works: when a work was complete, he underlined it in green ink. The diaries also contain information of a more routine, everyday nature and are prefaced by a summary of his substantial debts. The diary is neither a work of musical analysis nor an autobiography – it is far too fragmented and subjective for that; but it does offer a unique snapshot of Sibelius's rapidly shifting moods.

While in England Sibelius escaped from London and took a trip to Cheltenham – but it was not exclusively a tourist visit, as he conducted *Valse triste* and *Spring Song* there. After leaving London, he spent a few days in Paris before continuing to Berlin. He visited his surgeon, Fränkel, who examined him and found no recurrence of the tumour that had been removed the previous year.

The *String Quartet in D minor, 'Voces intimae'*, Op. 56, was finished on 15th April. He could now deliver another major work to Lienau, and pronounced himself satisfied with the result: 'It is something that induces a smile even at the moment of death', he wrote to Aino. This five-movement work is widely acknowledged as a masterpiece among twentieth-century quartets, and is moreover an undisputed highlight of Sibelius's 'dark, introspective' period. The earliest sketches, however, date from as early as 1899–1903. The sub-title *Voces intimae* comes from a copy of the score that Sibelius dedicated to Axel Carpelan: he wrote the words 'Voces intimae' by the rapt E minor chords at bar 21 of the slow movement.

Thematically, *Voces intimae* is a tautly integrated work that is wholly characteristic of its composer. The first movement is in sonata form – complete with a slow introduction, a meditative dialogue between first violin and cello, from which the main body of the movement grows organically. At times the rather measured pace lends the music a lyrical atmosphere, but the sense of direction and feeling of forward momentum are never lost. The brief second movement, a sort of mini-scherzo, follows without a break. Its thematic material is drawn almost exclusively from the first movement but is seen in a wholly different light: it is transformed into a mercurial flight of fancy that whisks us along at breakneck speed, ghostly and demonic by turns.

The third movement of the quartet represents its emotional core and has much in common with the *Fourth Symphony*. In scale, emotional range and thematic substance this movement closely resembles the slow movement of the symphony, though in fact its opening idea was drawn from the tiny unpublished *Adagio in E major* for piano, JS 13, written in 1907. The main scherzo is placed fourth, with a heavy rhythmic tread that rudely shatters the foregoing rêverie. What starts out as an earthy, pastoral dance soon grows in stature: Sibelian falling fifths, off-beat accents and motoric triplets alternate and combine with the simple opening theme in a richly inventive movement.

The finale has the same irrepressible energy and physical excitement as the tone poem *Lemminkäinen's Return*. In this movement Sibelius reuses a motif from the *Overture in A minor* of 1902. This is another example of the way he 'rescued' valuable motifs from works that had fallen into oblivion. In this case the *Overture* – which had been written in great haste to fill out the programme for the première of the *Second Symphony* – was unpublished and unlikely to be heard again.

The fair copy of the manuscript has a different ending from the printed version – an alternative, lighter-textured and rhythmically simpler version of the final bars in which the tempo rises to *Presto* before a rather abrupt final flourish. Sibelius must have replaced the final pages during the summer as the piece was published in September, even though it had yet to be performed.

In Berlin, during April and May, he completed the set of eight songs, Op. 57. With this opus he discharged his contractual commitment to Lienau. All of the poems are by Ernst Josephson, although they do not form an integrated cycle. As elsewhere in Sibelius's output the textures are sparer than before, the harmonies less opulent, although at times restraint gives way to searingly dramatic utterances. In keeping with this, many of the texts reflect the poet's preoccupation with death and decay. In the first of the set, *Älven och snigeln* (*The River and the Snail*), the off-beat piano motif of regular quavers, insistently rising and falling, impart a musical image of a rushing river. Set against this are characteristic Sibelian triplets in the declamatory vocal part. As the phrase structure remains relatively regular, however, these different rhythmic patterns do not destabilize the music. The second song, *En blomma stod vid vägen* (*A Flower stood by the Wayside*) is simple and poignant, in the manner of a folk-song, with an attractive vein of melancholy. The vocal line at the beginning of No. 3, *Kvarnhjulet* (*The Mill Wheel*), recycles a melodic line from the unfinished choral piece *Listen to the Water Mill* from 1906. The undulating motion in the piano part in the short opening *Con moto* section recalls *Älven och snigeln*, albeit with less syncopation; this time, however, it imitates the mechanical sound of a turning mill wheel. This soon gives way to a broad, eloquent and very Sibelian melody as the singer describes the wheel's old, overgrown and neglected predecessor. At the end of each verse the piano hints at the opening motif at the slower tempo. No. 4, *Maj* (*May*) has something of the Schubertian style found in *Jägargossen* of 1891, with a bright and cheerful character and easy-going 3/4 metre; only briefly does the writing become more expressive and dramatic.

No. 5, *Jag är ett träd* (*The Tree*), is justifiably held in high esteem. It starts with intense, fanfare-like piano flourishes that subside to an expectant, syncopated triplet groundswell. As in another recent Josephson setting, *Jubal*, the vocal line features a rising motif at the start of each verse and has a boldness that almost anticipates *Luonnotar*. In the last verse, the piano's spare, rhythmically simple chords seem to suggest the tree's longing for death. Next comes a ballad, *Hertig Magnus* (*Duke Magnus*), which looks in a wholly different direction. The story tells of a duke who thinks he hears a mermaid calling him from the waves of the Swedish Lake Vättern and throws himself into the water – a tale that had formed the basis of a full-length opera by the Swedish composer Ivar Hallström in 1867. Both the tempo marking of Sibelius's song (*Andantino quasi allegretto*) and the melodic line itself recall the slow movement of the *Third Symphony*. The seventh song, *Vänskapens blomma* (*The Flower of Friendship*) is one of two quite different settings Sibelius made of this poem. The vocal line is stately and dignified, and the firm piano chords of the accompaniment exude an air of confidence. The other setting (JS 215) – evidently written at the same time as Op. 57, although it is musically completely different – remained unpublished until 2005. It is sensitive but rather characterless, and Sibelius no doubt felt that the poem required a sharper profile. No. 8, *Näcken* (*The Watersprite*), inhabits an anguished world of dreams and fantasies. It is an impressive song with a threatening, unpredictable piano part. When the dreamer awakes in the last verse the mood changes abruptly: the capriciousness gives way to a solemn, lugubrious atmosphere.

Adolf Paul made a German translation of the poems for the Op. 57 songs, but Lienau rejected this firmly and instead commissioned Theodor Rehbaum to make new ones for the published edition. 'They should not be translations but rather totally new poems', Lienau wrote to Sibelius, although Paul's versions were in fact used as a reference.

Over the past decade Sibelius had given ample proof of his ability to write effective music for the theatre but so far had not specifically tackled the genre of ballet. He had not consciously avoided the genre – he did, after all, mention a projected ballet to Axel Carpelan in Tvärminne in 1902 – but nor had he gone out of his way to court it. Now the Toronto-born dancer Maude Allan suggested that Sibelius should write a ballet on ancient Egyptian themes. Allan was a colourful character. Some years earlier her brother had been convicted of a particularly unpleasant double murder and hanged. She herself moved to Europe and won extensive fame with her own production *The Vision of Salome* (1906), based on Oscar Wilde's play *Salome*, although it was banned in Munich (and later in England too, after many acclaimed performances) and earned her the reputation of being a dissolute character. This was compounded by the fact that a few years previously she had published *Illustriertes Konversations-Lexikon der Frau*, a sex manual for women. In 1918 she sued the English MP Noel Pemberton-Billing for libel after he had accused her of obscenity and in later years, in the USA, she appeared in several films. For Sibelius, a collaboration could have proved lucrative, but he seems to have been put off by the subject-matter itself and declined the offer.

In his absence Sibelius was not allowed to forget that his long-suffering family back in Finland was still desperately short of money. Aino had written to point out that 'we have here a whole collection of bills and demands and my head is simply spinning. I don't have the energy to look at them. I just think about you all the time and I don't have the will to stop myself crying.' Jean encouraged her to try to borrow money from her brother Eero, and assured her that 'at the end of the month I shall have plenty of money. The songs [Op. 57] are going to be good. I'm very busy with them, and otherwise too my work here is going so well... What have I done? Composed splendidly. And as a result they bombard my home, my sacred home with bills? And harass my wife? No!...' 'Smile! Eat porridge! Try to hold out! Soon the "dark night" will be over.'

After arriving back in Finland in late May, Sibelius wrote a major set of ten piano pieces – Op. 58 – which were rejected by Lienau but duly published by Breitkopf & Härtel. Now that Sibelius had freed himself from Lienau's schedules, he had decided to renew his contacts with Breitkopf and had signed a new contract with the firm's publishing manager, Oskar von Hase, whom he had first met back in 1898. Unusually for Sibelius's piano collections, this one seems to have been conceived and executed in a single burst of activity, and was completed at Ainola on 28th August. It had been almost five years since Sibelius had written a significant new piano work (as opposed to piano transcriptions or accompaniments), and the Op. 58 set clearly shows a development in his musical style. The piano writing itself has matured and sounds less 'orchestral'. The Finnish folk style and the *Kalevala* are rarely to be found; instead, elements of impressionism are combined with 'young classicism'. Despite all the clarity of texture and richness of imaginative vision, however, Op. 58 lacks the degree of concentration and compression, the unswerving focus on the essential that characterizes Sibelius's finest works from the next few years, from the little *Sonatinas* for piano to the mighty *Fourth Symphony*. Sibelius was not unhappy with the end result: 'It seems to me that the technique in these pieces is better than in others of their kind' (diary entry, 28th August). The pieces vary greatly in mood and length and, when heard as a whole, the group thus seems to lack focus and direction. Moreover, some of the thematic material itself is rather conventional and arguably ill-suited to the new expressive means. These factors may help to explain the comparative neglect of Op. 58.

In the first of the set, *Rêverie*, vague, impressionistic motifs gradually yield up a ruminative melody in which an 'S-motif' is a primary element. Gradually ideas of a more determined character emerge and briefly lend their colour to the main theme, but the final bars return to the ethereal mood of the beginning. The 6/4 main theme of the second piece, *Scherzino*, is characteristic of middle-period Sibelius – one might compare it with the song *Hertig Magnus* or even the slow movement of the *Third Symphony* – but the capricious way in which it is treated anticipates Sibelius's piano works from the mid-1920s. The composer claimed that it had 'something of the character of Benvenuto Cellini about it', no doubt an allusion to the colourful life of this sculptor, painter, goldsmith, soldier and musician from Florence (1500–71) rather than to Berlioz's opera.

Next comes *Air varié*, one of the rare examples of variation form in Sibelius's mature output. It is hard to share the enthusiasm of the pianist and composer Ilmari Hannikainen, who described it as the finest of Sibelius's piano pieces. The theme itself, unusually in Op. 58, has hints of the folk style, although the variations themselves, which follow each other seamlessly, are closer to 'young classicism'.

No. 4, *Der Hirt* (*The Shepherd*), is a sort of pastoral dance with 'young classical' overtones, but the compromise between these elements is uneasy. By contrast the fifth of the set, *Des Abends* (*The Evening*), is a pantheistic nature portrait with restrained thematic invention and a sustained, melancholy character. With a complete lack of pretence it conjures up a mood of quiet rapture. The following *Dialogue* is also successful, a vividly characterized question-and-answer session between motifs in the left and right hands (with characteristic syncopated accompaniment) that exhibits a greater sense of humour than many of the other pieces in the set.

No. 7 is a rather lumpy *Tempo di minuetto* which again reflects the influence of 'young classicism'; it is clearly a concert work rather than a piece for dancing. The eighth piece, *Fischerlied* (*Fisher Song*), is one of the most immediately attractive of the Op. 58 pieces – its main theme is not entirely dissimilar to that of the *Third Symphony*'s slow movement. With its barcarole-like 6/4 metre it has a fluency missing from its predecessor. Next comes *Ständchen* (*Serenade*), which opens with a bold, Spanish-sounding flourish and retains something of a theatrical character throughout. Last in the set is *Sommerlied* (*Summer Song*), a noble and grand nature portrait which brings the set to a dignified conclusion.

In July Sibelius started to compose music for the symbolist play *Ödlan* (*The Lizard*) by Mikael Lybeck. Sibelius and Lybeck were old friends, as they had both been members of the Euterpist group a few years earlier, and *Ödlan* was Lybeck's first play. He started work on it in 1907 and it was published in Stockholm a year later. On 25th November Sibelius wrote to the playwright: '*Ödlan* has made a profound impression upon me. It is poetic and has a unique style. I agree to compose the music for you as you request. With the finest of my artistry! Of course!' He decided to confine his contribution to two scenes, scored for a small group of strings placed backstage (Sibelius mentioned nine players – a curious choice as it implies two string players to a part, with all the problems of ensemble and tonal blend that such an ensemble creates – though he agreed to a minimum of six, including a solo violin; a note on the manuscript score suggests that in the end there were seven: two first violins [including soloist], one second, one viola, two cellos and one double bass). One of the motifs in the second movement is also found in a diary entry written on 7th March in London, where Sibelius writes about the *Voces intimae* quartet; this would strengthen the case for regarding *Ödlan* as a chamber piece rather than – as is sometimes claimed – an orchestral work.

The play is a struggle between good and evil for love and power, and exhibits all of the trappings of fairy-tale and exoticism characteristic of Symbolist dramas, as well as their preoccupation with death. Following the death of Count Ottokar, the 23-year-old Alban inherits the family estate. Alban is engaged to an innocent young girl named Elisiv but is courted by his alluring, power-hungry older cousin Adla (= Ödlan, the lizard). Elisiv ultimately dies, and Alban kills Adla.

The first musical number, for the end of Act II Scene 1, is brief, and it is here that the violin solo appears, as Alban plays a violin on stage at this point. Lybeck's stage direction here reads: 'the violin is no longer alone; an orchestra – a full orchestra – has joined in, and the notes pursue each other in an anguished lament that rises to desperation. It is as though the earth would tremble.' Sibelius – fully conscious that he was writing for a small ensemble rather than a full orchestra – had other ideas, and chose to write gentle, sensitive music. As he wrote to Lybeck in August 1909: 'After this enormous dramatic climax one cannot have "descriptive" music. It would be best to maintain the atmosphere you have created. On the other hand, in the dream scene I shall be more expansive.' The music for Act II Scene 3, 'Elisiv's feverish visions', is indeed more extensive, although it is similar in style and is based to some extent on the same thematic material. It starts before the curtain rises and continues throughout the scene but, as it is heard behind the dialogue, it is confined almost exclusively to a supporting function. It is predominantly quiet, with extensive chromatic writing and much syncopation, and at one point – like the *Swanwhite* music the previous year – offers a foretaste of similar writing in *Tapiola*.

In late September Sibelius took a trip that was to prove inspirational. He journeyed with his brother-in-law Eero Järnefelt to the Koli mountain in North Karelia, across the lake from Lieksa where he had spent his honeymoon seventeen years earlier. As one of the highest hills in the region, Koli was by then a popular destination among artists with an interest in the *Kalevala* and Karelianism, and there was already a hotel there to accommodate them. He confided in his diary: 'On Koli! One of the greatest impressions in my life. Planning "La montagne".' This visit to Koli is generally regarded as the impulse for the composition of the *Fourth Symphony*, a work that Sibelius dedicated to Eero Järnefelt – but it cannot be stressed too highly that the finished symphony is in no sense a travelogue. Indeed, motifs associated with mountains are frequently encountered in Sibelius's diaries, both in relation to his music and to his state of mind.

While working on *Ödlan*, which he completed on 15th October, Sibelius found time to compose music for Shakespeare's *Twelfth Night*, Op. 60: he had been asked by the Swedish Theatre to write two of the Clown's songs for a production to be premièred on 12th November. The play was performed in Carl Hagberg's Swedish translation and, in their original form, the songs were with guitar accompaniment. They differ vastly in mood and style. *Kom nu hit, död* (*Come Away, Death*) comes straight from the heart, its lamenting vocal line all the more profound for being so understated. Without degenerating into pastiche or even losing sight of his artistic individuality, Sibelius here manages to conjure up the spirit of Elizabethan music. By contrast *Hållilå, uti storm och i regn* (*Hey, ho, the Wind and the Rain*) is a strophic bagatelle. Shortly after completing the versions with guitar, Sibelius made arrangements of both songs with piano accompaniment. In the case of *Hållilå, uti storm och i regn*, he reduced the number of stanzas from the original five to two.

Whereas the *Twelfth Night* songs used a Swedish translation of Shakespeare's text, *Hymn to Thaïs* is a setting of an original English text by the Swedish-speaking Finnish businessman Arthur Borgström, and was a written as gesture of gratitude, as he had provided Sibelius with pecuniary help. Borgström sent Sibelius several versions of the poem, which had not yet been published, the last of which arrived in mid-September. It is a noble and powerful song even if Sibelius, whose English was at the time rather limited, sometimes struggles with the text.

Also from this period is the Christmas song *Giv mig ej glans, ej guld, ej prakt* (*Give me no Splendour, Gold or Pomp*), Op. 1 No. 4, to words by Zachris Topelius. It was probably composed for the Christmas albums *December, Jultidning för det Svenska Finland* (in Swedish) and *Sampo, Joululehti Suomen Kansalle* (in Finnish). A simple strophic song, originally for voice and piano, this has become one of Sibelius's best-loved compositions and is nowadays heard in innumerable arrangements – including several made by Sibelius himself in his old age. The theme itself is a derivation of a melody that he had used in the song *Segelfahrt* in 1899.

As the year drew to a close, Sibelius was hard at work on *In memoriam*, Op. 59, a large-scale funeral march for orchestra. He told Karl Ekman that the idea for the piece had come to him in Berlin in 1905, and mentioned to his daughter Eva that the piece was written in memory of Eugen Schauman. It is likely, therefore, that *In memoriam* may derive in part from the abandoned *Marjatta* oratorio, or from the proposed requiem for Schauman, or both. It should not be forgotten that Sibelius himself, in the aftermath of his throat operations, was still very susceptible to doubts about his own state of health. Whomever he had in mind, however, he chose as his models Beethoven ('*Eroica*') and Wagner (*Götterdämmerung*) rather than following the example of Robert Kajanus, who in his *Kullervo's Funeral March* had combined these influences with Finnish folk music. In the original version there is a short introduction, a wisp of melody from the violins and violas, answered by a few lugubrious chords, from which the main theme gradually emerges like the approach of a distant cortège. The march is in sonata form and does not hesitate to make effective use of the clichés of the funeral march genre: rattling percussion, waves of chromatic writing. He completed the piece – or so he thought – at home on 14th December, and sent it away to Breitkopf, who duly set to work on the score and parts.

It is worth considering whether or not *In memoriam* might contain any specific references to Schauman's assassination of Bobrikov. Bach might have filled such a piece with symbolic references, but Sibelius tended to portray historical characters and events with broader brushstrokes, as for instance in the *Press Celebrations Music* a decade earlier. Nevertheless, one could interpret the bleak opening bars as a symbol of Finland's repression (it distils an atmosphere similar to the opening of the tableau representing *The Great Hostility* in the *Press Celebrations Music*), the rising main theme as Bobrikov ceremonially arriving at the Senate House and ascending the steps, and the descending chromatic line followed by three 'knocking' quavers in the development as Schauman descending the stairs and firing the fateful three shots at the Governor-General.

Undeterred by Sibelius's rejection of her idea for an Oriental ballet a few months earlier, Maude Allan now proposed another joint venture – a ballet to be called *The Bear's Death Ceremonies*. Sibelius's debts were spiralling, but he had no real desire to commit himself to Allan's project. In December Axel Carpelan came to his rescue: together with his cousin Tor, Carpelan approached wealthy patrons, among them the Turku businessman Magnus Dahlström, and money soon started to arrive; further funds were to arrive during the spring. Sibelius thus felt able to turn down the ballet commission ('insufficient earnings for a major expenditure of time') and a lottery composition (mentioned in his diary on 29th November, though nothing more is known of the project), and turn his thoughts to the *Fourth Symphony*. Not for the first time, Sibelius appreciated not only Carpelan's altruism but also the intuition that led him to intervene just when mundane pecuniary considerations were threatening to deflect him from his chosen artistic course. 'I admire this fine talent. His capacity for judgement is exceptional', Sibelius wrote in his diary on 30th November.

CHAPTER 10

THE FOURTH SYMPHONY
AND EXPRESSIONISM: 1910–1912

1910

Nonetheless, the *Fourth Symphony* was not the first work to occupy Sibelius in 1910: a short, impressionistic orchestral tone poem, *The Dryad*, Op. 45 No. 1, was completed on 5th February. The title suggests the world of Greek mythology, to which Sibelius had already made reference in *Pan and Echo*. A dryad is a nymph that inhabits a forest or an oak tree, but unlike Sibelius's earlier work on such a theme – *The Wood-Nymph* – this is an aphoristic piece, with frequent changes of pulse and direction from the gentlest of atmospheric whispers to wild dance-like motifs. Its cool, other-worldly atmosphere has much in common with the *Oak Tree* movement from the later incidental music to *The Tempest*. There is no disguising the similarity between some of its motifs and ideas in the forthcoming *Fourth Symphony*. Lienau refused the piece but it was accepted by Breitkopf, and Sibelius wasted no time in preparing an effective piano arrangement.

As well as working on new pieces, Sibelius made a list of no fewer than eighteen earlier works that he was considering for revision. Some of them – the *Impromptu*, Op. 19, the cantata *The Origin of Fire* and movements from the *Press Celebrations Music* – were indeed soon to be reworked; others (the unpublished *Lemminkäinen* movements) had to wait much longer, but most (among them the second, fourth and fifth movements of *Kullervo*, and the *Piano Quintet*) would remain untouched.

It was not long before the proofs for *In memoriam* arrived at Ainola, and Sibelius immediately began to doubt the merits of the piece. In particular he felt that the instrumentation was poor. On 18th February he sent a telegram to Breitkopf, asking them not to print the work as he wished to make 'small modifications'; a week later he sent them a letter revealing that he wanted to give the entire piece 'a new form' and offering to recompense the publisher for the wasted work. Breitkopf replied that 'we very much liked the original version of the work' but agreed to destroy the plates. During the first weeks of March Sibelius set about the revision; he excised the atmospheric opening bars, softened the rhythmic contour of the main theme by removing the dotted rhythm from the up-beat, and adjusted the orchestration throughout. The final version was sent away on 20th March, and in May Sibelius wrote to Breitkopf: 'As for the funeral march, after much experimentation and playing through with the orchestra, I have now decided in favour of the new version. Compositionally and "melodically" it is, so to speak, quite like the earlier one – and so your favourable verdict is unaffected – but the instrumentation is now much more flexible and of a more noble character. This is my *firm* conviction.'

On 6th April Lybeck's play *Ödlan* received its première at the Swedish Theatre, with Sibelius himself directing the string ensemble. The reviews were complimentary about the music: Julius Hirn in *Nya Pressen* wrote: 'Mikael Lybeck has written how he imagined the music, and the master has understood him better than anybody. With beauty and nobility this melodramatic tone poem rises up ... reflecting the longing for the infinite and the inconceivable that is hidden in Alban's nervous, agitated fantasies.' Nevertheless, the play disappeared after a few performances. Quite how highly the composer regarded the score is questionable. In a letter from the previous November he had told Carpelan that it was 'one of the most exquisite works that I have written', but otherwise he seems to have recognized that it was not suited to concert performance. Professor Paul Klengel at Breitkopf & Härtel had already noted that 'the incidental music to *Ödlan* ... is conceived in a proximate relationship with the action on stage; on its own it will scarcely be comprehensible and will awaken no interest', a conclusion that Sibelius had in any case reached on his own. Shortly after completing the score he had written to Breitkopf: 'If, however, I turn the music into a fantasia or something of the kind, I shall be pleased to send you the manuscript,' and, a few days later, 'As for the music to *Ödlan*, I plan to write variations – symphonic ones – on the final theme. It is excellently suited to such an application.' But these plans came to nothing, and as late as 1936 Sibelius responded to an enquiry from Edition Wilhelm Hansen: 'As I said before, the music for *Ödlan* is impossible for anything except the theatre.'

During the spring Sibelius set about overhauling the *Impromptu* for women's voices and orchestra, adding a new introduction – with words from a different part of the Rydberg's poem – and a more effective concert ending. He also slimmed down the scoring, omitting trumpets and some of what had been a rich array of percussion instruments. As with the original score, he prepared a version with piano – it would be unjust to call it a piano reduction. The piano writing is in places a very free adaptation of the orchestral part, very much in Sibelius's middle-period piano style. 'The piano score is prepared in such a way that it can be used in performance if there is no orchestra available', he wrote to Breitkopf on 19th April. For now, however, the revised version remained unperformed. He also sent away a (presumably) revised version of *The Origin of Fire*, but that work had not yet attained its definitive form.

Voces intimae had been published the previous September but did not receive its first performance until 25th April 1910, at the Helsinki Music Institute. The players were Viktor Nováček and Sulo Hurstinen, violins, Carl Lindelöf, viola, and Bror Persfelt, cello. Sibelius did not attend the concert, though he had been present at some of the rehearsals. Nováček apparently had more success with this piece than with the *Violin Concerto*, as the reviews were favourable – in the words of *Helsingin Sanomat* (a newspaper that had emerged in 1905 as the direct successor to *Päivälehti*) 'without doubt one of the most brilliant contributions to the genre'.

A short trip to Viipuri in May offered Sibelius the opportunity to meet up again with Rosa Newmarch; together they saw the Imatra waterfalls, and she subsequently spent several weeks in Helsinki, with the composer as her guide to the city's sights. During this period Mrs Newmarch grew very fond of the entire Sibelius family, and she also started to collaborate with the composer in translating some of his song texts into English. 'He would play his songs to me; then suddenly, getting up, he would walk up and down the room and declaim the words in a rough but vivid translation, generally into German. I, catching their meaning, in breathless haste would put them down in English in a sort of impromptu shorthand to be worked up later. Some of them, I believe, have kept a little of the spirit infused into them by Sibelius himself.'

At the beginning of June plans were being laid for a forthcoming visit to Kristiania (Oslo); Sibelius envisaged a concert in which he could conduct his *Fourth Symphony* – if it was ready in time. On 9th June he wrote a revealing diary entry on the subject of orchestration: 'The "epic" in instrumentation. The "narrative". Don't interrupt the mood earlier than necessary. When scoring a work one should in principle beware of leaving a passage without string instruments. It will sound "ragged" – The different quality of the winds in different countries and cities, differently sized string sections and so on mean that the relationship between strings and wind is uncertain, variable and dependent on the circumstances. The sound is largely determined by the purely musical "setting", its polyphony and so on. Especially where dynamics are concerned.' He goes on to make a number of practical remarks that address the limitations of wind players in provincial orchestras, evidently based on his own experiences as a conductor.

In July Sibelius finished a set of songs that is in many ways a vocal counterpart to the Op. 58 piano pieces. The eight songs that make up Op. 61 – with words by some of his favourite poets, Tavaststjerna, Rydberg, Runeberg and Gripenberg – are among the least performed of Sibelius's works in the genre, perhaps because of their often cryptic musical style and lack of immediate audience appeal. Unusually, several of the numbers revisit musical material from earlier songs. For instance the first of the set, *Långsamt som kvällskyn* (*Slowly as the Evening Sky*) – a psychologically probing and deeply moving song to words by Tavaststjerna – draws on an earlier orchestral song, the *Serenade* (1895) to a poem by Stagnelius, which Sibelius had in fact considered revising a few months earlier. Instead of keeping the old text and orchestration, however, he adapted its material to a new context of evocative nature imagery. With its haunting melodic line and spare piano accompaniment, *Långsamt som kvällskyn* is one of the finest of Sibelius's middle-period songs.

The other songs in Op. 61 are far less appealing. The impression they convey is that Sibelius, in his haste to send them away to Breitkopf, was less rigorous than usual when it came to the selection and refinement of the musical ideas. Despite being a setting of Rydberg the second song, *Vattenplask* (*Lapping Waters*) has none of the pantheistic grandeur of *Höstkväll* or *På verandan vid havet*: it relies far too heavily on its natural-istic piano accompaniment, the vocal line itself being cumbersome and ordinary.

The next four songs are all settings of Tavaststjerna. No. 3, *När jag drömmer* (*When I dream*) is more characteristic, but the song does not really come to life until the third of its five verses, when the piano – at first confined to isolated notes or flourishes – starts to play a more active part in the proceedings. Beginning with a dactylic motif in the piano that recalls the finale of the *Violin Concerto*, the fourth of the set, *Romeo*, sets out in a more lighthearted vein. The poem alludes to the well-known image of Romeo serenading Juliet on the balcony. Like the song *Illalle* from 1898, it consists largely of slight variations on a single phrase, but with a greater emphasis on rhythm. No. 5, *Romans* (*Romance*), develops a motif from the previous year's *Hymn to Thaïs* in a declamatory style. That this quotation was intentional is indicated by the fact that Sibelius dedicated the *Romans* to Arthur Borgström, who wrote the text for *Hymn to Thaïs*. The sixth song, *Dolce far niente*, starts promisingly with a little piano fanfare that is transformed into an indolent tune by the singer. Unfortunately the melody soon loses direction. Sibelius worked on two more Tavaststjerna poems at this time – *Skuggornas ö* (*The Isle of Shadows*) and *Kärleks rim*

(*The Rhyme of Love*), presumably with a view to incorporating them into Op. 61, but neither setting was completed.

The seventh song, *Fåfäng önskan* (*Idle Wishes*), has words by Runeberg. Here the piano's incessant, virtuosic hemidemisemiquavers lend a restless agitation to the slow-moving, anguished vocal line. Sibelius himself feared that the song might be too Chopinesque: 'Do such broken chords and inherited modulations actually belong to anybody? One can easily change that sort of thing to the point where it is unrecognizable – especially concerning a "resemblance to Chopin". But is it not more dignified simply to acknowledge how one felt and thought, without reflection but with inspiration. – When (like you, Ego) one is forced to earn a crust with the "pen", it can't always be like nine-year-old wine.'[1] A much less threatening atmosphere is created in the last song in the group, a setting of Gripenberg's *Vårtagen* (*The Spell of Springtide*). Breitkopf & Härtel arranged for German and English translations to be made and published the entire Op. 61 collection without delay.

As soon as the songs were ready, Sibelius seems to have set off for the island of Järvö in Kyrkslätt (Kirkkonummi), south-west of Helsinki. The surroundings there were similar to those in Korpo, where he had spent the summers of 1886 and 1887, but this time he could only spare a few days to recharge his creative batteries – by swimming and making plans to redecorate Ainola. During the autumn, work continued on 'forging'[2] the *Fourth Symphony* – with the usual false starts and changes of plan that were an intrinsic part of his working method. There were plenty of distractions. He was holding discussions with the building committee for a new church designed by Lars Sonck in Helsinki's Kallio (Berghäll) district; the idea was for Sibelius to provide a melody for the church bells. He was also doing his best to support his friend Arthur Borgström's attempt to have some poetry published. In addition, he had been asked to provide a song for schoolchildren to commemorate the 100th anniversary of the birth of Uno Cygnaeus, 'the founder of the primary school in Finland' and, like Sibelius, a native of Hämeenlinna. It is unlikely, though, that a sixteen-bar march in C major for two-part children's choir will have cost the composer too many sleepless nights. With the title *Kansakoululaisten marssi* (*March of the Primary School Children*), JS 103, and an anonymous text (the author used the pseudonym 'Onnen Pekka'), it was performed in various Finnish schools on 10th October.

Sibelius had started to harbour doubts about *The Origin of Fire*, and asked Breitkopf to return the score. When it arrived in late September, he interrupted work on the finale of the *Fourth Symphony* to revise the cantata. In fact work on the symphony would have been interrupted anyway, as Sibelius had to conduct in Kristiania. The concert was held on 8th October at Gamle Logens Store Sal on Grev Wedels plass, one of the city's foremost cultural venues. As the symphony was not ready, *In memoriam* and *The Dryad* were now given their premières, alongside *Night Ride and Sunrise*, selections from *Swanwhite* and the *Second Symphony* (*Valse triste* was played as an encore). The concert received mixed reviews although the audience was well satisfied, as was Sibelius himself.

He then headed for Berlin, where he spent the rest of the month with Adolf Paul, although his diary entries display a degree of impatience both with his host and with the city in general. On 19th October he mentions '"carousing" in the evening' and the following day remarks 'Hard to keep feeling young without wine etc.'. One wonders if he had suffered a temporary lapse in what he called 'this frightful struggle against wine and cigars'. He heard new works by such composers as Rachmaninov ('a sense of sonority, culture, but it seems tame'), Arensky ('good, naïve'), Reger ('national, German, ornate and long-winded but, because of its German quality, good') and Debussy ('refined but, as I see it, "small"') in concert, visited Busoni, completed the revision of *The Origin of Fire* for Breitkopf and continued work on the *Fourth Symphony*.

In many ways the revision of *The Origin of Fire* is quite typical of Sibelius's method: a process of condensation and refinement. Fortunately he left the basic material intact: the orchestral introduction with its simple yet potent evocation of the total darkness of endless night, the expressive baritone solo – now less episodic, progressing in a single, concentrated span, although unfortunately also less colourful – and the robust choral section are clearly recognizable. A new transition between the solo and choral sections gives the choir a pitch reference for its exposed first entry, and the final chords of the piece have more character and impact. While revising the cantata Sibelius also prepared a version with piano accompaniment.

Back at home in early November, Sibelius realized that a further obstacle stood in the way of work on the symphony. This was an orchestral song for Aino Ackté, a setting of Edgar Allan Poe's poem *The Raven*, to be performed on a forthcoming tour in central Europe. He met up with Ackté in Helsinki on 8th November but it is clear from his diary that his plans for the song were vague: 'I'm curious to know what the result of our plans will be. I must produce a good piece of work.' A few days later he did attempt to work diligently on the song but had to admit that 'All my ideas are in a state of flux' and 'I have my doubts about *The Raven*.' Matters were not made any easier when his wife fell ill; on 19th November Sibelius took her to hospital in Helsinki, where he paid her frequent visits. Meanwhile Ackté increased the pressure by trying to confirm dates for the promised

European tour (not unreasonably, as it was only three months away). By December Sibelius had realized that the tour plans were hindering progress on the symphony. He noted in his diary: 'Working on *The Raven*... A pity that Symph IV is not coming to fruition' and, without further delay, stopped work on the song – much to the fury of Aino Ackté.

As had happened previously with Willy Burmester in the case of the *Violin Concerto*, Sibelius risked alienating a close ally and champion. This time, however, the consequences were less far-reaching. Perhaps Sibelius handled Ackté with more tact, or perhaps their relationship was already secure enough to survive such a crisis. At any rate, she continued to perform Sibelius's music and would soon receive ample compensation in the form of the orchestral song *Luonnotar*. As it turned out, the time Sibelius had devoted to *The Raven* was not entirely wasted: some of the material was used in the finale of the *Fourth Symphony*. By the end of December he could feel more confident, and wrote in his diary: 'The "big one", which I dimly perceived a year ago, is taking shape.'

1911

In the new year, however, work on the symphony slowed down. Sibelius spent several weeks at the beginning of January in Helsinki (staying first with a musician friend, Adolf Berlin, and later at a hotel), where he worked on two more orchestral movements for a revised version of Arvid Järnefelt's *Kuolema* at the National Theatre. Among other distractions the proposed bell melody for Kallio church had not yet been finalized, and on 18th January Sibelius suggested using the concluding bars of the *Second Symphony* for this purpose.

His next major undertaking, however, was a concert tour that began with a visit to Gothenburg on the west coast of Sweden in early February; strangely enough, he had not conducted his own music in Sweden previously. Gothenburg was a good place to start, as the town's symphony orchestra was then conducted by Wilhelm Stenhammar, who had developed a profound admiration for Sibelius and his music. Sibelius conducted two concerts, including such works as *Pohjola's Daughter* and the *Third Symphony*. The next stop was Latvia, where he conducted the recently founded Rīga Symphony Orchestra both in Rīga and in Mitau (Jelgava).

After the concert tour, Sibelius put the finishing touches to the two new *Kuolema* pieces, though in fact neither of them was newly composed. According to Kari Kilpeläinen, the exquisite *Rondino der Liebenden* (*Rondino of the Lovers*, later renamed *Canzonetta*), Op. 62a, is a slightly revised version of a piece written in 1906 – which no doubt explains its similarity of mood with the slow movement of the *Third Symphony*. The other piece, *Valssi-intermezzo* (*Waltz Intermezzo*, later renamed *Valse romantique*), Op. 62b, has its origins in sketches from the turn of the century. The *Valse romantique* made much less of an impression and after the rehearsals even Sibelius had to admit in his diary: 'the *Canzonetta* is charming. The *Valse* is all right but hardly a repertoire piece.' They were first performed when the play opened on 8th March 1911, conducted by Alexei Apostol; Sibelius noted afterwards that the music was 'a fiasco... inaudible'. Järnefelt's revisions to the play – especially to the second act – had rendered the second, third and fourth numbers of Sibelius's original score redundant and, apart from the two new pieces, only *Valse triste* (in its revised form) was now performed in the theatre. Breitkopf immediately set about publishing the new additions, plainly hoping to repeat the commercial success of *Valse triste*: 'The charming and readily comprehensible *Valse romantique* will be a pendant to *Valse triste*. We also very much like the beautiful, expressive melody of the *Canzonetta*.'

With the *Kuolema* pieces out of the way, Sibelius realized that he could no longer put off the new symphony: 'now or never', as he himself put it on 28th February. After a mighty struggle, he put the finishing touches to the work on 2nd April. (It must have been virtually complete before that, however, to allow time for the preparation of the orchestral parts and rehearsal.) He conducted the first performance of his *Symphony No. 4 in A minor*, Op. 63, at a concert in the University Hall the very next day. The entire concert consisted of relatively recent works: the first half contained *In memoriam*, the *Canzonetta*, *The Dryad* and *Night Ride and Sunrise*, and the symphony was heard after the interval. The arrival of a new Sibelius symphony was a major event and the evening was carefully staged: the YL choir was present to sing *Isänmaalle* and Pacius's *Suomis sång*, and Heikki Klemetti had prepared a congratulatory speech. But the audience's reaction was one of bewilderment, and the critics were no less perplexed. Klemetti himself wrote in *Säveletär* that: 'Everything seems strange. Curious, transparent figures float here and there, speaking to us in a language whose meaning we cannot grasp.' Evert Katila, writing a little later in *Uusi Suometar*, called the piece 'a sharp protest against the general trend in modern music ... the most modern of the modern.' As with the *Second Symphony*, some critics were keen to attach a programme to the work: in this case it was Karl Fredrik 'Bis' Wasenius, who claimed in *Hufvudstadsbladet* that 'the theme of the symphony is a journey to the celebrated mountain Koli near Lake Pielinen' and went on to provide a detailed programme – one that was robustly denied by Sibelius.

Sibelius had, of course, taken an enormous risk in writing such an uncompromising symphony as the *Fourth*. Nothing in his earlier music – not even the slow movement of *Voces intimae* – had given any clue that his next symphony would be so stubborn, or would yield so little to popular expectations and taste. His iconic status among his countrymen was assured, but with this work he offered nothing to raise the nation's morale. He could hardly have been surprised that it was greeted with a lack of comprehension – but at least it was received politely, despite Aino's later recollection that 'people avoided our eyes, shook their heads; their smiles were embarrassed, furtive or ironic. Not many people came backstage to the artists' room to pay their respects.' When the entire concert was repeated two days later, the hall was sold out.

Jussi Jalas underlined the symphony's pivotal position within Sibelius's output when he wrote in 1988: 'For us Finnish musicians, Sibelius's *Fourth Symphony* is like the Bible. We approach it with great respect and devotion. In this work Sibelius had seen the unfathomable tragedy of life's inconsistency, and given it expression boldly, by new means and in a new musical language.'[3]

Sibelius wrote to Rosa Newmarch that the *Fourth Symphony* was 'a protest against present-day music. It has nothing, absolutely nothing of the circus about it.' Certainly it is an enigmatic and challenging work, one in which we find a foretaste of Sibelius's late symphonic style where form and content are inextricably linked. Gone is the Romanticism of the first two symphonies and the Classical clarity of the *Third*; instead Sibelius wrote in a style that is resolute in its austerity, concision and concentration. Although he scored the work for full orchestra, he used it in a very economical fashion that is often compared to chamber music. The symphony is dominated by the interval of a tritone, *diabolus in musica*, first heard in the brooding opening notes, C–D–F sharp–E, which the composer himself said should sound 'as harsh as fate'. Sibelius is happy to follow formal conventions if they accord with the inner demands of his themes, but refuses to be a slave to traditional rules – and so, for the first time in one of his symphonies, the opening movement is slow, although it does retain a recognizable sonata-form structure. Its main theme is first heard from a solo cello, which establishes the key of A minor (in one sketch this theme is labelled 'Marche élégiaque'); the second group, which centres on F sharp, begins with forceful brass chords. The entire movement – indeed the entire symphony – is dominated by ideas that are motivically and harmonically closely related, and so, despite great variety in orchestration and tempo, everything in the symphony is interconnected. The development section begins with some of Sibelius's most tonally ambiguous music, followed by rising woodwind figures over a scurrying string backdrop, and the recapitulation is foreshortened, starting with high violins and the brass chords of the second group.

The scherzo, *Allegro molto vivace*, is placed second. Its playful oboe melody in 3/4 is answered by superimposed rising fourths from the violins, anticipating the opening horn signals of the *Fifth Symphony*. The music, almost like a quick waltz scene, hustles through several episodes of varying character, but the apparent civility of the entire scherzo section is exposed as a brutal fraud when the tempo is halved and the 'waltz scene' is nightmarishly transformed into a savage, desolate landscape, *Doppio più lento*. Was it a waltz at all? Sibelius was, after all, fascinated by waltzes and other dance music but – unlike Tchaikovsky – he never overtly used one in his symphonies. Moreover, not since the *Scène de ballet* of 1891 had he written a dance movement of such ambiguous, perplexing character. And what is the precise relationship of the two halves of the movement – scherzo and trio, scherzo and epilogue? The closing bars could well be seen as a distorted, miniature reprise of the scherzo material; but Sibelius gives us no clear answer. Such riddles are an essential part of the *Fourth Symphony*.

At the core of the symphony lies the third movement, *Il tempo largo*. This a good example of Sibelius using formal processes which are determined by the inner essence of the themes to such an extent that attempts at structural analysis are virtually redundant. Overall, the music works its way towards a broad statement of an ascending chorale-like theme, first heard as a two-bar phrase on the horns. The melodic contours and rhythms of this movement are closely related to the slow movement of *Voces intimae*, and indeed the main themes of both movements were originally sketched on the same piece of paper, scored for quartet.

Formally the finale, *Allegro*, is a sonata rondo. It starts with a rising motif, bright and carefree, derived from a similar idea near the end of the slow movement. The rising woodwind figures of the second group (in E flat, against A major in the strings – an uneasy juxtaposition of keys a tritone apart in place of the more conventional tonic/dominant relationship) are closely related to a motif from the first movement's development. These gain a pendant, a descending seventh; both ideas recur in the coda. Although Sibelius continues to use the orchestra sparingly, with solo contributions for cello, violin and clarinet, the movement does contain a part for glockenspiel.[4] Initially it plays an 'S-motif' without the first note, and later in the movement it plays the complete motif. A horn chorale theme, its rocking *ostinato* string accompaniment (which almost sounds like rapid, regular breathing) and the following syncopated chromatic passage all originate in sketches for the abandoned orchestral song, *The Raven*, and these ideas play an important part in the final climax – and also in the bleak coda, where motifs from the second group reflect upon the conflict that is now past. The symphony ends not in tragedy but in resignation, with repeated *mezzoforte* A minor chords. A year after completing the symphony, Sibelius noted in his diary: 'A reflection concerning the *Fourth Symphony*! The middle theme in the last movement could – when taken up by the horns – have been in double note values. That would have done more justice to the character of the horn. But in that case the whole thing would have taken on a different shape.'

A few days after the première of the symphony, Sibelius's relationship with Axel Carpelan turned briefly sour. A slight misunderstanding about a concert ticket wounded Carpelan's pride and led to a rift between the two men that was resolved only after a hasty exchange of letters in which Sibelius apologized unreservedly and Carpelan relieved himself of some long-standing grievances.

On 5th November 1910, while working on the *Fourth Symphony*, Sibelius had written in his diary that 'a symphony is not just a "composition" in the ordinary sense of the word. It is more of an inner confession at a given stage of one's life.' Having made his 'inner confession', though, where could he turn next? For a start he agreed to write music for Adolf Paul's play *Die Sprache der Vögel* (*The Language of the Birds*). Evidently he was unfamiliar with the play but was keen to help out his old friend. 'I have no idea how much I'll have to compose, but I'm keen to be of assistance to Paul', he wrote to Breitkopf.

It took some six weeks to make a fair copy of the symphony for publication. In the process he made some changes, the most important of which were the rescoring of the second half of the scherzo (which grew in length by 20 bars) and a reworking of some passages in the finale (which gained twelve bars).[5] Meanwhile an opera libretto turned up, written by Georg Boldemann, a German Sibelius enthusiast who lived in Copenhagen. Apparently the text was a conventional effort set in eighteenth-century France, but Sibelius did at least take a serious look at it before rejecting the project. He also needed to attend to practical matters. Aino was pregnant again and the family was running out of space at Ainola. The original architect, Lars Sonck, was consulted about the construction of an upper floor, and the builders soon started work on the first major renovation of the house. It is thus hardly surprising that Sibelius had little opportunity or inclination to concentrate on new compositions at this time. A visit to his sister Linda at the Pitkäniemi mental hospital in Nokia did little to cheer him up; he accompanied her to Kerava but noted in his diary on 8th June: 'Terrible depression. In her fate I see my own! – Visit her once in a while but never let her visit my own home. Hard words.' Aino gave birth to another daughter, Heidi, on 20th June, and the family enjoyed a spell of glorious midsummer weather.

On 4th August the music for *Die Sprache der Vögel* was ready. In the end Sibelius composed only one musical number, a *Wedding March* for orchestra, JS 62. Despite its title the piece is not really march-like in character, nor does it offer much scope to comply with the score's indication *con grandezza*. The scoring is unusual in that it omits both bassoons and horns but includes trumpets, trombones and numerous percussion instruments. The march was not used in any stage production that we know of, and probably remained unplayed until Esa-Pekka Salonen and the Finnish Radio Symphony Orchestra gave a studio performance on 21st September 1983.

Sibelius's eldest daughter Eva had left school at the end of the spring term, and during the summer became engaged to Arvi Paloheimo. The Paloheimo family lived at Kallio-Kuninkala, very close to Ainola, and Eva and Arvi had been friends for some years already. As an engagement present Sibelius wrote an *Étude* for piano, Op. 76 No. 2 – a charming and unpretentious little piece that is as far removed from the rigours of the *Fourth Symphony* as one could possibly imagine.

For the new, enlarged Ainola the Sibelius family decided that another servant was necessary, and their choice fell upon the eighteen-year-old Aino Kari, who was responsible for cleaning, washing and other household duties. Like the cook Helmi Vainikainen, Kari was to become part of the family, remaining at Ainola for the rest of her working life and retiring in 1968.

The refurbishments at Ainola were nearing completion, and Sibelius took a break from furnishing the new rooms by composing a short piece for women's choir to words by Walter von Konow. Despite its grand title of *Cantata*, this is an unassuming work (JS 107) designed for performance at the fiftieth anniversary celebrations of a girls' school (Heurlinska skolan) in Turku, where von Konow had taught history since the turn of the century.

In September Sibelius could move into a new study upstairs, where at last he could start work on a project that had been on his mind for almost two years: the fashioning of an orchestral suite – which he initially referred to as 'Suite caractéristique' – from the *Press Celebrations Music* of 1899. From the original score he selected and reworked the first, fourth and third tableaux respectively as *All'Overtura*, *Scena* and *Festivo*. The revisions were very successful: Sibelius refined the orchestration and removed some of the rough edges of the tableau versions without sacrificing the colourful, rather chivalrous tone of the originals. The suite, which was completed on 27th September, was eventually christened *Scènes historiques*, Op. 25, and Sibelius insisted in a letter to Breitkopf that it 'must be printed with the number I, as it is my intention to continue: a second suite, *Scènes historiques II*'.

At the end of September he managed to sell two little pieces for violin and piano, the *Romance in B minor* and *Perpetuum mobile* from 1890–91, to the publisher Apostol in Helsinki. It was unusual in the extreme for the mature Sibelius to exhume such early works; although a few of his early pieces were still listed for revision, most of them had by now been quietly forgotten. Neither the *Romance* nor the *Perpetuum mobile* differs greatly from his other violin pieces from that period, save in one important respect: when they were first composed, both had been published in journals, and they were thus to some extent already in the public domain. Before sending them off to Apostol, however, Sibelius subjected both pieces to a significant revision. In the case of the *Perpetuum mobile* this amounted to a recomposition based on the same thematic material (in which, as in the *Fourth Symphony*, the tritone is prominent). As the old title would have been inappropriate for the revised version, it was renamed *Epilogue*, although in deference to the works' origins an early opus number, 2, was assigned.

It may have been the sale of the two Op. 2 violin pieces to Apostol that suggested to Sibelius a white lie that he used to avoid an embarrassing conflict of interests. A new song, *Arioso*, Op. 3 (with words from Runeberg's poem *Flickans årstider* [*The Maiden's Seasons*]), was completed on 17th October and sold to Apostol the following day. To judge from Sibelius's diary, he worked on the version with string orchestra and the one with piano accompaniment at the same time. Apostol in turn offered the song to Breitkopf, who promptly wrote reprimandingly to Sibelius: 'We should like to know whether this is one of your older compositions. If not, you would surely have approached us directly, as you have been doing for some time, to our great pleasure.' Sibelius hurriedly replied that '*Arioso* is an old composition, written before 1890.' In fact he had planned to set this poem early in his career, and a sketch for the beginning has survived from around 1890–92 – but musically this is unrelated to the song from 1911 and, in any case, it was never completed. At any rate *Arioso* is a very fine song, with a vein of Nordic melancholy and string textures that have often been compared to Grieg.

A new choral piece saw the light of day in October: a setting of Ernst V. Knape's *Män från slätten och havet* (*Men from Land and Sea*), Op. 65a, for mixed choir *a cappella*. This work – which Sibelius referred to as a 'cantata' in his diary – was commissioned by Axel Stenius and 'Svenska Folkskolans Vänner' ('the Friends of the Swedish Elementary School') for a festival to be held in Vaasa the following June. Less austere in style than the *Fourth Symphony*, it is nevertheless a more challenging piece than many of Sibelius's choral songs – so much so that it was necessary for a string orchestra to accompany the choir *colla parte* at the first performance. That the choir numbered an astonishing 1,300 singers

may have contributed to this necessity. The subtle writing and refined
harmonies would, one assumes, have been ill-suited to performance by
a choir of such mammoth proportions. Although the text has patriotic
overtones ('Homeland, homeland, sunny and beautiful, you are in our
dreams by day and night'), the piece is no rabble-rousing chorus but rather
a tranquil tone poem for voices.

In late October Sibelius undertook another foreign trip. His first stop
was Berlin, which he found 'insufferable', and he continued the next day
to Paris, Here, despite not indulging in alcohol or tobacco, he managed
to live with all the extravagance of his student days, with the predictable
consequence that he soon ran out of money. He visited Versailles and the
Bois de Boulogne. As well as consorting with Finnish and Scandinavian
artists, including the painter Magnus Enckell and the Swedish composer
Emil Sjögren, he also spent some time with Rosa Newmarch, although he
could not afford to entertain her with his customary lavishness. As for
work, in addition to reading proofs for the *Fourth Symphony* he made
a revision of the patriotic chorus *Har du mod?*, 'completing' it on 6th
November (he revised it again a fortnight later), and reworked the choral
suite *Rakastava* (1894) for string orchestra, declaring it ready on 2nd
December.

This unpublished version of *Rakastava* differs markedly both from the
choral versions and from the ultimate score, and represents an intermediate
stage between them. The string writing is flexible and idiomatic, but the
motifs have not yet come to assume their final form. The solo violin and
cello contributions are differently configured, Sibelius has not yet decided
on the final keys for the movements, and the second movement – in this
version named simply *Die Geliebte* (*The Beloved*) – has not yet gained its
definitive ending: as in the choral versions, it leads straight into the last
movement.

Shortage of funds led Sibelius to move from the Hôtel de Malte to the
Hôtel Danube where, according to his diary, he lived 'amid the dirt and risk
of fire' and the *garçon* looked 'like a murderer', and then to the Hôtel de
la Grande Bretagne. Here he received the unwelcome news that Breitkopf
had rejected *Har du mod?* The concerts he attended included Strauss's
Salome, Franck's *Psyche* and Dukas' *Symphony in C major*, but in general
he was not greatly excited by what he heard. Even an introduction to the
influential critic M. D. Calvocoressi proved a disappointment: at a concert
where his music featured alongside that of Sjögren, Sibelius found that
his work was represented by only a few songs. To make matters worse,
they were apparently badly sung by Minnie Tracey (in later years Sibelius
disliked Tracey greatly). The occasion must have seemed like a re-run of
his disappointing visit to the Music Club in London two years earlier. On

this somewhat unsatisfactory note he left France for the three-day journey home, arriving in Järvenpää on his 46th birthday.

Having caught up with reading a number of reviews that had arrived during his absence – to his surprise, not all of them bad – Sibelius now busied himself in earnest with a second set of *Scènes historiques*, a task that would take him several months. In the meantime he had been harbouring doubts about the *Rakastava* suite. He had sent this away to Breitkopf from Paris at the beginning of the month but now demanded it back, writing to the publisher that 'the essence of this composition is good but the arrangement must be different'.

Less problematic was a short choral march for his local students' association in the province of Uusimaa – 'a unison [piece], a monumental one, one that lasts for centuries'. The region had previously had a marching song in the form of *Nylänningarnas Marsch* (*March of the People of Uusimaa*) by Henrik Borenius, but that was in Swedish and was rapidly falling from favour in a district that was becoming increasingly Finnish-speaking. Sibelius agreed to compose a march, but was unwilling to use the first choice of text, Erkko's poem *Uusimaa*, because it had already been set to music by Oskar Merikanto. The students' association thus organized a competition to write a new Finnish-language text, and the winner was a singing teacher named Kaarlo Terhi. In his diary Sibelius complained that 'he [Terhi] is lower-class and smells. How hard it is to be with such people.' Sibelius worked out the theme of his *Uusmaalaisten laulu* (*Song of the People of Uusimaa*), JS 214, before Christmas, although he did not finalize the piece until 21st January. The melody of Sibelius's song – originally for mixed choir, but arranged soon after its completion for male choir – is now displayed on the Järvenpää town sign beside the motorway from Helsinki to Lahti.

1912

On New Year's Eve Sibelius received the scores of *Rakastava* and *Har du mod?* back from Breitkopf. The revision to *Rakastava* made rapid progress and on 9th January the definitive score, Op. 14, was sent back to Germany. It met with rejection, however: by Breitkopf – on the grounds that it was a revision of an older work, by Lienau – on the grounds that music for string orchestra was no longer in fashion, and by another Berlin publisher, Zimmermann. In the end it was published in Helsinki by Axel Lindgren. The final adjustments to the score may have been accomplished quickly, but were nevertheless substantial: Sibelius added the timpani and triangle parts, changed the keys and registers, composed a new ending for the second movement and adjusted many motivic and textural details. The publishers' reluctance is hard to understand. The reworking retains and expands the thematic material of the choral original, but transforms it into very idiomatic, rhythmically subtle string writing that is wholly character-istic of the mature composer. As the first movement no longer needed to be singable, its 'ethereal polyphony' (Tawaststjerna) could be allowed to develop with great freedom. In the second movement the almost constant triplets of the melodic line combine with a *pizzicato* accompaniment to give the delicate theme a feeling of constant motion. The third movement features a solo violin and cello, assuming the roles that the vocal soloists had performed in the choral versions of the suite. The addition of a lengthy and turbulent transition passage between the original opening and closing sections, both of which are slow, adds weight and variety without destroying the pervasive mood of heartfelt melancholy.

As soon as he sent away *Rakastava*, Sibelius turned his attention briefly to poems by Viktor Rydberg: *Kyssen* (*The Kiss*) and *Goternas sång* (*Song of the Goths*, from *Dexippos*), but these plans came to nothing, although he was to return to *Kyssen* a few years later. His main focus of attention remained the *Scènes historiques II*, to which he referred in his diary as a 'Suite symphonique'.

Sibelius often felt that his colleagues and contemporaries received more than their fair share of honours and praise, but on 17th January he himself reveived a very flattering invitation. His old teacher Robert Fuchs was retiring from the Akademie für Musik und darstellende Kunst in Vienna, and Sibelius was offered the post of Professor of Composition. After the intrigues that had accompanied his attempt to secure a similar position in Helsinki when Richard Faltin retired in 1896, Sibelius must have felt a little anxious that history would repeat itself. In this case he was not even first choice to fill the vacancy, as both Richard Strauss and Max Reger had already turned it down. Within a few days the newspapers announced the offer, but Sibelius remained unconvinced.

Sibelius's aunt Tekla, one of his few remaining reminders of his childhood in Hämeenlinna, passed away and was buried on 4th February. Sibelius did not attend the funeral – the first time he had stayed away from a family burial. His attention was taken up instead with work on *Scènes historiques II*, Op. 66. In its overall proportions and three-movement layout the second set of *Scènes historiques* resembles the first but, unlike its predecessor, the new suite had no connection with the *Press Celebrations Music*. That is not to say, however, that all the music was newly written: themes from the *Love Song* can be traced back to two works from 1905 – the abandoned *Luonnotar* tone poem and *Cortège* – whilst the second half of *At the Draw-Bridge* is plainly recognizable from the third movement of the 1894 *Promotional Cantata*.

At this point he planned to place the three movements in the order *At the Draw-Bridge*, *Love Song* and *The Chase*, but in the completed work this order was reversed.

The exuberant style and colourful orchestration of *Scènes historiques II*, especially in *The Chase*, has more in common with Sibelius's works from the 1890s than with the introspective music of his middle period. As in the *Karelia* and *Press Celebrations* scores, Sibelius seems to evoke archaic, courtly scenes, although here he does so without specific historical subject matter.

The Chase functions as an overture to the suite. Stylized hunting fanfares (coloured by the presence of the tritone) are contrasted and alternated with music that might be said to depict galloping horses – although there is more rhythmic and textural variety, and less cumulative energy, than in the similar portrayal in *Night Ride and Sunrise*. If the tone colours of the music recall early Sibelius, the motifs themselves are by contrast forward-looking: the melodic line of the opening fanfare would be transformed and developed in the *Sixth Symphony*, whilst the syncopated woodwind idea that follows suggests the same symphony's scherzo. We know from a letter to Aino that Sibelius started to sketch a 'tone poem' called *La Chasse* in Berlin in 1909; at that time he predicted that it would be 'a lively and spirited piece, light in its colours'. The piece ends with a festive, ceremonial coda.

The middle movement is entitled *Love Song*.[6] The mood of the music is warm and serene, and the scoring is understated: Sibelius omits trumpets and trombones, though there is an important part for the harp. Above an early sketch of its opening theme, Sibelius wrote 'Aino'; this is the idea that had formerly been intended for *Luonnotar*. The last piece, *At the Draw-Bridge*, is divided into two main sections: the first is based on a playful, good-humoured theme for two flutes, whilst the second resembles a stately minuet. The thematic material from the 1894 *Promotional Cantata* is here reworked in a style redolent of the incidental music to *Swanwhite*. The orchestral texture is delicate: the strings play *pizzicato* for much of the piece, both when in an accompanying role (in the first part) and when playing the melodic line (in the second section). Sibelius once more does without trumpets and trombones, although he includes a part for triangle and (almost inaudible) tam-tam.

By the end of the month he had reached some decisions. He turned down the professorship in Vienna by telegram on 1st March, and a week later noted in his diary: 'Many of my compatriots and friends are surprised at my rejection of Vienna. As I see it, they cannot understand my patriotism and love of my own, independent work.' He did in fact already have long-term projects of such an independent nature in mind, and his diary alludes to 'a fifth symphony. A sixth symphony: "Luonnotar". It remains to be seen if these plans will endure.'

On 29th March Sibelius conducted a successful concert of his most recent music at the University Hall. Apart from the *Fourth Symphony* all of the pieces were premières: the *Scènes historiques II* (now in their final order), which he had only just finished in time, the definitive version of *Rakastava* and the revised version of the *Impromptu* for women's chorus and orchestra that he had prepared two years earlier. The entire programme was repeated on 31st March at the People's Hall; at a third concert in the Volunteer Fire Brigade Hall on 3rd April, the *Impromptu* was replaced by *Night Ride and Sunrise*. These concerts marked the twentieth anniversary of Sibelius's breakthrough with *Kullervo*, and at the concert in the People's Hall Kajanus presented Sibelius with a laurel wreath bearing the text 'Thank you for 20 years'.

Kajanus had a more immediate reason to feel grateful to Sibelius. A few months earlier, as one of a range of cuts in its cultural budget, the Senate had withdrawn state funding from the Philharmonic Society orchestra. Kajanus had travelled to St Petersburg to argue the orchestra's case; he met with Vladimir Kokovtsev, president of the Council of Ministers, with the intention of referring the matter up to the Governor-General, Frans Seyn. Unfortunately Kajanus had reckoned without the hostility that his trip would arouse in Helsinki: the Finnish nationals saw it as a humiliating act of appeasement, whilst the Swedish faction regarded it as a selfish exercise in self-promotion. Such was the resentment felt that his concerts were shunned and his place on the podium had to be taken by Selim Palmgren.

The Finnish State Music Committee was keen for orchestral music to be played in Helsinki, but felt that under the circumstances Kajanus no longer commanded sufficient respect or support, and therefore appointed his bitter rival Georg Schnéevoigt as conductor of the newly formed Helsinki Symphony Orchestra. The presence of two competing orchestras in one small city was a recipe for ill feeling. The Swedish community broadly supported Schnéevoigt, but Kajanus's friends were not about to desert him. An announcement was placed in several newspapers in mid-March stating that 'A continuation of the Philharmonic Society's activities – naturally reformed in accordance with our times – is... essential for the natural and undisturbed development of our young national music', and the signatories included Sibelius, Emmy Achté, the composer, reviewer and educator Otto Kotilainen, Heikki Klemetti, Akseli Gallen-Kallela (as Axel Gallén had been called since 1907), Eero Järnefelt and Pekka Halonen. It comes as no surprise that Sibelius sprang to Kajanus's side; after all, almost all of his major works had been premièred by the Philharmonic Society orchestra. In this context their competition for the university professorship in 1896–97 must have seemed like ancient history; Sibelius now had a chance to repay Kajanus for his years of support. 'He said that your music was like a religion to him', Aino had written to her husband three years earlier.

The entire situation was in danger of degenerating into a chaos of assertions, rumours and denials, but Sibelius had no real desire to antagonize the Symphony Orchestra. He thus made it known in *Hufvudstadsbladet* that 'if anyone believes that I have anything against Schnéevoigt, this view is based on a misunderstanding. I make him doubly welcome and wish him every conceivable success. What I regard as desirable is merely that the Philharmonic Society should not cease its activities that have been so important for our own music.'

There were also conflicts on the domestic front. The abrasive personality of Saimi Järnefelt, wife of Eero, had already been cited by Juhani Aho as a reason for his decision to move from Järvenpää back to Helsinki some months earlier.[7] The relationship between Saimi and Aino Sibelius, too, was uncomfortable. In early April they had a particularly unpleasant exchange during which, according to Sibelius's diary, 'Saimi insulted Aino so much that Aino fell to the ground in convulsions. And everything that she, Aino, had worked for was dismissed like a puff of breeze. We must get away! To live with such a raw and brutal person as Saimi as a neighbour is impossible for all of us.' With Aino's consent, Sibelius considered selling Ainola and moving to Paris, but soon abandoned such ideas. At this time he was in something of a creative lull, torn between dreams of fantasy, opera and symphony, as he himself acknowledged in his diary on 5th May: 'As a composer I am "in a period of expectation"... "First Fantasy for large orchestra, Op. 67"!! "Second" and so on!! That is where the solution may lie. – Opera?! Symphonies? Yes, yes, the matter must be approached calmly.' During the spring, though, he made progress with none of these projects. Instead he wrote the *Three Sonatinas* for piano, and decided to buy a horse!

Despite their brevity the *Three Sonatinas*, Op. 67, have received general acclaim as some of Sibelius's finest piano works. By comparison with the various dance movements and character pieces that proliferate in his output for the piano, the *Sonatinas* are more abstract. They are not miniatures *per se*, but rather highly condensed examples of larger forms.

The *Sonatina in F sharp minor* establishes the pattern for all three works: although the mood is by no means as bleak as in the *Fourth Symphony*, the motifs are if anything even more aphoristic, the lack of superfluous harmonic support even more apparent. The slow movement, in Sibelius's favourite slow 3/2-time, begins with measured dignity, at times calling to mind the slow movements of the *Fourth Symphony* and

Voces intimae, although the theme itself is closer to the hymn-like string passage from the *Seventh Symphony*. As in the symphony, the main theme later returns in more amply harmonized form. The sonatina ends with a tiny rondo.

In the *Sonatina in E major* the earthy, robust theme of the first movement, the gently lilting 6/4 melody of the *Andantino* and the dance-like main motif of the finale recall Sibelius's style as it had been in the 1880s or 1890s: indeed, parts of this work can be traced back to a sketch from 1898, now in the National Library of Finland, marked 'Celli/Tutti'. The way these ideas are used, however (such as the canonic treatment of the opening theme or the magical right-hand accompaniment in the slow movement), and the light textures, clearly identify it as the work of the mature Sibelius. The contrapuntal elements in the music may also reflect his lifelong love of Bach.

The third of the set, the *Sonatina in B flat minor*, has only two movements, although some would regard the *Allegretto* that starts at bar 39 of the second movement as sufficiently distinct to be counted as a separate movement. In fact such distinctions are immaterial because the entire sonatina is based on the same thematic material, heard in the opening bars, which is transformed with great variety and ingenuity, acquiring the character of a funeral march at the beginning of the second movement and later (in the *Allegretto*) becoming a manic, intense rondo. All three *Sonatinas* are dedicated to Sibelius's friend Martha Tornell, who was now also his daughter Katarina's piano teacher.

At the beginning of July the Sibelius family did leave Ainola – but not for a new life in Paris. Instead they spent a short holiday in Kuhmoinen by Lake Päijänne. While there Sibelius once again came to grips with *Har du mod?*

Breitkopf had been less than enthusiastic about the revision of *Har du mod?* that Sibelius had made in Paris the previous November, and had written to him: 'A pendant to *Song of the Athenians* would be very desirable in Germany. But if we may be frank, Op. 31 No. 2 cannot be compared with *Song of the Athenians*.' It is true that the 1911 version of *Har du mod?* inhabited a curious stylistic no-man's land: the melody itself was much the same as in the 1904 version, though with a few rhythmic alterations. By means of the orchestral accompaniment, however, Sibelius clearly tried to elevate this simple marching song into the realm of art music. The first verse is dominated by noisy, boldly chromatic tremolos, whilst the second features isolated chords reminiscent of the end of the third movement of *Kullervo*. Sibelius also made an arrangement of this version with piano accompaniment.

The 1912 revisions were quite a different matter, though from this point a certain amount of guesswork is required in order to follow the story. Over the next couple of years two new orchestral versions saw the light of day. Most probably only one of them was made in July 1912, but we cannot be certain which is which. In both, the choral part is little changed but a very attractive dance-like beginning and ending has been added. When he noted in his diary on 8th July that 'My mind is set on *Har du mod* and the gavotte', he was probably referring to the one and the same piece. At that time, though, he had not reached a firm decision about the piece's character – two days later he wrote: 'I imagine it as a march ... in Masonic style.' One of the two versions – presumably the earlier one – features an orchestra of modest proportions (though including piccolo and bass clarinet); with its clearly defined rhythms and gavotte-like additions it anticipates some of the writing in *Scaramouche*, while retaining something of the harmonic boldness of the 1911 score. Sibelius's patience with this simple marching song must by now have been wearing dangerously thin, but he could finally declare on 11th July: 'At last I'm through with it.' Sibelius also made a piano transcription, but – confusingly – this differs from the lightly scored gavotte version. The piano score appeared in print in December 1913.

He was not yet done with small pieces, however, as he still had to deliver the long-discussed bell melody for Kallio church in Helsinki. Even this seemingly insignificant piece involved more than its fair share of discussion and argument, as well as time-consuming visits to Helsinki; he finally found a satisfactory melody in late July (Op. 65b). Meanwhile the idea of writing another symphony refused to go away, although in the short term it was supplanted by what he referred to as 'a number of smaller compositions for violin and orchestra' – which would eventually become the *Two Serenades*, Op. 69.

It is often claimed that the mature Sibelius rejected and did his best to suppress his early music, and it is true that in later life he did adopt a negative attitude to much of his student output. No doubt much of his reluctance to release the scores stems from a concern that the pieces might be compared adversely to his later music, although practical considerations also played a part: the sheet music, if he had it at all, was not necessarily easy to locate. It would be quite wrong, however, to use Sibelius's caution as an excuse to disregard his early works, and in August 1912 he provided clear evidence that he had not dismissed them by selling the first three movements of the *Suite in A major* for string trio, JS 186 (which had been performed to some acclaim in the spring of 1889) to the publisher Lindgren, provisionally calling it his Op. 1. He made minor revisions to the score at this time – but to no avail, as the work did not actually appear in print.

On 19th July the horse arrived.

Sibelius's relationship with Aino Ackté, which had been strained by his refusal to complete *The Raven* the previous spring, was by now in better shape; it was for her that he orchestrated the piano accompaniment of the song *Hertig Magnus*, Op. 57 No. 6, completing it on 22nd August. The scoring is very sensitive, with a translucent quality that recalls the incidental music to *Pelléas et Mélisande* or *Swanwhite* (Sibelius revised the theatre score for *Swanwhite* that very month). The orchestral version of *Hertig Magnus* was long assumed to be lost; around 1935 Sibelius drafted a letter to the publisher Robert Lienau: 'since then the material has been on its travels. Here and there it has been performed. I have asked everywhere. But without success.' In January 1943 Lienau traced an orchestral score, but this subsequently went astray again, and was only rediscovered in 1994 by Fabian Dahlström in Lienau's collection of printed scores in Berlin.

Kallio church was to be consecrated on 1st September, and for the occasion Heikki Klemetti made a choral version of Sibelius's bell melody, to a text of his own devising. Sibelius was not exactly pleased – especially when the newspaper reports suggested that Klemetti had composed the melody! In his diary Sibelius complained: 'Klemetti's attempt at the bell tune for the inauguration annoyed me. I was furious but, after a couple of hours, became wholly indifferent to his impudence.' A few days after the ceremony, however, Sibelius made his own arrangement for mixed choir *a cappella*, retaining Klemetti's text. He also made a transcription for piano.

The duality of Sibelius's attitude to Robert Kajanus, even while the latter was struggling to save his orchestra, emerges clearly from a diary entry dated 7th September 1912: 'As for Kajus [= Kajanus], he is after all fighting for his life. And for his place in history. That part of the plan is to overshadow me is certain, though perhaps in his case unconscious. But I have one powerful weapon, which is that my works are in print. One day somebody will come across my art and will put its merits in the spotlight.'

Sibelius was asked to compose a piece on the theme of Magdalena and Christus (based on Dante's *Divina Commedia*) but nothing came of this. One commission he did accept – although he must later have regretted doing so – was to write music for the pantomime *Scaramouche* to a libretto by Poul Knudsen and Mikael Trepka Bloch for a production in Copenhagen; the Danish publisher Wilhelm Hansen would guarantee his fee and also expressed an interest in publishing the score. Sibelius's next commitment, however, was another visit to England, where he was to conduct at the Birmingham Music Festival. He would be among friends: Granville Bantock was the festival's director, and the main conductor was Henry Wood.

He set off on 18th September, and just over a week later was conducting a rehearsal at the Queen's Hall in London. Rosa Newmarch took him to Stratford-upon-Avon and then, on 1st October, in Birmingham Town Hall, Sibelius conducted his *Fourth Symphony*. In the same concert Elgar gave the première of his cantata *The Music Makers*. Sibelius's symphony was a challenge for the British audience and critics but its reception was far from negative: *The Times* critic wrote that 'it is music which stands apart from the common expression of the time ... the orchestration is almost disconcertingly new', whilst *The Musical Times* reviewer wrote that 'Sibelius's Symphony brought us into another world – one with which most of us are so unfamiliar that we stumbled in our endeavour to understand.'

Sibelius had every reason to be satisfied with his visit to England, but could not afford to linger, as on 11th October he was due to conduct the embattled Philharmonic Society orchestra in Helsinki. The concert was held in the unflattering acoustic of the National Theatre, though in Sibelius's own view it passed off 'with exceptional success'. At the end of the month Busoni visited Helsinki and Sibelius was full of praise for his piano recitals.

A project now came along that could have profoundly changed the course of Sibelius's career – an opera based on Juhani Aho's recent novel *Juha*. The libretto was prepared by Aino Ackté and had initially been offered to Erkki Melartin. Aho visited Sibelius on 3rd November and immediately wrote to Ackté that the composer had developed 'new ideas about how an opera should be composed. As I understand it, they are completely new and, in some respects, different from former operatic traditions.' At that time Sibelius suggested a timescale of several years for composing the work. It is unlikely, however, that he made any real progress with it.

In early November he completed two more piano pieces, the two *Rondinos*, Op. 68, which were published by Universal Edition in Vienna and may have been written in response to a letter from Universal some months earlier that asked Sibelius to write 'primarily piano music, rather than excessively large-scale chamber and orchestral music'. Despite the recent offer of a professorship, Sibelius was not well known in Vienna, and one is tempted to suggest that Universal's request showed not only a lack of knowledge of Sibelius's work to date but also a lack of comprehension of his strengths as a composer. This was (and to some extent still is) sadly typical of the Viennese attitude to Sibelius – as would soon be illustrated even more clearly when the *Fourth Symphony* was scheduled to be performed there. In both scale and substance the *Rondinos* closely resemble the *Sonatinas* that he had written a few months earlier. The first of them, in G sharp minor, is improvisational and ruminative; the

interval of a minor ninth adds a special poignancy to its melodic line, and
the climax of the piece is marked by a prominent, unexpected appearance
of an 'S-motif'. The second, in C sharp minor, offers sparkling textures,
strong dynamic contrasts and a quirky idiom in which snatches of dance-
like music are begun and then abruptly broken off.

The first of the *Two Serenades* for violin and orchestra was completed
on 23rd November. Sibelius's diary reveals that he once envisaged calling it
I gammalt hem (*In the Old Home*), presumably alluding to Tavaststjerna's
poem *I ett gammalt hem* (*In an Old Home*), but in the end decided against
doing so; this title was instead used for a piano piece eighteen months later.
This was Sibelius's first piece for violin and orchestra since the revision
of the *Violin Concerto* seven years earlier and, as Jaakko Kuusisto has
observed, 'the violin writing is extemely discreet, but the solo part may thus
demand even greater elegance and stylistic awareness'.[8] Like the concerto,
the serenade opens with a simple, dignified melodic line, but in general
its solo writing eschews overt showmanship and is skilfully integrated
with the orchestra; the music also has a pronounced modal flavour. As
in Sibelius's late orchestral music, the mood-changes in the piece appear
seamless: the placid opening yields to darker, more agitated music before
arriving at a serene and beautiful conclusion.

Before he could complete the second of the serenades Sibelius had
another important foreign engagement. As November drew to a close he
set off for Copenhagen to conduct the Royal Danish Orchestra at the Odd
Fellow Palace. At the concert on 3rd December the *Fourth Symphony*
proved as controversial as ever. Charles Kjerulf, writing in *Politiken*,
suggested that its proximity to chamber music might have justified the
title 'Sinfonietta'. At the post-concert reception the Danish composers
Louis Glass and Carl Nielsen paid their tributes. Although they were the
foremost Nordic symphonists of their generation, however, Sibelius and
Nielsen ('a false "friend"', according to Sibelius's diary) never developed a
particularly close relationship. Sibelius returned home in time for his 47th
birthday, but the day was spoilt by the arrival of unsympathetic reviews
from Copenhagen.

The very next day a letter arrived from Adolf Paul: 'I am so happy that
I can finally give you a libretto that will suit you, and will make your
music dance.' The text in question was *Blauer Dunst* (*Blue Mist*), a five-
act comedy in German for which Paul had engaged the Swedish author
and diplomat Count Birger Mörner to make a Swedish translation. At this
stage, however, he had only prepared the libretto of the first two acts.
Sibelius cautiously agreed to take part, but his enthusiasm – which had
been modest from the start – gradually waned over the next few months
and a year later the opera plan was quietly allowed to lapse.

Back at Ainola, Sibelius carried on with the second of the serenades for violin and orchestra, with a brief interruption on 13th December for the composition of a piano piece for a Christmas magazine named *Lucifer*. The piece in question, *Valsette*, is an unpretentious and elegant miniature (just 36 bars long), far more relaxed in nature than the *Sonatinas* and *Rondinos*. It was later included as the first piece of the *Pensées lyriques*, Op. 40.

If the *Fourth Symphony* had bewildered listeners wherever it had been played – even the polite Finnish audiences who were inclined to be well disposed towards Sibelius – it suffered a humiliating fate in Vienna. Felix Weingartner programmed the work at a subscription concert with the Vienna Philharmonic Orchestra on 15th December, but the orchestra refused to play the symphony and Weingartner was forced to replace it with music by Weber and Beethoven.

CHAPTER 11

A VISIT TO AMERICA: 1913–1914

1913

Around Christmas of 1912 a new rented piano arrived at Ainola, and Sibelius's first composition of the new year was another little piano piece, the *Chant sans paroles*, which he wrote in the first week of January and described in his diary as 'a pendant to the *Valsette*' (both pieces are in E minor). The two miniatures were sold to Westerlund in Helsinki without delay, and ultimately the new 'song without words' became the second piece in the Op. 40 collection. Two weeks later he added a third, the *Humoresque*, Op. 40 No. 3, in which a cheerful main theme is contrasted with a musette-like idea. Sibelius noted in his diary that this piece was 'in this easy style that I have reserved for Pelle W[esterlund]', a simple statement of fact that has unaccountably been seized upon by many commentators and held up as an admission of the music's inferiority. Two more piano pieces followed in early February, the *Berceuse*, Op. 40 No. 5, which has been eagerly sought out and arranged for various instrumental combinations on account of its beautifully sweet, tender melody – and a rococo-style *Menuetto*, Op. 40 No. 4.

At the request of the singer and singing teacher Anna Sarlin, an influential figure in Finnish music education, Sibelius prepared a series of four arrangements for women's or children's voices *a cappella* of his own works. The songs in question were *Soi kiitokseksi Luojan* (from the university degree cantata of 1897), *Nejden andas* (*The Landscape Breathes*, from the patriotic piece *Islossningen*), *Aamusumussa* (*Hail Princess*, from the late 1890s and originally for mixed choir) and *Terve Ruhtinatar* (from the *Coronation Cantata* of 1896). Only one of these, *Soi kiitokseksi Luojan*, can be dated with precision to early February – by means of a diary entry – but it seems reasonable to assume that the others were made at around the same time.

News of the *Fourth Symphony*'s fate in Vienna reached Sibelius in mid-January, to be followed a few weeks later by another setback. Over in Sweden, Stenhammar played the symphony twice with the Gothenburg Symphony Orchestra. The first concert was on 17th January, and a couple of weeks later, he wrote to Sibelius: 'I made the mistake of playing your symphony in one of our subscription concerts. The audiences at these concerts consist mostly of bourgeois people who lack any serious interest in music... And so something unheard of happened – as far as I know a unique event in the annals of Gothenburg's musical history: at the end of the symphony the few people who were politely applauding were drowned out by loud hissing.' It turned out that the culprits were artillery officers from the local garrison and, when Stenhammar performed the symphony again a few weeks later, it was more favourably received – but the Gothenburg critics were not won over. Sibelius was also concerned at the reception the symphony would receive in Berlin, where Busoni was planning to conduct it with the Blüthner Orchestra: 'I'm profoundly unhappy at the prospect, as the work is the first piece on the programme and he is no conductor', he noted in his diary. In fact Busoni cancelled the concert for personal reasons, though he did conduct the *Fourth Symphony* in Amsterdam in March. On 2nd March it also received its American première, with Walter Damrosch conducting the New York Symphony Orchestra: members of the audience made their escape between movements.

The second of the *Serenades* for violin and orchestra, in G minor, was finally ready on 10th February. Its atmospheric opening theme is lent special poignancy by evocative dissonances in the orchestra. This theme is contrasted with a more animated, trochaic idea that recalls the first part of *Night Ride and Sunrise* and, to a lesser extent, the finale of the *Violin Concerto*. As with its companion piece, the orchestration is light and lucid: trumpets and trombones are omitted. Those violinists who have played Sibelius's *Serenades* are full of praise for their delicacy and craftsmanship, but these finely crafted gems remain cruelly neglected in the concert hall.

Sibelius made plans for a 'character piece for small orchestra' to be called *The Knight and the Naiad* or, according to a later diary entry, *The Knight and the Elf*. Erik Tawaststjerna has suggested that this piece drew inspiration from Josephson's poem *Hertig Magnus*, which Sibelius had already set as a solo song in 1909 (and had orchestrated as recently as August 1912). He also started work on a new tone poem, *The Bard*, Op. 64. Unlike many new conceptions from this period, *The Bard* did not change title during the process of composition – right from its first mention in Sibelius's diary on 21st February, its name was determined. This suggests that it was drawn from a specific source of inspiration – most probably Runeberg's poem of the same name – although Sibelius himself tried to deny any such association. He conducted a preliminary version of *The Bard* on 27th March at the National Theatre and then spent almost a fortnight refining the piece before sending it away to Breitkopf. Sadly this version of the work no longer exists, but it elicited the comment from Breitkopf: 'we regard your composition as attractive, atmospheric music, but we cannot rid ourselves of the impression that it is only the introduction to a work of larger proportions, perhaps a suite. Would it not be advisable to assemble the suite first?' Otto Kotilainen wrote in *Helsingin Sanomat*: 'This new work is a veritable masterpiece which is a valuable addition to Sibelius's great works... As it progresses the strings move softly and with restraint, like gentle voices with which are combined the solo harp's colourful, delicate figures. The work concludes with a powerful, broad climax from the brass. As well as its masterful construction, the piece possesses a peculiar, rich colour.'

On 1st May, the day on which Finland traditionally celebrates the coming of spring, Sibelius wrote two Christmas songs to words from *Läsning för barn* by Zachris Topelius: *Nu står jul vid snöig port* (*Now Christmas Stands at the Snowy Gate*) and *Nu så kommer julen* (*Now is Christmas Coming*). They are very simple but melodically appealing strophic songs totally devoid of artistic pretensions, often assumed by casual observers to be early works on account of their inclusion as the first and second items in Sibelius's Op. 1; in a work list from 1915 Sibelius claimed that they were based on old themes from the 1880s.

The Bard now needed to be finalized, although Sibelius had still not decided whether it should stand alone or be combined with other music. He had already replied to Breitkopf's comments by proposing: 'as *Scènes hist. III* the tone poems: 1. *The Bard*; 2. *The Knight and the Elf*; 3. *Rondo* (conceived as a round dance)' and suggesting that the movements of the new suite would be longer and more involved than the previous *Scènes historiques* and would thus merit a higher fee. Several diary entries suggest that he then came to see *The Bard* in terms of 'an intrada to a rather longer *allegro*', and suggest that he was now working on 'the latter part – the new one'. By 8th June he regarded the work as complete and called it 'a triptych for orchestra'; in this form it was even sent away to Breitkopf, but Sibelius soon recalled it: 'I have made a terrible mistake by – without examining the matter – sending the piece to you immediately, and letting myself be influenced as regards its form. *The Bard* is neither a diptych nor a triptych, but as it was originally. Now the ending (that is, the last 22 bars) must be in the tonic, not the dominant.'

The Bard is among the shortest and most elusive of Sibelius's tone poems. It falls into two sections, which are closely related both in mood and in substance. Despite the presence of a prominent, almost soloistic harp part, the melodic material itself is very slight. Much of it appears in the opening bars: a rising motif (first heard on the clarinets and then on the harp), an undulating idea in semiquavers (violas) and a descending scale fragment (harp). These ideas gradually evolve and coalesce into gentle, slow-moving 'themes', one of which (played *tremolo* by the violas and cellos) has clear affinities with *Voces intimae*, reinforcing the chamber-music-like quality of the scoring. This, and the subtlety with which the ideas are developed, also invite comparison with the *Fourth Symphony*. In the second section the music becomes more agitated and rises to the work's one big climax, before dying away in a mood of resignation and tranquillity. This reticent little piece has won wide acclaim as one of the most profound and moving of Sibelius's tone poems.

What happened to the second and third movements of *The Bard*? If we believe Sibelius's correspondence and diaries we can assume that they were both substantial compositions – longer than the five or six minutes of the earlier sets of *Scènes historiques* – and that the last of them was some kind of rondo. Sadly it is not possible to identify the missing second and third movements although, as we shall see, there is good cause to speculate. In its definitive, one-movement form Sibelius sent *The Bard* not only to Breitkopf but also to Universal Edition and Zimmermann on 1st August, planning to initiate a bidding war; in the event both Universal and Zimmermann turned it down, and Breitkopf's first edition appeared the following May.

Meanwhile Sibelius had made a start on *Scaramouche*, the Danish ballet commission, but in his opinion it was a shameless imitation of the Viennese dramatist and novelist Arthur Schnitzler's *The Veil of Pierrette* (set to music by Ernst von Dohnányi in 1908–09, Op. 18), and he did not hesitate to inform Wilhelm Hansen of his views. Knudsen admitted a similarity, although he asserted that his own work had been planned before *The Veil of Pierrette* was finished. Perhaps in response to Sibelius's criticism, he continued to make revisions to his text after the latter had started work on the music. By now Sibelius found the entire project an irritation, and was deeply regretting having agreed to it. On 21st June he confessed in his diary: 'I ruined myself by signing the contract for *Scaramouche*. – Today things became so heated that I smashed the telephone. – My nerves are in tatters.'

On 10th June – Jean and Aino's own wedding anniversary – Eva Sibelius married Arvi Paloheimo after a two-year engagement. Some eighty guests descended upon Ainola for a celebration which, despite cool and changeable weather, was (according to Sibelius's diary) 'unforgettably atmospheric'.

To take Sibelius's mind off the Danish pantomime project there was also a commission from Horatio Parker. Born in Auburndale, Massachusetts, Parker had studied in America under George Whitefield Chadwick and in Munich under Josef Rheinberger, and was a prolific composer, nowadays best remembered for an oratorio called *Hora novissima*. He became a professor at Yale University in 1893, where his pupils were to include Charles Ives and Roger Sessions. Parker had come to Europe to commission a series of works from prominent composers for a series of of songbooks entitled *The Progressive Music Series*; he asked composers such as Stanford, Reger and Pierné for contributions, and Sibelius provided *Three Songs for American Schools*, JS 199. Parker selected the texts and sent them to Sibelius; curiously, none is by an by American author. Each of Sibelius's settings is for a different vocal combination. The first, *Autumn Song*, is for soprano, alto and piano and is a setting of the English clergyman, poet and historian Richard Watson Dixon; its sweet harmonies and lilting 6/8-metre call to mind Sibelius's small instrumental pieces from the 1880s. The second song, *The Sun upon the Lake is Low*, is a straightforward setting for mixed choir *a cappella* of words by the Scottish novelist and poet Sir Walter Scott, whilst the last, *A Cavalry Catch*, is a march-like piece for unison male voices and piano. The poet – another Scot, William Sharp – wrote the text under his usual pseudonym of Fiona MacLeod. Sibelius sent off these three short songs on 23rd June.

A month later he was working on a new score: *Luonnotar*, Op. 70.[1] This shared nothing but its name and *Kalevala*-derived subject matter with the tone poem from 1905 that evolved into *Pohjola's Daughter*. The new piece was an amalgam of orchestral song and tone poem and was composed for Aino Ackté to perform at the Gloucester Festival in England. It is thus tempting to imagine that *Luonnotar* might incorporate some of the motifs originally planned for the abandoned setting of *The Raven*, but there is no supporting evidence for such a theory. On the contrary, the opening theme of *Luonnotar* is derived from an idea hastily jotted down on 8th May 1909 in the Bar Riche on Unter den Linden, Berlin, and handed to his friend Eliel Aspelin-Haapkylä, a university professor and champion of Finnish literature and theatre.

The main phase of work on *Luonnotar* was a fairly concentrated period in July and August, and he finished the piece (at least provisionally) on 24th August. A brief interruption came in the form of a Christmas piece, the dance-like *Spagnuolo* for piano, JS 181, for publication in *Joulutunnelma* (*Christmas Mood*) and written on 6th August; as the title suggests, this tiny piece has a Spanish flavour. In addition, Sibelius took part in an ambitious excursion organized by his neighbour K. A. Paloheimo by motor car to various towns in south-western Finland (among them Forssa, Rauma and Turku), and was greatly taken by the sight of Lake Pyhäjärvi at Kauttua.

With its imaginative sonorities and a daring (and extremely difficult) vocal line, *Luonnotar* is an undisputed highlight of Sibelius's vocal œuvre. The text is his own rather free adaptation of the creation story from the first runo of the *Kalevala*. Luonnotar, daughter of the Heavens, comes to earth and roams the oceans for 700 years. Distressed by a great storm, she appeals to Ukko, chief of the gods. A scaup makes its nest on Luonnotar's knee, but she allows the nest to fall into the water and the shattered fragments of egg are transformed into the sun, the sky, the moon and the stars. The regular pulse of the quiet string semiquavers at the outset establishes a mood of expectancy by simple means that anticipate the opening of the *Fifth Symphony*'s finale – but, instead of proceeding to a richly noble second theme, the music dies away to accommodate the solo soprano. The orchestral accompaniment is sparse (indeed, the soprano's first bars are totally unaccompanied), although two harps and the interval of a second in the timpani writing provide bold touches of tone colour. Sibelius also made a version of *Luonnotar* with piano accompaniment which, in its own right, is a skilfully crafted song that goes well beyond what might be expected of a rehearsal score.

No sooner had he completed *Luonnotar* than Sibelius received another commission, through the mediation of Horatio Parker. Parker recommended Sibelius to the wealthy American patrons Carl Stoeckel and Ellen Battell-Stoeckel and in late August could approach the composer with a commission from the Stoeckels for a new symphonic poem – no more than fifteen minutes in length – to be premièred at the Music Festival in Norfolk, Connecticut the following year.

Sibelius himself did not go to England to witness the première of *Luonnotar* on 10th September. Aino Ackté was one of many soloists in an ambitious programme at Gloucester's Shire Hall, where the festival orchestra (made up largely of players from the London Symphony Orchestra) conducted by W. H. Reed played Hans Sachs's monologue from Wagner's *Meistersinger*, *Luonnotar*, Mozart's *Piano Concerto in B flat major* – played by Camille Saint-Saëns, Saint-Saëns's own aria *Mon cœur s'ouvre à ta voix*, the final scene from Richard Strauss's *Salome* (a special favourite of Aino Ackté's) as well as music by Dvořák, Sullivan, Debussy, W. H. Reed and Herbert Brewer. Ackté telegraphed to Sibelius to tell him that she had enjoyed no fewer than six curtain calls after *Luonnotar*.

Much of the rest of 1913 was spent composing *Scaramouche*, although Sibelius's diaries make little mention of the fact, apart from the occasional outburst of frustration ('*Scaramouche* is tormenting me. It will be the death of me', 28th September). In October he heard Carl Nielsen conduct at the University Hall in Helsinki; apart from Dvořák's *Cello Concerto*, the concert was devoted entirely to the Danish composer's music, the principal works being the *Helios* overture and the new *Sinfonia espansiva*, which Sibelius found to be 'a good work. But, as I see it, without compelling thematic material.' At least on this occasion Sibelius would concede that Nielsen – whom he had described at their previous meeting as 'a false "friend"', was 'a genuine artist'. Sibelius was similarly unimpressed by Elgar's *Falstaff*, which he heard in Helsinki in November and described as 'somewhat confused'.

In early November Sibelius took a break from *Scaramouche* to compose the brief but intense *Rêverie* for piano, Op. 34 No. 6. Its proximity to the ballet score is clearly evident from the main theme, with its emphatic, dotted rhythms, whilst the harp-like, arpeggiated accompaniment recalls *The Bard*.

On 27th November Heikki Klemetti and YL performed *The Captive Queen* in Helsinki, in an arrangement for male choir and orchestra. Although this is the first documented performance of the male-choir version, we cannot be sure that it was really the first time it was heard in concert, as it had been published by Lienau in November 1910. Sibelius could have prepared the arrangement at any time between 1906 and 1910; the manuscript is lost.

As the year drew to a close, a new chapter in Sibelius's creative life began: *The Oceanides*. The story begins with a projected suite for orchestra in three movements, of which only the second and third movements survive. At some later stage Sibelius wrote in pencil on the title page: 'Fragments from a Suite for Orchestra 1914 / Predecessor of *The Oceanides*', and he repeated his name and the date at the top of the first score page of the second movement. As the year 1914 was written in at a later stage, however, it is by no means sure that it is accurate; indeed, we have every reason to assume that the movements were written in 1913. The second movement occupies pages 26–38 of the manuscript, and the third movement (played *attacca*) pages 39–70, which indicates that the first movement was 25 pages long, assuming that the title page was unnumbered.

The thematic material of the second movement, *Tempo moderato* (E flat major), is unrelated to *The Oceanides*, but is instead shared with a piano piece with the somewhat unusual name *Till trånaden* (*To Longing*), JS 202, completed on 28th November 1913 and published in *Lucifer*. Its melodic outlines are very characteristic of Sibelius, with triplets and descending fifths at the ends of phrases. The piano piece is not a transcription of the orchestral movement (nor vice versa), but they are so closely related that they can, in practical terms, be regarded as siblings. In character the *Tempo moderato* might be compared to the various short movements that Sibelius composed as incidental music for plays.

In the longer third movement, marked *Allegro* and also based in E flat major, we find much of the material that was eventually used in *The Oceanides*: the main theme of the tone poem in the flutes, its answering motif (in the cellos at letter B of the final score), the 'wave-like' triplets from the strings and the harp theme (letter I in the final score) are among the ideas present, albeit in rather primitive, undeveloped form. The overall shape of the third movement is close to that of the published tone poem: the flute theme and harp motifs appear at corresponding places, and the main climax comes towards the end. The movement concludes gently, the merest hint of a fanfare motif (flutes, timpani) appearing in the otherwise peaceful closing bars. The third movement can thus be regarded as the prototype for the eventual tone poem.

The missing first movement of the suite is shrouded in mystery. It may be that Sibelius simply misplaced it – or destroyed it. But there is an intriguing possibility that it was a wholly different piece that has indeed survived in another form. The most likely candidate, for which there is a considerable amount of circumstantial evidence, is the tone poem *The Bard*.

As we have already noted, after the original version of *The Bard* was premièred Breitkopf remarked that the piece sounded like the first movement of a suite, whereupon Sibelius considered reworking it, first as an *Intrada and Allegro* and then as a triptych. Although the original version of *The Bard* is lost, the fair copy of the final version, made by an unknown copyist, occupies pages numbered 2–27, and would thus appear to be of very similar proportions to the missing first movement of the suite. The title and atmosphere of *The Bard* have suggested to some observers, among them Erik Tawaststjerna, that the tone poem was inspired by Runeberg's poem of the same name. One striking piece of inferential evidence links *The Bard* with the incomplete orchestral suite, and also supports the assumption that *The Bard* is inspired by Runeberg: in Volume 1 of Runeberg's *Collected Works*, the title *Till trånaden* (the name of the piano piece related to the second movement of the suite) appears prominently a page or so after the last stanzas of *The Bard*. The third movement of the suite's *Allegro* marking would, moreover, fit in with the composer's suggested 'Intrada and Allegro'.

The surviving movements of the suite are scored for a noticeably less extravagant orchestra than that used in either of the tone poem versions of *The Oceanides*, but virtually identical to that used in *The Bard*. They were premièred by the Lahti Symphony Orchestra conducted by Osmo Vänskä at the Sibelius Hall in Lahti in September 2002.

In late 1913 Christian Sibelius fell ill, and had to be hospitalized. Jean was seriously worried: 'In recent days I have been affected by the most profound sorrow. For a long time my beloved brother has been seriously ill with exhaustion (and anæmia). The risk to his life is still there, although now it is slight', he wrote in his diary on 28th October. In late November Christian went to recuperate at Ainola, much to the delight of the entire family. And yet, for all his concern for his brother, Sibelius still had his own career to think of, and the details of his forthcoming trip across the Atlantic needed to be arranged.

Scaramouche, Op. 71, was finally completed just before Christmas. Despite its ample proportions and the effort it had cost, this score has never won widespread acclaim, and performances remain few and far between. To be sure, Knudsen's pantomime was no masterpiece – but neither was Järnefelt's *Kuolema*. Maybe more significant, and very surprising bearing in mind the relatively clear-cut dance sections in the music, the composer never made a concert suite from the *Scaramouche* music, although he did plan to do so for a time in 1921. With Sibelius's approval, Jussi Jalas later prepared a condensed version of the score, preserving the original orchestration – at Sibelius's express wish – and playing continuously for about twenty minutes, but this too has failed to win a place in the repertoire.

The plot of *Scaramouche* is not especially subtle: set at a ball hosted by Leilon, it involves the seduction of his dance-loving wife Blondelaine by Scaramouche, a sinister black-robed, hunchbacked dwarf viola player. When the ball is over, Scaramouche returns to abduct her, but she kills him with Leilon's dagger. In the end Blondelaine dances with ever-increasing vigour until she falls dead (a stage situation not unlike that of *Valse triste*) and Leilon goes mad.

With the exception of the opera *The Maiden in the Tower*, *Scaramouche* is Sibelius's only continuous dramatic score, and it therefore raises the question of how an opera by the mature Sibelius would have sounded. His employment of what amounts to leitmotifs in the score is especially thought-provoking, given his ambivalent attitude to Wagner.

The score divides up the musicians into three groups: players on stage (the minstrels and, on occasion, Scaramouche), offstage (Scaramouche), and the main orchestra, which offers a musical commentary on the action. Sibelius employs only modest orchestral forces: double woodwind, four horns, one cornet, timpani, percussion, piano and strings. The omission of the heavy brass means that Sibelius has to depict the mysterious, supernatural qualities of Scaramouche with restraint. Thus melody and harmony are the dominant elements throughout; rhythm plays a subordinate role and there are few startling orchestral colours or virtuoso effects. The orchestration is sensitive, with a transparency akin to chamber music, and climaxes are not an end in themselves but a means to highlight the stage action.

According to research by Kari Kilpeläinen, some of the material used in *Scaramouche* can be traced back to sketches from 1905–06, and there are also parallels with a surviving sketch for *The Raven*. But the range of styles which had to be sewn together into an uninterrupted entity was large. The cheerless, apathetic minuet heard at the outset had to progress not only to a buoyant waltz, to the sweetly passionate *Andantino*, the reflective and tender flute solo and the ambiguous bolero, but also to the wild, charismatic dance music of *Scaramouche*. At times it was also necessary to produce descriptive effects by musical means (such as when the exasperated Leilon strikes the point of his dagger into a table, depicted orchestrally by two *fortissimo* chords). There was never any question of these elements being united into a score of symphonic cohesion, but this does not mean that *Scaramouche* is incoherent. Sibelius's unmistakable style is in itself a significant unifying factor, and his fingerprints – woodwind in thirds, phrases which end with a quick decoration followed by a rising or falling fourth or fifth, and so on – are present in almost every bar.

Between Christmas and the New Year Sibelius made highly sensitive and effective orchestral versions of the songs *Våren flyktar hastigt* (1891) and *Soluppgång* (1902), almost certainly for Ida Ekman who performed them in Turku the following March along with *På verandan vid havet* and (also for the first time) the orchestral version of *Arioso*.

1914

In the New Year Sibelius set off for Berlin. Among his first tasks there was the arrangement for solo piano of two sections – *Danse élégiaque* and *Scène d'amour* – of the still unperformed *Scaramouche*. He still felt drained from his work on the pantomime before Christmas, but needed to concentrate on the commission for America. He attended concerts featuring a wide range of repertoire, although he missed a performance of his own *Violin Concerto* given by Alfred Wittenberg with the Berlin Philharmonic Orchestra under Carl Panzner. 'According to Palmgren it went extremely well. But he looked so insincere that I fear the reverse was true', Sibelius wrote in his diary. He wrote home to Aino that 'I hear novelties every evening, and this is extremely dear and important to me.' Many of the works he heard, however, were pieces by minor composers and in private he dismissed them scornfully. Notable exceptions included Bruckner's *Fifth Symphony*, which 'moved me to tears' in a performance by the Berlin Philharmonic Orchestra under Arthur Nikisch; and works such as Mahler's *Fifth Symphony* and Schoenberg's *First Chamber Symphony* conducted by Hermann Scherchen aroused his interest. He articulated his reaction in his diary on 4th February: 'It is of course possible to see things in this way. But it is horrible to listen to. A result achieved through mental exertion. People whistled and shouted. Not for weak minds or so-called talented people. They would be sure to misuse it. Something big behind it. But it won't be Schoenberg who brings it off.'

All the same, the concerts Sibelius attended demonstrated to him quite clearly that he was was no longer in the vanguard of modernism and forced him seriously to reconsider his position and aims as a composer. Over the next few years he struggled to find a new direction for his symphonic thought. Form was to be increasingly determined by content, whilst retaining sufficient traditional features to make the music readily accessible to performers and audiences. This reappraisal took place to a large extent at a subliminal, intuitive level, but may help to explain why the *Fifth Symphony* took so long to reach its final state.

While in Berlin it was natural for Sibelius to look up his old friend Adolf Paul, who had fallen on desperately hard times. Indeed, by comparison with Paul, Sibelius was affluent. It was probably then that he finally made the fate of the *Blauer Dunst* opera plain; on 12th January Paul wrote to Birger Mörner, explaining that 'Sibelius still hasn't composed the opera. He didn't like the last act.'

Among the smaller works from the Berlin visit was a song, the Rydberg setting *Vi ses igen (Farewell)*, Op. 72 No. 1, which he sent to Breitkopf & Härtel on 24th January, declaring his intention to send a further four companion pieces over the coming months.

In January Sibelius also persuaded Breitkopf & Härtel to accept a set of four piano pieces that he had yet to write. He produced the first of these, *Ekloge (Eclogue)*, in Berlin, completing it on 9th February. If it is overstating the case to regard this little piece as a kind of preliminary study for what has become known as the Yale version of *The Oceanides*, it does at least spring from a similar expressive world. The *Ekloge* is full of gentle wave-like figures; its main theme starts with a long note followed by a swirling, decorative figure (similar to a woodwind device in the Yale version of *The Oceanides*, omitted from the final revision), and even the shape of its later ornamental motifs resembles the surging string-writing in the tone poem. The alternation between 9/4 and 6/4 time, with the crotchets often subdivided into triplets, gives the piece great rhythmic plasticity. The word 'eclogue' means 'poem' or 'pastoral dialogue', but this is more of a soliloquy than a musical conversation of the type Sibelius had written five years earlier in the sixth of his Op. 58 piano pieces.

Sibelius returned to Finland in mid-February and the remaining three piano pieces for Breitkopf were completed in Järvenpää on 4th March.

With the possible exception of its introductory flourish, *Sanfter Westwind* (*Soft West Wind*) contains no obvious illustrative effects, relying instead on a rocking 6/8 metre to imply a light breeze (the French title, curiously, is given as *Douce brise de l'Est!*). Like the *Ekloge*, this piece has hints of Impressionism; Sibelius had, after all, been exposed to Debussy's music on his recent trip to Berlin. The third piece, *Auf dem Tanzvergnügen* (*At the Dance*), is a lively polka in which the urbane main theme is set against a more bucolic idea. The slow introduction to the fourth piece, *Im alten Heim* (*In the Old Home*) leaves no doubt as to the identity of its composer. The music develops into a nostalgic waltz, interrupted abruptly by the solemn closing bars. The title – which, as we have seen, was originally considered for the first of the violin *Serenades* – presumably refers to a poem by Tavaststjerna, *I ett gammalt hem* (*In an Old Home*). The entire set was published with the rather Griegian title of *Four Lyric Pieces*, Op. 74.

At the same time he put the finishing touches to another song, the Topelius setting *Orions bälte* (*Orion's Girdle*), Op. 72 No. 2, which was also sent to Breitkopf. Sadly the manuscripts both of this song and of *Vi ses igen* were lost during the First World War.

Work continued on the Norfolk commission; the 'working title' for the piece at this stage was *Rondeau der Wellen* (*Rondo of the Waves*), which in due course was altered to *The Oceanides*. At the end of March Sibelius finished what had developed into a single-movement work in D flat major and, a few days later, sent off the score and parts to America. Shortly afterwards he received an official invitation to conduct it in America in June. (Later, on his departure from America, the composer left the manuscript of this version with his sponsor Carl Stoeckel. It eventually found its way into the library of Yale University and has thus come to be known as the Yale version.)

If the third movement of the fragmentary orchestral suite is a 'work in progress', the Yale version of *The Oceanides* is much more 'complete'; at the very least, Sibelius thought highly enough of it to present it to his American sponsors. Many of the motifs used in the third movement of the suite have for the Yale version been refined and expanded in duration, harmony and tonal colour, although they still have some distance to travel before attaining their final form. Compared with the suite movement, the Yale version also contains a number of new ideas. There are frequent 'wave-like' motifs from the woodwind and strings, and a more melodic theme that was re-used in the piano piece *Björken*. The gentle fanfare-like motif from the end of the suite movement is retained in the Yale version; indeed it is more clearly defined in the Yale score, where it is heard from the trumpets before it is played by the flutes.

In the Yale version, the musical ideas are presented in a different order from either the suite movement or the final version (which are strikingly similar in this respect); for instance, the theme played on the harps and *Stahlstäbe* in the final version is introduced by the harps alone right at the outset, where it is presented much more slowly. The appearance of the flute theme that serves as the 'main theme' of the suite movement and the final version is delayed by several minutes, and is thus much less prominent. The percussion writing in the Yale version is more colourful but less well integrated than in the final version; other motifs seem to anticipate the incidental music to *The Tempest* and even Sibelius's other great American commission, *Tapiola*. Osmo Vänskä, who conducted the world première performance of the Yale version with the Lahti Symphony Orchestra at the Sibelius Hall in Lahti on 24th October 2002, has aptly characterized the difference in mood between the Yale version and the final score by comparing the former to a large lake and the latter to a mighty ocean.

Sibelius plainly had severe doubts about the version of *The Oceanides* that he had despatched to America: a few days after sending the score, he embarked on a comprehensive revision of the piece. It is no exaggeration to say that he virtually recomposed the work using many of the former themes.

Good news came from Helsinki University: Sibelius was to be given an honorary Doctorate of Philosophy (which was presented while he was in America, and so Aino stood in for him at the ceremony), and a few days later he learned from Horatio Parker that he was to receive an honorary doctorate from Yale University as well. But Sibelius's spirits were at a curiously low ebb; he felt that he was letting Aino down with his unreliability, and inability to earn enough money to pay the family's debts. He chose to look yet again at *Har du mod?*, and on 17th April wrote out a fourth version for voices and orchestra. As mentioned previously, there is some confusion as to the order of the versions. If indeed the lightly scored gavotte version dates from 1912, by a process of elimination the 1914 score must be a more heavily orchestrated version that retains the gavotte-like framework. This version corresponds closely to the piano edition published the previous year and so we must admit the possibility that Sibelius used the published piano edition as the basis of the orchestral score. While contrary to his normal working practice, this is not wholly inconceivable, as he had done the same a few years earlier with the *Dance-Intermezzo*, Op. 45 No. 2.

At this time Aino Sibelius also tried to keep a diary; here she gives a vivid impression of the frenetic activity at Ainola as the date for Sibelius's departure drew closer: 'The trip to America is approaching. *Rondeau der Wellen* is not yet complete. Terrible haste. The trip is arranged for

1 Jean Sibelius with his sister Linda (left) and brother Christian (centre),
probably in 1876.

2 Christian Gustaf Sibelius, the composer's father.

3 Maria Charlotta Sibelius, the composer's mother.

4 Korpo gård.

5 Jean Sibelius, 1889.

6 Christian Sibelius, the composer's brother, around 1889.

7 Pehr Sibelius, the composer's uncle.

8 Jean Sibelius, 1896.

9 Axel Carpelan.

10 Sibelius standing in front of the fireplace at Ainola, 1905.

11 Jean Sibelius with Aino and three of their daughters at Ainola in the second decade of the twentieth century.

12 Jean Sibelius, 1915.

13 Jean Sibelius rehearsing for his 50th birthday concert in Helsinki, 1915.

14 Jean Sibelius playing the piano, 1927.

15 Sibelius acknowledging applause at his 70th birthday concert at the Exhibition Hall in Helsinki, 1935.

16 Jean Sibelius, c. 1935.

17 Jean Sibelius, 1930s.

18 Jean and Aino Sibelius, 1945.

Saturday. The score is only half-ready. The copyist, Mr Kauppi, is staying with us and writing night and day. Yesterday we found out that he [Jean] has to leave on Friday evening. It's unimaginable. We have to count every hour. Otherwise all the practical aspects remain completely unfinished. It is only because of Janne's energy that we are making progress... Yesterday evening we could not do anything practical any more but then Janne applied himself and forced himself to work. Still about twenty pages to go. We lit a lamp in the dining room, a chandelier in the living room, it was a festive moment. I didn't dare to say a word. I just checked that the environment was in order. Then I went to bed and Janne stayed up. All night long I could hear his footsteps, alternating with music played quietly. In the early hours he moved upstairs. The copyist sat up in his own room.'

When Sibelius set sail aboard the *Kaiser Wilhelm II* on 19th May, the tone poem was virtually ready. Admittedly he continued to make changes even after his arrival in America on 26th, but these last-minute adjustments must have been minor, as the orchestral parts had already been written out before he left Finland. After rehearsing the new work at Carnegie Hall, Sibelius was plainly very satisfied with it, as emerges from a letter to Aino: 'it's as though I had found myself, and more besides. The *Fourth Symphony* was the start. But in this piece there is so much more. There are passages in it that drive me crazy. Such poetry.'

In the definitive score Sibelius changed the main key of the work from the somewhat uncomfortable D flat major of the Yale score to a radiant and confident D major. Most of the 'new' thematic material that had been introduced for the Yale version was discarded in the definitive version. The original motifs that can be traced back to the suite version were further expanded and combined in a manner that defies analysis but possesses a profound inner logic; the sequence of the various thematic elements reverted to the order of the suite version. The orchestration is essentially the same as for the Yale version (there is one additional trumpet in the final score). The gentle fanfare motif at the end of both the suite and the Yale version is omitted from the final score. Formal analysis is no more rewarding in *The Oceanides* than in any other work by the mature Sibelius: Robert Layton describes it as a free rondo, whilst James Hepokoski sees it as an example of rotational form. Stylistically, it is often compared to Impressionism, although in fact the Yale score is much more Impressionistic than the final version.

In America, Sibelius enjoyed lavish hospitality and widespread acclaim; Carl Stoeckel treated him to meals in first-class restaurants and showed him the skyscrapers of New York. In Norfolk, too, he lived in style as Stoeckel's guest at his lavish home, known as the White House, and mixed with some of the most influential figures in American music. Despite his ineptness in pecuniary matters even Sibelius realized the vast commercial potential of the American concert scene, and he dreamed of turning this to his advantage. 'I have an enormous reputation here in America, and I believe that the proposed tour (as yet secret) of between forty and fifty concerts would be a great success. I could pay off my own debts and yours besides', he wrote to his brother Christian.

Even though Sibelius rehearsed at Carnegie Hall, he did not actually perform in New York or any other major American city. The concert venue for the Norfolk Festival was 'The Music Shed', a wooden concert hall that could accommodate an audience of 2,000. Sibelius was most impressed with the playing of the orchestra at his disposal, which drew its players from the New York orchestras and the Boston Symphony Orchestra, and the concert on 4th June (in the first half of which Sibelius conducted *Pohjola's Daughter*, movements from the *King Christian II* suite, *The Swan of Tuonela*, *Valse triste*, *Finlandia* and finally *The Oceanides*) was a resounding success – perhaps the greatest triumph that he would ever experience as a conductor. It was certainly helpful that the new tone poem was far more accessible in style than the *Fourth Symphony*, and the critics were ecstatic. Olin Downes referred to *The Oceanides* as 'the finest evocation of the sea which has ever been produced in music'. A week later Stoeckel took Sibelius to see Niagara Falls, after which it was time to prepare for the degree ceremony at Yale University.

Sibelius reluctantly returned to Europe aboard the *President Grant*, as he had a conducting engagement at the Baltic Exhibition in Malmö in southern Sweden, a short ferry ride away from Copenhagen. Aino and Ruth travelled down to the Danish capital to meet him, but the concert was cancelled 'right in front of my nose', as Sibelius indignantly noted in his diary. The exhibition focused on Germany, Denmark, Sweden and Russia, and the Swedish organizers, unwilling to antagonize the Russians, made the unpopular decision to incorporate the Finnish contribution into the Russian one. It was little consolation that the *Elegy* and *Musette* from *King Christian II* had been included at a Russian concert conducted by Vassily Safonov on 25th June.

CHAPTER 12

MINIATURES AND THE FIFTH SYMPHONY: 1914–1919

But by now heavier political clouds were beginning to gather over Europe. While he was on board the *President Grant*, Sibelius had heard the news of the assassination of Archduke Franz Ferdinand, heir to the Austro-Hungarian throne, in Sarajevo on 28th June. Events spiralled out of control and led to the outbreak of the First World War. A month later Austria-Hungary issued an ultimatum to Serbia and, unsatisfied with the response, declared war. The Russians started to mobilize their armies. On 1st August the Germans declared war on Russia, and a few days later invaded Belgium, an action which brought France and Britain into the war as well.

The outbreak of war did not immediately threaten Sibelius's personal safety, as Finland was remote enough to be spared direct involvement in the conflict. It did, however, have a profound effect upon his lifestyle and income. For one thing he had less opportunity to travel abroad, either for conducting engagements or to promote his work. As Finland was still nominally a Russian territory, his dealings with German publishers were at a stroke rendered much more problematic. Payments for performances of his music overseas dried up: as the war progressed, his income dropped to almost zero. In the circumstances he had little option but to play it safe and publish a number of new pieces locally, but Finnish publishers – who were themselves by no means immune to the effects of war – were more interested in undemanding miniatures that could readily be sold to enthusiastic amateurs than in profound orchestral masterpieces that required dedicated professional performance. It should, of course, be noted that Sibelius did not start writing miniatures as a consequence of the war: the Op. 74 collection and many of the pieces in Op. 34 and Op. 40, for instance, were already complete well before it broke out.

The status of the small pieces that Sibelius composed during this period has long been disputed. The traditional view is that they are worthless trifles that were composed with the sole aim of earning enough money to feed his family, and this view has no doubt discouraged performances of the pieces, at least outside Finland. In recent years, however, the music has become better known, not least through numerous recordings, and a more positive opinion has gained ground, not least among those pianists who actually play the music. Eero Heinonen, for instance, writes: 'No one would deny the primary importance of orchestral works in Sibelius's output, but when the composer said that he wrote piano pieces to make a living, this tells us of nothing but the motivation that each of us experiences at least sometimes in our everyday jobs. If we think that a composer's work is less valuable when he does it for money, we would have to denounce all of Bach's cantatas.'[1] Folke Gräsbeck remarks in a similar vein: 'What brilliant flash of intelligence leads people to keep repeating Sibelius's explanation to his children that he wrote some of his piano pieces so that they could have butter on their bread? With the possible exception of the wealthy Rossini in his old age, what composer has had any alternative but to work in order to support himself and his family decently? This, indeed, is not an original thought. It is time to bury this absurd criticism.'[2] Sibelius's diary entry from 15th August 1914 simply reflects the reality of the situation in which he found himself: 'Now I shall be fifty. How miserable it is that I must compose miniatures.' Nonetheless, the composer refused to dismiss the pieces: 'I know that they have some future', he told his secretary Santeri Levas many years later, 'although today they are almost entirely forgotten.'

A few months earlier the male-voice choir Muntra Musikanter had expressed an interest in new songs by Sibelius, and on 26th August the composer responded with the first of several new settings, *Herr Lager och Skön fager* (*Mr Lager and the Fair One*), Op. 84 No. 1. The text is by Fröding, who provided his poem with the subtitle 'a little song of how love comes and goes'. The five-part song has the character of a humoresque and is composed as a dialogue between the wily Mr Lager and a young lady who initially rejects him but ultimately succumbs to his charms.

Despite all the critical sniping, the set of piano pieces commonly known as 'The Trees', Op. 75, has become one of the most popular of Sibelius's piano works. The first three pieces were completed on 14th September 1914. The first, *När rönnen blommar* (*When the Rowan Blossoms*), opens with delicate, almost improvisatory figures – at one point clearly anticipating the melodic line of the song *Hennes budskap* from January 1918 – which gradually crystallize into a warm, Romantic melody. By contrast, the second piece, *Den ensamma furan* (*The Solitary Fir Tree*), launches straight into a theme stated emphatically in a dignified 2/4 time, with a massive, orchestral sonority and a noble demeanour comparable to *At the Castle Gate* from *Pelléas et Mélisande*. Later, however, the theme becomes more fragmented and its motifs are impressionistically decorated before tonal certainty is restored in the closing bars. The third piece, *Aspen* (*The Aspen*), contrasts two themes, starting with a gently rocking idea with a simple phrase structure and (later) *kantele*-like broken chords that suggest folk music, although the ethereal G sharp minor harmonies give lie to such a notion. The second theme meanders chromatically in the left hand, like a preliminary study for the bassoon solo in the first movement of the forthcoming *Fifth Symphony*. An early draft of *Aspen*, rather shorter than the final version, has survived with the provisional title *Ballade*.

The rest of Op. 75 followed in the next few weeks. The fourth piece is *Björken* (*The Birch*, completed at the beginning of October). Despite the title the inspiration came from water rather than trees: the piece is based on a theme that had been prominent in the Yale version of *The Oceanides* but which was discarded in its final revision. This is combined with a rocking motif similar to the accompaniment of the 'Raven' theme in the finale of the *Fourth Symphony*. In the second half of the piano piece, marked *misterioso*, the motifs are heard more gently and indistinctly. It is as though we are looking at the reflection of the tree in rippling lake water. Two more pieces were planned for the set, and both are waltzes. No. 5, *Granen* (*The Spruce*, finished on 23rd September), is measured and sonorous, and its main theme has points of contact with the famous *Romance in D flat major* from Op. 24. The sixth, *Syringa* (*The Lilac* – not usually classed as a tree, perhaps – 24th September), is quicker and was perhaps intended to relieve the serious mood of its predecessor and end the suite in a relaxed, affable mood. Five years later Sibelius revised both pieces; *Granen* remained in Op. 75, but *Syringa* was then transplanted into Op. 96 as *Valse lyrique*. The final Op. 75 thus contained just five pieces.

Curiously, the 'orchestral' piano style that Sibelius had apparently outgrown in Op. 58 and the *Sonatinas* returns with a vengeance in Op. 75 and some of the other wartime piano works. Several of the pieces have been orchestrated (for instance Gordon Jacob arranged a selection from Opp. 75, 76 and 85 for the ballet *The Lady of Shalott*, based on Tennyson's Arthurian poem, choreographed by Frederick Ashton and first performed at the Ballet Club in London on 12th November 1931). Sibelius himself made an orchestral version of *Syringa* in its later incarnation as *Valse lyrique*.

On 11th October Arvi Paloheimo visited Ainola, and his cigar smoke evoked for Sibelius 'all the poetry of my youth'. As if in musical response to this memory, he briefly revisited his earlier *Kalevala* style and the

following day made an arrangement for mixed choir of his successful song
Venematka (*The Boat Journey*) from 1893.

Meanwhile Sibelius had started to lay plans not for one new symphony,
but for two. In September he wrote to Axel Carpelan: 'I am still deep
in the mire, but I have already caught a glimpse of the mountain I must
surely climb... God opens his door for a moment, and his orchestra is
playing the *Fifth Symphony*' – but the deity was not to give up his secrets
lightly; the composition of the *Fifth* was to prove a monumental artistic
battle, which Sibelius later referred to as a 'struggle with God'. At this
stage the symphonies were in a very embryonic form. Indeed, the overall
arrangement, make-up and grouping of the themes of the *Fifth* and
Sixth Symphonies took a considerable time to become established in the
composer's mind, although their respective tonal centres of E flat major
and D minor became clear to him at a relatively early stage. Among the
ideas found in a sketchbook from the autumn of 1914, several are recognizable from the *Fifth Symphony*'s scherzo section, and another contains
the germ cell of the swinging horn theme in the finale. As in so many other
works, Sibelius found inspiration in nature. In November he noted in his
diary: 'A wonderful theme has come to me. The *Adagio* for the symphony
– earth, worms and privation – *fortissimos* and mutes, lots of mutes. And
the sounds are godlike!!' The *Adagio* movement did not materialize, but
these words are a very apt description of the E flat minor episode in the
finale of the *Fifth Symphony*, the first sketches of which are found amongst
ideas for the *Adagio* in Sibelius's jottings. One idea that found its way into
the symphony is labelled 'Bacchic Procession' in the sketches.

On 17th October Sibelius wrote to Aino Ackté and pulled out of the
project to write the opera based on Juhani Aho's *Juha*.[3] Another collaboration with Aho, the *Kalevala*-based ballet *Karhuntappajaiset* (*The Bear's
Death Rituals*), had been proposed during the summer, but in November,
no doubt with memories of *Scaramouche* very fresh in his mind, Sibelius
declared that he would not take part. As he had written to Axel Carpelan
on 27th July: 'I can't just become a *vielschreiber*. That would damage both
my reputation and my work... But why should I throw away on some "pas"
ideas that would work brilliantly in a symphonic setting?' Carpelan had
lent his support and replied: 'My firm advice would be to listen to your
inner promptings and not to take commissions from left, right and centre.
Follow your own star and stick to the symphonic path.'[4] As a listener
one might regret Sibelius's decision to decline both the opera and the
ballet. By doing so, however, he made a conscious choice to avoid major
commitments that would distract him from the *Fifth Symphony*.

The war may have restricted Sibelius's international appearances but he
could still make the most of the Helsinki cultural scene. He attended an

orchestral concert presenting works by the young Aarre Merikanto and also noted the emergence of the composer Moses Pergament. Sibelius's daughter Ruth, whose greatest wish was to pursue a career on stage and who had been engaged by the National Theatre the previous year, appeared there in Henry Kistemaeckers's play *L'Embuscade*. On the other hand his own works were absent from the Helsinki orchestral programmes that autumn. At least the feud that had been raging since 1912 had subsided: the Philharmonic Society orchestra and Helsinki Symphony Orchestra had merged in 1914 to form the Helsinki Philharmonic Orchestra, with Kajanus and Schnéevoigt sharing the conducting duties. With the outbreak of war, however, most of the foreign players had left; the new orchestra numbered only around forty musicians.

All the time the flood of miniatures continued. As the autumn progressed, Sibelius wrote a number of short piano pieces that subsequently found their way into an assortment of different opus groups. The *Arabesque* (6th October), Op. 76 No. 9, is a mercurial miniature scherzo, spontaneously ornamental in its exploitation of the keyboard's upper reaches yet following a pattern that we can trace back to the third movement of the *Hafträsk Trio* and the *Scherzo in E minor*, JS 165. The fanfare-like motifs and piano texture in the *Nouvellette* (19th October), Op. 94 No. 2, hark back to the *Intermezzo* from the *Karelia* music. Its down-to-earth nature is in stark contrast to the dreamy musings of the *Romanzetta*, Op. 76 No. 6, completed on the same day, where the left hand has a gently lilting yet slightly restless melody in 6/8 time above decorative right-hand figures. Sibelius returned to a more straightforward dance style in the Chopinesque *Valse* and an *Air de danse* in the style of a gavotte (25th October), Op. 34 Nos 1 and 2.

Three pieces dated 3rd November are quite different in style: the bright and cheerful *Mazurka*, Op. 34 No. 3, has an unambiguous melody and dance rhythm, whilst – unsurprisingly – the *Carillon*, Op. 76 No. 3, consists exclusively of bell effects, its 'uneven' rhythms in fact very precisely notated. The *Pensée mélodique*, Op. 40 No. 6, is bolder and more aphoristic, stylistically close to the *Piano Sonatinas*. The interval of a tritone figures prominently in its theme, as does a characteristic Sibelian triplet rhythm. The *Couplet* (Op. 34 No. 4) is more of a 'couplet' of verse than the 'humorous song' that the title is often taken to imply. Sibelius almost immediately had second thought about the piece, and revised it a week later – making more effective use of one if its principal motifs – before releasing it for publication.

Capriccietto (24th November, Op. 76 No. 12), is a peculiar piece that flutters around like a butterfly, without landing either on a tonal centre or a recognizable melody. *Rondoletto*, Op. 40 No. 7, is a vigorous polka that was referred to by Sibelius's daughters as a 'Walpurgis dance', although it was completed not on May Day Eve but on 7th December. On the same day, he finished a piece called *Boutade*, Op. 34 No. 5, which makes numerous light-hearted but ultimately unsuccessful attempts to break out into a full-blown Viennese-style waltz; the title means 'drollery'.

A rather larger piece, to which Sibelius initially referred as 'Lofsången' ('Song of Praise') and 'Lauda Sion', took shape in November. This turned into the *Cantique*, the first of the two *Serious Melodies*, Op. 77, and was scored in the first instance for violin and orchestra. The composer later gave it the Latin subtitle 'Laetare anima mea' ('Rejoice my soul'). Although Sibelius wrote very little overtly religious music, these names suggest an ecclesiastical atmosphere – and indeed, in a letter to the publisher Axel Lindgren, Sibelius wrote that 'the accompaniment could easily be positioned in a church gallery. An arrangement for organ and harp should be issued.' The version for violin and orchestra was completed on 1st December 1914 and an arrangement – not for organ or harp, but for violin and piano – soon followed.

The composition of *Cantique* seems to have spurred Sibelius on to write more music for the violin. On Christmas Day he wrote in his diary: 'a planned "Sonata I for violin and piano" as Op. 78. Perhaps! The idea has been with me for a long time – since the 1880s, when I wrote two such pieces.'

1915

Before Sibelius finished his 'sonata' several shorter pieces for violin and piano saw the light of day, and he envisaged a set of pieces for violin and piano called 'Pensées fugitives', a companion to the 'Pensées lyriques' for piano, Op. 40. On 9th January 1915 he completed what is probably his most popular work in this genre, the *Romance in F major*, Op. 78 No. 2, which no doubt owes its fame to its sweetly lyrical melody, reminiscent of Svendsen's *Romance*, Op. 26, and Elgar's *Salut d'amour*. In his diary the composer speculated: 'Perhaps it is *too* traditional?', but he volunteered, if a publisher so desired, to provide versions with orchestral accompaniment or with the viola as solo instrument. Having sold his *Valse triste* very cheaply, he was no doubt keen to cover himself in case the *Romance* achieved similar 'cult status'. Two weeks later he finished the *Rigaudon*, Op. 78 No. 4, a sturdy neo-classical dance. Like their later companion pieces in Op. 78, the *Romance* and *Rigaudon* were also issued in versions for cello and piano.

On 1st February 1915 another song for Muntra Musikanter was completed, *På berget* (*On the Mountain*), Op. 84 No. 2, to words by Bertel Gripenberg; the piece has the unusual time signature of 7/4. It must have been a thankless task to set such a florid text, and it is surprising that Sibelius agreed to do so. As the conductor Matti Hyökki has observed, 'the counterpoint progresses syllable by syllable and note by note, laboriously like a snowplough in a drift.'[5]

A visit from his son-in-law Arvi Paloheimo prompted Sibelius to confess to his diary on 23rd February that he was falling back into old habits. 'Smoked with him and drank a drop of red wine. The tobacco tasted excellent. But I don't think I could smoke much.'

On 12th March Sibelius finished his 'violin sonata' but, no doubt because of its modest proportions, eventually decided to publish it under the title of *Sonatina in E major*, Op. 80. There can be no doubt that the composition of this work – his only mature multi-movement piece for violin and piano – stirred memories of his youthful dreams and ambitions. 'Dreamed that I was twelve years old and a virtuoso. My childhood sky is full of stars – so many stars', he wrote in his diary while at work on the first movement. When he told his biographer Erik Furuhjelm that 'my violin sonata [*sic*] should really be played by a sixteen-year-old girl', might he also have remembered that in 1887, while on summer holiday in the idyllic countryside of Korpo, he had composed and dedicated his *Andante cantabile* in G major, JS 33, to the sixteen-year-old Ruth Ringbom?

Bearing in mind that at least some of his miniatures for violin and piano from this period are relaxed and gently nostalgic in mood, one might expect the style of the *Sonatina* to be similarly mellow. In fact, however, it fully reflects the changes his music had undergone in the intervening years and is more comparable with that of the *Sonatinas* for piano, Op. 67 (several commentators claim a particular affinity with the second piano sonatina, also in E major). Emotionally the violin sonatina is predominantly cool, even detached: even in the dance-like sections of the outer movements, the harmonies are often quite austere. Thematically, too, the work is unmistakably a product of the mature Sibelius: indeed, the main theme of the finale was originally intended for the finale of the *Sixth Symphony*.

Later that month, in a rare and no doubt welcome break from his wartime isolation, Sibelius set off for Gothenburg to give his first public concerts since the visit to America. Because of the war it was not advisable to travel by boat, and so he had to make the long trip overland, by train via Tornio and Stockholm, where he visited his brother-in-law Armas Järnefelt. Moving on to Gothenburg, he was well entertained by Stenhammar, and the trip cheered him up immensely. He visited the Gothenburg Art Gallery to see paintings by Ernst Josephson (whose texts Sibelius had set in his Op. 57 and elsewhere), and gave two concerts of his own works, mixing established compositions such as the *Nocturne* from *King Christian II*,

Lemminkäinen's Return and the *Second Symphony* with new ones, among them *The Oceanides* and the *Fourth Symphony*.

Shortly after his return, Ruth brought a visitor to Ainola. He was Jussi Snellman, an actor and director at the National Theatre. Born in 1879, he was fifteen years older than Ruth, and it was plain that she saw him as more than just a friend. Sibelius was initially horrified, writing in his diary on 4th April: 'Poor Ruth, who can't see beyond the end of her nose. He is a theosophist, a vegetarian and so on... What a terrible thought! ... And she wants to sacrifice her happiness in life for this old bachelor. He is 18 [*sic*] years older than her. I must act now!' As he became better acquainted with Snellman, however, his antagonism melted away.

Work on the symphonic projects continued. Sibelius transferred ideas to and fro between the *Fifth Symphony* and the *Sixth* (which he referred to at one stage as *Fantasia I*): even the swinging theme from the *Fifth*'s finale was at one stage tested in the finale of the *Sixth*. On 10th April he wrote in his diary: 'Spent the evening with the [fifth] symphony. The disposition of the themes: with all its mystery and fascination this is the important thing. It is as if God the Father had thrown down pieces of mosaic from heaven's floor and asked me to put them back as they were. Perhaps that is a good definition of composition.' Just over a week later he continued: 'Walked in the cold spring sun. Memories of old affronts and humiliations came back. Had powerful visions of the *Fifth Symphony*, the new one'; and, three days later, 'Just before ten to eleven I saw sixteen swans. One of the greatest experiences in my life. Oh God, what beauty! They circled over me for a long time. Disappeared into the hazy sun like a glittering, silver ribbon. Their cries were of the same woodwind timbre as those of cranes, but without any tremolo... Nature's mystery and life's melancholy! The *Fifth Symphony*'s finale theme.' The clear association of the swinging horn theme in the finale with swans in flight is corroborated by a later letter from Axel Carpelan (15th December 1916) which speaks of 'the incomparable swan hymn'.

On 26th April Akseli Gallen-Kallela celebrated his fiftieth birthday. Kajanus made a speech and Eino Leino produced a commemorative poem, but neither Sibelius nor Aino attended the birthday dinner; Sibelius sent a letter to which Gallen-Kallela replied with a typewritten note. In truth the old friends had grown apart. Sibelius was jealous of the press attention that Gallen-Kallela now received, and was in any case reluctant to break off his labours on the *Fifth Symphony*. The very next day the choral songs *På berget* and *Herr Lager och skön fager* were premièred by Muntra Musikanter conducted by Olof Wallin in the University Hall, but made little impact. Sibelius had high expectations but subsequently referred to the concert as a fiasco.

On 11th May the solo songs *Kyssen* (*The Kiss*), Op. 72 No. 3, and *Kaiutar* (*The Echo Nymph*), Op. 72 No. 4, were provisionally completed, although Sibelius made adjustments to the latter at the beginning of June. *Kyssen* is a Rydberg setting, but on this occasion the Swedish poet's words, about the power of a fugitive kiss, did not inspire Sibelius to give of his best: the song is agitated but relatively bland. A much bolder, more charac-terful vocal line is found in *Kaiutar*, one of Sibelius's few solo songs in Finnish, which one could almost regard as a 'mini-*Luonnotar*', although its text is not from the *Kalevala* but from a poem by Larin Kyösti. The melodic line itself has a close affinity with that of an earlier song, *Hållilå, uti storm och i regn* from *Twelfth Night*.

On 23rd May Sibelius became a grandfather when his daughter Eva in her turn produced a daughter, Marjatta (at this time his own youngest daughter, Heidi, was almost four). Another family celebration followed shortly afterwards, with the silver wedding of Eero and Saimi Järnefelt on 12th June. Although the Sibelius's relationship with Saimi Järnefelt had often been less than cordial, Jean composed a delightful duet for the occasion that was performed by Lena Järnefelt and Ruth Sibelius, with Aino at the piano (JS 192). He chose Runeberg's poem *Tanken* (*The Thought*), which he had already set as a choral song several decades earlier, but this time used a mellifluous melody in 6/4 time which downplays any political symbolism that the text might possess ('Do not complain, that like a prisoner you are bound to the earth; light as a bird, quick as light, you are freer than them both'), especially as the vocal parts are often in thirds. Such souvenirs had been Sibelius's stock-in-trade in the late 1880s and he had evidently not lost his touch. Three weeks later normal service was resumed when Saimi was once more rude to Aino, and Sibelius's daughter Katarina was reduced to tears by insults from the Järnefelt children (Sibelius pointedly refers to them in his diary as 'Saimi's children', and exclaimed ironically 'Marvellous neighbours!') but the following day it was Jean's turn to accept criticism from his brother Christian, who confiscated his cigars.[6] At least he was in better physical shape than Axel Carpelan, however, whose strength was at a low ebb. On a more positive note Sibelius discovered that Erik Furuhjelm was planning to write a monograph about him, to be published to coincide with his impending fiftieth birthday. Leevi Madetoja also proposed to write a biography, but abandoned the idea when no suitable publisher could be found.

A number of smaller compositions – and other matters, including a visit from Rosa Newmarch – distracted Sibelius during the summer months and he soon found himself in a race against time to complete the *Fifth Symphony*. Many of the pieces he wrote during the summer were for the violin, and the first of them, *Devotion* – the companion piece to *Cantique* in Op. 77 – was ready on 10th June; this time the setting for violin and piano was finished before the orchestral version. The underlying mood of this piece is one of anxiety, although the atmosphere is similarly devout; the composer later added the subtitle 'Ab imo pectore' ('From my very heart'). Unusually for Sibelius, the orchestral arrangement omits timpani. A rather astringent *Tempo di Menuetto*, Op. 79 No. 2, was completed at the same time; on 12th July it was followed by the *Impromptu*, Op. 78 No. 1, in which an *ostinato* bass with a pedal point on the note C not only lends a slightly Spanish flavour to the stylish, march-like theme (which is based on a repeated 'S-motif') but also recalls the orientalism that Sibelius had explored nine years earlier in his incidental music for *Belshazzar's Feast*. On 21st August he finished the *Souvenir*, Op. 79 No. 1, which starts with a thematic motif of a type of familiar from *Pohjola's Daughter*, although the main theme itself – which originates in the unfinished *Pianokompositioner för barn* of 1898–99 – has more the character of a Viennese salon piece.

A new choral piece was ready on 23rd June – the Fröding setting *Ett drömackord* (*A Dream Chord*) for male choir *a cappella*, the third in the Op. 84 group. Like the earlier works in the set (*Herr Lager* and *På berget*) this was composed for the Muntra Musikanter choir, and is a distinguished piece with slow-moving, often quiet chromatic writing. Formally it could be compared to *The Bard*, with two closely related sections, the second of which is slightly more animated and rises to a climax. The first verse describes the sound of bygone centuries with calm, almost static descending phrases resembling the bassoon lament from the first movement of the now imminent *Fifth Symphony*. The second verse, in which a victorious nobleman returns home, is more flowing in character, although its stately tempo is unchanged: Sibelius resists the temptation to include lively music to depict the 'people dancing a round' in Fröding's poem.

Muntra Musikanter had commissioned a new work from Sibelius, 'Unge Hellener' ('Young Hellenics') – a text from Rydberg's *Livslust och livsleda* that Sibelius had already set in his *Impromptu* for women's choir and orchestra from 1902 – but this never materialized. Instead, he turned his attention to another work from that period. Over the past few years Sibelius had in his diary returned to the possibility of revising *Sandels*, but now he began to have doubts. 'I have decided not to revise *Sandels*', he wrote. 'It can remain as a *document humain* from 1898.' Nevertheless he did make some minor changes a few days later, especially in the latter part of the work, but the overall shape and atmosphere of the piece were unaffected. So insignificant are the alterations, indeed, that one is tempted to suggest that they were undertaken only in an attempt to compensate Muntra Musikanter for the non-appearance of *Unge Hellener*.

Bearing in mind how little time was now left before the première of the *Fifth Symphony*, it is remarkable that Sibelius spent much of August working on minor pieces. The piano miniatures *Scherzando* and *Petite sérénade* were added to the Op. 40 set, as Nos 8 and 9 respectively; the former is a stylized polka, the latter a warm-hearted, Italianate melody that would by no means be out of place in a vocal piece. The next piece Sibelius wrote was in fact a song, a humorous setting of Fröding's *Tre trallande jäntor* (*Three Warbling Maidens*), JS 204, but within days he had second thoughts about the work and, presumably, destroyed it. A very brief, rather Schubertian setting of *Der Wanderer und der Bach* (*The Wanderer and the Brook*), Op. 72 No. 5, by Martin Greif (a pseudonym for Friedrich Hermann Frey) was ready on 19th August. The poem is a dialogue between a wayfarer and the stream rushing down to the sea. The last lines hint at the relationship between the transient nature of human life and the self-renewing power of nature, but Sibelius rightly resists the temptation to inflate this dainty little morsel into a weighty pantheistic utterance. *Der Wanderer* and a much earlier Runeberg setting, *Hundra vägar* from 1907, were now sent away to Breitkopf to complete the Op. 72 set of songs.

A good illustration of Sibelius's hypersentitivity is his reaction to an article by M. Touchard about Kajanus in *Hufvudstadsbladet* on 15th August: '[Kajanus] lists among his works rhapsodies, the symphonic poem *Aino, Kullervo* and *Sommarminnen* [*Summer Memories*]'. Having presumably forgotten that Kajanus had indeed written a powerful orchestral piece named *Kullervo's Funeral March*, Sibelius jumped to the conclusion that Kajanus had claimed *Kullervo* as his own work! At that time Kajanus still had the score of Sibelius's *Kullervo* in his possession – and had done for a decade (he had conducted the fourth movement in 1905). By an unfortunate coincidence, though, he had mislaid the manuscript, and was forced to admit this to Sibelius in a letter a few days after the newspaper article was published: 'I find myself faced by something wholly mystifying. Might some crazy manuscript collector have purloined the score? I cannot believe it should be so, but neither can I come up with a less silly assumption. In any case the score is not lost. It is too voluminous to go astray. It is just a question of remembering where I have hidden it, and I shall not tire in my search. You know how stubborn I am. Moreover, I haven't by any means given up hope.' Kajanus's persistence paid off, and a few months later the manuscript was duly deposited at the National Library of Finland.

By the beginning of September Sibelius had begun to realize that he needed to concentrate on the new symphony, and the tally of new miniatures fell substantially. Before finishing the symphony he completed just two more shorter pieces. One was another song for Muntra Musikanter, *Evige Eros* (*Eternal Eros*), Op. 84 No. 4, to a text by Bertel Gripenberg. Uniquely among the Op. 84 songs for male choir, this one requires a solo baritone, with an expressive, chromatic vocal line that – as in *Ett drömackord* – has similarities with the bassoon threnody from the *Fifth Symphony*. The other novelty was a *Mazurka* for violin and piano, Op. 81 No. 1, which has become one of Sibelius's most frequently played violin pieces. It owes its popularity to a combination of brash showmanship, with wide leaps and almost percussive *pizzicati* lending weight to the characteristic mazurka rhythms, and a melody that is athletic and unsentimental.

There can be no doubt that Sibelius was under great pressure to complete the symphony in time for his fiftieth birthday concert. On 13th October he wrote: 'Everything now in broad outline. Worried that I won't have time to work on the all the details and make a fair copy. But I must.' And, within the next few days, he did indeed send away the various movements of the symphony to the copyist. But Sibelius's own metaphor of 'pieces of mosaic from heaven's floor' is particularly apt with regard to this work as, in its original four-movement form, the symphony rather resembles an incomplete jigsaw puzzle. Sibelius has put together enough pieces to give some idea of the overall picture, but the finer details have yet to emerge and the final position of the elements within the overall picture has yet to be established. As a conscientious and self-critical artist Sibelius would not knowingly have presented a sub-standard work, but it is undeniable that the version of the *Fifth Symphony* performed on 8th December 1915 did not maximize its potential. For the purposes of the fiftieth birthday celebrations, perhaps this did not even matter. It was more important that he had a grand new symphony to present – one that would not prove as challenging or controversial as the *Fourth*.

Meanwhile the practical preparations for his birthday had to be made. There was uncertainty about where the celebratory concert should be held: Sibelius initially wanted to use the National Theatre but later changed his mind in favour of the University Hall – a wise choice, as its acoustic was superior. He accepted an invitation from his brother-in-law Armas Järnefelt to conduct the new symphony in Stockholm the following February, although in his diary he expressed reservations about the musical climate in the Swedish capital. 'This typical Stockholm philistinism in music!! Their – that is, the Swedes' – narrow-minded approach to every-thing that isn't immediately accessible. That Armas has managed to put up with them for so long is a mystery to me. – But Stenhammar is there – a God-fearer in this Sodom.'

In the midst of all the preparations another major Finnish orchestra work was premièred: Kajanus's elegant *Sinfonietta in B flat major*, which was first performed by the Helsinki Philharmonic Orchestra on 25th November. The work is dedicated to Sibelius, who nevertheless chose not to attend the première: at this busy and artistically challenging time he would have had no wish to be upstaged by Kajanus. Although the *Sinfonietta* has its stylistic roots in German Romanticism, the lightness and refinement of its orchestration indicate a shift in the composer's emphasis towards neo-classicism. Sibelius, of course, was pursuing a very different path.

On 6th December a chamber concert was arranged featuring works from all periods of Sibelius's career. His early music was represented by movements from the *String Quartet in B flat major*, his *Kalevala* style by the piano suite *Kyllikki*, his 'introspective' period by *Voces intimae* and his new music by the *Sonatina in E major*, played by the young violinist Richard Burgin.

When the great day arrived Sibelius was treated as a national celebrity, with newspaper articles, his portrait in shop windows and messages of congratulation from far and wide. His presents included a large number of paintings by Finland's leading artists (though not from Gallen-Kallela) and even a Steinway grand piano. As he had done a few months earlier for Gallen-Kallela, Eino Leino wrote a poem for the occasion. In lieu of the projected biography, Madetoja published an essay about Sibelius's music in *Helsingin Sanomat*. Sibelius himself took an orchestral rehearsal in the morning and hardly had a moment's peace for the rest of the day. The concert itself was a lavish affair at which the music competed for pride of place with a wide range of tributes. For Helsinki audiences the programme was completely new. First there was the Finnish première of *The Oceanides*, after which Robert Kajanus presented Sibelius with a ceremonial wreath. The *Two Serenades* for violin and orchestra came next; though they were several years old, they had not been played before, and Richard Burgin's performances were very well received. After that, Sibelius received a civic address bearing 15,000 signatures. The *Fifth Symphony* occupied the second half of the programme. It was greeted enthusiastically, and repeat concerts were held on 12th (at the National Theatre) and 18th December (at the University Hall).

The concert was followed by a banquet at the Stock Exchange building. Among the many tributes from leading Finnish cultural figures was a noble speech by Robert Kajanus in which he said that: 'As far as our Finnish music is concerned, it scarcely existed when Jean Sibelius struck his first powerful chords... Barely had we begun to till the barren soil, when a tremendous sound arose from the wilderness. Away with spades and picks. Finnish music's mighty springs came bursting forth. A great torrent burst forth to engulf all before it. Jean Sibelius alone showed the way.' One can only imagine that Sibelius's international colleagues and champions would have been delighted to witness his triumph, had the war not restricted their movements.

Like Beethoven, Sibelius knew how to surprise the audience at the first performance of his symphonies. If the classicism of the *Third* had been a mild disappointment (as had been the case with Beethoven's *Eighth*) and the harsh dissonances of the *Fourth* a painful shock, the *Fifth* must have come as something of a relief. But if it was less forbidding than the *Fourth Symphony*, the 1915 version of the *Fifth* was not yet the rich, colourful and life-enhancing work that it was to become.

The most obvious difference between the 1915 and 1919 scores is that the original version was in four movements rather than three; the first two movements of the original were combined to form the long first movement of the definitive score. The tempo markings often differ between the versions of the symphony, suggesting either that the composer changed the markings in order to clarify his intentions, or that he actually changed his mind as to the best tempo for the passages in question (or a combination of both). To confuse matters further, the original concert programme for the 1915 version contained different tempo markings for the movements from the preserved parts (the original full manuscript score no longer exists). The 1915 score contains fewer expressive markings – *ritardandi, accelerandi* and so on: either Sibelius consciously made the music more varied and flexible during his revisions, or he simply did not have time to notate all of his wishes before sending the score to the copyist, and relied on his abilities as a conductor to impart the desired light and shade. The *Fifth* is scored for the normal Sibelius symphony orchestra: double woodwind, four horns, three trumpets, three trombones, timpani and strings. In addition, the 1915 version requires a bass clarinet – an instrument which features in only one other Sibelius symphony, the *Sixth*.

The first movement of the original *Fifth Symphony* begins with a single *mezzoforte* chord from the clarinets and bassoons (the same chord that begins the first movement of the *Lemminkäinen Suite*: A flat, E flat, F, C), followed by rising woodwind figures. Unusually for Sibelius, the strings do not play at all in the opening pages. The flutes and oboes proceed with music derived from the rising motif, and the horns add one of the movement's most important motifs – two consecutive rising fourths. Only now do the strings enter, providing support for what might be termed the second group, which alternates between the first violins and woodwind, and ends with a sweeping upward gesture. The exposition now comes to an end by rising to an agitated climax, the strings and wind just out of synchronization, after which the tension is released by a rocking, wave-like motif. After this comes a passage described by some writers as the second part of a double exposition, and likened by others to an exposition repeat, ending with three somewhat tentative woodwind bars.

The ensuing development section is a lugubrious bassoon lament above murmuring strings. The strings and wind then seize upon the second group, investing it with a sorrowful dignity, the strings singing richly, the horns sighing wistfully, winding the movement down to its inconclusive final bars, in which the double basses and cellos play the now familiar superimposed fourths – but this time *pizzicato*, in preparation for the lighter textures of the scherzo movement, which follows after a fermata.

The first movement and scherzo are built from the same basic motivic material. The scherzo's opening pages have a pastoral quality – reinforced on occasion by a high, sustained *pianissimo* C flat from the second violins, a sonority familiar from the *Pastorale* from *Pelléas et Mélisande*. Compared with the final 1919 score, the 1915 version has far less feeling of growth and impetus; the tempo remains fixed at *Allegro commodo* until the appearance of a *Poco a poco più stretto* marking towards the end of the movement. At the final climax the brass hammer home the theme from the climax of the first movement's exposition, followed by a succession of rising fourths, and then the movement comes to an unexpected, rhythmically unsatisfying end.

The slow movement is based in G major and its thematic material would in the ensuing revisions be expanded in emotional range and arranged in a different order. The main theme, for instance, is heard from *pizzicato* violins alone in the 1915 version, whereas in the 1919 score *staccato* flutes and *pizzicato* violins alternate. Just as the first and second movements of the symphony are thematically linked, so too there are correspondences between the slow movement and finale. One string *pizzicato* passage in particular anticipates the scurrying string writing at the beginning of the finale. In the 1915 score the slow movement simply fades away, its harmony unresolved, very much in the manner of some of the short interludes in Sibelius's theatre scores – in particular his music to Strindberg's *Swanwhite* (in which, we should remember, the eleventh number contains a clear anticipation of this very movement).

The finale in the first version of the symphony is much longer than its equivalent in the final score: 679 bars compared with 482. It begins with a cascade of string writing, followed by a 'swan hymn' from the horns. In the final version, this horn theme is heard in counterpoint with a rich, songful theme (woodwind, cellos), but at this stage in the 1915 score the latter idea is heard only in fragmentary form. After a change of key to C major, the original version contains a savage trumpet interjection, a wholly unexpected *cri de cœur* that looks back to the tonal ambiguities of the *Fourth Symphony*. This trumpet motif is derived directly from the second group of the first movement, and after it the 'swan hymn' yields to a spectral reprise of the first theme of the movement. This is followed by a long, atmospheric but uneventful passage in which the violins bounce on and on, finally relieved by a woodwind variant of the counterpoint theme. After an impassioned passage in E flat minor, the key changes back to E flat major and the tempo slows to *Largamente molto*. In this last moment of respite before the symphony's overwhelming final climax, the trumpets play the 'swan hymn'. The violins here recall the earlier brutal trumpet interjection: the effect is now more resigned and tranquil, though no less heart-rending. And then, finally, the 'swan hymn' takes control and builds up towards the triumphant final pages. In the 1915 score there are five concluding chords from trumpets and trombones, the first four heard above sustained woodwind and horns and a string *tremolo*.

Numerous other concerts were held to honour Sibelius's fiftieth birthday. On 10th December Schnéevoigt and Kajanus joined forces for a concert including the first two symphonies and some orchestral songs. The same day, Karl Ekman (father of Sibelius's friend and biographer Karl Ekman Jr) conducted the Turku orchestra in a programme that also featured the *First Symphony*. And on 14th December the Muntra Musikanter choir joined the Philharmonic Orchestra for a concert at the University Hall that included the première of the song *Evige Eros*.

One of the complex aspects of Sibelius's character was the manner in which he combined the roles of a solitary nature-lover and a cosmopolitan *bon viveur*. And so, although he was honoured by all the presents, tributes and fine words, after a while he began to be worn down, noting in his diary 'I'm tired of this attention. I long to work. That's what gives life its dignity.' He was also aware that all the messages of congratulation in the world would not pay the bills: 'My debts won't get any smaller. It's a mystery to me, as I am earning good money and using a large part of it for repayments. Despite my reputation I don't get paid enough. Yes, yes!' This was confirmed in dramatic fashion in the immediate aftermath of the birthday celebrations, when the bailiffs tried to take away his new Steinway. Fortunately common sense won through and the instrument was left at Ainola. At Christmas the family had one more reason to be of good cheer: Ruth and Jussi Snellman announced their engagement.

1916

Soon after the celebrations had died down, Sibelius started to have doubts about his new symphony. It was normal practice for him to make small corrections and alterations to his scores after the first performance, in readiness for publication, but in this case he realized that something more drastic was called for. At that point he could not have known that the symphony would be submitted to a four-year process of revision during which he would change not only the outer form of the work but also its inner essence, moving away from the *Fourth Symphony*'s orbit towards a loftier, more sublime and yet more accessible style. He conducted the *Fifth Symphony* again at Folkets hus on 9th January (the programme was the same as at his birthday concert except that *The Bard* – given for the first time in its definitive form – replaced the *Two Serenades*).

Axel Carpelan's health was deteriorating: he contracted a lung inflammation and was, or so Sibelius thought, mortally ill. At this time Sibelius himself was suffering from ear trouble; he believed that he was going deaf and consulted a doctor. Such fears turned out to be nothing more than hypochondria, but provided a convenient excuse for him to cancel his planned conducting trip to Stockholm, even though the concerts had already been advertised (in the end they were conducted by Armas Järnefelt, and the *Fifth Symphony* was not included). Despite his comments the previous month, it is odd that Sibelius called off the visit. It would have proved a rare wartime opportunity to travel, and his trip to Sweden the previous year had been a great success. The reason seems to have been that he was keen to immerse himself once more in the *Fifth Symphony*. In his diary on 26th January he admitted that he was 'once more working on Symphony 5. Struggling with God. I want to give my new symphony a different, more human form. More earthy, more vibrant – the problem was that I myself have changed while working on it.'

In early February – to be precise on 5th February (Runeberg day) Sibelius learned from Ida Ekman that a collection had been organized to pay off a significant proportion of his debts. After an all-Sibelius concert (*The Swan of Tuonela*, *En saga*, *The Rapids-Rider's Brides* and the *Fourth Symphony*) conducted by Kajanus at the beginning of March, Sibelius received a further donation of 13,000 marks from the choral conductor, musical administrator and appeal court judge Emil Forsström.

Sibelius's former pupil Leevi Madetoja made his début as a symphonist with the Philharmonic Orchestra on 10th February with a three-movement work, dedicated to Robert Kajanus, that plays for some 25 minutes. In his review in *Hufvudstadsbladet*, Bis perceived the presence of Sibelius as a model, though 'not as a slavish imitation on the part of Mr Madetoja, but rather in pointing out the general direction'. Sibelius attended the concert and was impressed by the piece.

During the spring Sibelius took on a new composition pupil, Bengt von Törne, whom he met at a rehearsal for a performance by Kajanus of the *Fourth Symphony* and who would later record his memories in the book *Sibelius: A Close-Up*. One of Sibelius's earliest pieces of advice to von Törne was the often quoted line: 'Never pay any attention to what critics say... Remember, a statue has never been set up in honour of a critic!'

On 30th March and 2nd April Sibelius conducted the *Fifth Symphony* at concerts in Helsinki; it was not to be heard again in this form during the composer's lifetime. The first of these concerts also featured the premières of Nos 1 and 2, *Cantique* and *Devotion*, Op. 77, played not on the violin but in a new arrangement for cello – and, incidentally, in reverse order. The soloist was the Helsinki Philharmonic Orchestra's principal cellist, Ossian Fohström. (The cello part can also be combined with the composer's piano accompaniment.) By the time Edition Wilhelm Hansen published the works in 1922, however, the original solo part for the cello version of *Devotion* could not be found. A manuscript – possibly retained by Fohström after the première – found its way into the collection of the Russian philologist Andrei Rudnyev in St Petersburg, and this was returned to Finland in 1952. Most cello performances of *Devotion* have relied upon various conjectural transcriptions of the published violin part, but in recent years Sibelius's authentic cello part, in accordance with the Rudnyev manuscript, has started to be used once again.

During the early months of 1916, when he was not conducting or attending concerts, busy with family and friends or worrying about his financial predicament, Sibelius entertained almost exclusively symphonic thoughts. The generous donations he had received clearly relieved him of the pressing need to write pieces for immediate sale – but his regular income was still falling, and covered only a small fraction of his debts. In the second half of May, however, he suddenly returned to writing miniatures: he noted in his diary that he was 'working intensively on a number of little things. And am hoping that they will earn me some money.' On 9th June he listed no less than eight such pieces as complete, and they were sold forthwith to the publisher Lindgren.

Six of the eight pieces were for solo piano, and the first two were for a new opus group – Op. 85, all of which are based on flower themes. *Iris* (*The Iris*), No. 3, contrasts and ultimately interweaves improvisatory, whirling flourishes, like gusts of wind (an anticipation of the forest storms of *Tapiola*) with a regular, Bach-inspired motif that starts as a fugue but is never allowed to develop. Though it is notated in 6/4, *Oeillet* (*The Carnation*), No. 2, is by nature an amiable, gently nostalgic waltz. The remaining four found their way into the Op. 76 collection. *Pièce enfantine*, No. 8, shares its waltz character and its key of A flat major with *Oeillet*, but is a much livelier, even frivolous piece that plays for just one minute. *Harlequinade*, No. 13, lives up to its title and portrays the capricious humour of a *commedia dell'arte* jester; its opening phrase with its triplet and descending fifth is Sibelian to the core. The *Humoresque*, No. 4, is full of bustle and activity, and plays with motivic fragments without ever attempting to combine them into a coherent theme. *Elegiaco*,

No. 10, returns to a waltz-like idiom, but with a more intimate vein of melancholy.

The remaining two miniatures were for violin and piano, and were included in Op. 79. They are more ambitious than the piano pieces completed at this time and commanded a commensurately higher fee from Lindgren. In fact the *Danse caractéristique*, No. 3, with its spiky violin writing and unpredictable, nightmarish flights of fancy, could hardly be further removed from the honest directness of the *Pièce enfantine*. Virtuosity and showmanship are more to the fore here than in any of Sibelius's violin pieces since the *Violin Concerto*, and at the same time the piece clearly anticipates the more astringent style of his violin pieces from the 1920s. Its companion piece, *Sérénade*, No. 4, is a decorous piece with a genteel D major melody, although more fervent emotions surface briefly in its middle section.

On 23rd April the Senate awarded Sibelius a professorship, an honour to which he claimed to attach little weight. In any case he was distracted because his daughter Ruth had fallen off the horse, though she remembered nothing of the incident itself. Jussi Snellman visited her at Ainola, and the close attention he paid to his future wife made a good impression on Sibelius.

In mid-June Sibelius accepted a commission from Jalmari Lahdensuo, director of the National Theatre, to write a score for Hugo von Hofmannsthal's *Jedermann* (*Everyman*). Before he could get very far with this, however, there were family matters that required his attention. First of all there was a brief visit from Linda, on temporary release from the Pitkäniemi mental hospital. Sibelius tended to become depressed when he had contact with his sister, seeing in her situation a fate to which he himself could all too easily succumb. But he had to put aside his worries about his sister's health – and also that of his 'wonderful friend' Axel Carpelan, who was feeling 'weak and miserable' (according to Sibelius's diary entry of 21st June) – because he had a wedding to arrange. Ruth married Jussi Snellman on 21st July, and there was a lavish party to be organized.

To help fund the wedding, Sibelius sold five more piano pieces to Westerlund, and Jussi Snellman took them to the publisher on 4th July. A robust, high-spirited *Polonaise*, justifiably one of the most popular of Sibelius's character pieces, was eventually included as the last of the ten *Pensées lyriques*, Op. 40. The remaining four completed the Op. 34 collection. *Souvenir*, No. 10, has been described by Folke Gräsbeck as 'one of Sibelius's fabulously yearning, slow, minor-key waltzes'.[7] The restless, chromatic contour of the main theme takes its cue from the '*Lulu*' *Waltz* for cello and piano (1889). *Danse pastorale*, No. 7, also calls to mind Sibelius's early music: in its simplicity and brevity it could be compared to the thematic exercises of the 1880s. *Reconnaissance*, No. 9, is similarly concise, and is based on a descending D major scale motif in repeated semiquavers, seen by Eero Heinonen as a portrayal of 'mirthful laughter'. Finally there was *Joueur de harpe*, No. 8, where the piano imitates the sound of a solitary harp player, solemn and archaic, in the same spirit as the tone poem *The Bard*. Unfortunately Sibelius was a little too eager to celebrate. With his mother-in-law installed at Ainola for the wedding, he set off to Helsinki where he collected payment for the piano pieces on 7th July. Sibelius's gradual return to his old habits is demonstrated by the fact that he promptly spent much of the money on a drinking spree.

The wedding passed off smoothly – although Sibelius did not enjoy the punch – and he was soon back at work. His next project was a set of songs, Op. 86, composed in August for Ida Ekman. Originally the set included five songs of which the first, *Vårförnimmelser* (*The Coming of Spring*), is a Tavaststjerna setting: the arrival of springtime is, as we have seen, a recurrent theme in Sibelius's songs. This time he produced a relatively conventional piece based on variations of a single musical phrase. This consists of a bar of 2/2 followed by a bar of 3/2, resulting in a five-beat phrase, but despite this the song contains no trace of the *Kalevala* style or folk music. The second song, *Längtan heter min arvedel* (*Longing is my Heritage*), to words by Karlfeldt, is far more distinguished. This is a sublime song full of tranquil, understated melancholy. *Dold förening* (*Hidden Union*), No. 3, is very brief; the vocal line proceeds above a regular, metrical accompaniment. Carl Snoilsky's unassuming text deals with the theme of deceptive appearances. The gently undulating melodic line and restrained piano writing in *Och finns det en tanke?* (*And Is There a Thought?*), No. 4, lend a special poignancy to Tavaststjerna's touching poem on the theme of mortality, an effect intensified by the use of a tritone in the melody. The fifth song, *Sångarlön* (*The Singer's Reward*), another Snoilsky setting, is less impressive: its vocal line is not especially distinctive, and is moreover encumbered by some busy-sounding piano writing. A year later, perhaps in recognition of *Sångarlön*'s shortcomings, Sibelius added a sixth song to the Op. 86 set – a mesmerizing setting of Lybeck's *I systrar, I bröder* (*Ye Sisters, Ye Brothers*).

In September Sibelius had to focus on the music for *Jedermann*. This necessitated the occasional visit to Helsinki, for instance to see Jalmari Lahdensuo, who showed him a puppet presentation of the play – but such trips were not without their dangers, as he acknowledged in his diary: 'In town yesterday. Not without boozing... I must reduce my alcohol consumption to a minimum. The same goes for tobacco.' But despite such temptations he managed to complete this extensive score by 6th October.

Jedermann, Op. 83, is scored for the unusual combination of two flutes, oboe, two clarinets and bassoon, two horns, two trumpets, timpani, piano, organ, strings and mixed chorus with vocal soloists. Hofmannsthal had written a new version of this medieval morality play in 1911, and for the National Theatre's performance it was translated into Finnish by Huugo Jalkanen. Sibelius was experienced at writing music portraying allegorical figures, and the characters of Death, Good Works, Faith, the Devil and Mammon afforded him a further opportunity to demonstrate this skill. What was new here, however, was the overtly sacred motifs and symbolism that permeate the play. Religious allusions in plays such as *Swanwhite* had been incidental, but here they are central to the purpose of the play. Unlike in the projected *Marjatta* oratorio, where the Bible stories were filtered by being interwoven with Finnish mythology, the religious message in *Jedermann* comes direct and unadorned from central Europe.

The music for *Everyman* is one of the most uneven of all of Sibelius's theatre scores, ranging from light dance numbers to extended passages of delicate 'mood music' intended to accompany spoken text. The music is an integral part of the drama; it was never intended to be performed independently of the action on stage, and does not really work as a concert item unless at least some dialogue is included. The score is divided into sixteen musical numbers of which the first consists of a single chord (admittedly twice repeated)! This leads straight into a bleak, discordant number accompanying the scene where God summons Death and gives him the task of fetching Everyman, who lives a carefree, materialistic earthly existence; here the piano and bells establish the interval of a fourth which will prove important later in the score.

We then come down to earth for Everyman's banquet scene with his friends and his mistress, Paramour. The preparations are accompanied by gently bustling string writing (*Allegro*, No. 3), which is condensed into a four-bar dance motif (*Allegro comodo*, No. 3a). Next comes a strophic song (*Dance Song*, No. 4), performed by the arriving guests; this is one of the most attractive movements in the score. Its trochaic *pizzicato* string accompaniment above held woodwind and brass chords is reminiscent of *Peer Gynt's Serenade* from Grieg's famous incidental music. The fifth and sixth numbers are tiny pieces for mezzo-soprano – or rather isolated phrases, as they are respectively just six and four bars long. The following madrigal, however (*Maat ja metsät viheriöivät* [*Forests Are Becoming Green*], No. 7), is more characteristic on account both of its slow 3/2 metre and of its theme, which has similarities with runic melodies and is, indeed, very close to one of the main themes in Sibelius's *Karelia* music. During the lively song *Oi Lempi, armas Lempi* (*Alas, Alas, Lady Love*; No. 8) a tolling bell is heard, summoning Everyman to his death; then the melody of the madrigal returns, as a canon for the choir (No. 9). The tenth number, in a wholly characteristic Sibelian style, takes up and expands material from the banquet preparations, breaking off abruptly as Death arrives at the party to fulfil his mission.

In his hour of need Everyman is deserted by his friends. Only an ailing old woman, Good Works, is willing to accompany him. At this point in the score, Sibelius's music changes radically in character. To accompany the dialogue between Everyman and Good Works he wrote a long, meandering, chromatic piece of mood music (No. 11) – scored for muted strings and sinister, booming timpani – that evokes an uneasy atmosphere comparable to that in the music to *Ödlan* (1909). Gradually the intensity grows and motifs start to take shape. In the twelfth number Everyman encounters Faith; here the thematic strands coalesce further, acquiring a more definite profile. The thirteenth number accompanies the scene where a repentant Everyman sees his mother going to morning mass; here the organ chorale theme and Bach-like string writing allude to the clichés of religious music in a way that is most unusual for Sibelius. Everyman must still die, but at least his soul has been saved. Faith and Good Works prevent the Devil from reclaiming him: an expressive, chromatic string motif accompanies the Devil's futile attempts (No. 14). Everyman goes to his grave to the strains of solemn, processional music (No. 15), and in the last number a chorus of angels sings 'Gloria in excelsis Deo' while the male voices have a few bars of strange, very modern-sounding *Sprechgesang*, and the score ends (No. 16) with thematic references back to the very beginning. The first night of *Jedermann* was on 5th November 1916, conducted by Robert Kajanus; the music was well received as an integral part of the production.

The *Jedermann* commission had taken up valuable time that Sibelius might have preferred to spend revising the *Fifth Symphony* and so it was with a degree of inevitability that he noted in his diary on 23rd November: 'I'm working on the revision of the *Fifth Symphony*. And, again, I'm in a hurry. But – it *has to be* good.' A month later the revised symphony was ready.

We shall probably never be in a position to judge how successful the 1916 version of the *Fifth Symphony* was. Only a double bass part survives,[8] from which we can tell that the original first and second movements had now been joined together and were much closer to their final form – complete with the opening horn call and the final *Più presto* climax. The slow movement and finale (where the E flat minor episode was replaced by a *Vivace* passage in E flat major) were still some distance from their final form. The finale was even longer than in the 1915 version: 702 bars compared with 679.

Sibelius conducted the symphony for the first time on 8th December, his 51st birthday, at the Fire Brigade Hall in Turku, with the Turku

Musical Society orchestra; the programme also contained *En saga* and the *Rakastava* suite, and was repeated two days later. Carpelan had recently warned Sibelius that the Turku orchestra 'is now, to tell the truth, no longer good. The cellist is hopeless, horns are missing, the oboe and flute are weak, and so on.' Luckily it was reinforced by musicians from Helsinki for the concerts, and Carpelan at least was delighted with the result. Even though they had spent time together in Turku, he sent a letter of congratulation to Sibelius that makes it clear that he saw the new symphony in almost pictorial terms, as an extension of Sibelius's work as a nature poet: 'The sounds of your *Fifth* are still ringing in my ears, richer, more original and more beautiful than any nature symphony since Ludwig the Great. In the *Allegro molto* the mood and natural freshness are wonderful: a "midsummer night's dream"... the woodwind = creatures of nature, never before heard, and then this incomparable swan hymn!' One wonders what he would have made of *Tapiola*, had he lived long enough to hear it!

When Sibelius conducted the symphony in Helsinki the following week, however, it failed to make much impact. It may have been that the concert itself went less than perfectly. In his diary Sibelius wrote that it was 'not at all to my taste. No enthusiasm.' He even suspected that people were conspiring against him, and had somehow influenced the critic Bis who, in his review in *Hufvudstadsbladet*, found fault with the work's form, instrumentation and dissonant ending.

Robert Kajanus and Georg Schnéevoigt were no longer in direct competition as conductors, as Schnéevoigt had moved to Stockholm the previous year to take up the post of principal conductor of the Konsertförening orchestra (now the Royal Stockholm Philharmonic Orchestra). Kajanus celebrated his sixtieth birthday on 2nd December, and both Jean and Aino attended the dinner held in his honour.

At least Sibelius could take heart from the appearance of Erik Furuhjelm's biography (in Swedish) *Jean Sibelius: Hans tondiktning och drag ur hans liv* (*Jean Sibelius: His Music and Aspects of his Life*), which came out just before Christmas. Sibelius approved of the result, praising its conscientiousness and thorough research. The original intention had been for Furuhjelm's book to be published at the time of Sibelius's fiftieth birthday, but the delay had at least given the author a chance to examine the newly rediscovered score of *Kullervo*. The book gives a very sympathetic and detailed portrayal of the young Sibelius, and discusses many of the early chamber works that, already in 1916, were unknown even to Sibelius's most ardent admirers, among them the *String Quartet in E flat major*, the *Suite in D minor* for violin and piano, *Theme and Variations in C sharp minor* for string quartet and the *String Trio in G minor*. In due course a Finnish translation appeared, made by Leevi Madetoja.

1917

In the New Year Sibelius took another look at the *Fifth Symphony*, with a view to sending it to Armas Järnefelt for a performance in Stockholm. It did not take him long to realize the folly of such a plan, and on 6th January he wrote to Järnefelt: 'When I was composing my Sym. 5 for my 50th birthday, I was very pressed for time. As a result I spent last year re-working it – but am still not satisfied. And *cannot*, absolutely *cannot* send it to you.' Many composers would have given up after one revision, but Sibelius realized in his heart of hearts that the *Fifth Symphony* was not yet perfect. In pursuit of his symphonic ideals he was nothing if not tenacious, as the fate of the *Eighth Symphony* many years later was to prove. But he was not yet inclined to plunge into a further reworking of the symphony. Instead he turned to a song cycle for Ida Ekman, this time on the theme of flowers, and – also for Ida Ekman – made an orchestration of the popular *Demanten på marssnön*.

This was a period of tension in the relationship between Jean and Aino, and one does not have to look hard to find the reason. Sibelius simply lacked the self-control to keep away from alcohol, even if he was fully aware of the harm it was causing both to himself and to his family: 'It's hard to know about Aino. She's having a really hard time at the moment and is suffering terribly with me. Within me there sings an intimate, sad melody. [Illegible word] how we love each other. Aino longs for death as a relief' (diary, 21st January). His excesses were frequently followed by remorseful confessions in his diary. When Aino paid a fortnight's visit to Eva and Arvi Paloheimo, who were then living in Petrograd (formerly St Petersburg), Jean set off for the bright lights of Helsinki. 'In town the day before yesterday and yesterday. Boozing with the depression that follows. A frightful condition. Especially when, with my taste for drink, am doing myself harm both in my own eyes and in other people's. At home some illicit drinking to calm my nerves' (7th February). By the beginning of March things had become so bad that Sibelius was even considering divorce, although he admitted that neither he nor Aino had the courage to take such a step.

But he still needed to compose. Among the shorter pieces that saw the light of day in 1917, works for the violin occupy pride of place. While Aino was in Russia he completed the first of what would ultimately become six *Humoresques* for violin and orchestra. The neglect of these pieces in the concert repertoire is unaccountable, as they are sparkling, inventive works that not only show Sibelius at his best but also have immediate audience appeal. The fact that he could compose such gems at such a difficult time in his private life shows the danger of claiming too close a link between a composer's life and his works. According to Jussi Jalas, Sibelius intended the six *Humoresques* to form a suite, even though they were eventually split between two opus numbers (Op. 87 and Op. 89). Even when the solo writing is at its most flamboyant, it remains organically integrated with the orchestra. Sibelius considered calling them 'Impromptus' or 'Lyrical Dances', and the latter title suits their character well. *Humoresque No. 1 in D minor*, Op. 87 No. 1,[9] for instance, has the character of a mazurka. In its original form it was scored with particular delicacy, with muted strings throughout and harp, as well as double woodwind, four horns and timpani.

In the winter sunshine Sibelius bemoaned the world war and complained at the insincerity of his friends. Such worries are not reflected in a whimsical *Esquisse* for piano, Op. 76 No. 1, completed on 21st February. Even for this modest trifle Sibelius considered a range of titles, among them *Giroflée* (*The Gillyflower*) and *Pensée* (*The Pansy*), possibly with the intention of including it in his Op. 85 'flower' pieces.

Among the most deeply felt of Sibelius's wartime miniatures is a noble hymn in 3/2 time for violin or cello and piano. It is similar in mood to the earlier *Cantique* from the *Serious Melodies*, Op. 77, and this may be why titles that Sibelius considered included *Mélodie sérieuse* and *Preghiera* (*Prayer*). Finally, however, he settled upon the name *Religioso*, Op. 78 No. 3, and dedicated the piece to his brother Christian.

Internationally, 1917 was a cataclysmic year in world history, especially in Russia. In February – the very month when Aino chose to visit Eva and her husband – there were food riots in Petrograd, and the situation grew worse as the weeks passed. Facing rebellion among the armed forces as well as widespread public unrest, Tsar Nicholas II was forced to step down on 15th March.[10] News of his abdication reached Finland within days and was greeted with enthusiastic celebrations: whatever uncertainties the future held, political change in Finland too was now inevitable. In the Tsar's place came a Provisional Government which recalled the Governor-General, Frans Seyn, and annulled the February Manifesto of 1899, reversing all the steps taken to curtain Finland's autonomy. The Finnish parliament could also now meet again.

Both Jean and Aino were pleased to welcome Eva and her daughter Marjatta home from Petrograd, especially as Eva was once more pregnant. Sibelius's reaction to events in Russia, to judge from his diary, was somewhat laconic. 'Big changes afoot in Russia. Are we to be permitted to determine our own destiny? That is the big question. A heavy weight hangs over Finland' (16th March). The following diary entry makes no further mention of political developments, but merely records the completion of two more short pieces for violin and piano, the *Dance Idyll*, Op. 79 No. 5, and *Waltz*, Op. 81 No. 3. Neither piece shows any trace of the great events that were happening in the world; indeed both are whimsical in character. The gentle *Dance Idyll* has a rippling piano accompaniment that suggests waves lapping on a beach. Sibelius revised the piece before selling it to the publisher Lindgren in early April. The *Waltz* is an undemanding salon piece with an appealing D major melody that clearly comes from the same stable as the first woodwind theme of the *Second Symphony*. At times the piece takes on an almost improvisational quality – not least when the violin falls unexpectedly silent for a moment towards the end, as though the player could not remember his part! A similar spontaneity infuses the brief *Affettuoso* for piano, Op. 76 No. 7, written at the beginning of April.

Later that month Sibelius wrote two pieces for choir *a cappella*. The first of these was *Till havs* (*To Sea*), Op. 84 No. 5, written for the long-established male choir Akademiska sångföreningen ('Akademen'). Though it is ostensibly a sea song, Jonatan Reuter's poem, dating from 1895, is really a call to arms, and Sibelius set it as an energetic strophic song, march-like in character. Like several other similar marches in his output (e.g. *Har du mod?* and the later *Scout March*), the music proceeds in clear-cut, almost *staccato* rhythms with clear breaks between – and in some cases within – the phrases. Having completed a draft of the piece on 17th April, Sibelius went on to make some small revisions that served further to emphasize the rhythmic quality of the music. *Till havs* was included in the Op. 84 set of songs but is the only one of them not to have been written for Muntra Musikanter. A common factor, however, was the conductor Olof Wallin, who had directed Muntra Musikanter until the autumn of 1915 and who now conducted the première of *Till havs*, just days after its completion, with Akademen at a May Day's Eve concert at Helsinki's Kaivohuone.

On 21st April Sibelius put the finishing touches to another Reuter setting, *Drömmarna* (*The Dreams*), JS 64, this time for mixed choir and composed in response to a commission from Svenska Folkskolans Vänner (the Friends of the Swedish Elementary School). The smoothly flowing music reflects the generations that 'glide like reflecting streams' mentioned in the text; human life is transient but dreams remain constant through the ages. These choral pieces were anything but lucrative: for *Till havs* Sibelius received 200 marks, for *Drömmarna* just 100. By comparison he had received 500 marks for the first edition of *Affettuoso*, and 2,000 for the first of the violin *Humoresques*.

In May the second of the *Humoresques* for violin and orchestra, Op. 87 No. 2, was ready, a nervous, virtuosic piece in D major that almost has the character of a *moto perpetuo*. Its frenetic energy could well be compared with the second movement of *Voces intimae*, although the *Humoresque* is more extrovert; its throwaway ending is delightful. In the same key and

2/4 metre, but much more relaxed in tone, is the popular *Rondino* for violin and piano, Op. 81 No. 2, completed a few days later – although the latter was, according to Sibelius's diary, 'something for Pelle [Westerlund], as I need "loads of money" now'.

It is easy to underestimate how difficult conditions were in Finland during this period. Russian soldiers and sailors based in Helsinki were in a rebellious mood, made worse by the Finnish workers' propensity for murdering Russian officers. Among the Finns, riots and strikes were commonplace. Järvenpää was still isolated enough to be spared the worst of the unrest that affected the capital, but daily life remained a struggle, and food was in short supply. Sibelius referred to the situation as 'complete anarchy' (diary, 17th May), and it therefore came as a very pleasant surprise when, in mid-May, he received a leg of lamb as a present from the architect and amateur singer Torkel Nordman in Pori. In Swedish such a leg of lamb is known as a 'fårfiol' – a 'lamb fiddle' – and Nordman had imaginatively labelled it as such and packed it inside a violin case, rightly surmising that nobody would be curious if Sibelius were to be sent a violin! Sibelius responded by sending Nordman a newly composed song, *Fridolins dårskap* (*Fridolin's Folly*), JS 84, a wonderfully mellifluous strophic setting of a humorously nostalgic poem by Karlfeldt which alludes to such a leg of lamb (Sibelius discreetly omits the strophe which deals with Fridolin's amorous exploits). The melody itself has similarities with a hymn tune by Rudolf Lagi, *Jag lyfter ögat mot himmelen* (*I lift my eyes to heaven*). Sibelius regarded the piece as nothing more than a joke and was surprised at the popularity it achieved.

During the summer family celebrations proved a welcome distraction from the privations of wartime. On 10th June Sibelius and Aino celebrated their silver wedding anniversary in the company of Christian and Linda – a gathering that Sibelius described as 'very atmospheric'. Two new grandchildren arrived: Eva gave birth to her second child, a boy who was named Martti, and Ruth too bore a son, Erkki. The relationship between Jean and Aino was still tense, however. So too was the political situation, as Sibelius saw for himself when he went into Helsinki in early July.

In the meantime the set of six flower songs for Ida Ekman (Op. 88), begun already in January, had been finished. The composer himself called them a song cycle, although they draw on the work of two poets: Frans Franzén (a Swedish-speaking Finn, born in Oulu, who became Bishop of Härnösand, Sweden, in 1824) in the first three songs, and Runeberg in the others. They are undeniably modest pieces, but charming nonetheless. There is a clear stylistic distinction between the almost self-conscious intimacy of the Franzén settings and the wider emotional range of the Runeberg songs. Throughout the set Sibelius consciously avoided writing vocal lines that were technically challenging. He later recalled: 'The flower songs, Op. 88, were written for Ida Ekman's last concerts, when her voice was already past its best. In consequence the songs are not demanding, but clearly permitted Ida's intimate, intelligent and animated interpretation to emerge with full power and effect.' The vocal line in the first song, *Blåsippan* (*The Blue Anemone*) has obvious similarities with the violin part of the third *Humoresque* which was soon to be completed, whilst the piano part – which, as elsewhere in the set, is where any decorative writing is found – is a model of grace and propriety. The second, *De bägge rosorna* (*The Two Roses*) recalls movements from incidental music – *Mélisande* (*Pelléas et Mélisande*) or *The Maidens with Roses* (*Swanwhite*), although it is less waltz-like than either. The delicate, lilting melody of *Vitsippan* (*The White Anemone*) reflects the fragility of the flower as described in Franzén's poem. When we reach the first of the Runeberg settings, *Sippan* (*The Anemone*) we immediately find that the vocal phrases have a broader sweep and the piano part greater variety; again, individual motifs are related to ideas in the violin *Humoresques*. The metre and melodic shape, not to mention the solemnity and simplicity of the fifth song, *Törnet* (*The Thorn*), resemble a much earlier Runeberg setting, *Se'n har jag ej frågat mera*, from the early 1890s; indeed, the poems come from the same volume of poetry.[11] In the last song, *Blommans öde* (*The Flower's Destiny*), the piano carries the bulk of the musical argument whilst the voice has little more than an *obbligato* line to convey the text. One could almost imagine the piece performed as a melodrama, by narrator and piano. The vocal line, like the autumn flower described in the poem, has been sapped of all its vigour.

The flower songs were ready on 16th June, but the following months were unproductive and it was not until mid-September that Sibelius's next pieces saw the light of day. First of all there was a piano miniature, *Mandolinato*, JS 123, for publication in *Lucifer*. Despite its title, this dance-like piece does not really imitate the sound of the mandolin; instead, it builds on a rhythmic motif that is familiar from several other works from different phases of Sibelius's career, among them the *String Trio in G minor*, *Impromptu* for women's voices and orchestra, and *Musik zu einer Scène*.

A few days later he completed three more *Humoresques* for violin and orchestra. In *Humoresques No. 3* and *No. 4*, both in G minor, the supporting orchestra is confined to strings. *No. 3* has the character of a gavotte and features highly demanding double stopping and arpeggios for the soloist – although the technical fireworks are not an end in themselves, but are seamlessly integrated into the musical argument. Like a sponta-neous meditation above held chords in the orchestra, *No. 4* serves as a 'slow movement', melancholy and full of intensity. A highlight of the set is the *Humoresque No. 5*, a genuinely exuberant piece in E flat major, in which flutes, clarinets and bassoons are added to the orchestra; moreover, at one point the solo violin acquires an almost piccolo-like, whistling timbre by playing the main theme in artificial harmonics. The short–long–short syncopations in the main theme are reminiscent of the finale of the '*Korpo*' *Trio* of 1887.

One piece from 1917 that was not immediately mentioned in Sibelius's diary is the *March of the Finnish Jäger Battalion*. The 27th Royal Prussian Jäger Battalion consisted of some 1,900 Finnish patriot volunteers who had left their homeland illicitly, via Sweden, to undergo military training; they fought in the ranks of the German Army in the battles on the northern flank of the eastern front in 1916–17. In August 1917, while the battalion was based in Liepāja in Latvia, a competition was held among the troops to write the text for a regimental song; the winning entry, by Heikki Nurmio, was smuggled to Finland and secretly set to music as a simple yet robust march for male voices and piano by Sibelius, who withheld his name from the first edition, although at the end of the piece a date was written: his birthday. The first performance of a version with piano accompaniment took place privately in Helsinki on 23rd October 1917 and copies – some containing many errors – soon began to circulate. In purely musical terms the march is not remarkable, although it has tremendous verve and an infectious melody that has helped to secure it greater international renown than comparable works as *Song of the Athenians* or *Har du mod?*

In late September Katarina, then aged fourteen, started to attend a school in Helsinki; she stayed with Martha Tornell and returned to Ainola only once a week. Sibelius was saddened by her departure, and his mood was not improved by a visit from his sister Linda. Autumn was coming; the cranes departed. Any money that he managed to earn was devalued by raging inflation, and the situation at home and in Russia meant that he had to refuse an offer to conduct in Kiev. He was not in the right frame of mind to make further revisions to the *Fifth Symphony* or to proceed with the *Sixth*, and remarked in his diary: 'I am worn down by doubts about the form of my new things.'

And so, with seeming inevitability, he turned once more to the composition of miniatures. By the end of September he had produced a mysterious, aphoristic, syncopated *Berceuse* for violin and piano, Op. 79 No. 6, and a lighthearted piano piece named *Bellis* (*The Daisy*, but sometimes translated as *Bluebells*), Op. 85 No. 1, with a similar unaffected robustness as the *Étude* and *Pièce enfantine* from Op. 76. Maybe the composition of the six flower songs for Ida Ekman had reminded Sibelius that he had begun a set of piano pieces on flower themes the previous year; at any rate, he now carried on and completed *Aquileja* (*The Columbine*), Op. 85 No. 4, a couple of weeks later. The melodic line is kept so separate from the supporting figures in this charming piece that one could almost imagine it scored for a solo instrument and accompaniment in the style of the violin *Humoresques*. The Op. 85 set was completed in November with No. 5, *Campanula*, in which Sibelius seems to have taken his cue from the flower's common name – bellflower – and written a harmonically ambiguous carillon which only achieves a degree of stability in the gentle arpeggios in the closing bars.

If the proximity of the *Humoresques* was noticeable in *Aquileja*, it is even more pervasive in the song *I systrar, I bröder, I älskande par* (*Ye Sisters, Ye Brothers, Ye Loving Couples*), Op. 86 No. 6, that was also completed in November. The poem is by Mikael Lybeck, and Sibelius described it in a letter to the publisher Lindgren as 'one of the best *musical* texts that I have ever had'. The theme of the poem – that young people should enjoy love before it is too late – is not dissimilar to the central concept of *Våren flyktar hastigt*, but whereas the earlier song is lyrical and dramatic, the piano accompaniment in *I systrar, I bröder* lends the song a hypnotic, compulsive, even sinister quality. It was published together with the five songs written a year earlier for Ida Ekman.

On 25th October (7th November in the Gregorian calendar) Lenin and the Bolsheviks had risen up against Kerensky's provisional government in Russia's October Revolution, and the situation in Finland too was becoming increasingly tense. During the summer various armed groups had been constituted amongst the Finnish socialist and conservative factions, and efforts were now made to mobilize them. A week-long general strike took place in mid-November and it soon became clear that a major political change was imminent. Sibelius's diary mentions the impending general strike and what he saw as the socialist threat to 'us patriots' but, characteristically, was far more preoccupied with his own situation: 'There are moments in life when everything is blacker than black – darker than night. They say that time heals wounds. But what about those that cannot be healed? On the other hand life is so short. Is it really impossible to hold out? Certainly it is, but it's a struggle. – My beloved Aino, whom I love more than words can convey and who shares the struggle with me: how I am sorry for her from the depths of my heart. She gets so little joy from me. And so much deep misery. – I am terribly uneasy. – Strange that I myself should always be the source of all my suffering' (24th November).

On 6th December Finland proclaimed itself an independent country. For Sibelius – one would imagine – this ought to have been a cause for great celebration: everything that his music had come to symbolize was now a reality; the prophecy made with such clarity and passion in works such as *Islossningen* and *The Captive Queen* had now been fulfilled. But, at least at first, there is not a single word in the composer's diary about the declaration of independence. He writes instead of everyday matters – Aino going to Helsinki, Kajanus conducting the *Third Symphony*, a passing reference to his own 52nd birthday, and assorted revenues from local publishers. When he does eventually mention political developments several weeks later, it is in unspecific terms and with considerable apprehension: 'Anarchy on the increase. My unhappy country', and these sentiments are juxtaposed with trivialities: 'Aino in town to buy Christmas presents' (18th December).

Meanwhile the urge to compose symphonies was returning ('I have Symphonies VI and VII "in my head". And the revision of Symph V'), although it remained at this stage unfulfilled. This – in the same diary entry from 18th December – is the first specific mention of the *Seventh Symphony*, which must have been at the earliest planning stages. But first Sibelius returned to the poetry of his beloved Runeberg and wrote what would prove to be his last opus numbered song collection – Op. 90. These songs, like their predecessors in Op. 86 and Op. 88, were composed for Ida Ekman. First to be completed was *Morgonen* (*The Morning*), No. 3, on 4th December. Arpeggiated piano chords lend this song something of a bardic character, as does its relative uniformity of style. The rhythms and melodic contours have much in common with the song *Fågellek* written in Vienna in the spring of 1891 (both are in F major).

Just over a week later he finished the next two of the set. *Sommarnatten* (*Summer Night*), No. 5, starts out in a conventional, lyrical manner: the singer sits fishing by the lakeside all through a summer night, listening to the song of a thrush (an image that must have reminded Sibelius of the idyllic archipelago summers of his youth); piano arpeggios imitate the lapping waters. At the song's unexpectedly powerful climax we catch a fleeting glimpse of Sibelius the pantheistic nature poet ('And I raised my eyes, bright was the earth, bright the skies, and from the heavens, the shore, the wave') before he impishly lightens the mood when the singer remembers more earthly pleasures ('My girl came into my mind'). *Norden* (*The North*), No. 1, is generally reckoned to be the highlight of the set, and here Sibelius the nature enthusiast is very much to the fore. Bearing in mind Sibelius's love of swans it comes as no surprise that he responded sympathetically to a poem describing their reluctant migration: 'Migrating swans sail sadly towards the south, they search for food, yearning for home, they ply the southern seas, longing for our waters.' Above a gently discordant *ostinato* piano accompaniment, the vocal line moves with great freedom, as though imitating the swans' flight, and the whole song is composed as a single long *crescendo*, culminating in a resolution of the harmonic tension on the last word, 'heaven'.

Next to be written was *Hennes budskap* (*Her Message*), No. 2, another example of a song based on variations of a single phrase. In this case the phrase could be seen as illustrating the gusts of wind in the poem, bringing a sorrowful message from the singer's distant beloved. Although he listed it as complete on 16th December, Sibelius made a number of revisions to this song over the next two weeks before he was happy with it. A few days before Christmas he finished *Fågelfängarn* (*The Bird Catcher*), No. 4, a bright but rather forgettable song about an unsuccessful but still cheerful hunter. Finally, in the days between Christmas and New Year he concluded the Op. 90 set with *Vem styrde hit din väg?* (*Who Brought You Hither?*). The subject of Runeberg's poem is the unfathomable power that turns strangers into lovers, and Sibelius accords the subject great dignity by composing it in the slow 3/2 metre that he favoured for music of an exalted character and by incorporating numerous 'S-motifs'.

As 1917 drew to a close Sibelius was feeling an understandable creative frustration. He had produced a large quantity of miniatures but had completed no large-scale works all year. Very little of his output that year had involved an orchestra, and his symphonic dreams showed little sign of progress. He summarized his moods in a long diary entry in which he expresses his shame that friends had paid off his debts, while claiming (with no small portion of artistic vanity) that they could not understand his inner nature. On the other hand some of the deprivations caused by political events and his isolation at Ainola were genuinely vexing: he had not heard an orchestra for almost a year. It did not help that Aino was in a state of depression and unwilling to talk about her troubles. On 31st December Sibelius concludes: 'The end of 1917. *Can* anything be more tragic? There must be something good in me, to enable me to overcome my misery. Oh God!'

1918

Finland's new status was rapidly being acknowledged. Lenin's new Russian government recognized Finnish independence on 4th January, and so did Sweden and France; Germany followed suit two days later.

On 11th January Ilmari Vainio, a member of a Helsinki scout group named Metsänkävijät, asked Sibelius to provide a musical setting of a text that had been written the previous year by Jalmari Finne. A preliminary version of the *Scout March* was ready the next day. In fact Sibelius had not written a completely new piece but had re-used a short march that he had sketched for brass septet and percussion as early as 1897–99. Sadly, despite a passing melodic reference to the famous Christmas hymn *Adeste fideles* (*O Come, All Ye Faithful*), this little piece is formulaic and by no means matches the sparkle and charisma of the *Jäger March*. Meanwhile the *Jäger March* itself was attracting more attention. Unconfirmed reports indicate that it was performed publicly in Finland for the first time at an independence rally at the National Theatre on 13th January, alongside established patriotic favourites such as *Finlandia* and *Isänmaalle*. If so, it was presumably in the version with piano accompaniment. Performances with and without orchestra were given at the University Hall on 19th January, but that orchestration must have been made by somebody else: Sibelius does not mention the completion of the orchestral version until a week later, and his version was first heard on 20th April. At least he could now reveal that the *Jäger March* was his own work, a fact that was duly observed in the newspapers.

Finland was a divided country. On one side were the Socialists, the 'Reds', whose support came from the Finnish workers' movement and from a number of Russian soldiers who had remained in Finland. On the other were the 'Whites', with whom Sibelius's sympathies lay. The Whites were 'conservatives' whose groups of militia were formed into an army by General Gustaf Mannerheim and who gained the support of the Jäger Battalion and a corps of Swedish volunteers. On 28th January the Red Guards seized control of Helsinki and the unrest finally spilled over into civil war, in which both sides were guilty of atrocities. 'How shameful for our people and our country', Sibelius lamented in his diary on 28th January. The Reds' power base was in the south of Finland, where they controlled not only Helsinki but also the other major cities – Turku, Tampere and Viipuri – and thus Ainola was in an area that was firmly under Red control. The Whites, meanwhile, were based in Vaasa on the west coast.

The *Jäger March* soon became a recognized symbol for the Whites and, in a climate where murders and rumoured killings were commonplace, Sibelius realized that this made him a natural target for the Reds. Fortunately he was overestimating the local Red Guard's level of cultural awareness: they regarded him as a local celebrity rather than a threat. Nonetheless, when a curfew was introduced he was not exempt. '"Forbidden" to go out for a walk. Marvellous – but what has it got to do with my symphonies?' (diary, 5th February). Around this time he was working on the first movements of the *Fifth* and *Sixth Symphonies*, but also entertaining doubts about the form they should take, or indeed whether the very word 'symphony' had outgrown its usefulness.

As the civil war progressed, searches were made of properties in the Järvenpää area and checkpoints were set up throughout the district. Use of the telephone was restricted, only newspapers with Red affiliations were permitted, and Sibelius found himself confronted with all sorts of rumours and stories concerning the fate of other prominent White sympathizers. Christian Sibelius, then a senior doctor at the Lapinlahti mental hospital in Helsinki, was arrested for refusing to provide beds for Red Guard soldiers, but then released. Mikko Slöör, the brother-in-law of Gallen-Kallela, was said to have been murdered. This proved to be untrue, but Sibelius was perturbed to discover that a prominent Helsinki doctor named Gösta Schybergson had indeed been taken away and shot. In due course, on 12th and 13th February, Red Guard troops arrived at Ainola and searched the house for weapons. Sibelius was both affronted and ashamed: 'When I was forced to open the drawers and they could see this poor, needy house's "treasures" on display, I could scarcely contain my grief. A bunch of bandits, armed to the teeth, and me – a nervous, defenceless composer' (diary, 14th February). In fact he was not quite unarmed: he had a revolver hidden in the basement. Luckily it remained undiscovered.

In the end it became clear to everybody except Sibelius that it was no longer practical for him to stay at Ainola. Robert Kajanus secured permission to travel there and escort Jean and Aino, together with Katarina, Margarta and Heidi, back to Helsinki – and Sibelius was eventually persuaded. On 20th February they travelled in a procession of sledges, led by Kajanus, and the Sibeliuses were safely delivered to Lapinlahti mental hospital, where they were to spend several months with Christian and his family. Fortunately relations between Jean's family and Christian's (his wife Nelma and their four children Marjatta, Jussi, Rita and Christian) were excellent, but conditions were hard, and food was impossibly scarce. This time there were no deliveries of meat masquerading as musical instruments; Sibelius lost 20 kilos in two months.

In these inauspicious circumstances Sibelius composed his cantata *Oma maa* (*My Own Land*), Op. 92, for mixed chorus and orchestra. Its origins were described in the journal *Suomalainen musiikilehti* in 1955 by Armas Maasalo, who conducted the work's first performance: 'In 1918 the choir I conducted, the National Chorus, was preparing to celebrate its tenth anniversary and decided – despite the turbulent times – to turn to Jean Sibelius, no less, for an interesting new concert item... When, a couple of weeks later, a familiar voice on the telephone announced that the work requested by the choir was ready, I was greatly surprised – especially when the maestro, as though with a roguish twinkle in his eye, asked if I might possibly have the time to call in and take a look... The score was on the table. He asked me to look at it and explained that the quiet environment [at the hospital] near the big cemetery was favourable for his work. "I don't have any instruments at my disposal, but that doesn't matter," he added.'

Maasalo and his choir obtained the new piece on very favourable terms: Sibelius was to receive a deposit of 1,000 marks, but this was to be returned if the piece was subsequently sold to a publisher! Sibelius himself selected the text for *Oma maa*, and his choice fell upon a poem by Kallio, a text that had become very dear to him during the war years. To an uninitiated observer, Sibelius – engrossed in his work amid a cloud of cigar smoke – must have presented a curious sight. When the Red Guard inspected the hospital, a soldier dismissed him as one of the lunatics!

By the time Sibelius finished work on *Oma maa*, it was becoming clear that the Reds' cause was hopeless; on the day he finished the piece, 20th March 1918, he wrote in his diary: 'They speak of a decisive turning point in a few days. Perhaps tonight. Bombardments and so on.' Apart from the new cantata, however, he had written no music for some time, even though his feeling that he had 'been vegetating for almost four years' (diary, 23rd March) was rather overstating the case. At the beginning of April he busied himself with two small works for violin and piano, *Aubade* and *Menuetto*, Op. 81 Nos 4 and 5. Arpeggiated piano chords and violin *pizzicati* provide a bold touch of colour at the beginning of the *Aubade*, but the main body of the piece is a gently lilting 6/8 'souvenir' that could have been composed thirty years earlier – far removed indeed from the tribulations of war. The main theme of the *Menuetto* is more truculent, though its middle section relaxes into an ingratiatingly sweet, Viennese-style rêverie. These two pieces were sold to the publisher Westerlund.

Before long, the Whites could celebrate victory in Helsinki, and the Sibelius family could return to Ainola. Before leaving Helsinki they witnessed the bombardment of the city as German forces (who had landed at Hanko) and White militia joined forces to drive out the Red troops. Sibelius described the sound as 'strange but magnificent. I had never dreamed that there could be anything so powerful' (diary, 14th April). A few days later Kajanus conducted a celebratory concert for the German forces in the University Hall in Helsinki, and Sibelius also took up his baton to perform the *Jäger March*.

Magnus Gottfrid Schybergson, father of the murdered doctor Gösta Schybergson, asked Sibelius to set two poems by his late son, *Ute hörs stormen* (*Outside the Storm is Raging*) and *Brusande rusar en våg* (*The Roaring of a Wave*), as a memorial tribute. These works for male choir *a cappella* (JS 224) were the first pieces that Sibelius produced after returning home; he delivered them to the Schybergson family on 30th April. For occasional pieces they are of high quality, robust and direct. Surprisingly, given his credentials as a nature poet, Sibelius made no attempt to depict the howling storm or crashing breakers in the music, confining himself to a more straightforward choral style.

Although fighting continued elsewhere in Finland until mid-May, and
the ill-feeling engendered by the civil war would take many years to
subside, some aspects of life could now slowly return to normal. For a
start Sibelius could now appear as a conductor again, and on 9th May he
conducted a programme of his own music including *The Oceanides*, the
two *Serious Melodies* (with Ossian Fohström as soloist), and the *Second
Symphony*. But even if the hostilities were now drawing to a close, Sibelius
still feared that his prominence and White sympathies would make him
a target for murder. In late May he received news that Toivo Kuula, who
had been his pupil a decade earlier, had been killed in Viipuri. At a gala
to celebrate the city's liberation Kuula had become involved in a fight with
one of the Jäger troops and had been fatally shot; ironically, Kuula himself
was a committed supporter of the Whites. The sentiments Sibelius felt at
Kuula's death were no doubt prompted by his own insecurities: 'Today my
friend Toivo Kuula is being laid to rest in the cold earth. How infinitely
sorrowful is the fate of an artist! Lots of hard work, talent and courage
– life's courage – and then it's all over' (diary, 28th May). The passing of
Richard Faltin also severed a link with the past; Sibelius refused to attend
his funeral, noting in his diary: 'I can no longer attend funerals.'

In a famous letter to Axel Carpelan dated 20th May 1918 Sibelius
discussed his future plans. The letter reveals surprisingly little about the
works in question, but serves rather to confirm how radically Sibelius
changed his mind about their character and style during the long process
of writing them. 'Today I am busy with the *Fifth Symphony* in a new form
– virtually recomposed. First movement wholly new? Second movement
reminiscent of the old, third movement reminiscent of the former ending
of the first movement. Fourth movement: the old motifs but more tautly
developed. All in all, if I may say so, a vigorous intensification right to the
end. Triumphal. The *Sixth Symphony* is wild and passionate in character.
Dark, with pastoral contrasts. Probably in four movements, with the end
rising to a dark orchestral roar in which the main theme is drowned. The
Seventh Symphony – joy of life and vitality with *appassionato* sections. In
three movements; that last of them is a "Hellenic rondo". All this with due
reservation... Concerning the *Sixth* and *Seventh Symphonies* I may change
my plans, depending on the way the musical ideas develop. As always I am
a slave to my themes and submit to their demands.'

He could not rid himself of doubts concerning the *Fifth Symphony*.
'Will it be of interest any longer? It's out of step with today's taste which,
influenced as it is by Wagnerian pathos, seems to me to be theatrical, and
anything but symphonic' (diary, 3rd June). Clearly he was not yet certain
about his future direction as a symphonist. At least, however, work on
the symphony was making progress. Otherwise the summer of 1918 was

not a productive time. It was not until 20th September that Sibelius could sign off another work, and even then it was only a short song for male choir *a cappella*, a setting of three verses from Karlfeldt's witty poem *Jone havsfärd* (*Jonah's Voyage*), JS 100, a modern retelling of the Biblical story of Jonah and the whale. Despite its simplicity, this strophic piece (which Sibelius claimed to have written in half an hour) has an infectious humour and energy that lift it well above the routine. Like *Fridolins dårskap*, it was composed for Torkel Nordman, who this time had promised to send Sibelius lampreys! A few days later, in a wholly different idiom, he wrote the delicate piano miniature *Linnæa* (*The Twinflower of the North*), Op. 76 No. 11, with gently falling semiquaver figures seemingly depicting the fragile, bell-like flowers.

A supplement to the music magazine *Säveletär*, which had recently been relaunched after a break of seven years, included a new arrangement for voice and piano of *Kullervon valitus*, the baritone monologue from the end of the third movement of *Kullervo*. Sibelius worked forwards from the German-language arrangement he had made a quarter of a century earlier, but this time used the original Finnish text. This necessitated numerous alterations to the metre of the vocal line, which in the new version was closer but not identical to the 1892 orchestral work.

Times were still hard. In October the family horse had to be sold and the stable boy lost his job. That month Sibelius spent a few days in Helsinki. The first performance of *Oma maa* took place on 25th at the University Hall; Armas Maasalo conducted the Helsinki Philharmonic Orchestra and the Helsinki Nationalist Youth Mixed Chorus, as the National Chorus was then known. The reviews were polite rather than enthusiastic, although Evert Katila noted in *Uusi Suometar* on 26th October that 'Sibelius has found convincing expression for the beauty of Finland.' Indeed, the underlying character of the work is of serenity and optimism – so far removed from the upheavals of the civil war that, with hindsight, it is easy to interpret the work as portending, or at least aspiring towards a more peaceful future.

On 20th November the last of the *Humoresques* for violin and orchestra, in G minor, Op. 89d, was ready. In this piece Sibelius takes very character-istic material and presents it in a new way. Motifs that would have been at home in the finale of *Voces intimae*, *Lemminkäinen's Return* and even *Pohjola's Daughter* are woven together in the solo violin part above an unobtrusive and very economical accompaniment in which the strings' almost mechanical *staccato* is a prominent feature.

Jalmari Finne had delivered a revised text for the *Scout March* a few months previously, and Sibelius had worked on it with more effort than he probably cared to expend. 'How much forging such monumental things require', he noted ironically in his diary on 5th September. The final musical setting, for piano with text written above, was completed on 27th November. A version for mixed choir and orchestra was probably made at about the same time.

On 17th December Sibelius attended a concert, conducted by Kajanus, at which Leevi Madetoja's *Second Symphony* was premièred; once again Sibelius was impressed by his former pupil's work. After the concert he was waylaid by a young lyric poet named Jarl Hemmer for a lengthy and well-lubricated discussion about a libretto that Hemmer was writing for a cantata, *Jordens sång (Song of the Earth)*, that Sibelius had agreed to compose for the forthcoming inauguration of Åbo Akademi, the new Swedish-language university in Turku. The project was lucrative: Axel Carpelan had convinced the university authorities to agree to a fee of 6,000 marks. The founding of Åbo Akademi was a major milestone in Turku's history. The city had once been the capital of Finland, but the administrative centre moved eastwards to Helsinki after the country had been conquered by the Russians in 1809. For a while the university remained in Turku, but it too was relocated to Helsinki after a devastating fire in Turku in 1827; only now, after the civil war, were conditions right for a replacement to be established.

1919

On 11th January 1919, Sibelius's mother-in-law Elisabeth Järnefelt celebrated her eightieth birthday. For the occasion he wrote a strophic song, *Mummon syntymäpäivänä (Birthday Song to Grandmother)*. This was by no means intended for public consumption: the anonymous text, probably written by a member of the immediate family circle, is naïve, and the musical setting correspondingly unassuming.

Sibelius personally delivered *Song of the Earth* to Turku in February 1919; on this visit he saw Axel Carpelan for the very last time. The inauguration of Åbo Akademi was postponed from the spring until the autumn, however, giving the composer a chance to make some alterations. The commission was undoubtedly a prestigious one, but Sibelius's initial excitement ('We are going to return to the atmosphere in Turku from before the fire. I hope Jarl Hemmer is going to surpass himself. Anyway, I'm going to do it – I have to do it') soon waned. Perhaps he was nervous about the quality of performance that he could expect: after receiving a letter from the conductor of the Turku orchestra, Karl Ekman, Sibelius noted in his diary that 'the musical resources in Turku are impossible' (14th January). Moreover, Hemmer did not surpass himself: his text is verbose and pretentious. The poem falls into clearly defined sections, and the poet provided suggestions – which Sibelius basically ignored – for setting these as recitatives, solos or for mixed, male or female choir (at one point the score is unclear as to whether five solo voices or the full choral sections are required).

Despite the unpromising nature of the poem, Sibelius's music is immediately appealing and full of bright melodies – almost like a grander, more ceremonial version of Nielsen's *Springtime in Funen* (1921). Many years later he told Jussi Jalas: 'I composed the cantata for Åbo Akademi very reluctantly. Neither the text... nor the occasion itself filled me with enthusiasm. I did it only because I was being paid.' But Sibelius was hardly in a position to turn down the chance to earn a generous fee at a time when post-war inflation was taking its toll on his finances. He received his payment in mid-February, and was no doubt glad to have money at his disposal to pay for a new luxury – the connection of Ainola to the mains electricity supply.

By February 1919, Sibelius had abandoned the idea that he had expressed to Axel Carpelan the previous May for a new first movement for the *Fifth Symphony*, and wrote to the Baron: 'These days have been very successful. Saw things very clearly. The first movement of the *Fifth Symphony* is one of the best things I've ever written. Can't understand my blindness.' Soon after this, however, Carpelan's health declined sharply. From his sickbed he wrote to Sibelius on 27th February that 'as a whole both in form and musical substance ... the *Fifth Symphony* is altogether outstanding... Now I know that it will be a masterly symphony... This has weighed on me for more than two years. All my wretched days, I have put all my heart and soul behind your cause, even if it is only of limited help.' On 22nd March Carpelan sent a last postcard: 'Terrible pains which cannot be alleviated by any medicine... Dear and wonderful Janne, a long farewell and thanks. God's blessing now and always. A fraternal greeting to Aino. Thanks for *everything, everything*.' Two days later he was dead.

Far from being 'only of limited help', Carpelan's advice and support (on a pecuniary as well as an inspirational level) had been of the utmost importance to Sibelius for almost twenty years, and the composer was profoundly conscious of his loss. 'Axel is dead †. How empty life seems. No sun, no music, no affection –. How alone I am with all my music...' (diary, 24th March); 'Now Axel is laid to rest in the cold earth. It feels so immeasurably and profoundly sad. For whom shall I compose now?' (29th March).

Sibelius did not attend the funeral; he was represented by Aino, who laid a wreath on his behalf bearing the words 'Farewell, unforgettable friend; my art mourns.' Nor did he directly commemorate Carpelan's passing in music: in a way the *Fifth Symphony* was his requiem. Instead, a few days later, he produced a pallid *Mélodie* for piano, Op. 94 No. 5, in which a rather half-hearted fanfare-like idea introduces a gentle, halting theme that is at its best when it surrenders to nostalgic, 1880s-style harmonies.

On 22nd April the *Fifth Symphony* in its definitive form was virtually ready – but the following week Sibelius's worries were to surface one more time. In his diary he says that he has 'dispensed with the second and third movements of the symphony. The first movement is a symphony and *does not require any continuation*. That's where all my work started!!! Shall I call it "symphony in one movement" or symphonic fantasy! Fantasia sinfonica I?' This moment of doubt, however, was short-lived: 'The symphony will be as it originally was, in three movements. All are with the copyist ... A confession: reworked all of the finale one more time. Now it is good. But this struggle with God' (6th May).

With the symphony safely at the copyist's, Sibelius again wrote some small piano pieces. *Danse*, Op. 94 No. 1, is a robust little waltz, whilst *Consolation*, Op. 76 No. 5, is a dreamy little fantasy on a simple descending motif.

For Helsinki University's degree ceremony Sibelius wrote an *Academic March* for orchestra, JS 155. This is a surprisingly lyrical piece – certainly less ostentatious than the concluding march from the *Promotional Cantata* of 1894, and it has the same easy-going melodic inventiveness that Sibelius had displayed in the *Cortège* he had composed for Kaarlo Bergbom at the National Theatre in 1905 (both pieces are in the sunny key of D major). The performance at the ceremony in the University Hall on 31st May failed to meet with the composer's approval. 'Kajanus, who conducted, wanted – this is a fact – to ruin it. Even though I asked him for just the opposite, he took it so fast that all the *con grandezza* disappeared', Sibelius complained in his diary. Bouts of jealousy were of course by no means uncommon in Sibelius's relationship with Kajanus, and Sibelius cannot have forgotten that the original cause of ill will between them had been their competition for a teaching post at the same university more than twenty years earlier. Kajanus was also a convenient scapegoat: by claiming that the performance was below standard, Sibelius could excuse the lack of attention the piece gained either from the public or from the press. In fairness to Kajanus, any *grandezza* that the *Academic March* possesses is confined to the tempo marking – *Andante con grandezza*. If he did indeed ruin the piece by playing it too fast, he must have chosen a very radical tempo indeed.

A further sign that life was returning to normal was that in June 1919, after more than four years of relative isolation in Finland, Sibelius could once more travel abroad. Aino accompanied him to Copenhagen where he was to conduct at the Nordic Music Days. Similar festivals had taken place in Copenhagen in 1888 and Stockholm in 1897, but Finland had not previously been represented; in the coming years the festival was to be held rather more frequently. This time Kajanus was involved with the planning, and Sibelius was the 'senior partner' among a group of Finnish composers that included Erkki Melartin and Selim Palmgren (who scored a notable success with his *Third Piano Concerto*). Sibelius had initially been reluctant to go to Copenhagen: he had been asked to perform the *Second Symphony* – which indeed he did to great acclaim on 18th June, although he would have preferred to present the new version of the *Fifth* instead. The concerts took place at the Odd Fellow Palace with a hundred-strong orchestra made up of players from the leading Copenhagen orchestras. Sibelius was interviewed by a journalist from *Berlingske Tidende* and made the point very plainly that his new *Fifth Symphony* was absolute music, which he equated with 'musical thought'; for this reason any title for the piece would be superfluous. The same can, of course, be said of all Sibelius's symphonies (though of Carl Nielsen's four symphonies to date, three bore titles). Nonetheless, Sibelius and Aino – along with his old friend Stenhammar, and Kajanus and his wife – were invited to Nielsen's home for a meal, and on this occasion – according to Stenhammar's account of the evening – there was no tension between the two great symphonists.

Early in 1919 Sibelius's friend, the painter Oscar Parviainen, was admitted to hospital in Ulricehamn in Sweden, suffering nominally from 'heart symptoms', but in fact exhausted and desperate. From there he sent Sibelius a cry for help that June: 'Send me a couple of lines when you have time; I shall treat the music you send as a sacred gift and shall never put it to bad use.' A piano piece was an obvious response to this plea; it would probably be easy enough to find a piano in the hospital. Sibelius's first impulse was to dedicate a small piano piece that he was working on to Parviainen, and he even added the dedication 'To O. Parviainen from his old, faithful, grateful friend Jean Sibelius,' but he had second thoughts. The piano piece in question – the *Andantino 'Till O. Parviainen'* (To O. Parviainen), JS 201, was perhaps too lightweight and unfinished to do justice to their friendship, and so he composed a new piece, *Con Passione*, JS 53 – which, despite its extreme brevity, is more imposing and impassioned than the *Andantino*. The dedication was transferred almost verbatim to the new piece, which Sibelius then sent to Sweden. Parviainen was delighted: 'It was as though lightning had passed through me and I was alive again. A song of rejoicing from the angels of heaven!... You have sent me hope to live and to pray to the Gods in heaven – how can I thank you?'

Meanwhile the *Andantino* was returned to the pile of 'works in progress', from which it emerged in a more extended and polished form in late July as the *Sonnet*, Op. 94 No. 3. Around the same time Sibelius finished two of its companion pieces in Op. 94, *Berger et bergerette*, No. 4, and *Gavotte*, No. 6. *Berger et bergerette* is a pastoral miniature in ABA form that manages to unify the Op. 94 group by making subtle allusions to two of the other pieces: its outer sections have a rhythm and pianistic texture derived from the second theme of the *Danse*, No. 1, whilst the bucolic dance in the middle section has a similar rhythm and melodic contour to the fanfare motif at the start of the *Mélodie*, No. 5. The *Gavotte* – like the *Air de danse* from Op. 34 – is a pastiche of the eighteenth-century courtly dance style.

On 2nd August, at the behest of the publisher Westerlund, Sibelius returned to two piano pieces from the 'trees' suite of 1914, *Granen* and *Syringa*, and tried to combine them into a single waltz in ABA form with the title *Valse lyrique*. He was not happy with the result, however, and decided instead to rework *Granen* as a separate piece with a more florid writing and a more clearly defined rhythmic profile throughout. By 8th August he had also completed a revised and greatly expanded version of *Syringa*, again calling it *Valse lyrique* (although a few weeks later he also suggested that it should be called *Les Lilas, Valse pour piano*). Its themes are attractive, if not especially typical of Sibelius, and it is a sunny, carefree piece, more in the spirit of Tchaikovsky than Johann Strauss. Like Tchaikovsky's *Waltz of the Flowers*, Sibelius's 'waltz of the trees' culminates in an effective *stretto*.

During the autumn Sibelius had more peace and quite than usual at home in Järvenpää. After a riding accident his youngest daughter Heidi, then aged eight, caught scarlet fever and had to spend some time in hospital, and Aino stayed close by in Helsinki. The eleven-year-old Margareta was often out playing with the neighbours' children, although when she was at home she did play music with her father. The teenage Katarina was away at school.

Sibelius put the finishing touches to *Song of the Earth* at Ainola on 23rd September and conducted its first performance at the Old Academy Hall in Turku on 11th October with an *ad hoc* mixed choir and the orchestra of the Turku Musical Society; at the well-oiled post-concert celebrations he entertained his colleagues by playing the finale of the *Fifth Symphony* on the piano. *Song of the Earth* was performed again the following day.

It was finally time for the definitive *Fifth Symphony* to be premièred. On 24th November, in the presence of the first Finnish president, Kaarlo Ståhlberg, Sibelius gave the first of three sold-out and hugely acclaimed concerts featuring the new work. As usual he conducted the Philharmonic Orchestra at the University Hall. Despite his later indifference, Sibelius obviously thought highly enough of *Song of the Earth* to include it in the programme together with the *Six Humoresques* for violin and orchestra, played by Paul Cherkassky.

Although the definitive version of the *Fifth Symphony* omits the bass clarinet found in the 1915 score, it has richer, more sonorous orchestration throughout. The first movement now begins with a serene horn call, beginning with two rising intervals of a fourth, followed by the rising woodwind figures from the original score. Formally and thematically the movement progresses in a manner that is not very different from the 1915 version, but Sibelius has made vast strides in integrating and refining the raw materials: where the 1915 version was tentative and indecisive, the definitive version radiates confidence and colour. After the development section with its bassoon lament, Sibelius creates a tremendous feeling of expectation; the music builds up inexorably towards a climax (only at one point does Sibelius reduce the strings' dynamic level for a moment, perhaps as a reminiscence of the original version, a detail which is almost always ignored in performance) until finally we arrive at a change of key, to a radiant B major. The brass proudly intone the rising motifs from the beginning of the symphony; these are answered by the woodwind, and the scherzo (which functions to some extent like the recapitulation in a sonata form movement) is under way. The entire scherzo is a gradual *accelerando* to the final climax: after the brass have once again intoned the rising fourths, the movement is capped by a splendidly confident coda.

In the definitive version the thematic material of the slow movement is now presented not only in a different order, but also with greater variety of rhythm and tone colour. It is also rather longer – 212 bars compared to the original 171. In the 1915 version the main theme had been given to *pizzicato* violins alone, but in the 1919 score *staccato* flutes and *pizzicato* violins alternate. As the movement progresses, we observe not only that the strings now play much less *pizzicato*, but also that their melodic lines have become far more gracious and decorative. It may be that Sibelius reduced the music's reliance upon *pizzicato* as a result of the reservations expressed in Bis's review of the 1916 version. In the final score Sibelius made the thematic link between the string *pizzicato* passage before letter F and the beginning of the finale less obvious; although, by way of compensation, he added a clear allusion to the finale's 'swan hymn' in the double bass line later on. The definitive ending of the movement is quite different from the original – more elaborate and richly scored.

The finale in the final version of the symphony is much shorter than in either the 1915 or 1916 scores. As before, it begins with a cascade of string writing, followed by the 'swan hymn' from the horns. The hymn is now combined with a luxuriant theme on woodwind and cellos, which at the corresponding stage in the 1915 score had been heard only in fragmentary form. The most noticeable abbreviation in the 1919 score occurs in the passage between the return to the first theme and the episode in E flat minor; the music now has a better internal balance and a much more secure sense of direction. This time the symphony ends with six chords, widely (but very precisely) spaced, and played with maximum force by the entire orchestra – without doubt one of the most powerful and original symphonic endings ever written.

In a set of sketches from 1919, ideas from the outer movements of the *Sixth Symphony* were tried out in the context of a projected tone poem to be named *Kuutar* (*The Moon Goddess*), on a theme from the *Kalevala*. Here, a theme from the first movement was labelled 'Winter' and another, from the finale, 'The spirit of the pine tree'.

Autrefois is a setting of an occasional poem by Hjalmar Procopé that Sibelius wrote in the autumn of 1919 for the inauguration of the Gösta Stenman gallery in Helsinki on 1st December. The planned performance very nearly had to be cancelled, as Sibelius had managed to escape to a restaurant, where he was found just in time, rather the worse for wear (even though prohibition had been introduced in Finland some months previously). Half a bottle of champagne enticed him back, and cheered him up so much that he conducted the piece twice. It is a simple yet highly attractive pastiche of eighteenth-century pastoral scenes scored for two sopranos and small orchestra, and at the première it was indeed billed as *Scène pastorale*. The two verses of the song are framed by a gracious dance in the manner of a gavotte.

At the end of 1919 Sibelius could look back on a year of mixed fortunes: he was now able to conduct again, both at home and abroad, but the death of Axel Carpelan was a severe blow. Moreover, the only major works he had completed were *Song of the Earth* and the *Fifth Symphony*, and although the full glory of the symphony had now been revealed, it had cost more than its fair share of time and effort.

CHAPTER 13

THE SIXTH SYMPHONY: 1920–1923

1920

Sibelius's long-cherished desire to portray himself as an aristocrat suffered a setback in January 1920, when the journalist Eeli Granit-Ilmoniemi in *Helsingin Sanomat* published a portrait of Sibelius alongside that of one of his distant relatives, a carpenter named Ojanen. This article enraged Sibelius, who used it as an excuse to pour forth his woes about life in general to his diary on 9th February: 'When they started to pester me about my origins a few years ago, I knew how it would end... Everything is lost. It all paralyses me – I cannot work. And my debts are mounting. No improvement. I am growing old, and a new generation is coming with new ideals, capturing people's interest. Will the evening of my life find me idle and resigned, waiting silently for death?... How brutal is fate! It seems as if my mother would have known of my coming suffering. That would explain her infinitely melancholy expression when she looked at me. Oh, if only I could undo some things in my life! My dear mother! Why did you give me a life that I cannot live?'

Heikki Klemetti and the Suomen Laulu choir had proved assiduous champions of Sibelius's music, both in Finland and abroad. It was only with reluctance, however, that he agreed to write a work for them. In January 1919, while working on *Song of the Earth*, he had noted in his diary: 'And then there's the promise I made Klemetti regarding a piece for Suomen Laulu. He is by no means one of my "admirers". It annoys me that he only wants to use my name as a decoration. Whether I serve that purpose or not is better left unsaid.'

Time dragged on, and the promised choral piece failed to appear; Klemetti grew increasingly exasperated with Sibelius's delaying tactics.

Klemetti's wife Armi recalled: 'Heikki bombarded Sibelius time after time, as we really wanted to be able to perform this new choral work at our twentieth anniversary celebrations in the spring of 1920. In the end Heikki became quite depressed when Sibelius always replied to his profound wishes in the same way: "Yes, yes, I'll do it, but so far I haven't found a suitable text".' In the end Klemetti gave up, and it was only the intervention of Armi Klemetti, around Christmas 1919, that persuaded Sibelius to start work on the new cantata.

Initially Sibelius planned to set Aleksis Kivi's poem *Suomenmaa* but he later decided upon a somewhat verbose poem by Eino Leino: *Maan virsi* (*Hymn to the Earth*). This choice was unfortunate insofar as its title led people to believe that it was merely a Finnish translation of *Song of the Earth*. *Hymn to the Earth* is a patriotic piece but, in newly independent Finland, its patriotism is marked by serenity and the celebration of nature in the manner of *Oma maa* or indeed *Song of the Earth* rather than by the frustrated belligerence of *The Captive Queen*. Sibelius's disinclination to compose the piece is reflected in the music, which is by no means his finest work in this genre. Despite a promising, moody opening it rapidly degenerates into rather predictable sequences. Sibelius completed the work on 28th January 1920 and dedicated it to Klemetti. It was first performed at Suomen Laulu's anniversary concert on 4th April (Easter Sunday) of that year; the choir was joined by the Helsinki Philharmonic Orchestra under Klemetti's baton.

The paths of Sibelius and Eino Leino were soon to cross again – or rather to collide. In 1919 a *Kalevala* Society had been established in Helsinki, and on 16th February Sibelius went to a gathering also attended by Leino, Robert Kajanus, Eero Järnefelt and Pekka Halonen. Despite the prohibition laws, the drinks flowed freely and plans were discussed for the forthcoming celebrations on 28th February, *Kalevala* Day, when Sibelius was to conduct the cantata *The Origin of Fire*. By the early hours of the following morning Sibelius and Leino were discussing nobility and 'Swedishness'. This was a sensitive subject and the conversation soon turned into an argument. Sibelius, still angry about what he saw as Granit-Ilmoniemi's recent slurs on his ancestry, was keen to stress that both he and Leino were aristocrats. Leino countered by claiming that he himself was a Renaissance figure but Sibelius, on the other hand, was 'a rococo figure and descended from Häme peasant stock'. And so the bickering continued. They did not actually come to blows but on *Kalevala* Day Sibelius refused to conduct *The Origin of Fire*, claiming that he was suffering from rheumatism.

His rheumatism was not entirely fictional, however: it had plagued him a few weeks earlier when he had been preparing an orchestral version of the previous year's *Valse lyrique*. This relatively simple task cost him more effort than he had anticipated: he complained that his hand was shaky, and could be calmed only by drinking wine that he could ill afford. A potential solution to Sibelius's pecuniary woes seemed to present itself, however, when a letter arrived from the Norwegian pianist Alf Klingenberg, a friend of Sibelius from his studies in Berlin thirty years earlier. Klingenberg had emigrated to the United States and had been one of the founders of a music school in Rochester in 1913. Five years later the industrialist and philanthropist George Eastman, founder of the Eastman Kodak Company, bought the institute and presented it to the University of Rochester. Eastman was in the process of expanding the existing school to create the Eastman School of Music, which opened in 1921, and in the first three years of its existence Klingenberg was director of the new school. He suggested that Sibelius should become a professor of composition there, with sufficient free time to conduct as well. A few years earlier Sibelius would have jumped at such an opportunity but now he was strangely indecisive. 'Wrote to Alf Klingenberg... and decided to keep his proposal in reserve; one never knows how life will turn out' (diary, 29th February). Someone who might well have shared this sentiment was Alexander Siloti, who a few days later arrived in Helsinki with his family as refugees from Petrograd. In Helsinki he gave several concerts, at least one of which Sibelius attended, and the two men met socially as well.

Despite Sibelius's experiences with the *Kalevala* Society, he had lost none of his enthusiasm for the poem itself: he was still working on his *Moon Goddess* plan. This, however, would eventually merge with the *Sixth Symphony*. Meanwhile his earlier music was performed extensively in concert: Kajanus conducted all five symphonies in Helsinki and also took his orchestra to Paris, where – in a long programme devoted to a selection of Finnish composers – he gave the French première of the *Third Symphony*. In Copenhagen *En saga* was performed under the baton of Carl Nielsen. A Sibelius concert was planned in Sydney, but such was the strength of anti-German feeling in Australia that the music despatched from Germany by Breitkopf was confiscated by the customs authorities, and the Finnish consul, Kaarlo J. Nauklér, was accused of 'dealing with the enemy'! Eventually the authorities relented and the concert could take place. Sibelius's music was well represented at the Trade Fair in Helsinki in June/July, the first such event to be arranged in Finland: his music was featured at six concerts, and he himself conducted at four of them, sometimes sharing the podium with Kajanus.

Six years earlier Ivan Narodny, who had close ties to the opera and ballet scene in New York, had written a very positive article about Sibelius in *Musical America*. Now Narodny approached the composer with a proposal for two ballet scores. But after his experiences with *Scaramouche* Sibelius had no intention of accepting the commission and, in any case, the *Sixth Symphony* had started to take shape in his mind. He thus ruled himself out of the project by asking for the wholly unaffordable fee of $20,000.

Sibelius enjoyed a short summer break in his native Häme region in late July, visiting both Walter von Konow at Lahis gård and also his daughter Ruth at Annila, a villa in Sääksmäki owned by two great-aunts on Sibelius's mother's side. He corresponded with Rosa Newmarch in London about the prospect of a trip to England the following spring, suggesting that he should conduct the *Fifth Symphony* in London, and in September the plans for this trip were agreed.

In the autumn a set of *Six Bagatelles* for piano, Op. 97, was ready. As they are short and generally straightforward in style, these pieces have proved an easy target for those who seek to belittle Sibelius as a composer of piano music. Nevertheless the group contains some excellent examples of Sibelius's lighter style, and also many hints of his early style that are not merely reminiscences but are seen from the perspective of an older composer. Superficially these little pieces resemble the miniatures of Op. 34 and Op. 40. Compared with the wartime piano pieces, however, we can detect a shift in musical emphasis. In Op. 97 and its successor, Op. 99 (1922), dance forms are less dominant than before: Sibelius takes a step back towards the more abstract, aphoristic expression of the Op. 58 collection and this time keeps the scale of the pieces more modest. The first three were completed by mid-August and the remainder followed in October.

In this set Sibelius pays lip service to the concept of a cyclical work by naming both of the outer pieces *Humoreske*. The first opens with a sad, song-like theme in even note values that is first heard unaccompanied in the lower middle register; only later is it joined by a persistent syncopation. The piece remains ambiguous in expression throughout: is it a solitary lament or a capricious dance? No such doubts exist in the case of the second piece, *Lied*, in which gentility and sophistication go hand-in-hand with melodic warmth (the main theme is a series of 'S-motifs') and gentle humour. This may not be cutting-edge piano writing by the standards of 1920, but it is a delightful piece nonetheless. The third of the set, *Kleiner Walzer* (*Little Waltz*), has been compared to French ballet music although its flowing main theme could equally well be transplanted into the waltz Sibelius had composed for Betsy Lerche in 1889. By contrast the descending, stretto-like second idea anticipates a technique later used in the *Morceau romantique* of 1925. Music from the years 1892–93 is suggested by the fourth piece, *Humoristischer Marsch*: repeated rhythmic patterns and prominent short-long-short syncopations recall the second of the *Impromptus*, Op. 5 and the first movement of the *Piano Sonata* (both from 1893), whilst a motif based on a rising scale resembles the string accompaniment at the climax of *En saga*. The last two pieces in Op. 97 are more representative of Sibelius's late style: the fifth, *Impromptu*, is a wistful rêverie (an unpublished preliminary version contains an additional 21 bars in the middle section), whilst in the concluding *Humoreske II* the gentle, melancholy theme heard in the first few bars grows into a whirling dance but never shakes off a certain ambivalence of mood.

In autumn Sibelius revised his pastoral scene *Autrefois* from the previous year in readiness for publication. 'As for other languages, it would be best if a new text were written in the style of the 1760s', he wrote to Wilhelm Hansen in October. 'People have said that it might be a new *Valse triste*. But I don't share that view... The work is suited for any sort of arrangement.' Sibelius himself recommended that the vocal lines in *Autrefois* could be taken by two clarinets if no singers were available, and he also made arrangements for two sopranos and piano, and for piano solo (with the text written above the music). In addition there is a draft with piano accompaniment of the middle section, presumably made for rehearsal purposes before the première the previous year; the piano part is substantially different from the printed version, with a slow right-hand tremolo almost throughout. Curiously, the text was omitted from the first published edition of the orchestral score – apparently by mistake – and in consequence the piece is often referred to as a vocalise.

The invitation that Sibelius had received a few months earlier from Ivan Narodny in New York may have been easy enough to avoid, but Alf Klingenberg was not so easily dissuaded. He came to Europe in seach of staff for the Eastman School of Music in Rochester, and in mid-September arrived at Ainola to offer Sibelius a year's contract. The terms offered were reasonably generous, but Sibelius was still unwilling to commit himself, and several months of soul-searching ensued. In the meantime he accepted an offer to conduct three concerts in London the following February.

On 24th October, *Kullervo* by Armas Launis was premièred at the Finnish National Opera. Like Sibelius, Launis was born in Hämeenlinna and went on to study in Helsinki (in fact he numbered Sibelius among his teachers); by 1920 he was a professor of musical analysis and folk music at Helsinki University. Sibelius did not attend the première, though Aino and Katarina went to a later performance and reported back that the piece was a success. 'Strange that I didn't bring the myth to fruition', Sibelius wrote in his diary the following week: his own *Kullervo* lay forgotten and his opera plans had run into the sand.

Nor were his symphonic plans in the rudest of health. His diary entries from this period are littered with business dealings but the few mentions that there are of the *Sixth Symphony* suggest that progress was anything but satisfactory. Yet again its status as a symphony was called into question: 'Doubts about the symphony or "Runes symphoniques"' (25th November).

On Sibelius's 55th birthday his friends once more provided ample proof of their generosity. The tenor Wäinö Sola handed over a cheque for 63,000 marks, the result of a collection among Finnish businessmen. Had they known that he would immediately set off for a week's carousing in Helsinki, they might have been less generous!

For the Christmas magazine *Lucifer* Sibelius wrote *Små flickorna* (*Young Girls*), JS 174, a song to a text by his friend Hjalmar Procopé. It takes the form of a quick, salon-style waltz. The poem is a lighthearted description of the lifestyle of office girls in a big city – and Sibelius, here on unfamiliar territory, treats it with the flippancy that it deserves.

In December Sibelius also responded to a commission from an old schoolfriend, Allan Schulman, an achitect and the conductor of the male choir Viipurin Laulu-Veikot (W. S. B., 'the Singing Brothers of Viipuri'). Schulman himself had composed a parade song for the choir, using a text by Eero Eerola, a choir member and local publican. Now he asked Sibelius for an 'honour march' based on the same text, and the result was the *Viipurin Laulu-Veikkojen (W. S. B:n) kunniamarssi* (*Honour March of the Singing Brothers of Viipuri* [*W. S. B.*]), JS 219. Sibelius's setting was perhaps less straightforward than the choir had envisaged: when rehearsing it, they declared the piece to be 'different', though presumably they would have recognized the closing bars, which are almost a direct quotation from the end of *Isänmaalle*.

1921

On 3rd January Sibelius sent a telegram to Rochester and accepted the professorship. A few weeks later he set off on a major concert tour that was to take in eight concerts in England (often sharing the programme and podium with other composers and conductors) and four in Norway. On the way he stopped off in Berlin to visit Breitkopf & Härtel, before taking the train to Ostend where he caught a ferry to Dover. He spent over a month in England – from 6th February to 10th March – and, as always, he could count on the support of Rosa Newmarch, Henry Wood and Granville Bantock; at the beginning of the visit Mrs Newmarch arranged a reception at which Sibelius met Vaughan Williams. Another new but enduring friendship that he made on this visit was the pianist Harriet Cohen. Sibelius's profile was now high enough for him to be entertained by independent Finland's first ambassador to London, the former industrialist Ossian Donner.

Sibelius's schedule in England was nothing if not demanding. At his first concert, in the Queens Hall on 12th February, Sibelius conducted the British première of the *Fifth Symphony* to great acclaim. Three days later there was a reception in his honour at the Royal College of Music, where Sibelius conducted the college's orchestra in *En saga*. Next he went to the south coast to conduct the Bournemouth Symphony Orchestra in *Finlandia*, *Valse triste* and the *Third Symphony*. Two days later he was back at the Queen's Hall, conducting some shorter pieces at an afternoon 'ballad concert' that was repeated in the evening. The very next day he was up in Birmingham, conducting a long programme in which the principal works were *En saga* and the *Third Symphony*. On the way back to London he visited Oxford, where he saw the sights and dined at New College.

At the next Queen's Hall concert Sibelius conducted his *Fourth Symphony* and Ferruccio Busoni played Mozart's *Piano Concerto No. 23 in A major*, K 488, and his own *Indian Fantasy*. This was the last time that Busoni and Sibelius would meet, but for both men it was like turning the clock back more than thirty years. As Henry Wood later recalled: 'I could generally manage Busoni when I had him to myself, but my heart was always in my mouth if he met Sibelius. They would forget the time of the concert at which they were to appear; they hardly knew the day of the week... They were like a couple of irresponsible schoolboys.'[1] Quite how sympathetic the British audiences were to Sibelius's music is shown by a review of this concert in *The Times*: 'Having heard M. Sibelius conduct three of his symphonies in the last fortnight, the fifth and fourth in London and the third in Birmingham, we can have no hesitation in saying that this, No. 4 in A minor, is incomparably the finest. It stands out from its companions in its absolute directness of movement and simplicity of line. Its very simplicity is baffling.' Sibelius must have been overjoyed that the symphony that had been rejected by Vienna and hissed in Gothenburg was now held up as an example of his work at its very finest.

The next afternoon and evening Sibelius again conducted at the 'ballad concerts', this time with *The Oceanides*, the *Elegy* from *King Christian II* and *Valse lyrique* on the programme. The following week he was once again in the north of England, conducting *Finlandia* and *Valse triste* at the Free Trade Hall in Manchester. The British part of the tour ended on Sunday 27th February with two more 'ballad concerts' in London.

Sibelius discussed his possible move to America with Rosa Newmarch, and her reaction was as vehement as it was unequivocal. 'But I beg you not to squander your energies in teaching young Americans harmony and orchestration *à la* Sibelius... You are a composer, not a pedagogue; possibly the greatest creative musician of our times – and certainly one of the noblest and most individual. *That is your mission. Au diable les dollars!'*, she wrote to him on 7th March.

From London Sibelius took the train to Newcastle, from where he set sail for Bergen. Here he conducted the Harmonien orchestra on 21st March and visited Grieg's home, Troldhaugen, before taking the train to Kristiania for three more engagements. The programmes for the Norwegian concerts were less adventurous than those in England: neither the *Fourth* nor the *Fifth Symphonies* was included, and indeed the only recent work was *Valse lyrique*. Nonetheless, the concerts were sold out and he was introduced to Norway's King Haakon VII. Finally, at the beginning of April, an exhausted Sibelius could return home.

By the end of the month he had made a firm decision concerning America, and wrote to Alf Klingenberg announcing that he could not after all accept the offer. In the ensuing exchange of telegrams Klingenberg almost persuaded him to change his mind again, but on 9th May he gave his final verdict: he would stay in Finland. Less than a fortnight later he was back on the podium: the Nordic Music Days had come to Helsiniki and Sibelius's music was represented at a chamber evening (*Voces intimae*) and two orchestral concerts. The festival ended with an all-Sibelius programme on 28th May, where he conducted the *Fifth Symphony, Pohjola's Daughter*, a selection of *Scènes historiques* and *Hymn to the Earth*.

For some months Sibelius had been so busy travelling and conducting that he had composed nothing. The *Sixth Symphony* was nowhere near ready. An increasingly shaky hand made it a laborious task to write and, when he did put pen to paper, his first project was the *Suite mignonne* for two flutes and strings, Op. 98a. This is perhaps the most readily appealing of the three short suites for small orchestra that he composed around this time, and was completed on 29th June. Less overtly a pastiche than *Autrefois*, the piece nevertheless has a comparable pastoral character as well as a stylistic affinity with Tchaikovsky's ballet music. It also serves as an outlet for Sibelius's interest in dance music. For the listener the *Suite mignonne* may be straightforward, but for the players it is by no means easy to bring off in concert. As Gabriel Fauré said of the music of Mozart, it is 'particularly difficult to perform. His admirable clarity exacts absolute cleanness: the slightest mistake in it stands out like black on white. It is music in which all the notes must be heard.' The rhythmically ambiguous opening bars of the first movement, *Petite scène*, have a freedom that anticipates the opening of the *Sixth Symphony*, but the pulse soon becomes clear and the introduction yields to a stylish and cultured waltz. Since his student days Sibelius had been capable of writing captivating polkas, and the central *Polka* in the *Suite mignonne* is fresher and more ebullient than any of his pieces of this type since the *Allegro in D major* for piano trio from 1886. With its buoyant 6/8 pulse the third movement, *Epilogue*, trips along with easy-going charm, evidently untroubled by the (presumably coincidental) reference to the famous *Valse triste* melody at the phrase-ends. Only towards the end does the mood darken for a moment, before the closing bars return us to the jaunty atmosphere in which it began. Sibelius also made a piano transcription of the suite and both versions were published by Chappell in London, the firm's initial reluctance overcome by the enthusiastic advocacy of Rosa Newmarch.

It is strange that the pieces to which Sibelius returned most frequently over the years, making new arrangements and small adjustments, are frequently among his least innovative and musically insignificant – generally strophic songs and marches. This is certainly the case with the *Scout March* (1918) of which he made a new version for mixed choir and piano at some point during 1921.

On 10th August Aino celebrated her fiftieth birthday. Sibelius gave a speech in which he praised her patience and endurance: 'I, who owe you such an indescribable debt of gratitude, can affirm that without you my life would have broken down a long time ago, and my achievements would have been poorer and more trivial. It is no trivial matter to be married to a composer like me. The moments of light, when work is over, are thinly spread, and the struggle against the darkness of night is long drawn-out. It is truly remarkable that you have withstood these storms in our life.'

After the exertions of the spring, the rest of the year passed relatively uneventfully. Sibelius neither completed any new works of significance (though he worked on a waltz, the *Valse chevaleresque*) nor travelled far from home. In October he and Aino were honoured to be the guests of General Mannerheim, and he also spent time with his drinking buddies, not least at Kajanus's 65th birthday party. Sibelius was cheered by good reviews after Busoni conducted the *Fifth Symphony* in Berlin, but closer to home a feeling of insecurity was never far from the surface. 'I am thinking of getting rid of some of my old acquaintances, or "friends"', he wrote in his diary in October, and when he conducted at the centenary concert for the 'Societas pro fauna et flora fennica' in Helsinki on 1st November he imagined that half the orchestra was agitating against him, with the cellist Ossian Fohström as ringleader.

1922

At the beginning of 1922 Sibelius remained more concerned with the production of lighter music than continuing with the *Sixth Symphony*. In January he put the finishing touches to the *Valse chevaleresque* that had occupied him the previous November, working simultaneously on versions for orchestra and for solo piano, but decided to rework it after it was turned down by the publisher Chappell; in revised form it was accepted by Wilhelm Hansen. If we are to believe an interview given by Walter von Konow to *Stockholmstidningen*, this was the very same waltz that Sibelius had improvised in his presence in Florence years earlier but had then refused to publish. Aino Sibelius made no secret of her dislike for the piece, viewing it as a symbolic of her husband's worst alcoholic excesses. She may have been motivated to take such a view because Sibelius's drinking was once more a cause for concern, and was placing ever greater strain on their relationship. Whether the piece depicts sparkling regal jewellery, or whether its emphatic down-beats, complete with rattling side-drum, represent the hiccuping of the intoxicated composer on his way home from the Kämp, can be left to the listener to decide.

In January, at the request of the Turku male-voice choir Musices Amantes, Sibelius composed a 'male-voice quartet in the old, good style' (diary, 22nd January). This was a refined setting of Runeberg's *Likhet* (*Resemblance*), JS 121, a poem that he had already used in a solo song in 1890, although musically there is no link between the two settings. The presence of an A flat pedal point through much of the choral piece softens its otherwise essentially homophonic texture, adding depth and warmth.

On 7th February a *Suite champêtre*, Op. 98b, was ready and Sibelius immediately sent it away to the publisher Chappell, who refused it (Wilhelm Hansen agreed to publish it that April). 'Good in its own way' was Sibelius's own verdict in his diary on this three-movement piece for piano solo or string orchestra. The opening *Pièce caractéristique* is based on a simple march-like motif that seems to approach from the distance, gathering speed and intensity until it becomes a whirling dance; only at the climax does it yield to a few bars of more lyrical music. The title of the slow movement, *Mélodie élégiaque*, is wholly adequate to describe the essence of this Grieg-like piece. The finale, *Danse*, approximates to the folk style; in the orchestral version a solo violin offers a reminder of the earlier *Humoresques*.

In early 1922 a proposal was made to establish a new Masonic lodge in Finland – Suomi loosi 1. Freemasonry had reached Finland via Sweden in the mid-eighteenth century: the Lodge of St Augustin was founded in 1756, though it was shut down by the Russians in 1809. The founder members of the new lodge, among them the lawyer Toivo H. Nekton and J. E. Tuokkola, drew on their experiences of freemasonry in America. Among the list of candidates were Sibelius, General Mannerheim, Archbishop Gustaf Johansson, Lars Sonck, Pekka Halonen and Robert Kajanus. Sibelius was one of the first batch of 27 members to join, on 18th February. He attended meetings at least twice during the latter part of 1922 and even served as the lodge's organist. Nekton, a keen choral singer, suggested that 'Jean Sibelius will compose special, genuinely Finnish music for the lodge', but at this stage the idea came to nothing.

In March, Wilhelm Kempff visited Finland, appearing both as a pianist at the University Hall and as an organist at the neo-Gothic Church of St John. Sibelius thought that his Bach performances were 'unforgettable' (diary, 21st February), and was pleased to welcome the young German as his guest at Ainola.

As the year wore on, the *Sixth Symphony* finally became Sibelius's first priority. On 27th April he wrote in his diary: 'The "new work" is forcing its way out and I am not happy... I still have much, so much to say. We live in a time when everyone looks to the past... I'm just as good as they were. My orchestration is better than Beethoven's and I have better themes than his. But – he was born in a wine country – I in a land where *surmjölk* [curdled milk] is in charge.'

In May 1922 Sibelius heard that his ballet *Scaramouche* had finally been performed at the Royal Theatre in Copenhagen, conducted by Georg Høeberg – and had been well received. 'Here, once again, Sibelius has undeniably created a musical work that confirms his status as the most original and imaginative composer in the Nordic countries', according to the reviewer of *Social-Demokraten*. But by now Sibelius had other things on his mind. Shortly before receiving the news from Denmark, he had been informed by his brother's doctors that Christian was terminally ill, suffering from incurable anæmia. Naturally Jean was both saddened and concerned though, as so often, he viewed the situation in terms of its impact on his own state of mind: 'It is impossible to say what this will mean for me. Again I stand on the threshold of an unavoidable fate'; 'How profoundly distressing it is. My beloved brother!... my life is filled with constant anxiety for Christian' (diary, 3rd/22nd May).

Christian's illness distracted Sibelius from his symphonic work; he laid the *Sixth Symphony* aside and composed a set of short piano pieces, Op. 99, the very lightness and inconsequentiality of which can be seen as an attempt to escape from his personal worries. At first, in May, Sibelius wrote six pieces. The first, *Pièce humoristique*, alternates capriciously between 3/4 and 2/4, whilst the broken octaves in *Esquisse* (No. 2) present the performer with the challenge of convincing the listener that the first note does not come on the down-beat! The reflectiveness and gentle melancholy of *Souvenir* (No. 3) have an intimacy that may well reflect the composer's concerns about his brother. The fourth, *Impromptu*, which is not in any way milita-ristic despite its *Quasi marcia* marking, finds Sibelius in a brighter mood; its closing bars paraphrase *Oeillet*, the second of the 'flower' pieces, Op. 85.

Couplet (No. 5) has the character of an improvisation; its opening melody
has the charm of some of Elgar's music for children. The original finale to
the set, *Animoso*, focuses on a single rhythmic pattern; one suspects that
it might have drawn its inspiration in this regard from the scherzo of the
forthcoming *Sixth Symphony*, or from the doggedly persistent *Night Ride
and Sunrise*. In the piano piece, however, the rhythm is not trochaic but
rather dactylic, as in the first movement of Beethoven's *Seventh Symphony*.
At the beginning of June two more pieces were added. One was the
Tchaikovskian *Moment de valse* (No. 7), where the waltz theme grows
from inconspicuous beginnings into a grand melodic statement – proof that,
even in a small piece, Sibelius was prepared to use themes of great richness
and potential. The last piece in Op. 99 is *Petite Marche*, an irascible piece,
a Sibelian counterpart to Grieg's *March of the Dwarfs*.

Christian Sibelius died on 2nd July. According to *Hufvudstadsbladet*,
a piece for string quartet by Jean (the *Elegy* from *King Christian II*,
according to Christian's daughter Rita) was played at his funeral five
days later. Jean's feeling of loss was profound, and even in November he
complained that his grief was preventing him from composing.

In the months between Christian's death and the end of the year, Jean
produced just three works. Of these, the *Suite caractéristique*, Op. 100,
completed on 8th August, had been in progress at least since March, when
Sibelius mentioned it in a letter to the publisher Carl Fischer in New York.
The suite is available in versions for solo piano or for harp and strings; the
harp is not used soloistically, however, but merely to add tonal colour. The
Suite caractéristique betrays hardly a trace of Sibelius's personal worries.
It is a good-humoured and totally unpretentious work, and has thus drawn
much invective from those who refuse to acknowledge Sibelius's mastery
of lighter music. Like the *Suite mignonne* and *Suite champêtre* it has
three short movements. In his letter to Carl Fischer, Sibelius gave them the
descriptive titles *Danse passionée*, *Danse romantique* and *Danse chevaleresque*. Fischer rejected the piece, however, and when it was published
by Wilhelm Hansen these titles were not included. They do seem rather
ostentatious for such an unassuming work, but when he wrote the letter
Sibelius had not yet completed the second and third movements, and
his plans may have changed in the intervening months. The waltz-like
first movement, *Vivo*, is thematically very close to the *Allegro moderato*
section of the forthcoming *Seventh Symphony* and, as in this passage
from the symphony, incorporates a long, gradual *accelerando*. The second
movement, *Lento*, is dominated by gentle, sighing motifs, whilst the finale,
Comodo, is dominated by buoyant, dance-like rhythms.

In September Sibelius completed a lyrical *Novellette* for violin and
piano. Here he continued in the essentially warm, melodious style of many

of his wartime violin pieces rather than anticipating the much more acerbic works for the instrument that he would produce in the mid and late 1920s. His original plan to compose a number of companion pieces never materialized, and the *Novellette* thus stands alone as Op. 102.

The final work from 1922 was delivered in response to a request from Walter Parviainen for a 'festive cantata' to celebrate the 25th anniversary of a factory in Säynätsalo, near Jyväskylä, and was first performed at the anniversary celebrations held in the local school on 28th December of that year. Instead of writing a cantata, Sibelius supplied a relatively short piece for string quartet: *Andante festivo*, JS 34a. Its character is solemn yet impassioned, and it has been suggested that some of the musical material derives from sketches made in the early 1900s for the *Marjatta* oratorio.

Financial worries continued to plague the composer, and – no doubt remembering the success of his trip to America eight years earlier – he enquired from his Masonic friend Toivo Nekton whether the American market could be tapped. In December Nekton replied: 'All of these Americans are willing to accept so-called "small compositions" from European composers but, they claim, cannot sell symphonies. The best offer that I have received here came from Carl Fischer.' Sibelius paid heed to Nekton's advice, but this was not the time to be composing piano music. Despite the trauma of his brother's death and the ever-present worries about paying the bills, Sibelius was far from idle. On the contrary, he was now engrossed in the *Sixth Symphony*.

1923

During 1922 Sibelius's diary entries had become increasingly sporadic, and from 1923 onwards they cease to provide an accurate representation either of his activities or of his state of mind. On 14th January he noted the completion of the first three movements of the *Sixth Symphony* but after that there are no further entries for four months.

Sibelius conducted the Helsinki Philharmonic Orchestra in the première of his *Symphony No. 6*, Op. 104, on 19th February 1923, including in the same concert four of his recent lighter works – *Autrefois*, *Valse chevaleresque*, *Suite champêtre* and *Suite caractéristique*, along with *La Chasse* from the second set of *Scènes historiques*. The concert was repeated three days later.

On the whole the *Sixth Symphony* was received kindly. Evert Katila in *Helsingin Sanomat* described it as 'milder, less wide-ranging, more fragile in character. The *Fifth* is an imposing, celebratory drama, the *Sixth* a pure idyll. The *Sixth* is also a poem within the framework of a symphony … the overall mood is serene, gleaming like a bright Finnish late summer day.'

Heikki Klemetti described it as being 'not of the flesh, but of the spirit'. Among the dissenting voices were Leo Funtek and Karl Ekman, who complained of a lack of big climaxes and dramatic contrasts.

Of all Sibelius's symphonies, the *Sixth* is the most tranquil and most intimate. It is not unusual for his works to have a modal flavour, but here the influence of the Dorian mode is especially pronounced. Indeed, as the opening pages of the first, third and fourth movements have no key signature, it is arguably more suitable to call the piece a 'symphony in the Dorian mode' rather than a 'symphony in D minor' (the title page of the score omits any mention of a key).

Despite the use of bass clarinet (its only appearance in a Sibelius symphony, except in the 1915 version of the *Fifth*) and harp (which he had not used in a symphony since the *First*), the texture of the *Sixth Symphony* is dominated by the strings. The serene polyphonic opening is without parallel in symphonic music; a descending phrase right at the beginning and a rising theme first heard on the oboe soon afterwards provide the basic motivic material for the entire work, which in performance comes across as entirely seamless. Its raw materials are quintessentially Sibelian: woven into the polyphony as early as the second bar is the rhythmic pattern short–long–short that had featured prominently in his music since the 1880s, and in the ninth bar the lower first violin line includes the first of many 'S-motifs'. The tranquillity of the opening yields to more animated music, though the basic pulse remains the same. Not until the coda do *tremolos* in the lower strings and distant horn chords signal a darkening of the mood.

In the dreamy second movement the upper strings often play *divisi*, creating a luminous texture. The music has an uncommon rhythmic freedom, almost as though it were notated without bar-lines – not least towards the end, when the strings play *flautato* – a passage often compared with the 'Forest Murmurs' section of Wagner's *Siegfried*. Here the chirpy woodwind calls are mostly based on 'S-motifs'. In the manuscript Sibelius originally marked the movement *Andantino quasi allegretto*, then changed it to *Allegretto (e poco a poco più)* before finally settling on the published indication of *Allegretto moderato*. In total contrast, the brief scherzo is a crisp, down-to-earth piece with an insistent trochaic pulse reminiscent of the tone poem *Night Ride and Sunrise*.

The finale opens with a noble melody in regular phrase-lengths, played antiphonally by the woodwind/upper strings and lower strings. The phrases gradually lose their symmetry, however, and the music becomes increasingly urgent, rising to a frenzied culmination. In the aftermath of this climax we eventually arrive at a sublime chorale-like idea, which finally eases the symphony into silence.

Sibelius does not quote or compose explicit chorale themes. Instead, he alludes indirectly to religious concepts that had no immediate place in his vision of the symphony as absolute music. Despite his great admiration for Bach, Sibelius generally avoided composing overtly religious music in the traditional sense – though occasionally, such as in the incidental music for Hofmannsthal's *Jedermann*, he came close to this style. He was not deeply religious in the way his mother and sister were; his secretary Santeri Levas explains (referring to events in December 1946): 'the sun again peeped through the clouds, for the first time in ages. "How marvellous," said Sibelius, "even this weak sunshine is. What peace and deep devotion Nature can arouse in man!" Then we spoke about the astonishing sense of law in the universe, and an almost inconceivable harmony that makes every human effort seem tiny and senseless. "That," he concluded, "is precisely what I call God."'

After the première of the *Sixth Symphony*, Sibelius and Aino set out on a trip abroad that was part concert tour and part holiday. Things started well enough; their first port of call was Stockholm, where they arrived on 25th February. Even though Armas Järnefelt was still conductor at the Royal Opera, Sibelius had on this occasion been engaged by Schnéevoigt's Konsertförening orchestra. The venue was the Auditorium on Norra Bantorget – a large (1,751-seat) cinema that had been opened in 1914 and was also used as a concert hall, serving as the orchestra's base until the Stockholm Concert Hall was opened in 1926. The first concert, on 1st March, included well-established music – *En saga*, *Rakastava*, *The Swan of Tuonela* and the *Second Symphony* – whilst the second, four days later, included *The Oceanides*, the *Sixth Symphony*, *Pohjola's Daughter*, *The Rapids-Rider's Brides* (with the popular Swedish baritone John Forsell as soloist), extracts from *Pelléas et Mélisande* and *Finlandia*. In between there was a matinée with the *Elegy* from *King Christian II*, *Valse triste* and, again, *Finlandia*. On 6th March he conducted the same orchestra in the University Hall in Uppsala, in a programme that included the *First Symphony*, which he conducted in Stockholm again the next day. What little time was left between the concerts was filled with a more than usually generous round of official functions, dinners and receptions.

The concerts went well and even the normally vexatious Wilhelm Peterson-Berger found less to complain about than usual. In an interview with William Seymer for the newspaper *Svenska Dagbladet* Sibelius remarked about the new symphony: 'It is very tranquil in character and outline... and is built, like the *Fifth*, on linear rather than harmonic foundations. Furthermore like most other symphonies, it has four movements; formally, however, these are completely free. None of them follows the ordinary sonata scheme... I do not think of a symphony only as music in this or that number of bars, but rather as an expression of a spiritual creed, a phase in one's inner life.'

The Sibeliuses headed south to Italy, stopping off in Berlin to visit Adolf Paul. Their first stop in Italy was Rome, where the Finnish diplomat Herman Gummerus had arranged a matinée with the Augusteo Orchestra on 18th March. The choice of repertoire can hardly be described as adventurous: *Finlandia*, *Pelléas et Mélisande*, *The Swan of Tuonela*, *Lemminkäinen's Return* and the *Second Symphony*, but Italian audiences were not familiar with his music and it was probably wise to choose well-established works. Even so, the reviews were only average; for some of the critics Sibelius's world was remote and incomprehensible. In an interview with Alberto Gasco of *La Tribuna*, he tried to explain his position: 'For my part I must say that my music is not folkloristic; I have never used Finnish folk motifs for my own ends. I have composed much that is in the style of folk melodies, but the notes themselves have always come from my own imagination, or rather from my ardent Finnish heart... I dipped into the poetry and sagas of my native land and then sang my own tune, often enriching my soul with the *Kalevala*, which is an unfailing inspiration for an unspoiled Finnish artist.'

Jean and Aino continued south to Capri for a week's holiday. After that they retraced their steps and travelled via Rome and Berlin (where they tried to visit Busoni, who was too ill to receive them) to Sweden – this time not to Stockholm but to Gothenburg, where they were the guests of Stenhammar's sister-in-law Olga Bratt.

Two concerts were scheduled with the Gothenburg Orchestral Society, and the first took place on 10th April. On the programme were *Pohjola's Daughter* and the *Fifth* and *Sixth Symphonies*. Sibelius was on top form both at the concert itself, which was lavishly praised in the reviews, and at the reception afterwards, even if he did consume so much wine that he could not concentrate on a verbose eulogy from the Swedish composer and poet Ture Rangström, who the previous year had succeeded Stenhammar as principal conductor there.

The following morning Aino wrote to her daughter Katarina: 'Papa has rehearsed very well, is very calm, and all of his Helsinki nervousness has gone ... the concert yesterday was a great success... Papa is brilliant.' She might have been less inclined to send the letter if she had waited a few more hours, for it was at the concert that day – *Rakastava*, *The Oceanides* and the *Second Symphony* – that Sibelius embarrassed himself. The morning rehearsal went smoothly enough, but the organizers were unwise enough to allow him to escape to a restaurant during the afternoon, and there he stayed, eating oysters and drinking champagne. As the appointed start time of the concert approached he was taken back to the concert hall, by now rather the worse for wear. The concert duly began, but after a few bars Sibelius stopped – apparently believing that he was at a rehearsal! The music restarted and the rest of the performance passed without disturbance. But Sibelius's weakness for alcohol had now had a very visible effect on his work, and he was consumed by shame. After the concert he discovered a bottle of whisky in his pocket and angrily smashed it on the steps of the concert hall.

This incident did not prevent the listeners from displaying their enthusiastic approval, and would probably have been forgotten if Aino Sibelius had not been sitting among the audience. Many years later she told Erik Tawaststjerna: 'To my ears it all sounded like chaos; I was scared to death.'

From Gothenburg, the Sibeliuses returned to Finland, where one more conducting engagement awaited with the local orchestra in Viipuri, which had been rehearsed for the occasion by its regular conductor, Boris Sirpo. Sibelius had not conducted in Viipuri for many years and was now treated as a celebrity, with crowds awaiting his arrival at the railway station. The programme consisted of *Spring Song*, *Belshazzar's Feast* and the *Second Symphony*, and demand for tickets was such that the 400-seat hall was full and the audience spilled over into the stairways and vestibule. The following day the concert was repeated as a matinée, after which Sibelius set off for Helsinki, where he met up with Gallen-Kallela at the sixtieth birthday celebrations of their mutual friend, the author and publisher Wenzel Hagelstam, before returning to Ainola.

In the meantime two more countries had decorated him: he now held the Swedish Vasa Order and had been appointed Commendatore dell' Ordine della Corona d'Italia. Unfortunately such honours did not pay the bills, and inflation in Germany was becoming so severe that Sibelius's income from his German publishers was drastically reduced. He had at least joined GEMA (the German Authors' Rights Society), the oldest and best-known organization of its kind in Germany and the most important in economic terms, but in the short term the benefits were not significant.

During the summer the pianist Wilhelm Kempff again visited Finland and spent a few days at Ainola. According to Sibelius's daughter Katarina, Kempff spent much of the time playing for his host, and she made special mention of Beethoven's *'Hammerklavier'* Sonata.

CHAPTER 14

THE SEVENTH SYMPHONY
AND TAPIOLA: 1923–1926

The next big project was looming: the *Seventh Symphony*. Since he had written to Axel Carpelan five years earlier suggesting that the symphony would be characterized by 'joy of life and vitality with *appassionato* sections. In three movements; that last of them is a "Hellenic rondo"', his ideas for the work had developed beyond recognition. Manuscript evidence from the early 1920s proves that he then envisaged the work not in three movements but in four. Little can be established with certainty about the projected first or third movements, although the sketches imply that the music was centred in G minor. Most of the musical material found in the eventual single-movement *Seventh Symphony* derives from the planned second movement, an *Adagio* based in C major. Some of the faster music can be traced to the projected G minor finale.

It is likely that Sibelius made his decision to turn the *Seventh* into a one-movement work around this time of his trip to Sweden and Italy. The first draft of a single-movement *Seventh Symphony* evidently dates from 1923, though the ending was not yet fully worked out. Through the summer he worked on the symphony, at some point producing a further, more fully developed draft version – although here too the ending was absent. In fact he sketched and discarded several different endings to the symphony before arriving at the definitive version. One of these is even performable, although it should be stressed that – unlike the case of *En saga* or the *Fifth Symphony* – this is by no means an 'original version' but rather a solution that was decisively rejected by the composer. And no wonder: beginning after the last major climax in the work (8 bars after Z in the published score), the music digresses into a quiet, syncopated passage, *poco pressante*, that seems to lack any sense of direction, although the C major chords in the closing bars, *Adagio molto*, have satisfying power and breadth.[1]

On 6th November his financial difficulties were eased by the award of a 100,000-mark scholarship from the Kordelin Foundation in Helsinki: 'not just for the promotion of Finnish music and taking it along new paths, but also for making Finnish culture known throughout the civilized world'. The rest of the month was full of distractions that delayed work on the *Seventh Symphony*. Both Linda Sibelius and Eero Järnefelt celebrated their sixtieth birthdays – Sibelius described the latter event as 'a moving occasion for a fine person' (diary, 11th November) – and Stenhammar visited Helsinki to perform his own *Second Piano Concerto* at one of Kajanus's concerts. Sibelius treated his Swedish friend with great hospitality and one day, when Kajanus had invited them both to lunch at the Seurahuone, he took him to one side and asked: 'Would you do me the great honour of allowing me to dedicate my *Sixth Symphony* to you?'

1924

A year earlier, Sibelius had concentrated on completing the *Sixth Symphony* to the exclusion of other works. While working on its successor in late 1923, however, he had found time to start no less than ten piano pieces – Op. 101 and Op. 103, more ambitious in both scale and emotional range than the recent Op. 97 or Op. 99 collections; they were finished in early 1924. Although he offered some of them to Wilhelm Hansen first, it seems likely that Sibelius always intended to follow Nekton's suggestion and submit these pieces to Carl Fischer in New York; the Op. 103 set even has English as the principal language for its titles. These piano works mark the beginning of Sibelius's late period as a piano composer; the emotional world that they explore is clearly related to those of the *Sixth* and *Seventh Symphonies*. At a much earlier phase of his career, Sibelius had shown that, although he was normally reluctant to quote themes from his published music in other works, he had nothing against recycling material from forgotten occasional pieces or from abandoned projects. It is therefore by no means impossible that some of the ideas from the discarded first and third movements of the *Seventh Symphony* found its way into these piano works.

The *Romance*, Op. 101 No. 1, certainly has a weight of sonority and dignity that recalls the *Seventh Symphony*. Though it does without the symphony's polyphony, the principal motif of the *Romance* uses a dotted rhythm that is particularly reminiscent of the string passage near the beginning of the symphony, and the works moreover share the key of C major. A similar dotted rhythm, combined with a falling fifth, is also present among the more impressionistic sonorities – comparable with the second movement of the *Sixth Symphony* – that start the second piece,

Chant du soir. From the mists grows a solemn, chordal theme, not unlike *Andante festivo* (1922) in outline, and the piece ends in a mood of rapt, almost devout simplicity. It is the finale of the *Sixth Symphony* that is evoked in the motoric whirlwind of the third piece, named *Scène lyrique*, though its reticent, slightly melancholy opening idea – incorporating an 'S-motif' with an added top note – calls to mind the theme of the *Air varié* from Op. 58. The fourth piece, *Humoresque*, lives up to its title: after an opening cadenza-like flourish the music lurches along, like a drunkard heavily attempting to dance a mazurka. The concluding piece in Op. 101 is the deservedly popular *Scène romantique*. Here the opening theme, supported by evocative chords, would not be out of place in one of Sibelius's pantheistic nature portraits, but the mood is very charmingly lightened and humanized, without becoming trivial. It is as though a solitary dreamer were being gradually and perhaps reluctantly drawn into a world of warmth and social grace.

The Op. 103 set begins with *The Village Church*, which reuses material from the unpublished and still virtually unknown *Andante festivo*. In the piano piece, this material is more fragmented and forms the basis of a wide-ranging, often dark-hued fantasy in which it would be easy to imagine an organ-like chorale or the ringing of bells. The second piece, *The Fiddler*, is a sparkling portrayal of a folk fiddler. *The Oarsman* is a gentle if rather halting barcarole; this oarsman is clearly not in a hurry! Its parallel thirds are an 'orchestral' habit here transferred to the keyboard. Despite a few onomatopoeic touches the fourth piece, *The Storm*, is a pale anticipation of the vast storms that Sibelius would soon paint in *The Tempest* and *Tapiola*; it cannot be a preliminary study for *The Tempest*, however, as Sibelius had not yet received the commission for the theatre score. Finally comes *In Mournful Mood*, which Sibelius originally wanted to call *The Mourning Strain*, a pianistic equivalent of the orchestral funeral march *In memoriam*. The melody has an impressive sweep and, as in the orchestral march, the quiet beginning and ending lend the piece the character of a cortège. In the piano piece, though, Sibelius runs no risk of being accused of plagiarizing the funeral march from Beethoven's *Eroica*, a charge sometimes levelled at *In memoriam*.

Otherwise the opening months of 1924 were a period of concentrated work on the new symphony. Sibelius often worked at night, drinking whisky. Whether the whisky calmed his increasingly shaky hand (as he claimed) or exacerbated his tremors is a matter for conjecture; less debatable is the debilitating effect his lifestyle had upon Aino. 'How eternally tragic is the lot of an ageing composer', he wrote in his diary on 6th January. 'It [work] doesn't proceed with the same pace as it used to, and one's self-criticism grows to impossible levels.'

Aino's patience had in fact been strained beyond breaking-point. She wrote her husband a very direct letter that takes him to task for his weakness of character and fondness for alcohol – although at the same time it is clear that her concern stems from the profound love she felt for him. 'Dear Janne! – are you dear to me? – Yes.' She rightly judged that the written word would be far more effective than a frank discussion: 'I know that I cannot speak to you of these matters; you would not believe me and things would only get worse between us.' She states quite openly: 'I am unhappy', and tells him bluntly: 'if you don't change, you will surely go under... Try to break free from that which is dragging you down. Haven't you yourself noticed where it is leading? Even if you do complete a few compositions, they will be nothing compared to what you could otherwise achieve. Believe me.' Fearing a repeat of his escapades in Gothenburg the previous year, Aino refused to accompany him to Stockholm for the première of the *Fantasia sinfonica* / *Seventh Symphony*. The letter ends with a heartfelt plea: 'Pay heed to everything you have that is great and holy. I pray to you on bended knee, and I know that you can do it if you really want to. Your life companion.' This letter dented Sibelius's confidence so severely that he never openly discussed its contents. Its consequences, however, were wide-reaching. It would still be some time before he learned to moderate his drinking, but he could at least avoid public humiliation on his home territory: he would never again conduct a full-length public concert in Finland.

He was hardly cheered up by the death of Oskar Merikanto on 17th February. Merikanto was three years younger than Sibelius and had often written sympathetic reviews of Sibelius's music. Sibelius overcame his dislike of funerals and laid a wreath at the funeral service the following week at St John's Church in Helsinki, where Merikanto had been the organist since 1892.

The work that would ultimately be called the *Seventh Symphony* was finished on 2nd March, and first performed by the Konsertförening orchestra at the Auditorium in Stockholm – the only one of Sibelius's symphonies that was not premièred in Helsinki, though it was not actually billed as a symphony. The title plainly gave Sibelius some trouble; the manuscript score bears traces of the titles 'Fantasia sinfonica No. 1' and 'Sinfonia 7 continua'. For the première he opted for *Fantasia sinfonica*, which in the concert programme was corrupted to 'Fantasia sinfonico'.

On this visit Sibelius conducted three times. The first concert was on 24th March and included, in addition to the *Fantasia sinfonica*, the *First Symphony* and *Violin Concerto*. Aino's fears of a repeat of the drunken antics in Gothenburg the previous year proved groundless and the *Fantasia sinfonica* was well received, despite the very limited rehearsal time available. Strangely enough, this was the first time that Sibelius himself had conducted the revised version of his *Violin Concerto*, a work which had still not really become established in the repertoire; the adequate rather than outstanding soloist was Julius Ruthström. The concert was not sold out, but Armas Järnefelt and Stenhammar were both well pleased, as was Sibelius himself. Two days later Sibelius conducted the *Fifth Symphony* and *Snöfrid*, and Nils Grevillius conducted Adolf Wiklund's *First Piano Concerto* with the composer as soloist. The last concert, a packed matinée on 30th March at which the *Fantasia sinfonica* received its second performance, otherwise featured more popular music: three movements from *King Christian II*, *The Swan of Tuonela*, *Valse triste*, the *Romance in C major* and, inevitably, *Finlandia*.

A rising scale, *Adagio*, begins the *Fantasia sinfonica / Seventh Symphony*; the subsequent flute theme and stepwise falling and rising motif both date from the earliest identifiable sketches. The music settles into a long, chorale-like polyphonic passage in a dignified 3/2 metre, dominated by the strings. Sibelius said of this passage that it was 'as though before the face of God'. There follows a gradual increase in intensity until, with seeming inevitability, a majestic C major trombone theme grows organically out of the string music. This trombone theme occurs three times during the symphony and is one of its most important structural features.

The music subsides and, more than eight minutes into the work, we encounter the first change of pulse – a gradual quickening all the way to *Vivacissimo* – though even this is almost imperceptible at first. It is characteristic of late Sibelius that changes of pulse occur gradually, and nowhere is this better illustrated than in this symphony, where (at least without a score) it is barely possible to pinpoint any change of tempo with accuracy. The motivic material of the *Vivacissimo* section, astonishingly, seems to have been planned for an unfinished song, and leads into the second appearance of the trombone theme, now in a stormy C minor.

The tone lightens as we arrive at the dance-like *Allegro moderato*. Before Sibelius's plans for a four-movement *Seventh Symphony* came to light, this passage was often assumed to be the 'Hellenic rondo' he mentioned in his letter to Carpelan from 20th May 1918. The entire section is another gradual *accelerando* – this time reaching *Presto* before broadening into the third and final appearance of the trombone theme, back in C major, now richly orchestrated and delivered with great intensity. Reminiscences of motifs from the very beginning of the symphony dominate the coda (where there is also a progression recognizable from *Valse triste* that commentators love to point out, though it is presumably wholly coincidental), and the symphony ends with a mighty C major chord.

Despite the very different characters of the works as a whole, there are some striking parallels between individual motifs in the *Sixth* and *Seventh Symphonies*. These reflect not only the fact that he worked on them simultaneously, but also the short gap – just over a year – between their completion, the shortest interval between any two of his symphonies. If Sibelius continued with the working methods he had used for the *Fifth*, *Sixth* and *Seventh Symphonies*, he would surely at this stage already have set aside some themes or sketches for the *Eighth*. If this was the case, he must have been careful to dispose of any such material when he destroyed the *Eighth Symphony* in the 1940s. The only allusion that has possibly slipped through the net is a rather cryptic number 'VIII' alongside a few highlighted bars containing an ascending motif marked 'Trio' among sketches for the *Seventh Symphony*.[2]

The Stockholm trip had been more than satisfactory but, when he returned to Järvenpää, Sibelius was not in the best of moods. Indeed, his diary entries from the spring of 1924 – both before and after the Stockholm visit – are uncompromisingly bleak. 'My life will soon be over. How infinitely tragic to have to stop when one is just getting started'; 'The "ghastly spectre" within is consuming me'; 'This life in the kingdom of death, without vitality and without wonders... Where should I find life's joy when everything screams of life's misery? If I could arrange somewhere for Aino to live in town it would be easier for her. And I would wait for death in some out-of-the-way spot here in the country.' If the problem with Aino was to a large extent of his own making, in other respects his frustration is easy to understand. He was now fast approaching sixty and, over his long career, had developed into a figure of iconic importance for his country and, in public (not least when he was abroad), he was by and large treated with the respect and acclaim that he had earned. And yet, on a mundane level, it was still a struggle to pay the household bills: 'My economic situation is now frightful' (diary, 14th May). It must all have seemed terribly unfair. He now regretted having turned down the offer from the Eastman School of Music back in 1921.

In late May a party was arranged at Ainola. For understandable reasons Sibelius's daughters were normally discouraged from having too many friends to visit while he was in the throes of composing and so, by way of compensation, when a gathering was arranged, it was all the more lavish. Among Margareta's guests was a shy schoolboy and music student who had recently moved to Helsinki from Jyväskylä by the name of Jussi Blomstedt (he later changed his surname to Jalas). One can only imagine the young student's excitement, arriving at Ainola for the first time straight from a matinée at the Conservatory, at meeting a man whom he later described as 'a living legend'. Blomstedt was persuaded to play Liszt's *Sixth Hungarian Rhapsody* and soon established a cordial friendship with Sibelius – which was fortunate, as it was not long before he and Margareta (who was fifteen at the time of the party) fell in love; they married in 1929. Jalas later became a distinguished conductor whose interpretations of his father-in-law's music have a special authenticity.

Another musician with a special affinity for Sibelius's music was Martti Similä, who met the composer for the first time a few months later. He, too, became a close friend and loyal champion. In addition to his work as a conductor – of the Finnish National Opera, the Helsinki Philharmonic Orchestra and then the Lahti Symphony Orchestra – Similä was also a skilled pianist and composer, especially of film music.

By the beginning of July Sibelius had completed two small pieces for violin and piano that he called *Danses champêtres*, Op. 106. These mark the beginning of his last stylistic period as a composer of violin music. By contrast with his wartime miniatures they mark a significant toughening of style; henceforth his music for violin and piano would be characterized by greater acerbity of mood, more adventurous harmonies and a wider emotional range. The *Danses champêtres* have the character more of virtuoso studies than of conventional dances. The first of them is broad and majestic (*Largamente assai*), as though evoking a bleak and chilling landscape illuminated by flashes of lightning. As we pass through this countryside our attention is twice diverted to an earthy, bucolic polka (*Vivace*). At the end of the second dance, a sparkling *Alla polacca*, Sibelius cheekily parodies the slow movement of his own *Fifth Symphony*. These two dances were offered to the publisher Carl Fischer in New York along with the Op. 101 and 103 piano pieces.

On 27th July Ferruccio Busoni died in Berlin, after a long struggle against kidney disease. Sibelius had long regarded Busoni's abilities and insights as a pianist as quite extraordinary. Admittedly he had been less impressed by his friend's skills as a conductor and composer, but Busoni had been a loyal friend and champion since the 1880s and his passing must have come not only as a major blow in its own right but also a reminder that he, Sibelius, was growing old. On a more positive note, Sibelius and Aino hosted a happy (if expensive) event on 30th August: their daughter Katarina married Eero Ilves. At 37, Ilves was sixteen years older than his wife. By profession he was a bank manager, a circumstance which Sibelius was to turn to his advantage: for many years Ilves placed his financial knowledge at the composer's service.

Lauri Kuoppamäki, commissioner-general of the Finnish Industrial Fair, visited Ainola to deliver a commission for a piece to be called *Työn laulu* (*Song of Work*), a setting of words by V. A. Koskenniemi, which was supposed to be ready in time for the Industrial Fair's fifth anniversary celebrations the following summer. Sibelius started work on the piece at the end of December but it failed to fire him with enthusiasm and on 1st February he backed away from the project. On the other hand he did manage to complete another Koskenniemi setting, a strophic setting of the poem *Koulutie* (*The Way to School*), JS 112, for mixed choir *a cappella*. It is a charming, naïve piece in an easily flowing 6/8 time, though after the first few verses the simple melody does rather outstay its welcome. We do not know exactly when in 1924 it was composed; it was intended for (but did not not actually appear in) the fiftieth anniversary album of the educational authority in Oulu.

Prestigious bookings as a conductor were also flowing in. Sibelius signed a contract for a concert in Bergen the following April (although in the event he did not fulfil this commitment), and at a month's notice he also accepted an invitation to give a series of concerts in Copenhagen. He set off – once again without Aino – on 23rd September.

In Copenhagen Sibelius was accommodated in style at the Hotel d'Angleterre and (as he professed in a letter to Adolf Paul) drank only champagne. There were six concerts at the Odd Fellow Palace with the Copenhagen Philharmonic Orchestra between 1st and 8th October and, for good measure, they travelled across to Malmö in Sweden for an extra concert. With one exception the programme was basically the same: the *First* and *Seventh Symphonies* – the latter still under the name *Fantasia sinfonica* – along with *Finlandia* and *Valse triste* (in three concerts there was also *Valse chevaleresque*). The programme on 2nd October featured just one symphony – the *Fifth* – alongside four movements from *King Christian II*, the ubiquitous *Finlandia* and *Valse triste*, and one surprising rarity: the *Impromptu* for women's chorus and orchestra. Sibelius's visit attracted the attention not only of musicians (Carl Nielsen, Fini Henriques and Louis Glass were among those who went to hear him conduct) but also of statesmen and royalty: at one concert Sibelius was presented with the Order of the Dannebrog by King Christian X and Queen Alexandrine.

The *Seventh Symphony* had still not acquired its definitive name. Even though it was billed as *Fantasia sinfonica* in Copenhagen, at least one critic – in *Politiken* (2nd October) – called it *Symphony No. 7*. It is not known exactly when Sibelius made the definitive decision to number the work among his symphonies. Admittedly he used the new title in a diary entry dated 5th September 1924, but he reverted to the old name in a letter to Wilhelm Hansen on 25th February 1925 – though remarking: 'Best if its name is *Symphonie No. 7 (in einem Satze)*'. By May 1925 the engraving was complete, and the new name was fixed.

The concerts were sold out and received glowing reviews, as did the new work. In the case of *Nationaltidende* such a response was predictable, as the critic was Gunnar Hauch, a committed Sibelian who had been influential in organizing the entire trip. Sibelius clearly enjoyed Hauch's company, and even compared him to Axel Carpelan. Towards the end of this concentrated and strenuous trip, Sibelius became so exhausted that he had to take medical advice. In letters to Aino he explained that the doctor had advised him to give up conducting and to spend some months resting in Italy; he was also put on a diet and given sleeping pills. One wonders how much of this advice actually came from the doctor: after Aino's reprimands earlier that year Sibelius was in any case inclined to curtail his conducting, and he hardly needed much encouragement to visit Italy. He even considered travelling straight on to Italy and tried to persuade Aino to join him in Copenhagen for the onward journey. In the end, however, having spent all the money he had earned, he just went home.

Despite the success of the Copenhagen concerts, Sibelius soon sank back into despondency. Writing and conducting the *Seventh Symphony* had clearly depleted his energies – and this time there was no immediate prospect of completing another major work. In November he wrote in his diary: 'How incessantly arduous it is to grow old as an artist, and above all as a composer. It might be wisest not to have any friends. One would die alone, and that would be easier... [But] are you, Jean Sibelius, certain that you do not still have many fine works unwritten?' 'Alcohol is the only friend that never lets one down.'

1925

Sibelius's feelings of loneliness and depression persisted well into the new year. At least, though, he could take heart from the situation at Breitkopf & Härtel. The company was now recovering strongly after the war; an offer from Wilhelm Hansen to buy up Breitkopf's entire Sibelius catalogue was rejected outright, and the German firm was keen to acquire new works. Otherwise, during these months, he spent much time in the company of 'the only friend that never lets one down'; he admitted that he had started to partake of secret nightcaps, and he sought solace at Helsinki's most exclusive restaurants – either in the company of Eero Järnefelt and his friends at the 'Citronbord' ('lemon table') at the Kämp or, more worryingly, on his own.

Sibelius's urge to compose seems to have fallen away, and he put pen to paper only when he really had to. In mid-January he completed three more *Danses champêtres* for violin and piano, which he needed to send along with the earlier two to Carl Fischer in New York. The first of the new additions, *Tempo moderato*, is full of effective display writing for the violin. A rising motif, heard at the beginning, is whipped up into a vigorous and forceful dance, a storm that eventually blows itself out as the piece calms down before a final flourish. The main dance section in the middle of the next piece, *Tempo di Menuetto*, is framed by passages in which minuet-like rhythms are combined with a wide-ranging, almost improvisational melody. The last piece contrasts an earthy, march-like *Poco moderato* with a more nervous passage (*Allegretto*) which, with its note repetitions, is insistently memorable. Overall, the five *Danses champêtres* are a strikingly imaginative group of pieces which, in their ability swiftly to conjure up a wide variety of moods and characters, are stylistically closer to the incidental music for *The Tempest* than to the Olympian majesty of the *Seventh Symphony*.

In February he delivered four small pieces that had been commissioned by Heikki Klemetti for a volume of liturgical melodies, *Suomen evankelis-luterilaisen kirkon Messusävelmät* – 'religious things... he ordered them and had the right to get them' (diary, 17th February). Sibelius's lack of experience in writing conventional sacred music shows: he does not sound wholly at ease with the sacred texts here. Scored for liturgist, choir (i.e. congregation) and organ, the *Three Introductory Antiphons*, JS 110, are rather musty pieces, none of them thematically distinguished. The dominant rhythmic pattern in the first, *Palmusunnuntaina* (*On Palm Sunday*), can be traced back, via *The Rapids-Rider's Brides* and *En saga*, to the *Violin Sonata in F major* of 1889. The solo passages of the second, *Pyhäinpäivänä tai hautajaisjumalanpalveluksissa* (*On All Saints' Day*), owe an obvious debt to the polyphonic writing in the *Seventh Symphony* and incorporate an 'S-motif'; this piece is also designed for use at funerals. The last of the set is *Kristillisissä nuorisojuhlissa* (*General Prayers*), which makes a brief thematic allusion to the much earlier song *Se'n har jag ej frågat mera*. Though its invention is equally unmemorable, *Herran siunaus* (*God's Blessing*), JS 95, a song with organ, includes several of Sibelius's trademark devices; there is a slow 3/2 pulse (though it sometimes sounds like 6/4) and a prominent 'S-motif' in the very first bar. Isolated echoes can be heard of earlier music – there is even a hint of *Höstkväll* – whilst elsewhere the music anticipates future glories: several ideas, not least the setting of the word 'Amen', are uncannily close to the forthcoming portrayal of Prospero in *The Tempest*.

Later that month Sibelius reworked the *Scène d'amour* from *Scaramouche* for violin and piano. Such an arrangement had been requested by Wilhelm Hansen, with the subsequent clarification that it 'should ideally be easy, so that it can be played in a domestic context'. The double-stopped passages in this piece call to mind the *Aubade* from Op. 81 (1918). Sibelius wrote to Hansen that the *Scène d'amour* was 'almost a new piece', and he hoped that it would enjoy wide circulation. Another violin piece from this period makes use of closely related thematic material: *En glad musikant* (*A Happy*

Musician), JS 70. This work for solo violin (a poem by Ture Rangström is written in above the violin part) cannot be dated more precisely than 1924–26, but the similarity in style makes it quite possible that it dates from around the same time as the *Scène d'amour*.

On 9th March a benefit concert was held in Helsinki in aid of the Mannerheim Society for Children. At the personal request of General Mannerheim, who attended the concert, Sibelius was persuaded to break his self-imposed moratorium on conducting in Helsinki: he conducted *Belshazzar's Feast* and *Rakastava* with an ensemble from the Philharmonic Orchestra. As a surprise at the end of the concert he presented a novelty: the *Morceau romantique sur un motif de M. Jakob de Julin*, JS 135, based on a waltz theme by a friend of his, the industrialist Jakob von Julin, who was related to Mannerheim. A piano version of the piece dates from the same year; to judge from the style of the orchestral and piano writing, the piano piece came first. A copy of the manuscript, autographed by Sibelius and Mannerheim, was subsequently sold for the benefit of the children's charity.

Around this time, or perhaps slightly earlier, Sibelius wrote two songs for male choir *a cappella*, Op. 108, as a present for Eduard Polón – who, in 1898, had established Suomen Gummitehdas Oy (the Finnish Rubber Works), a company that manufactured shoes, boots and other rubber products and was one of the forerunners of today's industrial giant Nokia. The texts of the songs – *Humoreski* (*Humoresque*) and *Ne pitkän matkan kulkijat* (*Wanderers on the Long Way*) are by Larin Kyösti, from the collection *Kulkurin lauluja* (*Songs of a Wayfarer*). They both offer an idealized image of the wayfarer's life: in the *Humoreski* he takes life's trials in his stride, playing a little polska on his flute, whilst in *Ne pitkän matkan kulkijat* the wanderers come and go aimlessly, relying on God's bounty to feed them both physically and spiritually. Sibelius's settings have a wry humour that suits the texts very well.

In April Robert Lienau wrote and asked if Sibelius had any shorter orchestral works to offer in the style of *Pelléas et Mélisande* or *Belshazzar's Feast*. This prompted Sibelius to write back suggesting a suite from another theatrical score: 'A few years ago I wrote music for *Jedermann*. From this music I could put together a good suite. I shall write to you about it next season.' To Lienau this sounded like an excellent idea and he agreed enthusiastically. In the end, however, Sibelius never made a suite from the *Jedermann* music – although at around this time he did make piano transcriptions of the second, fourth and eighth numbers (*Episodio*, *Scena* and *Canzone*), presumably as an offshoot from this project.

Sibelius may have lost interest in a *Jedermann* suite when a new commission for theatre music arrived the following month. The Royal

Theatre in Copenhagen, along with the publisher Wilhelm Hansen, asked him for incidental music for a new production of Shakespeare's *Tempest*. At last he had found a major project that fired his imagination! But the time available was short: Hansen asked for the score by 1st September, just four months away, so that it could be rehearsed for a planned première at the end of the year. Sibelius set to work and delivered the music on time, although as it happened the first night was put back until 15th March.

The Tempest, Op. 109, is a vast score – as long as the complete *Scaramouche*, but scored for more lavish forces including vocal soloists, choir, large orchestra and harmonium. It is divided into no fewer than 34 musical numbers (including some brief pieces that are repeated) that are spread throughout the play, and with its great variety of moods, seemingly endless thematic invention and sparkling orchestration it represents the zenith of Sibelius's theatre music. In this score Sibelius experiments with spatial effects, placing the harp high above the stage and moving some instruments and the choir to different locations above and behind the stage for the best effect.

The producer in Copenhagen was Johannes Poulsen, and his view of Shakespeare's play (given in the Danish translation by Edvard Lembcke) was by no means conventional. Poulsen came to Helsinki and spent several weeks in a hotel with Sibelius, explaining his ideas and exploring the musical possibilities.

Poulsen omitted the scene from the beginning of the play in which, through Prospero's sorcery, a storm strikes the ship carrying Antonio, Alonso, Ferdinand, Sebastian, Gonzalo, Stefano, and Trinculo. The travellers are marooned on the island where the magician Prospero and his daughter Miranda have been living since Antonio usurped Prospero as Duke of Milan twelve years earlier. Here Sibelius was asked to write a stormy overture, at the climax of which the curtain rose to reveal the ship sinking. In his tone poems – notably in *The Oceanides* and the following year also in *Tapiola* – Sibelius wrote glorious 'storm music', but in those works it had to be fitted into a larger tonal and structural context. In *The Tempest*, unencumbered by such constraints, he could concentrate on a mighty, arguably unequalled portrayal of the crashing waves and howling winds, ultimately subsiding into a series of mysterious, apprehensive horn calls.

To calm Miranda's fears about the fate of the seafarers, Prospero assures her that they have survived. He tells her how his treacherous brother Antonio, in collaboration with with Alonso, King of Naples, banished him. With the assistance of the trusty Gonzalo, Prospero had managed to escape with his daughter and his books of magic. He puts her to sleep with a spellbinding berceuse for harmonium and harp (No. 2). Now

Prospero summons his servant Ariel (No. 3), who arrives in a flash of orchestral colour and explains how he arranged the storm and shipwreck; in the background we hear a soothing choral vocalise accompanied by harmonium and harp (No. 4). At Prospero's bidding, Ariel flies away (No. 5) and Prospero orders his other slave, the coarse and unwilling Caliban, to fetch firewood. Invisible to the others Ariel, singing the song *Come unto these yellow sands* (No. 6), fetches Ferdinand, Alonso's son, with whom Miranda immediately falls in love. Ferdinand believes that his father has perished, an impression that Ariel does nothing to dispel in the song *Full fadom five thy father lies* (No. 7). Its melody makes striking use of the tritone and imitates a tolling bell. Prospero accuses Ferdinand of being a traitor and imprisons him.

The interlude at the beginning of Act II (No. 8) is one of Sibelius's dignified hymns in a slow 3/2-time. If the string writing in its outer sections calls to mind similar music in the *Seventh Symphony*, the more lively middle part recalls the finale of the *Second*. The music is a character portrait of Prospero – but Prospero is not himself present at the beginning of the act. This is set in another part of the island, where the shipwrecked nobles are gathered. The next musical number is a portrayal of Ariel, disguised as an oak tree: he plays a haunting flute melody on a broken branch (No. 9). Ariel sings to Alonso and Gonzalo (*While you here do snoring lie*, No. 10), waking them from their slumber and thus protecting them from Sebastian and Antonio, who are plotting to murder them. Poulsen took an uncharitable view of Prospero's slave Caliban, regarding him as an uncouth savage, and Sibelius's character portrait (No. 11) with its oafishness and heavy tread faithfully reflects this interpretation. Encountering the jester Trinculo and the butler Stephano – who sings a drunken song (*I shall no more to sea, to sea*, No. 12) – Caliban mistakes Stephano with his 'celestial liquor' for a god and transfers his allegiance to him with a wild, rough-hewn song (*Farewell, master; farewell, farewell!*, No. 13).

At the beginning of Act III Sibelius combines musical devices familiar from the very beginning of his career – short–long–short syncopations and triplets – with a graceful, alluring melody to paint a beguiling picture of the naïve and unsuspecting Miranda (No. 14) as she talks to Ferdinand, who has been set to work carrying wood; they decide to marry. Meanwhile Caliban, Stephano and Trinculo, in a well-oiled condition, have dreamt up a plot to kill Prospero. Ariel leads them in a merry dance (No. 15) and they sing an ugly, boisterous canon (*Flout'em and [s]cout'em*, No. 16). Elsewhere, Antonio and Sebastian are still plotting to do away with Alonso and Gonzalo. Antonio is the subject of the next musical portrait, a swaggering 'dance of the devils'. Even when portraying the villain of the piece, Sibelius uses an 'S-motif' in the main theme of the number, though this later yields to a whirling dance as Prospero causes a banquet to be set out for the castaways by strange spirits, the 'Shapes' (No. 17). Before they can eat, however, Ariel appears in the guise of a harpy (No. 18); he reminds Antonio and Alonso of the shameful way they treated Prospero, and calls back the Shapes to take the food away (No. 19).

At the beginning of the fourth act Prospero is beginning to relent in his treatment of Ferdinand. Alonso still believes his son to be dead, and his sadness is the subject of a hushed, mournful E flat minor intermezzo (No. 20). The texture of the music is very similar to that of a number of minuets for string trio that Sibelius had written in the 1880s, but the slower tempo and restrained dynamics lend this simple music great emotional depth. Prospero commands Ariel to come (No. 21) and arrange a harvest festival in honour of Miranda and Ferdinand. The festival takes the form of a masque in which the spirits assume the shapes of Ceres, Juno, and Iris; Poulsen's production featured a rainbow here. After a brief song from Ariel (*Before you can say 'come' and 'go'*, No. 22) there is a lugubrious 'rainbow interlude' (No. 23), a waltz-like melodrama for Iris (No. 24), a song for Juno derived from the same musical material (*Honour, riches, marriage-blessing*, No. 25), a dance of the naiads in the form of an elegant minuet (No. 26) and a harvesters' dance, a sort of bucolic polka (No. 27). But Prospero's foes are still plotting against him. Ariel is sent away (Nos 28, 29 and 30) to create a distraction for the clumsy conspirators Caliban, Trinculo and Stephano, and these immediately forget their plans. Prospero sets the dogs on them and drives them away (No. 31).

A brief interlude (No. 31 bis) introduces Act V. Prospero tells Ariel to gather all his enemies together; their senses are to be restored, they will be forgiven, and Prospero himself will abandon his magic. He breaks his staff and casts his book of magic to the bottom of the sea. Poulsen's wish was for this to be accompanied by 'a lunatic music, followed by a solemn melody'. Sibelius fulfilled this wish with a violently dissonant, dramatic *Largo* that sounds like a nightmarish metamorphosis of the noble transition from the first movement of the *Fifth Symphony* and throws the ensuing hymn-like passage into sharp relief (No. 32). Prospero gives Ariel back his freedom, and Ariel sings in delight, his melody taken from the interlude that began the act (*Where the bee sucks, there suck I*, No. 33). With the arguments resolved and scores settled, Prospero invites all his guests to his home, and they set off in procession (No. 34). For this final procession – a polonaise – Sibelius reworked an idea from a long-forgotten work: the *Cortège* that he had written for Kaarlo Bergbom's retirement celebrations at the Finnish National Theatre in 1905.

Sibelius was able to work almost undisturbed on *The Tempest*: he was required to produce only one other piece of music during its gestation. In the summer King Gustaf V of Sweden paid a state visit to Finland, and Sibelius was asked to compose an organ piece to be performed at a special church service in the Nikolai church (now Helsinki Cathedral) on 22nd August. The organist there was John Sundberg, with whom Sibelius made contact in order to find out about the particular qualities of the organ, and it did not take him long to compose the *Intrada*, Op. 111a, which has become his best-known organ work and something of a display piece for Finnish organists. It is a measured and hugely dignified piece in a slow 3/2 time, very close both motivically and stylistically to the *Prospero* movement from *The Tempest*.

Jussi Jalas may have regarded his future father-in-law as 'a living legend' but his stature was not sufficient to tempt the Helsinki publisher Holger Schildts Förlag to accept a little song for mixed choir in late November. The piece in question, an attractive enough but by no means a distinctive work, is the *Skolsång (School Song)*, JS 172, with a text by Nino (rather than Johan Ludvig) Runeberg. The same author provided the words for the *Skyddskårsmarsch (Skyddskår's March)*, JS 173, a small march for male choir and piano *ad lib.*, written for a patriotic organization that had played a prominent role in the Civil War. After a few bars of introduction in which the choir imitates the sound of a side drum (the word 'fram' ['forward'] is conveniently prominent), the song conveys its heroic, fighting spirit in music that is uplifting and bright.

Sibelius had hoped that his sixtieth birthday would pass without undue ceremony. After the letter from Aino the previous spring he certainly had no intention of conducting a concert himself, but he had plenty of friends who were willing and able to do so. Kajanus, who had opened the concert season with an all-Sibelius programme, conducted a birthday tribute on 9th December featuring the *First Symphony*, *Swanwhite* suite and *Song of the Athenians*. Moreover, Sibelius's international fame was now sufficient for his sixtieth birthday to be celebrated at concerts in other countries as well. He spent his birthday with his immediate family at his daughter Eva Paloheimo's home in Liisankatu in Helsinki, but his whereabouts were by no means a secret. Finland's president, Lauri Relander, made an official visit and presented the composer with the Order of the White Rose of Finland. Other gifts offered more tangible benefits: a public subscription had raised the significant sum of 275,000 marks, and his state scholarship was raised from 30,000 to 100,000 marks per year. These sums, coupled with the increasing income he was now receiving from performances of his works, helped to provide him with a level of financial stability that he had never before enjoyed.

For *Lucifer* Sibelius composed *Ett ensamt skidspår (A Lonely Ski-Trail)*, JS 77a, a melodrama for speaker and piano. Gentle but insistent left-hand syncopations accompany a simple, fragile melody while the speaker recites Bertel Gripenberg's touching poem on the themes of mortality and solitude. Another poem by Gripenberg, a sonnet on the subject of nostalgia, formed the basis for the solo song *Narciss* (*Narcissus*), JS 140, more Romantic in expression than his earlier flower songs (some motifs and the syncopated accompaniment recall the *Romance in C major* for strings of 1904) and with an attractive vein of melancholy. Apart from arrangements of earlier works, this was to be Sibelius's farewell to the genre of song with piano.

1926

On 4th January 1926 a telegram arrived from the conductor Walter Damrosch in New York, with a commission for a new symphonic poem. Born in Breslau, Damrosch had emigrated to the USA in 1871 and had become a prominent figure on New York's musical scene as a conductor, composer and educator, who had given the first American performances of works by such composers as Wagner, Mahler, Elgar and Tchaikovsky – and also, on 2nd May 1913, of Sibelius's *Fourth Symphony*. Sibelius accepted with alacrity and set to work on a piece which, Damrosch requested, should be between fifteen and twenty minutes long. The choice of subject matter was left entirely to the composer, and the result would be *Tapiola*.

In late March Sibelius once more headed south, taking the sketches for *Tapiola* with him. Even though he was not proposing to give any concerts and the probability of alcohol-induced public humiliation was therefore slim, Aino decided not to accompany him. Curiously he chose not to stop off in Copenhagen to see *The Tempest* with his incidental music (the première was 16th March, conducted by Johan Hye-Knudsen); instead, his first port of call was Berlin where, predictably, he visited Adolf Paul and his family. Sibelius, who had so recently received generous financial donations, must have been saddened to find his friend in penury. But he could not dally in Berlin, as his ultimate goal was Italy, where he was to spend some time with his childhood friend Walter von Konow.

On arrival in Rome, Sibelius checked into the Hotel Grande Albergo Minerva, where for a while he locked himself away and worked on his new symphonic poem. Aino relayed to him news of how *The Tempest* had fared in Copenhagen: the music and stage sets won more acclaim than the production itself. On 27th March he was joined by von Konow, and together they celebrated von Konow's sixtieth birthday before travelling down to Capri. They visited the Blue Grotto: according to a letter from von Konow to Aino, Sibelius found that only a painter could capture its colours, but that the place itself was very musical. On 19th April they arrived back in Rome. Von Konow set off for Finland the following day, but Sibelius remained until the 24th to continue work on *Tapiola*. He stopped off in Berlin on the return trip as well, and did not arrive back home until the middle of May.

Väinön virsi (*Väinämöinen's Song*), Op. 110, for mixed choir and orchestra, is a *Kalevala* setting written during the spring of 1926. It was commissioned by the Society for Popular Education for a singing festival in Sortavala, where Robert Kajanus conducted its première on 26th June. Although composed at the same time as *Tapiola*, *Väinön virsi* does not share its thematic unity and concentration. The orchestral introduction sets the ceremonial tone for the entire work. When the choir enters, however, the orchestra retreats to a mostly accompanimental role; the choral writing itself is in the homophonic style that Sibelius had used in *Kalevala* settings since the beginning of his career. Towards the end there is a note of acerbity recognizable from the coda of the *Fourth Symphony*. *Väinön virsi* was the last cantata that Sibelius completed and, like his other post-war works in this genre, radiates optimism and national pride. The piece may be 'public' rather than 'private' Sibelius, but the subject matter was still close to his heart.

Around this time Sibelius began to nurture grand plans for the organ *Intrada* that he had composed the previous August. To judge from a manuscript in the National Library of Finland collection,[3] he proposed using it as the fourth movement of a five-movement organ suite: *Preludium, Interludium, Toos Hilarion Arioso* (*Hilario's Arioso*), *Intrada* and *Postludium*. For the *Interludium* and *Arioso* the manuscript contains only brief thematic sketches, and there is no evidence that he ever composed any more than that. Admittedly the manuscript contains no actual music for the *Intrada*, and so we cannot be certain that he planned to use the existing piece in the suite – but it is a logical and plausible assumption, especially as he did write the key signature of E major, which is correct for the earlier *Intrada*.

The *Preludium* and *Postludium*, JS 153, however, did progress further, and for each of them there is a complete draft (they were published in 2001 in an edition prepared by the composer and Helsinki Cathedral organist Harri Viitanen). The *Preludium* proceeds placidly and somewhat discursively in a flowing 6/4 time; its passing similarity in rhythm and melody to a motif from the seventh movement of *Swanwhite* (the fourth movement of the concert suite) is presumably coincidental. The opening theme of the *Postludium* shows clear similarities with the third of the Op. 67 *Sonatinas* for piano. The pieces are similar in proportions, style and even thematic invention to the *Masonic Ritual Music* from the following year.

In one important sense, the première of *Tapiola* was a leap into the unknown for Sibelius. Having conducted the premières of almost all his principal works himself, he had grown accustomed to being able to make last-minute revisions before the pieces appeared in print. Admittedly Sibelius was not present when Siloti premièred *Night Ride and Sunrise* in St Petersburg, but the printed edition did not appear until six months later. With *Tapiola* he faced the prospect of a major work being printed before its first performance – moreover a performance by another conductor, on another continent. Later revisions or improvements were thus out of the question. On 17th September he told Breitkopf & Härtel that he wished to make some cuts in *Tapiola*, but by then the work was already engraved.

It is often claimed that *Tapiola* is inspired by the *Kalevala*, but it would be closer to the truth to say that it was inspired by the vast Finnish forests. Forests, offering a point of contact with nature in its primordial glory, are perhaps Finland's greatest commercial asset and also occupy a central place both in the Finnish people's leisure activities and in the nation's culture. While composing this tone poem Sibelius proposed translating its title into English as *The Wood*, which Aino fortunately suggested changing to *The Forest*. In Finnish mythology Tapio is the god of the forest, and Tapiola is his domain, but this piece is not related to a specific *Kalevala* story. It is worth remembering in this context that the links between Sibelius's *Kalevala* pieces and the poem itself tended to be tenuous. Neither the *Lemminkäinen Suite* nor *Pohjola's Daughter* was originally conceived to illustrate the stories with which they became associated; the music was adapted to fit the story at a later stage. Sibelius also tried to play down any direct connection between the *Kyllikki* piano pieces and the *Kalevala*. The only unequivocal links are to be found in works that involve the human voice, from *Kullervo* through to *Väinön virsi*.

To explain *Tapiola*'s title for the benefit of musicians and audiences unfamiliar with Finnish mythology, Sibelius supplied a prose explanation of the title. Breitkopf & Härtel had this converted into the quatrain which, with the composer's approval, appeared in English, German and French in the score:

> *Wide-spread they stand, the Northland's dusky forests,*
> *Ancient, mysterious, brooding savage dreams;*
> *Within them dwells the Forest's mighty God,*
> *And wood-sprites in the gloom weave magic secrets.*

Sibelius had already given up conducting in Finland, and the autumn of 1926 brought his last conducting appearance abroad as well. His Danish champion Gunnar Hauch had invited him to Copenhagen, but the timing was awkward because Sibelius's concert, on 2nd October, was uncomfortably close to the 25th anniversary concerts of the Danish Concert Society and moreover clashed with a state visit by Finland's President Relander. The Danish composer Louis Glass, founder of the Concert Society, was understandably irritated and did not shy away from publishing a scathing article in the newspaper *Politiken*. Nonetheless Sibelius conducted the *Fifth Symphony*, the *King Christian II* suite, the *Impromptu* for women's voices and orchestra and *Finlandia* to a full house; *Valse triste* was the encore. The Danish audience found the symphony and the *Impromptu* rather difficult, but welcomed the lighter pieces enthusiastically.

Back at home it was time to put the finishing touches to *Tapiola* so that it could be sent to Damrosch in New York. On 5th November Breitkopf sent him the score and parts, hot off the press. Sibelius's own thoughts were already moving on, and on 12th September he noted in his diary that he was working on 'the "new one"': the *Eighth Symphony*. He also started work on the *Masonic Ritual Music* for tenor and harmonium that he had promised to write for the Finnish lodge.

Robert Kajanus celebrated his seventieth birthday on 2nd December, and both Gallen-Kallela and Sibelius gave speeches. Sibelius compared his old friend to a flame, and praised his ability to conduct at the age of seventy in a manner that was the envy of many thirty-year-olds.

The première of *Tapiola*, Op. 112, was set for 26th December, with the New York Symphonic Society orchestra at New York's Mecca Temple (now the New York City Center), a domed, neo-Moorish building that had been built three years earlier on West 55th Street between 6th and 7th Avenues. *Tapiola* is one of Sibelius's longest symphonic poems, with a duration of about eighteen minutes. Its themes are concise and so closely related to each other that several commentators have been tempted to regard the piece as monothematic. By Sibelius's standards the scoring is lavish, including parts for piccolo, cor anglais, bass clarinet and contrabassoon – though the only percussion required is timpani, and he does without harp or piano. Sibelius's handling of tempo and pulse is impressive: without a score, a listener would almost certainly assume that the underlying tempo was a slow one, but in fact, with the exception of the first twenty bars (*Largamente*), the work alternates between a basic *Allegro moderato* tempo and a fully fledged *Allegro*. A further remarkable feature is that the piece remains almost exclusively in the minor key right up to the final bars – a serene, sustained chord of B major.

In view of the scale and achievement of *Tapiola*, it has become fashionable to regard the work as an extension of Sibelius's symphonic output, an *ersatz* eighth symphony. This view is sustainable to the extent that the mature Sibelius reassessed his symphonic principles, working towards a form dominated by the musical content and towards the concept of the symphonic fantasy. Indeed, the *Seventh Symphony* is only slightly longer than *Tapiola*. On the other hand, *Tapiola* also marks the culmination of a quite different series of works: the symphonic poems with clear extra-musical associations. Also, unlike any of Sibelius's symphonies, *Tapiola* was written in response to a commission.

Walter Damrosch was delighted with *Tapiola*, writing to Sibelius after the première that it was 'one of the most original and fascinating works from your pen. The variety of expression that you give to the one theme in the various episodes, the closely-knit musical structure, the highly original orchestration, and, above all, the poetic imagery of the entire work, are truly marvelous. No one but a Norseman [*sic*] could have written this work. We were all enthralled by the dark pine forests and the shadowy gods and wood-nymphs who dwell therein. The coda with its icy winds sweeping through the forest made us shiver.' Critical reaction to the new symphonic poem, however, was initially muted; even Sibelius's great supporter Olin Downes, writing in the *New York Times* in April 1927, called it 'a work of style and manner rather than inspiration'. As the years passed, however, great Sibelius interpreters such as Koussevitzky, Beecham and Karajan helped to establish the work in the international concert repertoire, their performances confirming the verdict reached by Cecil Gray in his monograph on Sibelius as early as 1931: 'the culminating point of his entire creative activity, and a consummate masterpiece... Even if Sibelius had written nothing else this one work would be sufficient to entitle him to a place among the greatest masters of all time.'

CHAPTER 15

LIFE AND WORKS OF
THE LATER YEARS: 1927–1957

1927

If one is to believe the widely held claim about Sibelius's career, the 'Silence from Järvenpää' began immediately after *Tapiola*. This is not in fact the case: he produced less music than before, but certainly did not stop composing.

First of all he had still to keep his promise to the Freemasons, and the *Masonic Ritual Music* or *Musique religieuse*, Op. 113, was first performed on 12th January. This is one of Sibelius's most enigmatic and problematical works. It centres around a series of songs for tenor and harmonium, but Sibelius revised some movements and added some new ones in the 1940s, and thus the number and order of movements varies between the original manuscripts and the editions published in 1936 and 1950; some of the later additions require a male-voice choir. An English edition of the work was prepared by Galaxy Music Corp. in New York. A further edition from 1969 (twelve years after the composer's death!) even includes movements by other composers. It is thus almost impossible to arrive at a single definitive 'performing version'. Moreover, the Finnish Masons – as copyright holders in the music – have over the years been reluctant to release the work for performance or recording.

The *Masonic Ritual Music* begins with *Avaushymni* (*Opening Hymn*) for solo harmonium, after which come the songs, to texts by a wide variety of authors. *Suloinen aate* (*Thoughts be our Comfort*), No. 2, to Eino Leino's Finnish translation of words by Franz von Schober, maintains not only triple metre of the *Avaushymni* but also (at least at first) its intimate, even slightly aloof atmosphere. The third movement, *Kulkue ja hymni: Näätkö kuinka hennon yrtin* (*Procession and Hymn: Though*

Young Leaves Be Green), begins with a flowing forty-bar introduction for harmonium alone before the voice enters with a Bach-like chorale in long, even note values to words by the Chinese poet Bao Zhao, translated by Eino Tikkanen. The next movement, *Kulkue ja hymni: Ken kyynelin (Procession and Hymn: Who Ne'er Hath Blent His Bread with Tears)*, takes the form of a march with two trios. This time the words are by Goethe, again translated by Eino Leino. *On kaunis maa (How Fair Are Earth and Living)* is a reticent piece; the words by Aukusti Simelius are set to a succession of sighing phrases at a slowish tempo. No such inhibitions are found in the sixth piece, *Salem*, a jubilant, majestic hymn that seems to ignore Sibelius's new stylistic direction and revel in its straightforward, rich melody. With a text by Viktor Rydberg, originally written to celebrate the 400th anniversary of Uppsala University, this is the first of the Masonic songs to have words in Swedish. The text for the seventh piece, *Varje själ, som längtan brinner (Whosoever Hath a Love)* comes from the same source. In this movement, as in the piano piece *The Village Church* written a few years earlier, Sibelius quotes extensively from his own quartet piece *Andante festivo*, although in *Varje själ ...* he concentrates on the second theme of *Andante festivo*, which had not appeared in the piano piece. The 1927 version of the score ended with another harmonium solo, *Marche funèbre (Funeral March)*.

Even as a young child Sibelius had grown accustomed to living in financial difficulties, and the spectre of debt had pursued him throughout his adult life. But in early 1927 he finally paid off everything that he owed. To celebrate, he bought Aino an expensive leather coat, and the couple took a long holiday – the first time they had been abroad together since the ill-fated trip to Italy and Sweden four years earlier. This time their destination was Paris, and they stayed away for several months, returning in April. Staying at the Hôtel du quai Voltaire, Sibelius did his best to avoid other Finns; instead, he and Aino attended concerts of modern French music, which was much admired by the younger generation of Finnish composers and often included in Kajanus's concert programmes, as well as early music, which was then rarely heard. Sibelius was enjoying his newfound financial freedom, and wrote to his sister Linda: 'Now things are fine from a financial point of view, and I can concentrate on whatever I like. Isn't it wonderful?' Speaking of the wealth of impressions he had gained in the French capital, he remarked in an interview with Anna Levertin from the magazine *Suomen Kuvalehti*: 'even on my deathbed I shall surely still be curious about the direction that music is taking.'

On 25th April 1927 the first Finnish performance of the *Seventh Symphony* took place, under the baton of Robert Kajanus. In the same concert he gave the first Finnish performances of *Tapiola* and the *Tempest* prelude. Sibelius did not attend the concert; we can surmise that he did not want people to wonder why he was not conducting it himself. Nor did he go to Stockholm in May for the Nordic Music Days. He had not been consulted about the choice of programme and was represented only by the cantata *Hymn to the Earth*. This, and much of the other Finnish music that was played, was duly savaged by Peterson-Berger in his review.

In 1927 the Swedish-language Finnish hymnbook was revised, and the committee in charge asked Sibelius to contribute to the new edition. The result, delivered in early June, was the chorale *Den höga himlen* (*The Lofty Heaven*), JS 58a, composed for four-part mixed choir to a Swedish translation by Jacob Tegengren of a Finnish original by Simo Korpela.

By then Sibelius was at work on the selection and revision of material from *The Tempest* for concert use, but work did not progress with much fluency: what had proved an inspirational subject less than two years earlier now failed to arouse his enthusiasm. Moreover, his shaking hand made it physically uncomfortable to compose. 'It's like having to do my homework again', he noted in his diary on 17th May. No doubt his reluctance to come to terms with reworking the material explains why, of all Sibelius's orchestral selections from his theatre music, the concert suites from *The Tempest* are the least representative of the original score. That is not to deny that they contain music of genius, but by omitting some excellent numbers entirely, radically shortening others and changing the playing order in a way that no longer corresponds to the action on stage, Sibelius managed to devalue rather than enhance his original achievement.

The concert version consists of the overture (unchanged) and two suites of nine movements each; the first suite ends with a foreshortened variant of the overture in which the atmospheric closing section is omitted and the music ends abruptly at the height of the storm. The omission of the vocal parts – both solo and choral – from the theatre score was inevitable for concert use and does not in itself do harm to the essence of the music. On the other hand the removal of the contrasting middle section and *da capo* from the *Prospero* portrait leaves the movement rather short and insubstantial. Similarly, the bold and characterful main theme from the *Dance of the Devils* is omitted, and the resulting movement – renamed *Dance Episode* – provides a surprisingly lame conclusion to the second suite. While reshaping the music Sibelius made piano transcriptions of three movements, *Episode* (the portrait of Miranda), *Dance of the Nymphs* and *Scène*, sending them away to Wilhelm Hansen in June with the remark that 'the others would be easy to arrange as well'.

He delivered the first orchestral suite to Hansen at the beginning of July, with the second following a month later, but it was several years before the published edition appeared. In 1928 Sibelius declared that the version of the E flat minor *Intermezzo* (No. 20) from the second suite should replace the original in theatre performances – but this movement was virtually unchanged anyway (in the original score the dynamic level is *p*, in the suite *ppp*). To judge from a letter to Wilhelm Hansen from July 1929, he was considering exchanging other pieces too: 'When I get to see the theatre score for *The Tempest* I shall say which of the musical numbers should be replaced by their equivalents in the suites', but he never actually made up his mind, perhaps because in later years there was no demand for theatre performances with the complete music.

On 8th May Sibelius wrote laconically in his diary: 'Abused, lonely, all my real friends dead. Just now my prestige here is non-existent. Impossible to work.' This may have been an accurate reflection of his state of mind but it scarcely corresponded to the truth. Admittedly his brother Christian and Axel Carpelan were among those who had passed away, but Kajanus, Gallen-Kallela and his brothers-in-law Arvid, Eero and Armas Järnefelt were still very much alive – not to mention the greatest supporter of all: Aino. A more likely explanation for his faltering progress with the revisions to *The Tempest* becomes evident from his diary entries during the late spring and summer. As part of the same entry he noted: 'In order to be able to live at all, I must consume alcohol. Wine or wisky [*sic*]. That's the reason for all this.' But he had clearly decided that it was time to cut back drastically. Over the next seven weeks he made a record of his consumption of alcohol and cigars. Some days have the proud boast 'Sine alcohole', but his resolve could easily weaken: 'Days under the influence of alcohol. Depression.'

In September Sibelius received a visit from Olin Downes, the American critic whom he had previously encountered at the première of *The Oceanides* and who had been a committed Sibelian for many years. Downes was by now a music critic for the *New York Times* and his support was so vociferous that he later gained the nickname 'Sibelius's apostle'. Earlier that year Downes had unsuccessfully tried to tempt Sibelius to return to America for a concert tour, but the composer had refused on the grounds that he was 'closely engaged with new works'. When they met in September, Downes enquired about the 'new works', correctly assuming that Sibelius was working on the *Eighth Symphony*, but failed to elicit a detailed response: two movements were written down, the composer claimed, and the rest was in his head.

In November 1927 the National Theatre in Helsinki mounted a production of *The Tempest* with Sibelius's music, in the Finnish translation by Paavo Cajander and featuring Sibelius's daughter Ruth as Ariel. For this performance Sibelius added a brief epilogue (No. 34 bis) as an alternative for the existing cortège. Once more he turned to an unpublished orchestral piece for thematic inspiration; this time the donor work is *Cassazione* from 1904, and the passage he chose is a solemn hymn in his characteristic slow 3/2 time.

1928

In February Sibelius went to Berlin. Staying first at the Hotel Excelsior and then moving to the cheaper Hotel Moltke, he spent some time with Adolf Paul, went to concerts and worked hard on the *Eighth Symphony*. Writing home to Aino he claimed that 'my work will be wonderful. It just seems to take so long to get it finished. But then I'm not in any hurry.' On 9th March he heard a performance of the *Violin Concerto* by Ferenc von Vecsey with the Berlin Philharmonic Orchestra under Furtwängler, but the reviews were mixed. Sibelius returned to Finland later that month.

In August the opera singer Wäinö Sola proposed that Sibelius should compose a programmatic 'Imatra symphony' on the subject of the rapids in Imatra, where a new power station was being built. The composer was familiar with the rapids, having taken Rosa Newmarch to see them some years previously. Surprisingly Sibelius did not immediately reject the idea out of hand, although he raised a number of concerns regarding the cost of such a project and the relative neglect of his recent works for special occasions. On 20th August he even went to Imatra to discuss the project further with Sola and the chief engineer, Hugo Malmi, but in the end the venture came to nothing.

Wäinö Sola did, however, manage to extract one new work from Sibelius that year, for it was at his instigation that *Siltavahti* (*The Guardian of the Bridge*), JS 170, was composed. Two years earlier, while on tour in America, Sola had promised to ask the author V. A. Koskenniemi and Sibelius to write a piece for New Yorkin Laulumiehet, a male-voice choir made up of Finns living in New York. Koskenniemi was not interested in writing such a text and so Sola wrote his own and delivered it to Sibelius, who composed a stirring march for male choir *a cappella* (with an alternative version for solo voice and piano) in the autumn of 1928, in time for Sola to take it to America in person that October. Sola himself gave the first performance in New York on 22nd October.

Among the increasingly frequent international performances of his music, Serge Koussevitzky conducted the *Third Symphony* with the Boston Symphony Orchestra on 9th November, with such success that he soon programmed it again; two years earlier he had conducted the *Seventh*, which he had also kept in his repertoire. Koussevitzky now wrote to Sibelius and asked whether he had 'any new works which have not yet been performed'. He must have been hoping that Sibelius would announce the completion of the *Eighth Symphony*, but he was to be disappointed. Sibelius had nothing against being championed by such an eminent conductor and virtuoso orchestra, but he had no new compositions to offer. He did, however, promise to keep Koussevitzky informed of any progress. Even at this stage, however, his utterances on the subject of the *Eighth Symphony* were contradictory. In December he told Wilhelm Hansen that the symphony was still in his head – even though he had told Olin Downes more than a year earlier that two movements were already written down.

The encouragement and keen attention shown by Koussevitzky and Downes was in stark contrast to the vexatious ravings of Wilhelm Peterson-Berger in Stockholm. In December, after a performance at the Stockholm Concert Hall conducted by Ture Rangström, P.-B launched a vicious attack on the *Fourth Symphony*, which he found 'wanting in blood, colour, temperament and ideas'. Sibelius, as always sensitive to any kind of negative criticism, was deeply offended by Peterson-Berger's words.

1929

In early 1929 the Sibelius family celebrated two weddings. On 26th March Margareta married Jussi Blomstedt. Just over a month previously, on 17th February, Sibelius's niece Rita was also married at the German church in Helsinki. For this happy event the quartet piece *Andante festivo* was dusted off and played by a double string quartet; Margareta and Jussi were among the violinists. Other student orchestras in Helsinki subsequently performed the piece, although Sibelius did not actually make an orchestral arrangement until almost a decade later.

The early months of 1929 brought forth a stream of short pieces from Sibelius's pen. The *Five Esquisses* for piano, Op. 114, and the Op. 115 and 116 pieces for violin and piano were all composed by April, as was the *Suite for Violin and String Orchestra*, JS 185. These pieces make it apparent that Sibelius was on the threshold of a radical new stylistic period, in which the close thematic integration of the *Seventh Symphony* and *Tapiola* would yield to spikier motifs and more audacious harmonies. Even though he often gives the pieces titles that allude to the natural world, his approach to it is now predominantly conceptual rather than descriptive.

The immediate catalyst for writing the pieces came from the New York publisher Carl Fischer, who had written the previous October expressing an interest in 'works for piano, voice and piano and violin and piano... We would like to recommend that you write some characteristic numbers in the form of an orchestra [*sic*] suite, comprising from [*sic*] three numbers ... we have every reason to believe that an orchestral suite along these lines from your pen would be a very commercial proposition.'

The titles of the Op. 114 piano pieces all allude in some way to nature, though the music contains few specifically pictorial elements. They are closely related in mood and texture, though based on disparate melodic material. Even the tempi move within a narrow range. The set begins with *Maisema* (*Landscape*), which takes a theme not dissimilar to that of *Den ensamma furan* from Op. 75 and places it in a harmonic context typical of Sibelius's late style. In *Talvikuva* (*Winter Scene*) the thematic material appears alternately in folk-like, pastoral guise and in a heavier, gloomier incarnation. The undulating quavers in *Metsälampi* (*Forest Lake*) are a naturalistic touch unusual in Op. 114: they might portray the rippling waters of the lake. In *Metsälaulu* (*Song in the Forest*), similar quavers serve as part of the Impressionistic scenery from which a mournful melody emerges just once, in the middle of the piece. Finally, with *Kevätnäky* (*Spring Vision*), we return to a more stable melodic and harmonic environment.

The first piece of the Op. 115 set for violin and piano, *Auf der Heide* (*On The Heath*), is an effective piece of small-scale tone-painting. The thematic material is sparse: the violin sings its melancholy, lonely song above a modest piano accompaniment. At one point the music seems to suggest the cries of Sibelius's beloved migratory birds. The second piece, *Ballade*, is rich in incident. The highly-charged, ominous violin motif heard at the outset undergoes tortuous, virtuoso variations, searching for form and direction, before a 'fate' motif in the piano guides it towards a demonic dance, relaxing only in the final few bars. The *Humoresque* which follows is less dramatic though no less capricious. A few years earlier Sibelius might have used such themes in a jaunty dance, but here – except in the brief middle section, which is more Romantic in character – he remains aloof. In *Die Glocken (Capriccietto)* (*The Bells*), the muted violin plays a mysterious, fluttering line, like a moth around a flame, whilst the piano has rapidly tolling, bell-like effects. This weird and disturbing music ends abruptly and enigmatically.

Op. 116 continues where Op. 115 left off. The thorny, restless violin line of the first piece, *Scène de danse*, is a nightmarish parody of the conventional dance idiom; the piano's insistent, hollow syncopations only add to the menacing mood. This piece and its successor, *Danse caractéristique*, constantly startle the listener with jagged rhythms, 'modern' harmonies and violent changes of mood. The concluding *Rondeau romantique*, however, marks an unexpected return to the stylistic world of the wartime pieces: charming, exuberant, and as comforting as its companion pieces are bitter.

Unusually, all of the movements of the *Suite for Violin and String Orchestra*, JS 185, bear titles in English: *Country Scenery, Serenade:*

Evening in Spring and finally *In the Summer* – a clear sign that it was composed in response to Carl Fischer's suggestion. The music is characteristic of Sibelius's lighter style: rustic, dance-like and idyllic by turns, with a brilliant *moto perpetuo* as its third movement; on the other hand, its idiom is more advanced than that of the *Suites mignonne, champêtre* and *caractéristique*.

In the event Fischer published neither the suite nor the instrumental works that Sibelius offered him, writing on 7th September: 'We must reluctantly inform you that in view of the extremely unfortunate constellation in the music publishing field in the United States, it seems to us inadvisable at the present time to publish compositions of the high standard which you have sumbitted to us.' The composer subsequently marked the score of the *Suite for Violin and String Orchestra* 'Sketch. To be reworked!' Despite some pencilled corrections in the manuscript, this revision was never completed. He provisionally assigned the work the opus number of 117, but at various times thereafter he allocated the same number to the *Academic March*, *Andante festivo* and the choral piece *Karjalan osa*. In his final opus lists from 1951–52, no work is listed as Op. 117.

In May the ever-enthusiastic Olin Downes once more visited Ainola, and later in the year Sibelius welcomed the English conductor Basil Cameron, who tried to tempt the composer to conduct at the Hastings Festival the following January.

Not everything that Sibelius wrote in 1929 was intended for Carl Fischer. The strophic Christmas song for mixed choir *On lapsonen syntynyt meille* (*A Child is Born to Us*), JS 142, to a text by A.V. Jaakkola, was written early that year for the Finnish Lutheran Evangelical Society. In this otherwise unremarkable song Sibelius introduces an element of rhythmic ambiguity at the end of each phrase. The piece is sometimes sung to the alternative text *Nyt seimelle pienoisen lapsen* (*To the Crib of the Little Boychild*) by V.I. Forsman. Sibelius also revisited the Eerola text he had set almost a decade earlier for Viipurin Laulu-Veikot and wrote a wholly new version of their honour march. The second *Viipurin Laulu-Veikkojen kunniamarssi* (*Honour March of the Singing Brothers of Viipuri*), JS 220, was probably premièred by the choir the following April, conducted by Felix Krohn. Sibelius was also busy reading proofs for the concert suites from *The Tempest*, and decided to overhaul (and slightly shorten) the *Canon* in the first suite, sending the new version to Wilhelm Hansen on 14th November.

At the end of December the English writer Cecil Gray visited Helsinki and soon forged a close relationship with Sibelius. Shortly after this visit, Gray was to start writing a biography of the composer that set the tone for generations to come. Though dismissive of the piano music and (generally) the songs, Gray is full of praise for the orchestral music, in particular the symphonies. His book gives some idea of the devotion that Sibelius's music now inspired in the Anglo-Saxon countries and offers an uncanny premonition of his fate in Germany. There is so much in his book that belongs to the political and social climate of the 1930s, however, that some of Gray's arguments now seem fundamentally flawed. Arguing that 'German music ... is primarily rooted in song – romantic song – and consequently in spirit is fundamentally opposed to the symphonic style', Gray suggests that 'the Germans are in reality the last people in the world to arrogate to themselves, as they do, the supremacy over all other races in symphonic music ... this makes their patronizing attitude towards the symphonies of Sibelius particularly laughable ... it is precisely the long-winded, Teutonic thematic material of the German symphonists of the nineteenth century that prevents them from attaining to the monumentality and concentration of form, &c., which are the hall-mark of the true symphonic creations of the Finnish master.' He is especially scathing about Brahms, whose symphonic 'movements, however they are labelled, practically all seem to be *andante con moto*; he is incapable of writing either a true *allegro* or an *adagio* movement – above all a *scherzo*. He entirely lacks gaiety, verve, spontaneity, abandon, in default of which a symphony is necessarily incomplete and imperfect.'

In every other phase of Sibelius's career we can observe how his major – predominantly orchestral – works stand as the ultimate manifestation of his style at a given moment. If we were to judge his National Romantic works on the basis of the *Romance in D flat major* for piano, or his expressionist period on the basis of the Op. 61 songs, we should gain only a fragmentary notion of how powerfully he could express himself in a given idiom. When we come to this last stylistic period, however, we do not have this luxury, as the work that would have set the shorter works in context, the *Eighth Symphony*, was never to be made public.

1930

As early as 1928, Aino had noticed that Sibelius was more inclined to stay in Järvenpää than to go carousing. 'These days he is almost always at home, and hardly ever goes into town. He has become a real hermit. Just think: Janne, who used to be so sociable', she wrote to Linda. Now he was developing a taste for listening to the radio and gramophone records, and his public appearances were becoming fewer and further between, although he did attend a celebration at his old school in Hämeenlinna in May.

Pressure to deliver a new symphony was beginning to mount. Koussevitzky was continuing to explore Sibelius's symphonies with a performance of the *Sixth*, and he tried to persuade Sibelius to go and conduct in Boston. When this came to nothing, Koussevitzkty did at least hope for a new work to be premièred in the 1930–31 season. It says something for Sibelius's international fame that the loudest voices in the clamour for the *Eighth Symphony* came not from Finland but from America. Not that his old ally Robert Kajanus had forgotten him: in May 1930 the 73-year-old Kajanus was in London, making the first recordings of the *First* and *Second Symphonies* along with the outer movements of the *Karelia Suite* with the London Symphony Orchestra (billed simply as 'Symphony Orchestra') for the Columbia Gramophone Company, a project underwritten by a grant from the Finnish government. In the absence of any recordings by Sibelius himself of his symphonies, Kajanus's readings – despite their undeniable deficiencies in orchestral playing – have a vigour and authenticity that remain unchallenged.

On 7th July more than 12,000 people marched into Helsinki to show support for the Lapua Movement – an anti-Communist faction that had been founded the previous year and, to begin with, won wide support among the Finnish intelligentsia. Sibelius attended and was asked to write a song for the movement's followers, to a text that had been specially written by Aleksi Nurminen; in early August Bertel Gripenberg also suggested that Sibelius should write a 'Lapua march'. This spirited strophic song for unison male choir and piano was the only work that Sibelius completed in 1930, and is named *Karjalan osa* (*Karelia's Fate*), JS 108. It was first performed in Sortavala on 7th September. The opening piano flourish is based on an 'S-motif', whilst the melody itself is not dissimilar to that of the *Skyddskårsmarsch* from five years earlier. The Lapua Movement soon ran into trouble: it developed into a quasi-Fascist group that was held responsible for various murders and, after its supporters kidnapped ex-president Ståhlberg in October as part of a planned coup, its power base crumbled – though not before its champion, Pehr Evind Svinhufvud, had been elected president of Finland, taking office on 1st March 1931. Eighteen months later the Lapua Movement was banned.

1931

Akseli Gallen-Kallela visited Copenhagen in early 1931 to deliver a lecture. On his return journey, in Stockholm, he contracted pneumonia from which, on 7th March, he died. Gallen-Kallela's son-in-law, Armas Otto ('A. O.') Väisänen, asked Sibelius to write a piece for the funeral, which was to be held at the Johannes church in Helsinki on 19th March. Sibelius initially agreed, then had second thoughts – but Väisänen insisted that the order of service had already been printed and that it was too late to change the plans. In the event Sibelius not only provided a piece of music but even served as a pall-bearer – despite his deep-seated dislike of funerals.

The new piece was *Surusoitto* (*Funeral Music*) for organ, Op. 111b, and it was played at the funeral by Elis Mårtenson. In this work Sibelius shows that his new artistic direction need not always result in the acerbic tone heard in the Op. 115 and 116 violin pieces. Indeed, *Surusoitto* is calm and dignified throughout; it could hardly have been otherwise. Unsurprisingly, it bears some stylistic resemblance to the *Masonic Ritual Music*.

Surusoitto is by no means a miniature, and the question inevitably arises of how Sibelius managed to produce it in the space of just a few days. After Sibelius's death, the composer Joonas Kokkonen put it to Aino that *Surusoitto* might have used motifs that Sibelius had considered for the *Eighth Symphony*, a possibility that she also found plausible. It is demonstrably true that Sibelius had been working on the main theme of *Surusoitto* for several years: it appears in a set of manuscript sketches[1] alongside material that found its way into the Op. 114 piano pieces, *Suite for Violin and Strings* and other works. What seems less likely, however, is that Sibelius would have consciously used a part of the half-finished symphony in another work: this would go against all the precedents that he had established over almost fifty years. We are thus left with the possibilities either that he had already decided that the symphony was doomed (improbable at this early stage) or that he used motifs that had already been rejected in a symphonic context.

The beginning of *Surusoitto* bears a striking resemblance to the nineteenth of the [*33 Small Pieces*] for string quartet of 1888–89. This is most probably a coincidence, but there is evidence that Sibelius in his sixties was taking another look at musical ideas from the early stages of his career. A further manuscript sketch from Sibelius's late period[2] contains what appears to be a draft for a choral piece with the title *O Herra, siunaa* (*O Lord, bless us*), with a theme that is identical to that of the third movement of the *Piano Quintet* of 1890. In an article about possible sketches for the *Eighth Symphony*,[3] Nors Josephson puts forward this theme as a possible component of the symphony's second (slow) movement – a possibility regarded by the present author as remote. But plainly Sibelius was planning some sort of work that would require a religious text.

In April Sibelius set off for his very last trip abroad, with the intention of working on the *Eighth Symphony*. As with his very first foreign trip back in 1889, his destination was Berlin, where he stayed at an apartment belonging to Holger Boldemann, husband of Arvid Järnefelt's daughter Maija and son of his friend Georg Boldemann (there were evidently no hard feelings after Sibelius had turned down the elder Boldemann's opera libretto in

1911). To judge from his letters to Aino he made good progress with the symphony, but in late May he fell ill and was diagnosed with pleurisy. His doctor, Professor Zuekler, gave him an experimental medicine, Eutonon, which made him feel very much worse. The Boldemanns made sure that he stopped the treatment; as soon as he had recovered he hurried home to Finland.

On 10th August Sibelius wrote a piece for piano four-hands as a sixtieth birthday present for Aino. *Rakkaalle Ainolle* (*To My Beloved Aino*), JS 161, is a slow, mystical work; by starting end ending on the dominant it creates the bewildering impression of having neither beginning nor end. It is almost devoid of melody as such, but the boldness of its tonal language is astonishing, and it marks a significant development of the style of the Op. 114 pieces.

A few days later he was again engaged in a correspondence with Koussevitzky about the *Eighth Symphony*. This time Sibelius was hopeful that it would be ready to perform in Boston the following spring, and he continued to work on the piece during the autumn, feeling 'full of youth' (diary, 18th December). One of his few visits to Helsinki was for the celebration of Kajanus's 75th birthday. The concert included not only a selection of Kajanus's own works but also Sibelius's *First Symphony*, and afterwards Sibelius presented his friend with a laurel wreath inscribed: 'The laurel is for your compositions, the gold for your heart.'

1932–38

By the middle of January 1932 Sibelius had realized that he could not finish the *Eighth Symphony* in time for a concert that spring, and telegraphed to America with the news. It would seem likely, however, that it was by then approaching completion, as the composer suggested programming it that October instead. Koussevitzky – who was planning a complete Sibelius symphony cycle during the 1932–33 season – and Olin Downes were understandably eager to see the score, and so too was Basil Cameron in London, who had been promised the first European performance of the piece. And yet Sibelius was not to be drawn; on 14th July he wrote to Koussevitzky, suggesting that the *Eighth* should not yet be advertised as his work on it had suffered 'all sorts of interruptions'.

It is debatable how many 'interruptions' Sibelius really suffered, but in March he certainly had good reason to be distracted: his youngest daughter Heidi married Aulis Blomstedt. By profession Blomstedt was an architect, which in Sibelius's opinion meant that he could be reckoned to be an artist. On 28th April, after a reign of fifty years, Robert Kajanus finally stepped down as conductor of the Helsinki Philharmonic Orchestra, to be succeeded by his old rival Georg Schnéevoigt. Kajanus's last concert was given at the National Theatre and included Beethoven's *Ninth Symphony*. He was by now a sick man but still managed to travel to England in June for a second period of recordings with the London Symphony Orchestra: he set down Sibelius's *Third* and *Fifth Symphonies*, *Pohjola's Daughter*, *Tapiola* and the orchestral suite from *Belshazzar's Feast*. In April the *Fourth Symphony* had also been recorded for the first time, by Leopold Stokowski and a reduced Philadelphia Orchestra.

Schnéevoigt now joined the queue of conductors keen to perform the *Eighth Symphony*, and Sibelius promised him the work's Finnish première in the spring of 1933. Before that, of course, both Koussevitzky and Cameron would need to have played it, and that could not happen until he had finished writing it. In late October Sibelius promised to send the score to Koussevitzky in December, but Christmas came and went and no symphony appeared. On 17th January he was forced to send a telegram admitting: 'Regret impossible this season.'

If Sibelius needed any proof of Koussevitzky's capabilities as an interpreter of his symphonies, he was to receive it in the shape of the first recording of the *Seventh Symphony*, from a public concert with the BBC Symphony Orchestra given in May 1933. Admittedly the performance takes certain liberties with the score (not least the addition of a trumpet to the final cadence) but it has fierce intensity and concentration. For a decade this was to remain the only available recording of the *Seventh*.

A diary entry reveals that in May 1933 Sibelius was still working on the first movement of the symphony, but it was soon ready and was delivered to the copyist Paul Voigt. By 4th September, Voigt had finished and sent an invoice for his work thus far – 23 pages. Sibelius wrote to him saying that there should be a *fermata* at the end, after which the music would lead directly into a *Largo*. The entire symphony was to be roughly eight times as extensive as what had so far been delivered. After that, however, it becomes impossible to follow the symphony's traces.

If Sibelius believed that remaining at home would give him more time to compose and to relax, he was mistaken. The more he stayed put, the more he became a magnet for foreign visitors. He gained a reputation as a perfect host who was willing and able to converse on any topic except one: his own music. Journalists were tolerated politely despite their inquisitiveness on this very subject, but musicians, writers and diplomats were welcomed with genuine warmth. Guests with an even more immediate claim on his and Aino's attention were the members of his own family, which was rapidly growing in size as the five married daughters in their turn produced an increasing number of offspring.

As Sibelius's grandchildren became more numerous, the friends and confidants from his own generation were slowly dying out. His sister Linda died in 1932, as did his brother-in-law Arvid Järnefelt. The following year the painter Pekka Halonen, Sibelius's neighbour in Järvenpää, passed away. In the spring of that year Robert Kajanus, suffering from necrosis, had to have his left leg amputated and on 6th July 1933 he too died in hospital in Helsinki. Quite apart from the grief Sibelius and Aino felt on a personal level for them, their demise can hardly have had a positive effect upon the composer's creative work.

In November 1933, at the instigation of Cecil Gray, the *Intrada* and *Surusoitto* for organ were performed at a concert of the Organ Music Society in London. The Society asked for a theme for improvisation, and Sibelius duly supplied a nine-bar fragment in C minor. At the concert André Marchal's improvisation was well received, and the Society thanked Sibelius: 'In the opinion of many present, the highlight of the programme was the *Adagio* that was improvised on your theme.' This could easily have led to the publication of the *Intrada* and *Surusoitto* by Oxford University Press, but Sibelius refused both this offer and a similar one from Wilhelm Hansen five years later; maybe he still had hopes of completing the five-movement suite that he had been planning in 1925–26. The two pieces were eventually published by Westerlund in Helsinki in 1943 and 1955 respectively.

As we have seen, when Sibelius was a young man he had gone through a period during which he was very much motivated by Wagner. The influence of Wagner – for better and for worse – played a central part in the genesis of such works as the *Lemminkäinen Suite*, and helped to shape his style for years thereafter. In his later years, however, the composer went out of his way to emphasize that he was at best indifferent to Wagner's music, and as the years went by he repeated this claim to anybody who would listen. Karl Ekman ('Wegelius tried in vain to infect him with his enthusiasm for Wagner; neither then nor later ... did Wagner play any part for Sibelius'), Cecil Gray ('Sibelius would seem to be practically the only modern composer ... who has neither been influenced by Wagner nor, what amounts to very much the same thing, reacted violently against him'), Bengt von Törne ('Wagner's music has meant practically nothing to Sibelius; the influence of his orchestral idiom, even less') and even his private secretary Santeri Levas ('Richard Wagner ... was the one among the great German composers who had the least appeal for Sibelius ... from what Sibelius said to me the "Wagner complex" can hardly be taken very seriously and in any case he got over it very quickly') are among those who fell victim to this subterfuge. It is strange that Sibelius was so keen to dismiss Wagner when he made no attempt to conceal his admiration for such figures as Bach, Mendelssohn, Bruckner and Beethoven. According to Santeri Levas, he was certainly no fan of Brahms, so we cannot explain his attitude along partisan Brahmsian/Wagnerian lines. Did he retain some lingering shame that he had not been able to share the enthusiasm of Wegelius, Kajanus and Armas Järnefelt? Might he secretly have regretted not trying harder with his operatic plans? Or did he tacitly acknowledge that Wagner did indeed have a massive influence on his style and try to suppress such ideas to emphasize the uniqueness of his own creative impulse?

In 1934 Georg Schnéevoigt took the Helsinki Philharmonic Orchestra to London, and while there they recorded the *Fourth* and *Sixth Symphonies* together with *Luonnotar*, with Helmi Liukkonen as soloist. Of these recordings, however, only the *Sixth Symphony* was released at the time; the *Fourth* (recorded at a public concert) was not approved by the composer and was not issued until 1977. A copy of this recording, with comments from the composer, was sent to Sir Thomas Beecham, who followed Sibelius's guidelines scrupulously and in 1937 set down what is by general consent one of the most convincing versions of the symphony ever recorded. Schnéevoigt's London recordings must have made a profound impression on Sibelius: nine years later, after one of Schnéevoigt's concerts in Helsinki, he sent the conductor a telegram (22nd May 1943) with a sting in its tail: 'Dear Georg, heartfelt thanks for yesterday's concert. I hope sincerely that you could make gramophone recordings of the *Lemminkäinen*[4] and *King Christian Suites* and, of my symphonies, the *First*, *Second* and above all the *Seventh* – but not the *Fourth* or *Sixth*.' Schnévoigt never in fact recorded any of the works that Sibelius suggested.

In 1935, which was the centenary of the publication of the *Kalevala*, several skeletons emerged from the cupboard. The two unpublished movements of the *Lemminkäinen Suite*, *Lemminkäinen and the Maidens of the Island* and *Lemminkäinen in Tuonela*, were performed at two concerts in Helsinki under Schnéevoigt's baton. At this concert the scores from 1897 were used; these had been acquired in 1920 by the *Kalevala* Society in Helsinki. On 1st March Schnéevoigt also performed the published version of *Lemminkäinen's Return*, and on 8th March he added *The Swan of Tuonela* as well. In between, on 3rd March, he had resurrected part of an even earlier work, the third movement of *Kullervo*, at the newly built Exhibition Hall (Messuhalli) in Helsinki. On this occasion the baritone solo was entrusted to Wäinö Sola, a tenor.

Later that year a Finnish-language arrangement of the fourth of the Op. 1 Christmas songs, *En etsi valtaa, loistoa*, was made for the YL choir. In this version it was first performed by YL, conducted by Martti Turunen, at the Johannes church in Helsinki on 3rd December.

So what was happening with the *Eighth Symphony*? Ever since commentators noticed that the time when Sibelius ceased to produce major works coincided almost exactly with the repayment of the last of his debts, and that moreover this was when he started to receive more respectable royalties, it has been suggested that he needed the stimulus of financial pressure to force him to work. Perhaps there is some truth in this, but his lack of direct exposure to an orchestra played its part as well. One might make a comparison with the years of the First World War, when for Sibelius the composition of miniatures was a necessity for survival. At that time he had very little opportunity to travel, to conduct or even to hear orchestral music; and during those years he had produced very few orchestral works of any magnitude. Among the repercussions of his drunken antics in Gothenburg in 1923 was a reduction in his conducting work, and by the late 1920s he had in real terms given up completely. He gave up international travel after his illness in Berlin in 1931, and went less and less frequently to Helsinki; his great friend and champion Robert Kajanus was no more. Moreover Sibelius himself was no longer at the height of his physical powers; as his trembling hands made work more and more difficult, he grew ever more self-critical with respect to his own music. In these circumstances it should therefore come as no surprise that he did not issue a flood of new orchestral masterpieces. Financial security may have relieved him of the need to write shorter pieces and thus enabled him to concentrate on what he believed to be artistically valid; but it is not a wholly convincing explanation for his refusal to release the *Eighth Symphony*.

By 1935, Sibelius's status as an international icon was secure. His seventieth birthday in December was noted in newspapers all over the world, and tributes of all kinds flooded in. At the celebratory concert at the Exhibition Hall, Armas Järnefelt conducted *Finlandia*, the *First Symphony*, extracts from *The Tempest* and *The Captive Queen*. The concert, the first part of which was broadcast live as far away as America, was attended by Finland's former presidents Ståhlberg and Relander (though not by the president of the day, Svinhufvud, who was indisposed) as well as Mannerheim, now a Field Marshal, and was followed by a lavish banquet at which a live relay of the *Second Symphony* was heard, conducted by Otto Klemperer in New York. Sibelius's renown in the Nordic countries, Britain and America seemed to know no bounds, and even if he did not enjoy a similar acclaim in Germany – by then under Nazi rule – he was still prominent enough to be awarded the Goethe Medal. The seventieth birthday celebrations were, however, to be Sibelius's last major public appearance.

In 1937 Wäinö Sola suggested to Sibelius that he should capitalize on the great popularity and symbolic value of *Finlandia* by adapting its 'hymn' section as a new national anthem to replace Pacius's *Vårt land*. The

Finlandia Hymn had indeed already been sung to texts by both Jalmari Finne (1907) and Yrjö Sjöblom (1919). The composer was apparently reluctant to turn his tone poem into a song, and the following year he told Sjöblom that 'it is not intended for singing, but rather composed for orchestra. But if the world wants to sing, one cannot do anything about it'. Sola nonetheless sent Sibelius a text that he himself had written, either planned as an anthem or with a view to Masonic use. Sibelius was somehow persuaded to make the necessary setting, which he finished in on 4th April 1938, and the result was first sung (by a vocal quartet with harmonium *colla parte*) at the tenth anniversary meeting of St John's Masonic Lodge in Helsinki that December. The *Finlandia Hymn* with Sola's text was also incorporated into some editions of the *Masonic Ritual Music*, though its performance has not been confined to Masonic circles.

The dignified anthem *Salem* from the *Masonic Ritual Music* originally had words by Viktor Rydberg. At the request of the publisher Galaxy, the vocal part (with an English text [*Onward, Ye Peoples*] by Marshall Kernochan, suited for non-Masonic use) was adapted for choir by Channing Lefebvre. In 1938 Sibelius was asked to provide an orchestral arrangement of the harmonium accompaniment; the version for choir and orchestra was first performed on 11th May 1939 at the May festival of the University of Michigan in Ann Arbor, conducted by Earl Moore. The orchestral part doubles the melodic line and the piece can also be effectively performed without voices.

With the death of his brother-in-law Eero Järnefelt in Helsinki in November 1937, Sibelius became the last surviving member of the Tuusula artistic community. By this time, composers from the generation after his own were already old men: Erkki Melartin, ten years younger than Sibelius, had died in February of the same year.

By the summer of 1938 the volume of correspondence that Sibelius received was substantial enough for him to require a secretary. After several failed attempts to fill this position, including a young lady who became so agitated that she smashed the typewriter on her first (and last) visit to Ainola, Sibelius's son-in-law Eero Ilves suggested the name of Santeri Levas, who was at the time employed at Ilves's bank. This was the start of an association that lasted until the end of Sibelius's life. Not only was Levas diligent and conscientious in his professional capacity, but also he developed a close personal rapport with the composer; his recollections form an indispensable part of our impression of Sibelius's later years.

1939–49

On 1st January 1939 Sibelius was persuaded by Olin Downes to make his last appearance as a conductor – not at a public concert but for a live broadcast to the New York World Fair. The piece chosen was *Andante festivo*, which he arranged for string orchestra and timpani especially for the occasion. The 73-year-old composer had not conducted for more than a decade but now, with trembling hands, he performed the piece with the Finnish Radio Orchestra. Sibelius himself had just one rehearsal before the relay, although the orchestra had practised in advance. The occasion was recorded and is the only surviving documentation in sound of Sibelius's conducting. He played the piece slowly, with immense dignity and with a degree of rubato that will surprise many modern listeners.

The authentic recording of Sibelius conducting was published for the first time in 1995. Some years before that, an even more expansive performance had been released which purported to be the genuine article but was in fact a rehearsal recording released in error. In both recordings the work is played considerably more slowly than is usual today; presumably the conductor of this second recording – possibly Toivo Haapanen – had consulted Sibelius about the tempo before preparing the orchestra.

Sibelius now – finally – made his revision of the two 'lost' movements of the *Lemminkäinen Suite*, using the 1897 scores as his starting point. Unusually, the new version of *Lemminkäinen and the Maidens of the Island* became marginally longer than the original (564 bars against 557), but this statistic gives little idea of the scale of the revision. The reworking of the middle part of the movement alone is sufficiently extensive to rank this as one of Sibelius's biggest projects from his later years. In addition there are innumerable adjustments to the scoring elsewhere in the piece. Nonetheless, he was wise enough not to interfere too radically with the overall colour or shape of the work, which retains all the vigour and youthful enthusiasm of the 1890s. In its companion piece, *Lemminkäinen in Tuonela*, Sibelius now decided – or maybe confirmed his earlier decision of 1897 – to cut both the 32-bar chordal introduction and a lengthy passage from the *Molto lento* section, and similarly adjusted the scoring, though less conspicuously than in *Lemminkäinen and the Maidens*. At this point Sibelius changed the order of movements in the *Lemminkäinen Suite*, placing *The Swan of Tuonela* before *Lemminkäinen in Tuonela*.

In early June 1939 Sibelius and Aino rented a large flat on the third floor of a modern block in Helsinki – Kammiokatu 11 A 10; the intention was for this to become a winter residence, more convenient and manageable than Ainola, and they invested a significant sum in furniture for the apartment before moving in in September. The street – Kammiokatu – was later renamed Sibeliuksenkatu in the composer's honour. The move was principally for Aino's benefit, to allow her easier access to her children and grandchildren, and provide some of the modern luxuries that were unavailable in the country. For his part Jean enjoyed walking by the sea (his promenades would have taken him to what is now the Sibelius Park, past the site of the Sibelius Monument [Eila Hiltunen, 1967]). He had not really expected to be disturbed by noisy neighbours, but had reckoned without the vocal exercises of a young lady – a student of singing at the Conservatory – who was lodging with the elderly widow on the floor below. The widow had no idea who had moved in upstairs but was apparently well informed in cultural matters. One can only imagine her astonishment when Sibelius himself knocked unannounced at her door to enquire politely as to whether the student could limit the duration of her practice sessions!

During the summer of 1939, presumably at Kammiokatu, Sibelius made a new arrangement of *The Jewish Girl's Song* from *Belshazzar's Feast* for the American contralto Marian Anderson. But his sojourn in the city was to be short-lived. As the Second World War was gathering pace in continental Europe, Finland was drawn into the first of two conflicts – the Winter War and the Continuation War – that were inextricably linked with the wider hostilities. Leningrad was then only around 20 miles from the Finnish border, and the Russians were keen to persuade the Finns to move the border a little further away, and to give them access to the harbour at Hanko for a naval base. But the Finns were hardly likely to agree to such demands, especially after they saw how the Russians had grabbed whatever Polish territory they could after the Germans had invaded that country in September. On 30th November the Soviet Union attacked Finland: the Winter War had begun. An evacuation began and the Sibeliuses promptly went back to Ainola. Sibelius, conscious of his role as a national symbol and by now accustomed to a pace of life in which international travel played no part, made a point of politely refusing offers of refuge from abroad.

Meanwhile the first known performance of the definitive *Lemminkäinen Suite* in its final order (with *The Swan* placed second) had been given by the NBC Symphony Orchestra at Carnegie Hall in New York on 28th September 1939; once again, Schnéevoigt was the conductor. Breitkopf & Härtel agreed to publish the two newly revised movements, but the production process was interrupted by the Second World War. After the war Breitkopf tried to negotiate a production and distribution deal with its British partner, British & Continental Music Agencies, but this fell through. It was not until 1954 – a year after the first recording by the Danish National Radio Symphony Orchestra under Thomas Jensen – that the works appeared in print, and even then Sibelius had second thoughts and, too late, tried to request that they should be withheld until after his death.

During the summer, for the Laulu-Miehet male choir and its conductor Martti Turunen, the *Finlandia Hymn* was combined with a text by V. A. Koskenniemi that had recently been published in the collection *Latuja lumessa* (*Ski Tracks in the Snow*), dedicated to the invalids of the Winter War; some changes to the poem were necessary in order to suit the melody. Turunen conducted the first performance of this arrangement at the choir's 25th anniversary concert on 7th December.

The Winter War finished with the Moscow Peace Treaty of 12th March 1940. Despite being heavily outnumbered, the Finns had stood firm against Stalin's troops. Nonetheless, the peace terms were not advantageous for the Finns – the peace conceded significant territories in the east of the country to the Russians – especially a large area around Viipuri, which had commercial as well as political significance – and allowed for the establishment of a Russian naval base in Hanko. As a result, in the months that followed, Finland developed an ever closer relationship with Germany.

In the 'interim peace' between the Winter War and the Continuation War, Jean and Aino returned to their city flat; this time they arrived in September 1940 and stayed there for some nine months, a period that included the composer's 75th birthday. When the violinist Arvo Hannikainen was making preparations for a concert with the Helsinki Philharmonic Orchestra under Toivo Haapanen on 15th December 1940, the score for the first of the *Humoresques* for violin and orchestra (D minor, Op. 87 No. 1) was nowhere to be found. In the weeks before the concert, Sibelius thus wrote out a new one that differs in many details from the original of 1917. In the new score, for instance, the orchestral strings are unmuted, and there is no longer a harp. The solo violin part from 1917 had survived and was left unchanged (Sibelius's fair copy omits much of the solo line).

Jean and Aino – along with some of their grandchildren, as it was recommended that children should be evacuated from Helsinki – returned to Järvenpää on 12th June 1941, shortly before the outbreak of the Continuation War. The conflict was to last for more than three years, and in terms of Sibelius's everyday life, its ramifications resembled those of the First World War: he was deprived of his income from abroad, and food was once more in short supply. During this period Aino's skills in cultivating fruit and vegetables in the garden at Ainola were put to especially good use.

After a break of eight years Sibelius returned to his diary in 1943 and wrote: 'At my age I *cannot* excuse this primitive way of thinking – anti-Semitism and so on. My education and culture are ill suited to these times' (6th September). It should be noted that Finland did not subscribe to the virulent anti-Semitism of the Nazis: Jews were granted asylum in Finland and Jewish soldiers even fought in the Finnish army. In the spring of 1942, at the initiative of Joseph Goebbels, a Sibelius Society had been established in Germany. A German film crew had visited Ainola and Sibelius had been persuaded to record a radio message containing some carefully chosen platitudes about the Germans' 'great sympathy for my fatherland' and the 'union of fate' between Finland and Germany, 'the radiant land of music'. Sibelius was fully aware that he had not yet secured a place in the hearts of German audiences – 'I like Germany very much: only Germans like not Sibelius', he had told the American journalist Carleton Smith in 1930 – and his cause was not helped by the addition of a political dimension. It was to prove detrimental to his reputation as a composer that German audiences identified him as a Nazi sympathizer, however erroneous this belief was. Even though Finland chose to ally herself with Nazi Germany, Sibelius himself could not suppress his revulsion at Hitler's policies.

Around 1942 Sibelius made some new arrangements of the most popular of his Christmas songs. A version for solo voice and women's choir of *Giv mig ej glans...* (using the Finnish text, *En etsi valtaa, loistoa*) was probably made at the request of Heikki Klemetti's wife, the choir conductor Armi Klemetti, and arrangements for two female voices both of this song and of *On hanget korkeat, nietokset* were made that autumn for Aimo Mustonen, the composer of a popular march song for the Finnish troops in the Winter War.

In December 1942 Sibelius gave up the flat in Kammiokatu. For the previous eighteen months it had been used only for the occasional city visit and to accommodate guests – among them Armas Järnefelt, who once came from Stockholm to conduct the Helsinki Philharmonic Orchestra and managed to consume Sibelius's entire supply of cognac!

In February 1943 Sibelius had told Santeri Levas that 'I have a major work in progress and I should like to see it finished before I die'. As late as that autumn, he was preoccupied with the *Eighth Symphony*: 'The symphony is in my thoughts' (diary, 13th September). That October, however, with enemy planes visible in the skies over Ainola, he again set the symphony aside and worked on a new adaptation of his orchestral song *The Rapids-Rider's Brides* (1897) for male choir and orchestra, most probably at the suggestion of Martti Turunen, who conducted the first performance of the new arrangement eighteen months later.

Sibelius's old friend Adolf Paul died peacefully in Berlin on 30th September 1943. The very same day, Sibelius heard a radio broadcast from

Stockholm, conducted by Malcolm Sargent, including a performance of Vaughan Williams' *Fifth Symphony*, which had been premièred in London three months earlier and is dedicated 'without permission' to Sibelius. 'Culture and rich humanity! I am deeply grateful. Williams gives me more than anyone can imagine', Sibelius noted in his diary.

The Continuation War came to an end in September 1944, but for Sibelius a struggle of quite a different kind had entered its final phase. What he had in mind was a scorched earth policy with regard to many of his scores – a course of action that would leave his wife deeply shocked and the waiting world profoundly disappointed. As Aino later explained: 'In the 1940s we started a great auto-da-fé. My husband had collected a lot of manuscripts in a laundry basket and he burned them in the dining room fireplace. There went movements of the *Karelia Suite* – later on I saw the remains of torn-up pages – and much more besides. I didn't have the strength to watch this appalling sight; I merely left the room. Therefore I don't know exactly what he threw onto the fire. But, afterwards, my husband's manner was calmer and his spirits were brighter. It was a happy time.' It is extremely probable – though it cannot be proved – that the *Eighth Symphony* was among the scores consigned to the flames. On the other hand he did not destroy the manuscripts for dozens of important chamber works including the *'Hafträsk'* and *'Korpo'* Trios. We cannot determine exactly when this destruction took place, but a likely time frame would be between January 1944 and August 1945.[5]

The destruction of his manuscripts did not, however, mark the end of Sibelius's work as a composer. In October 1945, probably for Servi Musica Sacrae, a vocal quartet of clergymen, Sibelius reworked his hymn *Den höga himlen* for male voices and organ. The ensemble was planning a visit to Sweden to raise funds for the Swedish church in the immediate post-war period, and it is thus strange that this arrangement uses the original Finnish text by Simo Korpela rather than the Swedish translation by Tegengren that Sibelius had used eighteen years earlier in the *a cappella* song.

In October 1945 a reluctant Sibelius was persuaded to participate in a documentary for the Finlandia-Kuva film company – one of the relatively few occasions his lifestyle was captured on film. A four-man team spent two days at Ainola, filming both indoors and out, their work not helped by a power cut on the second day!

On 1st December 1945 Sibelius dedicated the song *Hymn to Thaïs* to Aulikki Rautawaara. The original song, which was still unpublished, had been written in 1909 and it would appear that the composer no longer possessed the fair copy of the manuscript. He did have a complete draft, however, and this formed the basis of no fewer than three copies made between December 1945 and 1948. These copies were written out by

Jussi Jalas and Aulikki Rautawaara and contain various improvements to the vocal line and text (at places where Sibelius's original setting of the English words was especially awkward), as well as some alterations in the piano part. It is not possible to tell how many of the changes were made at Sibelius's own instigation, although it is safe to assume that he gave his approval.[6] The revised version was published posthumously in 1963.

The composer's eightieth birthday brought a vast number of greetings and presents and, even though Sibelius did not take part in any public events, he found the celebrations tiring. As Santeri Levas recalled: 'When I arrived at Ainola, where every room was full of huge baskets of fragrant flowers, Sibelius received me in bed, something that had never happened before. "I don't feel well at all," he said. "I have been coughing blood, but that's only between the two of us. There's no need for my wife to know, for it would worry her a lot."' As things turned out, Aino found out anyway. December was always the month when the composer was at his weakest: he told Levas: 'The darkest weeks of the year, from my birthday until Christmas, when the sun is at its lowest, are always a difficult time for me. Immediately Christmas is over things improve and life is fun once more.' Levas, keen to discourage unnecessary rumours and press intrusion, had the foresight to maintain a discreet silence when Sibelius fell ill. For instance, he managed to conceal the fact that Sibelius suffered from cataracts in both eyes that were so severe that his optician advised him that there was no point in replacing his glasses (he had acquired reading glasses as early as January 1922 but made sure that he was never wearing them in photographs). In general, though, the composer's health remained good even in his last years: 'All the doctors who wanted to forbid me to smoke and to drink are dead. But I am quietly going on living. It's not every man of my age who can unhesitatingly eat and drink as I do.'

In late 1946 two unison male choir songs with organ accompaniment were added to the *Masonic Ritual Music*: *Veljesvirsi (Ode to Fraternity)* in October, and *Ylistyshymni (Hymn)* in December. Stylistically and thematically *Veljesvirsi*, with its clearly defined and regular melody, comes close to the dignified processional quality of *Varje själ ...* from the 1927 selection and thus also to *Andante festivo*. By contrast *Ylistyshymni* is far more of a study in texture and sonority, swelling from a withdrawn opening to a climax of great expressive power. These two movements are believed to be Sibelius's last original compositions – and although he did continue to refine earlier pieces, he confined himself to smaller-scale works, almost exclusively for either solo voice or choir.

The year 1948 was quite productive for such arrangements. In the autumn, to limit the spread of inferior third-party arrangements, Sibelius acceded to his publisher Fazer's request and made a version of the *Finlandia*

Hymn with Koskenniemi's text for mixed choir *a cappella*. In addition, he made further changes to his *Masonic Ritual Music* following the installation of a pipe organ in the Masons' hall the previous year. Of the movements from 1927 the two solo pieces, *Avaushymni* (*Opening Hymn*) and *Marche funèbre* (*Funeral March*) were revised, as was *Salem*. He also made some alterations in the two recently composed choral songs *Veljesvirsi* (*Ode to Fraternity*) and *Ylistyshymni* (*Hymn*). Finally there was an arrangement of the melodrama *Ett ensamt skidspår* (*A Lonely Ski-Trail*) for speaker, harp and strings (JS 77b). It has been suggested that this was a somewhat belated response to the death the previous year of Bertel Gripenberg, whose words accompany the music. The version with strings comes across as even more delicate and subtle than the piano original, and the piece was first heard in this form on 19th December at the University Hall, conducted by Martti Similä. The narrator was Ella Eronen.

In December 1948 Kalevi Kilpi of the Finnish Broadcasting Association came to Ainola to record a ten-minute radio interview. Sibelius was plainly ill at ease in front of the microphone: his answers are often reticent to the point of being uncommunicative. As far as possible he tried not to discuss his own music, but naturally he could not avoid the topic completely. As well as acknowledging the authenticity of Finnish interpretations, however, he did single out English and Swedish performances of his works for praise – though without naming specific musicians. 'It always seems to me that one should either live in the forest or in a big city. Here at Ainola, this silence is eloquent.' In August of the following year the Canadian photographer Yousuf Karsh came to Ainola and captured some of the most atmospheric pictures ever taken of the notoriously camera-shy composer.

1950–56

In January 1950 a new edition of the *Masonic Ritual Music* was produced by the Grand Lodge of Free and Accepted Masons of the State of New York. For this new edition Sibelius apparently revised the music yet again; this time the piano (rather than the harmonium or organ) is named as the first choice of instrument for the accompaniment.

In September 1951, for the last time, Sibelius rented a small flat in Helsinki, in the building where his daughter Eva lived (Välskärinkatu 7). He never actually lived there and it is unclear why he should have taken the trouble to acquire it. Markku Hartikainen's suggestion that he did so to protect Eva from the risk of having to take in lodgers during a period when accommodation in Helsinki was in short supply is very plausible.

At around this time, following the adoption of the piece as an official song of the World Association of Girl Scouts and Girl Guides – with texts in English by Gavin Ewart and in French by Francine Cockenpot – Sibelius made revisions to the version of the *Scout March* for soprano and alto voices with piano.

In June 1951 the Sibelius Week – forerunner of today's Helsinki Festival – was held for the first time. During the 1950s this event attracted artists of the highest international calibre: in its very first year Jussi Björling sang there and Isaac Stern played the *Violin Concerto*, and later performers included Sir Thomas Beecham, David Oistrakh and Eugene Ormandy.

In 1954 a request from the publisher Nordiska Musikförlaget in Stockholm brought forth yet another arrangement of the Christmas song *Giv mig ej glans ...*, this time for three-part boys' choir (with optional organ). By now, however, Sibelius found the physical act of putting pen to paper a great challenge.

During the Sibelius Week in June 1955 the list of visitors to Ainola grew appreciably longer when the entire Philadelphia Orchestra arrived along with its conductor Eugene Ormandy; Yehudi Menuhin, Elisabeth Schwarzkopf and Walter Legge also paid their respects. Schwarzkopf recorded only a handful of Sibelius's most popular songs but Walter Legge, her husband and a legendary recording producer, was for many years actively involved with the appearance of Sibelius's music on disc: he founded the HMV Sibelius Society and was responsible for classic recordings under such conductors as Beecham and Karajan. Menuhin recorded the *Violin Concerto*, but it would be idle to pretend that his performance does justice either to the music or to his own artistry. Ormandy, of course, had already proved himself to be a passionate and committed Sibelian; he had already recorded several of of the Sibelius symphonies – the *First Symphony* twice (1935 in Minneapolis and 1941 in Philadelphia). The orchestral members gathered around the front door of Ainola, and Sibelius – despite suffering from acute toothache – greeted them with the words: 'You are all outstanding artists.'

By now, however, Sibelius's powers were beginning to fade. 'The briskness and vivacity so typical of him had forsaken him', recalls Santeri Levas. 'Only his attachment to nature was as it had previously been.' Visitors were now discouraged and the composer's ninetieth birthday celebration was a family affair.

1957

In the late spring of 1957, Sibelius fulfilled the wish of the bass-baritone Kim Borg and made new orchestral arrangements of two songs. It seems curiously appropriate that one of them, *Kullervo's Lament*, was an extract from the work with which he had made his breakthrough sixty-five years earlier, whilst the other was appropriately valedictory: his setting of *Kom nu hit, död* (*Come Away, Death*) from Shakespeare's *Twelfth Night*, originally from 1909. By then Sibelius's hands were incapable of writing down the notes, and he dictated the orchestration to Jussi Jalas. Jalas also conducted the first performances, sung by Borg, at the University Hall on 14th June, as part of the Sibelius Week concert series.

During the summer Sibelius became increasingly introverted. Even though his family visited frequently, he seldom left the house and even lost his formerly keen interest in current affairs. Santeri Levas recalled: 'During his last months the master's home seemed strangely altered... The life force of its owner no longer irradiated the place. He was in retreat from life, and he knew well that his last hour would soon strike.'

When the end came, it had a quiet dignity yet also an almost choreographed quality, with a neat tying up of loose ends that would not disgrace a Hollywood film or a murder story. Sibelius had not seen cranes for some years, but on the overcast morning of Wednesday 18th September several flocks of cranes flew low over Ainola. 'There they come, the birds of my youth!', he exclaimed to his daughter Margareta. While Sibelius watched them from the verandah, one bird broke away from the others and circled over the house before rejoining its mates for the migration southwards.

The following day Sibelius discussed his *Third Symphony* on the telephone to the conductor Martti Similä. He also had a phone conversation with Sir Malcolm Sargent, who had arrived in Helsinki to conduct the *Fifth Symphony* with the Helsinki Philharmonic Orchestra the following evening – a performance that was to be broadcast. Unusually, he went to bed early, rather than waiting for the eleven o'clock radio news in Swedish.

When he woke up on the morning of Friday 20th, Sibelius felt dizzy, but still managed to read the newspapers in bed, according to his normal routine. He got up and dressed himself but at one o'clock, at the lunch table, he collapsed. The local doctor, Vilho Laine-Ylijoki – who had been Sibelius's physician since 1937 – interrupted his rounds and arrived at Ainola within a quarter of an hour to discover Sibelius slumped by the table. He correctly diagnosed a cerebral hæmorrhage, and the maid and the cook helped him to carry the composer to bed. As the afternoon wore on it was plain to those present that he was aware of what was happening. Eva and Katarina were summoned, and soon joined Aino at his bedside. He was able to speak a few words and when Katarina said to him: 'Father, Eva and Kai are here,' he replied: 'Eva and Kai.' They were his last words. He lapsed into unconsciousness again at four o'clock and, around nine in the evening, passed away. Meanwhile, in Helsinki, the performance of the *Fifth Symphony* was under way. Aino considered turning on the radio; according to Katarina: 'Mother had the illusion that, if the radio volume were turned up loud, perhaps he would wake up again. This was wishful thinking. Father was beyond reach.'

The newspapers the following day reported Sibelius's passing with major articles. His death notice, published on 24th September, bore the text 'My song is made of sorrows'. The following Sunday (29th) a private ceremony was held at Ainola; Jussi Jalas played piano versions of *Sydämeni laulu* and *Prospero* from *The Tempest*, and then the coffin was driven to Helsinki. As the procession drove the twenty-five miles to the capital, more and more cars joined and, in the end, the cortège was over a mile long. In Helsinki all the trappings of a state funeral awaited. Torches illuminated Senate Square outside the cathedral, and twelve musicians from the Radio Symphony Orchestra and Helsinki Philharmonic Orchestra bore the coffin inside. A minute's silence was observed, and at nine in the evening there was an opportunity for the public to pay their last respects; no fewer than 17,000 people did so. Students placed a guard of honour on the scene through the night.

On Monday 30th, after the wreaths had been laid (which took several hours), the funeral service itself took place. Helsinki Cathedral's altar was adorned with seven huge candles, one for each of the symphonies, and the service was conducted by Archbishop Ilmari Salomies. The music included several of Sibelius's hymn settings as well as several movements from *The Tempest*, *The Swan of Tuonela*, the slow movement of the *Fourth Symphony* and the funeral march *In memoriam*, conducted by Tauno Hannikainen. The composer Yrjö Kilpinen gave the funeral address. After the ceremony, two more wreaths were laid – by Aino and by President Urho Kekkonen – before the coffin was carried to the hearse by musicians including Einojuhani Rautavaara and Uuno Klami to the strains of the *Marche funèbre* from the *Masonic Ritual Music*.

The public lined the streets as the procession made its way back to Ainola, where Sibelius's coffin was carried by members of his family to a secluded corner of the garden – one of Jean and Aino's favourite spots, which they had nicknamed 'Rapallo'. Here he was finally laid to rest. At Aino's wish, while the coffin was being lowered, Erik Bergman conducted the combined forces of the YL and Akademiska sångföreningen choirs in *Sydämeni laulu*. Aino laid a wreath bearing the words: 'With gratitude for a life that has been blessed by your great art. Your own wife.'

Immediately after Sibelius's death, Eva Paloheimo had announced that the family knew of no unpublished works that were awaiting release. As the donation to Helsinki University of 1982 demonstrated, there were in fact a vast number of manuscripts at Ainola – but those were primarily of early works, some no doubt even forgotten by the composer, and the purpose of her statement was, of course, to prevent endless requests for the *Eighth Symphony*.

That winter Aino wrote to her brother Armas in Stockholm: 'Now I am alone here, nature in its white beauty is glistening outside, and the snow is whiter than ever before. Every day I devoutly visit the grave of my own friend, my own life companion. You probably know that the grave is very close by, near our house, and that in the evenings I can switch on the light from indoors to illuminate the grave and say goodnight to Janne from the window of my own room. Otherwise I wouldn't be able to cope. Our dear daughters are taking good care of me, and there is almost always somebody here. But I'm fine on my own too – I have so much to reflect upon; a great life lies behind me...'

CONCLUSIONS

Sibelius's personality was full of contradictions. On the one hand he was a solitary dreamer, a nature-lover and pantheist who was especially fascinated by the great migrating birds such as swans and cranes, and had a profound need for peace and quiet in which to work. On the other hand he was gregarious and flamboyant, a *bon viveur* who thoroughly enjoyed being in the limelight and felt fully at home being wined and dined in major cities. He mixed easily in high society even though, to his own great disappointment, he came from middle-class rather than aristocratic stock.

His lifestyle, when he had the chance to indulge it, was colourful and lavish: fine wines and champagne, cigars, exquisitely tailored suits and luxury hotels. As a direct consequence of this, for most of his career he was in debt. On the other hand his various homes – the properties he rented until 1904 and Ainola itself – were by no means disproportionate to his needs. His relationships with his wife Aino and with close artistic associates such as Robert Kajanus could be tempestuous, but were founded on a deep and enduring respect that allowed them to survive the crises that are perhaps inevitable when strong personalities meet.

Sibelius was well aware of his special gifts. His diary reflects his rapidly changing moods from 'In good spirits – again a Himalaya' to 'Have been in Hades' as well as his acute sensitivity to any kind of criticism. He was an avid reader of reviews even though he was often deeply wounded by what the critics wrote. In the end, though, he was his own severest critic, ever eager to withdraw or suppress works that he did not regard as meeting his own exacting standards. It was this self-critical attitude that brought about the destruction of the *Eighth Symphony*, but the very same trait forced him to keep on revising the *Fifth* until it was perfect.

His 91-year life began just months after the end of the American Civil

War and the assassination of Abraham Lincoln, and encompassed revolutions and two world wars. He saw his country develop from a province of imperial Russia into a proud nation that held aloft the torch of democracy and had even hosted the Olympic Games. This doctor's son from a small garrison town rose through the ranks to become not only 'foremost among those who have been entrusted with bearing the banner of Finnish music', as Karl Flodin had prophetically remarked in 1889, but a symphonist of truly worldwide stature whose works were compared to those of Bach and Beethoven.

And yet his work did not lack detractors. Even if we set aside the cantankerous ravings of Wilhelm Peterson-Berger in Sweden – a country that has generally been favourably disposed towards Sibelius – we cannot ignore the genuine hostility towards his music that grew up in France and (perhaps especially) Germany in the post-war years. In neither country had he ever enjoyed the same degree of public approbation that he could take for granted in the Nordic countries, England or America. In Germany it became commonplace for critics to misunderstand or misrepresent his intentions: Walter Niemann, writing a monograph for Breitkopf & Härtel in 1917, suggested that Sibelius was essentially an Impressionist whose symphonies lacked monumentality of form, organic development and inner logic. For influential figures such as Theodor Adorno and René Leibowitz, Sibelius was anathema: his steadfast refusal to follow the dogma of the Second Viennese School alienated him from a generation of German scholars and composers, whilst his insistence on following his own artistic path rather than the vagaries of musical fashion meant that he was never *à la mode* in France. Adorno's attacks were motivated as much by political posturing and a desire to uphold the German musical hegemony as by musical arguments;[1] Leibowitz even called Sibelius 'le plus mauvais compositeur du monde'. At least in Germany he could count on the advocacy of Herbert von Karajan, who insisted that Sibelius's *Fourth Symphony* should be included in his first concert as principal conductor of the Berlin Philharmonic Orchestra. But some of this antipathy rubbed off in England and America as well, and by the 1960s concert organizers in those countries were reluctant to programme any but the most popular of Sibelius's works.

Fortunately this proved to be only a passing phase. Today Sibelius's music is more popular than ever, and even in France and Germany he is rapidly gaining supporters. His work appeals not just to audiences who love to hear it, nor just to performers who love to play it, but also to composers who nowadays increasingly acknowledge the seminal importance of his music, while admitting that the paths he trod are so personal that his work can neither be continued nor copied by others. When in the late 1990s

Edward Clark, president of the UK Sibelius Society, invited composers from all over the world to comment on Sibelius's significance,[2] he received very positive contributions from such diverse figures as Thomas Adès, Sir Malcolm Arnold, Pascal Dusapin, Detlev Glanert and Mark-Anthony Turnage. Only Pierre Boulez refused to participate.

Sibelius's music is the result neither of pure calculation nor of unfettered instinct, but rather of a fusion of the two. Though constructed with infinite care, it conveys an impression of spontaneity which renders it resistant to textbook analysis. His sense of form is as much a product of emotion and experience as of rational processes, and he himself admitted a distaste for music that exists only to follow predetermined rules: 'I have not been able to avoid the impression that much, yes, too much, in present-day music has very little connection with life. The themes often seem artificial, the elaboration mechanical.' Small wonder, then, that he did not take the path of Schoenberg towards dodecaphony. Sibelius had even less time for composers who merely followed the prevalent musical trends. 'Mr I. S. [Stravinsky] is always imitating someone ... Technique in music is not learned in school from blackboards and easels. In that respect Mr I. S. is at the top of the class. But when one compares my symphonies with his stillborn affectations ... !', he remarked in 1949.

The architectural element in Sibelius's scores is connected at a fundamental level with its sources of inspiration and he himself was probably not fully aware of its ramifications. 'For each symphony I have developed a special technique. It should not be superficial, but it must stem from experience', he told Jussi Jalas in 1943. He had earlier remarked to Karl Ekman that 'I do not wish to give a reasoned exposition of the essence of symphony. I have expressed my opinion in my works', and had told Axel Carpelan that 'I am a slave to my themes and submit to their demands'. The highly personal manner in which Sibelius used his material made him virtually immune to any attempt at plagiarism. For him teaching was not a vocation, and he did not try to instil a specific set of procedural or artistic values in his pupils.

In his radio interview with Kalevi Kilpi in 1948 Sibelius offered the advice to younger composers: 'Never write a superfluous note; every note must live.' His music, seen as a whole, shows how effectively he himself applied this principle throughout his long and distinguished career.

NOTES

Note to Preface

1. Lecture at the 'Sibelius in Korpo' festival, July 2003.

Notes to Chapter 1

1. HUL 0525.
2. HUL 0540.
3. HUL 0541a.

Notes to Chapter 2

1. HUL 0771.
2. The essay 'First Meeting' in *Aulos*, 1925.
3. HUL 0670.
4. HUL 0657.
5. Folke Gräsbeck, commentary to BIS-CD-1022 (1999).
6. HUL 0796.
7. *Trio* bars 13–14, cf. *Symphony* bars 232–35.
8. Translated by William Jewson.
9. HUL 0765.
10. Letter to Axel von Bonsdorff, 13th August 1887.
11. Sibelius uses a similar device at the end of the slow movement of the original version of his *Violin Concerto*.
12. Letter to Pehr, 27th September 1887.
13. HUL 0797.
14. HUL 0768.
15. HUL 0661.
16. HUL 0579.
17. In the fragmentary second movement of the *String Trio in G minor*, JS 210 (1893/94), the *Impromptu* for women's voices and orchestra, Op. 19, and the orchestral *Musik zu einer Scène* (and its revised version, the *Dance-Intermezzo*, Op. 45 No. 2).
18. HUL 0581.
19. When Fabian Dahlström's catalogue of Sibelius's music appeared in 2003, with its

JS listing of the composer's works without opus number, the correlation between *Den lilla sjöjungfrun* and the independent movements had not yet been established; thus the *Allegretto* and *Più lento* bear separate JS numbers.
20. HUL 0620.
21. HUL 0654.
22. HUL 0661.
23. HUL 0640.
24. HUL 1179.
25. JSW VIII/4.
26. Sibelius must have been unaware that several Finnish composers had previously written music for string quartet; the works in question were admittedly not in general circulation. The earliest were six quartets by the classical composer Erik Tulindberg (1761–1814); these were probably written in Turku in 1781–84 but were not rediscovered until 1925.
27. HUL 0614–0616.
28. HUL 1029: apart from *Hur blekt är allt* and *Upp genom luften* this contains sketches for the chorale *Kyrie eleison* and an unidentified sketch in A flat major.

Notes to Chapter 3

1. Surviving settings are: *Der König träumte*; *Der Mensch ist in seinem Leben wie Gras*; *Die Todten werden dich Herr nicht loben*; *Die Wasser sahen dich* (fragment); *Er ist unser Herrscher*; *Gelobet sei dem Herrn*; *Halleluja Halleluja*; *Halleluja Amen*; *Herr Gott mein Heiland*; *Ich gehe hinein zum Altar des Gottes*; *Ich will deines Namens gedenken*; *Mein Herr ich rufe dich an*; *Sei mir gnädig*; *Sende dein Licht und deine Wahrheit*; *Tag des Herren*; *Was betrübst du dich meine Seele*.
2. Sibelius would have heard its original version; Kajanus revised the piece in 1916. It is erroneously referred to in some sources as a symphony.
3. 'Mein Freund Sibelius' II–III, *Völkische Beobachter* 28/29th January 1938.
4. Ibid. p. 82.
5. Schnedler-Petersen: *Et Liv i Musik*, Copenhagen 1946.
6. Cf. also the *Molto lento* section of *Lemminkäinen in Tuonela*.
7. HUL 0419, along with sketches for many other works.
8. HUL 0419.

Notes to Chapter 4

1. Lahti Symphony Orchestra / Osmo Vänskä, BIS-CD-800, 1996.
2. The texts come from Runo 40 of the *Kalevala*; in *Venematka* Sibelius set lines 1–16; for *Heitä, koski, kuohuminen* lines 23–40.
3. HUL 1220. The same sketchbook includes material for the *Piano Sonata*, the fourth of the piano *Impromptus*, and for later works including *Spring Song*, the *Ballade* from *King Christian II* and *Finlandia*.

Notes to Chapter 5

1. Sometimes known as *Andante lirico* – a title which seems to be wholly inauthentic.
2. Letter from Carpelan to Sibelius, 17th April 1902 – referring of course to the F major version.
3. The imposing City Theatre was built in 1913 as a home for Tampere's professional theatre company that had been established in 1904.
4. In a provisional opus number list (1902) in issue 31 of the journal *Euterpe*, the

Impromptu followed the *Romance in A major*. When the pieces were finally assembled in Op. 24, however, their order was reversed.
5. Note to BIS-CD-1485, 2006.
6. Interview with A. O. Väisänen (*Kalevalan vuosikirja I*).

Notes to Chapter 6

1. As we cannot exclude the possibility that *Marche triste* was written in 1900 rather than 1899, we should also consider the option that it was written after the death of Sibelius's daughter Kirsti. In such a context the nostalgic mood of the trio section would be very appropriate. Whether the outer sections are too aggressive for such a context must be left to the listener to judge.
2. Principally a complete draft score in the Sibelius Museum in Turku, apparently made in the middle of the revision process, and a fragment of the finale in the National Library of Finland (HUL 0123).

Notes to Chapter 7

1. HUL 1160.
2. *Vilse* had been composed in 1898 but was revised in the summer of 1902.
3. HUL 1539.
4. HUL 0450.
5. HUL 0822.
6. One waltz episode is even marked 'à la Betzy' (*sic!*).
7. English translation after *Helsingin Sanomat* international edition.

Notes to Chapter 8

1. A piano transcription of the main theme of this movement, in the brighter key of A major, has also survived in manuscript.
2. Quoted by Christian Jokinen, 'Tyrannicide: Heroism or Terrorism' (*The Eurasian Politician*, May 2004).
3. HUL 1528/2.
4. Kari Kilpeläinen dates this sketch, HUL 1313, to 1907–10, which is admittedly slightly later than *Marjatta*; the type of paper used precludes a date earlier than 1907.
5. HUL 1038.
6. See Timo Virtanen: 'L'aventure d'un héros' in *Sibelius Studies*, ed. Jackson/ Murtomäki, Cambridge University Press 2001.

Notes to Chapter 9

1. HUL 0230.
2. HUL 1314.
3. Not to be confused with the abandoned tone poem of the same name.
4. HUL 1191 and 1192.
5. In Bax's memoirs *Farewell, My Youth*, London 1943, p. 61.

Notes to Chapter 10

1. Diary entry, 28th July 1910. Sibelius often refers to himself as 'Ego' in his diaries.
2. The concept of 'forging' music is another recurrent theme in Sibelius's diaries.
3. Jussi Jalas, *Kirjoituksia Sibeliuksen sinfonioista*, Fazer 1988 p. 67.

4. This direction has given rise to some controversy. Whilst Sibelius's autograph score asks for 'Stahlstäbe' (suggesting glockenspiel), the published edition states 'Glocken' (tubular bells). There is the strongest evidence that Sibelius wanted a glockenspiel, and that he found the sound of the tubular bells 'too oriental'.
5. Cf. HUL 0304, fair copy of the entire score.
6. Sibelius also considered the titles 'The Falconers' ('Die Falkoniere') and 'Ritter-liebe' ('Knightly Love') for the second movement.
7. A more probable cause for Aho's move was his own marital complications: he had fallen in love with his wife Venny's younger sister, Tilly Soldan.
8. Article in the programme book for the Lahti Sibelius Festival 2004.

Note to Chapter 11

1. 'Op. 70' is mentioned in Sibelius's diary as early as 8th May, but Fabian Dahlström, editor of the diaries, suggests that he was in fact referring to *The Bard*, which then lacked a definitive opus number.

Notes to Chapter 12

1. Notes to his recording on the Finlandia label (8573-80773-2).
2. Article in the programme book for the Lahti Sibelius Festival 2003.
3. The process of turning Aho's novel *Juha* into an opera still did not run smoothly, however. The libretto was passed first to Ilmari Hannikainen and then Aarre Merikanto, who finally brought it to fruition in the years 1919–22, only to have it rejected by the Finnish Opera (it was ultimately given a radio performance in the late 1950s). In 1934 Leevi Madetoja also tried his luck; his version of *Juha* was performed the following year.
4. The ballet was subsequently taken up by Toivo Kuula (as *Karhunpeijaiset*).
5. Notes to the YL recording on the Finlandia label (0927-49774-2).
6. The diary entry of 25th June 1915 refers to 'läkaren' ('the doctor'), in all probability a reference to Christian.
7. Article in the programme book for the Lahti Sibelius Festival 2003.
8. A set of parts for the 1919 revision was, however, adapted from the 1916 set, with pages removed or pasted over the old ones.
9. In his biography of Sibelius, Erik Tawaststjerna claims that what we now know as *Humoresques Nos 2–6* were actually composed first, and that Sibelius renumbered the pieces after composing another such piece in November 1918. According to Fabian Dahlström, however, such a reordering was merely considered and never actually took place.
10. 2nd March according to the Julian Calendar that remained in use in Russia until 1918; 15th March according to the Gregorian Calendar.
11. Runeberg, *Lyriska dikter* (*Lyric Poetry*), Stockholm 1882.

Notes to Chapter 13

1. Sir Henry Wood, *My Life in Music*, London 1938, pp. 141–2.

Notes to Chapter 14

1. HUL 0354.
2. HUL 0362, page 2. This manuscript is dated by Kari Kilpeläinen to the period 1915–23. See also Nors S. Josephson, *On Some Apparent Sketches for Sibelius's Eighth Symphony*, Archiv für Musikwissenschaft, Jahrgang 61, Heft 1 (2004).
3. HUL 0829/2.

Notes to Chapter 15

1. HUL 1728.
2. HUL 1737, dated by Kilpeläinen to 1930–57; similar material is found without text in HUL 1739.
3. Nors S. Josephson, *On Some Apparent Sketches for Sibelius's Eighth Symphony*, Archiv für Musikwissenschaft, Jahrgang 61, Heft 1 (2004).
4. At that time two movements of the suite were still unpublished.
5. This case is convincingly argued by Vesa Sirén on the basis of notes made by Jussi Jalas.
6. See Jukka Tiilikainen, critical commentary to this song in JSW VIII/4, Breitkopf & Härtel 2005.

Notes to Conclusions

1. See Antti Vihinen, *Theodor W. Adornon Sibelius-kritiikin poliittinen ulottuvuus*, Helsinki University 2000.
2. Published in *The Forest's mighty God – A Celebration of Sibelius*, UK Sibelius Society 1998.

APPENDIX I

MUSIC EXAMPLES

Musical examples from Sibelius's early works

Sibelius's earliest works betray the influence of central European dance music:

[1] *Luftslott* for two violins, JS 65 (c. 1881) – first violin part.

[2] *Trio* for two violins and piano, JS 205 (1883) – first movement, violin part.

As the years passed, a variety of additional characteristics and influences became discernible:

[3] In the sonata-form first movement of the *Piano Trio in A minor*, JS 206 (1884), the second subject offers an early example of Sibelius's distinctive use of triplets.

[4] The rondo finale of the *Violin Sonata in A minor*, JS 177 (1884), has a lightness reminiscent of Bizet's *Jeux d'enfants*.

[5] The minuet of the *Piano Quartet in D minor*, JS 157 (1884) (piano part), is a model of Viennese classical elegance.

[6] A similar classical character in the opening theme of the *String Quartet in E flat major*, JS 184 (1885) (first violin part), is especially reminiscent of Haydn.

[7] The second movement of the 'opera' *Ljunga Wirginia* (1885) for violin, cello and piano four hands is a wild tarantella.

[8] The main theme of the *'Hafträsk' Trio*, JS 207 (1886), presented by solo piano, is much more dramatic and Beethovenian.

The influence of the 'Korpo' Trio

[9] This expressive triplet-based theme from the slow movement of the *'Korpo' Trio*, JS 209 (1887) (violin part), has striking counterparts in later works:

[10] in the first movement of the *Suite in E major* for violin and piano, JS 188 (1888);

[11] in the choral song *Sydämeni laulu*, Op. 18 No. 6 (1898);

[12] in the first movement of the *Violin Concerto in D minor*, Op. 47 (1903–04, rev. 1905).

Thematic experiments and applications

By comparing other pieces from the years 1888/89–1890 with later works, we observe the extent to which Sibelius's trademark motifs were present in his music even before he started to write for orchestra:

[13] *Moderato – Maestoso* for violin and piano, JS 132 (1888–89).

[14] *The Wood-Nymph*, Op. 15 (1895) (trombones)

The rhythms of the *Moderato – Maestoso* (Ex. 13 bar 2: short–long–short syncopation; bar 3: dotted rhythm on the penultimate beat) anticipate the confident theme in the opening section of *The Wood-Nymph*.

[15] *Moderato – Allegro appassionato in C sharp minor* for string quartet, JS 131 (1888–89).

[16] *Kullervo*, Op. 7 (1892) – first movement.

These two movements are similar in scale and their main themes are similar in contour, with a long (dotted) opening note.

[17] *Piano Quintet in G minor*, JS 159 (1890) – third movement

[18] *O Herra, siunaa*, sketch (early 1930s [?])

At the very end of his composing career, Sibelius considered reusing the main theme of the third movement of the *Piano Quintet in G minor* in a projected choral piece, *O Herra, siunaa*.

Descending fifths

Descending fifths have long been recognized as one of Sibelius's fingerprints, often found in conjunction with long (or repeated) opening notes and a decorative triplet (or similar):

[19] *'Hafträsk' Trio*, JS 207 (1886) – first movement;

[20] *The Swan of Tuonela*, Op. 22 No. 2 (1896, rev. 1897/1900) – cor anglais solo;

[21; 22] *Symphony No. 2 in D major*, Op. 43 (1902) –
first movement (woodwind) and third movement (oboe solo);

[23] *Violin Concerto in D minor*, Op. 47 (1903–04, rev. 1905) – first movement;

[24] *Pohjola's Daughter*, Op. 49 (1906) (cellos, basses);

[25] *Scaramouche*, Op. 71 (1913) – flute solo from Act II.

Pianokompositioner för barn, JS 148

Seven themes from the sketched *Pianokompositioner för barn* (*Piano Works for Children*), JS 148 (1899). These motifs found their way into other works as follows (as indicated by the symbol >):

[26] No. 1 > *Rosenlied*, Op. 50 No. 6 (1906).

[27] No. 3 > *Symphony No. 2* (1902) – first movement.

[28] No. 6 > *Kyllikki* for piano, Op. 41 (1904) – third movement.

[29] No. 7 > *Scout March*, Op. 91b (1918).

[30] No. 10 > *Har du mod?*, version for choir *a cappella*, JS 93 (1903–04).

[31] No. 20 > *Souvenir* for violin and piano, Op. 79 No. 1 (1915)

[32] No. 21 > Tableau 4 of the *Press Celebrations Music*, JS 137 (1899) and its revised version, *Scena* from *Scènes historiques I*, Op. 25 (1911).

Patriotic march themes

A characteristic of Sibelius's patriotic marches throughout his career was the use of abrupt phrase ends, as illustrated here by:

[33] *Isänmaalle* for male choir *a cappella*, JS 98 (original version, 1899).

[34] *Har du mod?* for male choir and piano/orchestra, Op. 31 No. 2 (1904, rev. 1911, 1912–14; version with piano from 1912 shown).

[35] *Uusmaalaisten laulu* for mixed choir *a cappella*, JS 214 (1912).

[36] *Till havs* for male choir *a cappella*, Op. 84 No. 5 (1917).

The 'S-motif'

Some examples of the 'S-motif' from the years 1899–1912:

[37] *Symphony No. 1 in E minor*, Op. 39 (1899, rev. 1900) –
first movement, clarinet introduction.

[38] *Finlandia*, Op. 26 (1899, rev. 1900).

[39] *Nocturne* for piano, Op. 24 No. 8 (1900).

[40] *Romance in D flat major* for piano, Op. 24 No. 9 (1901).

[41] *Symphony No. 2 in D major*, Op. 43 (1902) – third movement.

[42] *Den 25. Oktober 1902. Till Thérèse Hahl* for mixed choir *a cappella*, JS 60 (1902).

[43] *Rêverie* for piano, Op. 58 No.1 (1909).

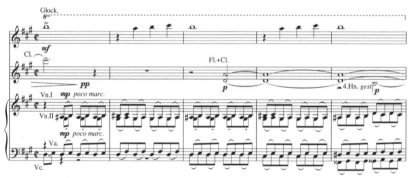

[44] *Symphony No. 4 in A minor*, Op. 63 (1911) – fourth movement.

[45] *Män från slätten och havet* for mixed choir *a cappella*, Op. 65a (1911).

[46] *Rondino No. 1* for piano, Op. 68 No. 1 (1912).

Rising motifs (1908–13) and laments (1914–19)

In Sibelius's middle period we find several examples of melodic lines which, unlike the 'S-motif' or the chromatic idea meantioned below, have a wide range, often greater than an octave. These are found especially (but by no means exclusively) in vocal music:

[47–49] The Josephson settings *Jubal*, Op. 35 No. 1 (1908), *Jag är ett träd* and *Vänskapens blomma*, Op. 57 Nos 5 and 7 (1909);

[50] *Symphony No. 4 in A minor*, Op. 63 (1911) – fourth movement;

[51] *Luonnotar* for soprano and orchestra, Op. 70 (1913).

A little later, in some of his smaller works from 1914–15, Sibelius experimented with chromatic writing that would figure prominently in the *Fifth Symphony*:

[52] *Aspen* for piano, Op. 75 No. 3 (1914).

[53] *Ett drömackord* for male choir *a cappella*, Op. 84 No. 3 (1915).

[54] *Symphony No. 5 in E flat major* (1919 version) – first movement.

Examples of the 'S-motif' in Sibelius's later music

[55] *Vem styrde hit din väg?* for voice and piano, Op. 90 No. 6 (1917). With its chordal piano accompaniment, this song is also a good example of Sibelius's 3/2 themes (see below).

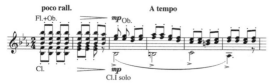

[56] *Symphony No. 5 in E flat major*, Op. 82 (1919 version) – third movement.

[57] *Lied* for piano, Op. 97 No. 2 (1920).

[58] *Symphony No. 6*, Op. 104 (1923) – second movement.

[59] *Tapiola*, Op. 112 (1926).

[60] *Karjalan osa* for male choir and piano, JS 108 (1930) – piano introduction.

The 3/2 themes

[61] The hymn-like string passage near the beginning of *Symphony No. 7*, Op. 105 (1924) – here from the violas – is often singled out for praise. Such dignified melodies in a slow 3/2-time, however, had been characteristic of Sibelius since the 1880s, for instance:

[62] in the suite *Trånaden* for piano and recitation, JS 203 (1887);

[63] in the *Hymn* (*Natus in curas*) for male choir *a cappella*, Op. 21 (1896, rev. 1898);

[64] the horn theme in the 'sunrise' section of the tone poem *Night Ride and Sunrise*, Op. 55 (1908);

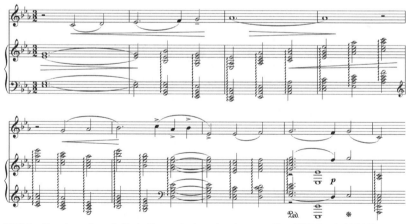

[65] in *Cantique* for violin/cello and piano/orchestra, Op. 77 No. 1 (1914).

By contrast the slow movement of the *Symphony No. 3* exploits the metrical contrast between 6/4 and 3/2. Sibelius himself is said to have conducted this movement in six and to have wished to emphasize its character as a genuine slow movement:

[66] *Symphony No. 3 in C major*, Op. 52 (1907) – second movement.

Music examples typeset by Jeffrey Ginn.

1–5, 8–11, 13–16, 19–22, 33, 34, 37–41, 43–47, 50, 51, 55, 57, 59, 62, 63:
© Breitkopf & Härtel, Wiesbaden. Reprinted by permission.
[Nos 1–5, 8, 9, 13, 15, 19, 33 and 62 are still unpublished and
are reproduced by kind permission of the Sibelius family.]

6, 10, 35, 36, 42, 60: Copyright © Warner/Chappell Music Finland Oy,
administered by Fennica Gehrman Oy. Printed with permission.

7, 18, 26–32: © the Sibelius family. Reproduced by kind permission.

12, 23, 24, 48, 49, 64, 66: © by Robert Lienau Publ., Frankfurt am Main (Germany)
[12 & 23: © 1905; 24: © 1906; 48 & 49: © 1910; 64: © 1909; 66: © 1907]

17, 25, 52, 54, 56, 58, 61, 65: Copyright © Edition Wilhelm Hansen AS,
Copenhagen. Printed with permission.

53: Published with acceptance by Sällskapet MM rf, Helsinki, Finland.

APPENDIX II

CATALOGUE OF WORKS BY JEAN SIBELIUS

At the time of writing (February 2007), research into Sibelius's music is continuing to reveal the existence of previously unknown works and fragments, although it is now unlikely that any more major works will come to light.

The titles of Sibelius's principal works have been established for many years but matters are far from clear when categorizing the less familiar areas of his output, and some inconsistency is thus unavoidable. The primary reference sources for this volume have been Fabian Dahlström's *Jean Sibelius: Thematisch-bibliographisches Verzeichnis seiner Werke* (2003 – including the JS numbered listing of Sibelius's works without opus number) and the ongoing research into Sibelius's fragments and unpublished works by Folke Gräsbeck. The fragments and shorter works which the composer left unnamed are so numerous that it would be confusing simply to list them by key or date, and I have thus followed Gräsbeck's example and provided them with unofficial 'working titles'. Such designations are given in square brackets.

Sibelius's opus numbers are a further source of confusion. He first made a numbered inventory of his works in 1896. The first list to bear opus numbers as such, however, dates from the following year, and this bears little resemblance to the final catalogue. After 1905 most first editions of Sibelius's works bore definitive opus numbers, but many other numbers were not allocated and, as Fabian Dahlström has observed in the above-mentioned *Verzeichnis* (which contains a detailed itemization of the development of the opus listing), 'he altered the numbering on numerous occasions. He also continued to revise his decisions as to which works should bear an opus number at all. The results... are extremely illogical from a chronological perspective. The development of the opus numbers is thus an expression of the re-evaluations that Sibelius sometimes undertook regarding the assessment and classification of his works.' By 1930–31 the register was approaching its final form, containing numbers from 1 to 116, although 'Op. 107' was never used in a published edition in the composer's lifetime; the last lists he made date from 1951–52.

Orchestral Music

Orchestral Music	JS / Opus No.	Date	Text
Overture in E major	JS 145	1891	
Scène de ballet	JS 163	1891	
Fäktmusik (Fencing Music) Lost	JS 80	1891	
En saga (original version)	Op. 9	1893	
Scenic Music for a Festival and Lottery in Aid of Education in the Province of Viipuri [Karelia] Simpler (preliminary?) version of Tableau VII	JS 115	1893	

Orchestral Music	JS / Opus No.	Date	Text
Scenic Music for a Festival and Lottery in Aid of Education in the Province of Viipuri [Karelia] *Completed by Jouni Kaipainen or Kalevi Aho* Overture I. A Karelian home. News of War (1293) *(2 solo folk singers)* II. The founding of Viipuri Castle (1293) III. Narimont, the Duke of Lithuania, levying taxes (1333) IV. Karl Knutsson in Viipuri Castle. Ballade (1446) *(baritone solo)* V. Pontus De la Gardie at the gates of Käkisalmi in 1580 VI. The siege of Viipuri (1710) VII/VIII. The reunion of Old Finland [Karelia] with the rest of Finland (1811)	JS 115	1893	I. Kalevala; IV. Swedish traditional
Karelia Overture	Op. 10	1893	
Karelia Suite I. Intermezzo. *Moderato* II. Ballade. *Tempo di menuetto* III. Alla marcia. *Moderato*	Op. 11	1893	
Impromptu in E minor *String orchestra*	arranged from Op. 5 No. 5	1893	
Scherzo [Presto] *String orchestra*	from Op. 4	1894	
Impromptu *String orchestra*	arranged from Op. 5 Nos. 5 & 6	1894	
Improvisation/Spring Song	[Op. 16]	1894	
Menuetto	JS 127	1894	
The Wood-Nymph (melodrama) *Recitation & orchestra*	Op. 15	1894–95	Viktor Rydberg
Spring Song	Op. 16	1895	
The Wood-Nymph (tone poem)	[Op. 15]	1894–95	
Lemminkäinen and the Maidens of the Island (original version)	Op. 22 No. 1	1896	
Lemminkäinen in Tuonela (original version)	Op. 22 No. 2 [later renumbered No. 3]	1896	
The Swan of Tuonela	Op. 22 No. 3 [later renumbered No. 2]	1896, rev. 1897 & 1900	
Lemminkäinen's Return (original version)	Op. 22 No. 4	1896	
Coronation March [from the Coronation Cantata of 1896]	from JS 104	1896	
Lemminkäinen and the Maidens of the Island (intermediate version) *Not performable*	Op. 22 No. 1	1897	
Lemminkäinen in Tuonela (intermediate version) *Not performable*	Op. 22 No. 2 [later renumbered No. 3]	1897	

Orchestral Music	JS / Opus No.	Date	Text
Lemminkäinen's Return (intermediate version)	Op. 22 No. 4	1897	
Symphony No. 1 in E minor (original version) I. *Allegro energico* II. *Andante (ma non troppo lento)* III. Scherzo. *Allegro* IV. Finale. *Quasi una fantasia* *Lost*	Op. 39	1899	
Press Celebrations Music I. Preludio II. Tableau 1. Väinämöinen delights Nature, and the peoples of Kaleva and Pohjola, with his song III. Tableau 2. The Finns are baptized IV. Tableau 3. Scene from Duke Johan's Court V. Tableau 4. The Finns in the Thirty Years War (1618–48) VI. Tableau 5. The Great Hostility (1713–21) Music played during the tableau VII. Tableau 6. Finland Awakes	JS 137	1899	
Finland Awakes (intermediate version)	from JS 137	1899	
Finlandia	Op. 26	1900	
Symphony No. 1 in E minor (final version) I. *Andante, ma non troppo – Allegro energico* II. *Andante (ma non troppo lento)* III. Scherzo. *Allegro* IV. Finale. *Quasi una fantasia*	Op. 39	1900	
Porilaisten marssi (March of the Pori Regiment) (arr.)	JS 152	1900	
Lemminkäinen's Return (final version)	Op. 22 No. 4	1900	
Symphony No. 2 in D major (version used at first performance; differs in some respects from published edition) *Fire-damaged manuscript* I. *Allegretto moderato* II. *Tempo andante, ma rubato* III. *Vivacissimo* IV. *Allegro moderato*	Op. 43	1902	
Symphony No. 2 in D major (published version) I. *Allegretto* II. *Tempo andante, ma rubato* III. *Vivacissimo* IV. *Allegro moderato*	Op. 43	1902	
Overture in A minor	JS 144	1902	
En saga (final version)	Op. 9	1902	
Cassazione (original version)	Op. 6	1904	
Musik zu einer Scène	[Op. 45 No. 2]	1904	
Romance in C major *String orchestra*	Op. 42	1904	
Cassazione (final version)	Op. 6	1905	
Cortège	JS 54	1905	
Pan and Echo	Op. 53	1906	

Orchestral Music	JS / Opus No.	Date	Text
[**Luonnotar**] (preliminary version of Pohjola's Daughter) *Fragment*		1906	
Pohjola's Daughter	Op. 49	1906	
Grevinnans konterfej (The Countess's Portrait) *Recitation & string orchestra*	JS 88	1906	Zachris Topelius
Dance-Intermezzo, transcription	Op. 45 No. 2	1907	
[**A major**] (same material as Ej med klagan) *Fragment*		1907 (?)	
Symphony No. 3 in C major: preliminary version of slow movement	[Op. 52]	1907	
Symphony No. 3 in C major I. *Allegro moderato* II. *Andantino con moto, quasi allegretto* III. *Moderato – Allegro (ma non tanto)*	Op. 52	1907	
Night Ride and Sunrise	Op. 55	1908	
In memoriam, funeral march (original version)	Op. 59	1909	
The Dryad	Op. 45 No. 1	1910	
In memoriam, funeral march (final version)	Op. 59	1910	
Symphony No. 4 in A minor (version used at first performance; differs in some respects from published edition) I. *Tempo molto moderato, quasi adagio* II. *Allegro molto vivace* III. *Il tempo largo* IV. *Allegro*	Op. 63	1911	
Symphony No. 4 in A minor (published version) I. *Tempo molto moderato, quasi adagio* II. *Allegro molto vivace* III. *Il tempo largo* IV. *Allegro*	Op. 63	1911	
Scènes historiques I I. All' Overtura II. Scena III. Festivo	Op. 25	1911	
Rakastava (The Lover) (preliminary orchestral version) *String orchestra* I. The Lover II. The Beloved III. Good Evening – Good Night!	Op. 14	1911	
Rakastava (The Lover) (published orchestral version) *String orchestra & percussion* I. The Lover II. The Path of His Beloved III. Good Evening!... Farewell!	Op. 14	1912	
Scènes historiques II I. La Chasse II. Love Song III. At the Draw-Bridge	Op. 66	1912	

Orchestral Music	JS / Opus No.	Date	Text
The Bard (original version) *Lost*	Op. 64	1913	
The Bard (final version)	Op. 64	1913	
Fragments from a Suite for Orchestra 1914 / **Predecessor of The Oceanides** *Fragments (?); first movement missing* II. *Tempo moderato* III. *Allegro*		1913–14	
The Oceanides (Yale version)	Op. 73	1914	
The Oceanides (final version)	Op. 73	1914	
Symphony No. 5 in E flat major (original version) I. *Tempo tranquillo assai* II. *Allegro commodo* III. *Andante mosso* IV. *Allegro commodo – Largamente molto*	Op. 82	1915	
Symphony No. 5 in E flat major (intermediate version) *Not performable* I. *Tempo molto moderato – Allegro moderato (ma poco a poco stretto)* II. *Andante mosso, quasi Allegretto* III. *Allegro molto*	Op. 82	1916	
March of the Finnish Jäger Battalion	Op. 91a	1918	[Heikki Nurmio]
Academic March	JS 155	1919	
Symphony No. 5 in E flat major (final version) I. *Tempo molto moderato – Allegro moderato* II. *Andante mosso, quasi allegretto* III. *Allegro molto – Largamente assai*	Op. 82	1919	
Valse lyrique (final version), transcription	Op. 96 No. 1	1920	
Autrefois (version with clarinets)	Op. 96b	1920	[Hjalmar Procopé]
Suite mignonne *2 flutes & string orchestra* I. Petite scène II. Polka III. Épilogue	Op. 98a	1921	
Valse chevaleresque	Op. 96c	1921–22	
Suite champêtre *String orchestra* I. Pièce caractéristique II. Mélodie élégiaque III. Danse	Op. 98b	1922	
Suite caractéristique *Harp & string orchestra* I. *Vivo* II. *Lento* III. *Comodo*	Op. 100	1922	

Orchestral Music	JS / Opus No.	Date	Text
Symphony No. 6 [in D minor] I. *Allegro molto moderato* II. *Allegretto moderato* III. *Poco vivace* IV. *Allegro molto*	Op. 104	1923	
Symphony No. 7 in C major (version with preliminary ending) [in one movement]	Op. 105	1923–24	
Symphony No. 7 in C major [in one movement]	Op. 105	1924	
Morceau romantique sur un motif de M. Jakob de Julin	JS 135a	1925	
Tapiola	Op. 112	1926	
Symphony No. 8 *Unscored sketches possibly for this work*	JS 190	1924–32 (?)	
Processional (No. 6 of Musique religieuse)	Op. 113 No. 6	1938	
Andante festivo *String orchestra & timpani*	JS 34b	1938	
Lemminkäinen and the Maidens of the Island (final version)	Op. 22 No. 1	1939	
Lemminkäinen in Tuonela (final version)	Op. 22 No. 3 [formerly num- bered No. 2]	1939	
Ett ensamt skidspår (A Lonely Ski-Trail) *Recitation & string orchestra*	JS 77b	1948	Bertel Gripenberg

Music for the Theatre

(all for orchestra unless indicated otherwise)

Music for the Theatre	JS / Opus No.	Date	Text
King Christian II, theatre score I. Elegy II. Musette III. Minuet IV. Fool's Song of the Spider *(baritone solo)*	Op. 27	1898	Adolf Paul
King Christian II, theatre score – additional movements Nocturne Serenade Ballade	Op. 27	1898	[Adolf Paul]
King Christian II, concert suite I. Nocturne II. Elegy III. Musette IV. Serenade V. Ballade	Op. 27	1898	[Adolf Paul]

Music for the Theatre	JS / Opus No.	Date	Text
Kuolema (Death), theatre score I. *Tempo di valse lente – Poco risoluto* II. *Moderato* (Paavali's Song: 'Pakkanen puhurin poika') *(baritone solo)* III. *Moderato assai – Moderato* (Elsa's Song: 'Eilaa, eilaa') *– Poco adagio (mezzo-soprano solo)* IV. *Andante* (The Cranes) V. *Moderato* VI. *Andante ma non tanto*	JS 113	1903	Arvid Järnefelt
Valse triste (from Kuolema), concert version	Op. 44 No. 1	1904	[Arvid Järnefelt]
Pelléas et Mélisande, theatre score I. Act I Scene 1: Prelude: *Grave e largamente* II. Act I Scene 2: *Andantino con moto* III. Act I Scene 4: *Adagio* IV. Act II Scene 1: Prelude: *Commodo* V. Act III Scene 1: Prelude: *Con moto (ma non tanto)* VI. Act III Scene 2: *Tranquillo* 'De trenne blinda systrar' *(mezzo-soprano solo)* VII. Act III Scene 4: *Andantino pastorale* VIII: Act IV Scene 1: Prelude: *Allegretto* IX. Act IV Scene 2 (no tempo marking) X. Act V Scene 2: Prelude: *Andante*	JS 147	1905	Maurice Mæterlinck, trans. Bertel Gripenberg
Pelléas et Mélisande, concert suite I. At the Castle Gate II. Mélisande IIa. At the Seashore III. By a Spring in the Park IV. The Three Blind Sisters V. Pastorale VI. Mélisande at the Spinning Wheel VII. Entr'acte VIII. The Death of Mélisande	Op. 46	1905	[Maurice Mæterlinck]
Belshazzar's Feast, theatre score I. *Alla marcia (Moderato)* IIa. Prélude: Notturno. *Andantino* IIb. The Jewish Girl's Song *(mezzo-soprano solo)* III. *Allegretto* IV. Dance of Life. *Commodo* V. Dance of Death. *Commodo* VI. Dance of Life (extract, more slowly) VII. *Tempo sostenuto* VIII. *Allegro* IX. Dance of Life (shortened) X. Dance of Death	JS 48	1906	Hjalmar Procopé
Scene with Cranes (from Kuolema)	Op. 44 No. 2	1906	[Arvid Järnefelt]
Belshazzar's Feast, concert suite I. Oriental Procession II. Solitude III. Nocturne IV. Khadra's Dance	Op. 51	1907	[Hjalmar Procopé]
Swanwhite: preliminary version of No. 9 *Fragment*	[JS 189]	1908	[August Strindberg]

Music for the Theatre	JS / Opus No.	Date	Text
Swanwhite, theatre score I. *Largo* II. *Commodo* III. *Adagio* IV. *Lento assai* V. *Adagio* VI. *Lento – Commodo – Lento – Allegro* VII. *Andantino* VIII. *Andante* IX. *Lento* X. *Moderato* XI. *Allegretto* XII. *Largamente* XIII. *Adagio* XIV. *Largamente molto*	JS 189	1908	[August Strindberg]
Swanwhite, concert suite I. The Peacock II. The Harp III. The Maidens with Roses IV. Listen, the Robin Sings V. The Prince Alone VI. Swanwhite and the Prince VII. Song of Praise	Op. 54	1908	[August Strindberg]
Ödlan (The Lizard) *String chamber ensemble* I. *Adagio* II. *Grave*	Op. 8	1909	[Mikael Lybeck]
Canzonetta (from Kuolema) *String orchestra*	Op. 62a	1911	[Arvid Järnefelt]
Valse romantique (from Kuolema)	Op. 62b	1911	[Arvid Järnefelt]
Die Sprache der Vögel (The Language of the Birds), wedding march	JS 62	1911	[Adolf Paul]
Scaramouche, theatre score [two acts, played continuously]	Op. 71	1913	[Poul Knudsen]
Jedermann (Everyman), theatre score *Mezzo-soprano, tenor, baritone, mixed choir, orchestra & organ* I. *Largo* II. *Largo* III. *Allegro* IIIa. *Allegro comodo* IV. Dance Song. *Tempo commodo* V. On riemussa hetket mennehet taas. *Tempo andante* VI. Kun vettä sataa. *Un poco con moto* VII. Maat ja metsät viheriöivät. *Tempo moderato* VIII. Oi, Lempi, armas Lempi! *Allegretto* IX. Maat ja metsät viheriöivät. *Tempo moderato* X. *Allegro molto* XI. *Largo, sempre misterioso* XII. *Adagio di molto* XIII. *Adagio di molto* (continued) XIV. *Largo e molto – Doloroso – Con grande dolore* XV. [*Lento*] XVI. Gloria in excelsis Deo. *Sempre dolce sin a Fine*	Op. 83	1916	Hugo von Hofmannsthal, trans. Huugo Jalkanen

Music for the Theatre	JS / Opus No.	Date	Text
The Tempest, theatre score *Soprano, mezzo-soprano, tenors, baritone, mixed choir,* *harmonium & orchestra* I. Overture II. Miranda is Lulled into Slumber III. Ariel Flies In IV. Chorus of the Winds V. Ariel Hastens Away VI. Ariel's First Song, with Introduction and Choir (Come unto these yellow sands) VII. Ariel's Second Song (Full fadom five) VIII. Interlude (Prospero) IX. The Oak Tree (Ariel) Plays the Flute X. Ariel's Third Song (While you here do snoring lie) XI. Interlude (Caliban) XII. Stephano's Song (I shall no more to sea) XIII. Caliban's Song (Farewell, master) XIV. Interlude (Miranda) XV. [Humoreske] XVI. Canon (Flout'em and [s]cout'em) XVII. Dance of the Devils XVIII. Ariel as Harpy XIX. The Devils Dance Out XX. Intermezzo XXI. Ariel Flies In XXII. Ariel's Fourth Song (Before you can say 'come' and 'go') XXIII. The Rainbow XXIV. Iris's Melodrama XXV. Juno's Song (Honour, riches, marriage-blessing) XXVI. Dance of the Naiads XXVII. The Harvesters XXVIII. Ariel Flies In XXIX. Ariel Hastens Away XXX. Ariel Flies In XXXI. The Dogs XXXIb. Overture to Act V Scene 8 XXXII. Ariel Brings the Foes to Prospero XXXIII. Ariel's Fifth Song (Where the bee sucks) XXXIV. Cortège XXXIVb. Epilogue	Op. 109	1925 XXXIVb: 1927	William Shakespeare, trans. Edvard Lembcke
The Tempest Prelude	Op. 109 No. 1	1925	[William Shakespeare]
The Tempest, Canon from Suite No. 1 (preliminary version)	Op. 109 No. 2 (fifth movement)	1927	[William Shakespeare]
The Tempest, Suite No. 1 I. The Oak Tree II. Humoresque III. Caliban's Song IV. The Harvesters V. Canon VI. Scène VII. Intrada – Berceuse VIII. Entr'acte – Ariel's Song IX. The Storm	Op. 109 No. 2	1927 (V. rev. 1929)	[William Shakespeare]

Music for the Theatre	JS / Opus No.	Date	Text
The Tempest, Suite No. 2 I. Chorus of the Winds II. Intermezzo III. Dance of the Nymphs IV. Prospero V. Song I VI. Song II VII. Miranda VIII. The Naiads IX. Dance Episode	Op. 109 No. 3	1927	[William Shakespeare]

Soloist (vocal or instrumental) and Orchestra

Soloist and Orchestra	JS / Opus No.	Date	Text
Serenad (Serenade) *Baritone & orchestra*	JS 168	1894–95	Erik Johan Stagnelius
Koskenlaskijan morsiamet (The Rapids-Rider's Brides) *Baritone (or mezzo-soprano) & orchestra*	Op. 33	1897	A. Oksanen
Se'n har jag ej frågat mera (Since then I have questioned no further) *Voice & orchestra*	Op. 17 No. 1	1903	Johan Ludvig Runeberg
På verandan vid havet (On a Balcony by the Sea) *Voice & orchestra*	Op. 38 No. 2	1903	Viktor Rydberg
I natten (In the Night) *Voice & orchestra*	Op. 38 No. 3	1903	Viktor Rydberg
Violin Concerto in D minor (original version) I. *Allegro moderato* II. *Adagio di molto* III. *Allegro (ma non tanto)*	Op. 47	1904	
Höstkväll (Autumn Evening) *Voice & string orchestra*	Op. 38 No. 1	1904	Viktor Rydberg
Höstkväll (Autumn Evening) *Voice & orchestra*	Op. 38 No. 1	1904	Viktor Rydberg
Violin Concerto in D minor (final version) I. *Allegro moderato* II. *Adagio di molto* III. *Allegro, ma non tanto*	Op. 47	1905	
Arioso *Voice & string orchestra*	Op. 3	1911	J. L. Runeberg
Hertig Magnus (Duke Magnus) *Voice & orchestra*	Op. 57 No. 6	1912	Ernst Josephson
Serenade No. 1 in D major *Violin & orchestra*	Op. 69a	1912	
Serenade No. 2 in G minor *Violin & orchestra*	Op. 69b	1913	

Soloist and Orchestra	JS / Opus No.	Date	Text
Luonnotar *Soprano & orchestra*	Op. 70	1913	Kalevala
Soluppgång (Sunrise) *Voice & orchestra*	Op. 37 No. 3	1913	Tor Hedberg
Våren flyktar hastigt (Spring is Flying) *Voice & orchestra*	Op. 13 No. 4	1913	J.L. Runeberg
Cantique (Laetare anima mea) *Violin & orchestra*	Op. 77 No. 1	1914	
Devotion (Ab imo pectore) *Violin & orchestra*	Op. 77 No. 2	1915	
Devotion (Ab imo pectore) *Cello & orchestra*	Op. 77 No. 2	1916	
Cantique (Laetare anima mea) *Cello & orchestra*	Op. 77 No. 1	1916	
Demanten på marssnön (The Diamond on the March Snow) *Voice & orchestra*	Op. 36 No. 6	1917	Josef Julius Wecksell
Humoresque No. 1 in D minor (original version) *Violin & orchestra*	Op. 87 No. 1	1917	
Humoresque No. 2 in D major *Violin & orchestra*	Op. 87 No. 2	1917	
Humoresque No. 3 in G minor *Violin & orchestra*	Op. 89a	1917	
Humoresque No. 4 in G minor *Violin & orchestra*	Op. 89b	1917	
Humoresque No. 5 in E flat major *Violin & orchestra*	Op. 89c	1917	
Humoresque No. 6 in G minor *Violin & orchestra*	Op. 89d	1918	
Autrefois (version with voices) *2 sopranos & orchestra*	Op. 96b	1919, rev. 1920	Hjalmar Procopé
Suite for Violin and String Orchestra I. Country Scenery II. Serenade. Evening in Spring III. In the Summer	JS 185	1929	
Humoresque No. 1 in D minor (revised version) *Violin & orchestra*	Op. 87 No. 1	1940	
Kullervon valitus (Kullervo's Lament) *Voice & orchestra*	from Op. 7	1957	Kalevala
Kom nu hit, död (from Twelfth Night), transcription *Voice & orchestra*	Op. 60 No. 1	1957	William Shakespeare, trans. C.A. Hagberg

Choir and Orchestra

Choir and Orchestra	JS / Opus No.	Date	Text
Herr du bist ein Fels (Lord, you are a rock) (version I) *Mixed choir & orchestra*		1889–90	–
Herr du bist ein Fels (Lord, you are a rock) (version II) *Mixed choir & orchestra*		1889–90	–
Herr erzeige uns deine Gnade (Lord, show us your mercy) (version I) *Mixed choir & orchestra*		1889–90	–
Herr erzeige uns deine Gnade (Lord, show us your mercy) (version II) *Mixed choir & orchestra*		1889–90	–
Kullervo *Baritone, mezzo-soprano, male choir & orchestra* I. Introduction. *Allegro moderato* II. Kullervo's Youth. *Grave* III. Kullervo and his Sister. *Allegro vivace* IV. Kullervo Goes to War. *Alla marcia [Allegro molto] – Vivace – Presto* V. Kullervo's Death. *Andante*	Op. 7	1892	Kalevala
Rakastava (The Lover) *Tenor, male choir & string orchestra*	JS 160b	1894	Kanteletar
Cantata for the University Graduation **Ceremonies of 1894** [Promotional Cantata] *Soprano, baritone, mixed choir & orchestra – Soprano part in third movement lost* I. *Molto maestoso ed adagio*. Syntyi kun maailmat II. *Allegro assai*. Kaskeksi korvet III. *Andantino*	JS 105	1894	Kasimir Lönnbohm
Cantata for the Coronation of Nicholas II *Mixed choir & orchestra* I. *Allegro*. Terve nuori ruhtinas II. *Allegro*. Oikeuden varmassa turvassa	JS 104	1896	Paavo Cajander
Laulu Lemminkäiselle (A Song for Lemminkäinen) *Male choir & orchestra*	Op. 31 No. 1	1896	Yrjö Weijola
Cantata for the University Graduation **Ceremonies of 1897** *Soprano, baritone, mixed choir & orchestra – Lost*	JS 106	1897	August Valdemar Forsman
Sandels (original version) *Male choir & orchestra*	Op. 28	1898	J. L. Runeberg
Athenarnes sång (Song of the Athenians) *Boys' & men's voices, woodwind, brass, percussion & double bass*	Op. 31 No. 3	1899	Viktor Rydberg
Islossningen i Uleå älv (The Breaking of the Ice on the Oulu River) *Recitation, male choir & orchestra*	Op. 30	1899	Zachris Topelius
Snöfrid *Recitation, mixed choir & orchestra*	Op. 29	1900	Viktor Rydberg
Impromptu (original version) *Female choir & orchestra*	Op. 19	1902	Viktor Rydberg
Tulen synty (The Origin of Fire) (original version) *Baritone, male choir & orchestra*	Op. 32	1902	Kalevala

Choir and Orchestra	JS / Opus No.	Date	Text
Har du mod? (Have You Courage?) (first version) *Male choir & orchestra*	Op. 31 No. 2	1904	J. J. Wecksell
Vapautettu kuningatar (The Captive Queen) *Mixed choir & orchestra*	Op. 48	1906	Paavo Cajander
Impromptu (final version) *Female choir & orchestra*	Op. 19	1910	Viktor Rydberg
Vapautettu kuningatar (The Captive Queen) *Male choir & orchestra*	Op. 48	1910 (?)	Paavo Cajander
Tulen synty (The Origin of Fire) (final version) *Baritone, male choir & orchestra*	Op. 32	1910	Kalevala
Har du mod? (Have You Courage?) (second version) *Male choir & orchestra*	Op. 31 No. 2	1911	J. J. Wecksell
Har du mod? (Have You Courage?) (third version) *Male choir & orchestra*	Op. 31 No. 2	1912	J. J. Wecksell
Har du mod? (Have You Courage?) (fourth version), transcription *Male choir & orchestra*	Op. 31 No. 2	1914 (?)	J. J. Wecksell
Sandels (final version) *Male choir & orchestra*	Op. 28	1915	J. L. Runeberg
March of the Finnish Jäger Battalion *Male choir & orchestra*	Op. 91a	1917	Heikki Nurmio
Oma maa (My Own Land) *Mixed choir & orchestra*	Op. 92	1918	'Kallio'
Scout March *Mixed choir & orchestra*	Op. 91b	1918	Jalmari Finne
Jordens sång (Song of the Earth) *Mixed choir & orchestra*	Op. 93	1919	Jarl Hemmer
Maan virsi (Hymn to the Earth) *Mixed choir & orchestra*	Op. 95	1920	Eino Leino
Väinön virsi (Väinämöinen's Song) *Mixed choir & orchestra*	Op. 110	1926	Kalevala
Processional (No. 6 of Musique religieuse) *Mixed choir & orchestra – Orchestral part arr. Sibelius; choir part arr. C. Lefebvre*	Op. 113 No. 6	1938	Marshall Kernochan
Koskenlaskijan morsiamet (The Rapids-Rider's Brides) *Male choir & orchestra*	Op. 33	1943	A. Oksanen

Chamber Music

Chamber Music	JS / Opus No.	Date	Text
Vattendroppar (Water Drops) *Violin & cello*	JS 216	1875 (?)	
Luftslott (Castles in the Air) *2 Violins*	JS 65	1881 (?)	
[Menuetto] in D minor *Piano trio*		1882–85	
[Andante] – Adagio – Allegro maestoso *Piano trio*		1883–85	
Trio 'in G major' *2 Violins & piano* I. *Andante – Allegro* II. *Adagio* III. *Vivace*	JS 205	1883	
Menuetto in F major *2 Violins & piano*	JS 126	1883	
Piano Trio in A minor I. *Allegro con brio* II. *Andante* III. *Menuetto*	JS 206	1884	
Sonata in A minor *Violin & piano* I. *Un poco lento – Più mosso quasi Presto* II. *Andantino* III. *Tempo di menuetto* IV. Rondo. *Presto*	JS 177	1884	
Quartet in D minor *2 Violins, cello & piano* I. *Andante molto – Allegro moderato* II. *Adagio* III. Menuetto IV. *Grave* – Rondo. *Vivacissimo*	JS 157	1884	
Andantino in C major *Cello & piano*	JS 40	1884	
Andante grazioso in D major *Violin & piano*	JS 35	1884–85	
Molto moderato – Scherzo *String quartet*	JS 134	1885	
[Scherzo] in B minor *String quartet – Completed by Kalevi Aho*		1885	
Sonata [movement] in D major *Violin & piano*		1885	
[Allegro] in C major *Piano trio*		1885	

Chamber Music	JS / Opus No.	Date	Text
String Quartet in E flat major I. *Allegro* II. *Andante molto* III. Scherzo. *Allegretto* IV. *Vivace*	JS 184	1885	
[Moderato] in A minor *Piano trio*		1885	
Ljunga Wirginia ('opera') *Violin, cello & piano 4 hands – Last movement completed by Kalevi Aho* I. *Moderato quasi andantino – Cantabile –* Recitativo II. *Prestissimo* III. *Largo* IV. *Andantino* V. *Allegretto* VI. *Allegro – Più vivo quasi Presto – Allegro con fuoco –* [Moderato]		1885	
[Moderato] – Presto – [Tempo I] in A minor *Violin & piano*	JS 7	1886	
[Menuetto] in D minor *Violin & piano*		1886	
[Andantino] in A minor *Violin & piano*	JS 8	1886–87	
[Andantino] in A major *Piano trio*		1886	
Piano Trio in A minor, 'Hafträsk' I. *Allegro maestoso* II. *Andantino* III. Scherzo. *Vivace* IV. Rondo	JS 207	1886	
Allegro in D major *Piano trio*	JS 27	1886	
[Étude] in D major *Violin solo*	JS 55	1886	
[Allegretto] in G major *Violin & piano*	JS 86	1886–87	
[Tempo di valse] in B minor *Violin & piano – Completed by Jaakko Kuusisto*	JS 89	1886–87	
[Mazurka] in A major *Violin & piano*	JS 4	1886–87	
[Andante molto] in C major *Violin & piano*	JS 49	1886–87	
[Aubade] in A major *Violin & piano*	JS 3	1886–87	
[Scherzino] in F major *Violin & piano*	JS 78	1887	
Andante cantabile in E flat major *Harmonium & piano*	JS 30b	1887	

Chamber Music	JS / Opus No.	Date	Text
Quartet in G minor *Violin, cello, harmonium & piano*	JS 158	1887	
[Four Themes]: G major, E flat major, A minor, E minor *String quartet*		1887	
Scherzo in E minor *Violin, cello & piano 4 hands – Completed by Timo Hongisto & Kalevi Aho*	JS 165	1887	
Andante cantabile in G major *Violin & piano*	JS 33	1887	
[Andante elegiaco] in F sharp minor *Violin & piano*		1887	
Andante molto in F minor *Cello & piano*	JS 36	1887	
Piano Trio in D major, 'Korpo' I. *Allegro moderato* II. Fantasia. *Andante – Andantino* III. Finale. *Vivace*	JS 209	1887	
Andantino in G minor *Piano trio*	JS 43	1887–88	
Serenata *2 Violins & Cello*	JS 169	1887	
Minuet and Allegro *2 Violins & Cello*	JS 128	1887	
Tempo di valse in G minor *Cello & piano – Piano part lost, reconstructed by Kalevi Aho*	JS 193	1887	
[Duo] in E minor *Violin & cello*	JS 68	1887	
[Theme and Variations] in D minor *Cello solo*	JS 196	1887	
[Sonata Allegro Exposition] in B minor *Violin & piano*	JS 90	1887	
[Menuetto] in E minor *Violin & piano*	JS 67	1886–87	
Suite in D minor (sometimes referred to as 'Sonata') *Violin & piano* I. *Un poco adagio – Andante* II. *Vivace* III. *Andantino* IV. *Vivacissimo* V. *Moderato* VI. *Quasi presto*	JS 187	1887–88	
Alla marcia in E minor *String quartet*	JS 16	1888	
Presto in F major *String quartet*	JS 154	1888	
Theme and Variations in G minor *String quartet*	JS 197	1888	

Chamber Music	JS / Opus No.	Date	Text
Allegretto in D major *String quartet*	JS 20	1888	
Andantino in C major *String quartet*	JS 39	1888	
[Lento] in E flat minor *Violin & piano*	JS 76	1887–88	
[Lento] in E flat minor *Cello & piano*	JS 76	1888	
Allegretto in E flat major *Violin & piano*	JS 22	1888	
[Allegretto] in A flat major *Piano trio*		1887–88	
Moderato – Maestoso in E flat major *Violin & piano*	JS 132	1887–88	
[Maestoso] in C minor *Violin & piano*		1887–88	
Allegretto in C major *Violin & piano*	JS 19	1888	
[Tempo di valse] in A major *Violin & piano*		1888	
Theme and Variations in C sharp minor *String quartet – Completed by Kalevi Aho*	JS 195	1888	
Piano Trio in C major, 'Lovisa' I. *Allegro* II. *Andante* III. *Lento – Allegro con brio*	JS 208	1888	
Suite in E major *Violin & piano* I. *Allegro molto moderato – quasi adagio* II. *Allegro molto* III. *Più lento quasi andantino* IV. *Allegro brillante*	JS 188	1888	
[Andante] in B minor *Cello & piano*	JS 91	1888	
Moderato in F major *Cello solo*		1885–89	
[Mazurka] in G minor *Cello solo*		1885–89	
Andante molto in B minor *Cello & piano*		1888–89	
[Andantino] in B minor *Cello & piano*	JS 92	1888–89	
[33 Small Pieces] *String quartet*		1888–89	

Chamber Music	JS / Opus No.	Date	Text
[Allegro] in G minor *String quartet*		1888–89	
Allegro [Sonata Exposition] in A minor *Violin & piano*	JS 26	1888–89	
Andante – Allegro *Piano quintet*	JS 31	1888–89	
Moderato – Allegro appassionato in C sharp minor *String quartet*	JS 131	1888–89	
Andante molto sostenuto in B minor *String quartet*	JS 37	1888–89	
Allegro in E minor *String quartet*	JS 28	1888–89	
Allegretto in A major *String quartet*	JS 17	1888–89	
Più lento in F major *String quartet*	JS 149	1888–89	
Adagio in F minor *String quartet*	JS 14	1888–89	
Andante – Allegro molto in D major *String quartet*	JS 32	1888–89	
Den lilla sjöjungfrun (The Little Mermaid) *String quartet & recitation – Fragment*	JS 59	1888–89	Hans Christian Andersen
Andantino in A major *Violin, viola & cello*	JS 38	1889	
Suite in A major *Violin, viola & cello – Violin part of fourth movement lost* I. Prélude. *Vivace* II. *Andante con moto* III. Menuetto IV. Air. *Andante sostenuto* V. Gigue. *Allegretto*	JS 186	1889	
Fugue for Martin Wegelius *String quartet*	JS 85	1889	
String Quartet in A minor I. *Andante – Allegro* II. *Adagio ma non tanto* III. *Vivace* IV. *Allegro*	JS 183	1889	
Canon in G minor *Violin & cello*	JS 50	1889	
Sonata in F major *Violin & piano* I. *[Allegro]* II. *Andante* III. *Vivace*	JS 178	1889	
Fantasy *Cello & piano – Piano part lost*	JS 79	1889	

Chamber Music	JS / Opus No.	Date	Text
Adagio in F sharp minor *Cello & piano*	JS 15	1889	
Tempo di valse in F sharp minor (Lulu Waltz) *Cello & piano*	JS 194	1889	
[Allegro] in D minor *Piano trio – Completed by Kalevi Aho*		1889	
Allegretto in B flat major *String quartet*		1889	
[Largamente, Fragment] in E minor *Violin & piano – Fragment*		1889–91	
Vivace [Scherzo] (alternative fourth movement for Piano Quintet in G minor) *Piano quintet*	(JS 159)	1890	
Piano Quintet in G minor I. *Grave – Allegro* II. Intermezzo. *Moderato* III. *Andante* IV. Scherzo. *Vivacissimo* V. *Moderato – Vivace*	JS 159	1890	
Romance in B minor (original version, also known as Grave) *Violin & piano*	Op. 2 No. 1	1890	
[Adagio] in D minor *Violin & piano*		1890	
Adagio in D minor *String quartet*	JS 12	1890	
[Larghetto, Fragment] in D minor *Violin & piano – Fragment*		1890–92	
String Quartet in B flat major I. *Allegro* II. *Andante sostenuto [Manuscript parts: Andante sostenuto; published edition: Andante molto]* III. *Presto* IV. *Allegro*	Op. 4	1890	
Minuet in F major *Violin & cello – Completed by Jaakko Kuusisto*		1891	
La pompeuse Marche d'Asis *Piano trio – possible alternative versions lost*	JS 116	1891	
Quartet in C minor [C major] *2 Violins, cello & piano*	JS 156	1891	
Perpetuum mobile *Violin & piano*	Op. 2 No. 2	1891	
[Allegretto] in E flat major *Piano trio – Completed by Jaakko Kuusisto*		1891–92	
Duo in C major *Violin & viola*	JS 66	1891–92	
Porilaisten marssi (March of the Pori Regiment) (arr.) *Piccolo, violin, viola and 'a few other instruments' – Lost*	JS 151	1892	

Chamber Music	JS / Opus No.	Date	Text
String Trio in G minor *Violin, viola & cello (Second and third movements incomplete)* I. *Lento* II. *Allegro* III. (no tempo marking)	JS 210	1893–94	
Rondo in D minor *Viola & piano*	JS 162	1893	
[Allegretto] in A major *Violin solo*		1891–94	
[Grave, Fragment] in D minor *Violin & piano*		1891–94	
Moderato *Kantele*	JS 130	1896–98	
Dolcissimo *Kantele*	JS 63	1896–98	
Lullaby [Waltz] *Violin & kantele*	JS 222	1899	
Malinconia *Cello & piano*	Op. 20	1900	
Violin Concerto in D minor (final version), transcription *Violin & piano* I. *Allegro moderato* II. *Adagio di molto* III. *Allegro, ma non tanto*	Op. 47	1905	
String Quartet in D minor, 'Voces intimae', preliminary ending to finale	Op. 56	1909	
String Quartet in D minor, 'Voces intimae' I. *Andante – Allegro molto moderato* II. *Vivace* III. *Adagio di molto* IV. *Allegretto (ma pesante)* V. *Allegro*	Op. 56	1909	
Romance in B minor (final version) *Violin & piano*	Op. 2 No. 1	1911	
Epilogue *Violin & piano*	Op. 2 No. 2	1911	
Cantique (Laetare anima mea) *Violin & piano*	Op. 77 No. 1	1915	
Romance in F major *Violin & piano*	Op. 78 No. 2	1915	
Romance in F major *Cello & piano*	Op. 78 No. 2	1915	
Rigaudon in D major *Violin & piano*	Op. 78 No. 4	1915	
Rigaudon in D major *Cello & piano*	Op. 78 No. 4	1915	

Chamber Music	JS / Opus No.	Date	Text
Sonatina in E major *Violin & piano* I. *Lento – Allegro* II. *Andantino* III. *Lento – Allegretto*	Op. 80 Op. 80	1915 1915	
Devotion (Ab imo pectore) *Violin & piano*	Op. 77 No. 2	1915	
Tempo di Minuetto *Violin & piano*	Op. 79 No. 2	1915	
Impromptu in A minor *Violin & piano*	Op. 78 No. 1	1915	
Impromptu in A minor *Cello & piano*	Op. 78 No. 1	1915	
Souvenir in D major *Violin & piano*	Op. 79 No. 1	1915	
Mazurka in D minor *Violin & piano*	Op. 81 No. 1	1915	
Devotion (Ab imo pectore) *Cello & piano*	Op. 77 No. 2	1916	
Cantique (Laetare anima mea) *Cello & piano*	Op. 77 No. 1	1916	
Danse caractéristique *Violin & piano*	Op. 79 No. 3	1916	
Sérénade in D major *Violin & piano*	Op. 79 No. 4	1916	
Religioso in G minor *Cello & piano*	Op. 78 No. 3	1917	
Religioso in G minor *Violin & piano*	Op. 78 No. 3	1917	
Valse in D major *Violin & piano*	Op. 81 No. 3	1917	
Dance Idyll in E minor *Violin & piano*	Op. 79 No. 5	1917	
Rondino in D major *Violin & piano*	Op. 81 No. 2	1917	
Berceuse in C sharp minor *Violin & piano*	Op. 79 No. 6	1917	
Aubade in D major *Violin & piano*	Op. 81 No. 4	1918	
Menuetto in D minor *Violin & piano*	Op. 81 No. 5	1918	
Novellette *Violin & piano*	Op. 102	1922	

Chamber Music	JS / Opus No.	Date	Text
Andante festivo *String quartet*	JS 34a	1922	
Danse champêtre No. 1: *Largamente assai* *Violin & piano*	Op. 106 No. 1	1924	
Danse champêtre No. 2: *Alla polacca* *Violin & piano*	Op. 106 No. 2	1924	
Danse champêtre No. 3: *Tempo moderato* *Violin & piano*	Op. 106 No. 3	1925	
Danse champêtre No. 4: *Tempo di Menuetto* *Violin & piano*	Op. 106 No. 4	1925	
Danse champêtre No. 5: *Poco moderato* *Violin & piano*	Op. 106 No. 5	1925	
Scène d'amour (from Scaramouche) *Violin & piano*	from Op. 71	1925	
En glad musikant (A Happy Musician) *Violin – Text written above the music*	JS 70	1925	Ture Rangström
Auf der Heide (On The Heath) *Violin & piano*	Op. 115 No. 1	1929	
Ballade *Violin & piano*	Op. 115 No. 2	1929	
Humoresque *Violin & piano*	Op. 115 No. 3	1929	
Die Glocken (Capriccietto) (The Bells) *Violin & piano*	Op. 115 No. 4	1929	
Scène de danse *Violin & piano*	Op. 116 No. 1	1929	
Danse caractéristique *Violin & piano*	Op. 116 No. 2	1929	
Rondeau romantique *Violin & piano*	Op. 116 No. 3	1929	

Piano Music
(all for solo piano unless indicated otherwise)

Piano Music	JS / Opus No.	Date	Text
Con moto, sempre una corda in D flat major	JS 52	1885	
[Andante] in E flat major	JS 74	1885	
[Menuetto] in A minor	JS 5	1885	
[Tempo di valse] in A major	JS 2	1885	
Scherzo in E major with Trio in E minor	JS 134	1885, arr. 1886	

Piano Music	JS / Opus No.	Date	Text
Scherzo in E major with [Trio] in A major	JS 134	1886	
[11 Variations on a harmonic formula] in D major		1886	
[A Catalogue of Themes, 50 Short Pieces]		1887	
Trånaden (Longing) *Piano & recitation* I. Tvenne lagar styra menniskolifvet / *Largo – Andante* II. Ser du hafvet? / *Andantino* III. Hör du vinden? / *Molto allegro – Andante – Adagio cantabile* IV. Hvad är våren? / *Allegro – Andantino – Moderato – Andante – Poco adagio – Allegretto* V. Menska, vill du lifvets vishet lära / *Largo*	JS 203	1887	Erik Johan Stagnelius
Andante in E flat major	JS 30a	1887	
[Aubade] in A flat major	JS 46	1887	
Au crépuscule in F sharp minor	JS 47	1887	
Tempo di menuetto in F sharp minor		1888	
Allegro in E major		1888	
[Moderato] in F minor		1888	
Vivace in E flat major		1888	
Andantino in C major		1888	
Andantino in B major	JS 44	1888	
Allegretto in B flat minor	JS 18	1888	
Allegro in F minor		1888	
[Waltz] in E major		1888	
Più lento – Tempo di valse in E flat major	JS 150	1888	
[Waltz, Fragment] in F minor *Fragment*		1888	
Allegretto in G minor	JS 24	1888	
Moderato – Presto in D minor	JS 133	1888	
[Allegro, Fragment] in E major *Fragment*		1888	
Largo in A major	JS 117	1888	
Adagio in D major	JS 11	1888	
Vivace in D minor	JS 221	1888	
[Interludium] in C minor		1888	
Andantino in E major	JS 41	1888	
[Two Sketches. Presto] in A minor	JS 6	1888	
O, om du sett (Oh, If You Had Seen) *Piano & recitation*	JS 141	1888	Ellen Hackzell
[Three Fugue Expositions] in D minor		1888–89	

Piano Music	JS / Opus No.	Date	Text
[Polka] in E flat major	JS 75	1888–89	
Florestan I. *Moderato* II. *Molto moderato* III. *Andante* IV. *Tempo I*	JS 82	1889	
Allegretto in E major	JS 21	1889	
Valse. À Betsy Lerche	JS 1	1889	
[Sonata Allegro Exposition] in D minor *Completed by Kalevi Aho*	JS 179a	1889	
[Two Sonata Sketches]		1889	
[Eleven Sonata Sketches]		1889	
[Sonata Allegro Exposition] in F minor *Completed by Kalevi Aho*	JS 179b	1889	
[Sonata Allegro Exposition] in C major	JS 179c	1889	
[Sonata Allegro] in E major	JS 179d	1889	
[Sonata Allegro Exposition] in C minor *Completed by Kalevi Aho*	JS 179e	1889	
Scherzo in F sharp minor	JS 164	1891	
Minuet in B flat major		1891	
Theme and Variations in C minor *Lost*	JS 198	1891	
[Waltz] in D flat major		1891–93	
[Polka, Fragment] in E minor *Fragment*		1890–92	
Piano Sonata in F major I. *Allegro molto* II. *Andantino* III. *Vivacissimo*	Op. 12	1893	
Impromptu No. 1 in G minor	Op. 5 No. 1	1893	
Impromptu No. 2 in G minor	Op. 5 No. 2	1893	
Impromptu No. 3 in A minor	Op. 5 No. 3	1893	
Impromptu No. 4 in E minor	Op. 5 No. 4	1893	
Impromptu No. 5 in B minor	Op. 5 No. 5	1893	
Impromptu No. 6 in E major	Op. 5 No. 6	1893	
Karelia Suite (movements I & II), transcription I. *Intermezzo. Allegro* II. *Ballade. Moderato*	from Op. 11	1893–97	
[Mazurka, Sketch] in D minor		1891–94	
Romance in A major	Op. 24 No. 2	1895	

Piano Music	JS / Opus No.	Date	Text
Impromptu in G minor	Op. 24 No. 1	1895	
The Wood-Nymph (transcription of final section)	[Op. 15]	1895	
Caprizzio in B flat minor		1895	
Allegretto in F major	JS 23	1895–96	
Lento in E major	JS 119	1896–97	
Allegretto in G minor [18 19/XII 97]	JS 225	1897	
Andantino in F major [Idyll]	[Op. 24 No. 6, preliminary version]	1897	
Minuet in B flat major		1898–1900	
King Christian II, transcription I. Elegy II. Musette III. Minuet IV. Fool's Song of the Spider	Op. 27	1898	Adolf Paul
[Three Sketches] (B flat minor, D flat major, C major)		1895–98	
[Largamente] in D minor		1897–99	
[Caprice in B minor]	[Op. 24 No. 3, preliminary version]	1898	
Caprice in E minor	Op. 24 No. 3	1898	
Romance in D minor	Op. 24 No. 4	1896–98	
Waltz in E major	Op. 24 No. 5	1898 (?)	
Idyll in F major (original version)	Op. 24 No. 6	1898	
Symphony No. 1 in E minor, extract from slow movement Fragment	[Op. 39]	1899	
Athenarnes sång (Song of the Athenians), transcription Text written above the music	Op. 31 No. 3	1899	Viktor Rydberg
Marche triste	JS 124	1899	
Andantino in F major (original version)	Op. 24 No. 7	1899	
Andantino in F major (final version)	Op. 24 No. 7	1899	
Pianokompositioner för barn (Piano Works for Children) (21 sketches)	JS 148	1899	
Finlandia, transcription	Op. 26	1900	
Nocturno	Op. 24 No. 8	1899	
Kavaljeren (The Cavalier)	JS 109	1900	
Romance in D flat major	Op. 24 No. 9	1901	
[Allegro] in G minor		1899–1903	
[Polka] in C minor, 'Aino'		1902–05	

Piano Music	JS / Opus No.	Date	Text
Barcarole in G minor	Op. 24 No. 10	1903	
Minun kultani kaunis on, sen suu kuin auran kukka (My beloved is beautiful, her mouth like a corn-cockle) (No. 1 of Six Finnish Folk-Songs)	JS 81 No. 1	1902–03	
Sydämestäni rakastan (I love you with all my heart) (No. 2 of Six Finnish Folk-Songs)	JS 81 No. 2	1902–03	
Ilta tulee, ehtoo joutuu (Evening is coming) (No. 3 of Six Finnish Folk-Songs)	JS 81 No. 3	1902–03	
Tuopa tyttö, kaunis tyttö (That beautiful girl) (No. 4 of Six Finnish Folk-Songs)	JS 81 No. 4	1902–03	
Velisuurmaaja (The Fratricide) (No. 5 of Six Finnish Folk-Songs)	JS 81 No. 5	1902–03	
Häämuistelma (Wedding memory) (No. 6 of Six Finnish Folk-Songs)	JS 81 No. 6	1902–03	
Minun kultani kaunis on, vaikk' on kaitulainen (My beloved is beautiful, even though her frame is slender)		1902–03	
Har du mod? (Have You Courage?) (first version), transcription *Text written above the music*	Op. 31 No. 2	1904	J. J. Wecksell
Adagio sostenuto in A major (Violin concerto, extract from slow movement) *Sketch*		1902–04	
Dance-Intermezzo	Op. 45 No. 2	1904	
[Adagio] in C major *Fragment*		1901–05	
Valse triste (from Kuolema), transcription (intermediate version)	Op. 44 No. 1	1904	
Valse triste (from Kuolema), transcription (final version)	Op. 44 No. 1	1904	
Idyll in F major (amended version)	Op. 24 No. 6	1904	
Kyllikki (Three Lyric Pieces) I. *Largamente – Allegro* II. *Andantino* III. *Comodo*	Op. 41	1904	
Pelléas et Mélisande, concert suite, transcription I. At the Castle Gate II. Mélisande III. By a Spring in the Park IV. The Three Blind Sisters V. Pastorale VI. Mélisande at the Spinning Wheel VII. Entr'acte III. The Death of Mélisande	Op. 46	1905	
Livets dans; Dödens dans (Dance of Life; Dance of Death) (from Belshazzar's Feast), transcription	from JS 48	1906	

Piano Music	JS / Opus No.	Date	Text
Adagio in E major	JS 13	1907	
Belshazzar's Feast, concert suite, transcription I. Oriental Procession II. Solitude III. Nocturne IV. Khadra's Dance	Op. 51	1907	
Pan and Echo, transcription	Op. 53	1907	
Rêverie	Op. 58 No. 1	1909	
Scherzino	Op. 58 No. 2	1909	
Air varié	Op. 58 No. 3	1909	
Der Hirt (The Shepherd)	Op. 58 No. 4	1909	
Des Abends (The Evening)	Op. 58 No. 5	1909	
Dialogue	Op. 58 No. 6	1909	
Tempo di minuetto	Op. 58 No. 7	1909	
Fischerlied (Fisher Song)	Op. 58 No. 8	1909	
Ständchen (Serenade)	Op. 58 No. 9	1909	
Sommerlied (Summer Song)	Op. 58 No. 10	1909	
The Dryad, transcription	Op. 45 No. 1	1910	
Étude in A minor	Op. 76 No. 2	1911	
Sonatina No. 1 in F sharp minor I. *Allegro* II. *Largo* III. *Allegro moderato*	Op. 67 No. 1	1912	
Sonatina No. 2 in E major I. *Allegro* II. *Andantino* III. *Allegro*	Op. 67 No. 2	1912	
Sonatina No. 3 in B flat minor I. *Andante – Allegro moderato* II. *Andante – Allegro*	Op. 67 No. 3	1912	
Ballade (preliminary version of Aspen)	[Op. 75 No. 3]	1912 (?)	
Kallion kirkon kellosävel (The Bells of Kallio Church), transcription	Op. 65b	1912	
Rondino No. 1 in G sharp minor	Op. 68 No. 1	1912	
Rondino No. 2 in C sharp minor	Op. 68 No. 2	1912	
Valsette in E minor	Op. 40 No. 1	1912	
Chant sans paroles in E minor	Op. 40 No. 2	1913	
Humoresque in C major	Op. 40 No. 3	1913	
Berceuse in D major	Op. 40 No. 5	1913	

Piano Music	JS / Opus No.	Date	Text
Menuetto in C major	Op. 40 No. 4	1913	
Spagnuolo	JS 181	1913	
Rêverie in E minor	Op. 34 No. 6	1913	
Till trånaden (To Longing)	JS 202	1913	
Danse élégiaque and Scène d'amour (from Scaramouche), transcription	from Op. 71	1914	
Ekloge (Eclogue)	Op. 74 No. 1	1914	
Sanfter Westwind (Soft West Wind)	Op. 74 No. 2	1914	
Auf dem Tanzvergnügen (At the Dance)	Op. 74 No. 3	1914	
Im alten Heim (In the Old Home)	Op. 74 No. 4	1914	
När rönnan blommar (When the Rowan blossoms)	Op. 75 No. 1	1914	
Den ensamma furan (The Solitary Fir Tree)	Op. 75 No. 2	1914	
Aspen (The Aspen)	Op. 75 No. 3	1914	
Granen (The Spruce) (original version)	[Op. 75 No. 5]	1914	
Syringa (The Lilac)	[Op. 75 No. 6]	1914	
Björken (The Birch)	Op. 75 No. 4	1914	
Arabesque in D flat major	Op. 76 No. 9	1914	
Nouvellette in F major	Op. 94 No. 2	1914	
Romanzetta	Op. 76 No. 6	1914	
Valse in D flat major	Op. 34 No. 1	1914	
Air de danse in E major	Op. 34 No. 2	1914	
Mazurka in A major	Op. 34 No. 3	1914	
Carillon	Op. 76 No. 3	1914	
Pensée mélodique	Op. 40 No. 6	1914	
Couplet in D major (original version)	Op. 34 No. 4	1914	
Couplet in D major (final version)	Op. 34 No. 4	1914	
Capriccietto	Op. 76 No. 12	1914	
Rondoletto in A flat major	Op. 40 No. 7	1914	
Boutade in A flat major	Op. 34 No. 5	1914	
Scherzando in A flat major	Op. 40 No. 8	1915	
Petite sérénade in B flat major	Op. 40 No. 9	1915	
Iris (The Iris)	Op. 85 No. 3	1916	
Oeillet (The Carnation)	Op. 85 No. 2	1916	
Pièce enfantine	Op. 76 No. 8	1916	

Piano Music	JS / Opus No.	Date	Text
Harlequinade	Op. 76 No. 13	1916	
Humoresque in C sharp minor	Op. 76 No. 4	1916	
Elegiaco in C sharp minor	Op. 76 No. 10	1916	
Polonaise in C major	Op. 40 No. 10	1916	
Souvenir in A minor	Op. 34 No. 10	1916	
Danse pastorale in A major	Op. 34 No. 7	1916	
Reconnaissance in D major	Op. 34 No. 9	1916	
Joueur de harpe in B flat minor	Op. 34 No. 8	1916	
Esquisse	Op. 76 No. 1	1917	
Affettuoso	Op. 76 No. 7	1917	
Mandolinato	JS 123	1917	
Bellis (Bluebells)	Op. 85 No. 1	1917	
Aquileja (The Columbine)	Op. 85 No. 4	1917	
Campanula (The Campanula)	Op. 85 No. 5	1917	
Linnæa (The Twinflower of the North)	Op. 76 No. 11	1918	
Scout March Text written above the music	Op. 91b	1918	Jalmari Finne
Mélodie in B major	Op. 94 No. 5	1919	
Danse in C major	Op. 94 No. 1	1919	
Consolation in C sharp minor	Op. 76 No. 5	1919	
Andantino 'Till O. Parviainen' ('To O. Parviainen')	JS 201	1919	
Con passione	JS 53	1919	
Sonnet in B flat major	Op. 94 No. 3	1919	
Berger et bergerette	Op. 94 No. 4	1919	
Gavotte in C major	Op. 94 No. 6	1919	
Valse lyrique (preliminary version; combination of Syringa and Granen)		1919	
Granen (The Spruce) (revised version)	Op. 75 No. 5	1919	
Valse lyrique (final version)	Op. 96 No. 1	1919	
Humoreske I	Op. 97 No. 1	1920	
Lied (preliminary version)	Op. 97 No. 2	1920	
Kleiner Walzer (Little Waltz)	Op. 97 No. 3	1920	
Autrefois Text written above the music	Op. 96b	1920	Hjalmar Procopé
Humoristischer Marsch	Op. 97 No. 4	1920	
Impromptu (preliminary version)	Op. 97 No. 5	1920	

Piano Music	JS / Opus No.	Date	Text
Impromptu (final version)	Op. 97 No. 5	1920	
Humoreske II	Op. 97 No. 6	1920	
Suite mignonne, transcription I. Petite scène II. Polka III. Épilogue	Op. 98a	1921	
Valse chevaleresque	Op. 96c	1921–22	
Suite champêtre, transcription I. Pièce caractéristique II. Mélodie élégiaque III. Danse	Op. 98b	1922	
Pièce humoristique	Op. 99 No. 1	1922	
Esquisse	Op. 99 No. 2	1922	
Souvenir	Op. 99 No. 3	1922	
Impromptu	Op. 99 No. 4	1922	
Couplet	Op. 99 No. 5	1922	
Animoso	Op. 99 No. 6	1922	
Moment de valse	Op. 99 No. 7	1922	
Petite Marche	Op. 99 No. 8	1922	
Suite caractéristique, transcription I. *Vivo* II. *Lento* III. *Comodo*	Op. 100	1922	
Romance	Op. 101 No. 1	1924	
Chant du soir	Op. 101 No. 2	1924	
Scène lyrique	Op. 101 No. 3	1924	
Humoresque	Op. 101 No. 4	1924	
Scène romantique	Op. 101 No. 5	1924	
The Village Church	Op. 103 No. 1	1924	
The Fiddler	Op. 103 No. 2	1924	
The Oarsman	Op. 103 No. 3	1924	
The Storm	Op. 103 No. 4	1924	
In Mournful Mood	Op. 103 No. 5	1924	
Morceau romantique sur un motif **de M. Jakob de Julin**	JS 135b	1925	
Jedermann (Everyman): Episodio, Scena and Canzone, transcriptions	from Op. 83	1925	[Hugo von Hofmannsthal]
Ett ensamt skidspår (A Lonely Ski-Trail) *Piano & recitation*	JS 77a	1925	Bertel Gripenberg

Piano Music	JS / Opus No.	Date	Text
The Tempest: Episode (Miranda); Dance of the Nymphs; Scène, transcriptions	from Op. 109	1927	[William Shakespeare]
Maisema (Landscape)	Op. 114 No. 1	1929	
Talvikuva (Winter Scene)	Op. 114 No. 2	1929	
Metsälampi (Forest Lake)	Op. 114 No. 3	1929	
Metsälaulu (Song in the Forest)	Op. 114 No. 4	1929	
Kevätnäky (Spring Vision)	Op. 114 No. 5	1929	
Rakkaalle Ainolle (To My Beloved Aino) Piano 4 hands	JS 161	1931	

Songs
(all for voice and piano unless indicated otherwise)

Songs	JS / Opus No.	Date	Text
Serenad (Serenade)	JS 167	1888	J. L. Runeberg
Song from 'Näcken' (The Watersprite) *Soprano, violin, cello, piano & recitation*	JS 138	1888	Gunnar Wennerberg
En visa (A Song)	JS 71	1888	Baeckman
Då världar ännu skapade ej voro (When Worlds Still Uncreated Were) *Voice, cello (?) & piano – Fragment*	JS 56	1888	–
Solen slog himlen röd (The Sun Reddened the Sky) *Fragment*		1888	–
Orgier (Orgies)	JS 143	1888–89	Lars Stenbäck
Skogsrået (The Wood-Nymph)	JS 171	1888–89	Viktor Rydberg
Höstkväll (Autumn Evening) *Fragment*		1888–89	Viktor Rydberg
Jag kysser dig ej (I shall not kiss you) *Fragment*		1889–91	–
Hjärtats morgon (The Heart's Morning)	Op. 13 No. 3	1891	J. L. Runeberg
Likhet (Resemblance)	JS 120	1890	J. L. Runeberg
Löjet var utan hem (The smile was homeless) *Fragment*		1890–91	J. L. Runeberg
Drömmen (The Dream)	Op. 13 No. 5	1891	J. L. Runeberg
Flickan gick en vintermorgon [Arioso] (The Maiden Went One Winter Morning) *Fragment*		1890–92	J. L. Runeberg
Sov in! (Go to Sleep!)	Op. 17 No. 2	1891–92	Karl August Tavaststjerna

Songs	JS / Opus No.	Date	Text
Frihet (Freedom) *Fragment*		1891–92	K. A. Tavaststjerna
Drick, De förflyga de susande pärlorna (Drink, the fizzling pearls are flying away) *Fragment*		1891–92	Frans Michael Franzén
Fågellek (Play of the Birds)	Op. 17 No. 3	1891	K. A. Tavaststjerna
Våren flyktar hastigt (Spring is Flying)	Op. 13 No. 4	1891	J. L. Runeberg
Jägargossen (The Young Huntsman)	Op. 13 No. 7	1891	J. L. Runeberg
Se'n har jag ej frågat mera (Since then I have questioned no further)	Op. 17 No. 1	1891–92	J. L. Runeberg
Den första kyssen (The First Kiss) *Fragment*	JS 57	1891–92	J. L. Runeberg
Tule, tule kultani (Come, Come, My Sweetheart) *(folk-song arrangement)*	JS 211	1892	Traditional
Under strandens granar (Under the Fir-Trees)	Op. 13 No. 1	1892	J. L. Runeberg
Kyssens hopp (The Kiss's Hope)	Op. 13 No. 2	1892	J. L. Runeberg
Till Frigga (To Frigga)	Op. 13 No. 6	1892	J. L. Runeberg
Kullervos Wehruf (Kullervo's Lament)	from Op. 7	1892–93	Kalevala, trans. F. A. von Schiefner
Melodrama from 'Svartsjukans nätter' (Nights of Jealousy) *Soprano, violin, cello, piano & recitation*	JS 125	1893	J. L. Runeberg
Koskenlaskijan morsiamet (The Rapids-Rider's Brides) *Baritone (or mezzo-soprano) & piano*	Op. 33	1897–99	A. Oksanen
Det mörknar ute (Outside it is growing dark)	Op. 1 No. 3	1897	Zachris Topelius
Fool's Song of the Spider (from King Christian II)	Op. 27 No. 4	1898	Adolf Paul
Vilse (Astray)	Op. 17 No. 4	1898, rev. 1903	K. A. Tavaststjerna
Illalle (To Evening)	Op. 17 No. 6	1898	A. V. Forsman
Svarta rosor (Black Roses)	Op. 36 No. 1	1899	Ernst Josephson
Men min fågel märks dock icke (But my Bird is Long in Homing)	Op. 36 No. 2	1899	J. L. Runeberg
Bollspelet vid Trianon (Tennis at Trianon)	Op. 36 No. 3	1899	Gustaf Fröding
Segelfahrt (Sailing)	JS 166	1899	Johannes Öhqvist
Souda, souda, sinisorsa (Swim, Duck, Swim)	JS 180	1899	A. V. Forsman
Den första kyssen (The First Kiss)	Op. 37 No. 1	1900	J. L. Runeberg
Andantino in E flat minor [preliminary version of Säv, säv, susa]	JS 42	1900	[Gustaf Fröding]
Säv, säv, susa (Sigh, sigh, sedges)	Op. 36 No. 4	1900	Gustaf Fröding

Songs	JS / Opus No.	Date	Text
Marssnön (The March Snow)	Op. 36 No. 5	1900	J. J. Wecksell
Demanten på marssnön	Op. 36 No. 6	1900	J. J. Wecksell
Flickan kom ifrån sin älsklings möte (The Tryst)	Op. 37 No. 5	1901	J. L. Runeberg
On hanget korkeat, nietokset (High are the Snowdrifts)	Op. 1 No. 5	1901	Wilkku Joukahainen
Lasse liten (Little Lasse)	Op. 37 No. 2	1902	Zachris Topelius
[Song in G major] (Preliminary version of Soluppgång)	JS 87	1902	[Tor Hedberg]
Soluppgång (Sunrise)	Op. 37 No. 3	1902	Tor Hedberg
Var det en dröm? (Was it a Dream?)	Op. 37 No. 4	1902	J. J. Wecksell
Lastu lainehilla (Driftwood)	Op. 17 No. 7	1902	Ilmari Calamnius
Höstkväll (Autumn Evening)	Op. 38 No. 1	1903	Viktor Rydberg
På verandan vid havet (On a Balcony by the Sea)	Op. 38 No. 2	1903	Viktor Rydberg
I natten (In the Night)	Op. 38 No. 3	1903	Viktor Rydberg
Harpolekaren och hans son (The Harper and his Son)	Op. 38 No. 4	1904	Viktor Rydberg
Jag ville, jag vore i Indialand (I wish I were in India)	Op. 38 No. 5	1904	Gustaf Fröding
En slända (A Dragonfly)	Op. 17 No. 5	1904	Oscar Levertin
Romans (Romance) *Fragment*		1905	K. A. Tavaststjerna
Les trois sœurs aveugles (The Three Blind Sisters) (from Pelléas et Mélisande)	Op. 46 No. 4	1905	Maurice Mæterlinck
Lenzgesang (Spring Song)	Op. 50 No. 1	1906	Arthur Fitger
Sehnsucht (Longing)	Op. 50 No. 2	1906	Emil Rudolf Weiss
Im Feld ein Mädchen singt (In the Field a Maid Sings)	Op. 50 No. 3	1906	Margareta Susman
Aus banger Brust (From Anxious Heart)	Op. 50 No. 4	1906	Richard Dehmel
Die stille Stadt (The Silent City)	Op. 50 No. 5	1906	Richard Dehmel
Rosenlied (Song of the Roses)	Op. 50 No. 6	1906	Anna Ritter
Erloschen (Extinguished)	JS 73	1906	Georg Busse-Palma
Judeflickans sång (The Jewish Girl's Song) (from Belshazzar's Feast) (first version)	Op. 48 No. 2b	1907	Hjalmar Procopé
Hundra vägar (A Hundred Ways)	Op. 72 No. 6	1907	J. L. Runeberg
Jubal	Op. 35 No. 1	1908	Ernst Josephson
Teodora	Op. 35 No. 2	1908	Ernst Josephson
Och skulle ditt hjärta jag fångat (And if I had captured your heart) *Fragment*		1908–10	–

Songs	JS / Opus No.	Date	Text
Älven och snigeln (The River and the Snail)	Op. 57 No. 1	1909	Ernst Josephson
En blomma stod vid vägen (A Flower stood by the Wayside)	Op. 57 No. 2	1909	Ernst Josephson
Kvarnhjulet (The Mill-wheel)	Op. 57 No. 3	1909	Ernst Josephson
Maj (May)	Op. 57 No. 4	1909	Ernst Josephson
Jag är ett träd (The Tree)	Op. 57 No. 5	1909	Ernst Josephson
Hertig Magnus (Duke Magnus)	Op. 57 No. 6	1909	Ernst Josephson
Vänskapens blomma (The Flower of Friendship) (preliminary version)	JS 215	1909	Ernst Josephson
Vänskapens blomma (The Flower of Friendship) (final version)	Op. 57 No. 7	1909	Ernst Josephson
Näcken (The Watersprite)	Op. 57 No. 8	1909	Ernst Josephson
Hymn to Thaïs (original version)	JS 97	1909	Arthur Borgström
Kom nu hit, död (Come Away, Death) (from Twelfth Night) (original version) *Voice & guitar*	Op. 60 No. 1	1909	William Shakespeare, trans. C.A. Hagberg
Hållilå, uti storm och i regn (Hey, ho, the Wind and the Rain) (from Twelfth Night) (original version) *Voice & guitar*	Op. 60 No. 2	1909	William Shakespeare, trans. Hagberg
Giv mig ej glans, ej guld, ej prakt (Give me no Splendour, Gold or Pomp)	Op. 1 No. 4	1909	Zachris Topelius
Kom nu hit, död (Come Away, Death) (from Twelfth Night) (revised version)	Op. 60 No. 1	1909	William Shakespeare, trans. Hagberg
Hållilå, uti storm och i regn (Hey, ho, the Wind and the Rain) (from Twelfth Night) (revised version)	Op. 60 No. 2	1909	William Shakespeare, trans. Hagberg
Långsamt som kvällskyn (Slowly as the Evening Sky)	Op. 61 No. 1	1910	K.A. Tavaststjerna
Vattenplask (Lapping Waters)	Op. 61 No. 2	1910	Viktor Rydberg
När jag drömmer (When I dream)	Op. 61 No. 3	1910	K.A. Tavaststjerna
Romeo	Op. 61 No. 4	1910	K.A. Tavaststjerna
Romans (Romance)	Op. 61 No. 5	1910	K.A. Tavaststjerna
Dolce far niente	Op. 61 No. 6	1910	K.A. Tavaststjerna
Fåfäng önskan (Idle Wishes)	Op. 61 No. 7	1910	J.L. Runeberg
Vårtagen (The Spell of Springtide)	Op. 61 No. 8	1910	Bertel Gripenberg
Arioso	Op. 3	1911	J.L. Runeberg
Nu står jul vid snöig port (Now Christmas stands at the snowy gate)	Op. 1 No. 1	1913	Zachris Topelius

Songs	JS / Opus No.	Date	Text
Nu så kommer julen (Now is Christmas coming)	Op. 1 No. 2	1913	Zachris Topelius
Luonnotar, transcription *Soprano & piano*	Op. 70	1913	Kalevala
Vi ses igen (Farewell) *Lost*	Op. 72 No. 1	1914	Viktor Rydberg
Orions bälte (Orion's Girdle) *Lost*	Op. 72 No. 2	1914	Zachris Topelius
Kyssen (The Kiss)	Op. 72 No. 3	1915	Viktor Rydberg
Kaiutar (The Echo Nymph)	Op. 72 No. 4	1915	Larin Kyösti
Tanken (The Thought) *2 voices & piano*	JS 192	1915	J. L. Runeberg
Tre trallande jäntor (Three Warbling Maidens) *Lost*	JS 204	1915	Gustaf Fröding
Der Wanderer und der Bach (The Wanderer and the Brook)	Op. 72 No. 5	1915	Martin Greif
Vårförnimmelser (The Coming of Spring)	Op. 86 No. 1	1916	K. A. Tavaststjerna
Längtan heter min arvedel (Longing is my Heritage)	Op. 86 No. 2	1916	Erik Axel Karlfeldt
Dold förening (Hidden Union)	Op. 86 No. 3	1916	Carl Snoilsky
Och finns det en tanke? (And Is There a Thought?)	Op. 86 No. 4	1916	K. A. Tavaststjerna
Sångarlön (The Singer's Reward)	Op. 86 No. 5	1916	Carl Snoilsky
Blåsippan (The Blue Anemone)	Op. 88 No. 1	1917	F. M. Franzén
De bägge rosorna (The Two Roses)	Op. 88 No. 2	1917	F. M. Franzén
Vitsippan (The White Anemone)	Op. 88 No. 3	1917	F. M. Franzén
Sippan (The Anemone)	Op. 88 No. 4	1917	J. L. Runeberg
Törnet (The Thorn)	Op. 88 No. 5	1917	J. L. Runeberg
Blommans öde (The Flower's Destiny)	Op. 88 No. 6	1917	J. L. Runeberg
I systrar, I bröder, I älskande par (Ye Sisters, Ye Brothers, Ye Loving Couples)	Op. 86 No. 6	1917	Mikael Lybeck
Morgonen (The Morning)	Op. 90 No. 3	1917	J. L. Runeberg
Sommarnatten (Summer Night)	Op. 90 No. 5	1917	J. L. Runeberg
Norden (The North)	Op. 90 No. 1	1917	J. L. Runeberg
Fågelfängarn (The Bird Catcher)	Op. 90 No. 4	1917	J. L. Runeberg
Vem styrde hit din väg? (Who Brought You Hither?)	Op. 90 No. 6	1917	J. L. Runeberg
Hennes budskap (Her Message)	Op. 90 No. 2	1917	J. L. Runeberg
Kullervon valitus (Kullervo's Lament)	from Op. 7	1917–18	Kalevala

Songs	JS / Opus No.	Date	Text
Mummon syntymäpäivänä (Birthday Song to Grandmother)	JS 136	1919	probably by a member of the Sibelius family
Pastorale (middle section of Autrefois; preliminary version) *2 sopranos & piano*	from Op. 96b	1919	Hjalmar Procopé
Autrefois *2 sopranos & piano*	Op. 96b	1920	Hjalmar Procopé
Små flickorna (Young Girls)	JS 174	1920	Hjalmar Procopé
Narciss (Narcissus)	JS 140	1925	Bertel Gripenberg
Siltavahti (The Guardian of the Bridge)	JS 170b	1928	Wäinö Sola
Den judiska flickans sång (The Jewish Girl's Song) (from Belshazzar's Feast) (second version)	JS 48 No. 2b	1939	Hjalmar Procopé
Hymn to Thaïs (revised version)	JS 97	1945–48	Arthur Borgström

Choral music a cappella

(or with piano/harmonium)

Choral Music	JS / Opus No.	Date	Text
Credo in unum Deum *Mixed choir a cappella*		1887	–
Allt hvad anda hafver (All that has breath) (version I) *Mixed choir a cappella*		1888	–
Allt hvad anda hafver (All that has breath) (version II) *Mixed choir a cappella*		1888	–
Gloria Deo in excelsis (Version I) *Mixed choir a cappella*		1888	–
Gloria Deo in excelsis (Version II) *Mixed choir a cappella*		1888	–
Kyrie eleison *Mixed choir a cappella*		1888	–
Säll är den som fruktar Herren (Blessed is he who fears the Lord) *Mixed choir a cappella*		1888	–
Morgonens och aftonens portar (The Gates of Morning and Evening) *Mixed choir a cappella*		1888	–
Svara mig Gud när jag ropar (Answer me, God, when I call) *Mixed choir a cappella*		1888	–
Ensam i dunkla skogarnas famn (Alone in the Depths of the Forests) *Mixed choir a cappella*	JS 72	1888	Emil von Qvanten

Choral Music	JS / Opus No.	Date	Text
När sig våren åter föder [Blomman] (When Spring Once More Comes to Life) *Mixed choir a cappella*	JS 139	1888	J.L. Runeberg
Tanke, se hur fågeln svingar (Imagine, See how the Bird Swoops) *Mixed choir a cappella*	JS 191	1888	J.L. Runeberg
Hur blekt är allt [Höstkvällen] (How Pale is All) *Mixed choir a cappella*	JS 96	1888	J.L. Runeberg
Upp genom luften [Kör av vindarna] (Up through the Air) *Mixed choir & piano*	JS 213	1888	Per Daniel Atterbom
Ack, hör du fröken Gyllenborg [Ballad] (Ah, Do You Hear, Miss Gyllenborg) *Mixed choir a cappella*	JS 10	1888–89	Ballad from Pernaja
Der König träumte (The King Dreamed) *Mixed choir a cappella*		1889–90	–
Der Mensch ist in seinem Leben wie Gras (Man is in his life like grass) *Mixed choir a cappella*		1889–90	–
Die Todten werden dich Herr nicht loben (The dead will not praise you, Lord) *Mixed choir a cappella*		1889–90	–
Die Wasser sahen dich (The Waters saw you) *Mixed choir a cappella – Fragment*		1889–90	–
Er ist unser Herrscher (He is our Lord) *Mixed choir a cappella*		1889–90	–
Gelobet sei dem Herrn (Praise be to the Lord) *Mixed choir a cappella*		1889–90	–
Halleluja Halleluja *Mixed choir a cappella*		1889–90	–
Halleluja Amen *Mixed choir a cappella*		1889–90	–
Herr Gott mein Heiland (Lord God my Saviour) *Mixed choir a cappell*		1889–90	–
Ich gehe hinein zum Altar des Gottes (I go in to the altar of God) *Mixed choir a cappella*		1889–90	–
Ich will deines Namens gedenken (I will remember Your name) *Mixed choir a cappella*		1889–90	–
Mein Herr ich rufe dich an (My Lord, I call to you) *Mixed choir a cappella*		1889–90	–
Sei mir gnädig (Be merciful to me) *Mixed choir a cappella*		1889–90	–
Sende dein Licht und deine Wahrheit (Send Your light and Your truth) *Mixed choir a cappella*		1889–90	–
Tag des Herren (Day of the Lord) *Mixed choir a cappella*		1889–90	–

Choral Music	JS / Opus No.	Date	Text
Was betrübst du dich meine Seele (Why are you troubled, my soul?) *Mixed choir a cappella*		1889–90	–
Vi kysser du fader min fästmö här? [Sonens brud] (Why Kiss You, Father, My Sweetheart Here?) *Mixed choir & piano*	JS 218	1889–90	J. L. Runeberg
Kullervo (movements III & V) *Baritone, mezzo-soprano, male choir & piano* III. Kullervo and his Sister. *Allegro vivace* V. Kullervo's Death. *Andante*	from Op. 7	1892	Kalevala
Venematka (The Boat Journey) *Male choir a cappella*	Op. 18 No. 3	1893	Kalevala
Heitä, koski, kuohuminen (Rapids, Cease Your Foaming) *Male choir a cappella – Completed by Erik Bergman and Erik Tawaststjerna*	JS 94	1893	Kalevala
Työkansan marssi (Workers' March) *Mixed choir a cappella*	JS 212	1893	Juhana Henrik Erkko
Soitapas sorea neito (Play, Pretty Maiden) *Tenor & mixed choir*	JS 176	1893–94	Kanteletar
Rakastava (The Lover) *Tenor & male choir*	JS 160a	1894	Kanteletar
Saarella palaa (Fire on the Island) *Male choir a cappella*	Op. 18 No. 4	1895	Kanteletar
Laulun mahti (The Power of Song) (arrangement of song by Jāzeps Vītols) *Tenor & male choir*	JS 118	1895	Aukselis, trans. J. J. Mikkola
Natus in curas [Hymn] (original version) *Male choir a cappella*	Op. 21	1896	Fridolf Gustafsson
Juhlamarssi (Festive March) (from the Promotional Cantata of 1894) *Mixed choir a cappella*	from JS 105	1896	Kasimir Lönnbohm
Italian Folk-songs (Ohi, 'Caroli'!; Trippole Trappole) *Mixed choir & (unknown) accompaniment – Only choral part survives*	JS 99	1897–98	Traditional
Me nuoriso Suomen (We the Youth of Finland) (from the University Cantata of 1897) *Mixed choir a cappella*	Op. 23 No. 1	1897–98	A. V. Forsman
Tuuli tuudittele (The wind rocks) (from the University Cantata of 1897) *Soprano, baritone & mixed choir*	Op. 23 No. 2	1897–98	A. V. Forsman
Oi toivo, toivo, sä lietomieli (Oh Hope, Hope, You Dreamer) (from the University Cantata of 1897) *Soprano & mixed choir*	Op. 23 No. 3	1897–98	A. V. Forsman
Montapa elon merellä (Many on the Sea of Life) (from the University Cantata of 1897) *Mixed choir a cappella*	Op. 23 No. 4	1897–98	A. V. Forsman
Sammuva sainio maan (The Fading Thoughts of the Earth) (from the University Cantata of 1897) *Mixed choir a cappella*	Op. 23 No. 5	1897–98	A. V. Forsman

Choral Music	JS / Opus No.	Date	Text
Soi kiitokseksi Luojan (We praise Thee, our Creator) (from the University Cantata of 1897) *Mixed choir a cappella*	Op. 23 No. 6a	1897–98	A.V. Forsman
Tuule, tuuli, leppeämmin (Blow, Wind, More Gently) (from the University Cantata of 1897) *Soprano & mixed choir*	Op. 23 No. 6b	1897–98	A.V. Forsman
Oi Lempi, sun valtas ääretön on (O Love, Your Realm is Limitless) (from the University Cantata of 1897) *Mixed choir a cappella*	Op. 23 No. 7	1897–98	A.V. Forsman
Kun virta vuolas (As the Swift Current) (from the University Cantata of 1897) *Mixed choir and percussion*	Op. 23 No. 8	1897–98	A.V. Forsman
Oi kallis Suomi, äiti verraton (O Precious Finland, Mother Beyond Compare) (from the University Cantata of 1897) *Mixed choir a cappella*	Op. 23 No. 9	1897–98	A.V. Forsman
Kuutamolla (In the Moonlight) *Male choir a cappella*	JS 114	1898	Aino Suonio
Carminalia (version A) *Three-part mixed choir (SAB) a cappella* I. Ecce novum gaudium II. Angelus emittitur III. In stadio laboris	JS 51a	1898	Anonymous
Carminalia (version B) *Two-part choir (SA) & organ (harmonium)* I. Ecce novum gaudium II. Angelus emittitur III. In stadio laboris	JS 51b	1898	Anonymous
Carminalia (version C) *Two-part choir (SA) & piano* I. Ecce novum gaudium II. Angelus emittitur III. In stadio laboris	JS 51c	1898	Anonymous
Sandels (original version), transcription *Male choir & piano*	Op. 28	1898	J.L. Runeberg
Natus in curas [Hymn] (final version) *Male choir a cappella*	Op. 21	1898	Fridolf Gustafsson
Sydämeni laulu (Song of my Heart) *Male choir a cappella*	Op. 18 No. 6	1898	Aleksis Kivi
Rakastava (The Lover) *Soprano, baritone & mixed choir*	JS 160c	1898	Kanteletar
Saarella palaa (Fire on the Island) *Mixed choir a cappella*	Op. 18 No. 4	1898	Kanteletar
Sortunut ääni (The Broken Voice) *Male choir a cappella*	Op. 18 No. 1	1898–99	Kanteletar
Sortunut ääni (The Broken Voice) *Mixed choir a cappella*	Op. 18 No. 1	1898–99	Kanteletar

Choral Music	JS / Opus No.	Date	Text
Min rastas raataa (Busy as a Thrush) *Mixed choir a cappella*	JS 129	1898	Kanteletar
Aamusumussa (In the Morning Mist) *Mixed choir a cappella*	JS 9a	1898	J. H. Erkko
Isänmaalle (To the Fatherland) (original version) *Male choir a cappella*	JS 98	1899	Paavo Cajander
Athenarnes sång (Song of the Athenians) *Boys' & men's voices a cappella*	Op. 31 No. 3	1899	Viktor Rydberg
Athenarnes sång (Song of the Athenians) *Boys' & men's voices, piano*	Op. 31 No. 3	1899	Viktor Rydberg
Athenarnes sång (Song of the Athenians) *Boys' & men's voices, piano & harmonium (ad lib.)*	Op. 31 No. 3	1899	Viktor Rydberg
Metsämiehen laulu (The Woodsman's Song) *Male choir a cappella*	Op. 18 No. 5	1899	Aleksis Kivi
Isänmaalle (To the Fatherland) (final version) *Mixed choir a cappella*	JS 98a	1900	Paavo Cajander
Terve, kuu (Hail, Moon) *Male choir a cappella*	Op. 18 No. 2	1901	Kalevala
Impromptu (original version), transcription *Female choir & piano*	Op. 19	1902	Viktor Rydberg
Kotikaipaus (Homesickness) *3 female voices*	JS 111	1902	Walter von Konow
Den 25 oktober 1902. Till Thérèse Hahl (I) (25th October 1902. To Thérèse Hahl [I]) *Mixed choir a cappella*	JS 60	1902	Nils Wasastjerna
Den 25 oktober 1902. Till Thérèse Hahl (II) (25th October 1902. To Thérèse Hahl [II]) *Mixed choir a cappella*	JS 61	1902	Nils Wasastjerna
Har du mod? (Have You Courage?) (preliminary version) *Male choir a cappella*	JS 93	1903–04	J. J. Wecksell
Veljeni vierailla mailla (My Brothers Abroad) *Male choir a cappella*	JS 217	1904	Juhani Aho
Sydämeni laulu (Song of my Heart) *Mixed choir a cappella*	Op. 18 No. 6	1904	Aleksis Kivi
On hanget korkeat, nietokset (High are the Snowdrifts) *2 voices & piano*	Op. 1 No. 5	1903–05	Wilkku Joukahainen
Ej med klagan (Not with Lamentation) *Mixed choir a cappella*	JS 69	1905	J. L. Runeberg
Listen to the Water Mill *Mixed choir a cappella – Fragment*	JS 122	1905–06	Sarah Doudney
Isänmaalle (To the Fatherland) (final version) *Male choir a cappella*	JS 98b	1908	Paavo Cajander
Impromptu (final version), transcription *Female choir & piano*	Op. 19	1910	Viktor Rydberg

Choral Music	JS / Opus No.	Date	Text
Kansakoululaisten marssi (March of the Primary School Children) *Mixed choir a cappella*	JS 103	1910	'Onnen Pekka'
Tulen synty (The Origin of Fire) (final version), transcription *Baritone, male choir & piano*	Op. 32	1910	Kalevala
Kantat till ord av W. von Konow (Cantata to words by W. von Konow) *Female choir a cappella*	JS 107	1911	Walter von Konow
Män från slätten och havet (Men from Land and Sea) *Mixed choir a cappella*	Op. 65a	1911	Ernst V. Knape
Har du mod? (Have You Courage?) (second version), transcription *Male choir & piano*	Op. 31 No. 2	1911	J. J. Wecksell
Uusmaalaisten laulu (Song of the People of Uusimaa) *Mixed choir a cappella*	JS 214a	1912	Kaarlo Terhi
Uusmaalaisten laulu (Song of the People of Uusimaa) *Male choir a cappella*	JS 214b	1912	Kaarlo Terhi
Har du mod? (Have You Courage?) (fourth version) *Male choir & piano*	Op. 31 No. 2	1912	J. J. Wecksell
Kallion kirkon kellosävel (The Bells of Kallio Church) *Mixed choir a cappella*	Op. 65b	1912	Heikki Klemetti
Soi kiitokseksi Luojan (We praise Thee, our Creator) (from the University Cantata of 1897) *Female/children's choir a cappella*	Op. 23 No. 6a	1913	A. V. Forsman
Nejden andas (from Islossningen i Uleå älv) *Female/children's choir a cappella*	from Op. 30	1913	Zachris Topelius
Aamusumussa (In the Morning Mist) *Female/children's choir a cappella*	JS 9b	1913	J. H. Erkko
Terve ruhtinatar (Hail Princess) (from Coronation Cantata) *Female/children's choir a cappella*	from JS 104	1913	Paavo Cajander
Autumn Song (No. 1 of Three Songs for American Schools) *Soprano, alto & piano*	JS 199 No. 1	1913	Richard Watson Dixon
The Sun upon the Lake is Low (No. 2 of Three Songs for American Schools) *Mixed choir a cappella*	JS 199 No. 2	1913	Sir Walter Scott
A Cavalry Catch (No. 3 of Three Songs for American Schools) *Male voices (unison) & piano*	JS 199 No. 3	1913	Fiona MacLeod
Herr Lager och Skön fager (Mr Lager and the Fair One) *Male choir a cappella*	Op. 84 No. 1	1914	Gustaf Fröding
Venematka (The Boat Journey) *Mixed choir a cappella*	Op. 18 No. 3	1914	Kalevala

Choral Music	JS / Opus No.	Date	Text
På berget (On the Mountain) *Male choir a cappella*	Op. 84 No. 2	1915	Bertel Gripenberg
Ett drömackord (A Dream Chord) *Male choir a cappella*	Op. 84 No. 3	1915	Gustaf Fröding
Evige Eros (Eternal Eros) *Baritone & male choir*	Op. 84 No. 4	1915	Bertel Gripenberg
Till havs (To Sea) (preliminary version) *Male choir a cappella*	[Op. 84 No. 5]	1917	Jonatan Reuter
Till havs (To Sea) (published version) *Male choir a cappella*	Op. 84 No. 5	1917	Jonatan Reuter
Drömmarna (The Dreams) *Mixed choir a cappella*	JS 64	1917	Jonatan Reuter
Fridolins dårskap (Fridolin's Folly) *Male choir a cappella*	JS 84	1917	E. A. Karlfeldt
March of the Finnish Jäger Battalion *Male choir & piano*	Op. 91a	1917	Heikki Nurmio
Ute hörs stormen (Outside the Storm is Raging) *Male choir a cappella*	JS 224 No. 1	1918	Gösta Schybergson
Brusande rusar en våg (The Roaring of a Wave) *Male choir a cappella*	JS 224 No. 2	1918	Gösta Schybergson
Jone havsfärd (Jonah's Voyage) *Male choir a cappella*	JS 100	1918	E. A. Karlfeldt
Viipurin Laulu-Veikkojen (W.S.B:n) kunniamarssi (Honour March of the Singing Brothers of Viipuri [W.S.B.]) *Male choir a cappella*	JS 219	1920	Eero Eerola
Scout March Mixed choir & piano	Op. 91b	1921	Jalmari Finne
Likhet (Resemblance) *Male choir a cappella*	JS 121	1922	J. L. Runeberg
Koulutie (The Way to School) *Mixed choir a cappella*	JS 112	1924	Veikko Antero Koskenniemi
Humoreski (Humoresque) *Male choir a cappella*	Op. 108 No. 1	1925	Larin Kyösti
Ne pitkän matkan kulkijat (Wanderers on the Long Way) *Male choir a cappella*	Op. 108 No. 2	1925	Larin Kyösti
Skyddskårsmarsch (Skyddskår's March) *Male choir & piano ad lib.*	JS 173	1925	Nino Runeberg
Skolsång (School Song) *Mixed choir a cappella*	JS 172	1925	Nino Runeberg
Den höga himlen (The Lofty Heaven) *Mixed choir a cappella*	JS 58a	1927	Simi Korpela, trans. Jacob Tegengren

Choral Music	JS / Opus No.	Date	Text
Siltavahti (The Guardian of the Bridge) *Male choir a cappella*	JS 170a	1928	Wäinö Sola
On lapsonen syntynyt meille (A Child is Born to us) *Mixed choir a cappella*	JS 142	1929	August Verner Jaakkola
Viipurin Laulu-Veikkojen kunniamarssi (Honour March of the Singing Brothers of Viipuri) *Male choir a cappella*	JS 220	1929	Eero Eerola
Karjalan osa (Karelia's Fate) *Male choir & piano*	JS 108	1930	Aleksi Nurminen
En etsi valtaa, loistoa (Give me no Splendour, Gold or Pomp) *Male choir a cappella*	Op. 1 No. 4	1935	Zachris Topelius, trans. ?
Finlandia Hymn *Male choir a cappella*	from Op. 26	1938	Wäinö Sola
Finlandia Hymn *Male choir a cappella*	from Op. 26	1940	V. A. Koskenniemi
En etsi valtaa, loistoa (Give me no Splendour, Gold or Pomp) *Voice & female choir*	Op. 1 No. 4	1942	Zachris Topelius, trans. ?
En etsi valtaa, loistoa (Give me no Splendour, Gold or Pomp) *2 female voices*	Op. 1 No. 4	1942	Zachris Topelius, trans. ?
On hanget korkeat, nietokset (High are the Snowdrifts) *2 female voices*	Op. 1 No. 5	1942	Wilkku Joukahainen
Finlandia Hymn (version in F major) *Mixed choir a cappella*	from Op. 26	1948	V. A. Koskenniemi
Finlandia Hymn (version in A flat major) *Mixed choir a cappella*	from Op. 26	1948	V. A. Koskenniemi
The World Song of the World Association of Girl Scouts and Girl Guides (Scout March) *Female choir & piano*	Op. 91b	1952	Gavin Ewart
Giv mig ej glans, ej guld, ej prakt (Give me no Splendour, Gold or Pomp) *Children's choir & organ*	Op. 1 No. 4	1954	Zachris Topelius

Miscellaneous Works

Miscellaneous Works	JS / Opus No.	Date	Text
Overture in F minor *Brass ensemble*	JS 146	1889	
Allegro *Brass ensemble*	JS 25	1889	

Miscellaneous Works	JS / Opus No.	Date	Text
Andantino and Minuet *Brass ensemble*	JS 45	1890–91	
Zirkusmarsch (Circus March) *Scoring unknown – Lost*	JS 223	1891	
Förspel (Prelude) *Brass ensemble*	JS 83	1891	
Jungfrun i tornet (The Maiden in the Tower), opera in one act *Soprano, alto, tenor, baritone, mixed choir & orchestra*	JS 101	1896	Rafael Hertzberg
Athenarnes sång (Song of the Athenians) *Boys' & men's voices, brass ensemble*	Op. 31 No. 3	1899	Viktor Rydberg
Tiera *Brass ensemble & percussion*	JS 200	1899	
March [preliminary version of Scout March] *Brass ensemble & percussion – Percussion part incomplete*		1879–99	
Kallion kirkon kellosävel (The Bells of Kallio Church) *Church bells*	Op. 65b	1912	
Herran siunaus (God's Blessing) *Organ – Text written above the music*	JS 95	1925	Numbers 6, verses 24–26
Palmusunnuntaina (On Palm Sunday) (No. 1 of Three Introductory Antiphons) *Liturgist (baritone), congregation & organ*	JS 110 No. 1	1925	from Psalms 23, 111 & 42
Pyhäinpäivänä tai hautajaisjumalanpalveluksissa (On All Saints' Day) (No. 2 of Three Introductory Antiphons) *Liturgist (baritone), congregation & organ*	JS 110 No. 2	1925	from Revelations 14 & Psalm 126
Kristillisissä nuorisojuhlissa (General Prayers) (No. 3 of Three Introductory Antiphons) *Liturgist (baritone), congregation & organ*	JS 110 No. 3	1925	from Ecclesiastes 12 & Gloria
Intrada *Organ*	Op. 111a	1925	
Preludium *Organ*	JS 153 No. 1	1926	
Postludium *Organ*	JS 153 No. 2	1926	
Avaushymni (Opening Hymn) (No. 1 of Musique religieuse; original version) *Harmonium*	Op. 113 No. 1	1927	
Suloinen aate (Thoughts be our Comfort) (No. 2 of Musique religieuse; original version) *Tenor & harmonium*	Op. 113 No. 2	1927	Franz von Schober, trans. Eino Leino
Kulkue ja hymni: Näätkö kuinka hennon yrtin (Procession and Hymn: Though Young Leaves Be Green) (No. 3 of Musique religieuse; original version) *Tenor & harmonium*	Op. 113 No. 3	1927	Pao Chao, (Bao Zhao), trans. Eino Tikkanen

Miscellaneous Works	JS / Opus No.	Date	Text
Kulkue ja hymni: Ken kyynelin (Procession and Hymn: Who Ne'er Hath Blent His Bread with Tears) (No. 4 of Musique religieuse; original version) *Tenor & harmonium*	Op. 113 No. 4	1927	Johann Wolfgang von Goethe, trans. Eino Leino
On kaunis maa (How Fair Are Earth and Living) (No. 5 of Musique religieuse; original version) *Tenor & harmonium*	Op. 113 No. 5	1927	Aukusti Simelius
Salem (No. 6 of Musique religieuse; original version) *Tenor & harmonium*	Op. 113 No. 6	1927	Viktor Rydberg
Varje själ, som längtan brinner (Whosoever Hath a Love) (No. 7 of Musique religieuse; original version) *Tenor & harmonium*	Op. 113 No. 7	1927	Viktor Rydberg
Marche funèbre (Funeral March) (No. 10 of Musique religieuse; original version) *Harmonium*	Op. 113 No. 10	1927	
Surusoitto (Funeral Music) *Organ*	Op. 111b	1931	
Theme for improvisation *Organ*		1933	
Suur' olet, Herra (You are Mighty, O Lord) *Male vocal quartet & organ*	JS 58b	1945	Simo Korpela
Veljesvirsi (Ode to Fraternity) (No. 8 of Musique religieuse) *Male choir & harmonium*	Op. 113 No. 8	1946	Samuli Sario
Ylistyshymni (Hymn) (No. 9 of Musique religieuse) *Tenor, male choir & harmonium*	Op. 113 No. 9	1946	Samuli Sario
Avaushymni (Opening Hymn) (No. 1 of Musique religieuse; revised version) *Organ*	Op. 113 No. 1	1948	
Salem (No. 6 of Musique religieuse; revised version) *Tenor & organ*	Op. 113 No. 6	1948	Viktor Rydberg
Marche funèbre (Funeral March) (No. 10 of Musique religieuse; revised version) *Organ*	Op. 113 No. 10	1948	

In 1950 Sibelius undertook further small revisions to the Musique religieuse, Op. 113.

A lost work provisionally named *The American Millers' Song* (JS 29) is mentioned in several of Sibelius's own work lists but no further details about the piece are known. Similarly, nothing is known of a lost work named *Snöfallet* (*The Snowfall*, JS 175) except that was composed for Jacob von Julin in September 1927.

APPENDIX III

SELECT BIBLIOGRAPHY

Reference works

Clark, Edward: *Sibelius Reflections*, United Kingdom Sibelius Society, London 2006

Dahlström, Fabian (ed.): *Jean Sibelius – Dagbok 1909–1944*, Svenska litteratursällskapet i Finland 2005

Dahlström, Fabian: *Jean Sibelius: Thematisch-bibliographisches Verzeichnis seiner Werke*. Including the JS-catalogue of works without opus numbers, Breitkopf & Härtel 2003

Ekman, Karl: *Jean Sibelius, en konstnärs liv och personlighet* (1935) (translated by Edward Birse as *Jean Sibelius, his Life and Personality*), Tudor Publishing Co., New York 1938

Furuhjelm, Erik Gustav: *Jean Sibelius. Hans tondiktning och drag ur hans liv*, Porvoo 1916

Goss, Glenda Dawn (ed.): *Jean Sibelius – The Hämeenlinna Letters*, Schildts förlag, Espoo 1996

Goss, Glenda Dawn (ed.): *The Sibelius Companion*, Greenwood Press, Connecticut 1996

Gräsbeck, Folke: notes for BIS recordings of Sibelius's music for piano (BIS–CD–1067, 1202 & 1272), violin and piano (BIS–CD–1022 & 1023), piano trio (BIS–CD–1292 & 1292) and piano quartet (BIS–CD–1182), BIS Records, Åkersberga 1999–2006

Gray, Cecil: *Sibelius*, Oxford University Press 1931

Jackson, Timothy L. and Murtomäki, Veijo (ed.): *Sibelius Studies*, Cambridge University Press 2001

Keane: Robert *The Complete Solo Songs of Jean Sibelius*, University of London 1993

Kilpeläinen, Kari: *The Jean Sibelius Musical Manuscripts at Helsinki University Library*, HUL / Breitkopf & Härtel 1991

Koskimies, Yrjö S.: *Janne Sibelius and his home town Hämeenlinna*, Hämeenlinna Sibelius Society 1990

Kurki, Eija: *Satua, kuolemaa ja eksotiikkaaa*, Helsinki 1997

Layton, Robert: *Sibelius*, Master Musicians Series, J.M.Dent & Sons, London 1965/78

Levas, Santeri: *Jean Sibelius, A Personal Portrait*, trans. Percy M.Young, J.M.Dent & Sons, London / WSOY, Porvoo/Juva 1972

Miettunen, Harri: *Finlandia*, article published in programmes of the Tampere Philharmonic Orchestra, on www.jeansibelius.net and in the United Kingdom Sibelius Society Newsletter No. 59 (2006). Translation: Jaakko Mäntyjärvi

Newmarch, Rosa: *Jean Sibelius, A Short Story of a Long Friendship*, Goodwin & Tabb, Boston 1939/London 1945

Rickards, Guy: *Sibelius*, Phaidon Press, London 1997

Sirén, Vesa: *Aina poltti sikaria*, Otava, Keuruu 2000

Talas, SuviSirkku (ed): *Sydämen aamu (The Heart's Morning)*: Letters from the engagement of Aino Järnefelt and Jean Sibelius, Suomalaisen Kirjallisuuden Seura (Finnish Literature Society), Helsinki 2001

Talas, SuviSirkku (ed): *Tulen synty* (*The Origin of Fire*): Aino and Jean Sibelius's correspondence, 1892–1904, Suomalaisen Kirjallisuuden Seura (Finnish Literature Society), Helsinki 2003

Tawaststjerna, Erik: *Sibelius*, Volumes 1–3 (translated by Robert Layton), Faber & Faber, London 1976/1986/1997

von Törne, Bengt: *Sibelius: A Close-Up*, London/Boston 1937

Virtanen, Timo: Jean Sibelius, Symphony No. 3 – Manuscript Study and Analysis, Studia Music 26, Sibelius Academy 2005

In addition, the website **www.sibelius.fi** *contains extensive information on Sibelius's life and work.*

Works of fiction with relevance to Sibelius

Aho, Juhani: *Yksin* (*Alone*), novella, 1890

Boswell, Simon: *The Seven Symphonies, A Finnish Murder Mystery*, Finnish Evolutionary Enterprises, Helsinki 2004

Carpelan, Bo: *Axel, A Novel*, trans. David McDuff, Carcanet Press, Manchester 1989 (from the Swedish edition by Bonniers, Stockholm 1986)

Paul, Adolf, *En bok om en människa* (*A Book about a Man*), novel, 1891

SELECT DISCOGRAPHY

Gramophone recordings of Sibelius's music have been appearing for more than a century and these have had a decisive – and generally positive – effect upon his reputation. Below is a list of recordings that give some idea of the wide range of interpretations that Sibelius's music has inspired; in making this admittedly subjective selection, I have concentrated primarily on artistic interest rather than on technical issues such as sound quality.

The earliest Sibelius recordings, from the very beginning of the twentieth century, were mostly of vocal music, and often featured the singers for whose voices he composed his songs – most notably Ida Ekman (1875–1942) and Maikki Järnefelt (1871–1929). Some thirty years later, the gramophone was well enough established for the ageing Robert Kajanus to travel to London to set down his authoritative interpretations of the *First*, *Second*, *Third* and *Fifth Symphonies* along with a selection of tone poems and other works. Since then, major contributions to the Sibelius discography have been made by a seemingly endless list of conductors: Sergei Koussevitzky, Anthony Collins, Eugene Ormandy, Sir Thomas Beecham, Herbert von Karajan, Sir John Barbirolli, Paavo Berglund, Sir Colin Davis, Neeme Järvi, Sir Simon Rattle, Leif Segerstam, Jukka-Pekka Saraste and Osmo Vänskä, to name but a few of the most distinguished figures. The *Violin Concerto* has been recorded by virtually every star violinist of the past few generations.

Paradoxically the songs and smaller-scale compositions fell out of favour and became rarities in the record catalogues until the early 1980s, when ground-breaking song collections performed by Tom Krause and Jorma Hynninen were issued. Although there have been numerous recordings of the string quartet *Voces intimae*, it was not until the 1990s that the rest of the chamber music started to attract wider attention, with recordings on the Ondine and BIS labels. In 2007 BIS started to gather together its Complete Sibelius recorded edition in a series of truly comprehensive and self-recommending boxed sets. BIS has also issued a 15-CD boxed set entitled 'The Essential Sibelius' which offers a substantial and carefully balanced overview of his production.

As many of the recordings listed below have been reissued many times in different couplings, the name of the record company is listed below, along with the (sometimes approximate) date of recording, but specific catalogue numbers are not given.

The Symphonies, Violin Concerto and Kullervo

Symphony No. 1   Symphony Orchestra / Robert Kajanus (1930) – HMV
London Symphony Orchestra / Anthony Collins (1952) – Decca
Philharmonia Orchestra / Paul Kletzki (c. 1956) – Columbia
Hallé Orchestra / Sir John Barbirolli (1966) – EMI
Lahti Symphony Orchestra / Osmo Vänskä (1996) – BIS

Symphony No. 2   Symphony Orchestra / Robert Kajanus (1930) – HMV
BBC Symphony Orchestra / Sir Thomas Beecham (1954) – HMV
Sinfonia of London / Tauno Hannikainen (1959) – World Records

Royal Philharmonic Orchestra / Sir John Barbirolli (1962) – RCA
Vienna Philharmonic Orchestra / Lorin Maazel (1964) – Decca
Gothenburg Symphony Orchestra / Neeme Järvi (1983) – BIS
Lahti Symphony Orchestra / Osmo Vänskä (1996) – BIS

Symphony No. 3
London Symphony Orchestra / Robert Kajanus (1932) – HMV
Finnish Radio Symphony Orchestra / Okko Kamu (1972) – DG
Boston Symphony Orchestra / Sir Colin Davis (1976) – Philips
Bournemouth Symphony Orchestra / Paavo Berglund (1977) – EMI
Lahti Symphony Orchestra / Osmo Vänskä (1997) – BIS

Symphony No. 4
London Philharmonic Orchestra / Sir Thomas Beecham (1937) – HMV
Berlin Philharmonic Orchestra / Herbert von Karajan (1960) – DG
Boston Symphony Orchestra / Sir Colin Davis (1976) – Philips
Gothenburg Symphony Orchestra / Neeme Järvi (1984) – BIS
Lahti Symphony Orchestra / Osmo Vänskä (1997) – BIS

Symphony No. 5
London Symphony Orchestra / Robert Kajanus (1932) – HMV
Philharmonia Orchestra / Herbert von Karajan (1960) – Columbia
Hallé Orchestra / Sir John Barbirolli (1966) – EMI
Philharmonia Orchestra / Sir Simon Rattle (1981) – EMI
Lahti Symphony Orchestra / Osmo Vänskä (1997) – BIS

Symphony No. 6
London Symphony Orchestra / Anthony Collins (1955) – Decca
Bournemouth Symphony Orchestra / Paavo Berglund (1973) – EMI
Boston Symphony Orchestra / Sir Colin Davis (1975) – Philips
Berlin Philharmonic Orchestra / Herbert von Karajan (1980) – EMI
Lahti Symphony Orchestra / Osmo Vänskä (1997) – BIS

Symphony No. 7
BBC Symphony Orchestra / Sergei Koussevitzky (1933) – HMV
Leningrad Philharmonic Orchestra / Evgeny Mravinsky (1965)
    – Melodiya
Hallé Orchestra / Sir John Barbirolli (1966) – EMI
Berlin Philharmonic Orchestra / Herbert von Karajan (1967) – DG
Lahti Symphony Orchestra / Osmo Vänskä (1997) – BIS

Violin Concerto
Jascha Heifetz / Chicago Symphony Orchestra / Walter Hendl (1959)
    – RCA
David Oistrakh / Moscow Radio Symphony Orchestra / Gennady
    Rozhdestvensky (1965) – Melodiya
Viktoria Mullova / Boston Symphony Orchestra / Seiji Ozawa (1985)
    – Philips
Leonidas Kavakos / Lahti Symphony Orchestra / Osmo Vänskä (1990)
    – BIS
Christian Tetzlaff / Danish National Symphony Orchestra / Thomas
    Dausgaard (2002) – Virgin Classics

Kullervo
Viitanen / Kostia / YL Male Voice Choir / Bournemouth Symphony
    Orchestra / Paavo Berglund (1970) – EMI
Hynninen / Rørholm / YL Male Voice Choir / Los Angeles
    Philharmonic Orchestra / Esa-Pekka Salonen (1992) – Sony Classical
Laukka / Paasikivi / YL Male Voice Choir / Lahti Symphony Orchestra
    / Osmo Vänskä (1997) – BIS

Tone Poems

En saga	Vienna Philharmonic Orchestra / Sir Malcolm Sargent (1961) – EMI London Symphony Orchestra / Antal Doráti (1969) – EMI Danish National Radio Symphony Orchestra / Leif Segerstam (1991) – Chandos Lahti Symphony Orchestra / Osmo Vänskä (2000) – BIS
The Wood-Nymph	Lahti Symphony Orchestra / Osmo Vänskä (1996) – BIS
Spring Song	Royal Liverpool Philharmonic Orchestra / Sir Charles Groves (1975) – EMI
Lemminkäinen Suite [incl. The Swan of Tuonela]	Philadelphia Orchestra / Eugene Ormandy (1978) – EMI Finnish Radio Symphony Orchestra / Okko Kamu (1975) – DG Los Angeles Philharmonic Orchestra / Esa-Pekka Salonen (1991) – Sony Classical Helsinki Philharmonic Orchestra / Leif Segerstam (1995) – Ondine Lahti Symphony Orchestra / Osmo Vänskä (1999) – BIS
Finlandia	Berlin Philharmonic Orchestra / Herbert von Karajan (1964) – DG Hungarian State Symphony Orchestra / Jussi Jalas (1974) – Decca Lahti Symphony Orchestra / Osmo Vänskä (1999) – BIS
Pohjola's Daughter	London Symphony Orchestra / Robert Kajanus (1932) – HMV Hallé Orchestra / Sir John Barbirolli (1966) – EMI Lahti Symphony Orchestra / Osmo Vänskä (2000) – BIS
Night Ride and Sunrise	Philharmonia Orchestra / Sir Simon Rattle (1981) – EMI
The Bard	London Symphony Orchestra / Sir Colin Davis (2000) – RCA
Luonnotar	Taru Valjakka / Bournemouth Symphony Orchestra / Paavo Berglund (c. 1973) – EMI Helena Juntunen / Lahti Symphony Orchestra / Osmo Vänskä (2005) – BIS
The Oceanides	Royal Philharmonic Orchestra / Sir Thomas Beecham (1955) – EMI London Symphony Orchestra / Antal Doráti (1969) – EMI Lahti Symphony Orchestra / Osmo Vänskä (2000) – BIS
Tapiola	London Symphony Orchestra / Robert Kajanus (1932) – HMV Berlin Philharmonic Orchestra / Herbert von Karajan (1964) – DG Boston Symphony Orchestra / Sir Colin Davis (1976) – Philips Lahti Symphony Orchestra / Osmo Vänskä (2000) – BIS

Theatre Music

King Christian II (suite)	Gothenburg Symphony Orchestra / Neeme Järvi (1983) – BIS
Kuolema (complete)	Soloists, Lahti Symphony Orchestra / Osmo Vänskä (1997) – BIS
Valse triste	Berlin Philharmonic Orchestra / Herbert von Karajan (1984) – DG Lahti Symphony Orchestra / Osmo Vänskä (1997) – BIS
Pelléas et Mélisande (suite)	Royal Philharmonic Orchestra / Sir Thomas Beecham (1955) – EMI

Bournemouth Symphony Orchestra / Paavo Berglund (1978)
– EMI
Gothenburg Symphony Orchestra / Neeme Järvi (1983) – BIS

Belshazzar's Feast (suite)   Norwegian Radio Orchestra / Ari Rasilainen (2001) – Finlandia
                               Records

Swanwhite (suite)   Gothenburg Symphony Orchestra / Neeme Järvi (1985) – BIS
                              Norwegian Radio Orchestra / Ari Rasilainen (2001) – Finlandia
                              Records

Scaramouche (complete)   Gothenburg Symphony Orchestra / Neeme Järvi (1990) – BIS

Jedermann (complete)   Soloists / Lahti Symphony Orchestra / Osmo Vänskä (1995)
                              – BIS

The Tempest (complete)   Soloists / Lahti Opera Choir / Lahti Symphony Orchestra /
                              Osmo Vänskä (1992) – BIS
                              Soloists / Opera Festival Choir / Finnish Radio Symphony
                              Orchestra / Jukka-Pekka Saraste (1992) – Ondine

Other Orchestral Music

Karelia (complete)   Soloists / Lahti Symphony Orchestra / Osmo Vänskä (1997)
                              – BIS
                              Soloists / Tampere Philharmonic Orchestra / Tuomas Ollila
                              (1998) – Ondine

Karelia Suite   Finnish Radio Symphony Orchestra / Okko Kamu (1975) – DG

Press Celebrations Music   Tampere Philharmonic Orchestra / Tuomas Ollila (1998)
                              – Ondine
                              Lahti Symphony Orchestra / Osmo Vänskä (2000) – BIS

In memoriam   Royal Liverpool Philharmonic Orchestra / Sir Charles Groves
                              (1973) – EMI
                              Lahti Symphony Orchestra / Osmo Vänskä (2000) – BIS

Rakastava   Hallé Orchestra / Sir John Barbirolli (1969) – EMI
                              Lahti Symphony Orchestra / Osmo Vänskä (2002) – BIS

Scènes historiques   Finnish Radio Symphony Orchestra / Jukka-Pekka Saraste
                              (1988) – RCA
                              Norwegian Radio Orchestra / Ari Rasilainen (2001) – Finlandia
                              Records

Serenades, Humoresques   Dong-Suk Kang / Gothenburg Symphony Orchestra / Neeme
[violin & orchestra]   Järvi (1989) – BIS
                              Christian Tetzlaff / Danish National Symphony Orchestra /
                              Thomas Dausgaard (2002) – Virgin Classics

Shorter Orchestral Works   [Suites mignonne, champêtre, etc.] Finlandia Sinfonietta /
                              Pekka Helasvuo (1985) – Finlandia Records
                              [Cortège, Musik zu einer Scène, etc.] Lahti Symphony
                              Orchestra / Osmo Vänskä (2000–03) – BIS

Chamber Music

Violin and Piano   (early repertoire) Jaakko Kuusisto / Folke Gräsbeck (1999)
                              – BIS, 2 separate CDs

	(later repertoire) Nils-Erik Sparf / Bengt Forsberg (1991, 1993) – BIS, 2 separate CDs
Cello and Piano	Torleif Thedéen / Folke Gräsbeck (1996) – BIS
Piano Trios	Jaakko Kuusisto / Satu Vänskä / Marko Ylönen / Folke Gräsbeck (2002) – BIS, 2 separate CDs
Piano Quartets	Jaakko Kuusisto / Satu Vänskä / Taneli Turunen / Folke Gräsbeck / Peter Lönnqvist / Harri Viitanen (2003) – BIS
Piano Quintets and	Jaakko Kuusisto / Laura Vikman / Anna Kreetta Gribajcevic / Joel Laakso / Folke Gräsbeck /
Melodramas	Monica Groop / Lasse Pöysti (2005) – BIS
String Quartets (complete)	Tempera Quartet (2004–05) – BIS, 3 separate CDs
Voces intimae	Fitzwilliam Quartet (c. 1980) – Argo
Chamber collections	(early repertoire) Pekka Kuusisto / Ernst Novacic / Jean Sibelius Quartet (etc.) (1994–95) – Ondine, 2 separate CDs

Piano Music

A series of recordings from the 1950s by Cyril Szalkiewicz, originally made for Finnish Radio, has been sporadically available commercially (Finlandia Records).

Complete recordings of the published piano music have since been made by Erik T.Tawaststjerna (1979–86; BIS), Annette Servadei (1992–94; Continuum/Olympia), Håvard Gimse (1997–2001; Naxos) and Eero Heinonen (1995–2000; Finlandia Records).

A fully comprehensive recording of the piano music by Folke Gräsbeck (BIS) is currently (2007) in progress.

Song Anthologies

Songs with piano	Ida Ekman / Maikki Järnefelt / Abraham Ojanperä (etc.): 'The Very First Sibelius Recordings' (1901–08) – Artie Music
	Jorma Hynninen / Ralf Gothóni (1980) – Finlandia Records, 2-CD set
	Tom Krause / Elisabeth Söderström / Irwin Gage / Vladimir Ashkenazy (1978–81) – Decca, 4-CD set
	Anne Sofie von Otter / Bengt Forsberg (1989, 1994–95) – BIS, 2 separate CDs
	Karita Mattila / Ilmo Ranta (1995) – Ondine
	Katarina Karnéus / Julius Drake (2001) – Hyperion
Orchestral songs	Kirsten Flagstad / London Symphony Orchestra / Øivin Fjeldstad (1958) – Decca [includes some third-party arrangements]
	MariAnne Häggander / Jorma Hynninen / Gothenburg Symphony Orchestra / Jorma Panula (1984) – BIS
	Soile Isokoski / Helsinki Philharmonic Orchestra / Leif Segerstam (2005) – Ondine [includes some third-party arrangements]

Choral Music

Choir and orchestra

Several collections from the Lahti Symphony Orchestra / Osmo Vänskä (2001–05; BIS) feature many of Sibelius's works for male choir and orchestra (with the YL Male Voice Choir) and mixed choir and orchestra (with the Jubilate and Dominante Choirs). There are also significant single-disc surveys of this repertoire from the Finnish National Opera Chorus and Orchestra / Eri Klas (1990; Ondine) and from the Ellerhein Girls' Choir, Estonian National Male Choir and Symphony Orchestra / Paavo Järvi (2002–03, Virgin Classics). The opera The Maiden in the Tower has been recorded by Neeme Järvi in Gothenburg (1983; BIS) and by Paavo Järvi in Estonia (2001; Virgin Classics).

Male choir a cappella

YL Male Voice Choir / Matti Hyökki (2001–02) – Finlandia, 2-CD set

Mixed choir a cappella

Jubilate Choir / Astrid Riska (1996–97) – BIS, 2 separate CDs
Tapiola Chamber Choir / Friends of Sibelius / Tapiola Choir / Hannu Norjanen / Kari Ala-Pöllänen (1996–97) – Finlandia Records, 2-CD set

DVDs: films and documentaries

Sibelius – The Christopher Nupen Films [The Early Years / Maturity and Silence]
    Christopher Nupen, narration / Swedish Radio Symphony Orchestra / Boris Belkin,
    violin / Elisabeth Söderström, soprano / Vladimir Ashkenazy, conductor/piano
    (1985/2006) – Allegro Films

Sibelius – a film by Timo Koivusalo
with Martti Suosalo and Heikki Nousiainen (Sibelius), Miina Turunen and Seela Sella
    (Aino)
(2003) – Artista Filmi / Buena Vista Home Entertainment

FAMILY TREE

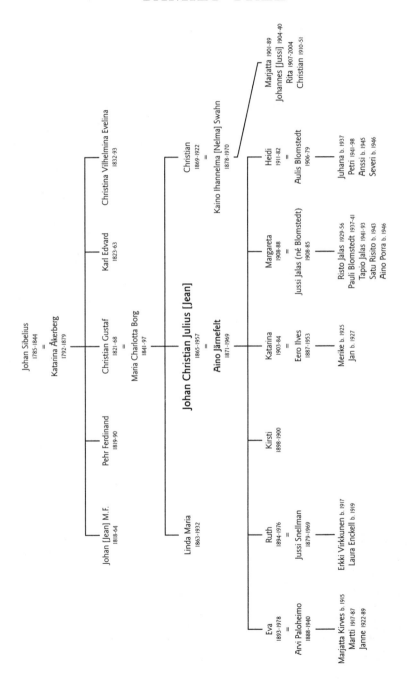

Johan Sibelius
1785-1844
=
Katarina Åkerberg
1792-1879

Christian Gustaf
1821-68
=
Maria Charlotta Borg
1841-97

Karl Edvard
1823-63

Christina Vilhelmina Evelina
1832-93

Pehr Ferdinand
1819-90

Johan [Jean] M.F.
1818-64

Christian
1869-1922

Johan Christian Julius [Jean]
1865-1957
=
Aino Järnefelt
1871-1969

Kaino Ihannelma [Nelma] Swahn
1878-1970

Marjatta 1901-89
Johannes [Jussi] 1904-40
Rita 1907-2004
Christian 1910-51

Linda Maria
1863-1932

Heidi
1911-82
=
Aulis Blomstedt
1906-79

Juhana b. 1937
Petri 1941-98
Anssi b. 1945
Severi b. 1946

Margareta
1908-88
=
Jussi Jalas (né Blomstedt)
1908-85

Risto Jalas 1929-56
Pauli Blomstedt 1937-41
Tapio Jalas 1941-93
Satu Risto b. 1943
Aino Porra b. 1946

Katarina
1903-84
=
Eero Ilves
1887-1953

Merike b. 1925
Jan b. 1927

Kirsti
1898-1900

Ruth
1894-1976
=
Jussi Snellman
1879-1969

Erkki Virkkunen b. 1917
Laura Enckell b. 1919

Eva
1893-1978
=
Arvi Paloheimo
1888-1940

Marjatta Kirves b. 1915
Martti 1917-87
Janne 1922-89

MAP OF SOUTHERN FINLAND

Map of southern Finland showing locations of importance to Sibelius. The post-war Russian border is shown.

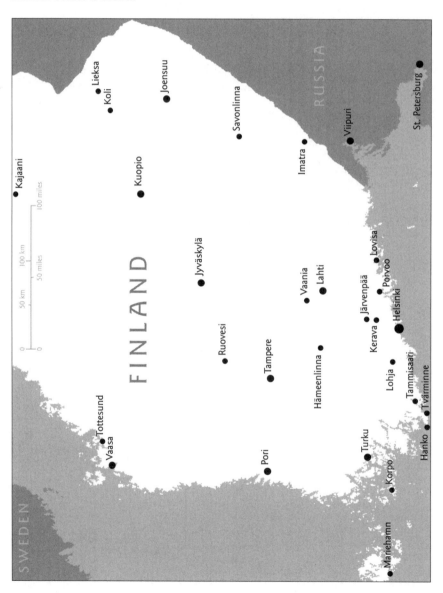

INDEX